High-Speed Networking
A Systematic Approach to High-Bandwidth Low-Latency Communication

High-Speed Networking
A Systematic Approach to High-Bandwidth Low-Latency Communication

James P.G. Sterbenz
and Joseph D. Touch
with contributions from
Julio Escobar
Rajesh Krishnan
Chunming Qiao

technical editor
A. Lyman Chapin

Wiley Computer Publishing

John Wiley & Sons, Inc.
New York • Chichester • Weinheim • Brisbane • Singapore • Toronto

Publisher: Robert Ipsen
Editor: Carol A. Long
Assistant Editor: Adaobi Obi
Managing Editor: Gerry Fahey

Text Design & Composition: UG / GGS Information Services, Inc.

Published by John Wiley & Sons, Inc.

Published simultaneously in Canada.

This publication is designed to provide accurate and authoritative information in regard to the subject matter covered. It is sold with the understanding that the publisher is not engaged in professional services. If professional advice or other expert assistance is required, the services of a competent professional person should be sought.

Library of Congress Cataloging-in-Publication Data:

Sterbenz, James P. G.
   High-speed networking: a systematic approach to high-bandwidth low-latency
   communication / James P.G. Sterbenz; with contributions from Joseph D. Touch
. . .[et al.] technical editor A. Lyman Chapin.
     p. cm. — (Wiley Networking Council series)
   "Wiley computer publishing".
   Includes bibliographical references and index.
   ISBN 0-471-33036-1
   1. Computer networks—Design and construction. 2. High performance computing. I. Touch, Joseph D. II. Chapin, A. Lyman. III. Title. IV. Series.

TK5105.5 .S743 2001
004.6—dc21   2001017642

Printed in the United States of America.

10 9 8 7 6 5 4 3 2 1

Wiley Networking Council Series

Series Editors:

Scott Bradner
Senior Technical Consultant, Harvard University
Vinton Cerf
Senior Vice President, MCIWorldCom
Lyman Chapin
Chief Scientist, BBN Technologies

Books in series:

To my wife Kris and daughter Katy

Contents

Networking Council Foreword

The Networking Council Series was created in 1998 within Wiley's Computer Publishing group to fill an important gap in networking literature. Many current technical books are long on details but short on understanding. They do not give the reader a sense of where, in the universe of practical and theoretical knowledge, the technology might be useful in a particular organization. The Networking Council Series is concerned more with how to think clearly about networking issues than with promoting the virtues of a particular technology—how to relate new information to the rest of what the reader knows and needs, so the reader can develop a customized strategy for vendor and product selection, outsourcing, and design.

In *High-Speed Networking: A Systematic Approach to High-Bandwidth Low-Latency Communication* by James Sterbenz and Joseph D. Touch, you'll see the hallmarks of Networking Council books—examination of the advantages and disadvantages, strengths and weaknesses of market-ready technology, useful ways to think about options pragmatically, and direct links to business practices and needs. Disclosure of pertinent background issues needed to understand who supports a technology and how it was developed is another goal of all Networking Council books.

The Networking Council Series is aimed at satisfying the need for perspective in an evolving data and telecommunications world filled with hyperbole, speculation, and unearned optimism. In *High-Speed Networking: A Systematic Approach to High-Bandwidth Low-Latency Communication*, you'll get clear information from experienced practitioners.

We hope you enjoy the read. Let us know what you think. Feel free to visit the Networking Council Web site at www.wiley.com/networkingcouncil.

Scott Bradner
Senior Technical Consultant, Harvard University

Vinton Cerf
Senior Vice President, MCIWorldCom

Lyman Chapin
Chief Scientist, BBN Technologies

Acknowledgments

First, acknowledgment to the people most responsible for getting me here: my parents Lois and Bert and grandparents Gratia and Jerome; my high school teachers Mr. O'Brien, Joe Hale, John Wiegers, and Herr Wallace Klein for cultivating my interest in science and teaching me how to think; my father Bert Sterbenz for getting me interested in digital logic early enough in my undergraduate education to rescue me from life as a chemical engineer; Mark Franklin for getting me interested in high-performance computer architecture as an undergraduate; IBM Rochester for giving me a personal System/370-158 and letting me muck around inside MVS solidifying my interest in operating systems; Jon Turner for insisting that his graduate students design VLSI chips and introducing me to fast packet switching; my advisor Guru Parulkar and committee members Jerry Cox, Gary Delp, and David Farber for believing in my unconventional ideas; and Peter O'Reilly, Craig Partridge, and Josh Seeger for getting me into stimulating research environments when IBM and GTE Laboratories successively shifted focus from research to advanced development. BBN has provided such an environment during the writing of this book.

Foremost, thanks to my wife Kris and daughter Katy, whose life was significantly impacted by time taken away from everyday family and household commitments. For over a year they altered their lifestyle, concocting all sorts of reasons to leave the house so I could concentrate on this task. Their sacrifice, support, and understanding have been incredible. Katy's response to my statement that I was almost done and would have lots more time to play soon was "Woo-hoo! That would be *wonderful*!" I look forward to many more hours playing with her stuffed Unicorn and Pegasus family. Kris will appreciate being able to walk through the house without having to avoid stacks of papers, journals, books, and marked-up chapter drafts.

I had thought about writing a high-speed networking book for some time, but it was not until Lyman Chapin approached me that I decided that the time and publication scenario were right. After considerable delay, and once Lyman was convinced *himself* that the book would actually happen, he spent many hours reading, correcting, and discussing form, content, and the principles. His insight and breadth of knowledge are impressive, and are reflected in the final pages. Fortunately, we live only 10 minutes away from one another in a rural suburb of Boston. Carol Long, whose initial enthusiasm turned to skepticism as I defied conventional management and scheduling techniques, and after many slipped deadlines, was surprised to actually get a book; I appreciate her understanding through some difficult times. Gerry Fahey was a delight to work with during the production phase, in spite of a production schedule that was intended for manuscripts in a greater state of readiness and in spite of the fact that I always forgot something during our phone conversations and would immediately call her back a second (or third) time.

I am grateful to colleagues in the IFIP Protocols for High-Speed Networks community, whose workshops in the 1990s not only provided a wealth of important references cited in the book, but also stimulating discussions that helped shape and sharpen my thinking. I'm particularly indebted to Harry Rudin, Marjory Johnson, Per Gunningberg, Martina Zitterbart, Bryan Lyles, Joe Touch, Christophe Diot, and Julio Escobar. I am similarly indebted to the IEEE Communications Society Technical Committee on Gigabit Networking community, in particular Dick Skillen, Nim Cheung, Rich Thompson, Sujata Banerjee, and Aloke Guha. While high-speed issues are now pervasive in all the networking we do, these intersecting communities of individuals are still deeply interested in high-speed networking. As the torch is passed to new leaders, the traditions will hopefully continue for another decade. Additionally, technical conversations over the last 15 years with Buddy Waxman, Ellen Witte Zegura, Lou Steinberg, Ken Calvert, Baiju Patel, Paul Skelly, Alden Jackson, and Rajesh Krishnan have had particular influence on my thinking, as well as providing stimulating nontechnical discussion.

I am indebted to the contributors to this book: Joe Touch helped refine the early outlines of all the chapters and the basic set of principles in Chapter 2, wrote the first draft of parts of Chapters 7 and 8, and contributed to Section 5.1. Julio Escobar not only contributed text on wireless networking in Chapters 3 and 5, but provided his networking insight throughout the book. While I learned far more about optical networking than I had expected, this would have not been possible without the contributions of Chunming Qiao to the optical networking text in Chapters 3, 4, and 5. Rajesh Krishnan began as a reviewer to the book, but his detailed and deep reviews became more of a systematic contribution than a review in the conventional sense. He made multiple careful passes through the entire text; contributed substantially to the structure and content of Chapters 2, 3, 7, and 8; helped me check the accuracy of numbers and formulas; and was an unbelievable storehouse of literature citations.

Joe Touch would like to thank the patience and consideration of Gail Schlicht, Leigh Connors, his parents Ralph and Filomena Touch, and friends (notably Theodore V. Faber) during the preparation of this book. They have provided abundant support and encouragement throughout this process.

Gary Delp reviewed my first large writing project (D.Sc. dissertation), and has done so again for my second significant project. He reviewed the majority of the book, providing significant insight reflected in these pages. Peter O'Reilly reviewed Chapters 1 and 2, contributing to the principles and the readability of the text. Martha Steenstrup reviewed and helped refine the sections on hierarchy. Ted Faber reviewed an early draft of Chapter 7, Alden Jackson reviewed portions of Chapter 5 and 7, and Kris Sterbenz helped improve readability. Of course, any inaccuracies or omissions that remain are solely my responsibility, and I would appreciate hearing about them.

Mark Allman, Bob Braden, Jerry Cox, Gary Delp, Aloke Guha, Alden Jackson, Mark Lucente, Bryan Lyles, Walter Milliken, Craig Partridge, Radia Perlman, Ram Ramanathan, Dennis Rockwell, Tushar Saxena, Martha Steenstrup, Tim Strayer, Rich Thompson, Greg Troxel, Jon Turner, Richard Vickers, and Buddy Waxman discussed issues and provided answers to questions that helped me refine the ideas presented. Vint Cerf and Dave Clark helped with their unpublished citations. Janet LeBlond sent many emergency packages when I was working at home, and Jennie Connolly was able to locate even the most obscure citation. Radia Perlman indicates in her book that one of her fears is forgetting people to be acknowledged. While she *is* on the list, I apologize in advance for anyone else I've forgotten.

James P.G. Sterbenz
jpgs@ieee.org
Hopkinton, Massachusetts

CHAPTER 1

Introduction

The discipline of high-speed networking came into its own in the mid-1980s with intense research, first in high-speed switching technologies, and then on how to eliminate end-system bottlenecks. In the late 1990s, high-speed networking became so pervasive that just about *everything* involved high-speed networking, and little was *only* about high-speed networking. The field is now mature enough that we can consider the complete range of issues needed to deliver high performance to distributed communicating applications.

This book provides a systemic and systematic description of the principles of high-performance network architecture and design—systemic because we are concerned with the performance of the entire networked system or systems and systematic because we will consider in turn all the factors that are required for high speed networking:

- Network subsystems (such as routers, switches, and end systems).
- The protocols that glue these subsystems together.
- The entire network as a complex *system of systems*.
- The end-to-end delivery of high-bandwidth, low-latency data to applications.
- Applications that use and drive the demand for high-speed networks.

This is not a book about any particular technology—but where appropriate, we will provide illustrative examples of particular aspects of particular technologies, ideas from the research community, and historical foundations. We will not assume that networking began with the Internet, and operating systems began with Unix.

1.1   Bandwidth and Latency

We define high-performance networking as having two fundamental character-istics: *high bandwidth* and *low latency*. The motivation for high-performance networks is to support high-performance distributed *applications*, including remote access by a user to an application located elsewhere. The key perfor-mance metric might be surprising until some thought is given to the matter: *delay*. If the total delay in transferring chunks of data between applications is zero, then there is no difference whether the applications and users are dis-tributed throughout a room or across the world. Note that we have not yet said anything about bandwidth.

1.1.1   Individual Delay

There are two components to this delay. The first is the time it takes to trans-mit a chunk of data out of the sending application, and the second is the time it takes to propagate across the network to the receiving application. If the chunk is only 1 bit long, then bandwidth doesn't matter very much; a 9600-b/s telephone connection will only impose a chunk transmission delay of 104 μs. Thus, the driver for high bandwidth between applications is the need to trans-fer large chunks of data with low delay. When applications are interactive, that is, in response to an action taken by the user, we want the request-response loop to complete quickly. Experience has shown that subsecond re-sponse time is necessary for reasonable productivity with interactive applica-tions, and approaching 100-ms response is desirable. For example, if we are requesting a 1-KB Web page, we need a data rate of 100 kb/s to transmit the page quickly enough.[1] If the page contains 1-MB high-resolution images, we need a data rate of 100 Mb/s. Therefore, low interapplication delay motivates the need for high-bandwidth paths between the applications.

Equally important is the delay component for propagation through the net-work, end systems, and application programs where the data is stored and ac-cessed. It is of little use to the end user if data is being transferred at 100-Mb/s rates along network links, but is suffering delays of seconds in servers, net-work nodes, or at the end systems. Similarly, the latency of control messages, supporting session or connection control, can be critical to application perfor-mance. In this case, we are concerned not only with the latency of a single

[1]We use the notation of lowercase b for bit, and uppercase B for byte, throughout this book.

end-to-end trip but also with minimizing the number of round-trip delays on which the application must wait.

Note that some applications, such as remote backup, are generally considered to require high bandwidth, but are not particularly sensitive to latency. This is still driven by the application delay, but it is the need to transmit terabytes or petabytes of data in a time frame of minutes to hours, rather than days to weeks. Some applications, such as real-time, two-way voice conversations and process control, need low latency alone.

Finally, some applications, such as interactive Web browsing with 100-ms response, require both high bandwidth and low latency. We will be most concerned with networks and applications that require *both* high bandwidth and low latency.

1.1.2 Aggregate Bandwidth

There are two ways of looking at bandwidth: on a per link or stream basis and in aggregate (with respect to a particular component, subnetwork, or application). We are concerned with both. We have thus far motivated the former, since designing systems to provide individual high-bandwidth, low-latency paths directly benefits individual applications. We are also concerned with the scalability of high-performance networks. Therefore, how to build large routers and switches and how to scale high-performance networks will also be a focus of this book. This requires that individual components such as switch elements be scalable and that signaling and routing algorithms are designed to avoid explosion in state and control messages. Hierarchy is an important way to help with this problem. Giganode networks are of concern in conventional networking among personal and enterprise computers. Teranode and petanode networks will be of concern as we move to ubiquitous computing and wireless networking, where an individual, residence, or office may each have tens to thousands of networked smart devices.

1.2 What Is High Speed?

In this book, we have generally avoided the use of a specific prefix multiplier such as *giga*bit, *tera*bit, *peta*bit, or *exa*bit. This is for two reasons. First, this is a book of architectural and design principles, not a snapshot of particular time frames or technologies. While the science of high-performance networking is still evolving, it is mature enough to codify principles that will continue to be valid as we move from gigabit to petabit networking and beyond. Second, the effective rate at which network components operate decreases as we move up the protocol stack and from the network core out to the end system. There are two reasons for this. The need for the network to aggregate vast numbers of high-performance interapplication flows dictates that the core of the network must be higher capacity than the end systems. Furthermore, it is easier to design components for high-speed communications whose sole purpose is networking than it is to optimize end systems with multiple roles and applications.

In the late 1990s, deployed link layers and multiplexors, such as Sychronous Optical Network (SONET), operated on the order of tens of gigabits per second, switches and routers at several gigabits per second per link, end system host–network interfaces in the range of 10 to 100 Mb/s, and applications typically on the order of several megabits per second. By the early 2000s, link bandwidth and switch bandwidth had increased an order of magnitude or two, but local access and end-system bandwidth continued to lag. The challenge of designing end-to-end systems that deliver high-bandwidth and low-latency performance to the application is one of the focuses of this book. We will consider techniques such as zero-copy transfer using memory mapping [Sterbenz 1990a] and masking the speed-of-light delay between applications [Touch 1989]. This requires a high-speed packet-switched [Turner 1986a] or optical infrastructure between the end systems.

1.2.1   High-Speed Technologies

Many of the principles described in this book are relatively independent of the core technology. However, in some cases, the choice among conventional electro-optical, all-optical, wireless, and satellite network subsystems can have profound impact in the network. Examples include the high latency of geosynchronous satellite links, long burst errors of wireless channel fades, and the inability for all-optical paths to buffer data. These aspects will receive specific attention as appropriate.

We will also consider the performance implications of active networking, which consists of introducing programmability and functionality into network nodes to provide enhanced services traditionally located in end systems.

1.2.2   Barriers and Constraints

There are several significant barriers to the deployment of high-performance networks, in addition to the specific problems of designing end-to-end systems to be high bandwidth and low latency.

1.2.2.1   Bandwidth-×-Delay Product

Designing systems with high bandwidth, particularly over wide area networks, provides a serious challenge. While we can design individual components and subsystems for high-performance, we cannot decrease the latency due to the speed-of-light signal propagation over distance. Thus, there will always be a latency component due to the speed of light, which is significant to end-to-end performance in wide area networks.

The *bandwidth-×-delay product*[2] refers to the amount of data in transit (r bit/s $\times$ d s $=$ rd bits). This has significant impact on the design of network components since rd bits of data must be handled in flight, and perhaps buffered in network components. The problem worsens as improving technology increases the bandwidth of optical links. As we begin to consider how to extend the Internet to interplanetary scales for the Mars and future Jupiter space missions [Cerf 1998], the prospect of petabits or exabits in flight is staggering. Furthermore, the design of protocols and applications for high-bandwidth-×-delay product is difficult, since over the interval that an application or protocol attempts to exert control, a large amount of data ($2rd$) may have flowed. By the time the control mechanisms take effect, the conditions that triggered them may no longer exist. Thus, when considering end-to-end protocols and applications, we will be just as concerned with high bandwidth-×-delay product networks as with bandwidth or latency alone.

1.2.2.2 Legacy and Heterogeneity

Two other barriers to the deployment of high-performance networks are of a more practical nature: legacy systems and heterogeneity. Although we might like to use the principles espoused in this book to start from scratch and design perfect high-performance networks, end systems, protocols, and application interfaces, this is clearly not practical. The world is full of legacy systems, and decades of experience have shown that it is very difficult to replace systems with a large installed base, particularly on which significant amounts of existing protocols and software rely. Even relatively minor changes like the introduction of multicast in the network and the transition from IPv4 to IPv6 can be quite painful. Proposals as drastic as the complete replacement of IP by ATM in the Internet are dead on arrival. Thus, this book will consider not only how to design new systems, protocols, and applications, but also how to use high-performance design principles to optimize existing network infrastructure and protocols, such as the Internet, Web, and TCP-based applications, with minimum impact.

A related barrier is that of heterogeneous applications and end systems, and results from several factors: Technological progress results in heterogeneous systems, even if only during a transition period (which is typically far longer than hoped). Heterogeneity also results from a desired variety in end-system applications and operating systems. Finally, heterogeneity results in the optimization of protocols and data formats to particular applications. As an

---

[2]Spoken as "bandwidth delay product."

example, the overhead in transcoding gateways in the network could be eliminated by using common data formats for all multimedia applications, but perhaps at a significant penalty in the end system and application itself, with considerable loss of flexibility to the end user.

1.3   Organization of This Book

Chapter 2 introduces the axioms and principles that guide the research, architecture, design, and deployment of high-speed networks. Chapters 3 and 4 then look at the network architecture as a whole. Chapter 3 considers high-speed network architecture, in particular topology, geography, and the location of functionality based on resource tradeoffs. Chapter 4 discusses network control and signaling. Chapters 5 and 6 consider how to design high-speed network components (links, switches, and routers) and end systems, respectively. Chapter 7 considers the end-to-end issues and transport protocols that interface to applications. Chapter 8 discusses high-performance applications and their interaction with the protocols. Finally, Chapter 9 looks ahead at the future of high-performance networking, as technologies and the contexts in which they are deployed change in foreseeable and unforeseeable ways.

Chapters 3 through 8 begin with the canonical system and protocol diagram shown in Figure 1.1, with the focus of each chapter highlighted.

Chapter 1—Introduction

Chapter 1 is a good place to state the sole criterion for deciding what topics to include in the rest of the chapters: *relevance to high-speed networking*. Very few books with the terms "high-speed" or "gigabit" in their titles are actually about the *issues and principles* of high-speed networking. Rather, they are about particular networking technologies [such as asynchronous transfer mode (ATM) or Gigabit Ethernet] or classes of applications (such as multimedia). Similarly, there are entire topics that we will only touch on briefly as they relate to high-speed networking, and resist the temptation to present more thorough coverage. Examples include quality of service, routing, and traffic management.

Illustrating with a common misconception, although a number of design decisions were made for ATM (allegedly for high-performance implementation), there is nothing inherently high performance about the ATM architecture and protocol suite *as a whole*. While we will discuss some of the important aspects (such as fast packet switching), we will use other aspects as a counterexample of how *not* to design high-performance networks (for example, small cell size and complexity of signaling and traffic management). Similarly, there is nothing inherently high bandwidth about multimedia applications. The

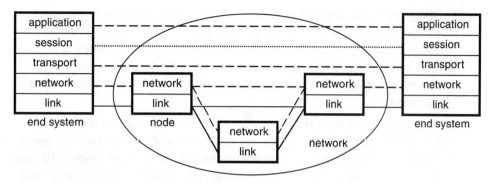

Figure 1.1   Network node and link architecture.

world is full of useful low-bandwidth video streaming, although interactive multimedia applications require low latency. Interactive data applications, such as Web browsing with high-resolution images and 100-ms response time, are far more bandwidth-intensive and latency-sensitive than video streaming.

Chapter 2—Fundamentals and Design Principles

Chapter 2 is the core foundation for the rest of the book, providing a set of axioms to guide our understanding of high-speed network architecture and design. Section 2.1 provides a brief history of networking. Section 2.2 discusses interapplication delay as the driver for high-speed networking, introduces an ideal zero-latency, infinite-bandwidth network model, and considers the barriers to deploying such a model. The axioms that will be described are as follows:

> **Ø. Know the Past, Present, and Future.**   Genuinely new ideas are extremely rare. Almost every "new" idea has a past full of lessons that can either be learned or ignored. "Old" ideas look different in the present because the context in which they have reappeared is different. Understanding the difference tells us which lessons to learn from the past and which to ignore. The future hasn't happened yet, and is guaranteed to contain at least one completely unexpected discovery that changes everything. On the other hand, we can prepare for the future by constantly reevaluating tradeoffs in the face of emerging technology, and questioning the basic assumptions of the present.

> **I. Application Primacy.**   The sole and entire point of building a high-performance network infrastructure is to support the distributed applications that need it. Interapplication delay drives the need for high-bandwidth, low-latency networks.

II. High-Performance Paths Goal.   The network and end systems must provide a low-latency, high-bandwidth path between applications to support low interapplication delay. We introduce an ideal network, and consider path establishment, path protection, store-and-forward avoidance, blocking avoidance, efficient transfer of control, and information assurance.

III. Limiting Constraints.   Real-world constraints make it difficult to provide high-performance paths to applications. These include the speed of light, limits on channel capacity and switching rate, heterogeneity, policy and administration, cost and feasibility, backward compatibility, and standards.

Section 2.3 presents the design principles and tradeoffs that form the basis of our approach for the research, architecture, design, and deployment of new communications and network technology.

IV. Systemic Optimization Principle.   Networks are *systems of systems* with complex compositions and interactions at multiple levels of hardware and software. These pieces must be analyzed and optimized in concert with one another. To this end, we discuss the need to consider the side effects of optimizations and the benefits of simple, open, and flexible architectures.

The Systemic Optimization Principle is the umbrella for the design principles in the rest of the book:

1. **Selective Optimization Principle.**   It is neither practical nor feasible to optimize everything. Spend implementation time and system cost on the most important contributors to performance.

2. **Resource Tradeoff Principle.**   Networks are collections of resources. The relative composition of these resources must be balanced to optimize cost and performance.

3. **End-to-End Arguments.**   Functions required by communicating applications can be correctly and completely implemented only with the knowledge and help of the applications themselves. Providing these functions as features within the network itself is not possible.

4. **Protocol Layering Principle.**   Layering is a useful abstraction for thinking about networking system architecture and for organizing protocols based on network structure.

5. **State Management Principle.**   The mechanisms for installation and management of state should be carefully chosen to balance fast, approximate, and coarse-grained against slow, accurate, and fine-grained.

6. **Control Mechanism Latency Principle**.   Effective network control depends on the availability of accurate and current information. Control mechanisms must operate within convergence bounds that are matched to the rate of change in the network and latency bounds to provide low interapplication delay.

7. **Distributed Data Principle**.   Distributed applications should select and organize the data they exchange to minimize the amount of data transferred and the latency of transfer and allow incremental processing of data.

8. **Protocol Data Unit Principle**.   The size and structure of PDUs are critical to high-bandwidth, low-latency communication.

For each of these principles, several refinement principles and corollaries are discussed. For example, while the Protocol Layering Principle indicates the benefits of layered protocols, we will need the corollary that Layering as an Implementation Technique Performs Poorly. The rest of the chapters will present refinements and contextual versions of these principles as appropriate.

Section 2.5 introduces some of the most important design techniques that will be used to support the principles:

- Scaling time and space
- Masking the speed of light
- Specialized hardware implementation
- Parallelism and pipelining
- Data structure optimization
- Cut-through and remapping

Finally, Section 2.6 provides a summary, complete list of axioms and principles, and suggestions for further reading.

Chapter 3—Network Architecture and Topology

Chapter 3 considers the overall architecture of the network. Section 3.1 discusses the issues that are important in engineering an entire network. This consists of the topology and structure to provide high-bandwidth, low-latency paths through the network and the impact of geography. Section 3.2 discusses how to achieve large scale in networks and the use of hierarchy to manage complexity. Then, Section 3.3 examines the resource tradeoffs between bandwidth, memory, and processing, constrained by latency requirements. This is important in determining the proper location of functionality and services that the network should provide. Finally, Section 3.4 presents a summary and list of principles introduced throughout the chapter.

Chapter 4—Network Control and Signaling

Chapter 4 describes control issues in high-speed networks. Section 4.1 considers signaling and control issues, examining the overheads involved in the spectrum of connectionless to hard connection-oriented networks, and the mechanisms used in optical networks. Section 4.2 considers traffic management and congestion control in high-speed networks. Section 4.3 describes the impact of dynamic paths on high-speed networks. Section 4.4 touches on issues important in the monitoring and control of high-speed networks. Section 4.5 summarizes and presents the list of principles introduced in Chapter 4.

Chapter 5—Network Components

Chapter 5 examines the components that make up the network: links and nodes. Section 5.1 considers issues in the design and use of high-speed links of a variety of technologies. Section 5.2 describes the functional components needed in switches and routers. Traditional Internet router design is presented, and the performance bottlenecks are discussed. Then Section 5.3 considers how to design high-bandwidth, low-latency connection-oriented fast packet switches. Section 5.4 delves into the internal structure of the switch datapath, considering the design of buffering schemes and scalable switch fabrics that minimize blocking and utilize cut-through paths. Section 5.5 considers how to apply the techniques of high-speed fast packet switching design to high-speed connectionless datagram switches. In particular, techniques for fast address lookup, packet classification, and scheduling, will be discussed. Section 5.6 considers higher-layer protocol processing and the design of high-speed active network nodes. Finally, Section 5.7 presents a summary, suggestions for further reading, and list of principles.

Chapter 6—End Systems

In Chapter 6, the discussion moves to the edge of the network, and considers how end systems must be designed to allow the end-to-end, low-latency, high-bandwidth communications. The end system is particularly sensitive to an understanding of where bottlenecks really lie and the resultant systemic optimization [Clark 1990]. Section 6.1 describes the organization of the end system as a whole and introduces the hardware and software components of concern. It also discusses the traditional layered I/O-based protocol implementation, and presents the ideal end-system implementation model, based on the ideal network model from Chapter 2. Section 6.2 describes protocol software and the host operating system for high-speed networking. Principles and techniques, such as critical path optimization, integrated layer processing (ILP), minimizing operating system context switches, and exploiting the virtual memory subsystem, are discussed. Section 6.3 discusses host architecture and organization. Particular emphasis is placed on processor–memory interconnects to support a nonblocking, high bandwidth path between the network interface and application memory. Section 6.4 describes the implementation of high-speed host–network interfaces, and the partitioning of functionality between hardware and software. Finally, Section 6.5 summarizes, reiterates the design principles, and provides some pointers for further reading.

Chapter 7—End-to-End Protocols

Chapter 7 considers the end-to-end communication on which distributed applications rely. This functionality is provided by transport protocols, which are of central importance to the chapter. Section 7.1 introduces the end-to-end functionality and mechanisms provided by transport protocol, and presents the end-to-end arguments. The end-to-end arguments are the key determinant of end-to-end functionality. The important issue of open- versus closed-loop feedback control is presented. The remaining sections examine the different end-to-end mechanisms in more detail. Section 7.2 discusses connection control, and Section 7.3 describes framing and multiplexing. Section 7.4 describes error control mechanisms, and Section 7.5 presents flow and congestion control mechanisms. The use of open-loop control and decoupling error from and flow control are key principles. Section 7.6 considers high-performance end-to-end data integrity and security mechanisms. Section 7.7 provides the summary and suggestions for further reading.

Chapter 8—Networked Applications

Chapter 8 returns us to the motivation for high-speed networks: high-performance applications and the interface to the protocols and network. Section 8.1 discusses the characteristics of high-speed applications and the criteria we will use to determine whether an application should be considered "high-speed." We classify applications as real-time, interactive, or deadline constrained. Section 8.2 describes applications by class: information access, telepresence, distributed computing, or a composition thereof, and relates them to the characteristics of the previous section. Section 8.3 explores how applications can adapt to less than desired network bandwidth and latency and, in particular, how to mask the effects of the speed-of-light delay. Section 8.4 describes the interaction of the application and the protocols and network, in particular application feedback and control mechanisms. Section 8.5 summarizes the chapter and principles.

Chapter 9—Future Directions and Conclusion

Chapter 9 concludes the book. Section 9.1 looks toward the future, with a discussion on how the relative changes in resource tradeoffs can fundamentally alter the ways in which networks and protocols are designed. Section 9.2 considers some of the technology and applications that show promise to enable and challenge high-speed networking in the future. Finally, Section 9.3 provides a brief conclusion to the book.

1.4   Who Should Read This Book

The author of this book assumes that the reader understands computer networks, computer architecture, and operating systems at the level that would be achieved by completing a rigorous undergraduate computer science or computer engineering curriculum. This book is intended for graduate students and professionals who wish to understand the principles of high-performance network design, and serves as a starting point to the vast body of literature describing original research on the subject. This book is particularly appropriate for use in a special-topics graduate course in high-speed networking.

While targeted to high-speed network design, we believe that the unique approach of stating axioms and design principles up front and then providing contextual refinements will provide insight into system architecture and design that transcends high-speed networking. This book provides examples of particular network and protocol technologies to illustrate high-speed network design principles, but it is not a comprehensive treatment of any particular technology.

CHAPTER 2

Fundamentals and Design Principles

This chapter presents the fundamental axioms and principles of high-speed networking that will set the stage for the rest of the book. Section 2.1 presents a brief history of networking and considers the defining characteristics of four generations of networking. We emphasize the importance of knowing the past in preparing for the future. Section 2.2 discusses high-performance distributed applications as the motivation for high-speed networks, presents an ideal network model that expresses the desired characteristics, and discusses the constraints that challenge this ideal.

All our efforts to design high-performance networks are attempts to get as close to the ideal high-bandwidth, low-latency network model as possible. Given the constraints of the real world and the laws of physics, we can approach but never reach this ideal.

The fundamental principles introduced in Section 2.3 express the conditions under which practical network architecture and design can most closely approach this high-performance network ideal. These principles will be used as the basis for context-specific versions in the chapters that follow.

We take a *systemic* as well as systematic view—that is, we recognize the network as a *system of systems*, and optimize the pieces that have the most impact on *overall* performance. While an approach often taken in the past is to concentrate on particular components and protocols and simply implement functionality in hardware, experience has shown that this does not necessarily improve interapplication performance. We will look at optimizing the critical path, resource tradeoffs, the end-to-end arguments, protocol layering, and the management of state.

Section 2.4 introduces the most important design techniques that will be used throughout the book to apply these principles toward our ideal network goal. These include scaling time and space, masking and cheating the speed of light, specialized hardware implementation, parallelism and pipelining, data structure optimization, and cut-through and remapping. Section 2.5 concludes with a list of the axioms and principles introduced in this chapter.

A note on terminology: We use the terms *end system* and *host* interchangeably for a computing platform attached to the network for the purpose of running applications. We use the term *node* for a system within the network that performs data routing, switching, or forwarding functions. Thus a node can be a switch, router, bridge, or link repeater; these terms will be used when the distinction matters. We use the term *link* to designate the connections between nodes. We use the term *path* to generically indicate a sequence of nodes and links through the network on which data or control information flows. A path can be a virtual circuit, connection, flow of datagrams, or datagram transaction; these individual terms will be used when the distinction matters.

2.1   A Brief History of Networking

The ability to make progress in science and engineering depends on understanding the past. Thus, we will begin with the first part of our first axiom:

Know the Past   *Genuinely new ideas are extremely rare. Almost every "new" idea has a past full of lessons that can either be learned or ignored.*

$\emptyset_1$

When an old idea surfaces in a new context, the important thing is to recognize what makes this context different from the context in which the idea's past resides. This suggests the following:

Know the Present   *"Old" ideas look different in the present because the context in which they have reappeared is different. Understanding the difference tells us which lessons to learn from the past, and which to ignore.*

$\emptyset_2$

A final corollary is required to counter the hubris engendered by all of this "knowing":

> **Know the Future**   *The future hasn't happened yet, and is guaranteed to contain at least one completely unexpected discovery that changes everything.*
>
> Ø₃

The history of networking and communications can be divided into generations [Sterbenz 1995], as summarized in Table 2.1. Each generation has

Table 2.1   Computer Network Generations

GENERATION	TIME FRAME	APPLICATIONS	TECHNOLOGY	PERVASIVENESS
1. Emergence	Through 1970s	Voice	Circuit-switched PSTN over copper wire RF	Universal
		Entertainment	Broadcast RF	Universal
		Data	Serial link over copper Modem	Very limited
2. Internet	1980s	Voice	Digital-switched PSTN Cellular mobile telephony	Universal
		Entertainment	CATV over copper coax	High
		Data	Store-and-forward packet	Corporate enterprise
			Gatewayed subnetworks	Research and education
			Transoceanic fiber optic cables Bent-pipe satellite links	
3. Convergence	1990s	Web Multimedia	Fast electronic packet switching over fiber IP-based global Internet Switched satellite networks	Very high (First world)
4. Scale Ubiquity Mobility	2000+	Mobile Ubiquitous	Wireless access network All optical networks (switches and fiber) Widely deployed transoceanic cable Widely deployed satellite networks	Global

distinctly different characteristics in terms of the scope of users and applications, the integration of various applications and media, and the enabling technology and tradeoffs.

2.1.1   First Generation: Emergence

The first generation lasted through roughly the 1970s and is characterized by three distinct categories: voice communication, broadcast entertainment, and data networking, each of which was carried by a different infrastructure. Voice communication was either analog circuit switched over copper wire in the public switched telephone network (PSTN), or analog radio transmission between transceivers. Entertainment broadcasts to radio receivers and televisions were carried by free space broadcast of radio frequency (RF) transmissions. Data communications was the latest entrant, and provided only a means to connect terminals to a host. This was accomplished either by serial link local communications (for example, RS-232, or Binary Synchronous Communications used on mainframes), or by modem connections over telephone lines for remote access; in both cases copper wire was the physical medium. Packet networking began to emerge in the wired network in ARPANET[1] and packet radio, primarily for military applications.

2.1.2   Second Generation: The Internet

In the 1980s a dramatic jump in the types and scope of networking occurred, but the three categories of communication (voice, entertainment, and data) remained relatively distinct. This period took us from the experimental ARPANET to the ubiquitous Internet.

While the end user of the voice network generally continued to use analog telephone sets, the internal network switches and trunks became largely digital. Transmission remained mostly over copper wire. Additionally, there was widespread deployment of digital private branch exchange telephone switches (PBXs) on large customer premises. Mobile communications emerged in the form of cellular telephony. The significant addition to the entertainment category of networking was the wide-scale deployment of cable television (CATV) networks for entertainment video over copper coaxial cable.

In data networking, we first saw the emergence of consumer access, but in the primitive form of bulletin board systems (BBSs) and consumer online services (such as America Online, CompuServe, and Prodigy). These were essentially first-generation networks made available to consumers, with modems

---

[1]Named after the Advanced Research Projects Agency of the U.S. Department of Defense, the funding sponsor.

connecting to a central server farm. The collection of research and education networks such as BITNET, CSNET, and UUNET, were collectively referred to as the Matrix [Quarterman 1989] before they began to join the Internet, unified by IP addresses, with the domain name system (DNS) symbolic addressing replacing bang paths.[2]

The growth in data networking for universities and the research community was significant during this period, for purposes of file transfer, remote login, electronic mail, and Usenet news. The technology employed was the packet-switched Internet utilizing the TCP/IP protocol suite. In the wide area, the backbone network consisted of store-and-forward routers connected by leased 56-Kb/s telephone lines. The NSFNET[3] upgraded the infrastructure to 1.5-Mb/s T1 lines, and ultimately 45-Mb/s T3 lines at the end of the second generation. In the local area, shared medium Ethernet and token ring networks allowed clusters of workstations and PCs to network with file and compute servers.

At the same time, but relatively distinct from this, connection-oriented corporate enterprise networks using protocols such as BNA, DECNET, and SNA[4] were widely deployed, along with the deployment of public X.25 networks (used primarily as corporate virtual private networks). Thus, even within data networking there were multiple incompatible architectures and poorly interconnected networks. Most of these networks used copper wire as the predominant physical medium.

It is important to realize that pioneering work was done in the computer architecture and operating systems in the 1960s and 1970s, and significant networking research and development were done in the context of the enterprise network architectures and protocols. The foundations of switching date farther back, to the emergence of relay-controlled railway interlockings and telephone switches. Thus, we state the first corollary to the Know the Past axiom:

Not Invented Here Corollary [1980s version]   *Operating systems didn't begin with Unix, and networking didn't begin with TCP/IP.*

                                                                                        Ø-A

2.1.3   Third Generation: Convergence and the Web

The third generation saw the emergence of integrated services: the merging of data, voice, and entertainment video on a single network infrastructure. With

---

[2]Bang path addresses required explicit mention of all host systems in the path, for example, `decvax!ihpn4!wucs!axon!jpgs` rather than the current form `jpgs@acm.org`.
[3]Named after the National Science Foundation, the funding sponsor.
[4]Burroughs Network Architecture, Digital Equipment Corporation network, and IBM Systems Network Architecture.

the advent of IP-telephony gateways, the PSTN started to become a subnet of the Internet. Network service providers scrambled to keep capacity ahead of demand in overprovisioned networks, since the quality of service (QOS) mechanisms to support real-time and interactive applications were just beginning to emerge.

The second generation was characterized by the packet-switched Internet, X.25, and enterprise networks. The third generation was characterized by an IP-based global information infrastructure (GII) based on fast packet-switching technology interconnected by fiber optic cable, with IP as the single network layer unifying previously disjoint networks.

The second significant characteristic is in the scope of access, with consumers universally[5] accessing the Internet with personal computers via Internet service providers (ISPs). Disconnected BBSs are a thing of the past, and online consumer services have become merely value-added versions of ISPs. The Internet went from being a kilobit kilonode network, through megabit meganode, approaching gigabit giganodes.

The final distinguishing characteristic of the third generation is the World Wide Web, which provided a common protocol infrastructure (HTTP), display language (HTML), and interface (Web browsers) to enable users to easily provide and access content. Web browsers became the way to access not only data in web pages but also images and streaming multimedia content. The rate of adoption of Internet connections vastly exceeded the rate of new telephone connections. In spite of the fact that the Internet and Web became the primary reason for users to have PCs, these devices were still not designed with networking as a significant architectural consideration.

Just as we needed to look beyond Unix in the 1980s, we need to look beyond what became the most common computing platform in the 1990s: the Intel x86 architecture PC running Microsoft Windows.

> **Not Invented Here Corollary [1990s version]**   *Operating systems didn't begin with Windows, and host architecture didn't begin with the PC and the x86 architecture.*
>
> **Ø-B**

However, in this case, the marketing model has limited the impact. Researchers require an open platform with freely available source code for the operating system and protocol stack, and thus Unix variants are still the platform of choice for the vast majority of networking research. The lack of open interfaces and source code on commercial routers and switches is a signifi-

---

[5]At least in the developed first world with some inroads into the second- and third-world nations. While we firmly believe that the benefits of technology should not be limited by geographic boundary or economic class, this is unfortunately not the case, but is beyond the scope of this book. The metric used for universal network access should be that it approaches the penetration of the telephone and radio receiver.

cant hindrance to the research, development, and trial deployment of new protocols and algorithms.

2.1.4   Fourth Generation: Scale, Ubiquity, and Mobility

The first decade of the new millennium inaugurates a new network generation, which will apparently be characterized by orders of magnitude increase in network scale, and by the ubiquity of mobile wireless computing devices. The third generation was largely a wired network; the fourth generation will be largely wireless at the edges, with access to a high-speed optical backbone infrastructure, including optical switches.

Advances in the interface between biological and microelectronic interfaces, and the benefits of applying micro- and macrobiotic behavior and organization techniques to networks may begin to emerge, or may be a characteristic of the fifth generation.

Ubiquitous computing, smart spaces, and sensor network research suggest that individual users will carry tens to hundreds of networked devices. These will perhaps include a personal node for computing and communications to other individuals, and a wireless network of wearable I/O devices and sensors (environmental and biological). Rooms and vehicles will consist of perhaps thousands of embedded sensors and networked computing platforms. Thus we need to consider teranode and petanode networks. There are profound implications to high-speed networking. The aggregate wireless bandwidth demanded will vastly exceed the capacity of the shared medium using third-generation protocols and techniques, and the highly dynamic nature will stress routing and control protocols. The ability to manage power among the massive number of autonomous wireless devices and to do high-speed networking where power is a constraint will be a major challenge.

We will see not only end systems, the sole purpose of which is networking, but also a blurring of functionality between end systems and network nodes. In mobile networking, many devices will serve both as application platforms and as switches or routers.

While the capacity in processing, memory, and bandwidth will dramatically increase, the tradeoffs will continue to shift. This is the subject of Chapter 9. The relative decrease in the cost of processing enabled the field of active networking, which may play a significant role in the fourth generation. We note that speed-of-light latency will continue to be a significant challenge, and increasingly so as we begin to build the Interplanetary Internet, initially for the Mars missions, but with an eye toward the Jupiter system.[6]

---

[6]Terrestrial latencies can generally be bounded in the subsecond range required for interactive response, but interplanetary latencies are in the range of minutes to hours; see Table 3.1 for details.

So we end with this fourth part of our first axiom, which amplifies the third part:

Prepare for the Future   *Simply knowing the past does not prepare us to understand the future. We must constantly reevaluate tradeoffs in the face of emerging technology and question the basic assumptions of the present.*

$\varnothing_4$

While we can't predict exactly what will be the next killer app, or what fundamental discoveries will take place, we can do our best to prepare for what is likely to come, and be prepared to adapt to the things we can't predict.

2.2   Drivers and Constraints

This section describes the fundamental drivers and constraints for high-performance network infrastructure. High-performance communicating applications are the reason to produce high-speed networks. The goal we would like to achieve is an ideal network with unlimited bandwidth and no latency, to allow delay-free transfer of data among applications. If it were possible to easily achieve the ideal network, there would be no need for this book. Unfortunately, there are a number of constraints that make it difficult to approach an ideal network.

2.2.1   Applications

Applications are the whole point of doing networking:

Application Primacy   *The sole and entire point of building a high-performance network infrastructure is to support the distributed applications that need it.*

I

This doesn't mean that we can predict the next killer app to determine the direction of high-speed networking. In fact, being too narrow in application target can just as easily lead us down the wrong path when subsequent killer apps do appear. Thus, it is important to research, design, and deploy high-speed network infrastructure, and see what applications will actually emerge.

Field of Dreams versus Killer App Dilemma   *The emergence of the next "killer application" is difficult without sufficient network infrastructure. The incentive to build network infrastructure is viewed as a "field of dreams" without concrete projections of application and user demand.*

I.1

Thus, we have a "field-of-dreams" versus "killer-app"[7] problem. In some cases government agencies are willing to build the infrastructure on the anticipation that "[If you] build it[,] they will come" [Robinson 1989]. An example of this was the NSFnet and high-performance computing and communications (HPCC) initiatives, funded by the U.S. government.

The most important distributed application metric of interest to us is *delay*.

Interapplication Delay   *The performance metric of primary interest to communicating applications is the total delay in transferring data. The metric of interest to users includes the delay through the application.*

I.2

If communicating applications are able to transfer data with essentially zero delay, then they behave like applications running on a single computing system, and we do not have a high-speed networking problem to solve. In reality, we must be concerned with applications that communicate with one another across significant distance through a network. The interapplication delay introduced by such a network consists of two components:

1. The delay involved in transmitting the bits at a particular rate. For a chunk of data b bits in size along a path of bandwidth r bits/s, the delay[8] is $t_b = b/r$. By increasing the bandwidth of the path, we can reduce this component of latency. This delay occurs at least once, when the chunk of data is transmitted by the sending application. It also occurs every additional time that it is transmitted out of h store-and-forward hops, or each c times a per byte operation takes place (such as copies between buffers in memory or manipulating in place), for a total of $1 + h + c$ times.

2. The delay t_p along a path consists of the latency incurred as the bits flow along a distance due to the speed of light, and delays through transmitting end system, all of the intermediate nodes in the network, and the receiving end system.

---

[7]Field of Dreams: "Build it and they will come," from the 1989 movie *Field of Dreams*; this variant of chicken-and-egg is quoted from Marjory Blumenthal.
[8]We will use the variable D for delay or latency throughout this book and uppercase variables for the aggregate and lowercase (d or t for time) for contributing components.

Thus, the total interapplication delay can be expressed as

$$D = (1 + h + c)b/r + t_p$$

To reduce the delay between applications we need to be concerned about the bandwidth and latency of a path, as well as the number of hops or copies, which affect latency. We will revisit these formulas and their components in more detail in subsequent chapters.

Network Bandwidth and Latency   *Bandwidth and latency are the primary performance network metrics important to interapplication delay.*

                                                                        1.3

Applications vary in their sensitivity to delay. Some applications have tight real-time delay requirements, such as remote process control and voice. Interactive applications such as Web browsing have somewhat looser constraints, but require delay bounds of subsecond with preferred bounds on the order of 100 ms to be truly interactive.

Other applications do not have tight latency bounds in the conventional sense, but the size of the data is so significant that to be useful the bandwidth is the usual way of thinking about the requirement. Examples include remote backup of data and network distribution of movies and television content. In these cases, to meet a practical delivery constraint of minutes to hours, bandwidth must be high.

For certain paths, especially those that include error prone (for example, low signal-to-noise ratio wireless links), link retransmissions contribute to the path delay. This could be viewed as an additional latency problem, or as a lower effective bandwidth problem. The latter perspective is generally better, because the problem responds better to bandwidth-intensive measures [for example, forward error correction (FEC) over greater bandwidth] than to latency reduction attempts measures (for example, finding shorter paths).

Finally, we need to consider how important high-speed communication is to the applications on a particular system, and how this feeds into the design and cost tradeoffs.

Networking Importance in System Design   *Communication is the defining characteristic of networked applications, and thus support for communication must be an integral part of systems supporting distributed applications.*

                                                                        1.4

While this is obvious for network components whose sole purpose is to perform communications processing, it is frequently overlooked in the design of general-purpose end systems such as PCs. Although a significant, if not primary, application of many consumer PCs is to browse the Web, networking performance is secondary to processor clock rate, memory size, and disk capacity in marketing-driven architecture. The rule of thumb has been that a maximum of 10 percent of the cost of a PC can be consumed by the network interface, but this should not be a factor that constrains the importance of networking in the modern world.

2.2.2   The Ideal Network

We can now consider what we want from the network (which for this discussion includes the end systems running the communicating applications). The ideal network is one that is completely transparent to communicating applications. In particular, the network directly connects applications with unlimited bandwidth ($R = \infty$) and no latency ($D = 0$), as shown in Figure 2.1. Thus, the applications cannot tell the difference between executing on the same host from executing on different hosts connected by the ideal network.

This ideal, of course, is unattainable, and the point of this book is to understand how to design and engineer networks that approach this ideal, and what the barriers are. We need to decompose this high-level ideal model to the next level of granularity before we can begin to understand how close we can come to the ideal case.

Figure 2.2 shows the ideal network architecture. Applications run on their respective CPUs in memory (M) without interfering with the interapplication communications. The applications are connected to one another by the ideal network ($R = \infty$ and $D = 0$), which is decomposed into a set of switches that fully interconnect the end systems with no blocking of communications traffic. Clearly, the switches themselves must also have the characteristics $R = \infty$ and $D = 0$.

In looking at the decomposed pieces (network, nodes, end systems, end-to-end protocols, and applications), we must remain ever mindful that the goal is to achieve an end-to-end high-performance path between applications. While these (and further) decompositions are necessary to get a handle on the problem, they cannot be done in isolation; this will be the subject of Section 2.3.

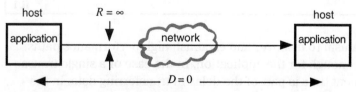

Figure 2.1   Ideal high-speed network.

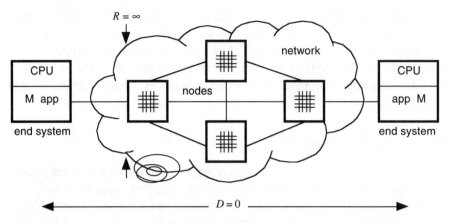

Figure 2.2 Decomposed ideal network model.

Thus, we can begin to see what we want the network to support: end-to-end high-performance paths between communicating applications, in support of low Interapplication Delay (I.2).

> **High-Performance Paths Goal** *The network and end systems must provide a low-latency, high-bandwidth path between applications to support low interapplication delay.*
>
> II

Indeed, this is the focus of the rest of this book, and we will examine how to achieve this in the various pieces: network architecture and organization in Chapter 3, network nodes (switches and routers) in Chapter 4, end systems in Chapter 5, end-to-end protocols in Chapter 6, and the application interface in Chapter 7.

We will introduce some corollaries to the High-performance Paths Goal that will help guide us in achieving the best architecture and design possible:

> **Path Establishment Corollary** *Signaling and routing mechanisms must exist to discover, establish, and forward data along the high-performance paths.*
>
> II.1

We need a mechanism to discover and establish high-performance paths, and to do it quickly enough for the application. In the case of a single transaction, this establishment time is part of the delay in transferring data. In the case of longer application associations such as collaborative sessions, the establishment time may have distinct and more relaxed time constraints, on the order of several seconds.

Path Protection Corollary   *In a resource-constrained environment, mechanisms must exist to arbirtrate and reserve the resources needed to provide the high-performance path and prevent other applications from interfering by congesting the network.*

II.2

Once we have discovered a high-performance path, we may have to guarantee that it will remain that way for the life of the application association. There are two ways to accomplish this. We can vastly overengineer the network, so that the probability of traffic from different applications interfering and congesting the network is insignificant. While bandwidth is cheap, it is not free, and shows no sign of being free in the foreseeable future. History has shown that application demand fills the available pipes, and this will be particularly the case for RF wireless access links, which are limited in available radio spectrum. Thus, the second approach is to have quality of service (QOS) mechanisms that reserve resources when a path is established, ensure that applications do not exceed the agreed traffic rate, and block the admission of applications that would exceed the capacity of network links and nodes. These mechanisms vary from fine-grained deterministic guarantees, through tight statistical bounds, through course-grained weak guarantees, to best-effort, carrying traffic as available in excess of reserved resources. We will discuss the tradeoff between overengineering and QOS complexity in Chapter 3.

We must be concerned with things that directly affect latency. Recall our delay equation from the previous section: $D = (1 + h + c)b/r + t_p$. The delay of transmitting the object of size b is multiplied for each hop at which it must be store-and-forwarded, or copied between buffers in memory. These delays are a critical component in the end-to-end latency, and we will strive to eliminate them.

Store-and-Forward Avoidance   *Store-and-forward and copy operations on data have such a significant latency penalty that they should be avoided whenever possible.*

II.3

The best we can possibly do is the single transmission delay at the sending system, resulting in a zero-copy system [Sterbenz 1990a], but application semantics may constrain this to an additional copy, as described in Chapter 6. The other serious impact on latency is when there is blocking in what should be a low-latency, high-bandwidth path. This occurs when data must be buffered in queues because paths interfere with one another toward the same destination, or there is back-pressure limiting the ability to transmit data on a link. These delays are a critical component that we must try to eliminate.

> **Blocking Avoidance**   *Blocking along paths should be avoided, whether due to the overlap of interfering paths, or due to the building of queues.*
>
> II.4

Another factor that limits the ability to provide a high-performance path is contention for a shared channel. This can occur in shared medium networks, such as traditional Ethernet, token ring, and wireless. It can also occur when a bus is used as interconnect backplane for a network node or end system. While shared medium channels have useful properties, such as the inherent ability to broadcast, they limit scalability. Thus, we need to ensure that channel contention does not limit scalability.

> **Contention Avoidance**   *Channel contention due to a shared medium should be avoided.*
>
> II.5

There are a number of control mechanisms that are needed in networking, for such things as the establishment and forwarding of data, management of traffic, routing of paths, control of congestion, and the execution of parts of the protocols. It is essential that mechanisms on which the critical path transfer of data is dependent be efficient, and that the interactions and transfer of control between domains of control be efficient.

> **Efficient Transfer of Control**   *Control mechanisms on which the critical path depends should be efficient. High overhead transfer of control between protocol-processing modules should be avoided.*
>
> II.6

Finally, recalling the Application Primacy (I), there are levels of service that are required for the applications to be able to use the network.

> **Path Information Assurance Tradeoff**   *Paths have application-driven reliability and security requirements which may have to be traded against performance.*
>
> II.7

Some of these translate directly into the Network Bandwidth and Latency (I.3) metrics that have already been introduced. For example, an unreliable link may have an error rate high enough that retransmissions or an added forward error correction (FEC) code reduces the effective bandwidth and increases latency. Block coding for voice in the Internet introduces significant delay. Other aspects of information assurance cannot be directly translated in this manner. For example, if the reliability of high-speed network nodes is so poor that paths cannot even be established much of the time, we cannot deliver high-speed networking to the applications. Similarly, there may be requirements for security and privacy that significantly reduce performance.

2.2.3   Limiting Constraints

We have now discussed the High-Performance Paths Goal (II) driven by Application Primacy (I). Unfortunately, we must now consider the constraints that make this goal difficult to achieve, which will give us plenty to consider in the subsequent chapters.

Limiting Constraints   *Real-world constraints make it difficult to provide high-performance paths to applications.*

III

The most fundamental constraint is the latency contribution due to the speed-of-light propagation along a path. We can reduce the interapplication delay by increasing the bandwidth and decreasing the latency of individual components such as the end system and intermediate nodes. Unfortunately, we cannot decrease the speed-of-light latency between two points, barring fundamental new discoveries in physics.

Speed of Light   *The latency suffered by propagating signals due to the speed of light is a fundamental law of physics, and is not susceptible to direct optimization.*

III.1

While we can't beat the speed of light, we will do our best to live with it by engineering direct long-haul network paths, and avoiding unnecessary round trips. These issues are discussed in Chapters 4 and 6. Furthermore, by caching, prefetching, and predicting, we can mask the effects of the speed of light, as will be discussed in Chapter 8.

Channel Capacity   *The capacity of communication channels is limited by physics. Clever multiplexing and spatial reuse can reduce the impact, but not eliminate the constraint.*

III.2

Communication channels, such as wires, fiber optic cables, and free space have physical limits on capacity. Clever coding and multiplexing techniques can increase the efficiency of channel utilization but not exceed physical limits. Spatial reuse allows increased aggregate capacity in the presence of spatial locality. In some cases, spatial reuse is easy to implement, for example, by increasing the number of fiber optic cables in parallel. In some cases, channel capacity is a difficult constraint, particularly for wireless communication where free space is a shared medium channel with limited radio spectrum.

Switching Speed   *There are limits on switching frequency of components, constrained by process technology at a given time, and ultimately limited by physics.*

III.3

The rate at which logic, memory, and transmission components can switch limits the bandwidth of communication systems. There are fundamental physical limits on the switching speed of electronic, optical, chemical, and biological systems. The practical limit is generally related to the particular technology (for example, CMOS and GaAs semiconductors) architecture (for example, SRAM versus DRAM), and fabrication process. Generally, a cost tradeoff (discussed next) determines how the limits should be applied to a particular system. In some cases, switching speed is optimized against channel capacity, for example, in determining the optimal number of wavelengths and per wavelength data rate in wavelength division multiplexing (WDM) transmission.

There are other constraints that affect the design and deployment, and while of less direct concern to this book, are important to understand and keep in the background throughout. When particularly relevant, we will explicitly refer to the following constraints:

Cost and Feasibility   *The relative cost and scaling complexity of competing architectures and designs must be considered in choosing alternatives to deploy.*

III.4

In the end, the decision to deploy a particular network technology is driven by a cost versus benefit tradeoff. When consumers, corporate entities, or governments are willing to pay for a particular service, it will be deployed at the corresponding level. This affects *when* a particular deployment takes place as the cost of technology decreases, and we will generally not be concerned with this issue.

We are, however, concerned with picking solutions which have relatively low economic cost, and which scale well, rather than more expensive alternatives. For example, while it might be possible to design a high-speed workstation host–network interface as an array of expensive microprocessors, there are other solutions which are competitive in performance, but an order of magnitude lower in cost.

We are also concerned with designs that scale well, and thus we will explicitly discuss the complexity of network nodes and overall network architecture. For example, we can design a crossbar nonblocking switch that contains n^2 switch elements for n ports. As n gets large, we should consider multistage interconnection networks that have a complexity of only $n \cdot \log_2(n)$ switch elements. (We will discuss this in Chapter 4).

> **Heterogeneity** *The network is a heterogeneous world, which contains the applications and end systems that networks tie together, and the node and link infrastructure from which networks are built.*
>
> **III.5**

Heterogeneity is a fact of life, allowing diversity and technological substitution. The applications and end systems that networks tie together are heterogeneous due to user preference and specialization in functionality. The node and link infrastructure of which networks are built is also heterogeneous due to network provider preference and emerging technology. While a certain degree of heterogeneity is necessary and desirable, it challenges performance. The network architecture and protocols should mediate in an efficient manner to deliver high performance to applications.

> **Policy and Administration** *Policies and administrative concerns frustrate the deployment of optimal high-speed network topologies, constrain the paths through which applications can communicate, and may dictate how application functionality is distributed.*
>
> **III.6**

In a perfect world, networks are deployed in a way that globally optimizes infrastructure. This ceased to be the case for the U.S. telephone network in the 1970s with the AT&T divestiture, and the U.S. Internet in the 1990s with the decommissioning of the NSFNET. While competition has clear benefits in driving costs down, the result is neither universal access nor global optimality, except to the degree required by regulation. In Chapter 4 we will consider the impact of network topologies that are not optimal. Furthermore, policies frequently dictate where traffic between communicating applications may or may not go, particularly based on security concerns, such as avoiding a competitor's network or hostile nations. Routing, signaling, and QOS mechanisms need to consider policy constraints, and deliver high-performance service to applications in spite of these constraints.

> **Backward Compatibility Inhibits Radical Change**   *The difficulty of completely re-placing widely deployed network protocols means that improvements must be back-ward compatible and incremental. Hacks are used and institutionalized to extend the life of network protocols.[9]*
>
> **III.7**

Backward compatibility has always been a concern to computer systems vendors; it is difficult to make changes that require a wholesale replacement of installed software. In the consumer PC market, users are lured to get new versions of software with new features, but this happens over a period of time. Network protocol software is less visible to the end user, more pervasive in end systems and network nodes, and must interoperate to allow nodes to communicate.

Thus, change in network architecture is pushed to be incremental and forward compatible. The location of the protocol directly affects how easy it is to replace. Replacing TCP with an incompatible new transport protocol would be nearly impossible to do, since virtually all systems on the Internet would be affected. It is somewhat easier to replace components and protocols within the network, particularly when the effect can be localized to part of the net, such as a single service provider or small set of servers. This is how routing protocols such as border gateway protocol (BGP) are currently upgraded in the Internet.

The failure of ATM to replace IP, and the delay in deploying IPv6 as a replacement for IPv4, are examples of this constraint. The ability to layer hack upon hack, and for them to become institutionalized, is sobering. Just when we thought that IPv6 would be required to solve the limited address space in IPv4, network address translation (NAT) [Dutcher 2001] hacks have further postponed the necessity of IPv6.

Progress can be made in spite of backward compatibility issues; the canonical example is Ethernet, which has changed considerably from its original 10-Mb/s incarnation, through 100BaseT, Gigabit, and 10Gigabit. The original carrier sense, multiple access, collision detect, and exponential back-off are now irrelevant; QOS is being added; and 8B/10B coding has replaced Manchester. Example 5.2 discusses this in detail. Even though ATM over SONET were scalable standards from the beginning, the ubiquitous deployment of Ethernet helped contribute to its dominance to the desktop.

> **Standards Both Facilitate and Impede Dilemma**   *Standards are critical to facilitate interoperability, but standards which are specified too early or are overly specific can impede progress. Standards that are specified too late or are not specific enough are useless.*
>
> **III.8**

---

[9]Eventually, the replacement may be substantially different from the original while keeping the same name. An instantiation of this is a statement commonly made by cynics: "We don't know what the transport and network layer protocols of the future Internet will look like, but they will be *called* TCP and IP."

Standards are an important way to codify design principles and produce interoperable systems with predictable behavior. Since networking is all about the interoperation of systems and protocols, networking standards are particularly important. After research indicates that a new approach should be taken, there is significant incentive to produce early standards so that multiple vendors can begin producing interoperable network components and software. It is also important to produce open standards so that individual software and component vendors do not push their own agendas and create multiple incompatible de facto standards.

Unfortunately, standards are frequently an *impediment* to progress. Standards are often defined prematurely, before research and prototyping have discovered all of the implications of an architecture that should affect the standards. The standards process of the International Telecommunications Union (ITU), for example, values agreement among its primarily government-owned postal, telephone, and telegraph (PTT) agencies above all else, including technical superiority. One of the most appalling consequences of this is the ATM cell payload size of 48 bytes, which was chosen as the average of the final competing proposals of 32 and 64 bytes (discussed in Example 2.2).

Standards that overspecify also impede progress, particularly when they specify the internal implementation of systems, rather than their externally visible behavior. Finally, standards that are codified too late are useless and irrelevant. Formal standards that are released after de facto standards take over are irrelevant.

2.3   Design Principles and Tradeoffs

So far, we have presented the axioms that we must Know the Past and Prepare for the Future ($\emptyset$), that Application Primacy (I) motivates for the High-Performance Paths Goal (II) in the network, and we have discussed Limiting Constraints (III) in achieving this. We are now ready to present the final axiom and two high-level corollaries, which will serve to cover the design principles that we will use throughout the book:

Systemic Optimization Principle   *Networks are* systems of systems *with complex compositions and interactions at multiple levels of hardware and software. These pieces must be analyzed and optimized in concert with one another.*

IV

The fundamental axiom that will guide our analysis and design of networks is that they are complex systems that must be considered as a whole. It makes no sense to optimize part of the network or a network component without considering the overall impact on network performance, and without ensuring that individual optimizations work together to enhance performance in concert.

An important factor in considering optimizations is the granularity over which the optimization applies. The range of time intervals is vast, covering many orders of magnitude (at least 10^{18}), from years for protocol deployment, through days or months for network configuration, to small fractions of a second for bit transfer time:

- Protocol deployment
- Network configuration
- Network management interval
- Session establishment and lifetime
- Connection/flow establishment and lifetime
- Packet/frame transfer
- Cell transfer
- Byte transfer
- Bit transfer

Fortunately, the modular, layered, and hierarchical principles we will introduce in the rest of this section help isolate these concerns from one another. We will highlight the granularities of concern in the subsequent chapters, as appropriate for particular aspects of high-speed networking.

Consider Side Effects   *Optimizations frequently have unintended side effects to the detriment of overall performance. It is important to consider, analyze, and understand the consequences of optimizations.*

$$IV_1$$

Optimizations frequently have unintended side effects that impact performance in other ways. Optimizing a particular component or aspect of a system virtually always comes at some cost elsewhere. If the balancing costs are not considered, the *overall* performance may actually decrease. While it is important to analyze systemic effects of optimizations in advance, this is very hard to do in complex systems of systems, and not all of the consequences of optimizations are likely to be discovered until deployment. Testbeds and phased deployments can help catch side effects before wide-scale deployment; this further complicates the Standards Both Facilitate and Impede Dilemma (III.8).

Keep it Simple and Open   *It is difficult to understand and optimize complex systems, and virtually impossible to understand closed systems, which do not have open published interfaces.*

$$IV_2$$

Simplicity in architecture and design of networks, protocols, algorithms, and components can pay off in two ways. First, complex systems are difficult to understand, optimize, maintain, and enhance. Lessons in computer architecture and software engineering have taught us that simplicity and regularity make it easier to produce high-performance systems. This is particularly true as systems evolve, where each incremental enhancement provides diminishing return, to the point where only a complete redesign will straighten things out. If this is an implementation of a protocol, it is an inconvenience to the developer. If it is the protocol design itself, it may not be practical to do the rework at all, due to Backward Compatibility Inhibits Radical Change (III.7).

Furthermore, closed monolithic systems are the antithesis of how we have learned to structure and design systems, and are particularly egregious in the network environment. Operating systems need to be modular with documented open interfaces so that network protocol functionality can be understood, optimized, and enhanced. Network nodes, such as routers and switches, need open published interfaces for signaling and control for similar reasons. Unfortunately, this is not the direction that operating system and router vendors are taking. Their goal often appears to be to maximize profit and market dominance. The open software movement in general, and the open signaling and architecture research initiatives in particular, attempt to move the field back toward robust and flexible networks that can evolve.

The second way in which simplicity must be considered is in the tradeoff between overengineered simplicity and optimal complexity, which will be addressed in detail later (Design Corollary 2B).

System Partitioning Corollary   *Carefully determine how functionality is distributed across a network. Improper partitioning of a function can dramatically reduce overall performance.*

IV$_3$

We have to be careful not to impose networking overhead by improperly distributing an application. We have already pointed out that networking is driven by application and user needs, and in many cases the location and partitioning of functionality is dictated by the physical location of users. However, given this constraint, there is a significant quantity of underlying application functionality and interaction with the network that may be arbitrarily partitioned to reside on user end systems, at servers, or within the network. We must make sure that this partitioning is not done in a way that challenges the ability to provide a high bandwidth path or makes an application appear to be high-speed when it doesn't need to be.

> **Flexibility and Workaround Corollary**   *Provide protocol fields, control mechanisms, and software hooks to allow graceful enhancements and workarounds when fundamental tradeoffs change.*
>
> **IV$_4$**

Technology improves, tradeoffs change, and new applications emerge that drive changes and new functionality in network architecture and protocols. What is optimal at a particular point in time is likely not to be in the future, but Backward Compatibility Inhibits Radical Change (III.7) prevents us from making progress if radical replacement is required. Thus, protocols should have data structures and fields to allow changes, negotiation of new options, and additions in a backward-compatible manner. Similarly, the specification of control mechanisms should be such that these can evolve over time in a graceful way.

The rest of this section will present the next level of refinements of the Systemic Optimization Principle (IV), that is, the detailed design principles. To simplify the numbering scheme, these principles omit the leading roman numeral IV, but any arabic numbered principle can be assumed to be a subprinciple of IV, for example, Design Principle 2 rather than IV-2.

2.3.1   Critical Path

In a systemic view of optimization, the most important thing is to understand which optimizations have the most significant impact on the system as a whole.

> **Selective Optimization Principle**   *It is neither practical nor feasible to optimize everything. Spend implementation time and system cost on the most important contributors to performance.*
>
> **1**

Network components (end systems, network nodes, and links) are not free and unlimited, nor are the pieces of which they are constructed, such as processors, memory, disk, and interface electronics. Trying to optimize everything to a particular degree comes at the cost of further optimizing the pieces that really matter, both in terms of time and effort in architecture, design, and implementation, as well as in the cost of deploying systems. Thus, we need to carefully consider what matters, how much it matters, and apply optimization effort accordingly.

> **Second-Order Effect Corollary**   *The impact of spatially local or piecewise optimizations on the overall performance must be understood; components with only a second-order effect on performance should not be the target of optimization.*
>
> **1A**

In particular, any component that has only a second-order effect (<10 percent) on performance is not a candidate for optimization. This can be viewed either in terms of other components or the total performance. For example, consider a network path consisting of four segments, with relative latencies of $50 + 2 + 25 + 10 = 87$. The one link that clearly *doesn't* need attention is the second, which contributes only $2/87 = 0.02$ of the total latency. Completely eliminating this delay doesn't significantly affect the overall latency. Similarly, upgrading a single link from 1 Mb/s to 10 Mb/s is a waste of resources if there are already 100-Mb/s links (with similar latency, error, jitter, and cost characteristics) that form parallel paths. Finally, this corollary indicates that we need to be far more concerned with optimizing the latency through wide area networks than LANs; the speed of light latency of the former is a significant fraction of a 100-ms interactive delay budget.

On the other hand, the latency through LANs cannot be ignored. Distributed processing and feedback control applications can have extremely tight latency bounds. This constraint has been felt even with relatively primitive third-generation networks of workstations (NOWs).

Critical Path Corollary *Optimize implementations for the critical path, in both control and data flow.*

1B

A related corollary is based on a data flow view, and examines the operations that must take place to transfer the data between the communicating applications. Operations that happen frequently have proportionally more impact on the overall performance, and are candidates for optimization. This is related to the concept of a software fast path, but is broader in implications; a fast path might be a technique to implement part of a critical path.

It is useful to consider control and data flow separately. Clearly, *data transfer functions* that are part of the normal data flow are part of the critical path, that is, we can view the end-to-end path between applications as a sequence of operations on the critical path. Optimization of operations not on the critical path, such as the processing of exceptions and errors is misdirected. There are three important observations to make:

1. *Transfer control functions* such as flow control and framing must be considered part of the critical path, even though they may occur at a larger granularity (for example, application frame versus packet versus byte).

2. The critical path may not be strictly serial; it may be formed by parallel branches, which rejoin before the data has reached the destination application.

3. Dependencies are important; even if an operation happens relatively infrequently, if subsequent data flow would be held up, this infrequent operation must be considered part of the critical path. For example, if only 1 percent of the packets need a particular data transformation applied, we might generally not consider this function to be part of the critical path and worthy of optimization. On the other hand, if packet sequence must be maintained, then subsequent packets will be delayed whenever this occasional operation occurs. We must either consider it part of the critical path or find a way to redesign the critical path to remove the slow operations.

It is important to note the relationship of the Critical Path Corollary and the Second-Order Effect Corollary (1A). The Critical Path Corollary tells us on which operations the critical end-to-end data flow depends, based on the frequency of these operations and dependencies. The Second-Order Effect Corollary tells us if—and how much—these functions need to be optimized based on their relative contribution to performance.

Functional Partitioning and Assignment Corollary   *Carefully determine what functionality is implemented in scarce or expensive technology.*

1C

The result of applying Design Principles 1A and 1B is a determination of what needs optimization and by how much. This can guide us on how to implement within a particular technology, such as what functionality to put in a software fast path or hardware pipeline.

Typically, we have a variety of implementation technologies to choose from, and the faster technology is generally more expensive. Thus we have a functional partitioning and assignment problem, for example, software versus hardware, memory versus cache versus registers, semicustom versus fully custom VLSI, or complementary metal oxide semiconductor (CMOS) versus gallium arsenide (GaAs) semiconductor technology. Thus we use the Second-Order Effect Corollary (1A) and Critical Path Corollary (1B) to determine what needs optimization, and the Functional Partitioning and Assignment Principle to determine the implementation technology based on the relative costs and benefits.

This can be crucial from a packaging standpoint, as there may be a finite amount of chip or circuit board area, or fast memory available, among which functionality must be partitioned. This is similar to the problem of trading off CPU versus cache memory area in high-performance VLSI processor design.

2.3.2   Resource Tradeoffs

Our next design principle recognizes that we must balance the utilization of resources to achieve optimal cost and performance.

> **Resource Tradeoff Principle**   *Networks are collections of resources. The relative composition of these resources must be balanced to optimize cost and performance.*
>
> **2**

The most obvious resources to consider in network deployment are the triple of bandwidth, processing, and memory $\langle B, P, M \rangle$. A simple example, described in more detail in Example 3.5, is the ability to trade bandwidth for memory in the location of cached movie content. If bandwidth is free and unlimited, but memory is very expensive, we minimize the memory requirements and have a single copy of each movie at central servers and blast to users each time it is viewed. If bandwidth is expensive and memory free and unlimited, then we minimize the bandwidth by sending every movie that a user will ever watch for indefinite storage.

It is important to note that the functions that govern these tradeoffs are not necessarily linear, nor are they always continuous. For example, increases in processing power and memory capacity are exponential in nature. The increase in processor frequency follows a relatively smooth curve with small and frequent increases in capacity. On the other hand, memory capacity is a step function whose points match an exponential curve only at the interval at which capacity is multiplied by four.

Other performance metrics limit our freedom to balance these resources, and are better viewed as constraints. The most important of these is latency (D), but others include jitter, error rate, power consumption, and heat dissipation. Latency is such an important constraint due to the speed-of-light propagation delay. It is important to note, however, that we can trade constraint values against resource utilization. For example, by increasing the bandwidth we can lower the loss rate by forward error correction, and lower the effective interapplication latency by presending all data likely to be needed within a round-trip time. We will thus be most interested in resource/constraint tuple $\langle B, P, M \mid D \rangle$.

> **Resource Tradeoffs Change**   *The relative cost of resources and the impact of constraints change over time, due to nonuniform advances in different aspects of technology.*
>
> **2A**

It is extremely important to be aware that the relative cost of resources changes over time, and this dramatically affects optimal network architecture and protocol design. For example, first-generation networks were designed assuming that bandwidth was relatively expensive. With the advent of optical fibers and fast packet switching, bandwidth became relatively cheap during the third generation. In the fourth generation, processing and memory have become significantly cheaper, reversing the tradeoff. While it may be hard to modify protocols quickly to the tradeoffs, we need to be aware of the potential for change. Network topology and engineering should be as flexible as possible to allow the optimal placement of resources as tradeoffs change.

> **Optimal Resources Utilization versus OverEngineering Tradeoff**   *Balance the benefit of optimal resource utilization against the costs of the algorithms that attempt to achieve optimal solutions.*
>
> **2B**

If resources are very expensive, then complexity in architecture and implementation may be required, but as noted by Keep It Simple and Open (IV_2), this comes at other costs. As an example, in an environment where bandwidth is expensive and thus a scarce resource, complex, fine-grained quality of service mechanisms to ensure optimal bandwidth utilization of the network are in order. This was the approach taken with ATM traffic management. This also requires the memory and processing required to store detailed link state metrics and process the admission control and QOS-based connection routing algorithms. On the other hand, when bandwidth is relatively cheap, it makes more sense to have simpler, coarser-grained QOS mechanisms with some overprovisioning of bandwidth to account for the inaccuracy of the algorithms. Finally, if bandwidth is free and unlimited, QOS mechanisms to optimize bandwidth and prevent congestion are not needed at all.

Note that cost includes the projected cost of upgrade, and benefit includes the factor of useful life. Parts that are very difficult to upgrade must be overengineered for the beginning of their life to delay the time at which they become the bottleneck. Examples of this are transoceanic cables and last-mile residential wiring. Because the fixed cost is so high, it makes sense to greatly overengineer the bandwidth based on current requirements to allow for future growth in traffic.

> **Support for Multicast**   *Multicast is an important mechanism for conserving bandwidth and supporting network control protocols, and should be supported by the network.*
>
> **2C**

Multicast is a service that depends on resource tradeoffs, which will be examined in Example 3.4. It is important to note here that multicast conserves bandwidth on links and through nodes, and reduces processing requirements in end systems by allowing them to transmit only a single copy of data. This comes at the cost of the complexity of implementing support for multicast in network nodes and protocols.

Furthermore, a number of network control mechanisms and protocols rely on multicast for efficient operation, such as network to link layer address translation. Thus, multicast should be supported by local area link protocols and network protocols and nodes.

2.3.3 End-to-End versus Hop-by-Hop

There are two ways in which particular protocol functionality can be implemented: end-to-end (E2E) or hop-by-hop (HBH), as shown in Figure 2.3.

This is a particularly critical issue in determining what functionality goes in the end-to-end transport protocol, versus the hop-by-hop data transfer link protocol, and will be extensively discussed in Chapter 7. We will thus introduce the End-to-End Arguments here, rephrased somewhat from its original form [Saltzer 1981, 1984].

End-to-End Argument   *Functions required by communicating applications can be correctly and completely implemented only with the knowledge and help of the applications themselves. Providing these functions as features within the network itself is not possible.*

3

This argument states that end-to-end services cannot be provided solely by the composition of hop-by-hop services. We might first think that $f = f_1 \circ f_2 \circ f_3$ as shown in Figure 2.3.[10] This is not really the case, since we cannot control

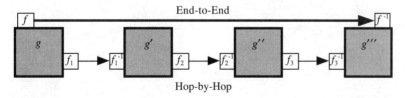

Figure 2.3   End-to-end versus hop-by-hop.

---

[10]Compostition of functions is indicated by the ∘ operator.

what happens between the boundaries of the hops, In reality we have $f = g \circ f_1 \circ g' \circ f_2 \circ g'' \circ f_3 \circ g'''$. A simple example of this is the use of encryption for data confidentiality. This function cannot be performed "in the network," since if the data is in the clear at any point between their end-systems source and destination, there is no confidentiality.

Hop-by-Hop Performance Enhancement Corollary   *It may be beneficial to dupli-cate an end-to-end function hop-by-hop, if doing so results in an overall (end-to-end) improvement in performance.*

                                                                                        3A

Since the end-to-end functionality cannot be provided as a composition of hop-by-hop functionality, it is generally a duplication of functionality, which comes at increased cost and perhaps reduced performance. This is not always the case, however, and functionality that *increases* the end-to-end performance of mechanisms *should* be done hop-by-hop. An example is that while hop-by-hop error control can't replace end-to-end error control, it may lower the probability of end-to-end errors significantly with a reduction in the frequency and latency of end-to-end retransmissions. This situation is the one that is faced, for example, by networks with error-prone wireless links.

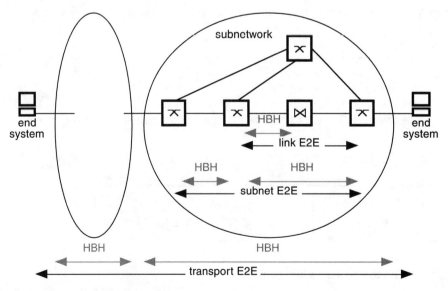

Figure 2.4   Endpoint recursion.

> **Endpoint Recursion Corollary** *What is hop-by-hop in one context may be end-to-end in another. The End-to-End Arguments can be applied recursively to any sequence of nodes in the network, or layers in the protocol stack.*
>
> **3B**

Generally, end-to-end is used in the context of associations between applications on end systems, and it is the transport layer protocol that implements end-to-end functionality. These issues will be considered in detail in Chapter 7. The relative notion of end-to-end (E2E) with respect to hop-by-hop (HBH) does not only apply between end systems, as shown in Figure 2.4.

With respect to the network nodes, flows between switches or routers can be viewed as end-to-end, while links between link repeaters (or bridges) are viewed as hop-by-hop. Similarly, within a network, link protocol functionality is hop-by-hop with respect to the end-to-end network layer. An internetwork consisting of multiple subnets can view each subnetwork layer 3 protocol as hop-by-hop with respect to the entire network. In each of these cases, the question is whether to place functionality end-to-end or hop-by-hop and the next lower layer of recursion.

2.3.4   Protocol Layering

Layering has long been a model for specifying and implementing communications networks; very early protocol suites such as SNA used layered models. The evolution of the layered model resulted from the way communications networks are organized:

1. *Physical layer* for waveforms, bit coding (for example, NRZI), and modulation (for example, QAM) over wire, fiber, or radio[11]

2. *Link layer* for framing and hop-by-hop data assurance across a link (for example, HDLC and SONET[12])

3. *Network layer* for addressing, routing, and signaling among switches, gateways, and routers (for example X.25 IP, and ATM)

4. *Transport layer* for data transfer between end systems (for example TCP and TP4), including end-to-end flow and error control

This layering has the benefit that protocols for a particular layer can be implemented on the components of that layer, without generally affecting the design of protocols or components of other layers. Note that higher-layer *systems* must terminate lower-layer *protocols*, as shown in Figure 2.5.

[11]Non-Return to Zero, Invert on ones and Quadrature Amplitude Modulation.
[12]High-Level Data Link Control and Synchronous Optical NETwork.

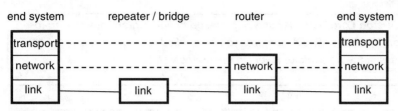

Figure 2.5 Layering based on component type.

The end system terminates the link and network layers in addition to the transport layer; the switch terminates the link layer in addition to the network layer.

Layering provides a useful service abstraction which isolates functionality, allows asynchronous operation, and independent replacement and upgrading of components, whether hardware (as in Figure 2.6) or protocol software. Layering provides a way of structuring systems to avoid monolithic architectures that are difficult to understand, debug, and upgrade.

Protocol Layering Principle   *Layering is a useful abstraction for thinking about networking system architecture and for organizing protocols based on network structure.*

4

This separation of communications protocol functionality is extremely useful, and led to the desire to standardize layer functionality and interfaces. A layered framework for communications protocols was developed, the ISO open systems interconnection (OSI) model [ISO7498], which refined the func-

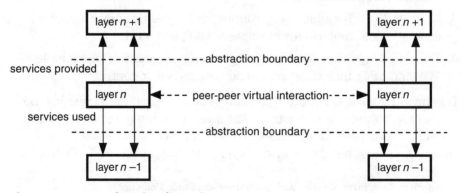

Figure 2.6 Layered service abstractions.

tionality of existing layers and defined additional layers:

5. *Presentation layer* provides reformatting data for heterogenous applications

6. *Session layer* control structure for communication between applications; session management between cooperating applications

7. *Application layer* for applications using communications services

It is critical to understand layering from three different perspectives:

- As an *abstraction* to think about network design and architecture

- As an *architectural division of protocols* based on the functional requirements of network components, network topology, end systems, and applications

- As a *mechanism for implementation* of protocol functionality

Unfortunately, many implementers of the OSI specification confused these three aspects, in particular protocol *specification* and *mechanism*. The OSI layered structure is shown in Figure 2.7.

There are two types of information flows:

Peer-to-peer protocols, which specify the data encapsulation (header and trailer) into protocol data units (PDUs) as well as the format of control messages. These are shown as dotted lines in Figure 2.5. Each PDU consists of a header, payload, and optional trailer. For example, we use TH

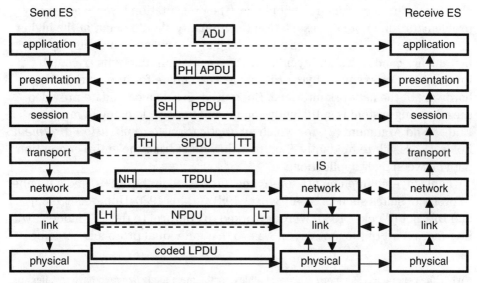

Figure 2.7 OSI protocol layers and data units.

for transport header, TT for transport trailer,13 and TPDU for transport PDU. Each layer has a protocol specification and packet format that is completely independent of the layers above and below it.

Inter-layer calls, which specify the inter-layer flows as data is passed up and down the protocol stack. For example, a network layer PDU (NPDU) is passed to the link layer, which generates and encloses the NPDU payload by a link header (LH) and link trailer (LT), forming a link PDU (LPDU). As PDUs flow up the protocol stack, the corresponding headers and trailers are stripped and processed. Thus, Figure 5.4 shows a sending ES (end system) passing PDUs down its stack, and then sends data out the physical medium. Each layer 3 IS (intermediate system—switch or router) receives the packet, pushes it up to the network layer for processing, and then back down the stack to be sent to the next hop. Finally, the receive ES pushes the PDUs up the stack so that the application receives the APDU. If there are layer-2 components, such as bridges or multiplexors, there is a similar flow, but only up to the link layer.

The first observation is that there are many individual steps in passing data between communications applications. The "obvious" way to implement these layers in the end system was to have a process per layer, with each process performing the encapsulation/decapsulation and processing for its corresponding layer. IPC (interprocess communication) was used to copy PDUs between protocol processes. This follows naturally to a specification that treats individual layers as asynchronous protocol engines.

It is also important to consider carefully where in the architectural hierarchy that a particular function should go. The presentation layer is especially problematic, and not all presentation functionality should occur at the higher layers. While functions such as natural language translation and display formatting are candidates for layer 6, some presentation functions are much lower level. For example, byte ordering is a candidate for implementation in hardware at the network interface. Encryption is also a candidate provided the operating system is sufficiently secure and trusted, keeping in mind the End-to-End Argument (3), for which an *application-to-application argument* holds. Users will redundantly encrypt if they don't trust the entire encryption path between their applications.

Highly layered implementations came into vogue in the 1980s, and a number of protocol suites such as SNA [Cypser 1981, Atkins 1980, Hoberecht 1980] and DECnet [Wecker 1980] were reworked to conform to the OSI model layer interfaces. Part of the motivation was so that individual protocols could be-

---

13While the general case supports trailers at all layers, the most likely layers to have a trailer are the transport and link layers.

come ISO standards within the layered framework, as well as jumping on the anticipated OSI bandwagon.

This leads to extraordinarily inefficient protocol processing, for reasons discussed in detail in Chapter 5. It also resulted in a general revolt in the network research community against layered systems in general for example, [Crowcroft 1992], and the OSI model in particular, just as many vendors were completing OSI based reimplementation (or at least repackaging) of their protocol suites.

It is important to make the distinction between layering as an *abstraction* and protocol *architecture* based on network structure, and as an *implementation* technique in a particular system.

> **Layering as an Implementation Technique Performs Poorly**   *Layered protocol architecture should not be confused with inefficient layer implementation techniques.*
>
> **4A**

This is one of the few places where we will talk about implementation techniques in a design principle. In this case, we need to explicitly state that architectures and protocol specifications must not prescribe inefficient implementations.

It is important to note that we didn't talk about layering in the end-to-end discussion; the End-to-End Argument (3) is independent of protocol layering. Rather, the determination of the protocol division among link, network, and transport layers is based on the structure of networks consisting of links, the collection of network nodes, and end systems, respectively. Thus the relationship between layering and end-to-end principles exists to the degree that particular protocols have end-to-end versus hop-by-hop significance.

> **Redundant Layer Functionality Corollary**   *Functionality should not be included at a layer that must be duplicated at a higher layer, unless there is tangible benefit in doing so.*
>
> **4B**

This corollary is very similar to Hop-by-Hop Performance Enhancement Corollary (3A). In fact, if the higher layer we are talking about is end to end with respect to the lower layer, 3A and 4B are equivalent (for example, transport and link layers). This is not necessarily the case, however. For example, we may be considering end-to-end versus hop-by-hop services that do not correspond to layers at all, such as along subnetwork segments all in the domain of the network layer protocol. Conversely, we may be considering functionality in the application and transport layers, both of which are terminated in the same pairs of end systems.

Now that we have talked about how *not* to design layers, we can begin to consider the principles that *should* be used to provide the benefits of layered abstraction and protocol division.

Layer Synergy Corollary   *When layering is used as a means of protocol division, allowing asynchronous processing and independent data encapsulations, the processing and control mechanisms should not interfere with one another. Protocol data units should translate efficiently between layers.*

4C

While layering allows useful independence between protocol specification, we need to be careful. The data formats and control mechanisms should not interfere with one another to reduce performance. This can actually be quite a challenge. A simple example is that TCP provides a congestion control mechanism called *slow start*, which slowly increases the data rate. This mechanism is targeted toward the traditional best-effort traffic model of the Internet. If TCP is run over a hard connection with QOS guarantees, such as that provided by ATM, slow start limits performance by not initially transmitting at the committed rate. Therefore, it would make sense for TCP to negotiate with the network layer to determine the right options to use. But if the TCP connection runs over concatenated best-effort and hard connection segments, we are left with the least common denominator in end-to-end behavior.

We could imagine picking a base model of behavior to help guide us in compatible layer models, but Resource Tradeoffs Change (2A) tells us that whatever model we choose may be obsolete in the future. To the degree that we do base our decisions on a common model, we should recognize that the network layer is the core, since it provides the global scheme for addressing, routing, and signaling. This leads to the Internet hourglass protocol stack, as shown in Figure 2.8 [Cerf 1983a, Clark 1988, NRC 1994].

Hourglass Corollary   *The network layer provides the convergence of addressing, routing, and signaling that ties the global Internet together. It is essential that addressing be common and that routing and signaling protocols be highly compatible.*

4D

IP is the network layer protocol of the global Internet, with various transport protocols above and link layer protocols below. When other network layers are deployed (such as ATM), they are subnetworks under IP, resulting in stacked layer 3 protocols. While there are occasions when this is necessary,

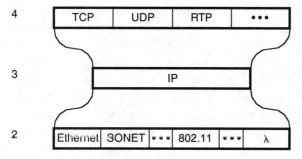

Figure 2.8   Hourglass Internet protocol model.

it is generally inefficient and adds considerable complexity to network control.[14]

An important guideline in implementing layers in a particular component, such as a network node or end system, is to efficiently perform the layer processing. By performing all of the data encapsulations at once, the inefficiencies of interlayer calls are eliminated. We will discuss techniques for integrated layer processing (ILP) in Chapter 6, since the end system must terminate the entire protocol stack.

Integrated Layer Processing (ILP) Corollary   *When multiple layers are generated or terminated in a single component, all encapsulations/decapsulations should be done at once, if possible.*

4E

One of the effects of layering systems is that information in lower layers may be abstracted or hidden to the higher layers. Sometimes this is a good thing; for example, an application does not need to know everything about what is happening at the network layer and have access to all of the link state and routing tables. Sometimes, this can be a bad thing, and we must be careful that layering does not obscure important properties, particularly path characteristics to the application. This particular issue will be discussed in Chapters 5 and 7.

Balance Transparency and Abstraction versus Hiding   *Layering is designed around abstraction, providing a simpler representation of a complicated interface. Abstraction can hide necessary property or parameter, which is not a desirable property of layering.*

4F

---

[14]IP was originally conceived as an *inter*network protocol *intended* to run over heterogeneous network layers. The protocol stack in [Cerf 1983a] shows distinct internetwork and network layers. Sometimes, the internetwork layer was called *layer 3.5* in this context.

The interface mechanism between layers should also be flexible, and chosen with high-performance in mind. In the case of protocol layering in an end system, this can frequently be an optimization of the protocol stack with some isolation between the network and applications. However, in the case of the interface between the higher-layer protocols (transport and session) and application, it is critical to provide a range of interfaces, so that applications can choose the one that optimizes performance. In some cases multiple interface types should be simultaneously provided at a given interface, for example, synchronous and asynchronous.

> **Support a Variety of Interface Mechanisms**   *A range of interlayer interface mechanisms should be provided as appropriate for performance optimization: synchronous and asynchronous and interrupt-driven and polled.*
>
> 4G

The provision of both interrupt-driven and polled asynchronous support is particularly important. Interrupt-driven interfaces are critical when asynchronous notification from below is required, particularly at infrequent or unpredictable intervals. The servicing of interrupts comes at considerable overhead, however. When information can be periodically requested (and is in a stable location), polled interfaces can eliminate the interrupt service overhead.

> **Interrupt versus Polling**   *Interrupts provide the ability to react to asynchronous events, but are expensive operations. Polling can be used when a protocol has knowledge of when information arrives.*
>
> 4H

Finally, interfaces between layers should be designed for scalability. We need to plan for bandwidth, latency, number of end systems, and number of network nodes to scale over many orders of magnitude. Address fields need to have enough bits to account for this, and parameters that range over many orders of magnitude need both precision multiplier and order-of-magnitude exponent fields.

> **Interface Scalability Corollary**   *Interlayer interfaces should support the scalability of the network and parameters transferred among the application, protocol stack, and network components.*
>
> 4I

EXAMPLE 2.1: ATM AND THE REVENGE OF LAYERED SYSTEMS

In spite of the knowledge that highly layered implementations were a bad thing, and that ATM was supposed to support high-performance communications, that is exactly what has happened with ATM systems. ATM grew out of research into fast packet switching, as will be described in Chapters 3, 4, and 5, and is a complete layer 3 protocol, including addressing, routing, and signaling.[15] However, since much of the world already ran applications designed for TCP over deployed IP networks (as well as SNA and X.25), the dream that ATM would become the global information infrastructure never came to fruition.

On the other hand, ATM networks were widely deployed due to their ability to provide a high bandwidth switched backbone. Due to the extremely small ATM cell size (48-byte payload + 5-byte header), there was already an adaptation layer to segment and reassemble application frames (this is essentially a sublayer just below the transport layer).

The result of this is an IP over ATM kludge, as shown in Figure 2.9. (The cell headers are depicted by 0 or 1, indicating the SDU type; Example 5.4 shows the format of ATM cells.) Since ATM was designed as a fully functional network layer that would replace existing layer 3 protocols, no attempt was made for packet formats or control mechanisms to be compatible with the TCP/IP protocol suite (or any other). Thus, not only are there 5 layers handling transport, network, and link functionality, but they are extremely incompatible in encapsulation and control mechanisms. Understanding the inefficiencies of TCP/IP over ATM has been the subject of much analysis, for example, [Moldklev 1994, Romanow 1994].

Similarly, the entertainment video sector uses MPEG-2 to stream video-on-demand content, and the MPEG (motion picture experts group) defined a set of transport layer protocols (MPEG transport stream) and connection management schemes (DSM-CC) not very compatible with anything else.

2.3.5   State and Hierarchy

One of the critical issues in high-speed network and protocol design is how to manage the state on which decisions are based. State is used to determine the routing and QOS given to flows of packets, and is critical in end-to-end flow

---

[15]In spite of those who claim that ATM is a link layer in the context of IP over ATM; in this case IP is a network layer operating over *another* network layer for which its own addressing, routing, and signaling mechanisms are redundant or underused.

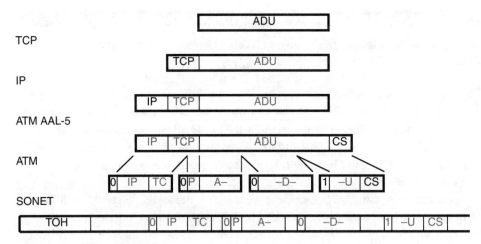

Figure 2.9   TCP/IP over ATM.

and error control. There are a range of possibilities that vary between approximate coarse-grained state and accurate fine-grained state, and we must make tradeoffs between them.

State Management Principle   *The mechanisms for installation and management of state should be carefully chosen to balance fast, approximate, and coarse-grained against slow, accurate, and fine-grained.*

5

We will refine this tradeoff in the following corollaries and tradeoffs, but the theme for high-speed networks will be that the ability to make quick decisions is as important as the accuracy of the state information. This is particularly true if bandwidth is cheap enough to overengineer the network to compensate for the suboptimality, as described in the Optimal Resources Utilization versus Overengineering Tradeoff (2B).

We will consider three degrees of state in the following discussion:

Stateless. No state is maintained; decisions are made instantaneously based on the information available, with no memory for future decisions.

Soft state. State is installed when conditions warrant, and is removed after a period of time for which the state is unused. Soft state must be continuously refreshed.

Hard state. State is explicitly installed by signaling and remains until explicitly removed.

The advantage of hard state is that once that state is installed, decisions can be made quickly based on precomputed values, such as the output port for a particular connection identifier. The disadvantage is that it takes time to set up the state, and if a node fails, recovery is more difficult. State inconsistencies (which can be introduced by a number of error scenarios) persist until explicitly repaired. Furthermore, if state is not properly removed, it can accumulate and require garbage collection mechanisms to determine when stale state has been inadvertently left in place. On the opposite end of the spectrum, stateless systems do not require that state be installed before data can flow, but decisions must be made for every data unit. Thus we have a tradeoff.

Hard State versus Soft State versus Stateless Tradeoff   *Balance the tradeoff between the latency to set up hard state on a per connection basis versus the per data unit overhead of making stateless decisions or of establishing and maintaining soft state.*

5A

If the data flow is long, then the overhead of state establishment amortized over the life of the data flow is insignificant; but if the flow is a short transaction, the overhead may be unreasonable, particularly in a wide area network. There are various middle grounds to install soft state and to send data opportunistically in parallel with state installation. Properly designed soft state systems have the advantage of stability, self-repair, and removal of stale state information. The middle ground is generally preferable to either extreme, as is usually the case for tradeoffs.

The other important consideration is the granularity of the state maintained: whether it is very fine grained (for example, per flow) or aggregated into larger units.

Aggregation and Reduction of State Transfer   *Aggregation of state reduces the amount of information stored. Reducing the rate at which state information is propagated through the network reduces bandwidth and processing at network nodes, which comes at the expense of finer-grained control with more precise information.*

5B

As an example, core backbone network nodes may have millions of flows passing through them at a time. If routing and traffic management were handled on a per flow basis, the amount of memory needed to store the information would be excessively expensive. Furthermore, the ability to extract the per flow state per packet at line rate would be extremely difficult. Aggregating flows into traffic classes and forwarding classes significantly decreases the cost and increases the performance of the core backbone.

Mechanisms that can be used to abstract and reduce the amount of state information moving through the network include:

Temporal abstraction of state information, which consists of aggregating state over the life of a larger granularity, for example, per connection or flow rather than per packet, or over a long-lived sequence of flows.

Spatial abstraction of state information, which consists of aggregating state over a set of network nodes or applications; this comes at the expense of fine-grained precision and control of the individual nodes or applications.

Frequency reduction of state information distribution, either by lengthening the period, or increasing the importance of an event or threshold of change that triggers updates.

Limiting extent of distribution, for example, the distance that state updates propagate.

Compression of state information.

An important technique that combines some of these mechanisms is to abstract information into a hierarchy of clusters in the network.

> **Hierarchy Corollary**   *Use hierarchy and clustering to manage complexity by abstracting and aggregating information to higher levels and to isolate the effects of changes within clusters.*
>
> **5C**

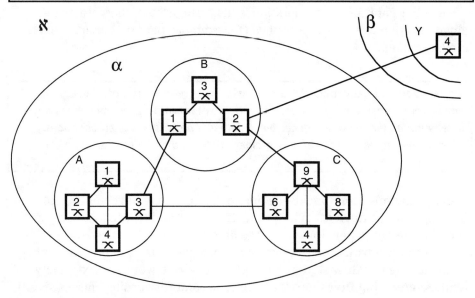

Figure 2.10   Hierarchical clustering.

Figure 2.10 shows an example of hierarchical clustering. Nodes are grouped into clusters in a multilevel hierarchy. For examples, nodes 1, 2, 3, and 4 in the bottom left are part of cluster A, which is part of 2nd level cluster α, which is part of 3rd level cluster א. At the lowest level, there is complete information among the peer nodes, but as we proceed up, the hierarchy state is abstracted. So, for example, while node א.α.A.2 has full state on the other nodes in cluster א.α.A, it only has aggregate state information on the nodes in clusters א.α.B and א.α.C. Similarly, as a part of second-level cluster א.α, it has no information about the node in the top left corner, except the state aggregated at the א.β level. Clustering will be most important when considering network topology and architecture, and will be revisited in Chapter 3.

Scope of Information Tradeoff *Make quick decisions based on local information when possible. Even if you try to make a better decision with more detailed global state, by the time the information is collected and filtered, the state of the network may have changed.*

5D

In high-speed networks it is critical to make decisions quickly, due to the high bandwidth-×-delay product. There are so many bits in flight through the network path that if decisions require round trips to the edge of the network or collecting large amounts of global state, the conditions that triggered the need for the decision may well have gone away before the decision is made. This is generally due to the dynamic bursty nature of application traffic. If nodes are also mobile, dynamic topology shifts the tradeoff even further to the need to make quick ap proximate decisions.

Assumed Initial Conditions *Use reasonable assumptions based on past history or related association to establish initial conditions for the installation of new state.*

5E

When new state is installed, some information may be explicitly supplied by the establishment mechanism. For example, parameters of a connection SETUP message may provide sufficient information to fully establish the state. In many cases, however, state accumulates or evolves over time; this is particularly the case for soft-state mechanisms. Initial conditions can be assumed based on past history or other similar state. For example, the parameters applied to a soft-state flow can be based on parameters recently used for a similar flow between the same pair of endpoints. This can significantly reduce the time to steady state, as discussed in Section 7.2.2.

Minimize Control Overhead   *The purpose of a network is to carry application data. The processing and transmission overhead introduced by control mechanisms should be kept as low as possible to maximize the fraction of network resources available for carrying application data.*

5F

Control mechanisms distribute state and other information among network nodes and end systems. The overhead of control messages represent a "tax" on the data-carrying capacity of the network; every control message sent from one node to another potentially displaces or delays a data message. An important design goal for high-speed networks is therefore to minimize control overhead.

2.3.6 Control Mechanisms

Control messages are used to distribute state through the network, to establish and modify paths, and to convey information among network nodes and end systems. It is essential that control mechanisms operate efficiently on a time scale commensurate with the rate at which the network changes, so that current state is available when and where it is needed. This requires both low latency for the transmission of control messages among network nodes and rapid convergence of distributed control algorithms to a consistent shared state.

Furthermore, data transmission frequently relies on control message exchanges to establish session, connection, or flow state. The latency of message exchanges must be bounded such that application service requirements are met.

Control Mechanism Latency Principle   *Effective network control depends on the availability of accurate and current information. Control mechanisms must operate within convergence bounds that are matched to the rate of change in the network and latency bounds to provide low interapplication delay.*

6

The following corollaries provide a set of refinements that indicate the different ways in which latency can be controlled in the exchange of control information and convergence of state.

> **Minimize Round Trips**   *Structure control messages and the information they convey to minimize the number of round trips required to accomplish data transfer.*
>
> **6A**

Control message exchanges should be structured to minimize the number of traversals through the network. The overriding goal is to reduce the number of round-trips between end systems and network resources that are required before a useful exchange of data can occur. In many cases, the number of round-trips can be reduced to 1 for a request/response sequence and 0.5 for a sender initiated transfer of data.

There are a number of techniques that can be brought to bear to reduce message transfer, which include the use of hop-by-hop acknowledgments, ranges of parameters for negotiation, and the overlap of control and data:

Hop-by-hop acknowledgments. Three-way handshakes are necessary for the reliable establishment of sessions and connections, but are a significant source of latency, since a SETUP/CONNECT/ACK message sequence must be exchanged before data can flow. Similarly a RELEASE/ RELEASED/ACK message sequence must occur before a connection is torn down; this is important in the case of reserved resources that must be released before another connection can be established. Conventionally, these messages have end-to-end (E2E) significance, as shown in Figure 2.11a.

Note that if a message is lost (SETUP along the first hop in Figure 2.11a), the sender has no way of knowing this until a timer t_{RTT} expires, indicating when the connection request *should* have been acknowledged from the destination.

By issuing acknowledgment messages on a hop-by-hop (HBH) basis for the essential end-to-end messages (PROCEEDING for SETUP and ACK for CONNECT) latency may be significantly reduced, as shown in Figure 2.11b. A timer t_{HBH} is run at each hop which is likely to be considerably shorter than t_{E2E}. This is particularly important in unreliable networks in which control messages may be dropped (for example, wireless) and in highly loaded networks where the probability of connection blocking is high (ameliorated by the next technique).

Parameter ranges. When control exchanges are used to negotiate path characteristics or end-system capabilities before a session, connection, or flow can be established, it is critical that the number of end-to-end message exchanges be minimized. If a single set of parameters is sent with the path SETUP message, the *first* network node along the path that cannot support the resources needed will REJECT the path establishment attempt. This introduces several problems. If the REJECT message

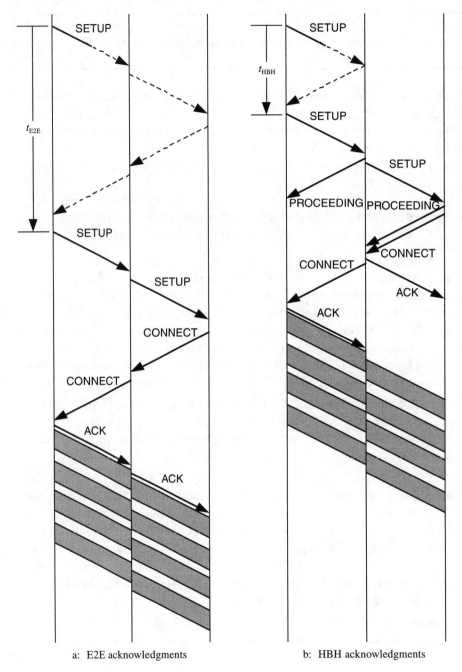

a: E2E acknowledgments   b: HBH acknowledgments

Figure 2.11   Hop-by-hop acknowledgments.

doesn't return the resource bound that could have been seized, the initiating system can only guess at what the next attempt should be. But even if the REJECT message does contain a resource bound, the sending system has no idea of whether this bound has changed in a dynamic network, or what resources *subsequent* nodes along the path can support, or whether the destination end system has the required capabilities. Thus, in loaded network, a series of attempts may be necessary before a session association or connection path can be established, involving multiple round-trips, as shown in Figure 2.12a.

A key technique is to provide a *range* of parameters that can be incrementally negotiated, or in the case of parameters that cannot be expressed as a numerical range, alternate parameter sets. This allows each hop along the path to adjust the parameters to meet its capabilities, as shown in Figure 2.12b. In this example, the first node reduces the resource request to 8, and the receiving end system to 5, which is returned in the acknowledgment. The request is denied only in the case that the minimum value of a range or all parameters of a set (for example, content-type encoding) cannot be met along the entire path.

Overlap of control and data. A final technique to reduce the number of round-trip times is to *overlap* the establishment messages with data transfer. There are a number of specific applications of this technique. In the case of sender-initiated transfer, data can be optimistically sent before acknowledgments have returned; this is described in Section 4.1.4. In the case of request/response (particularly transactions), the request information can be appended to the SETUP message; this is described in Section 7.2.2.

Exploit Local Knowledge   *Control should be exerted by the entity that has the knowledge needed to do so directly and efficiently.*

6B

Control should be exerted by the entity that has sufficient knowledge of conditions to be able to most directly exert the desired control, without multiple control relays and message exchanges to other nodes. For example, redirection of a request to a Web cache is best handled by the entity that knows how to locate the cache. In the case of a well-advertised static cache infrastructure, the client browser may have this information and most efficiently direct the request. In the case of dynamic active caching, nodes deep within the network may be the only ones with sufficient knowledge to redirect the request.

When state is distributed throughout the network, techniques that cache or continuously update distributed information can relieve the need for nodes to request and wait for control information.

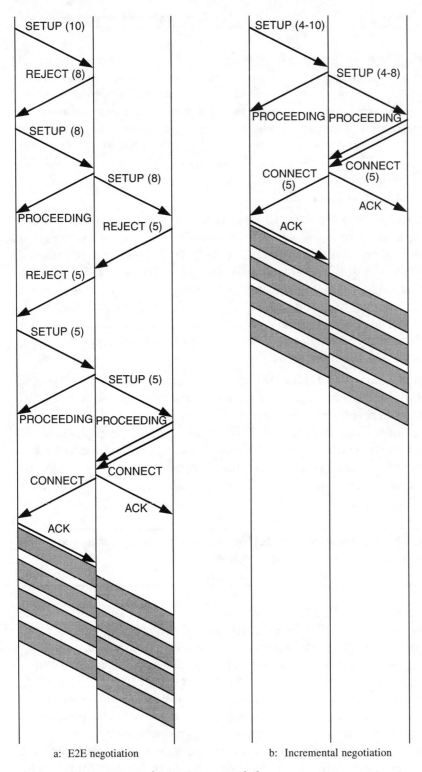

a: E2E negotiation   b: Incremental negotiation

Figure 2.12   Incremental parameter negotiation.

> **Anticipate Future State**   *Anticipate future state so that actions can be taken proactively before repair needs to be performed on the network that affects application performance.*
>
> **6C**

Anticipation of future network state is an important technique to reduce the latency penalty of reacting to conditions after the fact. The canonical example is congestion avoidance. By anticipating impending congestion, control can be exerted which minimizes loss and prevents congestion collapse. Reacting to congestion after it has happened can take many round-trips to recover and for applications to again transfer useful data. The interval of anticipation should be sufficient to account for reaction time of individual nodes, as well as the time to propagate control messages to the node or end systems that need to be controlled.

> **Open- versus Closed-Loop Control**   *Use open-loop control based on knowledge of the network path to reduce the delay in closed-loop convergence. Use closed-loop control to react to dynamic network and application behavior.*
>
> **6D**

Control can be based on either open-loop or closed-loop feedback. Open-loop control relies on state installed in the sender to regulate behavior, as shown in Figure 2.13a. Open-loop control is based on some a priori knowledge of the network path characteristics such as bandwidth, latency, and loss rates. Note that *open-loop* is the standard control theoretic term although there is no loop at all. Open loop is derived from "opening" a closed loop such that there is no feedback.

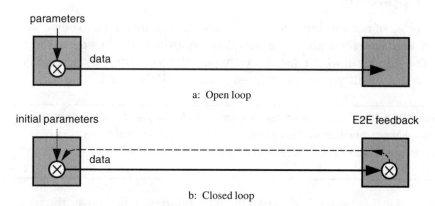

Figure 2.13   Open- and closed-loop feedback control.

Closed-loop feedback control depends on ongoing feedback from the network layer protocols and components to adjust the behavior of the sender, as shown in Figure 2.13b. Closed-loop control is most commonly exerted end-to-end by transport protocols. End-to-end control mechanisms are discussed in depth in Chapter 7.

Separate Control Mechanisms   *Control mechanisms should be distinct, or the information conveyed explicit enough, so that the proper action is taken.*

                                                                                        6E

There are a number of distinct, but interacting, control mechanisms that apply to network at a variety of levels: overall network topology and structure, paths between communicating end systems, and individual network nodes. While it is impossible to completely separate them, it is essential that they are distinct enough to convey the proper information to the entities under control. Implicit information is subject to misinterpretation, which can result in the wrong actions being taken. The consequences of this improper reaction can result in multiple round-trips to infer the action that *should* have been taken, and at worst making conditions in the network *worse*. For example, inferring congestion by packet loss is efficient only if congestion is the *only* source of loss. If losses are caused by an error-prone wireless channel, for example, the proper response is to retransmit or increase the level of FEC, both of which increase the offered load. If congestion is the source of loss, however, increasing the offered load can drive the network into saturation and congestion collapse.

It is therefore important to separate mechanisms where practical, and explicitly convey information necessary to exert proper control.

2.3.7   Distribution of Application Data

While the point of networking is to allow distributed applications to communicate, there is frequently flexibility in how data is partitioned and where data is located. The manner in which distributed applications partition and exchange data can have a significant effect on Interapplication Delay (I.2).

Distributed Data Principle   *Distributed applications should select and organize the data they exchange to minimize the amount of data transferred and the latency of transfer and allow incremental processing of data.*

                                                                                        7

We can divide this principle into two main corollaries, which cover the way in which application data is partitioned and structured and the location of data for low latency access.

> **Partitioning and Structuring of Data**   *Whenever possible, data should be partitioned and structured to minimize the amount of data transferred and the latency in communication.*
>
> **7A**

By properly partitioning data, the amount of data that needs to be transferred can be minimized. Furthermore the way in which application data is divided affects the latency of access. Sometimes these two factors must be balanced. For example, larger data transfers may result in data being properly located without the latency of additional request/response loops.

Data that is structured to be incrementally processed can also result in lower latency. For example, to meet 100-ms interactive response bounds, Web browsers should be able to process data in small enough chunks that an initial screen can be displayed, even before an entire long page is fetched.

> **Location of Data**   *Data should be positioned close to the application that needs it to minimize the latency of access. Replication of data helps to accomplish this.*
>
> **7B**

By locating (or maintaining a copy of) data close to where it is needed, the access latency can be reduced. Many of the techniques introduced in Section 2.4 and described in Chapter 8 exploit this principle, such as caching and prefetching.

2.3.8   Protocol Data Units

Given a particular Partitioning and Structuring of Data (7A) previously described, distributed applications communicate by exchanging this data. The size and structure of the protocol data units (PDUs) and the control fields that identify them is an important contributor to the ability to process efficiently and maximize the throughput of the data. This in turn allows us to optimize Bandwidth and Latency (I.3): Latency is minimized since the data is structured to reduce the processing time, and bandwidth is maximized since the number of PDUs processed per unit time is increased.

> **Protocol Data Unit Principle**   *The size and structure of PDUs are critical to high-bandwidth, low-latency communication.*
>
> **8**

We can subdivide this principle into three corollaries that relate to the size and granularity of the PDUs that traverse the network, the organization of PDU headers and trailers, and the ability to scale with performance.

> **PDU Size and Granularity**   *The size of PDUs is a balance of a number of parameters that affect performance. Trade the statistical multiplexing benefits of small packets against the efficiency of large packets.*
>
> **8A**

The size and structure of PDUs have a profound influence on the ability for network nodes to process at high rates and on overall application and network performance. Frequently, local and global optimizations are at odds with one another. Important factors include PDU size, whether PDUs are fixed in size or are of variable length, and the range over which they can vary.

Small PDUs allow finer control of delay and greater multiplexing efficiency, but challenge the ability for nodes and end systems to process them at high rate due to the short interarrival time. Large PDUs are more efficient due to less header overhead, but can interfere with other flows making it difficult to provide service to real-time and interactive applications. Furthermore, while fixed size packets allow simpler switch design, it comes at the expense of less flexibility, the difficulty of choosing the optimum packet size, and the overhead of fragmentation and reassembly. These issues will be introduced in Section 2.4.5 and discussed in detail in Section 5.3.3.

> **PDU Control Field Structure**   *Optimize PDU header and trailer fields for efficient processing. Fields should be simply encoded, byte aligned, and fixed length when possible. Variable length fields should be prepended with their length.*
>
> **8B**

The goal is to simplify the processing of control structures. In the case of software implementation, the number of instructions to parse, decode, and generate PDU headers and trailers can be considerably reduced. In the case of hardware implementation, the complexity of the logic elements that decode and generate PDU headers and trailers can be significantly simplified.

Byte alignment and simple encoding facilitate this. In the case of multibit fields, their isolation allows independent processing. In the case of flags, bit vectors are less complex to process than highly encoded codepoints. It is frequently worth sacrificing compactness of fields for efficiency in processing. This tradeoff must be carefully considered in every case.

Fixed-length fields are simpler to process, and allow templates for headers and trailers to be stored in memory and manipulated in hardware. The processing of variable-length fields can be considerably more complex, and require time-consuming buffer management schemes to deal with changing field size. In the case of fields that are only occasionally needed, well-defined *option subheaders* can be use. In the case where there is a compelling reason to make a field a variable length, a length field or pointer should be provided to easily locate the next field without complex pattern hunting.

Scalability of Control Fields   *PDU header and trailer fields and structure should be scalable with data rate and bandwidth-×-delay product.*

8C

It is just as important to support future application demands as current ones. This means that we need to be concerned that protocols and mechanisms scale with bandwith, and the resulting increase in bandwidth-×-delay product. There are a number of PDU control fields whose length is related to bandwidth, latency, and the bandwidth-×-delay product. For example, timers need to have enough bits to account for RTT. Sequence numbers need to have enough bits to ensure uniqueness as the bandwidth-×-delay product increases. The protocol mechanisms and corresponding header fields should be either insensitive to data rate or be designed to explicitly scale (as for example, SONET). A concrete example of these issues will be presented in Example 7.9.

2.4   Design Techniques

This section introduces the most important general techniques that will be used to guide the architecture and design of high-speed networks in the subsequent chapters, subject to the principles described in the previous section.

2.4.1   Scaling Time and Space

Recall that our primary goal is to reduce Interapplication Delay (I.1). There are two obvious ways to achieve this:

1. Speed up the clock so that data are processed and transferred at a higher rate; this is the bandwidth component of a high-performance path.

2. Move communicating applications and data closer together so that the latency of the transfer due to the speed of light is reduced. This is the main latency component of a high-performance path over long distances.

To some degree, we can do both of these, and in fact we do the first one all the time. As individual technologies improve and new technologies appear, the clock rate of end systems and network nodes continually increases. If we could *uniformly* speed up all the components of a system by increasing the clock rate, we would be done, and not need the rest of this book [Partridge 1990a].

There are two problems with this approach, however. The first problem is that while technology is improving, it is not improving uniformly, and we have noted that Resource Tradeoffs Change (2A). The second and more important problem is that we would have to speed up everything, including the velocity of data transmission between communicating applications. Clearly, the Speed of Light (III.1) prevents this, putting clear limits on the ability to scale performance with clock rate, particularly in wide area networks. If we could reduce the distance that data must travel correspondingly, we could achieve the same effect. Short of putting unreasonable constraints on applications, we cannot do this directly.

2.4.2   Cheating and Masking the Speed of Light

While we can't reduce the speed-of-light latency or demand that communicating applications be close to one another, we can use some techniques to mask the effect of geographic distribution. These will be discussed in more detail in Chapter 8.

2.4.2.1   Prediction

Prediction consists of running predictive algorithms locally to predict remote behavior and reduce the need for high-latency synchronization operations to update state. This can consist of predicting application state to improve the effective interapplication delay. It can also be used by the network itself to predict the behavior of other nodes and the network in aggregate to improve the stability and accuracy of routing and traffic information. Finally, in the case of mobile nodes, motion prediction can be used to more quickly adapt routing to dynamic network configurations.

2.4.2.2   Caching and Mirroring

Mirroring consists of geographically distributing copies of information to reduce the latency of access and reduce aggregate bandwidth in the network. Caching is the dynamic version of mirroring, and is typically demand driven, that is, data is cached when accessed on the assumption that it will be needed again, or in the cases of network caches, by someone else near by. Caches may also be preloaded with content that is expected to have frequent access.

2.4.2.3   Prefetching and Presending

Prefetching and presending exploit locality in data-referencing behavior; when a particular piece of data is used, related data is fetched in anticipation that it will also be needed. Spatial locality fetches adjacent data, such as all of the other files in a directory or other virtual memory pages in a segment. Temporal locality fetches data by following a reference chain, for example, virtual memory pages in the instruction sequence or by following HTML links in web pages.

2.4.2.4 *Autonomy*

By increasing the ability of systems to operate autonomously, we may reduce their reliance on latency-critical information. This still may require periodic resynchronizations as in the case of predictive algorithms.

2.4.2.5 *Code Mobility*

In some cases it is more efficient to dynamically move modules of executable program code to reduce the interprocess communication (IPC) bandwidth and latency. For example, it is more efficient for a Web browser to download a Java applet that performs interactive graphics manipulations than to exchange a long series of messages across a high-latency link. The Scope of Information Tradeoff (5D) guides us in making a decision.

2.4.3 Specialized Hardware Implementation

One of the standard techniques to increase performance is to implement a function in custom hardware rather than as software on a general-purpose processor. While this may speed up a particular function, it comes at substantial cost and must be done with care. A restatement of Functional Partitioning and Assignment Corollary (1C) in this context indicates that putting a particular function in hardware does not necessarily speed up the entire system, and may be done at the expense of more important optimizations.

2.4.4 Parallelism and Pipelining

Parallelism and overlap in processing provide a way to increase the throughput of a system, which in our case translates to increased bandwidth. Any parallel decomposition requires an understanding of the dependencies of operations on one another. This can be done by creating a partially ordered dependency graph [Feldmeier 1993].

An example graph is shown in Figure 2.14 for some functions that might be performed at a receiving end system. This partial order indicates that the decryption must come before data decompression, but that error detection can occur in parallel with the other sequence of operations.

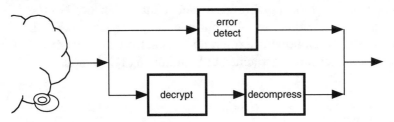

Figure 2.14   Protocol dependencies.

2.4.4.1   Parallel Operations

The simplest form of parallelism is to duplicate function and run in parallel. This can be done when a bit-serial communication link is considerably faster than the ability of a network node or end system to perform operations at link rate. This simplest form of parallelism is in fact done all the time, by converting between bit-serial links and byte wide paths within nodes and end systems, providing an easy 8:1 speedup factor.

Larger-grained parallelism can be considered, for example, packet parallel or connection/flow parallel processing. Such parallelism can be implemented in either hardware or software. Hardware implementation suffers from a cost-scaling problem: as we implement n-parallel functionality on the network interface, the cost goes up by a factor of at least n. We very quickly exceed Cost and Economic Feasibility (III.4), and such schemes are difficult to manage and control even for small n. This is not to say that this sort of parallelism should not be considered, but it must be judiciously applied. Generally, pipelining, described later, is a better technique since it decomposes and specializes processing, rather than duplicating it.

Software parallelism must also be considered very carefully. When protocol processing is parallelized on a uniprocessor, for example, a conventional end system, the parallelism is likely to degrade performance. Since we have only a single processor, operations are happening concurrently, but not simultaneously, and we have added the overhead and complexity of interoperation communication and synchronization. We will discuss these issues in detail for end systems in Chapter 6.

2.4.4.2   Pipelining

A standard technique for speedup in high-performance systems is to pipeline operations. By dividing an operation into an n-stage pipeline, n data units can simultaneously occupy the pipeline for a speedup of n times over monolithic implementation. Pipelining is particularly applicable where a common sequence of specialized operations is applied, which are amenable to hardware implementation. An example 5-stage pipeline is shown in Figure 2.15a. At each time step, a packet is shifted into the pipeline, and the packets already in the pipe are shifted to the next stage in lock step. This means the slowest stage is the bottleneck dictating the pipeline clock cycle time. In the case that one function is significantly longer than others, attempts should be made to divide it into multiple sequential steps; we have done so in the example by dividing f_2 into two stages f_{2a} and f_{2b}.

Figure 2.15b shows the overlap in processing as packets flow through the pipeline. Pipelining can be implemented at various granularities of data unit, although we have shown packet-level granularity in the example. If packets are large and variable in size, then a smaller granularity is preferable, temporarily fragmenting the packet while it travels through the pipeline. The degree of functional decomposition can also vary, from high-level functions, such as checksum and encryption, to fine-grained implementation of these functions.

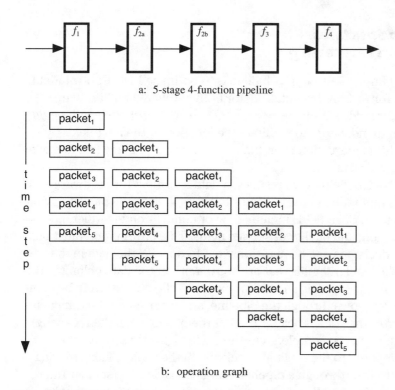

a: 5-stage 4-function pipeline

b: operation graph

Figure 2.15   Pipelined processing.

Some functions are easy to pipeline, some are considerably more challenging, and the capability to apply pipelining to a particular situation depends on the ability to match data granularity with the decomposition of pipelineable functions.

2.4.4.3 Combination of Techniques

We can combine various parallelization techniques as practical. Indeed, the example of Figure 2.10 indicates that a pipelined implementation of this graph might have two parallel branches.

2.4.5 Data Structure Optimization

There are a number of implementation techniques that dictate how protocol data units (PDUs) should be structured for high-speed networks, guided by the Protocol Data Unit Principle (8). We are concerned with data structures amenable to processing by high-performance components, as well as minimizing the mismatch between network and end-system formats.

2.4.5.1 Data Structures for Fast Processing

The first general implementation technique is to optimize PDU Control Field Structures (8B) for fast implementation, for both software and hardware. Header and trailer fields should be easy to decode, and variable length fields should have length indicators to facilitate the location of the next field. Byte alignment of fields is more important than conservation of a few bits in packet headers and control structures.

The order of control fields with respect to data is critical for hardware pipelines. Fields that indicate the behavior to be *applied* to the packet payload belong in the header. Such fields include flow or connection identifier, addressing information, and quality of service fields. This information must be decoded before decisions can be made on what to do with the data in the payload following the header. Fields that are *dependent* on the data belong in the trailer, such as checksum. This allows, for example, the checksum to be computed as the packet flows through the pipeline, and inserted on the transmitting side, long after the packet header has left the pipeline. On the receiving side, the checksum can be completed as the payload passes through the pipeline and compared to the original checksum in the trailer. This ordering allows a packet to flow through a pipeline that is considerably smaller than the packet length; violating this ordering requires that the entire packet be available for the duration of processing.

In the case that a protocol specification does not adhere to this ordering, there are ways to compensate. An intermediate wrapper consisting of the proper ordering of fields can be placed around the PDU for fast processing. For example, TCP, which has a header checksum, can be wrapped with an internal trailer with a copy of the checksum for processing by high-speed pipelined host–network interfaces.

2.4.5.2 *Packet Size*

PDU Size and Granularity (8A) is a critical issue that impacts performance in a number of places, and balancing these local optima to determine optimal packet size is extraordinarily difficult. In the context of this discussion, we are concerned with the *minimum* packet size. The smaller the PDU, the smaller the packet interarrival time, which results in less time to make control decisions for a particular packet before the next one arrives. The packet processing rate (packets per second) is a performance measure directly tied to packet size. Extremely large packets (frequently called *jumbograms*) allow control decisions to be made at relatively low performance. As the packet size decreases, these decisions must be moved from general-purpose processors, to high-speed embedded controllers, to fast specialized hardware. Furthermore, the smaller network packets are with respect to application data units, the more overhead is consumed on fragmenting and reassembling them. These issues will be discussed in more detail in Chapters 5 and 6.

If packets are fixed sizes (for example, ATM cell), they should be a power-of-2 bytes in length to fit well in standard memory chips in network node and host interface buffers. If they are variable size, the maximum should not be just over the power-of-2 size. This results in a decision on whether the entire packet or just the payload should be sized this way (the former is better for network nodes and the latter for end systems). A reasonable compromise is to size both header/trailer and payload as powers of 2, for example, 128B payload + 16B header. In this case the control information can be split and stored in separate memory. It is important to consider the control structures as well as the data in determining packet size.

Fragmentation and reassembly are inefficient and should be avoided [Kent 1987]. Multiplexing is also inefficient, and layered multiplexing should be avoided [Tennenhouse 1989].

2.4.5.3 *Matching End-System and Network Formats*

Another challenging problem is matching PDU structure to the somewhat different requirements of network nodes and end systems. Fixed size packets are better for some switch designs, as discussed in Section 5.3.3. However the

EXAMPLE 2.2: ATM CELL SIZE AND FORMAT

ATM provides us with an extraordinary example of how *not* to format and size packets, given that ATM was supposed to be optimal for fast packet switching at high link rates. ATM cells are 53 bytes long: 48 bytes of payload plus 5 bytes of header. Neither of these is a power of 2, and only the payload size is even a multiple of 8. As mentioned before, this was the result of a political compromise by a standards body. The fact that the cell size is so small was dictated by the desire to keep jitter small enough to eliminate the need for echo-cancellation when used to transport voice, and at a particular data rate. That this point-optimization was made reflects the influence that the European telephony community had over the standards process.

The extremely small cell size means that the interarrival time was so short (2.73 μs at OC-3 and 682 ns at OC-12) that it forced control logic to be implemented in VLSI rather than by network interface microcontroller software. This was coupled with an extremely complex interface requiring segmentation and reassembly. This imbalance with the technology of the early 1990s pushed the availability of commodity ATM UNIs (user-network interface) back by a year or two, which allowed time for 100-Mb/s Ethernet to become the technology of choice for LAN deployment.

problem with a fixed size packet is which size should be used, and should it scale with the data rate of the link, perhaps by powers of 2. For example, 40-byte TCP ACKs require 2 ATM cells. Variable size packets are a better match for application data units, but packets that are too large can have detrimental delay and jitter impacts on other flows in the network. Furthermore, even though application data units are variable size, the way in which they are stored in end systems may not be. Pages and cache lines are fixed size, and these may be more important units of granularity in moving data between the end system and network interface.

The encoding of data may be different between the end system and network, and even between communicating end systems; the simplest example of this is incompatible byte ordering within words. So while we will consider the best packet format and size in the context of network node and end systems, we need to be aware that compromises are necessary and that the PDUs should be organized for efficient transformation between the two realms.

2.4.6   Latency Reduction

In Store-and-Forward Avoidance (II.3), we indicated that the store-and-forward and copying of data could be a significant contribution to latency. Two important techniques can be used to avoid this latency hit.

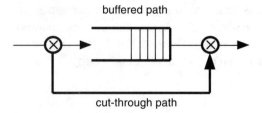

Figure 2.16   Cut-through paths.

2.4.6.1   Cut-Through Paths

In Chapter 5, we will describe fast packet switch architectures that are designed to allow data to flow through without requiring a store-and-forward operation. First-in–first-out (FIFO) buffers are still needed, at the output of the switch and perhaps within the switch elements when there is contention for an outgoing link. When the outgoing path is available, the queue latency can be avoided by providing a cut-though path to bypass the buffer, as shown in Figure 2.16.

2.4.6.2   Remapping

In end systems, one of the predominant datapath delays that we will be concerned with is the copying of data between the network interface and application memory. Copying a block of data requires an instruction loop stepping through

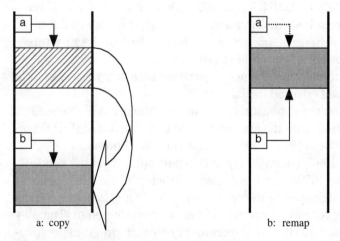

Figure 2.17   Copying versus remapping of data.

the block (or a multiple cycle block transfer instruction), as shown in Figure 2.17a copying from a to b. We can get the same effect by remapping, and manipulating pointers with far less overhead, as shown in Figure 2.17b. In this case, we merely alter the contents of pointer b to have the same effect as a copy.

2.5   Summary

This chapter has laid the foundation for the rest of the book. We have provided a look at the past and toward the future of networking that will be expanded in Chapter 9. We discussed the application motivation for an ideal high-bandwidth, low-latency network, and discussed the constraints that make this difficult to achieve. We then presented the design principles and generic implementation techniques that will be used in subsequent chapters. After recommendations for further reading, a full list of the axioms and principles presented in this chapter is presented.

2.5.1   Further Reading

There are a number of good networking textbooks that provide the background needed for this book, including [Davies 1979] for historical perspective, [Schwartz 1987] and [Bertselcas 1992] for an analytical slant, and [Tannenbaum 1996], [Keshav 1997], [Peterson 1999], [Stallings 2000a], and [Kurose 2000]. For an understanding of the Internet protocol suite, [Comer 1991, 1993, 2000] and [Stevens 1994, 1995, 1996] are comprehensive starting points that should lead to the wealth of online information in Internet RFCs. A history of the Internet from the ARPANET beginnings is given by [Salus 1995] and [Leiner].

In the spirit of the Not Invented Here Corollary (Ø-A and Ø-B), [Piscitello 1993], [Cypser 1991], [Meijer 1982], [Green 1982], [Sunshine 1989], and [Perlman 2000], should be consulted for an understanding of a number of different protocol suites. A comprehensive, accessible understanding of the structure of the U.S. telephone network is provided in [Rey 1983].

An understanding of the art and science of performance analysis is essential and is extraordinarily well covered in [Jain 1991].

A useful perspective on the evolution of the state of the art in high-speed networking can be gleaned from the six volumes in the 10 years of IFIP Protocol for High-Speed Networks [Rudin 1989b, Johnson 1991, Pehrson 1993, Neufeld 1995, Dabbous 1997, Touch 2000], and in particular from the snapshots provided by [Rudin 1989a, Sterbenz 1995, Sterbenz 2000]. A discussion of the role of ATM in a high-speed Internet led by Schulzrinne is presented in [Sterbenz 1995]. Further research papers in the area are collected in [Tantawy 1994a, 1994b] and [Spaniol 1994]. U.S. government research program perspectives are in [Leiner 1988 and Partridge 1990b, 1994b].

One of the few books with the word "gigabit" in the title that actually does address issues of importance to high-speed networking is [Partridge 1994a], which has a wealth of examples. Papers that present early perspectives on high-speed networking include [Clark 1990], [Parulkar 1990a], and [Partridge 1993b].

The Corporation for National Research Initiatives (CNRI) managed gigabit testbeds of the 1990s [CNRI 1996] and spawned a multitude of interesting programs. The testbeds were Aurora [Clark 1992], Blanca [Terstriep 1996], Casa, Vistanet [Stevenson 1992], and Magic. A wide variety of perspectives in high-performance computing and communications is collected in [Foster 1999].

KEY AXIOMS

$Ø_1$. **Know the Past**   *Genuinely new ideas are extremely rare. Almost every "new" idea has a past full of lessons that can either be learned or ignored.*

$Ø_2$. **Know the Present**   *"Old" ideas look different in the present because the context in which they have reappeared is different. Understanding the difference tells us which lessons to learn from the past and which to ignore.*

$Ø_3$. **Know the Future**   *The future hasn't happened yet, and is guaranteed to contain at least one completely unexpected discovery that changes everything.*

$Ø_4$. **Prepare for the Future**   *Knowing the past isn't sufficient to prepare for the future. We must constantly reevaluate tradeoffs in the face of emerging technology, and question the basic assumptions of the present.*

Ø-A. **NIH Corollary [1980s version]**   *Operating systems didn't begin with Unix, and networking didn't begin with TCP/IP.*

Ø-B. **NIH Corollary [1990s version]**   *Operating systems didn't begin with Windows and host architecture didn't begin with the PC and x86 architecture.*

I. **Application Primacy**   *The sole and entire point of building a high-performance network infrastructure is to support the distributed applications that need it.*

I.1. **Field of Dreams versus Killer App Dilemma**   *The emergence of the next "killer application" is difficult without sufficient network infrastructure. The incentive to build network infrastructure is viewed as a "field of dreams" without concrete projections of application and user demand.*

I.2. **Interapplication Delay**   *The performance metric of primary interest to communicating applications is the total delay in transferring data. The metric of interest to users includes the delay through the application.*

I.3. **Network Bandwidth and Latency**   *Bandwidth and latency are the primary performance metrics important to interapplication delay.*

I.4. **Networking Importance in System Design**   *Communication is the defining characteristic of networked applications, and thus support for communication must be an integral part of systems supporting distributed applications.*

II. High-Performance Paths Goal   *The network and end systems must provide a low-latency, high-bandwidth path between applications to support low interapplication delay.*

II.1 Path Establishment Corollary   *Signaling and routing mechanisms must exist to discover, establish, and forward data along the high-performance paths.*

II.2. Path Protection Corollary   *In a resource-constrained environment, mechanisms must exist to arbitrate and reserve the resources needed to provide the high-performance path and prevent other applications from interfering by congesting the network.*

II.3. Store-and-Forward Avoidance   *Store-and-forward and copy operations on data have such a significant latency penalty that they should be avoided whenever possible.*

II.4. Blocking Avoidance   *Blocking along paths should be avoided, whether due to the overlap of interfering paths or due to the building of queues.*

II.5. Contention Avoidance   *Channel contention due to a shared medium should be avoided.*

II.6. Efficient Transfer of Control   *Control mechanisms on which the critical path depends should be efficient. High overhead transfer of control between protocol-processing modules should be avoided.*

II.7. Path Information Assurance Tradeoff   *Paths have application-driven reliability and security requirements that may have to be traded against performance.*

III. Limiting Constraints   *Real-world constraints make it difficult to provide high-performance paths to applications.*

III.1. Speed of Light   *The latency suffered by propagating signals due to the speed of light is a fundamental law of physics, and is not susceptible to direct optimization.*

III.2. Channel Capacity   *The capacity of communication channels is limited by physics. Clever multiplexing and spatial reuse can reduce the impact but not eliminate the constraint.*

III.3. Switching Speed   *There are limits on switching frequency of components, constrained by process technology at a given time, and ultimately limited by physics.*

III.4. Cost and Feasibility   *The relative cost and scaling complexity of competing architectures and designs must be considered in choosing alternatives to deploy.*

III.5. Heterogeneity   *The network is a heterogeneous world, which contains the applications and end systems that networks tie together and the node and link infrastructure from which networks are built.*

III.6. Policy and Administration   *Policies and administrative concerns frustrate the deployment of optimal high-speed network topologies, constrain the paths through which applications can communicate, and may dictate how application functionality is distributed.*

III.7. Backward Compatibility Inhibits Radical Change   *The difficulty of completely replacing widely deployed network protocols means that improvements must be backward compatible and incremental. Hacks are used and institutionalized to extend the life of network protocols.*

III.8. Standards Both Facilitate and Impede Dilemma   *Standards are critical to facilitate interoperability, but standards which are specified too early or overspecify impede progress. Standards that are specified too late, or underspecify, are useless.*

KEY DESIGN PRINCIPLES

IV. Systemic Optimization Principle   *Networks are systems of systems with complex compositions and interactions at multiple levels of hardware and software. These pieces must be analyzed and optimized in concert with one another.*

IV$_1$. Consider Side-Effects Corollary   *Optimizations frequently have unintended side effects to the detriment of performance. It is important to consider, analyze, and understand the consequences of optimizations.*

IV$_2$. Keep It Simple and Open Corollary   *It is difficult to understand and optimize complex systems and virtually impossible to understand closed systems, which do not have open published interfaces.*

IV$_3$. System Partitioning Corollary   *Carefully determine how functionality is distributed across a network. Improper partitioning of a function can dramatically reduce overall performance.*

IV$_4$. Flexibility and Workaround Corollary   *Provide protocol fields, control mechanisms, and software hooks, to allow graceful enhancements and workarounds when fundamental tradeoffs change.*

1. Selective Optimization Principle   *It is neither practical nor feasible to optimize everything. Spend implementation time and system cost on the most important contributors to performance.*

1A. Second-Order Effect Corollary   *The impact of spatially local or piecewise optimizations on the overall performance must be understood; components with only a second-order effect on performance should not be the target of optimization.*

1B. Critical Path Corollary   *Optimize implementations for the critical path, in both control and data flow.*

1C. Functional Partitioning and Assignment Corollary   *Carefully determine what functionality is implemented in scarce or expensive technology.*

2. Resource Tradeoff Corollary   *Networks are collections of resources. The relative composition of these resources must be balanced to optimize cost and performance.*

2A. Resource Tradeoffs Change   *The relative cost of resources and the impact of constraints change over time, due to nonuniform advances in different aspects of technology.*

2B. Optimal Resources Utilization versus Overengineering Tradeoff   *Balance the benefit of optimal resource utilization against the costs of the algorithms that attempt to achieve optimal solutions.*

2C. Support for Multicast   *Multicast is an important mechanism for conserving bandwidth and supporting network control protocols, and should be supported by the network.*

3. End-to-End Argument   *Functions required by communicating applications can be correctly and completely implemented only with the knowledge and help of the applications themselves. Providing these functions as features within the network itself is not possible.*

3A. Hop-by-Hop Performance Enhancement Corollary   *It may be beneficial to duplicate an end-to-end function hop-by-hop, if doing so results in an overall (end-to-end) improvement in performance.*

3B. Endpoint Recursion Corollary   *What is hop-by-hop in one context may be end-to-end in another. The End-to-End Argument can be applied recursively to any sequence of nodes in the network, or layers in the protocol stack.*

4. Protocol Layering Principle   *Layering is a useful abstraction for thinking about networking system architecture and for organizing protocols based on network structure.*

4A. Layering as an Implementation Technique Performs Poorly   *Layered protocol architecture should not be confused with inefficient layer implementation techniques.*

4B. Redundant Layer Functionality Corollary   *Functionality should not be included at a layer that must be duplicated at a higher layer, unless there is tangible benefit in doing so.*

4C. Layer Synergy Corollary   *When layering is used as a means of protocol division, allowing asynchronous processing and independent data encapsulations, the processing and control mechanisms should not interfere with one another. Protocol data units should translate efficiently between layers.*

4D. Hourglass Corollary   *The network layer provides the convergence of addressing, routing, and signaling that ties the global Internet together. It is essential that addressing be common, and that routing and signaling protocols be highly compatible.*

4E. Integrated Layer Processing (ILP) Corollary   *When multiple layers are generated or terminated in a single component, all encapsulations/decapsulations should be done at once, if possible.*

4F. Balance Transparency and Abstraction versus Hiding   *Layering is designed around abstraction, providing a simpler representation of a complicated interface. Abstraction can hide necessary property or parameter, which is not a desirable property of layering*

4G. Support a Variety of Interface Mechanisms   *A range of interlayer interface mechanisms should be provided as appropriate for performance optimization: synchronous and asynchronous and interrupt-driven and polled.*

4H. Interrupt versus Polling   *Interrupts provide the ability to react to asynchronous events, but are expensive operations. Polling can be used when a protocol has knowledge of when information arrives.*

4I. Interface Scalability Corollary   *Interlayer interfaces should support the scalability of the network and parameters transferred among the application, protocol stack, and network components.*

5. State Management Principle   *The mechanisms for installation and management of state should be carefully chosen to balance between fast, approximate, and coarse-grained versus slow, accurate, and fine-grained.*

5A. Hard State versus Soft State versus Stateless Tradeoff   *Balance the tradeoff between the latency to set up hard state on a per connection basis versus the per data unit overhead of making stateless decisions or of establishing and maintaining soft state.*

5B. Aggregation and Reduction of State Transfer   *Aggregation of state reduces the amount of information stored. Reducing the rate at which state information is propagated through the network reduces bandwidth and processing at network nodes, which comes at the expense of finer-grained control with more precise information.*

5C. Hierarchy Corollary   *Use hierarchy and clustering to manage complexity by abstracting and aggregating information to higher levels, and to isolate the effects of changes within clusters.*

5D. Scope of Information Tradeoff   *Make quick decisions based on local information when possible. Even if you try to make a better decision with more detailed global state, by the time the information is collected and filtered, the state of the network may have changed.*

5E. Assumed Initial Conditions   *Use reasonable assumptions based on past history or related associations to establish initial conditions for the installation of new state.*

5F. Minimize Control Overhead   *The purpose of a network is to carry application data. The processing and transmission overhead introduced by control mechanisms should be kept as low as possible to maximize the fraction of network resources available for carrying application data.*

6. Control Mechanism Latency Principle   *Effective network control depends on the availability of accurate and current information. Control mechanisms must operate within convergence bounds that are matched to the rate of change in the network and latency bounds to provide low interapplication delay.*

6A. Minimize Round-Trips   *Structure control messages and the information they convey to minimize the number of round-trips required to accomplish data transfer.*

6B. Exploit Local Knowledge   *Control should be exerted by the entity that has the knowledge needed to do so directly and efficiently.*

6C. Anticipate Future State   *Anticipate future state so that actions can be taken proactively before repair needs to be performed on the network that affects application performance.*

6D. Open- versus Closed-Loop Control   *Use open-loop control based on knowledge of the network path to reduce the delay in closed-loop convergence. Use closed-loop control to react to dynamic network and application behavior.*

6E. Separate Control Mechanisms   *Control mechanisms should be distinct, or the information conveyed explicit enough, so that the proper action is taken.*

7. Distributed Data Principle   *Distributed applications should select and organized the data they exchange to minimize the amount of data transferred and the latency of transfer and allow incremental processing of data.*

7A. Partitioning and Structuring of Data   *Whenever possible, data should be partitioned and structured to minimize the amount of data transferred, and the latency inn communication.*

7B. Location of Data   *Data should be positioned close to the application that needs it to minimize the latency of access. Replication of data helps to accomplish this.*

8. Protocol Data Unit Principle   *The size and structure of PDUs are critical to high-bandwidth, low-latency communication.*

8A. PDU Size and Granularity   *The size of PDUs is a balance of a number of parameters that affect performance. Trade the statistical multiplexing benefits of small packets against the efficiency of large packets.*

8B. PDU Control Field Structure   *Optimise PDU header and trailer fields for efficient processing. Fields should be simply encoded, byte aligned, and fixed length when possible. Variable-length fields should be prepended with their length.*

8C. Scalability of Control Fields   *PDU header and trailer fields and structure should be scalable with data rate and bandwidth-$\times$-delay product.*

CHAPTER 3

Network Architecture and Topology

This chapter is concerned with the overall network architecture and organization issues of network topology and routing (Figure 3.1). Network signaling and control, as well as related session control issues, are covered in Chapter 4. Subsequent chapters consider individual components: Chapter 5 is concerned with the design and architecture of individual components in the network such as links, routers, and switches; Chapter 6 is concerned with the design of high-performance end systems.

Figure 3.2 shows the refinement of our ideal model, expanded to show the network components. In this chapter we will be concerned with the arrange-

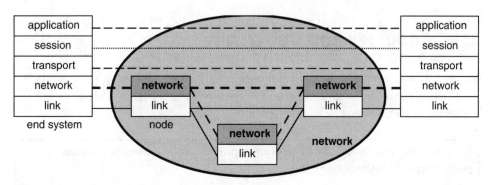

Figure 3.1   Network architecture and protocols.

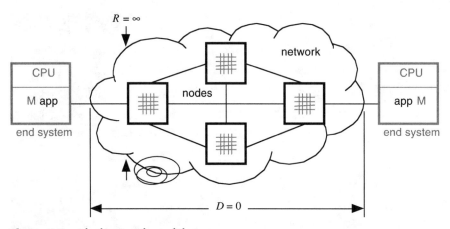

Figure 3.2   Ideal network model.

ment and organization of these components to provide a high-bandwidth, low-latency path between the edges of the network enabling a high-speed interapplication path.

This chapter is organized as follows: Section 3.1 discusses the issues that are important in engineering an entire network. This consists of the topology and structure to provide high-bandwidth, low-latency paths through the network. Section 3.2 examines the issue of how to scale high-speed networks to support large numbers of end systems, and to support dense configurations of mobile wireless nodes. The primary principles will be based on the use of hierarchy to manage complexity. Section 3.3 examines the resource tradeoffs among bandwidth, memory, and processing, constrained by latency requirements. This is important in determining the proper location of functionality and services that the network should provide. Finally, Section 3.4 presents a summary and list of principles introduced throughout the chapter.

3.1   Topology and Geography

We will now consider the physical location and interconnection of nodes in a high-speed network, beginning with the network refinement of the High-Performance Path Goal (II):

> **Network Path Principle**   *The network must provide high-bandwidth, low-latency paths between end systems.*
>
> **N-II**

Unless bandwidth is free and unlimited, we need a mechanism to protect a high-performance path from interfering traffic. Quality of service (QOS) mechanisms provide these guarantees; we will consider these issues in Chapter 4.

First, we will consider the basic issues in the structure of high-performance networks: topology, latency, and bandwidth. Networks consist of a set of *nodes* connected by *links*. Network nodes include switches, routers, bridges, and gateways; we will use the term *node* generically when it is not necessary to distinguish between switches and routers.

3.1.1   Scalability

A number of topologies can be used to connect a set of network nodes, the most general being an arbitrary mesh, as shown in Figure 3.3a. In this case, network nodes are arbitrarily connected by point-to-point links. If the nodes and protocols support a general mesh architecture, any desired topology can be deployed in particular cases, such as stars, trees, and rings.

Early local area network (LAN) technologies used a shared channel medium that dictated specific topologies, in particular a ring for Token Ring and fiber distributed data interface (FDDI) and bus for Ethernet, as shown in Figure 3.3b. Shared-medium channels have the nice property that broadcast is an inherent capability of the technology. Wireless LANs have a quasibroadcast property within a certain range dictated by transmission power and noise. Furthermore, dual-ring networks are fault tolerant to a link cut or node failure.

There are two major problems with these constraining shared-medium topologies, however. First, it is easier to wire a LAN as a mesh of interconnected stars, unless building topology happens to match the bus or ring of the chosen LAN technology. Second, and most important in the context of high-speed networking, a shared-medium does not scale well with

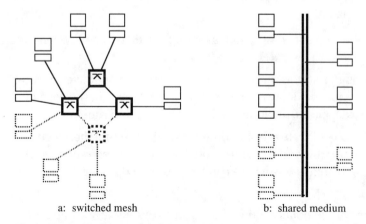

a: switched mesh   b: shared medium

Figure 3.3   Scaling networks.

bandwidth and node count. Each node shares a fraction of a fixed channel bandwidth; as the node count increases, the fraction available per node decreases.

On the other hand, mesh networks move the contention from a single shared channel to multiple nodes (switches or routers), which are interconnected with point-to-point links. Network nodes can be designed to be scalable in capacity and degree of connectivity, within packaging and technology limits. Furthermore, when the scalability limit of a particular node is reached, the network can be scaled by adding additional switches and links, as shown by the shaded node and links in Figure 3.3a. Thus, virtually all network technologies now are intended for deployment as an arbitrary mesh of point-to-point links. This includes modern deployments of Ethernet, which maintain the Ethernet medium access control (MAC) protocol for compatibility with the majority of desktop systems but do not use a shared-medium on the link.

Early optical networks were of the *broadcast and select* type, with edge nodes broadcasting on a particular wavelength to all receivers. The receivers had tunable filters to receive only the desired signal. The utility of this technology is limited to a LAN environment, using a star coupler switch. Scalability is limited in the number of wavelengths available in the shared-medium, the power requirements to broadcast wavelengths, and the relatively slow speed at which the receiving filters can tune.

Scalability of Mesh Topologies   *Mesh network technologies scale better than shared medium link technologies.*

N-II.4

3.1.2   Latency

Latency is one of the key measures of high-performance, and consists of three contributing components:

1. The delay t_p due to the speed-of-light traversing the distance between nodes.

2. Delay t_r or t_s though network nodes (router or switch, respectively), consisting of the forwarding delay t_f and queuing delay t_q, and in the case of store-and-forward routers, an additional object reception time t_b.

3. Delay due to the object transmission time t_b, that is, the time between the arrival of the first bit and the time enough data has been received to begin processing which is b/r, where b is the protocol data unit size and r the data rate.

In this chapter, we will be concerned with how network geography and topology contribute to latency, and thus will concentrate on the speed-of-light component and the *aggregate* node delay due to the number of hops imposed by topology. In Chapter 4, we will explicitly use these delays to examine the tradeoffs between different signaling mechanisms to minimize end-to-end delay. The design of network nodes to keep t_r and t_s low will be the subject of Chapter 5. Techniques that increase data rate and thus minimize t_b will be discussed throughout the book. Determination of packet size will be discussed in a variety of contexts in subsequent chapters.

Figure 3.4 shows a network consisting of several nodes and links (the thickness of the line indicates differences in bandwidth, which will be important in the next section). The key observation is that the end-to-end latency D of a network path is the sum of the latencies of the individual hops:

$$D = \Sigma d_i$$

The delay d_i of each hop consists of the latency through the internode network link and the delay within the nodes at each end. In this example, the latency along the path 1→2→3→6 consists of the latencies due primarily to the speed-of-light along the links 1→2, 2→3, and 3→6, *and* the latencies due primarily to queuing delay through the network nodes 1, 2, 3, and 6. We will consider the individual contributors to latency in the following sections, but for now note that the path 1→4→5→3→6 is longer in geographical distance and has more hops than the path 1→2→3→6. However, if the queuing delay in node 2 is long, this shorter path may actually have the longer delay.

> **Network Latency Principle**   *The latency along a path is the sum of all its components. The benefit of optimizing an individual link is directly proportional to its relative contribution to the total end-to-end latency.*
>
> **N-1A/**

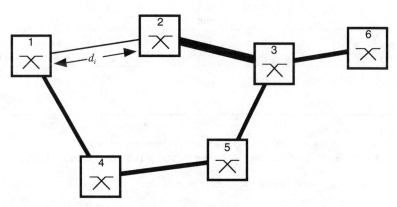

Figure 3.4   Delay along network paths.

3.1.2.1 Geography and the Speed of Light

The fundamental factor influencing latency over long-distances is the speed-of-light, $c = 3 \times 10^5$ km/s. For optical fiber, the actual propagation velocity is approximately $0.7c$; for wire, it is $0.6c$ to $0.95c$, depending on the physical medium (Table 5.1). The immediate observation is that with a circumference of approximately 40,000 km, it takes a communication signal about 200 ms to circle the earth.[1] Given the desire to satisfy interactive applications with 100-ms response time, we can see an immediate challenge. Higher-layer protocols

Table 3.1 Round-Trip Propagation Delays and Bandwidth-×-Delay Products

TYPE	DISTANCE	CHANNEL	RTT	BANDWIDTH-×-DELAY PRODUCT		
				1 Mb/s	1 Gb/s	1 Tb/s
DAN,SAN*	100 m	Wire/fiber RF/IR	1 μs	$\frac{1}{2}$ b	500 b	500 kb
LAN	1 km	Wire/fiber RF	10 μs	5 b	5 kb	5 Mb
MAN	100 km	Fiber	1 ms	500 b	500 kb	500 Mb
Transcontinental WAN	5,000 km	Fiber	50 ms	25 kb	25 Mb	25 Gb
Global WAN	20,000 km	Fiber	200 ms	100 kb	100 Mb	100 Gb
LEO satellite[†]	2 × 1,000 km 3000 km FP	RF	25 ms	12 kb	12 Mb	12 Gb
GEO satellite	2 × 36,000 km	RF/laser	480 ms	240 kb	240 Mb	240 Gb
Earth/moon	400,000 km	RF/laser	2.5 s	1.2 Mb	1.2 Gb	1.2 Tb
Earth–Mars[‡]	55–400 × 10^6	RF/laser	6–45 min	1.3 Gb	1.3 Tb	1.3 Pb
Solar system (Jupiter diameter)	10^9 km	RF/laser	2 hr	3.6 Gb	3.6 Tb	3.6 Pb
Solar system (Pluto diameter)	10^10 km	RF/laser	20 hr	36 Gb	36 Tb	36 Pb

*Desk area network, storage area network.
[†]The satellite distances are shown as orbital altitudes, and thus need to be multiplied by 2 for the uplink/downlink pair for *each* direction. LEO latencies are dependent on both altitude and footprint (FP) diameter.
[‡]Bandwidth-×-delay product is for worst-case, one-way latency (20 min).

[1]We are concerned with order-of-magnitude precision for purposes of this discussion.

and applications will generally be concerned with the *round-trip time* (RTT), which is the time it takes for a message to propagate to the destination and back. Table 3.1 lists the approximate RTTs for a number of network distances, as well as the one-way bandwidth-×-delay products at three data rates, which we will refer to later.

Table 3.1 indicates the degree to which distance latency matters for various network scopes. The distance latency component for LANs and MANs (metropolitan area networks) is so small relative to the individual network node delays in network nodes that the topology and distance of the links is not a significant concern (assuming that the number of hops is reasonably bounded, as will be discussed shortly). For WANS (wide area networks), however, careful network topology engineering becomes quite important. Furthermore, interactive applications requiring subsecond response time are not very sensitive to LAN or MAN delays, which are orders of magnitude lower than 100 ms, even if the topology is not optimal. On the other hand, physical topology is critical in wide area networks.

In the case of wide area networks, about all the *network* can do is to provide relatively straight paths between distant nodes. For example, a sensible North American backbone topology would not be a star centered in Chicago, shown in Figure 3.5. Traffic between Boston and New York would have to travel 2500 km and take 12 ms via Chicago, rather than the 1.5 ms along a 300-km direct link.

Similarly, the routing algorithms must forward packets or establish connections along paths short enough to meet application demands; a sensible routing of traffic between New York and Boston is not likely to include nodes in Tokyo or Sydney. Unfortunately, administrative concerns of service

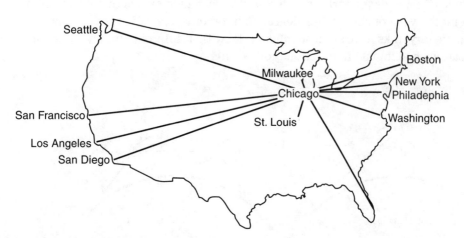

Figure 3.5 Star backbone topology.

providers frequently result in very ugly network routing topologies. We will address this later.

An even greater challenge to latency-sensitive applications is provided by satellite links, but they are generally not very high-bandwidth. Low earth-orbiting (LEO) satellites introduce latencies similar to those of transcontinental WANs. Geosynchronous earth-orbiting (GEO) satellites introduce latencies in excess of that of an intercontinental WAN. Satellite networks may consist of a single satellite which relays between two earth stations, called *bent pipe links* (shown in Figure 3.6a), or a mesh of satellites containing on-board switches (shown in Figure 3.6b).

On-board switching allows LEO satellites to avoid multiple satellite uplink/downlink traversals for long-distance communications. An alternative architecture for LEOs calls for multiple bent-pipe up- and downlinks, for example, between a terminal and a gateway located in the same region (or country), which is connected to the terrestrial wired network. This not only eliminates the complexity of switching onboard the satellites but also avoids regulatory issues of long-distance rights in many countries. It can be seen from Table 3.1 that several LEO hops do not exceed the latency of a terrestrial global WAN.

Finally, note that the latencies involved in the entire Earth system, including the moon, are only an order of magnitude above those of terrestrial networks, and thus the protocol issues do not change significantly. On the other hand, the links involved in an interplanetary Internet suffer latencies ranging from minutes to hours. Current Internet protocols are not designed to deal with latencies of this magnitude. Furthermore, until each planetary system is blanketed by complete satellite coverage, channels will be subject to occultation fades, requiring scheduling of link availability.

The added latency of space links also has significant impact on application design, which will be discussed in Example 8.1. At the low end, latencies are a couple of seconds for earth–moon round trips, which means that while 100-ms interactivity is not achievable, degraded interactive operation is possible. Interplanetary links have such significant delay that different latency-aware applications and human interaction modes will be required.

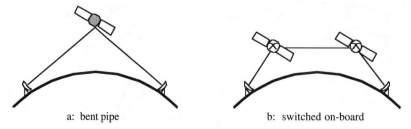

a: bent pipe   b: switched on-board

Figure 3.6 Satellite network topology.

EXAMPLE 3.1: THE VISION AND TRAGEDY OF IRIDIUM

In the 1990s a global network of 66 LEO satellites, called *Iridium*[2], were deployed [Lemme 1999]. Iridium was a network of 66 polar orbit satellites, orbiting at 780 km. Each satellite had 48 spot beams, resulting in 1,628 cells covering the earth, with 174 full duplex channels each at 2,400 b/s [Tannebaum 1996].

The "field of dreams" launching a global LEO communications infrastructure was truly visionary. Unfortunately, the deployment was *tunnel* visionary. Rather than deploying Iridium as a reasonably high-speed data network, the application driver was telephony: global telephone and fax capability. By the time Iridium was deployed, cellular telephony was ubiquitous throughout much of the densely populated world, with service and telephones available at a fraction of the cost of Iridium service.

The market for people communicating from mountain tops was not very big, and they already had conventional satellite phones. Iridium was shut down in 1999. Appallingly, less than 10 years after permission was granted by the FCC, the fate of Iridium satellites is uncertain, in what must surely qualify as the greatest communications fiasco of all time.

3.1.2.2 Topology and Number of Hops

We have discussed the distance component of latency. The second factor influencing network latency is the number of hops traversed, due to the forwarding and queuing delay in nodes. If we choose the path with the fewest number of hops h_{ij} for all pairs of end systems i and j, then the longest of these paths $\max(h_{ij})$ is the *diameter* of the network.

As will be discussed in Section 5.2.2, traditional IP routers store each packet in memory before a forwarding decision can be made. This latency can be significant, and the number of such hops needs to be tightly bounded for latency-sensitive applications.

Network Diameter Principle   *The number of per hop latencies along a path is bounded by the diameter of the network. The network topology should keep the diameter low.*

N-1A*h*

Fast packet switches, however, impose significantly lower delay; we can expect that a typical switch node will incur on the order of 1 to 10 ms.

---

[2]The atomic number of iridium is 77, the number of satellites originally planned. This was changed to 66, the atomic number of dysprosium. Needless to say, the network wasn't renamed.

Thus, we should target network paths to consist of several tens of nodes; many tens or hundreds of hops would have a significant impact on latency.[3]

3.1.3 Bandwidth

Bandwidth is the other key performance measure for high-speed network, and we will now consider the effect of network topology on bandwidth.

Geographic distance does not directly affect bandwidth, as it did latency.[4]

Our example network, repeated as Figure 3.7, shows a network consisting of several nodes and links of varying bandwidth (denoted by thickness of the line). The key observation is that the end-to-end bandwidth R of a network path is constrained by the *lowest rate* link r_i:

$$R = \min{(r_i)}$$

Thus, in this example the path 1→4→5→3→6 consists of a sequence of medium-bandwidth links. Even though link 2→3 is high-bandwidth, this does not help provide a higher-bandwidth path between nodes 1 and 6, since the overall path is constrained by the low-bandwidth link 1→2. It does no good to the end system applications to have a mostly high-bandwidth network, in which there is a low-bandwidth bottleneck.

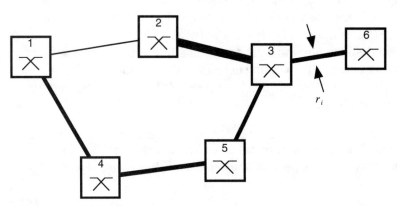

Figure 3.7 Bandwidth along network paths.

[3]When the intranode delay is significant relative to the distance latency. For interplanetary links, for example, we can introduce a few hundred hops with no significant effect on the end-to-end delay.
[4]Electronic, electromagnetic, and optical properties limit distance for a given power budget without signal regeneration, but this can be made relatively transparent above the link layer.

> **Network Bandwidth Principle**   *The maximum bandwidth along a path is limited by the minimum bandwidth link or node, which is the bottleneck. There is no point in optimizing a link that is not a bottleneck.*
>
> **N-1A***b*

3.1.3.1   Parallelism

While physics sets a lower bound on the latency between two points, we can increase the bandwidth by engineering. There are two techniques that we can consider to increase bandwidth above that available on a single path: striped links and multiple paths. *Striped* links refer to spreading data units (bits, bytes, or packets) across parallel links following the same path. This is an option only if there is plenty of aggregate bandwidth in the network, but the individual link rates are low. This requires that the skew between packets across the stripes be kept low enough to maintain packet sequence, unless the end-to-end protocol supports resequencing. Even if end-to-end resequencing is supported, there is additional control complexity and performance degradation in doing this. For example, if packets are striped per byte along a set of parallel links traversing parallel switch planes, the switches will not be routing in lock step unless the skew can be tightly controlled across the set of planes. This means that separate control will be needed, in effect replacing parallel switch data path planes with complete switches. Buffering and traffic shaping could be used to recover skew at each hop, but this adds latency and complexity. For this reason, virtually all network links are bit-serial, with striping limited to very specialized applications.

The other option is to route different packets belonging to a single end-to-end application along multiple distinct network paths. This presents a significant challenge to the end-to-end protocols, which must be responsible for managing the multiple flows, and for resequencing packets with extremely large skew. In general, it is far simpler to engineer the network to provide sufficient bandwidth, but in special circumstances these techniques may be necessary.[5]

It is important to note that this discussion applies to increasing the bandwidth of a *single* end-to-end path. The use of multiple links between network nodes as a network engineering technique to increase the aggregate bandwidth above that available on a particular link is a valuable technique that is commonly used.

---

[5]For example, to get more bandwidth from legacy residential access lines, such as interfaces which terminate two ISDN channels or multiple xDSL lines to get greater throughput than is available on a single line.

3.1.3.2   *Bandwidth-×-Delay Product*

We have discussed low latency and high bandwidth individually, but of course a high-performance network must supply *both*. The highest-bandwidth path through a network may not be the same as the lowest-latency path. In Figure 3.7 the low-latency path passes through node 2, but the higher-bandwidth path passes through nodes 4 and 5.[6]

Thus, it is the responsibility of the network engineer to ensure that paths exist that are high-bandwidth *and* low latency. It is the responsibility of the routing algorithms and QOS mechanisms to deliver paths that meet particular application requirements. In the case of bandwidth, this may require careful reservation of resources and load balancing so that sufficient bandwidth remains available as the network becomes loaded, or that connections/flows are rearranged to satisfy the QOS demands of new connections/flows.

The number of bits in flight along a link is referred to as the *bandwidth-×-delay product*. One of the side effects of long-distance high-bandwidth links is that the bandwidth-×-delay product can become extremely large. This is important to any feedback control mechanism, and mainly affects end-to-end protocols, which will be discussed in depth in Chapter 7. It also affects the network interface at the end systems, which must lock or buffer large amounts of information until returning acknowledgments indicate that retransmission will not be necessary.

A benefit of engineering a network for low latencies is to help relieve the end-to-end protocols from dealing with this problem. In some cases, however, there is nothing that can be done to reduce the bandwidth-×-delay product. For example, a 5,000-km transcontinental OC-192 link (10 Gb/s) has a bandwidth-×-delay product on the order of 240 Mb. Current deep-space links are relatively low-bandwidth and thus do not have bandwidth-×-delay products in excess of terrestrial networks. Future interplanetary links based on free space laser communications could have incredibly high-bandwidth-×-delay products of terabits or petabits, providing significant new challenges to network design. For these situations, especially those where bandwidth is not a constraint, a strategy to consider consists of relying heavily on forward error correction (FEC) techniques. This allows recovery from lost information at the receiver, within certain operating parameters, minimizing or avoiding the need for retransmissions.

3.1.4   Virtual Overlays and Lightpaths

So far we have discussed the effect of the physical topology on latency and bandwidth. Frequently, a *virtual* topology is overlaid on the physical network,

---

[6]Assuming that the delay *through* node 2 is not the bottleneck.

obscuring the physical topology from network layer routing. There are a number of reasons to construct overlay networks:

Virtual private networks (VPNs). VPNs are created as overlay networks to give the appearance and security of a private LAN or extranet using shared network infrastructure. VPNs are frequently used for LAN interconnection in corporate intranets, and allow the entire VPN to reside on the inside of a firewall connected to the rest of the Internet (for example, [Yuan 2001]).

Secure overlay sessions. To provide secure group communications, session control mechanisms may set up a variety of point-to-point and multicast network layer connections. In response to session dynamics, the topology and characteristics of the network layer connections need to adjust to maintain high-performance path characteristics, as for multicast connections. If some of the connections are mobile, these adjustments must also be made, as described in Section 4.3.1.

Datagram overlays meshes. One technique for avoiding the overhead of connection setup for transactions and short datagram flows in connection-oriented networks is to overlay a permanent connection mesh. Datagrams can then traverse paths along the mesh, without waiting for the round trip of `SETUP/CONNECT` signaling. In the case that a flow is longer lived, it can be move to a dedicated connection or flow with reserved resources [Parulkar 1990b, Mazraani 1990].

Lightpaths. Optical networks provide lightpaths, which are a wavelength routed overlay on top of the physical optical network topology. Due to the constraints in wavelength assignment, these paths do not necessarily correspond to the shortest physical path between endpoints, as will be described shortly.

In some cases there may be multiple levels of overlay. Routing along the overlay paths does not correspond directly to the routing that would take place on the level below (physical topology on the lowest layer). All of the refinements of the Network Path Principle (N-II) apply to the overlay topologies, and requires that bandwidth and latency information based on the topology overlaid on the physical network is available as part of the forwarding or connection routing process. Since overlay paths between two end systems may be longer than the shorted physical path, the overlay versions of the Network Latency Principle (N-1Al) and Network Diameter Principle (N-1Ah) are particularly important. Overlay topologies need to be reconfigured, as necessary, to provide the required high-performance paths to applications.

> **Network Overlay Principle**   *Overlay networks must provide the same high-performance paths as the physical networks. The number of overlay layers should be kept as small as possible, and overlays must be adaptable based on end-to-end path requirements and topology information from the lower layers.*
>
> **N-IIo**

A large number of overlay levels complicates the ability to do this. For example, a VPN may be overlaid on an IP network, overlaid on an ATM permanent virtual connection (PVC) mesh, overlaid on lightpaths, overlaid on the physical topology.

3.1.4.1 Path Multiplexed Wavelength Routing

Wavelength-routed networks allow optical lightpaths to traverse multiple hops without electrical conversion, as is necessary for SONET. Such lightpaths provide a high-bandwidth, low-latency pipe that is transparent to bit rate and coding format, with the potential to reduce the number of expensive electronic equipment such as SONET cross connects (XCs) and add/drop multiplexors (ADMs). Wavelength-routing optical switches based on opto-mechanical, acousto-optic, or thermo-optic technologies are currently too slow for efficient packet switching. Thus we have two problems to consider: how to overlay lightpaths on the physical network topology and how to efficiently transfer data in a circuit-switched mode. The latter issue will be covered in Section 4.1.5.

In the early fourth-generation (2000s), all-optical wavelength conversion and time-slot interchanging technology is not mature. Thus we will consider wavelength routing in which the switches are not generally capable of wavelength conversion; this is referred to as *path multiplexing*, which may be spatial in the form of wavelength division multiplexing (WDM) or temporal in the form of time division multiplexing (TDM).

A critical problem is how to assign the overlay lightpaths to preserve the high-performance path characteristics along the overlay. In this case, the problem is to assign a set of lightpaths, such that no optical link l_{ij} between switches i and j is carrying more than one lightpath of a particular wavelength λ_n. To the degree possible, we exploit spatial reuse of wavelengths.

For example, in Figure 3.8, two lightpaths are established between switches 1 and 6 and between 2 and 6. Distinct wavelengths λ_1 and λ_2 must be used since both lightpaths share link l_{36}. Lightpaths between switches 4 and 2, as well as between 5 and 6 can both use λ_3 since there is no common link. If a limited number of wavelength converters is available, we must be additionally concerned with the optimal placement of the converters in the

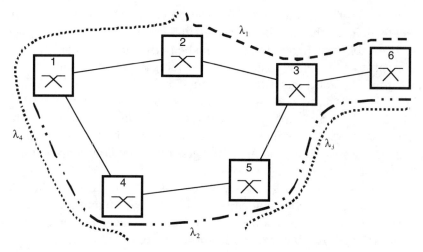

Figure 3.8 Wavelength routing and assignment.

network to maximize the spatial reuse in wavelength assignment. For example, placement of a wavelength converter on the edges of highly aggregated links partitions the wavelength assignment problem to smaller optimizations on each side.

If traffic patterns are very dynamic, a long-lived static assignment of lightpaths may not be sufficient, and a WDM layer may be needed to dynamically reassign wavelength assignments, similar to second-generation (1980s) digital circuit switched networks and third-generation (1990s) switched virtual circuit networks, over which aggregated flows will be carried.

Early research on lightpath establishment assumed centralized control, but distributed control improves scalability and reliability, as in electronic networks. Distributed control can use global information [Ramaswami 1996] or only local information [Qiao 1996]. WDM networks provide additional challenges in determining the tradeoff between global versus local state. There may be hundreds of wavelengths that are being dynamically assigned, each of which may have many TDM slots carrying data flows. Thus, the dynamicity and magnitude of flow information may exceed that of electronic networks.

If only local link state information is maintained, tentative reservation of a block of available wavelengths may yield a higher success probability than reserving just one wavelength at a time. In this case a wavelength group reservation is propagated hop-by-hop from the source, with the anticipation that at least one of them will be available all the way to the destination. When the destination is reached, all of the tentative wavelength reservations are released at each hop, other than the one that will be used.

The tradeoff between local and global information can be balanced by using the clustering techniques that will be described in Section 3.2.2.

Dynamically establishing lightpaths may also be performed in a manner similar to multiprotocol label switching (MPLS) (using the mechanisms described in Chapters 4 and 5); this is multiprotocol lambda switching (MPΛS). After an IP flow is recognized, a lightpath can be established for all future IP packets of the flow. In early fourth generation (2000s) packet over wavelength (POW) IP lightpath overlays, the number of required wavelengths is relatively small, approximately 4 to 64 depending on the granularity of flow aggregation in the backbone [Bannister 1999].

As time progresses, the need for more wavelengths will increase, but the number of wavelengths available in dense wavelength division multiplexing (DWDM) systems is rapidly increasing. On the other hand, even dynamic path multiplexing wavelength routing is not efficient in two cases:

1. Bursty traffic does not efficiently use a lightpath circuit or TDM slot in a lightpath. This motivates optical burst switching (OBS), discussed in Section 4.1.5.

2. For transactions and short flows, the lightpath reconfiguration time can be significant. This motivates the use of wavelength converters, which is discussed next.

3.1.4.2   *Link Multiplexed Wavelength Routing*

Optical switches which provide wavelength conversion at each switch eliminate the need for continuous lightpaths. This is called *link multiplexing*. Link multiplexing eliminates the need to make global decisions on wavelength assignment, since each assignment can be made by a pairwise local negotiation with neighbor switches, as is done for ATM virtual path/virtual connection (VP/VC) assignment.

It is worth noting that the performance advantage of link multiplexing over path multiplexing under distributed control can be much more significant than under centralized control. This suggests that using the costly wavelength converters may be justifiable in WDM networks using distributed control.

3.1.5   Practical Constraints

The geography and topology considerations discussed thus far have assumed that links can be arbitrarily laid between nodes to provide needed bandwidth and minimal latency. This is generally true within continental boundaries, but oceans (and occasionally mountain ranges) can present formidable barriers to high-bandwidth fiber optic cable. Transoceanic cables continue to be laid, and available bandwidth is catching up to that within land masses. As mentioned before, satellite links have a role, but are relatively low-bandwidth and high latency.

3.2 Scale

We have so far discussed the topology of high-speed networks without considering the *scale* of networks, in terms of node count. We are concerned with networks consisting of billions or trillions of end systems.[7] This leads to the question of what topologies and routing architectures are needed to support extremely large-scale high-speed networks.

3.2.1 Network Engineering

First, we need to consider the relevant network engineering parameters and characteristics:

Size n. The number of communicating end systems.

Diameter h_{max}. The maximum shortest path (measured in hops) between any pair of end systems.

Degree k. The number of adjacent nodes to which a given switch or router is connected.

Node count s. The total number of network nodes (switches and/or routers).

Path diversity. The number of parallel paths available between node pairs, providing redundancy in the case of link or node failure, as well as additional bandwidth availability.

Aggregation. The concentration of bandwidth in the core of the network and the number of end-to-end paths.

These parameters and characteristics determine our ability to provide the low-latency, high-bandwidth paths we have been discussing. To keep latency low we must limit h_{max} so that the per hop node delays do not dominate the speed-of-light delays or exceed the application latency budget. As previously indicated, this means the design target for h_{max} should be on the order of 10 hops. To keep bandwidth high, we need to ensure that the topology does not limit the design space for high-performance routers and switches. Chapter 5

---

[7]Ubiquitous computing research suggests that individuals will have tens to hundreds of nodes each, which along with a global sensor grid indicate a Global Information Infrastructure of at least trillions of nodes.

Table 3.2 Topology Parameters

TOPOLOGY	PARAMETER			
	DEGREE	# NODES	DIAMETER	AGGREGATION
Sparsely connected	Low	High	High	Low
Densely connected	High	Low	Low	High

discusses issues in scaling switches and routers, but we note here that there are packaging and performance limits on the size of nodes. It is reasonable to consider high-performance switches with thousands of ports, but probably not millions of ports. In the early fourth-generation (2000s) scaling $k = O(1024)$ is a reasonable upper bound to consider.[8]

This now allows us to explore the range of topologies that fall within this space. To connect the end systems we insert a mesh of switches. Table 3.2 shows the magnitude of parameters for two classes of network topologies, shown by example in Figure 3.9.[9]

Traditional data networks were sparsely connected, consisting of a semiregular mesh of low-degree nodes. An example sparse network connecting 16 end systems is shown in Figure 3.9a, with $k_{max} = 4$, $s = 11$, and $h_{max} = 6$. Sparsely connected networks scale poorly in both node count s and hop count h, and are unsuitable for large high-performance networks.

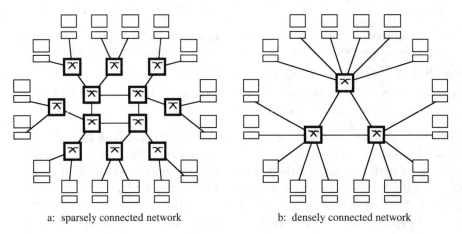

a: sparsely connected network   b: densely connected network

Figure 3.9 Degree of connectivity.

[8][Turner 2000] argues for very large switches to minimize overall cost, with per switch port dominating.

[9]Note that the nodes in Figure 3.9a are more sparsely connected, even though the density of nodes shown in the confines of the figure is higher.

Network topologies must scale the number of switches in a cost-effective way, such as $s = O(n/2k)$ for k sufficiently large to keep hop count reasonably low.[10] For high-speed networks we can consider the case of densely connected topologies with a few high degree switches.[11] An example network that somewhat more densely connects 16 end systems[12] is shown in Figure 3.9b, with $k_{max} = 8$, $s = 3$, and $h_{max} = 3$.

This leads to significant aggregation of bandwidth and flows in the network core, which must be limited to remain below the capacity of practical high-bandwidth links. To reduce this aggregation, additional switches can be deployed providing multiple paths between end systems. Thus, network engineering (typically based on simulation) is needed to determine a reasonable topology and connectivity, and the proper tradeoff among s, h, and k for a given network scenario.

3.2.2 Hierarchy

Large network scale presents an additional problem that cannot be solved by the network engineering exercise described previously. To provide QOS guarantees to applications, routing algorithms must know the state of the network to select a path that meets the desired latency and bandwidth requirements, as well as to avoid congesting paths already in use. This requires that each node have a topology and link state database for the entire network. As the network scale increases, the size of the database explodes, as does the bandwidth consumed to flood the network with the link state updates that keep the per node databases current and consistent.

Hierarchy is the standard way to manage complexity, and allows routing and link state information to be bounded by abstracting information at larger granularities. Thus, the network is divided into clusters of nodes [Kleinrock 1977, Steenstrup 2001]. The optimal engineering parameters are highly dependent on the situation, but a rough rule of thumb is that cluster sizes should be on the order of 10 to 100 nodes, with a degree of connectivity around 10. While a full discussion of hierarchical network design is beyond the scope of this book, we will introduce the concept of clustering before we concentrate on the high-speed networking implications.

Figure 3.10 illustrates hierarchical clustering. Nodes A.1, A.2, A.3, and A.4 in 1st level cluster A have full topology and link state information about one another. Information about all other clusters is abstracted, however. For example, nodes in cluster A know that there is an intercluster link A–C, and that A.3 is

---

[10]This figure is highly dependent on the topology, but $n/2k$ provides a guide based on a tree topology.

[11]The extreme case of this is a single switch in a star topology network, but it is clearly impractical to consider a single switch with billions or trillions of ports.

[12]A really dense network would consist of the range $128 < k < 1024$, but is difficult to show in a small figure.

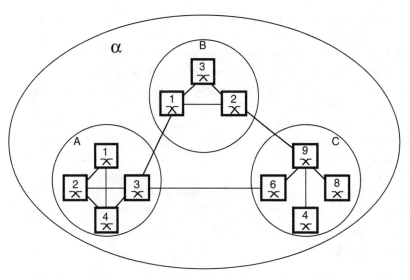

Figure 3.10   Hierarchical clustering.

the node that provides that connectivity, but have no other information about the topology or link state of nodes *within* cluster C. In this example we have created a 2nd level consisting of clusters A, B, and C. Similarly, these form a 3rd level cluster α, which can be similarly abstracted recursively for as many levels as needed. This sort of routing hierarchy is used in research protocols such as Nimrod [Steenstrup 1993p] as well as by the ATM PNNI [ATMF 1996p].

While this sort of hierarchy is important in any large complex network, it is especially critical in a densely connected high-speed network, in which there is very high aggregation of routing paths in the core. First, it limits the bandwidth of flooding link state and topology updates and the processing required in the switches. Second, connection and flow setup are more efficient due to significantly smaller topology and link state tables in the nodes.

End system addresses are frequently represented as hierarchies for administrative reasons. These hierarchies do not necessarily have any relationship to the network topology or routing hierarchy. There may be significant performance benefits when the addressing hierarchy matches the routing cluster hierarchy, due to the lack of address–cluster translation.

3.2.2.1   Configuration and Self-Organization

We have considered the topology of complex high-speed networks, without considering how this topology is established. Traditionally, this has been done in a static manner, with addresses and hierarchical structure manually assigned. This has been acceptable, since the network configuration time scale has been the longest, by orders of magnitude. As networks become more complex and dynamic, we must consider self-organizing networks, which automatically bootstrap and continually optimize a routing hierarchy. In mobile wireless networks, it is impractical to statically configure networks, particularly when the rate of mobility exceeds the rate at which off-line configurations can be determined. A sequence of protocols and algorithms is necessary [Abowd 2000], consisting of:

Neighbor discovery (using beacons which announce the presence of nodes).

Link formation and management based on the exchange of identity and characteristics.

Federation into a network layer routing and addressing hierarchy; this can be purely a network layer connectivity structure based on the link reachability, or constrained by higher-level concerns, such as building topology, organizational structure, security domains, and application communication patterns.

Topology optimization and maintenance in the face of node mobility and traffic patterns.

One key performance issue is that the self-organization protocol suite must be efficient enough to form networks on demand with a delay that is acceptable to users. For example, in a ubiquitous computing environment, when several individuals come together, we expect the network to self-organize in the time frame of seconds, but not minutes.

Similarly, optimization of the topology must occur in the same time frame as the mobility of the nodes that are driving topology and clustering changes. The mobility of nodes may be measured in terms of dwell time at a single network attachment point; if the dwell time is appreciably larger than the transient times in the network protocols (routing updates after topology changes, flow control convergence, server transaction times), the situation is manageable. This is relatively easy to do with slow-moving nodes, such as individuals walking, but becomes extremely challenging with fast-moving nodes, such as supersonic aircraft.

Hierarchical organization also serves as a strategy in this situation, particularly if mobility in local scales is higher than in wider scales. In this manner, the most frequent topological changes introduced by mobility lead to state updates only within the lowest cluster within the hierarchy, and the transient times refer to local dynamics with much shorter path times. In mobile networks with shared medium channel access, however, the appropriate design and implementations of self-configuring hierarchical organization are not simple. The degree to which protocol actions in one path affect other paths sharing an access medium is typically much greater than in wired networks, and the control stabilization dynamics become more complex.

3.2.2.2   Geography and Locality

We have described clustering as a technique to manage complexity in high-speed networks. Network engineering concerns suggest that we should also have a hierarchy that matches the geographical scope and implementation technology of the networks. This serves to isolate network engineering and technology choices, as well as match natural bandwidth aggregation characteristics to wide area long-haul networks.

Figure 3.11 shows such a hierarchy, based on the subnetwork type and geographical scope. At the bottom of the hierarchy are personal (body), desk (DAN), home, and local area networks, to which end systems are directly attached. These are connected together by metropolitan (MAN) and regional networks. Finally, a wide area network (WAN) forms the core backbone. Each one of these network clouds may *also* consist of an internal hierarchical clustering to manage its own internal complexity, as described previously.

Network Hierarchy Principle   *Use hierarchy and clustering to manage network scale and complexity and reduce the overhead of routing algorithms.*

N-5C

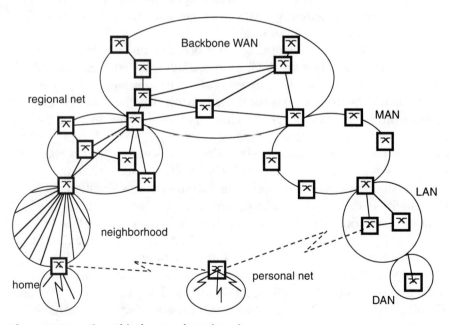

Figure 3.11   Hierarchical network engineering.

3.2.3   Bandwidth Aggregation and Isolation

Hierarchical organization allows bandwidth to be managed in two important ways: *aggregation* and *isolation*. First, backbone WANs carry the aggregation of a vast number of end-to-end traffic flows. Thus, they can be optimized to this task, as a mesh of very high-bandwidth links connecting interconnecting metropolitan and regional networks. By aggregating individual flows or connections into groups, the complexity of the forwarding decisions can be dramatically reduced. This can be done in an explicit address partition (as described in Example 3.2) or examining high-order address bits (as will be described for high-speed IP switch implementations in Section 5.5.2).

Similarly, networks low in the hierarchy can be engineered to meet the bandwidth and channel characteristics of end systems, as well as the technology choices dictated in particular deployments (such as optical fiber versus RF wireless).

EXAMPLE 3.2: ATM VIRTUAL CONNECTION HIERARCHY

ATM was designed with a two-layer virtual connection switching hierarchy consisting of virtual channels (VCs) inside virtual paths (VPs). The ATM cell format (shown in Figure 5.21) has a connection identifier field divided into a high-order 12-bit VP identifier and a low-order 16-bit VC identifier. The intent is to divide the network into a hierarchy consisting of LAN VC switches and core backbone VP switches as shown in Figure 3.12.

Each LAN attaches end systems to a collection of VC switches, each of which is capable of switching 2^{16} = 64K virtual connections.[13] The idea is to assign each pair of edge LANs a distinct virtual path (or several VPs divided by traffic class). The core switches then switch bundles of VCs in each VP, and examine only the high-order VP identification bits. This limits the size of the forwarding tables to a maximum of 2^{12} = 4K entries, instead of the 2^{28} = 256M maximum entries that would be needed to switch on the entire VP + VC connection identifier.

Multiprotocol label switching (MPLS) [Rosen 2000, Davie 2000] generalizes this to an *n*-level aggregation hierarchy by allowing label stacking of arbitrary depth, and is one of many examples of applying technology originally developed in non-IP fast packet switching contexts to the Internet. Example 5.5 examines MPLS in more depth.

---

[13]VP and VP identifiers have local hop-by-hop significance, thus 64K is *per* switch; the network can have many more connections.

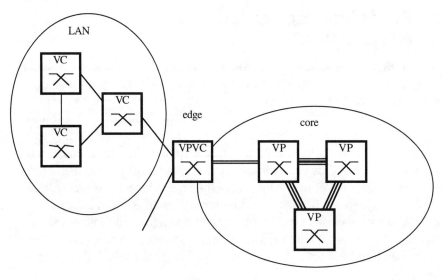

Figure 3.12 ATM virtual connection hierarchy.

Second, hierarchy serves to isolate bandwidth. In many cases, the lowest layers of the hierarchy have inherently high spatial locality in traffic patterns, for example, in an individual's wearable computing body area network, a home network, or desk area network (within an office). Many LANs also exhibit high locality of traffic, as in a small business intranet. This sort of hierarchy serves to keep traffic isolated from other subnetworks, as well as from entering higher layers in the hierarchy. In cases where high-bandwidth traffic is exchanged among a particular set of nodes, the network hierarchy can be engineered to specifically exploit this, and reduce the load on other parts of the network.

Hierarchy to Aggregate and Isolate Bandwidth *Use hierarchy to manage bandwidth aggregation in the core of the network, and to isolate clusters of traffic locality from one another.*

N-5B

3.2.4 Latency Optimization

Hierarchical network architecture also provides the ability to optimize latency, in terms of both geographical distance and number of hops. For example, the backbone WAN can be engineered as a densely connected mesh to provide low latency (2 or 3 hops) and high bandwidth with the node degree matching the number of MAN access points. Similarly, MAN technology and topology can be optimized to bound the latency for the particular situation independent of the WAN topology and engineering. By carefully engineering the maximum number of hops at each layer of the hierarchy, we can ensure the total end-to-end latency remains bounded by tens of hops.

Hierarchy to Minimize Latency   *Use hierarchy and cluster size to minimize network diameter and resultant latency.*

N-5C*I*

To some degree, this is a tradeoff. The diameter of a flat network of low degree is high. Adding hierarchy decreases the diameter, but only if done carefully. As topology information is abstracted, the routing algorithms do not have global control or ability to minimize the number of hops traversing each cluster.

To the degree that network topology can be simplified to create regular structures, the number of levels in the hierarchy can be reduced. The optimal tradeoff between a flat network and maximum hierarchy minimizes the diameter and its effect on latency.

3.2.5   Wireless Network Density

So far, we have discussed network scale in terms of the overall node count. This is, in fact, the measure of concern for networks connected by wire and fiber optics. In the context of wireless networks, we also need to be concerned with the *density* of the network. In this case the density measure is in terms of nodes/area, but it is directly related to the notion of a densely connected network discussed in Section 3.2.1. This is because for a given transmit power (assuming omnidirectional antennas), the degree of connectivity k increases as the distance between nodes decreases.

The trend toward higher spatial density in wireless networks is driven by the increasing availability and functionality of small embedded mobile wireless nodes. Furthermore, as wireless-capable devices with substantial processing power become smaller, their portability and potential spatial density increase. This means that for fixed devices, connectors and wires impose greater logistics and real estate penalty on the infrastructure within this volume, motivating the use of wireless links.

Furthermore, as bit rate r goes up, bit duration $1/r$ decreases. Thus, for a given received power level, the bit energy (power $\times$ $1/r$) is reduced and the bit error rate goes up. Increasing transmitter power is one solution, but this option is unattractive for power-constrained portable, ubiquitous devices, and increases the likelihood of undesired interference with other devices. Another option for wireless Internet access is to shorten the wireless access link by providing more wireless Internet gateways. There are other ways to attack the problem, but distance remains a fundamental constraint. This is particularly important from energy-constrained portable devices into the network (rather than in the opposite direction), and has the side effect of favoring asymmetric paths between the mobile host and network.

Ironically, wireless networks, which have traditionally been considered lower-bandwidth networks, have the potential to deliver higher bandwidth than fiber optic networks using short-link free-space propagation. This is because over short distances, line-of-sight operation becomes feasible, and the atmospheric attenuation over the visual optical spectrum is very low. Thus, short-link systems may use large portions of the optical spectrum plus at least the microwave spectrum, surpassing the capacity of optical fiber, at the expense of significant design challenges.

Wireless networks typically share an open channel within which individual links must contend for bandwidth, and nodes must be able to distinguish which links to decode and receive. If the internode spacing is too small with respect to the reach of the transmitters, the resulting degree of connectivity is so high that the aggregate bandwidth far exceeds the available channel capacity, as shown in Figure 3.13a.[14] This is the same issue that we considered at the beginning of the topology discussion, but we can't merely decide how to lay point-to-point wires in a wireless network. Conventional approaches include medium access control (MAC) and coding techniques.

MAC protocols allow multiple nodes to contend for the shared channel. While MAC protocols can be optimized to particular situations, at best we are deciding how to divide limited spectrum among a given number of links.

Clever *coding techniques*, such as spread spectrum, can increase the number of links in a given channel. In spread spectrum techniques, multiple transmissions share the same spectrum (at the same time in the same location).

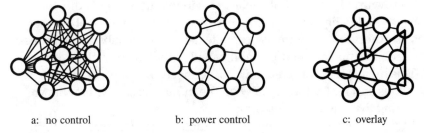

a: no control   b: power control   c: overlay

Figure 3.13   Density control.

[14]We have not used the same graphic here as in other figures for network nodes since mobile wireless nodes typically serve as both end system and switch or router. This will be discussed in Chapters 5 and 6.

Each spreads the power required for its transmission over a greater frequency spectrum than its individual transmission rate requires, but it does so in a manner that renders its signal relatively transparent to the other transmissions, looking like low-level background noise. This effect is often characterized as a spread spectrum processing gain, representing the apparent reduction in interference power achieved by the spread spectrum in well-designed systems. Gains in the range of 10 to 100 are common in commercial systems. The method facilitates uncoordinated simultaneous transmissions over the same spectrum and location, simplifying channel access methods. Since an RF shared medium tends to couple the dynamics of paths sharing this medium in ways that are more complex than the coupling experienced by paths sharing queues at a node, spread spectrum techniques often simplify higher-layer protocol dynamics too. The penalty is not only higher-bandwidth wireless interfaces than necessary for the data rates but also wasted bandwidth when the simultaneous transmissions are fewer than the spread spectrum gain design. These inefficiencies have motivated the design of adaptive gain spread spectrum systems.

One approach to the solution to a highly dense network is to increase spatial reuse of the spectrum by forming a less densely connected multihop network, which can be done in three ways:

1. **Directional antenna.** By aiming the antenna along the path of particular links, channel contention can be reduced. This technique is easier to accomplish with fixed wireless nodes than highly mobile nodes. A primitive version of this is used to increase spatial reuse in cellular telephone networks, dividing cells into sectors. In fact, adaptive array antenna technology is capable of tracking mobile nodes by sensing the reduction in received power as the mobile moves, and changing the orientation of the array antenna beam until a power increase is detected. The orientation is adjusted by controlling the electrical behavior (coherence) of all the antennas that make up the array. Speed of tracking and cost-effectiveness remain limitations of this technology.

2. **Power control.** Fast power control has been commercially deployed. The power level changes can be exercised many times per session, per packet, and even per bit. As the density of a network increases, we dynamically decrease the transmission power to limit the distance over which signals can interfere with one another [Ramanathan 2000]. The tradeoff involved in larger hop delay versus multiuser interference has been studied in the context of ad hoc networking and earlier in packet radio networks [Kahn 1978]. Least interference routing [Stevens 1988] and other schemes have been designed to mitigate the effects of density.

We will use power control to illustrate the density control concept. Recall that Figure 3.13a shows a dense network with long-range signals interfering with one another. This reduces the per link bandwidth between pairs of nodes, and stresses MAC contention mechanisms, including the per node processing overhead in detecting and discriminating the proper transmission.

Figure 3.13b shows the case in which transmission power has been reduced to create a multihop network within the given geography. The power should be low enough to keep the degree of connectivity low to avoid channel contention and control receiver overhead. On the other hand, the degree of connectivity must be high enough so that the loss of a link (due to channel fade or mobility) keeps the network connected. Thus, we want to continuously maintain a biconnected graph, in which at least two distinct paths exist between any given pair of nodes.

In very large networks, the number of hops to distant nodes becomes large. This results in excessive routing overhead in nodes and latency due to the per hop forwarding delays, as was discussed in the context of wired networks. As is so often the case, we have a tradeoff that must be optimized: low-bandwidth without density control versus longer latency in the multihop network with bandwidth control. In multihop wireless networks, the forwarding delays when resource reservations are not in use will tend to be worse than in wired networks. This is because the forwarding delay must allow for the dynamics of hop-by-hop retransmission and contention back-off behavior to stabilize the contention channel in case of local overload. This is a consequence of unarbitrated contention; arbitration, however, is not easy if the network must accommodate mobile nodes.

3. **Overlay construction.** The solution is to construct an overlay in which some links are higher power and longer distance, as shown in Figure 3.14c. This keeps contention for the shared channel low, while allowing distant nodes to communicate with low per hop latency. Multiple levels of this hierarchy are possible, and may be done in conjunction with a hierarchical clustering to manage complexity in the conventional sense, for networks that are both large in node count, as well as dense.

As mentioned earlier, such hierarchical organization can also be used to confine protocol state changes due to mobility in networks where mobile nodes are common. Thus, effective hierarchical self-organization algorithms and protocols are essential for mobile ad hoc networks.

Density Control to Optimize Degree and Diameter   *Use density control and long link overlays to optimize the tradeoff between dense low-diameter and sparse high-diameter wireless networks.*

N-5C*w*

3.2.6   Practical Constraints

Practical constraints, including administrative policies and the realities of commercial network deployment, severely complicate the effort to achieve the ideal hierarchical network model.

3.2.6.1   Policy-Based Routing

Policy-based routing [Clark 1989b, Steenstrup 1993a] refers to the inclusion of administrative policy in determining how network paths may be set up for particular end systems or applications. Examples of such policies include:

- Don't route traffic through an untrusted country or competitor's network.
- Route traffic through a particular network provider due to a contractual relationship.
- Route traffic only through highly secure nodes.
- Avoid a particular set of routes because they are historically unreliable.

These policies add routing constraints to the standard routing and QOS mechanisms that we would use to get a high-bandwidth, low-latency path for an application. About all we can do is note that to provide high-performance in this context, the network needs to include high-bandwidth, low-latency paths in the acceptable set of routes based on policy, and that the routing and QOS mechanisms support policy-based parameters.

3.2.6.2   Network Provider Deployment

The Internet was historically a hierarchical system, and in particular the NSFNET of the early 1990s fit this model well with a national backbone connecting regional networks to which campus and corporate research LAN clusters could attach. Unfortunately, the situation has become considerably more complex and difficult to control. The Internet now consists of a number of geographically overlapping backbone mesh networks deployed by large network providers. These peer with one another in places dictated more by administrative and rights-of-way concerns than with the goal of providing high-speed network infrastructure to end systems. Regional and metropolitan networks are similarly deployed by multiple providers, in some cases by the same providers deploying backbone networks.

Figure 3.14 shows an example of three backbone network providers A, W, and S. A connection between end systems 1 and 2, which are located in geographically close cities on the east coast of the United States, must traverse long-distance links to a city in the midwest in which networks A and S happen to peer with one another.

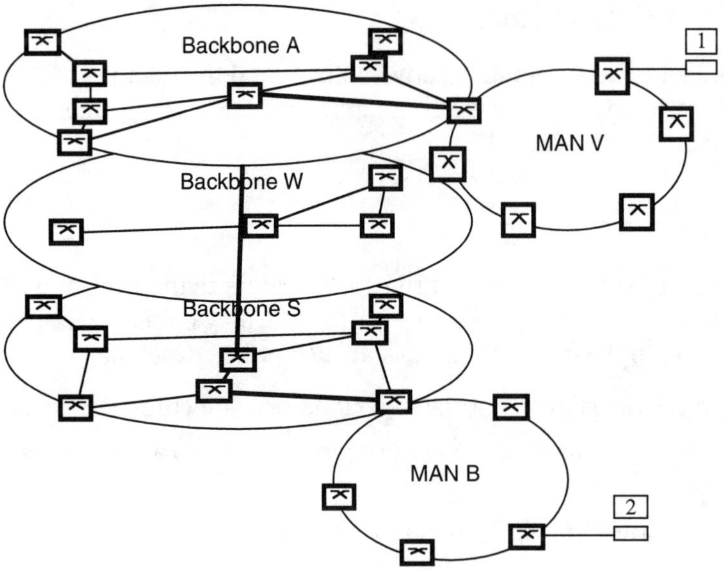

Figure 3.14 Multiple provider infrastructure.

The result is an extremely complex topology in which it is difficult for end users and applications to have access to the sort of controlled latency that we would expect a hierarchically designed network to provide. This is particularly a problem when communicating users subscribe to different network providers.

> **Administrative Constraints Increase the Importance of Good Design** *Policy and administrative constraints distort the criteria that govern the application of many high-performance network design principles. The importance of good (principled) design is elevated when these constraints are present.*
>
> **N-III.2**

We need not allow the real-world constraints applied by administrative concerns and policy to defeat the goal of high-performance networking. The motivation of Application Primacy (I) to meet the High-performance Paths Goal (II) still drives the design and deployment of high-speed network infrastructure. It makes it all the more challenging, and increases the importance of applying the principles to get the desired result.

3.2.6.3 Hybrid Networks

No single network technology is right for all situations, even at a given point in time. Fiber optic networks are best for high-bandwidth communication in a fixed infrastructure, where the costs of laying cable are practical. Even within

EXAMPLE 3.3: WHEN IS A HOP NOT A HOP?

When it is a POP. As the Internet moved to commercialization after decommission of the NSFNET in the mid-1990s, backbone service providers established access nodes to the network called POPs (points of presence) and connections between one another in the form of public Internet network exchanges (INXs) and private peering points. The explosion in demand for network service severely strained the capacity of POPs, particularly in the number of access links. Commercially available routers tended to have on the order of 64 to 128 ports, rather than the thousands necessary. POPs then became small network clouds in themselves with sparse connectivity (as in Figure 3.10a). This had three effects. First, instead of suffering a single router hop between an access network and backbone, there were perhaps 10 hops/POP[15] resulting in a significant latency hit. Second, this blurred the ability to have a clean hierarchical division at the POP. Third, the peering architecture is static and manually configured restricting dynamic traffic management.

As the fast packet switch technology developed for ATM finally became integrated into IP switches, POPs could be replaced by single routers supporting thousands of links. This had the ripple effect of severely straining BGP-4, the Internet routing protocol of the day, which was not initially designed as a scalable hierarchical routing protocol [Dube 1999, Scudder 1999]. Transparent optical backbones have the same straining effect on nonscalable routing protocols [Krishnan 2000].

this context, switching/routing technologies vary based on a number of trade-offs. Where fixed infrastructure is difficult to deploy, or mobility is needed, wireless and satellite networks are necessary. As technology changes, link, node, and entire subnetwork technologies are replaced. During transitional phases the complexity and heterogeneity are all the more significant.

In some cases, technologies are a good match for particular parts of the hierarchy shown in Figure 3.11. For example, fiber optics are generally appropriate for backbone WAN and regional/MAN networks. Wireless networking technologies are appropriate for personal and home networks. However, there will always be a need for mixed technologies. Examples include wireless and satellite links as part of backbone and regional networks to hard-to-reach areas and a variety of technologies for local and residential access networks. This has two implications. First, we have to carefully engineer the network to provide needed high-bandwidth, low-latency paths in the face of heterogeneous subnetworks and complex topologies as previously discussed. Second, gateways or interworking units (IWUs) may be required between subnetworks, as shown in Figure 3.15.

---

[15]Rather than one hop on POP [Geisel 1963].

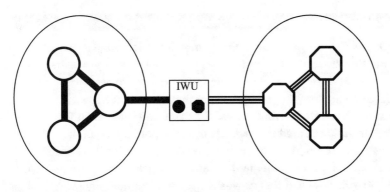

Figure 3.15   Interworking of heterogeneous subnetworks.

IWUs perform three functions. First, the IWU is responsible for both control and data transformation. In the case of data transformation, we require that it transform packet formats between the two subnetwork types. Assuming that each of the subnetworks has packet formats optimized for high-speed processing, this should be relatively easy to do. Fragmentation and reassembly may be required, however, and this can be a costly operation, in terms of latency and processing requirements in the IWU.

The second function is to transform control and signaling messages. If the two subnetworks have similar control mechanisms, this can be a relatively easy task, for example, a frame relay/ATM IWU. On the other hand, if the mechanisms are quite different, this can be complicated and difficult to do at low latency.

The third function is to map routing and link state information between the two subnetworks. The ability to do dynamic routing and traffic management between the two domains is extremely challenging, and helps motivate the Hourglass Corollary (4D).

3.3   Resource Tradeoffs

So far, we have considered a number of network design issues critical for high-bandwidth and low latency, In this section, we will consider the importance of engineering the proper tradeoffs among resources.

Network Resource Tradeoff and Engineering Principle   *Networks are collections of resources. The relative composition of these resources must be balanced to optimize cost and performance and to determine network topology, engineering, and functional placement.*

N-2

3.3.1   Bandwidth, Processing, and Memory

There are three types of resources that need to be considered in the design of any computing or communications system: bandwidth, processing, and memory. The tradeoffs among these resources are critically important in understanding how to design high-performance networks. The ability to provide these resources, in turn, is determined by their relative costs. We will describe these costs by the triple $\langle B, P, M \rangle$. To optimize the combination, we need to define an objective function $f(\beta(B), \pi(P), \mu(M))$, which captures the characteristics and cost function of each resource for a particular scenario.

EXAMPLE 3.4: MULTICAST

A simple example of these tradeoffs is the utility of multicast [Dalal 1978, Kadoba 1983] in the network. While it seems obvious that multicast is a useful service, this fact is based on resource tradeoffs: multicast conserves network bandwidth. If bandwidth and memory were free and unlimited, the network would have adequate bandwidth and buffers to support n point-to-point connections for a $1:n$ multicast, resulting in a worst-case bandwidth of nr on a link, as shown in Figure 3.16a. Furthermore, since there are n flows, n times as many buffers and routing table entries must be reserved in routers, and the end system involved in the multicast group must have n times the processing capability np.

One model for multicast consists of constructing a spanning tree connecting all the nodes in the multicast group carrying a single multicast flow, as shown in Figure 3.16b. Thus, the maximum bandwidth on a link is r, with buffers for only one connection and only a single routing table entry in each node.[16] Furthermore, the processing requirements on the end system generating the multicast are now reduced to p. Another way to look at this is that for a given network capacity, a network supporting multicast enables higher-bandwidth applications than would be the case for a point-to-point network.

If the nodes are involved in an $n:n$ multipoint-to-multipoint communication, the impact is more dramatic. Without multicast, $n^2 - n$ point-to-point flows are required, as opposed to the n point-to-multipoint flows and 1 multipoint-to-multipoint flow. In general, networks do not support multipoint-to-multipoint communications due to the difficulties of flow/connection management and resource reservation. This capability is provided in special cases, however; for example, with videoconferencing reflectors, which serve as the root of the spanning tree to multiple clients.

[16]Although multicast routing table entries are somewhat more complex and must indicate all egress ports.

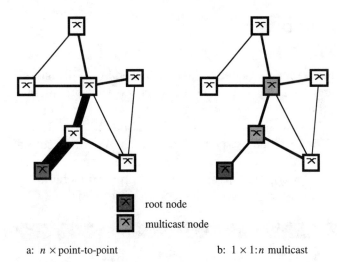

root node

multicast node

a: $n \times$ point-to-point

b: $1 \times 1:n$ multicast

Figure 3.16 Multicast efficiency.

3.3.2 Latency as a Constraint

We have considered the optimization of bandwidth, memory, and processing resources. We have not yet considered additional constraints important to the system. The most important of these, particularly in the context of high-speed networks, is *latency*. Although latency isn't a resource in the conventional sense, it is a critical characteristic of the network that must be considered in engineering resource tradeoffs.

Recalling the VOD example in the last section, we determined an optimal depth for caching of content. We did not consider whether or not the content was located close enough to the end system so that the response time to requests (initial and modification of the stream characteristics) is sufficiently small to meet interactive service requirements. It may be that content must be cached closer to the edge of the network than indicated by Figure 3.17 to meet the latency constraint. This is more likely to be an issue for highly interactive applications, such as Web browsing, than for moderately interactive applications such as movies on demand. Thus we need to expand our objective function to consider the latency constraint: $f(\beta(B), \mu(M), \pi(P) \mid \lambda(L))$.

There are a number of important applications with stringent latency bounds. These include applications traditionally considered best effort, such as Web browsing (which requires latency bounds on the order of 100 ms to be *interactive*), to extremely tight requirements for process control and interactive gaming. Application demands will be discussed in detail in Chapter 8.

EXAMPLE 3.5: CONTENT CACHE LOCATION

The problem of where to cache movies for a video on demand (VOD) service [Nussbaumer 1995] provides a good example of how resource tradeoffs can give us concrete assistance in network engineering. There are two extreme cases to consider. For the first case, assume bandwidth is expensive and memory is free: $\beta(B) = \infty$, $\mu(M) = 0$.[17] In this case the proper policy is to keep a copy of every movie on each end system computer (or set-top box). Thus, the bandwidth cost to the network in viewing a movie is zero since it already resides on the end system.[18] On the other hand, if bandwidth is free and unlimited, but memory is expensive, $\beta(B) = 0$, $\mu(M) = \infty$, then we should keep a single copy of each movie in the network and stream it to an end system when it is requested. Since bandwidth is free, we can afford to dimension the network so that content can be rapidly delivered whenever requested, even if everyone in the world is making simultaneous accesses.

Since neither of these extremes reflects reality, the proper answer lies in between the scenarios just described; movies should be cached throughout the network, with more popular movies cached in more places, and closer to the end user. We can show this by plotting curves for the cost of memory and bandwidth as a function of depth in the network, as shown in Figure 3.17.

Assume a spanning tree overlaid on the network is used for distribution of movies. If there is a single server, it resides at the root of the tree. User set-top boxes reside at the leaves of the tree. As content is replicated, the servers move down the tree; for example, in a binary tree the number of servers doubles as their location increases in depth.

As this happens, total bandwidth requirements decrease linearly and memory requirements increase exponentially, as shown by the dashed curves in Figure 3.17. By defining an objective function f summing the two costs, we get the aggregate cost, shown by the bold line. The minimum of this curve indicates the proper depth I_{opt} at which to store content in the tree.

Thus, we can determine the proper engineering of the network and applications by optimizing an objective function $f(\beta(B), \mu(M), \pi(P))$, where β, μ, and π are the functions reflecting the relative scaling of bandwidth, memory, and processing, respectively.

---

[17]This example is not particularly sensitive to the cost of processing, except to support the size of the server, which we will ignore.

[18]For this example, we ignore the costs of initially getting the copy to the end system, which is a different policy. In actuality, popular movies may be prebroadcast to all end systems at low rate when they become available, and unpopular movies loaded once on demand to particular end systems and then archived indefinitely.

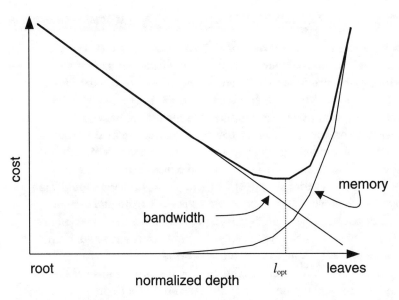

Figure 3.17 Optimization of bandwidth versus memory.

3.3.3 Relative Scaling with High Speed

We have discussed how to use resource tradeoffs and constraints to engineer networks and applications, but have not yet directly considered how this applies to high-speed networks. So we must ask the question, "What happens to the relative scaling of the cost of these resources as network speed increases?"

High-speed networks drive the cost of bandwidth down. Different technologies deployed in backbone, residential access, and corporate LAN networks complicate the situation, and do not track one another over time. Similarly, we know that Moore's law reduces the cost of computing and memory.

As we have discussed before, the one thing that does not scale is the speed-of-light component in latency. This has two significant ramifications:

1. The latency constraint becomes relatively more important as network bandwidth increases.

2. Since the bandwidth-×-delay product increases, the buffering requirements in routers and switches correspondingly increases.

We will consider how the future of high-speed networking might be affected by the long-term relative costs of processing, memory, and bandwidth in Chapter 9.

> **Resource Tradeoffs Change and Enable New Paradigms**   *The relative cost of resources and constraints changes over time due to nonuniform advances in different aspects of technology. This should motivate constant rethinking about the way in which networks are structured and used.*
>
> **N-2A**

An example of such a shift is the enabling of active networking due to the decrease in the cost of processing and memory.

3.3.4   Active Networking

Conventionally, processing within network nodes consists of forwarding or switching packets, and memory utilization consists primarily of routing tables, topology and link state databases, and packet buffers. General program execution is reserved for end systems.

Moore's law is driving down the cost of processing and memory to such a significant degree that it has become reasonable to consider what we could do by introducing intelligence into the network nodes.[19] This has led to the field of active networking [Tennenhouse 1997, Bhattacharjee 1998c].

Active networking (AN) can be divided into two flavors:

Strong AN.   Users inject *capsules* of code, which traverse the network for execution in active nodes. This is the form in which AN was first proposed. Strong AN raises a number of significant policy, resource, and security concerns that question its long-term viability.

Moderate AN.   Code is dynamically provisioned into active nodes by network providers.[20] This allows the deployment of new services and protocols without traditional software upgrades in network nodes. One of the things that can be provisioned, however, is an interpreter that can execute user capsules.

One of the first examples of active network processing was to perform active congestion control on MPEG-2 streams [Bhattacharjee 1998b]. When a node detects impending congestion, rather than random dropping of video packets, B and P frames are dropped, while I frames are passed. This results

---

[19]Intelligence in the network is not a new idea, and is well established in the PSTN in the form of the *intelligent network* (IN). IN, however, is a very specific architecture and protocol set based on the structure of the telephone network, the lack of intelligence in end systems, and SS7 protocols. While some of the goals are similar in spirit, in particular dynamic provisioning of new services, IN is not applicable to data networking with intelligent end systems.

[20]The term *strong AN* was coined by Bobby Bhattacharjee in the sense of strong AI; *moderate AN* was coined by James Sterbenz since "weak AN" didn't sound like a good name for the field of pursuit in which we were engaged.

in substantially better performance to the application. It does, however, require that the active node be able to filter packets on arbitrary criteria, and snoop into and modify higher-layer protocol fields and data.

Active networking has three high-performance objectives:

1. Do not interfere with normal (nonactive) networking. This can be done either by deploying additional active nodes in the network that do not interfere with conventional network paths and flows or by designing the active nodes in a manner that does not affect normal fast-path forwarding.

2. Perform active network processing at high-performance.

3. Provide new or enhanced services that improve the high-performance aspects of the network. Examples of such services include active congestion control, which can increase the effective bandwidth of a network, and active caching, which reduces the latency of content access to applications while optimizing the utilization of network resources [Bhattacharjee 1998b].

We will discuss the active node design aspects of the first two points in Section 5.6.2.

3.4   Summary

This chapter has considered the design and architecture of the high-speed network as a whole. We first presented the ideal network model. We then described the topology and geography issues that govern our ability to provide low-latency, high-bandwidth paths between the nodes at the edge of the network. Latency is the sum of the component delays and bandwidth is the minimum of the component rates. We then considered these issues in the light of overlay networks, with particular emphasis on optical network lightpaths. To address the problems of scaling high-speed networks, we considered the basic parameters and presented the benefits of hierarchical clustering. Finally, we stepped back and considered the network as a set of resources to be balanced against one another and optimized to determine the placement of functionality.

3.4.1   Further Reading

[Meijer 1982] provides an outstanding survey of second-generation (1980s) network architectures, including X.25, SNA, DECNET, Burroughs BNA, and Univac DCA. [Green 1980, 1982] and [Sunshine 1989] provide broad coverage of second-generation networking with survey papers on specific network issues, as well as papers targeted to particular technologies. In addition to [Cerf 1983a], early papers on the Internet architecture include [Crocker 1969], [McQuillan 1977], [Cerf 1974, 1983b] and [Postel 1980, 1981a]. The OSI architecture is described in [Folts 1983, Day 1983].

A wealth of information on routing in general is in [Steenstrup 1995], on routing performance in [Bohem 1969, Rudin 1976], on IP routing in particular in [Huitema 2000], and on mobile wireless hierarchy and routing in [Ramanathan 1996, 1999], and [Steenstrup 2001].

Optical networking is comprehensively covered by [Mukherjee 1997, Ramaswami 1998, Stern 1999, Sivalingam 2000, and Kartalopoulos 2000], which have extensive references to the research literature.

There is a vast body of literature on ATM and B-ISDN networks. The definitive monographs are [dePrycker 1995] and [Händel 1998], both of which have extensive references to the original literature, as well as to ITU and ATM Forum standards. A comprehensive coverage of the ATM architecture and protocol suites is covered in [Black 1999, 1998a, 1998b]

KEY NETWORK TOPOLOGY PRINCIPLES

N-II. Network Path Principle   *The network must provide high-bandwidth, low-latency paths between end systems.*

N-II.4. Scalability of Mesh Topologies   *Mesh network technologies scale better than shared medium-link technologies.*

N-4B. Redundant Functionality in the Network   *Balance the independence offered by layering against the inefficiencies of multiple and interfering implementation of the same function.*

N-1A*l*. Network Latency Principle   *The latency along a path is the sum of all its components. The benefit of optimizing an individual link is directly proportional to its relative contribution to the total end-to-end latency.*

N-1A*h*. Network Diameter Principle   *The number of per hop latencies along a path is bounded by the diameter of the network. The network topology should keep the diameter low.*

N-1A*b*. Network Bandwidth Principle   *The maximum bandwidth along a path is limited by the minimum bandwidth link or node, which is the bottleneck. There is no point in optimizing a link that is not a bottleneck.*

N-1Io. Network Overlay Principle   *Overlay networks must provide the same high-performance paths as the physical networks. The number of overlay layers should be kept as small as possible, and overlays must be adaptable based on end-to-end path requirements and topology information from the lower layers.*

N-5C. Network Hierarchy Principle   *Use hierarchy and clustering to manage network scale and complexity and reduce the overhead of routing algorithms.*

N-5B. Hierarchy to Aggregate and Isolate Bandwidth   *Use hierarchy to manage bandwidth aggregation in the core of the network and to isolate clusters of traffic locality from one another.*

N-5Cl. Hierarchy to Minimize Latency   *Use hierarchy and cluster size to minimize network diameter and resultant latency.*

N-5Cw. Density Control to Optimize Degree and Diameter   *Use density control and long link overlays to optimize the tradeoff between dense low-diameter and sparse high-diameter wireless networks.*

N-III.2. Administrative Constraints Increase the Importance of Good Design   *Policy and administrative constraints distort the criteria that govern the application of many high-performance network design principles. The importance of good (principled) design is elevated when these constraints are present.*

N-2. Network Resource Tradeoff and Engineering Principle   *Networks are collections of resources. The relative composition of these resources must be balanced to optimize cost and performance and to determine network topology, engineering, and functional placement.*

N- 2A. Resource Tradeoffs Change and Enable New Paradigms   *The relative cost of resources and constraints changes over time due to nonuniform advances in different aspects of technology. This should motivate constant rethinking about the way in which networks are structured and used.*

CHAPTER
4

Network Control and Signaling

This chapter is concerned with network control and signaling, including session control and traffic management, and, when paired with Chapter 3, covers the network layer issues. Subsequent chapters consider individual components in the network: Chapter 5 is concerned with the design and architecture of individual components in the network such as links, routers, and switches; Chapter 6 is concerned with the design of high-performance end systems.

From a protocol perspective, we will be concerned with network layer processing necessary for high-speed networks. The network layer consists of routing, signaling, and addressing (Figure 4.1). Recall that in Chapter 2 we discussed the range of processing granularity and the effect of the time interval on high-speed network design:

- Protocol deployment
- **Network configuration**
- **Network management interval**
- **Session establishment and lifetime**
- **Connection/flow establishment and lifetime**
- Packet/frame transfer
- Cell transfer
- Byte transfer
- Bit transfer

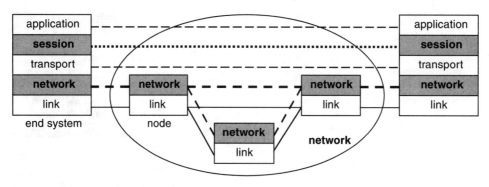

Figure 4.1 Network architecture and protocols.

Network nodes (switches and routers—Chapter 5) and end systems (Chapter 6) are concerned with data units such as bytes, cells, and packets. In this chapter, we are most concerned with connections, flows, and sessions, listed in boldface in the preceding list. These operate on time scales ranging from one to many orders of magnitude longer than those associated with packet, cell, or byte transfers.

These are units of control processing, rather than data processing, and present different challenges. In particular, we must ensure that the network control mechanisms support connection and flow establishment and management with sufficiently low latency for applications, especially in support of interactivity. The one exception is end-to-end issues for data flow between end systems, which will be covered in Chapter 7. In some cases issues are present at multiple layers (for example, congestion control), and will be discussed from a hop-by-hop perspective in this chapter, and from the end-to-end perspective in Chapter 7.

Figure 4.2 shows the ideal network model with the inside of the network expanded. In this chapter we will be concerned with the control, signaling, and management to establish and maintain high-performance paths, given the topology to support a high-performance path, as discussed in Chapter 3.

This chapter is organized as follows: Section 4.1 considers signaling and control issues, examining the overheads involved in the spectrum of connectionless to hard connection-oriented networks and for optical networks. Section 4.2 considers traffic management and congestion control in high-speed networks. Section discusses the issues in dynamic network topologies that motivate path rerouting. Section 4.4 considers issues in monitoring and management. Finally, Section 4.5 presents a summary and list of principles introduced throughout the chapter.

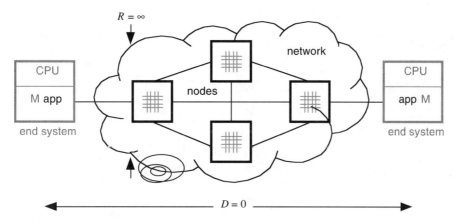

Figure 4.2   Ideal network model.

4.1   Signaling and Control

We will now examine signaling and control for high-speed networks. This is particularly important in connection-oriented networks (such as ATM) where explicit signaling is required to set up connections before data can flow. It is also an issue for higher-layer control protocols (for example, session control) and for signaling in connectionless networks, such as resource reservation protocol (RSVP) in IP networks. We will consider the tradeoffs in overhead in connection-oriented and connectionless networks, and examine intermediate solutions, such as the accumulation of flow state in connectionless networks. We will also examine burst switching, which is particularly important in optical networking.

In this section, we will depict the latency of packets and signaling messages through networks using packet flow diagrams, as shown in Figure 4.3.

Two network hops are shown, 1→2 and 2→3. The relative distance between nodes is depicted by the horizontal spacing of nodes (x_{12} and x_{23}). Time progresses downward; the slope of the line is the velocity of light in a particular medium, kc, where k is the medium-dependent multiplier (for example, 0.7 for optical fiber). Thus, the time to transmit a bit between nodes i and j is $t_p = x_{ij}/kc$. The transmission of signaling messages is shown by directional arrows, but a block of data b bits long is shown by a shaded parallelogram; the time to transmit or receive the bits b in a block is the transmission delay $t_b = b/r$, where r is the data rate.[1] Thus, a parallelogram is thick because either the data block is large or the link is slow. Delays at

---

[1]Signaling messages are generally short relative to data transmission, and their length in bits can be ignored in this analysis.

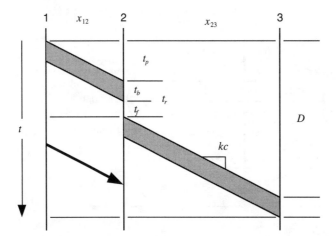

Figure 4.3 Packet flow diagram and parameters.

network nodes are shown by a step in the packet flow, and indicated by t_r or t_s (router or switch delay), depending on the context.[2] The components that may contribute to t_r or t_s (depending on the scenario) include the forwarding delay (which includes the time to label swap or do an address lookup) t_f, and the queuing delay t_q.

The analyses that follow are rough approximations with a number of simplifying assumptions to show significant tradeoffs between the different modes of transmission and signaling.

4.1.1 Circuit and Message Switching

First-generation (<1970s) networks used two techniques to transfer information through the network. Since these form the basis for the mechanisms used in high-speed networks, we will provide a brief introduction. We will then discuss their disadvantages, which require modifications of the basic schemes for use in high-speed networks.

4.1.1.1 Circuit Switching

Circuit switching is the mechanism used in the public switched telephone network (PSTN) to establish and transfer calls. It consists of explicitly establish-

---

[2]We will begin with the conventional usage of the term *router* for the store-and-forward datagram case and *switch* for the connection-oriented fast packet switch case. In later scenarios of fast datagram switching (Section 4.1.4) the distinction between the two is not particularly important.

ing a physical end-to-end connection that is dedicated to each pair of communicating devices (traditionally telephones), as shown in Figure 4.4.

A signal is used to establish the circuit, labeled SETUP in the forward direction and answered by CONNECT in the reverse direction. Note that this signal may be analog (as is the case in analog telephony) or digital; digital control

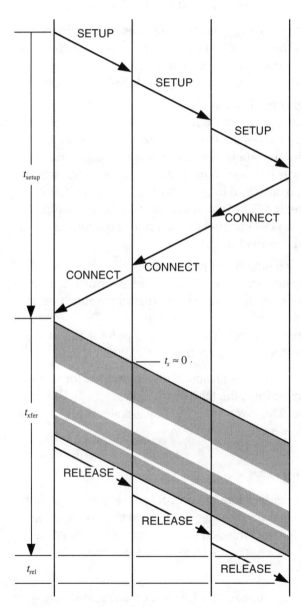

Figure 4.4 Circuit switching.

messages may be either out-of-band, as is the case for SS7 (signaling system number 7) [Russell 2000] in the digital telephone network, or in-band, as is the case for ATM networks.[3] While Figure 4.4 shows information transfer in only one direction, circuit switches typically switch full-duplex lines. In this case, we could superimpose the backward circuit on top of the forward flow. At the end of the transfer, a RELEASE signal propagates along the connection telling the switches to tear down the circuit; it can be initiated from either side. There are three important characteristics to note from this diagram:

Setup latency. A round-trip latency t_{setup} is required to establish the circuit. This latency is tolerable in the case of long-lived connections, such as telephone calls, or noninteractive media on demand, but may not be acceptable for short transactional messages across wide area networks.

Lack of multiplexing efficiency. The circuit is held until explicitly released, and during the connection there is no opportunity to multiplex other traffic on the circuit. This results in underutilization of resources, shown by the white gaps in the data transfer. In first-generation analog telephone networks, this was the case along physical links. In the second generation (1980s), digital trunks and long distance (class 4) switches used time division multiplexing (TDM) to share bandwidth on multiple virtual circuits, but within a TDM channel unused time slots during silence intervals still wasted bandwidth.

Low switch latency. There is insignificant propagation delay through switches in the case of physical circuits relative to the interswitch links: $t_s \approx 0$, as shown in Figure 4.4. In the case of TDM digital circuits, there is only the delay through digital logic time slot interchanges (TSIs), which is small in properly engineered switches. The important point is that there is no buffering or store-and-forward delays in switch nodes (t_b, t_q, $t_f = 0$)

The setup latency is a disadvantage in high-speed data networks for a number of applications such as transactions; the lack of multiplexing efficiency is a disadvantage for bursty traffic. The low switch latency is a significant advantage over message switching, as described next.

4.1.1.2 *Message Switching*

In message switching, messages (either data or control) are sent as a unit, hop-by-hop through the network. The entire message is received and stored at each node, until it can be scheduled for transmission on the appropriate outgoing link, as shown in Figure 4.5, which depicts the transfer of three messages.

---

[3]ATM signaling is in-band with respect to the physical link, but may be out-of-band with respect to individual virtual connections.

We can observe three characteristics of message switching in the figure:

No setup latency. There is no need to explicitly signal the establishment of a path; the message can be sent whenever the end system is ready.

Store-and-forward latency. Each node must receive the entire message, determine which outgoing link will get to the next hop, and hold the message until the link is available. This means that the end-to-end latency includes the time for the switch to make the forwarding decision and the length of the message $t_b + t_f$ at *each* hop.

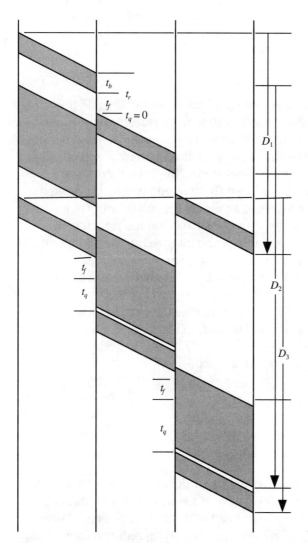

Figure 4.5 Message switching.

Queuing latency. While messages can be multiplexed on the links, there will be substantial queuing delays when there is large variance in the size of the messages, even in a relatively lightly loaded network. Note that the first two messages in Figure 4.5 are able to leave the node after the forwarding delay t_f. The third message, however, is subjected to queuing delay t_q, which increases at each hop due to the much longer second message. Thus, the latency for the third packet D_3 is substantially longer than for the first D_1. While we show a sequence of messages between a pair of points, this effect will occur whenever messages contend for the same outgoing link in a network node. Thus large message cross traffic is detrimental to short message traffic. This problem can be severe in heavily loaded networks with message sizes spanning many orders of magnitude (tens of bytes for transactions to megabytes for file transfer).

4.1.2   Packet Switching

The solution to the multiplexing inefficiency of circuit switching and the queuing delays of message switching is packet switching [Kleinrock 1961, Baran 1964, Davies 1967]. By dividing data transmissions into packets, a number of concurrent communicating applications are statistically multiplexed on a link. By providing reasonable bounds on the packet size, the queuing delays of message switching can be substantially reduced (but not completely eliminated).

Packet switching comes in two flavors, based on the relationship to circuit or message switching. *Datagram forwarding* is based on the principle of breaking long messages into shorter packets and interleaving them with one another. At each network router node, a per datagram decision is made to determine the next hop in the path. Virtual circuit packet switching is based on setting up multiple virtual circuits, which interleave packets to share the same physical path. Connection state is used to streamline the packet-forwarding decision at each node, and a per packet connection identifier is used to fetch the state at each packet switch node.

Thus, we can list a spectrum of control mechanisms:

- Message switching
- Datagram forwarding
- Virtual circuit packet switching
- Circuit switching

In this section, we will discuss datagram forwarding and concentrate on the overhead that results from store-and-forward. Store-and-forward virtual circuit switching suffers the *additional* overhead of virtual circuit setup latency t_{setup}, described in Section 4.1.1, with only slight benefit in reduced forwarding overhead.

In traditional datagram networks, packets are immediately sent through the network without the requirement for any explicit setup of the network path. Routing algorithms run asynchronously on a relatively long time scale to keep forwarding tables up to date.

Thus, we are not concerned here with the routing algorithms themselves, but merely in the overhead required to forward packets. Mechanisms to minimize the overhead of forwarding decisions will be discussed in Section 5.5.2. At each hop, packets are read into memory, and then the header is examined and compared to the forwarding table to determine the next hop router and outgoing link. Once this decision has been made, the packet can be written to the correct output interface. Such a flow is shown in Figure 4.6.

The time taken for a packet to traverse h hops consists of the propagation delay of each hop $\Sigma_h t_p$, the delay at each of the $h - 1$ routers $(h - 1)t_r$, and the delay of transferring the packet into the end system t_b. Since this is store-and-forward routing, the delay at each node t_r consists of the time to transfer the

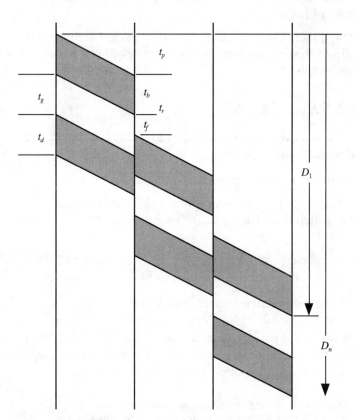

Figure 4.6 Conventional datagram forwarding.

packet into the router t_b, the routing lookup and forwarding delay t_f, and queuing delay[4] t_q, that is, $t_r = t_b + t_f + t_q$. Thus the total delay for a single packet is

$$D_1 = ht_b + \sum_h t_p + (h - 1)(t_f + t_q)$$

For a stream of n packets, we have to add the time taken for the additional packets to be transmitted, $(n - 1) \max(t_g, t_r)$, where t_g is the interpacket gap. The total delay to traverse the network is then

$$D_n = (n + h - 1)t_b + (n - 1) \max [(t_g - t_b), (t_f + t_q)] + \sum_h t_p + (h - 1)(t_f + t_q)$$

We can make four observations from this formula:

1. As the packet size increases, the delay t_b increases significantly, since it must be stored at each hop: ht_b.

2. As the length of the flow n increases, the importance of the distance latency t_p, forwarding delay t_f, and queuing delay t_q decreases in relative importance: $n \gg h$.

3. In long-haul networks the distance latency t_p is relatively important; in LANs the forwarding delay t_f (and perhaps queuing delay t_q) dominates (for the same number of hops).

4. If the forwarding and queuing delays exceed the interpacket arrival time $t_r > t_g$, the forwarding delay dominates and the number of hops h contributes significantly to the latency.

4.1.3   Fast Packet Switching

Traditional datagram-forwarding virtual circuit packet switching architectures suffer from a number of performance problems:

- The store-and-forward latency of packets is significant.

- It is difficult to design a high-performance store-and-forward router, throttling the rate at which links can operate (keeping t_b large for a given packet size).

- Resource reservation mechanisms were not present, making it difficult to provide QOS guarantees to applications such as multimedia streams.

The way to deal with these inefficiencies was to design fast virtual circuit packet switches, which make rapid switching decisions based on a connection identifier in the packet header, and merely swap the label [Kulzer 1984, Turner 1986]. The label swap is performed as the packet enters the switching fabric, and thus store-and-forward operation is not necessary. Packets can *cut*

---

[4]The queuing delay due to contention for an outgoing link or nonuniform packet sizes is not shown in the packet flow diagram; the formulas assume uniform packet lengths and that t_b does not dominate due to very large packets, in which case this degenerates to the message switching case.

through the switch, unless there is blocking in the switch fabric or contention for an output port. We will attempt to minimize the probability of these events by the switch design techniques presented in Chapter 5.

This means that signaling messages are required to set up the connections (and reserve resources) through the network, as for circuit switching. Interleaving of packets from multiple virtual connections provides statistical multiplexing gains.

4.1.3.1 Connection Signaling

There are two types of signaling messages: those with end-to-end significance[5] and hop-by-hop acknowledgments. End-to-end messages traverse the entire network to perform the connection setup, modification, and teardown. It is essential to ensure the delivery of signaling messages in a reasonable time. Thus, whenever a signaling message is sent to the next hop, a timer is started corresponding roughly to the round-trip time plus signaling processing at the next hop. When a node receives a message, it returns an acknowledgment to the sender. If the sending node does not receive the acknowledgment before the timer expires, the original signaling message is resent. Note that this is a critical way to reduce latency. If the hop-by-hop acknowledgment were not used, a sender of a signaling message would have to wait for the response to propagate through the *entire network*, rather than just the next hop, to determine if retransmission was necessary. Thus, we have Minimized Round Trips (6A) with the effect of a three-way handshake [Tomlinson 1974] with only a single round-trip end-to-end delay.

Figure 4.7 shows a typical connection setup signaling flow and data-transfer phase. A SETUP message is sent by the source, and traverses the network. At each switch node in the network, the following occurs:[6]

- The signaling message is decoded.

- The connection routing protocol uses the destination address and information in the topology and link state database to determine the outgoing link.

- Traffic parameters are used to determine if the switch and outgoing link have sufficient resources to support the connection; if not, the connection is denied and a RELEASE message is returned to the source.[7]

- PROCEEDING acknowledgment is returned to the last hop, to ensure delivery of the SETUP message; if a timer expires before PROCEEDING is received, the SETUP is retransmitted.

- The SETUP message is propagated to the next hop.

---

[5]Recall from the Endpoint Recursion Corollary (3B) that the scope of this "end-to-end" association may be limited to part of the network, for example, spanning just a subnetwork.
[6]This example is similar to ATM signaling, but is generally applicable to any hard-connection state network.
[7]Or, in some cases, a crankback mechanism may be used to go back to the last hop to attempt a different connection routing.

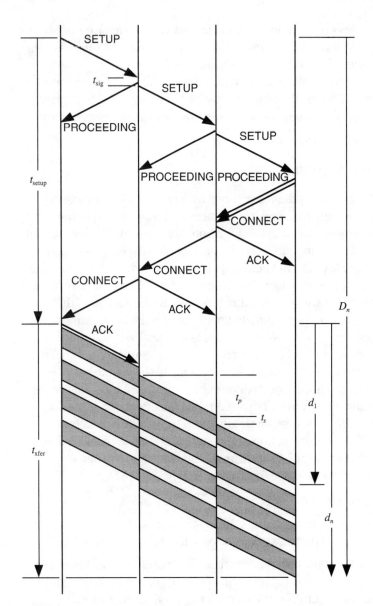

Figure 4.7   Connection-oriented switching.

At each node there is latency to process the signaling message t_{sig}. When the SETUP has propagated to the destination, a CONNECT message is returned to the source. At each switch node, resources provisionally reserved are committed. This takes some time but less than the forward signaling latency. An ACK acknowledgment is returned in response to each CONNECT message to ensure its delivery.

Once the CONNECT message has returned to the source, data transfer may begin. Thus, the latency to set up a connection is the sum of the round-trip propagation delay through the network and the signaling delays at each switch:

$$t_{\text{setup}} = 2\sum_h t_p + (2h - 1)t_{\text{sig}}$$

For this analysis, we assume that signaling messages are small and their transmission time is negligible ($t_h = 0$); that t_{sig} is the average of forward and reverse signaling delays, which includes the delay in turning the SETUP around to CONNECT at the destination; and that packet sizes are uniform.

The data transfer phase is calculated in a manner similar to the datagram router, with one significant difference. In the optimal case, the delay at each switch t_s consists *only* of the forwarding decision and queuing delay $t_s = t_f + t_q$, without the need to completely read the packet in before the forwarding process begins. This is the case when there is no contention among inputs for a particular output port, otherwise substantial queuing delay must be added. The ability to cut through the switch is shown in Figure 4.7 by the overlap of the data transfer parallelograms in successive hops. Thus, the delay for a single packet to traverse the network is

$$d_1 = t_b + \sum_h t_p + (h - 1)t_s$$

As before, for a stream of packets we add the transmission times of the additional $n - 1$ packets, and the total time is

$$t_{\text{xfer}} = d_n = nt_b + (n - 1)\, t_g + \sum_h t_p + (h - 1)t_s$$

Finally, we can add the signaling and data transfer components to get a total latency of

$$D_n = t_{\text{setup}} + t_{\text{xfer}} = nt_b + (n - 1)\, t_g + 3\sum_h t_p + (2h - 1)t_{\text{sig}} + (h - 1)t_s$$

When the data transfer is complete, a RELEASE and RELEASE COMPLETE message exchange occurs to tear down the connection and free resources. This exchange does not directly affect the latency under consideration, but does affect the ability of other connections to be established. We can now make some observations:

1. It takes *three* end-to-end latencies to accomplish the data transfer, which is one extra round-trip time greater than datagram forwarding. In the case of a LAN, this may be insignificant relative to the application response time requirements; in the case of a WAN, this latency may be a significant problem.

2. For a single packet transfer, for example, a transaction request, the signaling overhead dominates and may be intolerable. For a long data stream, the signaling overhead is amortized over the entire transfer.

3. Fast packet switches are designed for high data rate links, thus the packet transmission time t_b is relatively small for a given packet size. Thus for long streams of packets, the extra round-trip connection setup is amortized across the lower latency of the forward data transfer.

We have addressed the concerns with conventional datagram forwarding, but at some cost.

- The store-and-forward latency of a conventional router has been eliminated and the bandwidth has been increased, at the cost of the latency suffered to explicitly set up the connection.

- Resource reservation mechanisms can be deployed to provide QOS guarantees to applications such as multimedia streams.

- Neither of these improvements makes transactions go faster, but a permanent virtual connection mesh can be used to provide a pure best-effort datagram service without suffering the latency of connection establishment per datagram.

> **Connectionless versus Connection Tradeoff**   *The latency of connection setup must be traded against the reduction in end-to-end data transfer delay due to the elimination of store and forward delay, and faster transmission due to nodes capable of increased bandwidth.*
>
> **N-5A**

We have seen that connection setup can have a significant effect on delaying the data-transfer phase, particularly due to the speed-of-light delay in wide area networks. Thus, the goal is to minimize the number of round-trips that must be taken by signaling messages before data transfer begins.

Clearly, we don't want to suffer *multiple* round-trips in a control establishment, and the simple point-to-point connection setup described has only one round-trip. There are more complex signaling scenarios that may not be as simple, for example, multicast flow establishment. This issue will be discussed with respect to session control later in this section.

4.1.3.2   *Signaling Complexity*

In connection-oriented high-speed networks, it is essential to keep the signaling latency t_{sig} reasonably small. Signaling operations can be quite complex, and it is important that they do not dominate the overall latency. There are two key ways to achieve this.

First, the format and encoding of the signaling messages should be simple enough to allow fast decoding and processing of the message. Control fields should be in byte increments and fixed size when practical; they should have a corresponding length field when variable size is necessary. Byte granularity bit vectors should be used for control flags, rather then complex coded fields.

Second, signaling messages should fit into a single control packet. If this is not the case, then a reliable fragmentation/reassembly protocol must operate between each hop, adding overhead. This is a case where the End-to-End Arguments (3) applies. The signaling state machines cannot assume that another node will respond to a message, whether or not it is reliably delivered by the underlying protocol. Thus, signaling protocols must implement reliability at the control message level using timers and retransmissions, regardless of the reliability of the message transport mechanisms. There are cases where transport reliability mechanisms enhance performance, however. An example is to apply forward error correction (FEC) to signaling messages on noisy wireless links. This is the application of the Hop-by-Hop Performance Enhancement Corollary (3A).

Efficiency of Signaling   *Signaling messages should be simple in coding and format and fit in a single packet to minimize the latency in processing. The signaling protocol should be robust to lost messages.*

N-8B

EXAMPLE 4.1: ATM SIGNALING

The basic flow of signaling messages in ATM is quite sensible, and the hop-by-hop acknowledgments minimize the latency impact of dropped signaling messages. The main concern here is simply the round-trip latency of hard-connection setup.

Unfortunately, ATM signaling messages themselves are extremely complex, both in parameters and encoding. This is an unfortunate legacy from SS7 signaling, on which ATM is based. Furthermore, due to the extremely small cell size, signaling messages cannot fit into a single cell (and couldn't even if the messages were considerably simpler). Thus, a complex hop-by-hop signaling ATM adaptation layer (S-AAL) is required which segments signaling messages into cells, and reliably reassembles cells back into the signaling message, requesting retransmission of lost cells when needed. This violates the Efficiency of Signaling (N-8B) principle. ATM switches deployed in the mid-1990s were typically capable of only a few hundred to a thousand connection establishments per second.

4.1.4 Intermediate Control Mechanisms

We have begun to build a spectrum of control and signaling mechanisms, ranging from autonomous messages to circuits. The varieties of packet switching presented still present significantly different mechanisms: store-and-forward datagrams and connections with hard predetermined state. We can further refine the spectrum, concentrating on the way in which state information is established on the flow of data:

- Per message forwarding (message switching)
- Per packet conventional datagram forwarding
- **Data-driven soft state accumulation**
- **Control-driven soft state distribution**
- **Optimistic connection establishment**
- **Fast reservation**
- Explicit virtual connection setup (fast packet switching and virtual circuit switching)[8]
- Explicit physical connection setup (circuit switching)

Thus we need not accept the disadvantages of datagram forwarding and virtual connection setup, and will explore the intermediate mechanisms in bold font.

Network Path Establishment   *The routing algorithms and signaling mechanisms must be capable of forwarding datagrams or establishing connections on sufficiently high-performance paths and with low latency to meet application demands.*

N-II.1

State accumulation and distribution are mechanisms to speed up datagram networks by enabling fast packet switching; fast reservations and optimistic connection establishment are mechanisms to reduce the latency overhead in connection-oriented networks. In all of these schemes, we get the benefits of the higher data rates associated with fast packet switching, without the latency of connection setup, at least for a significant number of the packets in a long flow.

---

[8]Fast packet switching avoids the need to store-and-forward; in both cases, connections are explicitly set up.

4.1.4.1   Soft State Accumulation

It is possible to modify the basic datagram forwarding scheme to address the inefficiencies of store-and-forward datagrams, and to enable the construction of datagram switches. This can be done in one of three ways:

1. Adding a flow identifier to the datagram header, which is the index into the forwarding table.

2. Prepending labels to the datagram, enabling fast label swapping, as described in Section 5.3.2.

3. Putting a source route in the packet header, as described in Section 5.5.2.

The first two methods are broadly applicable; for example, IPv6 uses a flow identifier and multiple label switching (MPLS) performs label swapping. The ability to exploit source routing is more problematic, however. While source routing allows simple processing at the node (popping the next hop off the forwarding stack in the header), it requires the end system to have current knowledge about network topology and link state, and precompute the route. This is generally not a favorable tradeoff. Furthermore, network providers generally do not expose this information outside their administrative boundaries. There are some special cases where source routing might be considered as an option.

By using a flow identifier or label swapping, datagrams can be switched in the same manner as fast packet switching, eliminating the per hop store-and-forward latency and increasing bandwidth. These mechanisms will be described in Chapter 5. *Soft state* is introduced into the router in one of two ways:

Control driven. Signaling is used to set the state in conjunction with the routing protocols. Unlike the case of explicit signaling, this is done asynchronously by forwarding equivalence classes (FECs), which are sets of packets that get forwarded to the same next hop (for example, based on destination address). This provides the benefits of connection setup without requiring the overhead of the signaling round-trip before each data transfer (for example, [Rekhter 1997]).

Data driven. The router must recognize that a set of traversing packets is associated with a *flow*, in which case, label or flow-switching entries are established and label information exchanged with other routers. Until this happens, conventional store-and-forward routing takes place [Newman 1996]. The router may also propagate signaling messages along the flow path to inform other routers that a flow has been recognized.

The state is referred to as *soft*, because it is not needed to forward packets, but rather is introduced as necessary to increase the forwarding efficiency and times out if not explicitly removed.

Figure 4.8 shows a flow in which the first four packets are forwarded in the conventional manner; the latency in routing mode is t_r. Once the router recognizes a flow (based, for example, on a particular source/destination address

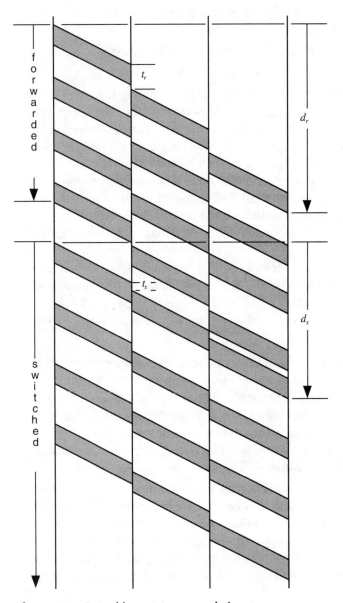

Figure 4.8   Data-driven state accumulation.

pair), it can change modes into fast packet switching. The switching latency is then $t_s < t_r$, and end-to-end delay in transferring a single packet is $d_s < d_r$.

4.1.4.2   Overlapped Control and Data

We can approach the middle ground in the signaling spectrum from the connection-oriented side as well. One of the main problems with connection-oriented protocols is the round-trip latency for connection setup before data can be transferred. A solution to this problem is to overlap the setup signaling with data transfer, on the expectation that sufficient resources will be available and the reservation will be successful.

Overlap Signaling Messages with Data Transfer   *To reduce unneeded end-to-end latency, signaling messages should be overlapped with data transfer.*

N-6A

4.1.4.1.1   Initial Best-Effort Phase

One way to accomplish this is to optimistically send data shortly after the connection setup message, with the expectation that there are sufficient network resources to handle the data and that the connection will actually be established. Until the connection has been established and resources reserved, data is transferred on a best-effort basis, as in the traditional Internet. This is shown in Figure 4.9.

As in the case of conventional connection establishment, a SETUP message is issued. After a delay, which is an estimate of the SETUP message processing time along the entire path Σt_{sig}, the data is optimistically sent.[9] A COMMIT message is returned, indicating that the connection establishment was successful and resources committed along the entire path. As for conventional connection establishment, if resources cannot be committed, a RELEASE message is returned, indicating that resources are not available to establish the connection.

4.1.4.1.2   Fast Reservation

Alternatively, the network nodes may do a fast reservation procedure [Hui 1988, Ohnishe 1988, Cidon 1990, Turner 1991, Suzuki 1992, Boyer 1982, 1994] so that by the time the first packet reaches the node the resources are already reserved. In this case, the delay should be long enough to allow

---

[9]The data should not arrive at a node unless the signaling message has already propagated to the next node. Thus, the sum of the signaling delays should be used as the estimate, since data packets may cut through individual nodes faster than the signaling delay.

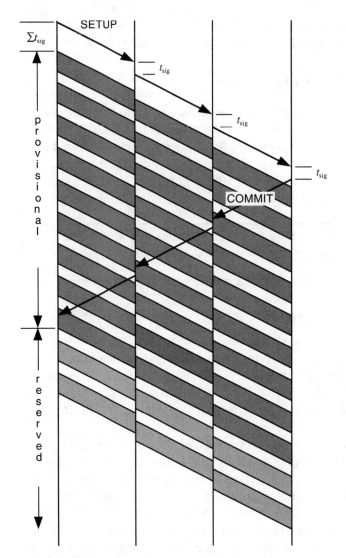

Figure 4.9   Optimistic connection establishment.

the per hop tentative reservation to actually occur, in addition to the signaling message processing. If the reservations occur along every node to the destination, the return COMMIT signaling message commits the tentative reservations.

Unlike the best-effort case, resources are reserved at each hop, but this is a provisional reservation, since there is no assurance that the reservations can be made the rest of the way to the destination.

4.1.5   Fast Circuit and Burst Switching

We presented fast packet switching as the solution to the inefficiencies of circuit and message switching, but it is not the only solution to consider. It is now time to return to circuit switching and consider how to directly deal with its inefficiencies. There are two situations in which traditional circuit switching makes sense:

1. Traffic is not very bursty, that is, the average and peak data rates are similar. Circuits can be established and resources reserved without the inefficiencies of wasted bandwidth on a physical path or in TDM slots.[10]

2. The time for the switch to select paths is very long relative to the time to receive a packet t_b, and therefore the unit of data that is switched should be longer than in packet switching.

If a significant fraction of the traffic is bursty, conventional circuit switching wastes bandwidth, but packet-switched virtual circuits can still provide some of the benefits if there are resource reservation mechanisms. This is done by providing per virtual circuit or flow reservations (in fine granularity integrated services mechanisms such as provided by ATM and Internet integrated service model intserv [Zhang 1993, Wroclawski 1997]), or coarse granularity service differentiation (such as the Internet differentiated service model diffserv [Blake 1998, Kilkki 1999]). The statistical multiplexing gain for bursty traffic can be achieved in other traffic classes. The traffic management styles will be described in Section 4.2.

Conventionally, circuit switching also suffers from the overhead of connection setup, but as we showed for optimistic connection establishment, there are fast reservation mechanisms that can be applied, leading to *fast circuit switching* [Easton 1982] and *burst switching* [Amstutz 1983]. There isn't universal agreement on the distinction between the terms *fast circuit* and *burst switching*. The original usage in the context of the PSTN considered fast circuit switching to be on a dedicated link with path establishment separated from talk spurt reservation, and burst switching multiplexed on TDM slots with simultaneous path selection and burst reservation. In optical networking, the term *burst switching* is used in all cases.

The relative merits of fast packet switching using statistical multiplexing (asynchronous transfer mode) and fast circuit switching using synchronous transfer mode can be debated [Kümmerle 1978, O'Reilly 1987, Joel 1996]. Although it is the asynchronous transfer mode[11] of fast packet switching that has

---

[10]The partitioning of the efficiency space between circuit and packet switching based on the number of flows and per flow utilization is quantified in [Thompson 1996].

[11]We intentionally avoid the use of the acronym ATM, due to its common use as the name of a specific protocol suite, which happens to use asynchronous transfer mode as the multiplexing technique.

generally prevailed for electronic switches, it is possible to dynamically reserve resources in a fast circuit switched TDM network [Wu 1987, Lindgren 1994, Bohm 1996]. The benefits are simpler traffic management and tighter control over latency, at the cost of coarser granularity in bandwidth reservations (incremental in number of slots) and perhaps less efficient utilization of network bandwidth.

It is the second situation listed earlier that motivates burst switching in optical networks. In the fourth generation (2000s), optical switches are controlled by electronics, with only the datapath switched in the optical domain. Since the rate at which switching operations can occur is relatively slow, these almost-all-optical networks are not capable of packet switching. Thus, we will concentrate on burst switching for optical networks [Turner 1999, Qiao 1999]. Chapter 9 will mention the prospect of all-optical packet switching networks in the fifth generation, which could use the techniques we have already described for fast packet and datagram switching.

There are four variations of burst switching: *tell-and-go* (TAG), and its variant *in-band-terminator* (IBT), and *reserve-a-fixed-duration* (RFD), and its variant *just-enough-time* (JET). In all four variations, fast reservation is similar to fast reservation optimistic connection establishment, but at the burst level.

4.1.5.1   *Open-Ended Reservations*

TAG (tell-and-go) is depicted in Figure 4.10. A SETUP control packet is sent on a separate control channel to reserve bandwidth and set the path through switches. The data is then sent along the established path, as for optimistic connection establishment, but no CONNECT response is needed. Each burst may consist of a sequence of packets; multiplexing efficiency is maximized by avoiding interpacket gaps in the burst.

At each switch, there is the delay t_{sig} to decode the SETUP message, after which it can be sent to the next hop. Additionally, there is a delay t_{set} to set the data path between input and output ports on the switch. Note that the initial delay t_{delay} between the injection of the SETUP message and the transmission of the data burst must account for the accumulating t_{sig} delays at each hop.[12] If the reservation cannot be made (at all or in time), packets are generally dropped, although it is possible to do a fast conversion to the electronic domain to buffer single packets in the case of contention for an output port.

At the end of the burst, a RELEASE message is sent along the control channel to release the path resources; this is called *open-ended* reservation. It is

---

[12]This is also the case for optimistic virtual connection establishment, but only to the degree that $t_{sig} > t_s$, since fast packet switches delay the data, unlike optical burst switches for which $t_s \approx 0$.

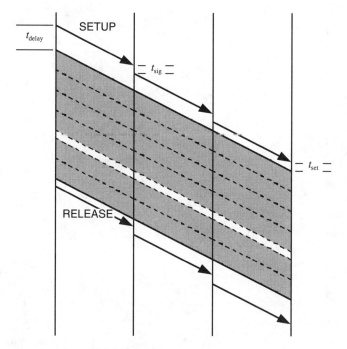

Figure 4.10   TAG burst switching.

also possible to use soft state to maintain the burst path, by sending periodic REFRESH control messages to keep the path alive.

In in-band terminator (IBT), each burst has an in-band burst header and trailer to indicate the beginning and end of the burst, respectively, as shown in Figure 4.11. This makes IBT look like message switching, but with reservations and the switch cut-through of circuit switching.

IBT has the advantage of not requiring out-of-band signaling, but requires that the burst packets be delayed enough at each hop to decode the header, do the fast reservation, and set the path, $t_{\mathrm{sig+set}}$. This delay is accomplished by fiber delay lines at each input controller. IBT also has the advantage of *immediately* releasing the switch reservation and path at the end of the burst.

4.1.5.2   *Closed-Ended Reservation*

The third variation of burst switching, RFD (reserve a fixed duration) [Mei 1997], is shown in Figure 4.12. RFD is distinguished from TAG by the explicit signaling of the expected burst duration t_B as a parameter of the SETUP message; this is a *closed-ended* reservation and does not require a RELEASE message.

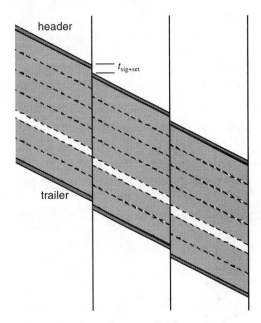

Figure 4.11 IBT burst switching.

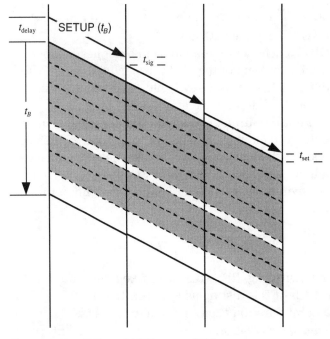

Figure 4.12 RFD and JET burst switching.

One of the advantages of using closed-ended reservation is that it facilitates intelligent resource allocation, when used in conjunction with a large enough offset time. Packets are grouped into bursts at the edge of the optical subnetwork, and more optimal link- and path-multiplexing assignments can be performed, as described in Section 3.1.4. This can eliminate the need to buffer packets in the optical switches due to contention for output ports, which in the early fourth generation (2000s) is impractical in the optical domain, and expensive in the electronic domain.

JET (just-enough-time) [Yoo 1997] is a variant of RFD, which explicitly calculates and signals the delay between the SETUP and burst t_{delay} to *each* switch. This has the potential for even more efficient resource utilization and wavelength assignment, allowing tighter interburst scheduling.

4.1.5.3 Closed- versus Open-Ended Reservation

As is so often the case, the choice of which signaling mechanism performs the best is a tradeoff [Qiao 1999]. The tradeoff between open- and closed-ended reservations lies in the ability to predict the burst length. Closed-ended reservation is most efficient when the burst lengths are either predictable in advance (such as for a long-lived flow with uniform packet lengths) or the memory penalty and latency hit of buffering at the ingress of the optical network to perform intelligent wavelength assignments are not too severe.

It is possible to consider a hybrid scheme that adds to RFD or JET the ability to explicitly signal connection RELEASE (as in TAG) if the burst is shorter than predicted or signal REFRESH if the burst is longer than anticipated.

4.1.6 Multicast Flows

So far we have considered only the issues associated with point-to-point connections. As mentioned in Chapter 3, multicast [Dalal 1978, Kadaba 1983] is an important way to conserve bandwidth in the network and processing at the end systems. The establishment of a multipoint flow involves many of the same basic issues as the establishment of a point-to-point flow, but is considerably more complicated, due to the requirement for a state establishment mechanism and the greater control message overhead. We will discuss state establishment here, and defer the control message overhead issue to Section 4.2.

State is required to establish and maintain a multicast tree, even in an otherwise stateless datagram network. The Network Path Principle (N-II) applies to multicast, but in this case to a spanning tree rather than a linear path. The problem is to globally optimize the assignment of the multicast tree to network links; this is an NP-complete problem to which heuristics must be applied [Waxman 1988]. The model used to establish the multicast tree can have a profound effect on performance, particularly in the case of very large multicast groups.

Figure 4.13a shows a small multipoint tree consisting of a root end system R and two leaf end systems 1 and 2. There are two ends from which additional group members can be added. In *root initiated join*, the root system is responsible for adding the new leaf to the tree. This requires a priori knowledge of the leaf to be added, or an additional signaling request to the root requesting to be added. The advantage is simplicity; to request joining a multipoint group a node only need send a JOIN-REQUEST message addressed to the root node of the multipoint tree. Then, ADD signaling messages propagate from the root down to the leaf, adding new links and nodes to the tree when necessary. This scheme is most appropriate for small groups, particularly when a single node or end system has predetermined knowledge of the group members. The loading of hierarchical caches (described in Section 8.3.1) is an example of when root control of the multicast tree is appropriate, assuming the root cache has knowledge of the cache hierarchy.

Root-controlled multicast does not scale at all well to large dynamic groups, due to the increasing signaling load on nodes closer to the root. This limits the rate at which the root can adapt to dynamic group behavior (join and leaves). Root-initiated join was first used for ATM point-to-multipoint connections, due to its simplicity.

A more scalable approach is for the leaf node to request membership in the group by sending a JOIN message to the tree; this is called *leaf initi-*

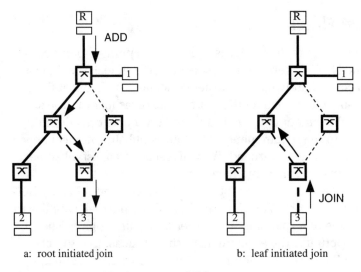

a: root initiated join   b: leaf initiated join

Figure 4.13   Multipoint tree establishment.

ated join, shown in Figure 4.13b.[13] This requires multipoint group addresses and routing, which are capable of finding an efficient route to the tree. This can be an extremely complex problem, dependent on the addressing scheme. If the multipoint address is that of the root node, and addresses match a clustering hierarchy (as in Figure 2.8), a joining node can relatively easily find the lowest layer in the group hierarchy to which its address matches. The leaf-initiated join mechanism is used in IP multicast [Deering 1989, 1991] (called *receiver initiated*), but unfortunately IP multicast uses a distinct address space that does not assist nodes in finding an optimal route to the group. Leaf initiated join was later added to ATM multipoint connection signaling to deal with the scaling problem for large multicast groups.

> **Root versus Leaf Multicast Control**   *Root multicast control is appropriate when a single entity has knowledge of the multicast group. Leaf-controlled multicast is needed for large dynamic groups.*
>
> **N-6B**

A compromise between the two extremes is to use a hierarchy of subroot nodes [Perlman 2000]. In this case, the multipoint group is clustered, and a leaf node that wishes to join the group sends a JOIN-REQUEST to the nearest multipoint cluster leader. This scheme can be efficiently combined with a hierarchical addressing hierarchy, as described in Section 3.2.2.

4.1.7   Session Control

A *session* is an association among multiple-user applications that involves a number of transport layer flows, connections, and/or transactions. Session control protocols such as session invitation protocol (SIP) [Handley 1999] initiate and control sessions. For example, a collaborative session may consist of a number of users, and involve multipoint audio-video connections, and a variety of data connections for shared whiteboard and document editing. Thus, the session layer is a control plane layer between the transport and application layers.[14] Session control must support dynamic multiparty multiconnection behavior, including SESS-JOIN/SESS-LEAVE and SESS-MERGE/SESS-SPLIT operations.

The high-performance issues in session control [Sterbenz 1996b] are similar to those of connection control; the latency of session establishment must be small enough to meet user and application requirements. Similarly,

---

[13]Root-initiated join and leaf-initiated join are called *centralized* and *decentralized*, respectively, by [Perlman 2000].

[14]Which happens to correspond roughly to the position of the OSI session layer, but not to OSI-defined functionality.

the response to dynamic behavior of the participants must be of sufficiently low latency. There are two concerns to consider: avoiding round trips in the session control protocol and associated connection/flow control mechanisms, and the location of session resources to be within reasonable latency bounds.

4.1.7.1   Avoiding Round Trips

At the highest level, session control protocols require an ESTABLISH/ESTABLISHED control message flow analogous to the SETUP/CONNECT procedure discussed for connection control protocols, as shown in Figure 4.14.

The main difference is that instead of directly reserving network resources, requests are being made to transport layer protocols to establish network connections or flows, or application address associations are being established for datagrams and transactions.

Session protocols have several characteristics that limit the ability to establish in a single round trip:

- Iterative negotiation between parties; for example, the destination user conditionally rejects the session request with countercriteria that must be negotiated with the requestor.

- Establishment of multiple transport layer connections, each of which may be multileg (multiple layer 4 "hops," for example, a two-leg connection between a sending user and transcoder and between the transcoder and the receiving user).

- Serial dependencies of the connection setups within a session.

So while we can't guarantee that only a single round trip will be involved, there are several techniques to minimize the total number of round trips in the session and network layer protocols before user applications can begin communicating:

- Establish as many connections/flows as possible in parallel.

- Begin connection SETUP as soon as the SESS-REQUEST message has propagated through the network, before the SESS-ESTABLISH message, as shown in Figure 4.14; this is accomplished by pushing parameters in the SESS-REQUEST message that can be used by the remote side in SETUP parameters, saving an end-to-end latency.

- Send ranges of parameters and lists of acceptable criteria for negotiation, as is done in ATM with desired and acceptable QOS parameters.

- Cache information on the location, characteristics, and preferences of the communicating applications in a local profile.

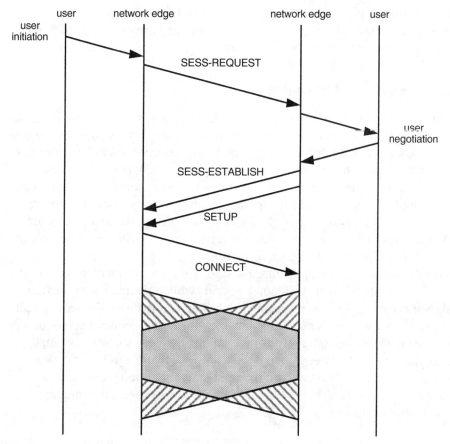

Figure 4.14   Session control signaling.

Complex session negotiations can involve a number of distributed parties, servers (for example, directories and Web servers), and resources (for example, transcoders and reflectors). Applying these optimizations can reduce tens of round-trip latencies to several.

In some cases, connections are expensive to set up, in terms of latency to the application and complexity to the network. An obvious example of this is multicast trees, but semipermanent virtual circuits in some subnetwork technologies or connections that use gateways also qualify. In this case, intelligence in session control can be exploited to reuse these layer 3 connections from session to session, rearranging when necessary rather than setting them up from scratch.

Session–Connection Interlayer Awareness   *Session control awareness of network layer control parameters allows the overlap of session and control signaling to reduce overall latency.*

N-4F

These techniques of connection reuse and pushing connection parameters in the session message to avoid an end-to-end latency are examples of the use of interlayer awareness to enhance performance.

4.1.7.2 *Location of Resources*

Sessions may involve a variety of resources in the network, for example, audio mixers and video transcoders for a collaborative session. Thus, a resource discovery protocol must determine where the best resources are before connection and flow establishment at the network layer can take place. The first concern here is to minimize the latency of discovery. Resource discovery algorithms should rely on location information cached near the users to avoid the algorithmic complexity and latency of locating resources each time they are requested. This is similar to using control-driven flow forwarding protocols to increase the efficiency of datagram forwarding.

Secondly, the discovery algorithms need to find resources which are located close enough to meet the latency bound (while meeting the other functional requirements of the applications, including bandwidth). For example, if two users need a transcoder to communicate, the session control protocol will need to discover a transcoder that is geographically close to, or between, the users to stay within the latency budget and set up a two-legged connection. Choosing a transcoder in New York to connect users in Delhi and Bombay would not be a good choice, if a transcoder with the needed functionality were available in Madras.

4.2   Traffic Management

Traffic management is an important aspect of network control, allowing network providers to optimize the deployment of resources and providing end users and applications with desired levels of service. These mechanisms are most important in networks where bandwidth is scarce; in a vastly overengineered network there is no need to worry about congestion control or optimality of traffic management.

There are two conflicting goals in the provision of network services to end users:

1. Provide sufficient resources to deliver the required quality of service (QOS) to the end-user application. This includes measures such as bandwidth, latency, jitter, and loss rates.

2. Minimize the network resources necessary to support the required level of QOS. This is both a local optimization as well as a global networkwide optimization.

These are generic goals that are applicable to all networks, not only high-speed networks, and detailed discussion of the mechanisms that can be used to achieve them is beyond the scope of this book. We will focus here on how resource reservation and congestion control apply to high-speed network design.

Mixed traffic types can be supported by a network infrastructure in several very different ways:

Distinct networks. This was the situation through the second generation (1980s), with distinct network infrastructure for the PSTN, entertainment broadcast of video, and data networks. Distinct networks have the advantage of allowing each network's technology, topology, and protocols to be optimized for the traffic characteristics of a particular application class. They have the significant disadvantage of traditionally having distinct end systems (telephone set, television, and computer), or requiring end systems to have multiple network interfaces, and make it difficult for applications to mix the media types. As the Internet subsumes the PSTN as a subnetwork and replaces the CATV (cable television) infrastructure except as an access network, this model of infrastructure is disappearing in the fourth generation (2000s).

Virtual network partitioning. It is possible to create the effect of distinct networks on a common network infrastructure by partitioning switch and link resources into multiple noninterfering and noninteracting overlays. This is probably the worst of all worlds, since unless resources are very cheap, the proper partitioning is a difficult network engineering exercise, and the end-system and application problems are the same as in the distinct network case. Some saving in network infrastructure may be achieved by virtual network partitioning.

Differentiated services. Differentiated services refers to a coarse granularity differentiation of traffic classes in the network. It can be viewed as a more integrated form of virtual distinct networks, and a coarse-grained traffic class aggregation of integrated services.

Integrated services. This is the vision of a single integrated infrastructure originally proposed as integrated services digital network (ISDN) for the PSTN and then by broadband ISDN (B-ISDN) and ATM. In this model, a single network infrastructure supports integrated data, voice, video, and other media and application types (such as sensors and transactions), supporting QOS and resource reservations at arbitrary end-to-end granularity. It is critical that integrated services mechanisms scale when aggregated in the core network.

We will discuss the two important ways to manage traffic in a high-speed resource-constrained network: *resource reservation* and *congestion control*.

EXAMPLE 4.2: INTERNET AND ATM SERVICE MODELS

The second-generation (1980s) Internet provided only a best-effort service model. The only way to get any performance guarantees was to get a dedicated fixed-capacity end-to-end grade of service, similar to leasing a dedicated circuit in the PSTN; this provides only the coarsest granularity of service. Integrated services [Wroclawski 1997] for the Internet was proposed, using RSVP [Zhang 1993] as a reservation protocol to install soft state in routers, and requiring resource reservation mechanisms in the routers. The number of traffic classes is relatively small: controlled load, guaranteed QOS, and best effort. Unfortunately, the per flow RSVP model doesn't scale to the vast aggregation of flows necessary in the Internet backbone [Mankin 1997]. Thus a differentiated services model [Blake 1998] was proposed. This has the advantage of the coarse granularity in the backbone, but lacks the per flow guarantees needed by many applications. A hybrid hierarchical approach of using integrated services at the edge and differentiated services in the core is an approach to this dilemma [Bernet 1998, Eichler 2000].

B-ISDN and ATM were designed to be integrated service networks from the beginning, and scalable routing private network node interface (PNNI) [ATMF 1996p] and traffic management [ATMF 1996t] mechanisms were designed to provide a multitude of traffic classes: initially constant bit rate (CBR), real-time variable bit rate (VBR-rt), nonreal-time variable bit rate (VBR-nrt), and unspecified bit rate (UBR)—best effort . To better support Internet traffic, available bit rate (ABR) and guaranteed frame rate (GFR)—best effort with a minimum bandwidth guarantee were added. The mechanisms are scalable due to the two-level hierarchical aggregation (VCs in VPs) described in Example 3.2, by abstracting the user-signaled parameters to a smaller set in the link state databases, and by using the clustering techniques described in Section 3.2.2. However, the attempt to optimally utilize network resources (far beyond the capability of most applications to predict their own traffic patterns) results in significant algorithmic and signaling complexity in the switches. This is a case where recognizing that bandwidth is cheap enough to allow some overengineering, and simplifying the traffic management and number of classes would probably have sped the deployment of dynamic ATM networks. By the time switched virtual circuit (SVC) ATM networks with traffic management were just beginning to be deployed in the mid third generation (1990s), the future of ATM was already threatened.

Both IP and ATM traffic management are examples of the difficulty in finding the balance in the Scope of Information Tradeoff (5D). They are examples of the fallout of the ATM and IP communities not ever really converging and high-speed networking technology developed initially in the fast packet switching and ATM context being adapted to the IP-based Internet.

4.2.1 Resource Reservation

QOS policies and protocols allow applications and users to specify performance requirements to the network such as bandwidth, latency, jitter, and error rate requirements. These may be hard requirements that the user needs to be willing to use a network service or a desired target for application performance.

> **Network Path Protection** *QOS mechanisms must be capable of guaranteeing bandwidth and latency bounds, when needed.*
>
> **N-II.2**

The QOS mechanisms interact with the routing protocol to find a path through the network that can support needed resources. The network must then translate the QOS request into a set of resources reserved along the path, including bandwidth through links and network nodes and buffers allocated in switches and routers.

This resource reservation serves four important purposes, which we will consider in the context of networks that have a high aggregate bandwidth, as well as the impact of individual high-bandwidth application flows.

1. As already discussed, it is desirable to be able to commit to meeting a level of service to applications. Specific examples of high-bandwidth, low-latency applications will be given in Chapter 8.

2. In order to make guarantees to applications, application flows must be protected from one another. Thus, it does no good to ensure that a particular application can get a high-performance path through the network if other application flows can steal these resources. Therefore, in addition to providing resource guarantees to applications, it is equally important to provide resource bounds to application flows. This is done by shaping traffic to maintain conformance to the traffic contract as it flows through the network[15] and by policing traffic to discard traffic in excess of the contract.[16]

3. If the network is not capable of accepting new traffic without adversely affecting existing reservations, *admission control* prevents the establishment of additional connections or flows. This is particularly important in the case of individual high-bandwidth connections. Admission control may feed back the availability of resources to allow tolerant applications to make another attempt with a less aggressive resource specification.

---

[15]As flows interact with one another and are buffered within nodes, the interpacket spacing is altered (Figure 5.25); traffic shaping restores the traffic pattern to that specified in the traffic contract between the application and network.

[16]Traffic in excess of the contract may be allowed to pass as best effort traffic if additional network capacity is available, but discarded if network resources are fully booked.

4. Reserving network resources allows a network provider to provide only the amount of network infrastructure for which customers are willing to pay. This allows far less overengineering of the network.

If bandwidth is extremely cheap, then it is cost-effective to overengineer networks so that QOS and resource reservations are unnecessary. There is no evidence, however, that bandwidth will ever be cheap enough relative to demand for this to be a viable long-term option. On the other hand, it is important to realize that the mechanisms we are discussing may be extremely complex and have a substantial implementation cost, in terms of the amount of state needed, message bandwidth, and algorithmic processing complexity in network nodes. When the granularity of reservation is low and aggregation in number of paths is high, QOS algorithms may have substantial difficulty scaling. Thus, we need to balance the desire to optimally allocate resources with the cost to implement the protocols and algorithms. Aggregating flows by class and subnetwork address can relieve the scaling problems. Furthermore, when some individual applications demand significant fractions of the bandwidth available, the problems of optimal flow assignment can be significant.

Optimal Resource Utilization versus Overengineering Tradeoff *Balance the tradeoff of optimal resource utilization and its associated complexity and cost against the cost of suboptimal resource utilization resulting from overengineering the network*

N-5A

Thus, a combination of some network overengineering is warranted in combination with tractable QOS protocols and algorithms.

Mobile environments present a major challenge to resource reservation. Unless the rate of mobility is low (or the trajectory is predictable), the resource reservation mechanism has little time to reserve the resources before topology and traffic characteristics change. Moreover, there is no guarantee that the resources to be found in the new available paths will be able to match the QOS that was contracted in the original path that was set up for communications. A network may choose to be conservative when committing resources in regions where mobile nodes operate, and give priority to maintaining connections. This is similar to protocols in cellular architectures that must maintain call continuity. The problem then becomes one of efficient use of resources, balanced against overengineering of scarce radio spectrum.

4.2.2 Network-Based Congestion Control

The goal of the preceding section was to provide a network infrastructure capable of guaranteeing high-bandwidth, low-latency paths to applications.

There are several reasons why we still need to consider the possibility of congestion in network nodes and at the access to links:

1. Since most high-speed applications typically do not have deterministic and uniform traffic demands, this guarantee is necessarily a statistical one,[17] even in networks with strict guarantees like ATM, unless connections are allocated and policed at peak rate. The degree to which the admission control algorithms underbook or overbook resources is typically tunable, and if resources are overbooked, congestion may occur.

2. In some networks, QOS mechanisms are not supported. *Best-effort* traffic is that which is carried without an explicit traffic contract. Internet traffic is traditionally carried as best effort (whether or not applications would benefit from QOS reservations),[18] and we need to ensure that application demands do not drive the network into congestion.

3. In networks with coarse-grained traffic mechanisms, such as the Internet differentiated service model, the resource reservation mechanisms may not prevent congestion without significant overengineering.

4. Even networks that provide a rich set of guaranteed service classes typically offer a best-effort traffic class. Some applications, such as email, need no guarantees at all. Thus, we need to ensure that traffic that is offered on a best-effort basis does not drive the network into congestion.

Congestion control can be tied to end-to-end error control, in which case lost packets at the end system are an indication of congestion; this is implicit congestion notification. In high-speed networks, decoupling error control from flow and congestion control has significant benefits, discussed in detail in Section 7.5. We are then left with the decision on whether or not to do congestion control in the network, end-to-end, or both. Since applications must be able to react and adapt to congestion, there is clear need for this functionality above the network layer.

Congestion Control in the Network Improves Performance   *Even though the end-to-end protocols must perform congestion control, there is substantial performance benefit in assistance from the network.*

                                                                                             N-3A

Due to the high bandwidth-$\times$-delay product and the dynamic nature of application-offered traffic, there is substantial benefit for the network to avoid and quickly react to ameliorate congestion. This reduces the amount of data

---

[17]Specific application examples will be covered in Chapter 8, but, as an example, interactive Web browsing is extremely bursty, with little predictability of burst size or interarrival time.
[18]Intserv and diffserv traffic engineering are later additions to the Internet architecture.

lost, both in flight and injected before the end system can react. The Hop-by-Hop Performance Enhancement Corollary (3B) tells us that this is a case where congestion control at both the transport and network layers is a reasonable thing to do.

4.2.2.1 Congestion Signaling

In high-speed networks, we are particularly concerned with the ability of the network to react quickly to congestion. For example, if an OC-192 link is 110 percent congested, approximately 1 Gb/s of data will be lost. Furthermore, the condition that triggered the congestion may be gone by the time that notification has reached the edge of the network.

We will concentrate here on the case where congestion control is independent from error control, and signaled by network nodes. We refer to this as *explicit congestion notification* (ECN), which may be either forward or backward, as shown in Figure 4.15.

Forward congestion notification (FECN) involves tagging data packets in-band with a congestion flag $C = 1$. The destination end system or network edge must decode the congestion bit, and turn around a **CONGESTION** notification message to the sender. This scheme is necessary if a network node has no way of sending a message back to the source address, as is the case in ATM where cells don't carry the source address. The disadvantage is that a full round-trip time is required before the source of the traffic can back off and

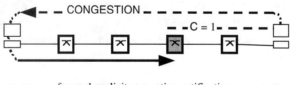

a: forward explicit congestion notification

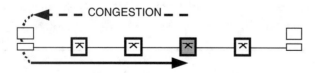

b: backward explicit congestion notification

Figure 4.15 Explicit congestion notification.

remaining data in the pipe clear out, as shown in Figure 4.15a. Additionally, it takes some time for the end systems to turn around and react to the congestion notification. In our congested OC-192 link example, assuming a 5,000-km diameter WAN, this results in excess of 500 Mb of data lost.[19]

Backward congestion notification (BECN) is preferable since it takes on average only a single end-to-end latency, without the end-system turnaround delay, as shown in Figure 4.15b. The network layer protocols and nodes must be able to support the generation of out-of-band signaling messages to the source of the traffic (for example, an ICMP[20] source quench message). This reduces the data lost on our example to a bit over 250 Mb on average (depending on the location of the node in the network).

4.2.2.2 Multipoint Flow Control

We have noted the signaling overhead based on the style of multipoint tree establishment in Section 4.1.6, but we need to also be concerned with control overhead on an established tree. If every leaf of the multipoint group were to engage in conventional end-to-end error and flow control mechanisms with the root, we have a significant scaling problem at the root end system. Thus, error and flow control need to be done more carefully, with the participation of nodes in the network. This makes the separation of error control from flow and congestion control all the more important. By using open-loop rate control mechanisms that determine the proper rate to send packets at each network node based on the capabilities of downstream nodes and receivers, we can avoid the message overload problem near the root. Similarly, error control mechanisms for reliable multicast are very challenging, and benefit from participation of network nodes in the multipoint tree. This issue is considered again in Section 7.4.3.

4.2.2.3 Congestion Avoidance

While it is important to respond quickly to congestion, it is better to *avoid* it entirely. Data lost due to congestion generally must be retransmitted, adding further to the likelihood of congestion. When the QOS mechanisms and resource reservation do not prevent congestion, then it is best for the network nodes to anticipate and prevent congestion on a local basis. Impending congestion is detected when queues in switches and routers begin to build up due to high loading within the node or on the output link to other nodes.

---

[19]These are rough back-of-the envelope calculations for bandwidth-×-delay product, and additionally don't account for the fact that data are dropped at packet granularity rather than uniformly per bit or consider the effect of end-to-end protocol interactions.
[20]Internet control message protocol [Postel 1981c] is the control protocol for IP.

When this happens, nodes should drop packets until queue occupancy drops to an acceptable level. Random early detection (RED) [Floyd 1993] is a mechanism that arbitrarily drops packets when a queue threshold is exceeded. Since the transport layer will need to recover from dropped packets end-to-end, it is important to drop at transport protocol data unit (TPDU) or frame granularity. Thus, in the case of cell relay networks (such as ATM), when a cell is dropped, the entire frame containing the cell should be dropped. This is referred to as early packet discard (EPD) [Romanow 1994], and requires that congestion avoidance look far enough ahead to drop entire frames of ATM cells. Partial packet discard (PPD) [Armitage 1993] provides some of the benefit by dropping remaining cells in the frame, without requiring the look-ahead.

Avoid Congestion and Keep Queues Short   *Avoid congestion by network engineering, traffic management with resource reservation, and by dropping packets. Buffers should be kept as empty as possible, with queuing only for transient situations, to allow cut-through and avoid the latency of FIFO queuing.*

N-II.4

Such a local reaction has the advantage of reducing the immediate congestion situation without waiting for end-to-end feedback. Explicit congestion notification is still desirable, however, since the source of the congestion may continue overloading the network until it is throttled.

Congestion control mechanisms introduce concerns about fairness, however. Simple congestion mechanisms like RED do not discriminate between the application that is causing the congestion and well-behaved applications. Applying these mechanisms at a finer granularity; for example, per traffic class, can help somewhat, but this is still a significant tradeoff.

Congestion Control Fairness versus Complexity   *The lack of fairness in simple congestion control and avoidance mechanisms must be traded against the complexity of fair implementations.*

N-2Bc

4.2.2.4   Hop-by-Hop Flow/ Congestion Control

In Section 7.5 we will discuss end-to-end flow and congestion control in detail. The distinction between flow and congestion control is subtle, but important. Flow control is used to regulate the transmission of a sender to match the receiver. Congestion avoidance and control are used to regulate the transmission of a sender to match the capacity of the network. Generally, flow control is implemented end-to-end, as open-loop rate control (Section 7.5.2) or closed-loop feedback control (Section 7.5.3). Open-loop rate control assumes that admission control limits the traffic so that congestion is very unlikely to occur. Closed-loop feedback control requires congestion avoidance mechanisms to participate in throttling the sender when its transmission rate exceeds the capacity of network nodes and links.

An alternative is to perform *hop-by-hop* flow/congestion control at each network node. Hop-by-hop control is more locally reactive to points of congestion caused by the multiplexing of flows, since it is these points that directly throttle the traffic from their upstream neighboring network node. One possibility is to perform hop-by-hop rate control [Mishra 1992] with rate negotiations occurring between each switch node. This allows dynamic rate adaptations based on local conditions, but takes a couple of round-trip times to converge. The advantage over end-to-end dynamic rate schemes (Section 7.5.5) depends on the length of the hop. The reactivity over a short LAN hop where the bandwidth-$\times$-delay product is a small fraction of the overall path provides a significant advantage. The advantage over a long WAN segment where the bandwidth-$\times$-delay product is very high is more limited.

Credit-based hop-by-hop flow control [Kung 1993, 1995] has the property of avoiding congestion, since *every* node ensures that its buffers cannot be overrun by regulating the traffic from its upstream neighbor. It is a dynamic window scheme (Section 7.5.4) operating on a hop-by-hop basis. Each node maintains a per VC *credit balance*, which limits the number of cells that can be transmitted.[21] Downstream nodes send credit resource management cells upstream to adjust the credit balance. This scheme thus applies backpressure, only allowing traffic than can be accepted and ensuring zero congestion loss. The problem is the complexity of implementing per connection of flow credit computations, which caused the ATM forum to choose end-to-end dynamic rate control for ABR (Example 7.7). The increasing capabilities of VLSI processing, however, have dramatically increased what can be implemented in switch input and output processing.

We will revisit congestion (and flow) control from a switch perspective in Sections 5.3.5 and 5.5.4 and from an end-to-end perspective in Section 7.5.

4.3   Path Routing Dynamics

Over the life of a connection or flow, topology and traffic characteristics can change, indicating that the connection or flow route should be modified. Two

---

[21]The credit-based scheme was designed to count cells for ATM, but could be adapted to packets by counting bytes.

significant causes of these route dynamics are dynamic multipoint group membership and network node mobility.

4.3.1 Multipoint Groups

Dynamic multipoint connections are particularly susceptible to decreasing optimality of the spanning tree topology over time. The Network Path Principle (N-II) applies to multicast, but in this case to a spanning tree rather than a linear path. The problem is to globally optimize the assignment of the multicast tree to network links; this is an NP-complete problem to which heuristics must be applied [Waxman 1988]. However, once a reasonable multicast tree has been established, successive JOINs and LEAVEs of end systems can alter the topology so that the tree diverges from optimality.

Figure 4.16a shows a multipoint tree, with a root end system R that is the source of the multicast, and four leaf nodes, numbered in the order in which they joined the tree. If nodes 2 and 3 leave the multicast group, we are left with a very inefficient topology. First, messages are propagating to the router that was directly attached to end system 2, even though there are now no listeners; thus bandwidth is wasted. We need to prune the tree back to a network node that is actually needed by the current multicast group, as shown in Figure 4.16b. Second, the path R→4 involves five hops; a significantly shorter path exists. Thus we should reroute long stubs of the tree that can be reached in fewer hops and shorter geographic distance, reducing latency and further reducing the aggregate delay.

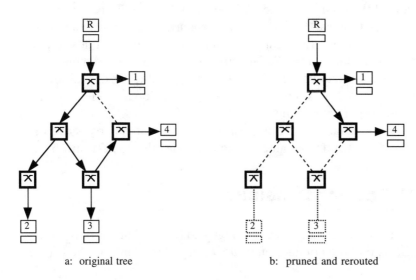

a: original tree   b: pruned and rerouted

Figure 4.16   Multipoint dynamics.

4.3.2 Node Mobility

Another way in which dynamic behavior can change the topology of networks is when mobile wireless nodes move with respect to one another, resulting in long latencies and inefficient use of spectrum for shared medium networks.

In Figure 4.17a, an intermediate node in a connection is moving away from the end nodes. This increases the distance latency beyond the requirements of the application using the connection. Thus, it is necessary to reroute the connection to a shorter path, as shown in Figure 4.17b.

A significant issue is the time it takes to perform the rerouting and the impact on the end-to-end protocols and application. A rerouting may result in significant misordering of packets, since once the cutover is made to the new shorter path, packets will arrive before those still in transit that are on the longer path. If the end-to-end protocols are not robust to misordering of packets, a large burst error will occur and require retransmission of the packets.

For connection setup procedures that install connection state information along the connection path, mobility presents the additional problem of having to reconstruct the appropriate connection information along the new path, sometimes requiring the whole path to be torn down first. Connection-oriented protocols must be reconsidered carefully in mobile environments. *Elastic virtual circuits* reroute themselves in response to node mobility [Ramanathan 1998].

Dynamic Path Rerouting   *Dynamic behavior can require adjustments to topology to maintain a high-performance path. The overhead and frequency of topology maintenance must be traded against the lack of optimality.*

                                                                              N-2B

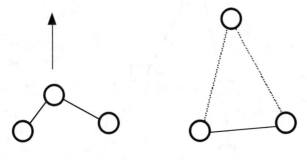

a: original configuration   b: reconfigured

Figure 4.17   Node mobility.

EXAMPLE 4.3: MOBILE IP AND CELLULAR TELEPHONY

Both mobile IP and cellular telephony suffer from the inability to optimally reroute in the face of node mobility. In the case of cellular telephony, while the home location register (HLR) is involved in the call setup (shown by the dashed control line), signaling establishes a short path directly to the mobile terminal via the switch associated with the visitor location register (VLR) connected to the closest tower V, as shown in Figure 4.18a. Once the connection is established, however, there is no dynamic adaptation to mobility. As the mobile node moves, the path can telescope as the mobile node roams to new switching centers. Even if the mobile node moves geographically close to the other end of the connection, toward a remote tower R, the call is still routed through the VLR-associated switch.

In the case of mobile IP, mobile nodes use a foreign agent (FA) to receive an address, but communications must still pass through the home agent (HA) in one direction, regardless of the latency, as shown in Figure 4.18b.

In spite of the impact on latency in both cases, and the bandwidth inefficiencies for high-speed data transfer in the mobile IP case, neither scheme allows dynamic direct routing of the data path. In the case of mobile IP one of the directions optimized, but this comes at the cost of triangle routing along two paths of potentially very different latency characteristics.

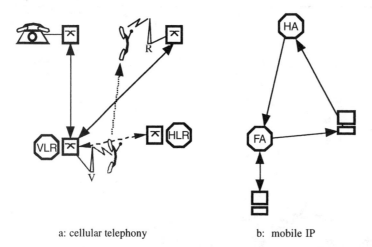

a: cellular telephony   b: mobile IP

Figure 4.18 Mobile IP and cellular telephony telescoping.

4.4   Monitoring and Management

Network management, in the traditional sense, occurs at the longest granularity, and thus in itself is not a topic for high-speed networking. There are significant implications that high-speed networks impose on monitoring, management, and control, however. In particular, monitoring and control must occur on the same granularity as the corresponding data units. There are two significant issues that are important in the management of high-speed networks.

First, things happen very quickly in high-speed networks, and thus the management interval is *very* long relative to changing network conditions. This means that mechanisms, such as congestion control, need to happen in real time, and nonintrusively within network nodes, as opposed to being reactive from an external management control. Furthermore, traditional network management tasks that were done in near real time by a human operator are now not possible, as data rates and bandwidth have increased by many orders of magnitude, but the reaction time of humans has not.

Second, network management and capacity planning require statistics from the network. At high data rates the size of such statistics can be beyond the capacity of node storage and of management systems to process the data. For example, collection of packet statistics for small 40B packets on a 10-Gb/s OC-192 link results in approximately 3 million records/s per link; for 1K × 1K switches, this translates to more than 3×10^9 records/s per switch. The only solution is for network nodes to do local sampling and data reduction in real time, with hardware assistance in the network node. Packet-level statistics must be abstracted; flow/connection level statistics are less problematic.

Network Monitoring Locality   *Network monitoring functions must be built into the critical path to provide nonintrusive local filtering and aggregation of statistics.*

N-1B

Intelligent monitoring and management schemes that are tied into the real-time fault monitoring and congestion control mechanisms in network nodes provide some relief, and active networking technology may be exploited to this end.

Thus, we can enumerate the set of functions that node management, monitoring, and control should support, starting at the hardware level:

1. Node hardware must provide the facilities to sample, accumulate, and average important packet-level statistics, and make them available to management and control subsystem in the node.

2. Node control software must provide per flow and connection statistics to the management and control subsystem.

3. As discussed in the specific context of congestion control, all forms of monitoring and control should be done locally, when possible. Another example consists of monitoring and local rerouting when a link fails. Nodes should propagate this information to other affected nodes for their action, without the latency of external control loop from a human operator at a network management station.

4. Nodes should have the ability to perform data aggregation and reduction from other nodes to provide monitoring information to other nodes and to an external network management station or operator. Concast (reverse multicast) [Calvert 1999a] can provide the network layer routing infrastructure to support this.

EXAMPLE 4.4: ACTIVE NETWORK MANAGEMENT

An example of a network management scenario is shown in Figure 4.19.

Active probes [Jackson 2000] are multicast into the network on a multicast tree shown by the dashed arrows (the same tree as in Figure 3.17). These probes are programs that monitor packet and connection/flow level statistics for a variety of conditions and events, including congestion, traffic anomalies, intrusion detection, denial-of-service attacks, and faults. When a probe is triggered by a particular condition, it takes local control action on the node, determines the set of adjacent nodes affected, and sends control messages to their management and control systems.

As appropriate, statistics and information are filtered, reduced, and aggregated along a concast tree shown by the solid arrow and sent to the appropriate system for networkwide analysis and archival.

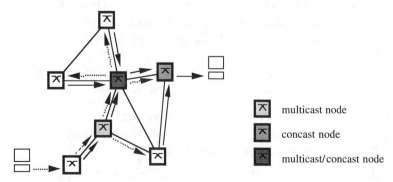

                multicast node

                concast node

                multicast/concast node

Figure 4.19   Active monitoring and control.

4.5   Summary

This chapter has considered the control and signaling of high-speed networks. We first described circuit and message switching, and the inefficiencies of each, followed by store-and-forward datagram packet switching in the traditional Internet. We then looked at virtual connection fast packet switching as a means to support high-speed networking. Intermediate fast datagram switching and optimistic virtual connection switching were described, providing the benefits of both. Then, we looked at burst switching for optical networks. The discussion moved to traffic management, considering QOS mechanisms to protect high-performance paths, as well as congestion control and avoidance mechanisms. We observed that it is best to avoid congestion entirely, and when it occurs, the network should explicitly signal the offending end systems. Then we considered the issues in dynamic network topologies, such as multicast and, due to mobility, the required rerouting of connections and flows. Finally, we considered the requirements high-speed networks impose on management and monitoring.

4.5.1   Further Reading

Many of the further reading suggestions in Chapter 3 apply to this chapter as well. Additionally, [Bosse 1998], [Onvural 1997], and [Black 1998] provide extensive information on signaling in telecommunication and ATM networks. The variety of datagram fast-switching proposals are covered in [Davie 1998], with comprehensive coverage of MPLS in [Davie 2000].

Internet integrated and differentiated service models are considered in depth in [Durham 1999] and [Kilkki 1999] and general issues in [Shenker 1995]; a comprehensive treatment of ATM traffic management is [Giroux 1999].

Multicast communication is broadly covered in [Diot 1997] and [Wittmann 2001] with a wealth of references; IP multicast in particular is covered in [Maufer 1998]. Wireless telephony and personal communications are covered in [Garg 1996], ad hoc networking in [Perkins 2001], and mobile IP in [Perkins 1998].

AXIOMS AND PRINCIPLES

N-5A. Connectionless versus Connection Tradeoff   *The latency of connection setup must be traded against the reduction in end-to-end data transfer delay due to the elimination of store-and-forward delay, and faster transmission due to nodes capable of increased bandwidth.*

N-8B. Efficiency of Signaling   *Signaling messages should be simple in coding and format and fit in a single packet, to minimize the latency in processing. The signaling protocol should be robust to lost messages.*

N-II.1. Network Path Establishment   *The routing algorithms and signaling mechanisms must be capable of forwarding datagrams or establishing connections on sufficiently high-performance paths and with low latency to meet application demands.*

N-6A. Overlap Signaling Messages with Data Transfer   *To reduce unneeded end-to-end latency, signaling messages should be overlapped with data transfer.*

N-6B. Root versus Leaf Multicast Control   *Root multicast control is appropriate when a single entity has knowledge of the multicast group. Leaf-controlled multicast is needed for large dynamic groups.*

C-4F. Session–Connection Interlayer Awareness   *Session control awareness of network layer control parameters allows the overlap of session and control signaling to reduce overall latency.*

N-II.2. Network Path Protection   *QOS mechanisms must be capable of guaranteeing bandwidth and latency bounds, when needed.*

N-5A. Optimal Resource Utilization versus Overengineering Tradeoff   *Balance the tradeoff of optimal resource utilization and its associated complexity and cost against the cost of suboptimal resource utilization resulting from overengineering the network.*

N-3A. Congestion Control in the Network Improves Performance   *Even though the end-to-end protocols must perform congestion control, there is substantial performance benefit in assistance from the network.*

N-II.4. Avoid Congestion and Keep Queues Short   *Avoid congestion by network engineering, traffic management with resource reservation, and by dropping packets. Buffers should be kept as empty as possible, with queuing only for transient situations to allow cut-through and avoid the latency of FIFO queuing.*

N-2Bc. Congestion Control Fairness versus Complexity   *The lack of fairness in simple congestion control and avoidance mechanisms must be traded against the complexity fair implementations. The impact of unfairness is mitigated by the infrequency of effect if the simple congestion avoidance mechanisms prevent congestion most of the time.*

N-2B. Dynamic Path Rerouting   *Dynamic behavior can require adjustments to topology to maintain a high-performance path.*

N-1B. Network Monitoring Locality   *Network monitoring functions must be built into the critical path to provide nonintrusive local filtering and aggregation of statistics.*

CHAPTER 5

Network Components

We discussed how to achieve a high-performance path through the network in Chapters 3 and 4. In Chapter 3 we discussed the topology and organization of components in the network; this chapter describes the architecture and design of the components themselves shown in Figure 5.1. These components consist primarily of links and switches.

In Chapter 4, we were concerned primarily with the relatively long granularity processing events associated with per connection and flow operations and network control. The events of most concern in this chapter are significantly smaller grained, such as the packets, cells, and bytes that are necessary to transfer and switch data through the network. These are highlighted in the following list:

Protocol deployment

Network configuration

Network management interval

Session establishment and lifetime

Connection/flow establishment and lifetime

Packet/frame transfer

Cell transfer

Byte transfer

Bit transfer

We again return to the decomposition of the ideal network model, shown in Figure 5.2.

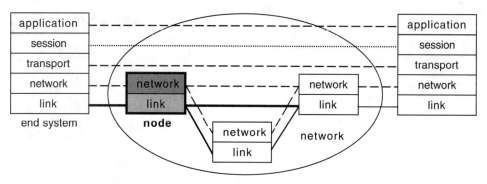

Figure 5.1   Network node and link architecture.

We are now concerned with the individual components, and thus the ideal link or network node has no latency and unlimited bandwidth: $R = \infty$ and $D = 0$. The ideal network node has the additional property that the number of ports is not constrained: $n = \infty$.

This chapter is organized as follows. Section 5.1 discusses high-speed link characteristics and protocols. While the focus of this book is not on the physical and link-layers, it is important to understand the link characteristics and technologies available to construct high-speed networks. Section 5.2 describes the generic functionality that network nodes must provide, and discusses the implementation and performance problems in early Internet routers. Section 5.3 describes the design of high-speed connection-oriented fast packet switches, which form the basis for high-speed network nodes. Section 5.4 examines the core of high-speed network nodes: the switch fabric. Section 5.5 extends fast packet switch design to support the additional functionality required to forward datagrams. Section 5.6 provides a brief discussion on higher-layer protocol switching and high-performance active network nodes. Section 5.7 concludes with a summary and suggestions for further reading.

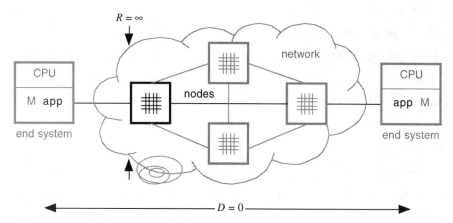

Figure 5.2   Ideal network model.

5.1 Links

This section discusses high-performance physical and link-layers, which form the building blocks for high-speed networks. The link-layer is an orphan of high-speed network architecture. Designers often have an appreciation and background in the physical layers or upper-layer protocols, but often not both. In the link-layer these two foci intersect, where good design combines the strengths of both.

Network Link Principle *Network links must provide high-bandwidth connections between network nodes. Link-layer protocol processing should not introduce significant latency.*

L-II

Section 5.1.1 introduces the various transmission media and describes characteristics important to high-speed networking. Section 5.1.2 considers link technologies classified by point-to-point, multiplexed, and shared medium, with concrete examples of SONET and Ethernet. Section 5.1.3 describes the components that exclusively perform physical and link-layer processing, such as regenerators, bridges, hubs, and layer 2 switches. Finally, Section 5.1.4 considers link-layer issues that impact the higher-layers in high-speed network design.

5.1.1 Physical Transmission Media

The physical characteristics of the transmission medium determines the basic properties of the network. We will first consider these basic properties and the important characteristics of bandwidth, latency, and bandwidth-×-delay product that result. Then, we will consider the important characteristics of wired, fiber optic, and wireless transmission media.

5.1.1.1 Physical Properties

There are several fundamental physical properties that drive the design of the physical and link-layer in the network and affect performance at higher-layers:

Signal propagation velocity. The speed at which a signal travels. Electromagnetic signals, including radio and photonic signals, propagate at the speed-of-light, which varies depending on the medium used for transmission. Propagation speed is not related to symbol rate, which is commonly called the "speed" of a link. In a vacuum, electromagnetic radiation propagates at approximately $c = 3 \times 10^5$ km/s. The velocity through a particular medium is limited by the index of refraction n: $v = c/n$. In air the velocity of light is very close to one. The index of refraction of glass fiber optic cable is in the range of 1.45 to 1.48, thus the velocity of light is approximately $0.68c$ [Palais 1998]. The *fastest* transmission mediums are space ($1.0c$), and the atmosphere and some coaxial cable (very near $1.0c$). The *slowest* transmission mediums are fiber optic and twisted wire pair, at about two-thirds the speed of light.

Link length.   The distance over which signals propagate. In the case of point-to-point links, this is simply the link length. In the case of shared medium networks, it is typically the longest path through the network. The length of a link is limited by physical properties such as attenuation and noise. There are a number of link-layer control protocols (such as ARP [Plummer 1982] that are dependent on the length of concatenated point-to-point links.

Symbol Rate.   The number of coding symbols transmitted per second, specified as the baud rate. This rate is limited by the rate at which transmission interfaces can switch.

Encoding.   The way in which data bits (binary digits) are encoded for transmission physical layer, for example, NRZI or QAM (nonreturn to zero insert on ones or quadrature amplitude modulation) and the way in which data is framed for the link-layer. The key implication of the physical layer encoding is the number of bits per symbol (bits per baud which may be more or less than 1) and the coding delay. Data is grouped into frames on the link, so that the receiver can recover basic information that will be used by higher-layers to delineate protocol data units. In some cases, this framing is impacted by the physical characteristics of the media (for example, the Ethernet preamble, discussed in Example 5.2).

5.1.1.2 High-Speed Network Characteristics

The physical properties of the transmission medium and connection topology determine the important parameters about which we are concerned in high-speed networking:

Latency   The time required for a message to travel from source to destination. This is composed of the sum of propagation delay (time for the front of the signal to travel the required distance) and transmission delay (time for the frame to be sent), as described in the Network Latency Principle (N-1Al).

Bandwidth   Commonly used in the networking community to refer to the data rate,[1] which is the bit rate determined by the baud rate (symbol/s) multiplied by the coding rate (bit/symbol).

---

[1]As opposed to the definition from physics and electrical engineering, which is the amount of spectrum used; we will follow the networking convention in this book.

Bandwidth-×-delay product. The number of bits in transit between source and destination in the physical medium. It is the product of the propagation delay and the bandwidth of the link.

Finally, there is one very important constraint to consider: power. Power is important in two ways: First, the power consumed by many microelectronic technologies (such as CMOS) is a function of the switching rate. Thus, a higher data rate consumes more power. Second, the distance over which a signal propagates is related to the power. In the case of a wire, higher voltage generally allows greater propagation distance; in the case of fiber optics, it is the power emitted by the laser; and in the case of a wireless link, it is the transmission power. Particularly for mobile devices, power is limited, either due to the need to minimize battery consumption or due to limited ambient power available.

Table 5.1 summarizes the important properties for the transmission mediums we will discuss in this chapter.

5.1.1.3 Wire

The traditional medium for communication links is copper wire. The data rate that can be transmitted depends on the physical construction of the wire (coaxial, shielded twisted pair, unshielded twisted pair), the coding scheme, the distance, and crosstalk from other wires in a cable bundle. Coaxial cable is the highest bandwidth, followed by shielded twisted pair. Unshielded twisted pair (UTP) supports the lowest bandwidth, but data grade category 5 is capable of 100 Mb/s over LAN distances.

High-bandwidth residential access is more problematic, due to the poor wiring infrastructure in the legacy PSTN. Asymmetric digital subscriber line

Table 5.1 Transmission Medium Properties

TYPE	MEDIUM	FREQUENCY RANGE	VELOCITY	DELAY	TYPICAL ATTENUATION
Wire	Twisted pair	0–1 MHz	0.67c	5 s/km	0.7 dB/km*
	Coax	0–500 MHz	0.66–0.95c	4 s/km	7.0 dB/km†
Optical fiber	Glass	120–250 THz 1,700–800 nm	0.68c	5 s/km	0.2–0.5 dB/km
Wireless	Microwave	1–300 GHz			
	Infrared	0.3–428 THz	1.0c	3.3 s/km	$1/r^2$
	Visible	428–750 THz			

*At 1 kHz
†At 10 MHz
Note: Data from [Palais 1998, Glover 1998, Personick 1985].

(ADSL) uses PSTN infrastructure between the residence and central office to provide downstream data rates on the order of 1 to 10 Mb/s, with upstream rates about one-tenth of the downstream [Maxwell 1999]. Very high-speed DSL (VDSL) reuses only the wire in the neighborhood into the residence, which allows higher-bandwidth due to the shorter lengths: up to about 50 Mb/s, depending on the configuration. The hybrid fiber coax (HFC) CATV (cable television) infrastructure is also used to deliver broadband access to residences, but is a shared medium and the cable plant is designed for a highly asymmetric bandwidth allocation. The bandwidth available to an individual user is highly dependent on configuration and contention among multiple users; 10 Mb/s downstream and 300 kb/s upstream is typical for an uncongested network [Ciciora 1999, Maxwell 1999].

5.1.1.4   Fiber Optics

Fiber optic links are used for the highest data rates, due to their ability to transmit high signal frequencies over a much longer distance than electric wire. Fiber optic cable is typically constructed of a glass[2] core doped with material that increases its refractive index, surrounded by a glass cladding doped with material that decreases the refractive index. The difference in refractive index causes the light beam to reflect along the edge of the core and propagate through the fiber.

Signals traveling through a fiber are subject to two effects that constrain the propagation of signals:

1. **Attenuation**. Measured in decibels per kilometer, attenuation is due to material absorption, Rayleigh scattering[3], and imperfections in the waveguide geometry. These effects limit the usable spectrum to the 800- to 1700-nm range for a usable bandwidth of approximately 20 THz [Stern 1999].

2. **Dispersion**. Consists of smearing of waveforms over distance, and results in the limit of the *bandwidth-×-distance product*. The higher the data rate, the shorter the intersymbol period, and thus the tighter tolerance for pulse edges. There are three types of dispersion:

   - *Intermodal dispersion*, in which the different reflection modes travel different distances through the fibers, resulting in a variance in velocity

   - *Chromatic dispersion*, in which different wavelengths travel different velocities

   - *Polarization mode dispersion*, in which different polarization states propagate at different velocities

---

[2]Other materials, such as plastic, may be used for low-cost, short-distance applications.
[3]Scattering caused by varying index of refraction due to variable molecular density of the fiber.

The bandwidth of a single fiber far exceeds the switching capabilities of transmission electronics. Thus, multiplexing techniques (described in Section 5.1.2) are needed to exploit a significant fraction of the bandwidth available on a single fiber. The ultimate usable bandwidth of a fiber is very much an open question, as new devices and technologies, such as optical code division multiple access (CDMA), evolve.

There are a variety of fiber optic cable types, and the choice has significant impact on the physical layer coding and multiplexing schemes that can be used. The earliest deployed fiber optic cables are called *multimode*, since the diameter of the fiber core (50 to 85 μm) is large enough that the signal travels through the fiber in different reflection *modes*, resulting in significant intermodal dispersion. Therefore, the longer the link, the more a single coding symbol is dispersed in time. Multimode fiber is thus limited in data rate, and requires frequent signal regenerators along the cable (typically every few kilometers). Multimode fiber in the 850-nm operating region is economical for short-distance applications, however, such as in the LAN environment.

A significant enabler to high-bandwidth communication over long distance was the development of erbium doped fiber amplifiers (EDFAs) and *single mode* fiber in the early 1980s, using the 1,310-nm band, which has a significantly smaller core (8 to 10 μm), and acts as a waveguide with all of the light traveling in a single mode. The elimination of modal dispersion enabled transmission of hundreds of megabits per second over tens of kilometers; the limiting factor became the signal attenuation over distance. The 1,550-nm band was then used due to its better attenuation characteristics, but suffers from chromatic dispersion.

Dispersion shifted fiber is engineered to have zero chromatic dispersion at 1,550-nm, and is suitable for a single-channel transmission of very high rate (for example, 40 Gb/s and above) over a long distance. It is not suitable for wavelength division multiplexing (WDM) (Section 5.1.2), due to strong interference among multiple channels. Single-mode dispersion-compensated fiber can operate over the entire 1,310 to 1,610-nm band, and is suitable for WDM with a large number of channels.

5.1.1.5 *Wireless*

Wireless communication consists of signals that do not propagate through a manufactured waveguide and includes radio and optical communications, plus any other wireless transmission technologies that may emerge (for example, magnetic coupling). Distance attenuation, line-of-sight requirements for microwave frequencies and beyond, and lack of control over the channel signal-to-noise ratio have contributed to the reputation of wireless links as a low-bandwidth technology. However, many of these restrictions do not apply to several scenarios of interest, including short-link architectures.

5.1.1.5.1   Spectrum Available

The wireless communication spectrum includes the radio frequency spectrum and the optical spectrum. Bands of 10 to 100 MHz over 10-km distances have become available to individual users throughout the world (for example, through unlicensed spread spectrum). The unregulated industrial, scientific, and medical (ISM) bands in the United States include 900 MHz (902 to 928), 2.4 GHz (2.4000 to 2.4835), and 5.8 GHz (5.725 to 5.850). Note that the higher-frequency bands have broader spectrum allocations (26, 83.5, and 125 MHz, respectively) supporting more channels of a given bandwidth. The 2.4-GHz band has been reserved to unregulated use worldwide. With appropriate coding and modulation techniques over channels that are not overcome by noise, 1 Hz of spectrum can carry more than 1 bit/s of data. Thus, for radio-based systems, several to tens of megabits per second are feasible expectations even beyond a campus area system; greater rates are achievable in smaller or more controlled environments.

Satellite transmission has traditionally been in the microwave frequencies: the 1 to 4 GHz L and S bands, particularly for mobile earth stations, and the 4 to 20 GHz C, X, and Ku bands for higher-bandwidth fixed stations. The lower-bandwidth 400- MHz to 1-GHz VHF and UHF frequencies have been used for LEO applications. As technology advances, the frequencies have extended into the millimeter wavelengths. In the late 1990s the 20- to 40-GHz Ka band came into use. Beyond that, the Q and V bands to nearly 100 GHz are available as transmission capabilities increase [Elbert 1999].

Even greater bandwidth is available through optical means in the visible or infrared portions of the spectrum [Lambert 1995]. Spectrum ranges for optical transmission are generally specified as wavelength rather than frequency (product of wavelength and frequency are equal to the velocity of propagation $\lambda f = v$). In Table 5.1 we have included frequencies to emphasize the extremely high-bandwidth potential of optical links. Infrared wireless transmission is typically in the 800- to 900-nm range, corresponding to 333 to 375 THz with a spectrum width of 41 THz.

However, there are many significant challenges in utilizing this bandwidth, including detector noise, background source interference for the several spectral bands of interest, the high cost of coherent detection optical systems, and the sensitivity to line of sight considerations. For fixed-location links or for short-link systems, it is possible to control some of these variables and provide high rate links comparable to the spectrum available in optical fibers. The problem then is more one of cost-effectiveness than of capacity limitations.

5.1.1.5.2   Signal Propagation

In free space, over distances greater than a few wavelengths of a propagating electromagnetic signal (for example, radio signals or optical signals), the power received by an antenna decreases with distance to the transmitting antenna as $1/r^2$, due to the greater spread of the transmitted energy.

In the presence of obstacles, another phenomenon that affects the received power comes into play. *Multipath interference* occurs when signals reflected off objects are received mixed with the primary signal. Multipath interference is dependent on distance when the number of obstructions increases. Thus, in environments with partially or fully reflecting surfaces, such as buildings in a city or metal cabinets in an office, we can expect that the received power will be lower than $1/r^2$. It is often represented as $1/r^x$, where x represents the equivalent attenuation power law and is greater than 2. For dense urban environments, x tends to approach 4, while for rural environments x is closer to 2. If the line of sight between transmitter and receiver is much shorter than the potential reflection paths, which is more applicable to the short-link case, the contribution from reflection paths is much lower intensity or can be separated due to their arrival difference in time. If the delay is greater than the duration of the symbol used as the basic element of communications, separating out multipath interference is simpler. This forms the rationale for multipath-robust systems proposed for digital television broadcast.

Receive power can also fade through the change of physical characteristics in the link. For mobile communications, the path between transmitter and receiver is constantly changing, with obstacles entering and leaving the path. This can happen in fixed wireless communications if mobile objects can transit across or near the link. Additionally, ambient noise for certain bands can vary depending on time of day, due to atmospheric conditions that affect electromagnetic propagation or with solar phenomena like the sun spot cycles that particularly affect satellite links. These factors lead to short- and long-term fade episodes. There are techniques to deal with most known situations, but they vary in cost-effectiveness. To higher-layer protocols, fades manifest as random, time-varying link capacity, which can be characterized statistically with different degrees of success, but which distinguish them from wired links.

5.1.1.5.3   Antennas

Multipath interference is the result of the superposition of direct and reflected signals. This can be exploited if it is possible to control the signals to some extent. Instead of letting the signals add randomly at a receiver, the system controls their time of arrival so that they add up constructively; the energy that would otherwise be spread in multiple directions can be concentrated in the direction of a receiver. This is done with time-delay methods in multipath receivers, but can also be accomplished by electrical means in directive antennas, whose shape or elements concentrate transmitter energy in specific directions, achieving power gains equivalent to factors of thousand or millions, at the expense of little strength in other directions. With these power gains, noise and multiuser interference are easily overcome. This technology works with both transmitting and receiving antennas. The difficulty with this

Table 5.2 Link Technologies

PHYSICAL MEDIUM	LINK TECHNOLOGY	APPLICATION	FREQUENCY	RANGE	DATA RATE
Wire	Ethernet	LAN	Baseband	500 m*	10 Mb/s
				100 m	100 Mb/s
				100 m	1 Gb/s†
	ADSL (twisted pair)	Residential access	25 kHz–2 MHz	10-1 km	1-10 Mb/s^D 0.16-0.8 Mb/s^U
	VDSL (twisted pair)		0.3–30 MHz	1.4-0.3 km	13-52 Mb/s^D 1.5-6 Mb/s^U 13-26 Mb/s^S
	HFC (coax)		50–1,000 MHz^D 5–40 MHz^U	160 km	27-38 Mb/s^D 0.32-10 Mb/s^U
	T-carrier	MAN WAN	Baseband	1–5 km	1.5 Mb/s 45 Mb/s
Fiber	Ethernet	LAN MAN	1,700–800 nm	2 km‡	100 Mb/s 1 Gb/s 10 Gb/s
	SONET	MAN WAN	1,610–1,310 nm	1,000 km	155 Mb/s 622 Mb/s 2.4 Gb/s 10 Gb/s 40 Gb/s

Wireless RF	802.11	LAN	2.4 Ghz	30–400 m	1-11 Mb/s
			5.8 GHz		6-54 Mb/s
	Bluetooth	personal	2.4 GHz	10 m	732 kb/s
	LMDS	residential access	24, 28 GHz (US) 28, 40 GHz (EU)	3-5 km	36 Mb/s^D 8–26 Mb/s^U
	point-to-point microwave	campus MAN	900 MHz 2.4 GHz 5.8 GHz	10 m-50 km	1-100 Mb/s
	satellite	WAN space relay	.4-1 GHz L,S: 1-3 GHz C,X,Ku: 3-20 GHz Ka: 20-30 GHz	$3–13 \times 10^3$ km§	622 Mb/s¶
Wireless Optical	802.11	LAN	900-800 nm	10 m	1Mb/s 2 Mb/s
	IrDA	short link LAN	900–800 nm	2 m	1 Mb/s 4 Mb/s 16 Mb/s
	point-to-point laser	campus MAN space relay interplanetary	4,000–800 nm	>10 m	622 Mb/s¶

*Thick wire coax.

†Requires four pairs of category 5 STP (shielded twisted pair).

‡Multimode fiber; single mode fiber can support considerably longer distances.

§ Dependent on satellite footprint.

¶ Highly variable—reflects data rate acheived in 2001.

D indicates downstream and U indicates upstream rates when asymmetric.

s indicates bandwidth *each* direction when symmetric.

Note: Data from [Bray 2001, Ciciora 1999, Cioffi 1999, Elbert 1999, Gagnaire 2000, Maxwell 1999, Nordbotten 2000, Palais 1998, Papir 1999, Spurgeon 2000, Williams 2000]

technology is that it is sensitive to orientation, so mobile systems are typically assisted by pointing control systems.

For high-speed networks, powerful and highly directional antennas have a role in backbone networks, because the channel and node locations are relatively static. For the local access to residences, the ability to cope with mobility, the need for simple installation, and the need for low cost makes inexpensive omnidirectional antennas more attractive.

5.1.2 Link Technologies

We have discussed the different types of physical mediums; these are used as the basis for link technologies, which are the combination of a particular physical medium and link-layer protocol mechanisms. Link technologies can be divided into three broad classes: point-to-point dedicated, point-to-point multiplexed, and shared medium.

Table 5.2 summarizes the important properties for a number of the link technologies we will discuss in this section.

Link Protocol Scalability Principle   *Link protocols should be scalable in bandwidth, either variably or in discrete intervals (power-of-2 or order-of-magnitude). Header/ trailer lengths and fields that relate to bandwidth should be long enough or contain a scale factor.*

L-8C

Note that some link protocols, such as SONET (Example 5.1), are designed to scale with bandwidth. Other link protocols, such as Ethernet (Example 5.2), are tied to specific data rates, and require a reworking of the standard with each new generation. Wireless protocols are more likely to *require* data rate specific physical medium dependent standards, due to the need to allocate frequency spectrum.

5.1.2.1   Point-to-Point Dedicated Links

The most straightforward way to use a link is for it to consist of a dedicated point-to-point connection between nodes. This is space division of the network, as shown in Figure 5.3.

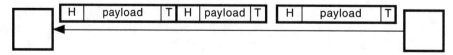

Figure 5.3   Point-to-point dedicated link.

EXAMPLE 5.1: SONET

Synchronous optical network (SONET) [Goralski 2000] is the most deployed WAN link technology. SONET uses a synchronous framing structure, and is an optical version of the electronic T-carrier transmission technology historically used in the PSTN. Synchronous digital hierarchy (SDH) is the almost identical European equivalent, but uses different terminology and data rates.

SONET is a synchronous protocol, in which a payload floats within a synchronous payload envelope (SPE), as shown in Figure 5.4. The SONET frame consists of a header, containing section overhead (SOH) and line overhead (LOH) subheaders. SONET sections are located between signal regenerators (perhaps 10 km apart), which examine only the LOH. SONET lines are the links between SONET layer 2 components [multiplexors, add/drop multiplexors (ADMs), or cross-connects], as well as the interfaces on layer 3 switches (for example, ATM or IP). The SOH/LOH is collectively called the *transport overhead* (TOH), and can be considered to be the part of the SONET link-layer header needed only by SONET equipment. A pointer in the LOH indicates the beginning of the path overhead (POH), which is the header to the payload floating in each SPE. The POH can be considered to be the part of the link-layer header needed by higher-layer components, such as switches.

The base rate in SONET is synchronous transport signal (STS-1), which is approximately 45 Mb/s, equivalent to the DS-3 data rate for the T-3 carrier. The header is organized as columns of nine rows. STS-1 has three columns for a total of 27 bytes. The POH consumes another column of 9 bytes in the SPE. Thus, the payload has 86 columns for a total of 774 bytes. The total 810-byte frame interval is 125 μs at the STS-1 data rate of 51.84 Mb/s. This is designed to maintain time slot synchronization for PCM voice in the PSTN.

SONET was designed to scale by multiplexing the base STS-1 frame structure and rate, and thus the size of the header and payload is dependent on the data rate. The lowest rate for which optical transmission is specified is optical carrier (OC-3) at 155 Mb/s, which is three times the STS-1 rate. An STS-3/OC-3 frame contains three full sets of transport overhead columns, for a total of nine columns, and in the multiplexed form, three sets of POH columns and three sets of interleaved payload columns.

In data networking, we are generally more interested in multiplexing at the network layer, and want high data rate links (rather than a bundle of low data rate links). In this form, called *concatenated*, there is only a single POH column and payload. Concatenated SONET links are denoted by appending a "c" to the designation.[4]

(Continues)

---

[4]Technically, this is only done for the electrical domain, for example, STS-3c, since concatenation, or lack thereof, is transparent to the optical domain. We follow common usage in Table 5.2, which refers to the link as OC-nc. Note that in the data networking world, the default assumption has become concatenated circuits, and thus when one refers to an OC-192 link, OC-192c (really STS-192c) is assumed.

(Continued)

An OC-3c frame thus has $3 \times 3 = 9$ columns of TOH for a total of 81 bytes, a POH of 9 bytes, and payload of 260 columns or 2,340 bytes. The base rate of SDH is STM-1, equivalent to OC-3. As the data rate increases by factors of 4, so does the transport overhead and payload size, as shown in Table 5.3. For reference the maximum possible ATM payload rate is included (which does not include the AAL dependent overhead).

There are two main problems with SONET. While SONET was designed to be scalable, it was designed primarily as a multiplexing scheme. Thus, the header increases in size, even though it is not needed for concatenated data links.

Second, the requirement to process multiplexed SONET paths (including multiplexed subrate virtual tributaries for 1.5 Mb/s T-1 and fractions thereof) makes SONET transceivers very complex. In the late 1990s deployments of packet over SONET (POS) [Malis 1999, Manchester 1998] began. PPP is used to frame IP packets for transmission in a variety of link protocols, and thus POS is layered as IP over PPP over SONET, with multiple PPP frames in a SONET SPE.

The need for SONET itself in the Internet is under question and simpler options are being explored, including transporting IP (perhaps IP in PPP frames) directly over the optical physical layer [called packets over wavelength (POW)] [Anderson 1999, Bannister 1999]. Two trends resist the deployment of POW. First, it is not necessary to support all of the complexities of SONET for data networking. A simple version of SONET network interfaces (sometimes called *SONET lite*) is adequate, and reduces some of the concern. Second, there will be a need for conventional SONET equipment to support the PSTN for a very long time. The use of a common network infrastructure for both the PSTN and Internet means that SONET is not threatened in the near future. The longer-term experience of POS on OC-192 and OC-768 links, and the rate at which voice traffic moves to IP will partially determine the longevity of SONET.

Link-layer payloads are transmitted along the links, encapsulated into a framing structure so that the receiver can recognize the location of the payload and to support desired point-to-point protocol functionality, such as error checking and perhaps reliable hop-by-hop delivery. Examples of common link protocols are ISO high-level data link control (HDLC) [ISO 3309], point-to-point protocol (PPP) [Simpson 1994], and SONET.

5.1.2.2   Multiplexed Links

In some cases, it makes sense to multiplex multiple virtual links onto a single physical link in a deterministic manner. The physical link is divided into channels, which are deterministically assigned to communicating nodes.

Table 5.3   SONET Link Characteristics

| LINK TYPE | | | | | SONET | ATM |
SONET	SDH	RATE	TRANSPORT OVERHEAD	PAYLOAD	PAYLOAD RATE	PAYLOAD RATE
STS-1	STM-0*	51.84 Mb/s	27 B	774 B	49.54 Mb/s	44.87 Mb/s
OC-3c	STM-1c	155.52 Mb/s	81 B	2,340 B	149.76 Mb/s	135.63 Mb/s
OC-12c	STM-4c	622.08 Mb/s	324 B	9,387 B	600.77 Mb/s	544.09 Mb/s
OC-48c	STM-16c	2.49 Gb/s	1,296 B	37,575 B	2.40 Gb/s	2.18 Gb/s
OC-192c	STM-64c	9.95 Gb/s	5,184 B	150,327 B	9.62 Gb/s	8.71 Gb/s
OC-768c	STM-256c	39.81 Gb/s	20,736 B	601,335 B	38.48 Gb/s	34.85 Gb/s

*STM-0 is commonly used, but not part of the STM standard.

Other than the channel assignment process, the link appears as a dedicated point-to-point link.

When the capacity of a transmission medium vastly exceeds the individual bandwidth requirements, multiplexing is used to share the transmission resource. Economies of scale in transmission equipment, cable, and right of way are exploited. The PSTN multiplexing hierarchy is the canonical example of this, historically using time division multiplexing (TDM), as shown in Figure 5.5a.

Data networks multiplex packets (or bursts) at the network layer to achieve the same effect, with far more flexibility than a fixed multiplexing hierarchy.

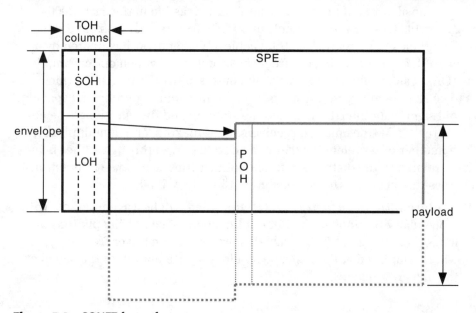

Figure 5.4   SONET frame formats.

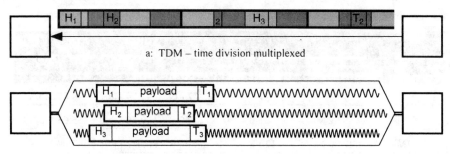

a: TDM – time division multiplexed

b: WDM – wave division multiplexed

Figure 5.5 Multiplexed links.

Optical networks provide a challenge, however, because the bandwidth capacity of a fiber vastly exceeds the rate at which network layer components can operate. Through the use of wavelength division multiplexing[5] (WDM), many high-bandwidth channels can share a single fiber optic strand, as shown in Figure 5.5b. Note that it is possible to combine multiplexing techniques and TDM in a WDM channel.

The total bandwidth utilization on WDM link is the product of the number of channels and the rate per channel. In the late 1990s, four to eight OC-192 SONET channels (10 Gb/s), multiplexed at different wavelengths onto a single fiber optic link, were widely deployed. This gave the transmission capacity of an OC-768 link (40 Gb/s), even though OC-768 transmission equipment was not yet ready for deployment.

WDM transmission of over 1 Tb/s per fiber is feasible in the early 2000s, using over 100 OC-192 rate channels or 40 OC-768 rate channels,[6] and the trend continues to increase. The total achievable bandwidth is limited by a number of factors, including the frequency range over which optical amplifiers (OAs) can produce flat gain and the output power of the OAs (which has to be shared among all the channels), the minimum interchannel spacing to avoid significant interference, and the stability and the wavelength selectivity of the WDM transmitters, receivers, multiplexors, and demultiplexors.

The number of wavelengths that can be transported through a fiber is inversely related to the distance, due to nonlinearities that cause interactions and cross-talk between the wavelengths [Chraplyvy 1990]:

Stimulated Raman scattering. Occurs when a light wave interacts with molecular vibrations in the fiber optic medium, scattering photons at a longer wavelength. When a signal is present at the lower frequency, it will be amplified at the expense of a loss in attenuation of the signal at the higher frequency.

---

[5]Which is just a form of frequency division multiplexing.
[6]Frequently called dense WDM (DWDM) due to the order-of-magnitude increase over the first WDM deployments.

Stimulated Brillouin scattering. Occurs when a light wave interacts with acoustic waves in the fiber optic medium, causing a loss in energy transferred to the reverse direction.

Carrier-induced cross-phase modulation. Causes phase shifts because light travels faster when other signals are present. This limits the product of the number of wavelengths and power *per* wavelength to approximately 21.

Four-wave mixing (FWM). Occurs when three closely spaced wavelengths λ_1, λ_2, and λ_3, induce a fourth new sum and difference wavelength $\lambda_i + \lambda_j - \lambda_k$, for i, j, and k each equal to 1, 2, or 3; nine such combinations are induced. When WDM wavelengths are evenly spaced, crosstalk will occur from the induced signals.

The power limits of stimulated Brillouin scattering and FWM are independent of the number of WDM channels, but FWM impacts the spacing of wavelengths. Stimulated Raman scattering significantly limits the power of transmitters for large numbers of wavelengths (hundreds to thousands). As the transmission power is limited, amplifiers and regenerators are required more often along the fiber.

5.1.2.3   Shared Medium Links

Shared medium links arise either because sharing the medium is an unconfined space or because the choice is made to share a confined media such as wire. In this case, only a single data transfer at a time can use the shared medium, or a *collision* will occur that garbles the data, as shown in Figure 5.6.

The important high-speed networking implication of shared mediums is that bandwidth must be divided among all the systems on the network. There are two significant architectural implications that are not present with point-to-point links: the need for addresses and the need for a medium access control (MAC) protocol.

Since multiple end systems (and perhaps also some network nodes) are attached to the shared medium, a mechanism is needed to discriminate the system for which a frame is intended. This is done by assigning MAC addresses to the attached systems. All systems need to listen to the shared medium, waiting

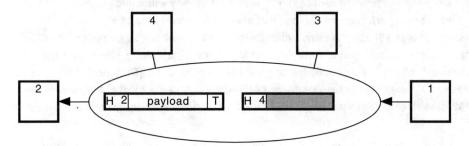

Figure 5.6   Shared medium link.

for frames for which it is the intended receiver. Figure 5.6 shows system 1 transferring a frame to system 2, followed by (and sharing the medium with) a frame addressed for system 4.

We also need a way to arbitrate for access to the shared medium; this is the role of the MAC protocol. A MAC protocol should ensure that there is either fair sharing of the medium or sharing in a desired manner with QOS support.

Medium Access Control Principle   *The MAC protocol should efficiently arbitrate the shared medium, in either a fair manner or with the desired proportion.*

L-II.2

A number of early LAN technologies, such as CSMA/CD Ethernet and token ring, used shared mediums. This provided flexibility and incremental extension, without requiring central infrastructure. When the channel capacity significantly exceeded the demands of a large number of attached systems, this worked well. As demand for channel capacity increased, the better Scalability of Mesh Topologies (N-II.4) drove the move from shared medium networks to point-to-point meshes. This is chronicled in Example 5.2, and also noted in the discussion on bridges, hubs, and switches in Section 5.1.3.

EXAMPLE 5.2: THE EVOLUTION OF ETHERNET

Ethernet has become, by far, the most ubiquitous link-layer technology for connecting computers and networked peripherals to LANs. Ethernet was designed in 1973 [Metcalfe 1976] as a way for multiple end systems (initially Xerox Alto workstations) to communicate by connecting to a shared coaxial transmission media. Ethernet was based on some of the ideas of the Aloha packet radio network [Abramson 1970], with the addition of a more sophisticated MAC (media access control) scheme, called carrier sense multiple access/collision detect (CSMA/CD). Each attached system waits for the shared medium to be silent before transmitting itself (CSMA) as well as listening for interference during its transmission (CD), which can occur if multiple systems happen to begin transmission at the same time (or within the propagation diameter of the network). When a collision is detected, the transmitters cease, and *back off* for a random period of time, to reduce the likelihood that they will collide again.

This scheme performs well in the local area with several tens of attached end systems [Boggs 1988], with fairly uniform delay through about 50 percent offered load, rapidly increasing at around 80 percent offered load[7] [Molle 1994]. Ethernet was standardized in essentially the original Digital Intel Xerox (DIX) form [IEEE802.3], and became the dominant LAN technology in the third generation (1980s) with only the token ring [IEEE802.5] as a significant competitor.

---

[7]Explained in Figure 7.22 as the knee and cliffs of the curves, respectively. This means that offered loads should remain below about 50 percent to maintain low latency.

The format of an Ethernet frame is shown in Figure 5.7a. A preamble field consists of alternating 1 and 0 bits, terminated by an 11 sequence at the end of the start frame delimiter (SFD). This provides time for network interfaces to recognize that a packet is on the wire and begin processing the frame. The preamble is followed by a 14-byte MAC header, which includes 48-bit source and destination MAC addresses. These must be resolved to network layer addresses. In the TCP/IP protocol suite this is performed by the address resolution protocol (ARP), and an ARP cache on the network interface performs the per packet IP to Ethernet address resolution during Ethernet frame encapsulation. A type/length field typically indicates the length of the frame. The MAC header is typically followed by an 8-byte logical link control (LLC) header in [IEEE802.2]) and subnetwork access protocol (SNAP) header, which demultiplex to the proper higher-layer protocols. The payload ranges from 38 to 1,492 bytes, and is padded to the 38-byte minimum (rarely necessary with the addition of IP and transport layer headers). Finally, a 4-byte FCS (frame check sequence) CRC (cyclic redundancy code) link trailer is added. The extension trailer is used only at data rates above 100 Mb/s and is described later.

The correct operation of the CSMA/CD MAC protocol requires an interrelationship between a number of protocol and network design parameters. In particular, the *slot time* is defined as an upper bound on the acquisition time of the channel and upper bound on the length of a frame fragment generated by a collision, and is the retransmission scheduling quantum. The slot time must be larger than the sum of the round-trip time along the full length of the physical medium and the maximum jam time (when a source detects a collision, 32 bits of jam sequence are transmitted following the preamble to ensure that other end systems detect the collision). The original Ethernet standard specified a slot time of 512 bit times which corresponded to a maximum cable length of 2,800 m.

The Ethernet scheme worked well and adapted to a variety of physical media following the original thick coaxial cable (10BASE5), including thin coax (10BASE2) and twisted pair (10BASE-T). Longer cable runs and isolation of traffic were accomplished by connecting Ethernet segments by bridges, which relayed packets between the segments. The preference for star wiring patterns and desire for easier network installation and maintenance resulted in the wide deployment of Ethernet hubs using twisted pair cable and modular RJ-45 connectors. The demand for increased bandwidth resulted in the large-scale replacement of hubs with Ethernet switches, allowing each end system to have access to the entire 10-Mb/s channel bandwidth, without sharing in the medium.

Thus, although Ethernet began as a shared medium technology, the typical deployment has become a point-to-point mesh, due to the Scalability of Mesh Topologies (N-II.4). To maintain compatibility in all environments, 10-MB/s Ethernet adapters all implemented the full CSMA/CD MAC protocol, even

(Continues)

(*Continued*)

though it is not needed in point-to-point full duplex deployments with separate transmit and receive paths for each end system.

As demand increased above the 10-Mb/s rate, the challenge shifted on what to use as a replacement for 10BASE-T. Unlike SONET, Ethernet was not inherently scalable in data rate, due to the dependence of network diameter, packet sizes, and slot time imposed by the CSMA/CD MAC protocol. For a while, it looked as though SONET OC-3 at 155 Mb/s might become the next widely deployed LAN technology, as various proposals for 100-Mb/s Ethernet variants were debated in the standards organizations. In the end, the failure of ATM over SONET to the desktop in the LAN environment (described in Example 6.2) and the increased cost of fiber optic cable deployment provided the needed time for the 100-Mb/s standards to converge. Furthermore, and there was no standard way to run IP directly over SONET in the mid-1990s. The 100BASE-T (as well as 100BASE-F for fiber) rely on the original medium dependent parameters. The slot time is also 512 bit times, which reduces the maximum distance of an Ethernet segment by roughly an order of magnitude to 205 m. Given the propensity to use point-to-point wiring technologies and due to length constraints dictated by physical wiring characteristics (100 m for twisted pair), it was not deemed necessary to change the interrelationship of parameters.

As the demand for bandwidth continued to increase, the issue of increasing Ethernet bandwidth was again addressed in the late 1990s. The historical trend of scaling by orders of magnitude was followed, resulting in 1000BASE-X standards, which uses the FCS (Fiber Channel Standard) 8B/10B line coding for fiber and FCS copper cable, as well as a 1000BASE-T, which uses five-level pulse amplitude modulation (PAM5) split over four twisted pairs. This eliminated the need for the preamble field, but it is retained for protocol compatibility. Reducing the maximum segment length by another order of magnitude to 20 m was clearly unacceptable, however. Thus, the slot time was increased to 512 B (an eight-fold increase), and an extension field was added to the end of the header, which is used to ensure that frames are at least 512 B long. Due to the overhead that this imposes on short frames (depicted in Figure 5.7b), frame bursting is employed, which allows sources to send successive frames after the first frame (with extension if necessary), up to a maximum of 64K bit times after the beginning of the frame, shown in Figure 5.7c. In full-duplex mode, however, neither carrier extension nor frame bursting is used, since there is no contention for the channel. Since the vast majority of gigabit Ethernet deployments use switches, it is unclear if frame burst mode will ever be used, but it is included in a continuing philosophy of compatibility.

In the early 2000s, work has begun on defining a 10-Gb/s Ethernet standard, which is likely to have payload sizes compatible with OC-192 SONET.

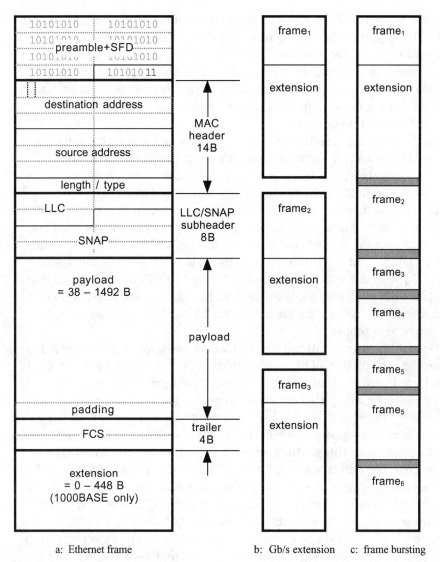

a: Ethernet frame   b: Gb/s extension   c: frame bursting

Figure 5.7 Ethernet frame formats.

5.1.2.3.1 Wireless Links

Wireless links can be either shared medium or point-to-point using directional antennas. Point-to-point links exploit spatial reuse, but do not benefit from inherent multicast capabilities (Section 5.1.4), and are more difficult to use in mobile applications. Spatial reuse can also be exploited in shared mediums by reducing the transmission power, either in an ad hoc manner or by dividing the network into cells.

In a shared medium, the MAC protocol arbitrates contention for the channel. Digital cellular telephone systems initially used time division multiple access (TDMA), which divides channels into time slots. Cellular digital packet data (CDPD) supports rates of tens of kilobits per second. The IEEE 802.11 standard [IEEE802.11] for wireless data networks uses a CSMA MAC protocol (with no collision detection due to the difficulty of detecting other radios while transmitting). Data rates of 1 and 2 Mb/s are specified, in the 2.4-GHz microwave band (frequency hopping or direct sequence spread spectrum), and using infrared light transmission.

Clearly, there is a demand for much higher wireless data rates, but this is constrained by the carrier frequency and other factors described in Section 5.1.1. Tens of megabits per second are achievable in the microwave bands, and thus third-generation cellular technology is targeted to 10-Mb/s links, using direct sequence spread spectrum code division multiple access (CDMA). Through use of more sophisticated coding (8-chip complementary code keying), the 802.11 data rate has been increased to 11 Mb/s [IEEE802.11b], using direct sequence spread spectrum, but remaining in the 2.4-GHz band. Data rates up to 54-Mb/s are specified in the 5-GHz band [IEEE802.11a]. Initial deployments of short-link technologies, such as Bluetooth [Bray 2001, Miller 2001], have low data rate (732.2 kb/s) and small MAC address spaces (eight devices active per picocell).[8]

A variety of point-to-point wireless link technologies is available for LAN interconnection and MAN applications. Microwave links in the 6- and 11-GHz microwave band have long been used for intercity PSTN links. For example, the 3A-RDS carrier provides the equivalent of a T-3 circuit at 45 Mb/s, with typical relay tower spacing of 10 to 40 km [Rey 1983], but the vast majority of PSTN microwave links have been replaced by SONET fiber optic links. Microwave links in the unregulated ISM bands (in the United States 900 MHz, 2.4 GHz, and 5.8 GHz can be used to provide tens of megabits per second. Distances can range from inter-building for campus LAN interconnections to tens of km for MAN applications. Local multipoint distribution services (LMDS) [Sari 1999, Nordbotten 2000] provides line-of-sight capabilities in the range of 3 to 5 km, using the 24- and 28-GHz licensed bands in the United States and the 28- and 40-GHz bands in Europe. LMDS technology can support digital broadcast and data applications at aggregate data rates up to around 2 Gb/s. Typical rates for downstream channels are 36 Mb/s and for upstream channels are 8 to 26 Mb/s.

---

[8]Bluetooth was specified by an industrial consortium requiring membership. The data rate is targeted toward very inexpensive implementations (U.S. $5.00) and integration with embedded controllers; higher data rates are under discussion. The 3-bit address space is an inexplicable architectural decision that is woefully inadequate for the tens to hundreds of devices *per* individual that will be required for personal area networks.

Infrared and visible laser links provide the potential for much higher-bandwidth links, since the modulation is not constrained by carrier frequency. The IrDA standard [IrDa 1998, 1999, Williams 2000] provides for short-link (~1-m) transmission at 1.152, 4, and 16 Mb/s, using pulse position modulation (PPM). Power is constrained by laser safety requirements, limiting the link distance. In the early 2000s, OC-12 rate (622-Mb/s) free space laser links have been deployed.

Time varying conditions, such as noise and channel fades, are a key characteristic of wireless channels, particularly in mobile communications. Adaptive techniques play a significant role in exploiting the maximum channel bandwidth with minimum power, as channel conditions change. Parameters to adapt include transmission power, data rate, forward error correction (FEC) rate, spread spectrum parameters, and amount of receiver processing to reconstruct the signal[Escobar 1990, Pursley 1999].

Multiuser detection is another technique to increase the link rate. A multiuser detector simultaneously tracks signals from multiple transmitters. It uses these signals, which may contain errors, to subtract noise from and isolate the desired signal, improving its bit error rate characteristics.

5.1.2.3.2   Satellite

As the sensitivity of receivers and the directionality of transmitters continues to improve, the potential role of satellite links is expanding from backbone network to user access.

Geostationary earth orbit (GEO) satellites are positioned in orbit locations that remain above a fixed point on the ground at an altitude of 36,000 km. Their height means that approximately one-third of the circumference is illuminated by a GEO link. Three GEO satellites are sufficient to cover most of the Earth (except for the poles), and most communications involve a single hop, and at most two. The NASA advanced communications technology satellite of the late 1990s was capable of supporting OC-12 (622-Mb/s) data rates [Acosta 1999]. The biggest challenge with GEO satellites is the long latency of approximately 240 ms per uplink/downlink hop, which uses half of a subsecond interactive response budget for a round-trip of 480 ms. Furthermore, the effects of errors can add significantly to the latency problem. It is thus critical that GEO satellite links have sufficient FEC to reduce the probability of end-to-end retransmission to acceptable limits. The high-bandwidth-×-delay product can challenge higher-layer protocols not designed with this in mind [Partidge 1997, Allman 1999c, Allman 2000a]. Practical challenges in deploying satellite links include the cost of satellite launch and the difficulty of equipment upgrade. It is thus crucial to properly anticipate future needs, to avoid the fate of Iridium (Example 2.1).

As described in Section 3.1.2, low-earth-orbiting (LEO) satellites have a link latency on the same order as long-haul terrestrial links, and thus have the potential to provide global coverage to areas not served by fiber optic cable. Furthermore, the proximity to the surface of the Earth means that, for the same power and antenna gains, higher transmission rates can be sustained, suitable for consideration as part of a high-speed network infrastructure. This is achieved at the expense of a constellation of satellites covering the Earth, since LEO satellites cannot be positioned in a stationary location where needed. In the early 2000s, LEO satellite constellations supporting 10-Mb/s data channels are under consideration.

5.1.3   Link-Layer Components

This section will briefly describe some of the components that perform link-layer processing exclusively. Note that all network nodes and end systems also perform link-layer processing, since they terminate communication links.

Link-Layer Components   *Link-layer components must sustain the data rate of the link, while not introducing significant delay.*

L-IIc

5.1.3.1   Amplifiers and Regenerators

When the distance between switch nodes or end systems exceeds the reach of a point-to-point link, it is far more cost effective to install a device that performs only physical or link-layer restoration of the signal. These components are particularly needed for long-haul links and in sparsely populated environments.

There is a range of signal restoration that can be employed. The most basic is an amplifier, which restores the signal level in the analog domain, shown in Figure 5.8a. Optical amplifiers are particularly cost effective, since they restore the level without regard to wavelength. Erbium doped fiber amplifiers (EDFAs) can be located up to a few hundred kilometers apart and restore all the wavelengths in a WDM transmission link. EFDAs operate in the 1,550-nm band with a pump laser at 980 or 1,480 nm multiplexed into an Er^{3+} doped length of fiber, and produce typical gains of 25 dB [Ramamurthy 2000a]. Praseodymium doped fluoride fiber amplifiers can be used in the 1,310-nm band.

Over a long enough distance, amplification is not enough, and the signal must be regenerated in the digital electronic domain, as shown in Figure 5.8b. Regeneration and reshaping (2R) are transparent to bit rate; regeneration with retiming and reshaping (3R) performs clock recovery as well. Electronic regeneration is required in optical links every few thousand kilometers, due to wave-

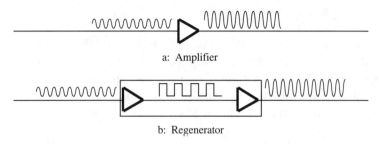

a: Amplifier

b: Regenerator

Figure 5.8 Amplifiers, regenerators, and repeaters.

form degradation from chromatic dispersion and nonlinear effects such as four-wave mixing.

Electronic regeneration of WDM signals is very expensive, due to the need for one optical/electronic/optical conversion circuit for each wavelength. This motivates research in the area of ultra-long-haul WDM transmission and all-optical 3R.

Not all repeaters are in the optical domain. Microwave transmission links were the link of choice in long-distance telephony in the first generation (through the 1970s), with repeater towers located to maintain line-of-sight transmission.

Bent pipe satellite links, shown in Figure 5.9, are another example of a link-layer component. The satellite receives, regenerates, and transmits link-layer frames. It is also possible for satellites to act as switch nodes, as shown in Figure 3.7

5.1.3.2 Multiplexors and Cross-Connects

As indicated in Section 5.1.2, link-layer multiplexing can be used to aggregate multiple virtual links onto a single physical link. Multiplexors (and demultiplexors) serve this function, aggregating and disaggregating TDM or WDM channels. Traditional multiplexors, as used in the PSTN, form a hierarchy combining T-carrier TDM channels.

SONET is typically deployed in a ring configuration, and the multiplexing/demultiplexing on/off the ring is performed in a single device called an *add-drop multiplexor* (ADM). Rings can be connected by a *cross-connect*, which is a Layer 2 switch that maintains a relatively static configuration.

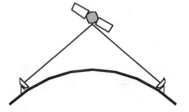

Figure 5.9 Bent pipe satellite link.

5.1.3.3 *Optical Wavelength Converters*

As described in Section 3.1.4, WDM networks provide lightpaths through the network, over which circuit or burst switching can be used. Lightpaths are used because the ability to convert wavelengths in the optical domain is beyond the reach of fourth-generation (1990s) technology. Cost-effective wavelength converters would allow their placement at switches, enabling wavelength converting switches.

Wavelength converters can be implemented as O/E/O devices, which convert through the electronic domain, but this does not exploit the advantages of optical switching by eliminating the electronic devices for each wavelength.

All optical wavelength converters are possible which use cross-modulation or coherent effects techniques [Ramamurthy 2000b]. Cross-modulation converters use the input signal to modulate a laser at the desired output frequency. Coherent effect converters use the nonlinear effects of fiber to produce a difference frequency, similar to that described for FWM in Section 5.1.1.

5.1.3.4 *Hubs and Bridges*

As discussed in Sections 5.1.1 and 5.1.2, a number of early LANs used shared medium wires, in particular, Ethernet and the token ring. The physical length limit, and in some cases topology considerations, led to the development of *bridges* to connect LAN segments. The first bridges were promiscuous, repeating all frames received to all other attached segments, depicted in Figure 5.11a.

As the demand for network access and bandwidth increased in the 1980s, shared medium LANs became saturated with traffic. A simple modification to the basic bridge consists of filtering frames, such that the only traffic that is forwarded to another segment is frames addressed to an attached system; this is depicted by the multiplexors in Figure 5.11b. These *learning bridges* observe the source address on incoming traffic to determine to which segments various systems are attached.

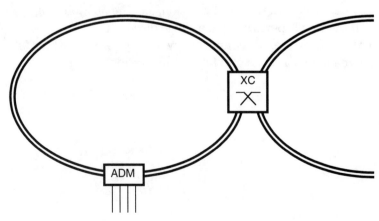

Figure 5.10 SONET dual-ring topology.

EXAMPLE 5.3: SONET ARCHITECTURE

The SONET dual-ring architecture is shown in Figure 5.10. Access to the ring is provided by ADMs that provide several lower data rate links multiplexed into the ring. For example, an OC-192 (10 Gb/s) ADM may have several OC-12 (622 Mb/s) or OC-48 (2.4 Gb/s) ports. Rings are connected by cross-connects (XC), which interconnect SONET channels between rings. The configuration of ADMs and cross-connects is static and provisioned by the network operator.

The SONET ring architecture was originally designed for metropolitan area network (MAN) deployment to support the public switched telephone network (PSTN). The primary motivation for the dual-ring architecture is to provide automatic protection switching (APS), which recovers from a node failure or fiber cut (generally called a *back hoe fade*); 50 μs is the standard recovery time. When a link or node (ADM or XC) fails, the adjacent nodes wrap the ring around, allowing full connectivity among the remaining nodes, albeit with a latency penalty. This is important to the telephone network, which is not otherwise robust to link failures. When a link goes down, the call is terminated, and telephone switches cannot automatically reroute around failed nodes.

SONET rings have significant deployment in wide area networks, in which case the recovery time is necessarily longer due to the speed-of-light propagation delay. A mesh network is generated by deploying overlapping rings with cross-connects; for example, a 3 × 3 array of interconnected nodes can be generated by four interconnected rings. Data networks are also run on top of the existing SONET ring infrastructure, but this has some significant implications for high-speed networks. First, the latency penalty of a SONET ring wrap can be significant, particularly in the case of wide area rings with diameters on the order of 1000 km. Second, Internet protocols are designed to route around link failures. Thus, APS is supplying functionality redundant to that of higher-layer protocols. The End-to-End Argument (3) suggests that we question this duplication of functionality. Note that in the third generation Internet (1990s), routing protocols do not converge quickly enough to be transparent to failures; thus APS is providing functionality that perhaps should be provided at a higher layer, but is not.

Topological and management considerations also caused a deviation from the traditional LAN installations. Building topologies were often not a good match for the linear topology of Ethernet or the circular topology of token ring LANs. Furthermore, the integrity of the network was exposed as the physical medium snaked through user offices. Thus, the star topology used for telephone wiring was adopted, and a *hub* served as the center of the star in a wiring closet, as shown in Figure 5.11c. Bandwidth is still shared among the hub ports, although hub sections can be bridged together to increase capacity.

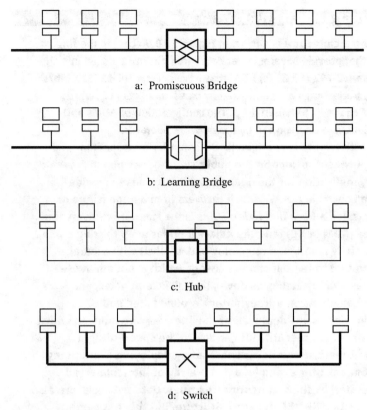

a: Promiscuous Bridge

b: Learning Bridge

c: Hub

d: Switch

Figure 5.11   Hubs, bridges, and switches.

As the demand for traffic increased, the logical extension was to replace the hub with a layer 2 *switch*, which only forwards frames to the systems to which they are addressed. This is depicted by the thick line to end systems in Figure 5.11d. This technique uses space division to exploit the Scalability of Mesh Topologies (N-II.4).

5.1.4   Support for Higher Layers

This section describes several areas that impact the interaction with, and performance of, higher layers, particularly the network layer.

5.1.4.1   Loss Characterization

It can be important for the characteristics of a link to be known to upper layers. If the characteristics are known in advance, they may be used to help determine how paths are established and what error control mechanisms can be used (for example, FEC over a lossy wireless link).

> **Loss Characterization Principle**   *Provide long-term and dynamic information on the reason for loss to higher-layer protocols so that end-to-end mechanisms respond appropriately.*
>
> **L-4F**

When congestion is inferred by end-to-end loss (as for TCP, Section 7.5.4), transport layer mechanisms can significantly benefit from explicit information distinguishing losses due to error-prone channels from losses due to congestion [Dawkins 2000].

Furthermore, due to the shared medium of wireless channels, end-to-end protocols cannot distinguish between physical layer throughput problems, like poor signal-to-noise ratio and channel contention problems. In both cases, data is lost, but unless physical layer devices can pinpoint the existence of a physical layer problem, it is difficult to determine at what layer the problem must be solved. This problem is compounded in mobile networks, in which the topology is dynamic.

Improper response due to this lack of information from lower layers can have a significant performance impact. For example, if a wireless node increases transmit power due to losses assumed to be due to a channel fade, but the losses are due to interference from other transmissions, the interference will only worsen.

Since the time scale of per hop link-layer can be many times less than an end-to-end round-trip time (RTT), it is better that the corrective measures be taken at the lowest layer that can best react to the problem. This is particularly important when a small portion of the path has significantly different error characteristics from the rest of the path. The interaction of physical, MAC, link, network, and transport layers is a challenge in high-speed networks, however, in part due to the amount and dynamicity of state.

One strategy is to use adaptive link-layer protocols capable of tracking and reacting to physical and MAC layer problems to stabilize the perceived link characteristics, so that higher-layer protocols have time to converge and provide good performance. If the link-layer protocols are sufficiently capable of communicating long-term conditions up to higher-layers, routing and traffic management can take proactive measures to adapt to the anticipated situation before the worsening conditions escape the dynamic range of adaptivity of the link-layer protocols.

5.1.4.2   Filtering

There are several capabilities that are best done in the lowest levels, at the highest speeds, and with the least protocol layering overhead. These capabilities can be emulated in higher-layer protocols in software, but usually only with substantial overhead and decrease in performance. They include filtering, broadcast, and multicast.

Filtering consists of discarding incoming frames that are not destined for higher-layer processing.[9] This includes frames not destined for this node or frames that this node is neither willing nor prepared to accept. The former case can occur on broadcast networks, where all nodes see all frames, regardless of the destination address, or where multicast packets are sent to nodes not tuned in to a particular multicast group.

When link-layer frames [and the higher-layer protocol data units (PDUs) that they encapsulate] are sent where they are not used, resources are wasted. As PDUs are processed in higher levels of the protocol stack, increasing resources are used, including buffer space, hardware channel capacity, and software processing capacity. The most effective strategy is to discard unwanted data as quickly as possible, in as low a layer as possible [Karn 2000].

> **Early Filtering Principle**   *Filter the incoming data not destined for a node as early as possible and discard as much as possible at each layer.*
>
> **L-4f**

5.1.4.3 Broadcast Support

A number of protocols and mechanisms benefit from broadcast, multicast, and anycast transmission, especially in support of LANs. Examples include address resolution protocol (ARP) and dynamic host configuration protocol (DHCP) [Droms 1997], which automatically obtains an IP address for an end system. Broadcast sends information to every destination on a subnetwork, multicast sends information to a subset of destinations on a network, and anycast sends information to at least one node of a set [Partridge 1993a]. The ability to broadcast is generally confined to a single subnetwork to limit the traffic.

Shared medium LANs support broadcast natively; all systems receive a single packet transmitted in the common channel. Similarly, multicast is directly supported by broadcasting with selective filtering.

> **Link-Layer Multicast Principle**   *Shared medium links provide native support for broadcast, essential for higher-layer control protocols and in support of multicast applications. Nonbroadcast point-to-point mesh LANs should provide broadcast and multicast support.*
>
> **L-2C**

---

[9]Filtering in the more general sense consists of examining a packet to determine its disposition, which may also consist of passing it somewhere else for processing, described in Section 5.5.3.

In subnetworks that do not have a native broadcasting capability, it must be supported by the network layer. This involves significantly more complexity than native broadcast.

5.2   Switches and Routers

We have discussed high-speed links; this section moves to consideration of the network nodes to which the links attach. The distinction between the terms *switch* and *router* is historic. Connection-oriented networks, including the PSTN and X.25 data networks, used the term *circuit* and *packet switch*, respectively. Once a circuit or connection is set up, data can be efficiently switched based on hard state, as described in Section 4.1.3. With the advent of connection-oriented fast packet switching, the term *switch* remained in use for connection-oriented networks.

In the second-generation networks (1980s) and the third-generation (1990s) Internet, packets were *routed* through the network nodes with no predetermined state. At each hop, a routing table was consulted to determine the most appropriate next hop based on the destination address in the packet. Thus, the term *router* is frequently used in the context of the IP based Internet.[10]

In reality, routing algorithms run in both connection-oriented and datagram networks to inform the nodes about network topology. Thus, it is better to talk about packets being *switched* through the nodes by looking up the output port in a *forwarding* table, which is populated by the *routing* algorithm. This is the terminology we will use throughout this book. We will, however, use the historical term *router* when describing early IP router organization in the rest of Section 5.2.

Additionally, the layer of protocol that is being switched impacts the terminology used. A link-layer component that connects multiple shared medium segments is called a *bridge*, but if it performs switching on the MAC address it is called a *layer 2 switch*, as described in Section 5.1.3. Network components that terminate the transport layer are called *layer 4 switches*, and those that terminate the application layer are called *application layer gateways*, or *layer 7 switches*. Unless qualified, we use switch in the layer 3 context, and *node* will refer to any of these components.

Network Node Principle   *Network nodes must support high-bandwidth, low-latency, end-to-end flows, as well as their aggregation. High-speed network nodes should provide a scalable number of high-bandwidth, low-delay interconnections.*

N-II

---

[10]Originally the term *gateway* was used, and is still part of the names of routing protocols such as border gateway protocol (BGP).

In the remainder of this section, we will first introduce the functional components needed in a network node. Then, the architecture of traditional second- and third-generation store-and-forward routers is presented, focusing on performance issues. Finally, we present the ideal node component of the ideal network model (Figure 5.2). This will be used as the target for optimizations in subsequent sections.

5.2.1 Switching

Figure 5.12 shows the functional components in a network node (switch or router). It is important to note at this point that we are enumerating the necessary *functions*, without yet indicating whether these functions are *implemented* in software or hardware and whether or not they need to be part of the critical path for high-speed networks.

The functions can be divided into two major categories, based on the granularity of operation:

1. Switching operates on a per packet basis.

2. Signaling occurs on a per flow or connection granularity.

3. Routing can occur on a per flow or connection granularity, when a connection route is being determined, and on a longer time granularity affecting many flows, such as topology and link state exchanges.

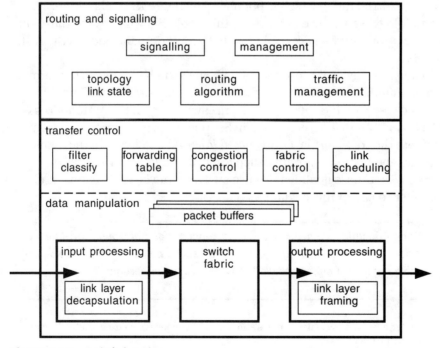

Figure 5.12 Switch functions.

5.2.1.1 Switching Functions

The *per* packet switching functions can be further divided into two categories: data manipulation and transfer control.[11]

1. **Data manipulation functions.**   Read and modify data and operate *per* byte or *per* packet. The functional blocks that perform data manipulation are

   Input processing.   Responsible for getting packets from the input ports, performing the link-layer decapsulation, and consists at least of some queueing to speed match the locally clocked switch to the link.

   Switch fabric.   Responsible for directing the packets that have arrived to the proper output port of the node.

   Output processing.   Responsible for sending packets on outgoing links, after performing link-layer framing. At the very least, some queuing is required to properly time the packet output.

   Packet buffers.   Hold packets which either need network layer processing or until they are able to be scheduled for an outgoing link. Depending on the switch design, packet buffering can be associated with input processing, the switch fabric, or the output processing. Some switches have no buffers at all; examples are traditional circuit switches and some optical burst switches.

   Link-layer decapsulation and framing.   Perform the hop-by-hop link-layer protocol processing on incoming packets before the switching can occur and then on outgoing packets before transmission to the next hop. In the case of shared medium links, particularly wireless, this includes medium access control (MAC) functions.

2. **Transfer control functions.**   Control operations that are directly related to the *per* byte or *per* packet transfer of data. Functional blocks that perform transfer control consist of:

   Filtering and classification.   Applied to determine the type of each packet so that it can be transferred through the proper path in the switch. This includes diversion of a control packet and determination of the appropriate determination of queue in the case of differentiated services. In the case of active network nodes, some packets are diverted from the normal datapath into the active processing path.

   Congestion control.   Performs the *per* packet traffic control functions, including rate policing, traffic shaping, and discard policy.

---

[11]Using the terminology from [Clark 1989a] applied to end systems, as described in Section 6.2.1.

Forwarding table. Provides the core control function that determines on which output port the packet needs to leave to get to the next hop along the path to the destination.

Output scheduling. Necessary to properly time the departure of packets on the outgoing link, particularly when multiple packets contend for a particular link at the same time and to meet QOS requirements.

5.2.1.2 *Routing and Signaling Functions*

The *per* flow or connection and longer time granularity functions consist of:

Management. Provides the network management interface and functionality to network management tools and operators, such as statistics collection, management information base (MIB) support, and command and control interfaces.

Signaling. The functionality that allows network layer control messages to be exchanged between nodes, as described in Chapter 4. Examples include signaling messages that update and synchronize topology and link state, connection management messages, and explicit congestion notification.

Topology and link state. Used to store information on the state of the network to allow the routing algorithm to make reasonable choices on how paths should be routed.

Routing algorithms. Use network topology and link state information to determine the nodes through which paths should flow, and load this information into the forwarding table. In the case of connectionless datagram networks, the routing protocol operates asynchronously with individual flows to keep the table loaded with entries. In the case of connection-oriented networks, the routing algorithm runs at each connection setup to load the appropriate information into the forwarding table. In the case of soft state flow switching (Section 4.1.4), routes are established when flows are signaled (control driven) or identified (data driven).

Traffic management. Responsible for reserving resources in the switch to particular paths or groups of paths, and in the case of guaranteed QOS classes, performing admission control so that resources are not overbooked.

Note that not all switches have all this functionality; for example, pure best-effort datagram routers do not have traffic management functionality, and it is possible for topology information to be incorporated directly into the forwarding table.

5.2.2   Traditional Store-and-Forward Routers

Traditional second-generation (1980s) store-and-forward routers (supporting the network architecture described in Section 4.1.2) used a bus-based computer system with multiple network interfaces (NIs), as shown in Figure 5.13.

The NIs terminate the network links, and typically perform layer 2 link and MAC processing (such as Ethernet, token ring, or T-carrier leased line). Incoming packets are copied from the incoming NI, across the system bus, and into main memory, where the network layer buffers reside. All network layer processing is performed in software, including header decode, forwarding decision, data integrity checking (for example, checksum verification), and scheduling for the outgoing NI.

There are three significant points of contention that limit the performance and scalability of this architecture.

1. All packets suffer the store-and-forward delay t_b, as described in Section 3.1.2.

2. Packet buffers contend for and share the same memory and processor. Thus, the forwarding delay t_f is constrained by the number of forwarding operations that must occur concurrently.

3. The system bus is the switching fabric, and all packet transfers must traverse the bus *twice*, on input and output, and for each ingress/egress NI pair. The bus bandwidth significantly constrains the number of NIs that

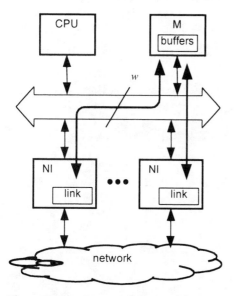

Figure 5.13   Store-and-forward router.

can be attached to a single router. Note that the CPU must *also* contend for the bus to do network layer processing on the buffers in memory, against the packet transfers between buffer memory and the NIs.

There are incremental optimizations to this architecture that provide some performance improvement. Direct memory access (DMA) is a mechanism that allows block transfers across the bus to memory without the programmed I/O (PIO) involvement of the CPU, as described in Section 6.1.4 in the context of end systems. This increases the bandwidth and efficiency of the transfers.

5.2.2.1 *Third-Generation Routers*

The most significant optimization that can be made to this basic architecture is to eliminate the shared CPU and memory as a source of contention among the various network links. This is done by distributing and offloading the network layer protocol processing to the NIs, as shown in Figure 5.14. This architecture was used in the NSFNET routers of the mid-1990s.

Packets are moved between NIs across the bus using *third-party* transfers, without going through main memory. In this case, the bus must support multiple controllers called *bus masters*, and each network interface needs bus master capability. Each network interface contains a network interface processor (NIP) that performs the network layer processing, along with buffer memory for packet processing.

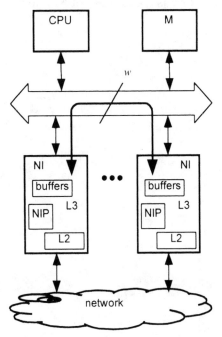

Figure 5.14 Third-party bus forwarding.

While this significantly reduces the contention for a single memory and distributes the processing to each NI, this architecture still requires a store-and-forward hop on the NI. Furthermore, a single bus as the interconnect between all NIs limits scalability; this issue will be discussed in detail in Section 5.4.2.

Now that we have discussed traditional router architectures, it is time to return to the ideal model, which will be the goal for fast packet switch architectures.

5.2.3   Ideal Switch Architecture

In Chapter 2 we introduced an ideal end-to-end model for low-latency, high-bandwidth communication, and showed the network refinement in Figure 5.2. Recall that two of the primary factors in designing low-latency systems are Store-and-Forward Avoidance (II.3) and Blocking Avoidance (II.4), by using such techniques as cut-through and pipelining.

Figure 5.15 shows the ideal switch. As in the case of the ideal network, there is unlimited bandwidth and no latency: $R = \infty$ and $D = 0$. Additionally, we want nodes to scale as large as necessary so as not to constrain the network topology choices discussed in Chapter 3. Thus we show an unlimited number of ports: $n = \infty$.

The goal we will try to achieve is to completely avoid any packet-based latency, in particular eliminating the store-and-forward latency and avoiding queueing delays. This is the network node version of Store-and-Forward Avoidance (II.3):

Store-and-Forward and Queueing Delay Minimization Principle   *Store-and-forward delays should be avoided, and per packet queuing should be minimized. In the ideal case, nodes should pipeline and cut through packets with zero per packet delays.*

S-II.3

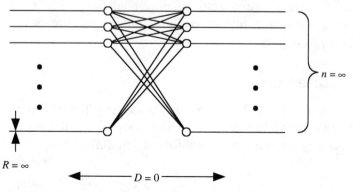

Figure 5.15   Ideal switch model.

Thus, we will discuss switch and router architectures that approach this ideal. We will discuss connection-oriented switch architecture in the next section, the switch fabric itself in Section 5.4, and extensions to support fast datagram switches in Section 5.5.

5.3 Fast Packet Switches

In the mid-1980s, the goal of the high-speed networking community was to increase network link bandwidth by a couple orders of magnitude beyond that supported by the store-and-forward IP router architectures described in Section 5.2.2, to OC-3 (155 Mb/s) and OC-12 (622 Mb/s) rates.[12] Since conventional datagram forwarding was too complicated to consider at these data rates in the technology of the time, fast packet switching was proposed [Kulzer 1984, Turner 1986, Coudreuse 1987]. By substantially reducing the complexity of packet processing, hardware implementation of the switching function was possible.

There are four key motivations that drove fast packet switching:

1. Dramatically simplifying packet processing and forwarding lookups by establishing connection state, as described in Section 4.1.3.

2. Eliminating the store-and-forward latency described in Section 5.2.2.

3. Eliminating the contention of the general-purpose computer bus as the switching medium, as described in Section 5.2.2.

4. Adding the ability to provide QOS guarantees to emerging multimedia applications, facilitated by resources reservations for connections.

The remainder of this section discusses the architecture and organization of connection-oriented fast packet switches. Section 5.3.1 introduces the high-level architecture and functional blocks. Section 5.3.2 describes the input processing and label swapping. Sections 5.3.3 and 5.3.4 discuss packet size and structure, respectively, which have significant effect on the ability to switch efficiently. Section 5.3.5 describes switch traffic management. Section 5.3.6 considers the partitioning of functionality among hardware and software and among different technology choices.

5.3.1 Switch Architecture

The architecture of a fast packet switch is shown in Figure 5.16. The goal is to blast packets through the switch without the delays of blocking due to contention in the switch fabric or need for store-and-forward buffering. Fast

---

[12]The U.S. HPCC (high-performance computing and communications) Gigabit Testbed program had a target of supporting OC-12, which "rounded up" to 1 Gb/s.

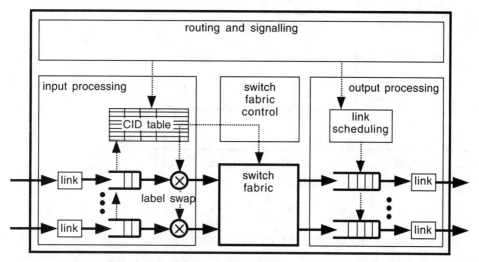

Figure 5.16 Connection-oriented fast packet switch.

packet switches are based on maintaining connection state to simplify the per packet processing as much as possible, so that the data path can be efficiently implemented in hardware.

> **Fast Packet Switch Critical Path Principle** *Simplify and optimize per byte and per-packet data manipulation and transfer control functions for implementation in a hardware critical path. State maintained per connection streamlines per packet processing.*
> **S-1Bc**

Thus, implementation of the per byte packet data manipulation functions (input processing, the switch fabric, and output processing) is in optimized fast hardware. Transfer control functions, which operate per packet, are also optimized, generally for hardware implementation.

5.3.2 Input and Label Processing

Packets arrive from incoming links and flow into the input processing block. Link-layer (and perhaps MAC) processing strips link-layer encapsulation (the link block in Figure 5.16). The packets then shift into input queues, the connection identifier (CID) field is stripped from the packet header and is used as an index into the CID table, as shown in Figure 5.17.

CIDs are locally negotiated hop-by-hop when connections are established, which prevents the need for global knowledge in CID assignment. Furthermore, this means that the CID table is densely populated with only the number of entries deemed necessary *per* switch, which allows a simple direct index lookup and implementation in relatively expensive fast memory.

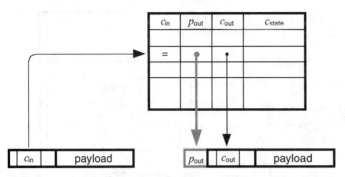

Figure 5.17 Label swapping lookup.

Thus a given connection will have an associated tuple $\langle c_{in}, c_{out} \rangle$ at each switch node. The CID entry for c_{in} indicates what the CID is for the next hop c_{out} that must be swapped into the CID field in the packet header; this is called *label swapping*. The CID entry also contains a field indicating the outgoing port p_{out} of the switch to use, along with other relevant connection state. The outgoing port number can be used in two ways. It may be used to set the path through the switch fabric. Some switch fabrics are *self-routing*, in which case p_{out} is prepended to the packet in an internal switch header to guide the packet through the fabric; this is described in Section 5.4.4.

A label swapped path is shown in Figure 5.18. In this example, each switch has four ports, p_0 is on the left and p_1, p_2, and p_3 on the right numbered from

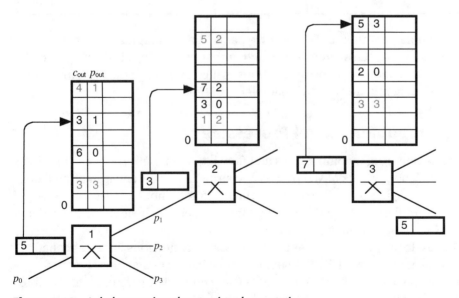

Figure 5.18 Label swapping along a virtual connection.

top to bottom (as shown for switch 1). As the depicted packet moves to the right, the label c_{in} is used to index into the table for each switch. The corresponding table entry contains the new label c_{out} that is swapped into the header, and egress port p_{out} along which the packet is forwarded. The tables also contain entries for the reverse path in dark text. Note that only the $\langle c_{out}, p_{out} \rangle$ *combination* need be unique in the table; it is possible for the same label to be assigned to multiple *outgoing* connections from a given switch (for example label 3 in switch 1); it is only the *incoming* labels that need to be unique. This can be accomplished during the connection establishment phase by the downstream node assigning the labels used by an upstream node.

Once packets have been directed to the proper output of the switch fabric, they are queued for output, and then go through link encapsulation and framing (and perhaps MAC) for transmission.

This architecture has two important improvements over the traditional router design described in Section 5.2.2:

1. By pipelining packets through the input processing, switch fabric, and output processing, the store-and-forward delay is eliminated. The granularity of pipelining may be considerably smaller than a packet. For example, the queue shown in the input processing need only be a per byte shift register that delays the packet long enough for a hardware-based index to return the new CID label and output port. Depending on the switch fabric architecture, the leading edge of the packet may be able to leave the switch before the trailing edge has arrived, if there is no blocking in the switch or contention for output links; this is called *cut-through* [Kermani 1979].

2. Conventional next hop lookup based on destination address is a relatively complex operation, as described in Section 5.5.2. By using connection SETUP to install the connection state in the CID table, this lookup can happen more quickly, resulting in a higher throughput measured in packets per second. The retrieval of connection state c_{state} also allows the packet to be classified in other ways, such as determination of the queue and policy for appropriate QOS, subsuming the packet classification process described in Section 5.5.3. This translates to the ability to support higher-bandwidth links for a given packet size.[13] This is particularly important for small packets, such as TCP control packets and Web requests.

Connectionless versus Connection Tradeoff   *The latency of connection setup must be traded against the increase in packet processing rate and resultant bandwidth increase achievable due to the less complex label swapping.*

S-5A

---

[13]And is the justification for the narrow packet flow trapezoids in Figure 4.7.

5.3.3 Packet Size and Variability

The size and structure of packets have significant impact on the performance of fast packet switches. There are several aspects to consider:

- Fixed versus variable length packets
- Packet size and variability
- Header and trailer structure

The first two items relate to the manipulation of entire packets, and will be discussed here. The last item relates to the ability to efficiently process individual fields within the packet, and the impact of such fields on protocol processing, and will be discussed in Section 5.3.4.

5.3.3.1 Fixed Cells versus Variable Packets

Packets can be allowed to either vary in size or be fixed at a particular length; fixed size packets are frequently called *cells*. Packet switches designed to relay cells are also called *cell switches* (for example, ATM switches and IP switches that use an ATM switch core). Each scheme has advantages.

Fixed size cells generally make switch design significantly easier, allowing cells to be pipelined in lock step through the queues and the switch fabric. Allowing packets to vary in size requires pipeline stages to be sized for the maximum packet size (which adds latency and is inefficient in buffer utilization), or significantly increases control and scheduling complexity. This is particularly true for multistage interconnection networks, described in Section 5.4.4.

The most challenging problem with fixed size cells is determining the proper cell size. This is a relatively simple local optimization to make for a particular switch technology, fabric architecture, and data rate. Globally optimizing this based on application traffic patterns, end system internal data structure (buffers, pages, cache lines), host–network interface design, link technologies and data rates, and across multiple switches is challenging, indeed.

There are two advantages of variable size packets. First, a global predetermination of packet size is not necessary. If the wrong choice is made (as was the case for ATM), the performance implications can be significant and irreversible once standardized. Second, up to reasonable packet lengths (discussed in the next section), segmentation or fragmentation is not necessary. Application data units (ADUs) can be directly transported through the network, and application layer framing (ALF), discussed in Section 7.3.2, can be more efficiently employed.

5.3.3.2 Packet/Cell Size

Packet size is an issue whether packets are fixed in size or allowed to vary over some range in size. In particular, a reasonable upper bound is needed to avoid the long latencies for short real-time packets backed up behind long packets (described in the context of message switching in Section 4.1.1). Furthermore, there are practical limits on the ability to buffer very long packets (commonly called *jumbograms*).

Similarly, packets that are too short present problems, due to the imposed packet processing budget, shown in Table 5.4. When packets are small and data rates high, the time to make control decisions about a packet in the input processing portion of the switch is limited. For example, at 10 Gb/s with 32 B packets there is only a budget of 25 ns to decode the header, look up the CID, label swap, and either prepend a header or set switch state before the next cell arrives. This problem can be ameliorated by using a parallel multicell pipeline, but this considerably increases the complexity of input processing hardware. Since packets *must* be processed at line rate, the combination of packet time and processing complexity directly determines how fast the packet processing hardware must be, and, in the limit, determines whether a particular data rate is feasible.

Furthermore, when packets are short, the relative overhead contributed to the header is high; long packets amortize the header overhead. When packets are small, optimizing the header length is more important, but this may come at the cost of efficient encoding (discussed in the next section) or by entirely eliminating typical fields (for example, sequence number, as was done for ATM cells). On the other hand, in the case of fixed size cells, the amount of internal fragmentation due to wasted space in the last cell of a stream is smaller for shorter cells.

The advantage of short packets is that interflow multiplexing delays are reduced. In the case of real-time interactive media, such as voice communications, this can be a significant issue, for example, in determining whether echo-cancellers are needed.

The fact that Resource Tradeoffs Change (2A) can also affect the choice of packet size. If bandwidth is free and unlimited, there is no reason to restrict

Table 5.4 Packet Processing Budget

	PACKET SIZE			
RATE	1 B	32 B	128 B	1 KB
100 Mb/s	80 ns	2.5 μs	10 μs	80 μs
1 Gb/s	8 ns	250 ns	1 μs	8 μs
10 Gb/s	800 ps	25 ns	100 ns	800 ns

packet size for efficient statistical multiplexing. Very high-bandwidth transparent optical networks motivate this. Objects, such as files, Web pages, and high-resolution images could be transferred in single very large packets (jumbograms). There are application reasons, however, to keep packets small, and it is desirable to Structure Data to Meet Interactive Response Bounds (A-7A), so that applications can incrementally process arriving data, as described in Section 8.1.2.

5.3.3.3 *Packet Granularity*

An important consideration is the granularity in packet size. In the case of fixed size cells, this relates to the size chosen. In the case of variable size packets, this is the granularity over which the size can vary. Important granularities are

  Byte.   Virtually all end-system and network protocol processing is in at least 8-bit byte (or octet) units. Thus, packet header, trailer, and payload sizes should be a multiple of 8 bits in length.

  Word.   Most end-system processing is done in at least word granularity, typically 32 or 64 bits (8 or 16 bytes). For example, cache lines are typically in multiple of end-system words to hold entire instructions and operands. Thus, payload sizes should be in 32-bit multiples to sensibly match end-system granularities.

  End-system data unit.   Some efficiencies may be exploited if the size of the payload is matched to important end system structures, such as system buffers or virtual memory pages. Since these structures and sizes vary among end systems, it is not practical to match all of them. Choosing a power-of-2 length that maps to an integer fraction or multiple can reduce the overhead of translating between end-system packet buffers and network packet payloads. It also results in less internal fragmentation in end-system buffers and larger buffering capability (in number of packets) for a given quantity of memory.

  Power-of-2 commodity memory.   Commodity memory components are usually produced in power-of-2 increments, with the density increasing by a factor of 4 in each subsequent technology improvement. Power-of-2 packet size makes it less likely that expensive custom memory components or application specific integrated circuit (ASIC) cells will be needed in switch nodes (as well as in end systems).

The challenge is determining *which* part of the packet should be power-of-2 granularity—the individual components or the entire packet. From an end-system perspective, it is the application data unit (ADU) that is important, from an end system network interface it is the transport protocol data unit

(TPDU), and from the network node perspective, it depends on the switch design. Generally in high-speed switches the control and data are separated; that is, header/trailer information will be stripped from the packet payload, and thus having a complete packet [network protocol data unit (NPDU)] that is a power-of-2 is less important. It may make sense for the header (and perhaps trailer) to be powers of 2. For example, a 148-B packet might consist of a 16-B header, 128-B payload, and 4-B trailer.

An additional consideration determining packet granularity is based on ADU and protocol mechanisms. The main distinction is between data transfer and control. Data transfer involves relatively large units. Control consists of signaling such as transaction requests, transport protocol acknowledgments, congestion notification, and connection setup messages. Thus, large packets are favorable to efficient data transfer, but waste bandwidth if they transport much smaller control messages.

Table 5.5 summarizes the tradeoffs in packet variability and size. The preceding discussion and Table 5.5 clearly indicate that there is no ideal choice, but rather a complex tradeoff of multiple orthogonal characteristics.

Packet Size and Variability Tradeoff *Packet size is a balance of a number of parameters that affect performance. Trade the statistical multiplexing and fine-grained control benefits of small packets against the efficiency of large packets. Trade the benefits to switch design of fixed cell size against the overhead of SAR and efficiency of variable packet size. Multiple discrete packet sizes increase flexibility at the cost of additional switch complexity. Hop-by-hop SAR localizes packet size optimizations at the cost of additional per hop delay and complexity.*

S-8A

There are a couple of middle grounds to consider, however. These include limited discrete variability and hop-by-hop segmentation and reassembly.

5.3.3.3.1 Discrete Packet Sizes

Some of the advantages of variable packet sizes, without all the hardware complexity, can be achieved by limiting the packet sizes to a small number of discrete increments. This provides the advantages of not forcing a global decision on packet size, while simplifying the packet processing in the switches over the completely variable case. Packets can be an integral length of a base number (for example, 64B, 128B, 192B, 256B . . .), or a progression of power-of-2 sizes (for example, 64B, 128B, 256B . . .). The switch can still operate as a pipeline in lock step at the granularity of the smallest packet size, with larger packets spanning multiple time slots. Depending on the switch design, this may require internal buffering at the granularity of the largest packet. During connection setup time, the cell size for a

Table 5.5 Summary of Packet Size Tradeoffs

ISSUE		CELL		VARIABLE PACKET		HYBRID
		SMALL	LARGE	CONTINUOUS	DISCRETE	HBM SAR
Size optimization		Global	Global	None	Per flow	Local
Hardware complexity	Pipelining	Simple	Simple	Complex	Moderate	Variable
	Packet interarrival	Short	Long	Variable	Variable	Variable
	SAR	E2E	E2E	None	None	HBH
Overhead	Header	High	Low	Variable	Variable	Variable
	Pipe synchronization	Low	High	N/A	Variable	Variable
	Internal fragmentation	Low	High	None	Variable	Variable

particular connection can be negotiated end-to-end, allowing proper resource reservation in the switch. The power-of-2 scaling can be tied to link
bandwidth, for example, 64-B cells for an OC-3 (155 Mb/s) link, 256-B cells
for an OC-12 (622 Mb/s) link, 1-KB cells for an OC-48 (2.4 Gb/s) link, and 4-
KB cells for an OC-192 (10 Gb/s) link. This has the advantage of keeping the
packet time relatively constant, so that increasing data rates do not result
in increased packet processing rates and the associated need for faster
packet processing control logic.[14]

Note that this does not solve the problem of efficiently transporting control messages and transaction requests at high data rates without wasting
bandwidth. It may be desirable to support a small packet size (for example,
64 B) for control messages, even if other packets are a larger incremental
size.

5.3.3.3.2 Hybrid Hop-by-Hop Segmentation and Reassembly

In a cell-based network, the transmitting end system must segment application data units into cells, as shown in Figure 5.19a. Cells pass through the network, and the receiving end reassembles the cells into application data units.
This process is called *segmentation and reassembly* (SAR), and can be done
by the application (ALF, discussed in Chapter 8), or by the transport protocol.
ATM performs this in the ATM adaptation layer (AAL), which resides just
below the conventional transport layer.

The compromise is to send variable size packets on the links, but to do
SAR at each switch in the network, as shown in Figure 5.19b. This has the
advantage of not requiring global predetermined (or even end-to-end per
flow) agreement on cell size. Each switch can SAR using the internal cell
format and size appropriate for its queueing and switch fabric architecture
and link speed. Note, however, that this has not improved the ability to
statistically multiplex at a fine granularity along individual *links*; the delay
and jitter of a flow is still subject to cross traffic based on the largest
packet size.

Hop-by-hop SAR requires that variable size packets be chopped and encapsulated into cells, each of which has an internal header so that the
packet can be reassembled at the output after switching. This process adds
complexity and latency to the datapath not present in simple fast packet
switched networks. If the SAR hardware can be economically implemented
to keep up to line rate, this is a reasonable thing to consider and is one way
to implement IP switches [Parulkar 1995, Esaki 1995, Newman 1996,
Basturk 1999].

---

[14]The need for this depends on the way in which Resource Tradeoffs Change (2A) and the relative tracking of processing speed and bandwidth.

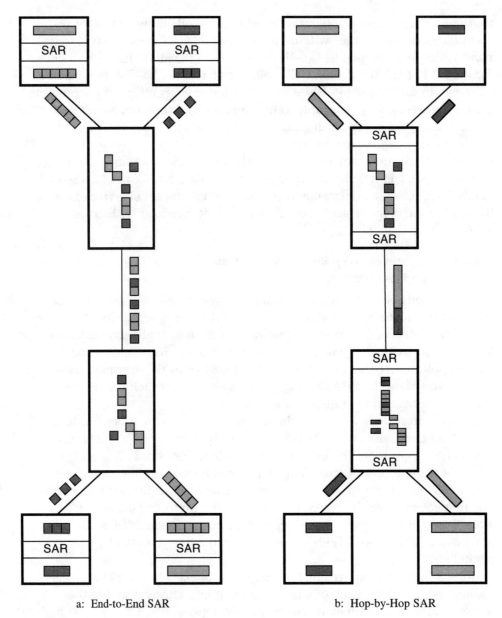

a: End-to-End SAR   b: Hop-by-Hop SAR

Figure 5.19 E2E versus HBH SAR.

5.3.4   Packet Structure

Packets consist of a header, payload, and perhaps a trailer, as shown in Figure 5.20.

The contents of the fields necessarily depend on the protocols and technology in use, but some general guidelines and typical fields are worth discussing:

Header.   The header should contain fields that are necessary to process the packet *before* it enters the switch fabric:

protocol id.   It may be necessary to identify a protocol type or version, which affects the interpretation and processing of subsequent fields. It is essential for this to be explicit to avoid complex pattern matching and interpretation rules.

packet type.   It is necessary to distinguish the type of processing that must be performed on the packet; generally the types are data and control. Data packets are forwarded through the datapath. Control packets are used for signaling, traffic management (such as congestion notification), and fault management. The important control subtype is whether

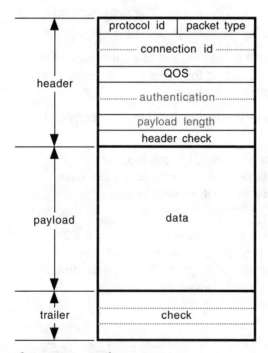

Figure 5.20   Packet structure.

or not it is a hop-by-hop control packet, such as for signaling, that must be pulled from the datapath or an end-to-end control packet, such as for congestion notification and fault management, that must be passed along the datapath.

connection identifier. The connection (or flow) identifier is used to quickly retrieve associated state. In the case of connection-oriented switching, the **connection identifier** indexes into the CID table to label swap and to determine which outgoing switch port to use. Furthermore, additional connection state is used to determine the *per* connection behavior and treatment of packets, for example, QOS and policy-based classification. In the case of connectionless datagram switching, the **flow identifier** is used to help look up outgoing port and perhaps retrieve soft state.

QOS bits. While per connection QOS state is maintained in the CID table, packets may be marked with a type of service or priority to indicate the treatment of *individual* packets within a connection. For example, the switch may mark packets nonconforming to the traffic contract as subject to discard (Section 5.3.5), and the application may assign priorities to packets indicating relative preference to discard under congestion (Section 8.3.2).

authentication. There may be authentication or capability information indicating the source of the packet or rights to use the data.

payload length. If variable-length packets are in use, the length of the packet needs to be in the header, so that logic does not have to hunt for the end of the packet by pattern matching.

header check. An integrity check on the header should be provided to protect against bit errors.

Payload. The payload is the data portion of the packet, generally a transport protocol data unit (TPDU), but in the case of tunneled or multiple network layers, it may be another network layer encapsulation.[15]

Trailer. The trailer should contain information to be inserted *after* the payload has passed through the pipeline, so that the entire packet does not need to be manipulated in place. This is essential to allow cut-through if a packet can be longer than the data

---

[15]The Hourglass Principle (4D) argues that multiple network layers, such as IP over ATM, are a bad idea in high-speed networks.

pipeline in a node. In generating the packet at the source, trailer information is computed as the payload passes through the pipeline and is inserted at the end. In reading the packet at intermediate hops, the trailer information is computed and compared against the expected value in the trailer. Additionally, trailers may be needed to perform an end-of-frame indication, which is useful in some link and MAC protocols.

check   The payload should have an integrity check, such as a cyclic redundancy check (CRC), to protect against bit errors.

Packet Control Field Structure   *Optimize packet header and trailer fields for efficient processing. Fields should be simply encoded, byte aligned, and fixed length where possible. Variable-length fields should be prepended with their length.*

S-8B

The format of these fields should be amenable to high-speed processing. Fields should be byte aligned, and control fields (such as type and QOS bits) should not have complex encoding. Variable-length header or trailer fields should be avoided but, if present, should have a length indicator at the beginning of each such field to avoid complex parsing. Option subheaders can be employed, in which case there should be a simple mechanism (option length) that allows nodes to skip the option header and locate the payload. Note that these formatting issues apply to protocol encapsulations regardless of the layer (link, network, transport) to allow efficient hardware processing.

5.3.5   Traffic Management

In general, quality of service and traffic management are not high-speed networking issues per se; however, the Path Protection Corollary (II.2) indicates that QOS mechanisms and resource reservations are needed to guarantee high-performance if bandwidth is not unlimited and free.

Switch Traffic Management   *In a resource-constrained environment, switches must support admission control with resource reservations to provide guaranteed-service traffic classes and policing to prevent other traffic from interfering.*

S-II.2

EXAMPLE 5.4: ATM

The ATM cell format was a compromise of the standards process, whose size was driven by the international telephony community, as indicated in Section 2.2.3 describing the Standards Both Facilitate and Impede Dilemma (III.8). The small cell size of 53 bytes demanded implementation in leading-edge hardware, due to the small packet processing budget (see Table 5.3). In particular, the processing budget for 53 B at the OC-3 data rate of 150 Mb/s (after SONET overhead) is 2.8 μs, and at OC-12 rate of 600 Mb/s is approximately 700 ns. This was far too fast for any interface implementation other than fully custom VLSI in the late 1980s. Had the packet been larger (a 512-B payload was proposed in [Turner 1988]), it is likely that interfaces would have been available earlier. This is particularly the case for end-system interfaces, which also perform the relatively complex SAR (segmentation and reassembly) functions. The availability of commercial SAR chips lagged the availability of user–network interface chips (UNI) by more than a year.

The ATM cell format is shown in Figure 5.21. Due to the small cell payload size (chosen as the average of the European proposal of 32 B and the U.S. proposal of 64 B), the header length was kept as small as possible to minimize the header overhead ratio. The virtual connection and virtual path identifiers (VCI and VPI) consume 28 bits. As described in Section 3.2.2 (and shown in Figure 3.13), ATM defines a two-layer address hierarchy, allowing VP switches to switch bundles of VCs transparently. The header also contains a 1-byte header check (HEC) and 4 control bits. The packet type indication (PTI) encodes whether the packet is control or data, and contains a bit to indicate explicit congestion (described in Sections 4.2.2 and 7.5.4), and discriminates between several types of management and control cell types. Cell-loss priority (CLP) is used to mark packets subject to discard when congestion is anticipated.

There was no room to even consider a sequence number that would not wrap in flight (Section 7.4.2). Thus, cells are required to be delivered in sequence, which eliminates switch designs (including multicast) that do not preserve sequence, prevents network path diversity within a connection, and dramatically reduces the ability to stripe cells over parallel links due to the tight intercell skew required.

Due to the small cell size, an ATM adaptation layer (AAL) was defined, which segments and reassembles AAL frames to cells at the end systems. Four AALs were originally defined, according to traffic class. The AAL designed to transport data was AAL3/4,[16] which had a per cell AAL header of 2 bytes and trailer of 2 bytes, leaving only 44 B of payload. The AAL header and trailer

---

[16]A merger of the original AAL-3 and AAL-4 formats which were almost identical.

consisted of a segment type (first cell, middle cell, last cell, or only cell), a 4-bit sequence number (not long enough to be useful), a multiplexing ID, a length indicator, and CRC-10 on the payload.

The reaction to such a complex and inefficient AAL standard was the proposal of a new data AAL called SEAL (simple and efficient adaptation layer) [Lyon 1991], that was adopted by the ITU as AAL-5 after it was clear that it would be the only data AAL that would actually be used in the United States. This required the allocation of 2 codepoints in the ATM cell PTI field: one which indicates a cell that is not the last [source data unit (SDU) type 0, shown in Figure 5.21a] containing 48 B of payload, and one codepoint indicating that the cell is the last or only cell in a frame (SDU type 1, shown in Figure 5.21b), and contains a CRC-32 checksum for the entire frame. AAL-5 simplifies the AAL processing as much as possible, provides robust error checking, [Greene 1992] and maximizes the payload efficiency.

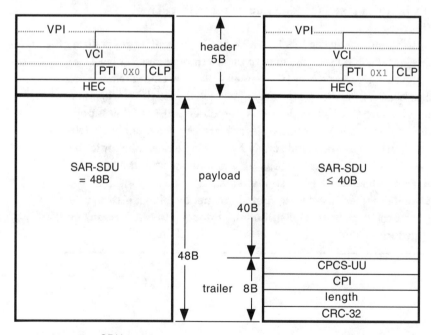

a: other cells – SDU type 0   b: last cell – SDU type 1

Figure 5.21 ATM cell format.

EXAMPLE 5.5: MPLS

Multiprotocol label switching (MPLS) [Viswanthan 1998, Rosen 2000a] provides a way to enable fast packet switching using conventional datagram protocols such as IP, as described in Section 4.1.4. This is accomplished by prepending an MPLS *shim header* to the existing network layer header (but inside the link-layer header), which serves the purpose of allowing nodes to forward a datagram according to the label in the MPLS shim header. This provides the performance benefits of connection-oriented label swapping (once state has been established for a particular flow) without requiring changes to existing network layer protocols such as IP. This includes all the benefits of fast retrieval of flow state, including packet classification in support of QOS and policy-based routing and virtual private networks (VPNs).

Figure 5.22a shows an MPLS shim consisting of a single 20-bit label. Associated with each label is an 8-bit TTL hop count, an S bit which is set to indicate the last (or only) label in the stack, and 3-bit COS, which may be used for class of service in support of differentiated services.[17] In this case, each label switched router (LSR) performs a label swap, as described in Section 5.3.2; this preserves the other flow information (COS and TTL). At the edges between distinct MPLS domains, a label pop/push pair may be performed, in which case the ingress domain can install new COS information.

MPLS also supports stacked labels, which can be viewed as generalizing the ATM two-layer (VPI/VCI) hierarchy idea to an arbitrary number of levels, as shown in Figure 5.22b. For example, when an MPLS switch at the edge of a higher-layer cluster is reached, it pushes a new label onto the stack, and uses this label to forward through its cluster. At the other end, the label is popped leaving the original label for the lower-layer hierarchy. A sequence of networks at the same level can be traversed simply by pushing a new label onto the stack at the entry to each new subnetwork immediately after the same level label had been popped by the last subnetwork.

Labels are distributed in a source routed manner by a label distribution signaling protocol, such as label distribution protocol (LDP) [Anderson 2000] or RSVP-TE [Awduche 2000].[18]

---

[17]Officially listed as "experimental" in [Rosen 2000b], but intended for class of service by MPLS designers.

[18]Which uses the same signaling protocol as RSVP resource reservation, but is otherwise unrelated to RSVP.

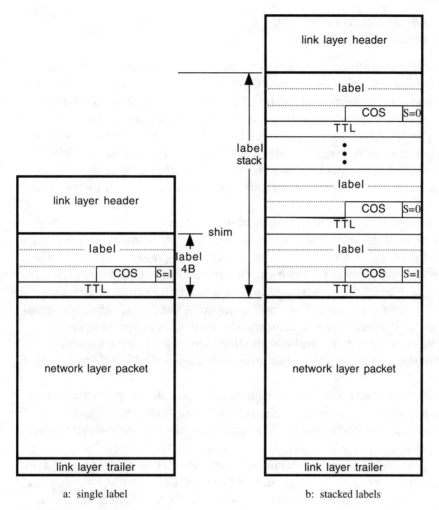

a: single label   b: stacked labels

Figure 5.22   MPLS shim format.

Section 4.2.2 describes hop-by-hop congestion control mechanisms and Section 7.5.4 describes end-to-end mechanisms. Switches must be capable of implementing congestion control and resource reservation. When these mechanisms interfere with the critical path, they need to be engineered with high performance in mind. We will consider two classes of mechanisms. First, efficient traffic characterization is necessary to ensure that traffic is not injected into the switch at a rate in excess of the agreed traffic contract, so the switch can perform traffic shaping at the output to restore the desired characteristics. Then, we will consider congestion avoidance and control, including connection admission control and discard policies.

5.3.5.1 Leaky Bucket Policing and Traffic Shaping

As discussed in Section 4.1.3, packet switching exploits statistical multiplexing gains to utilize the channel more efficiently than circuit switching. If traffic were constant rate, resources could be allocated to connections as relative shares of link and switch bandwidth. A number of applications generate high-rate bursty traffic, and allocation at peak bandwidth would significantly under-utilize the channel or conversely block users and applications that could otherwise share the bandwidth. Thus, we want to be able to allocate at a rate between peak and average rate. This issue will be discussed in more detail in Section 7.5.2.

From the switch standpoint, a simple traffic model needs to exist on which to base resource reservation at connection SETUP, and a way to police traffic in the input processing section, and shape traffic at the output scheduler. The leaky bucket [Turner 1986a] provides such a model, shown in Figure 5.23.

The goal is to enforce three parameters on a bursty flow: peak rate r_p, average rate r_a, and a burst factor. The greater the burst factor, the more conservative the resource allocation, since burst collision results in more queueing delay. In this description, we will assume fixed size cells, but the algorithm can be implemented (with somewhat more hardware complexity) for variable size packets.

The leaky bucket algorithm operates as follows to enforce average rate and burst: Each time a cell enters, a token is placed in a FIFO queue called the *bucket*. The bucket is drained at the average rate r_a. As long as the cell arrival rate is less than r_a, they will be allowed to pass, since the bucket will not overflow. A threshold in the bucket regulates the maximum burst size; as long as threshold is not exceeded, cells are allowed to pass. Cells that arrive when the bucket has passed the threshold are either discarded or, if there is excess capacity in the switch and outgoing link, may be marked as nonconforming cells

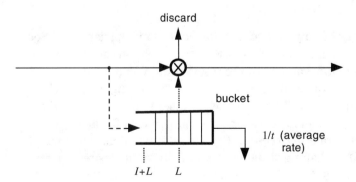

Figure 5.23 Leaky bucket.

that are a candidate for later discard if congestion is experienced down-stream. A short leaky bucket that holds a single token can be used to regulate peak rate (bursting above peak rate is not permitted).

Variants of the leaky bucket can be used to regulate variable-length packets (bytes must be counted instead of number of packets) and to smooth traffic (by queuing the packets instead of tokens and draining at average rate). Passing the packets through a queue also allows the leaky bucket to shape traffic at the output. The leaky bucket algorithm can be used to schedule packets from buffer memory (from a transmitting host [Sterbenz 1992] or a shared memory switch).

5.3.5.2   *Congestion Avoidance*

Connection-oriented networks rely on the reservation of resources to guarantee QOS and to keep the probability of congestion very low.

Congestion Avoidance and Control   *Bound offered load by admission control, traffic policing, and traffic shaping. When impending congestion is detected by building queues, notify sources to throttle. When congestion occurs, drop end-to-end frames if larger than network packets.*

S-6Cc

There are four congestion avoidance mechanisms to be performed hop-by-hop by connection-oriented fast packet switches:

1. Connection admission control (CAC) ensures that only connections are admitted for which resources are available [Turner 1988].

2. Traffic policing at the switch input ensures that individual connections do not exceed the traffic contract [Turner 1988].

3. A congestion notification bit can be set in the packet header to notify the source that congestion is impending and that it should throttle its transmission rate [Turner 1988].

4. Traffic shaping at the switch output ensures changes in connection traffic characteristics within the switch, such as jitter and burst amplification, are removed so that the traffic conforms to the rate specification at each hop in the network.

The algorithms used to reserve resources and compute virtual connection routes can be quite complex. The more traffic parameters that are signaled in the SETUP message, the more parameters that are kept in the link state database for the switch, and the more optimal the resource reservation process attempts to be, the more processing is required for connection SETUP and resource reservation.

> **Overengineering versus Optimality**   *Optimal traffic management policies use processing and memory, which also adds latency to connection establishment; trade these costs against the bandwidth wasted by over overengineering and overprovisioning the network.*
>
> **S-2B**

If bandwidth is relatively inexpensive, it is better to overprovision the network and use simpler conservative resource allocation algorithms. An overbooking factor may be tunable to compensate as part of the network engineering process. If resource reservations are too overbooked, congestion can result.

5.3.5.3   Congestion Control

Although connection-oriented fast packet switches are engineered to avoid congestion, it can occur. First, overly aggressive reservation strategies or overbooking can lead to congestion. Second, connection-oriented networks carry best-effort traffic (see Example 7.7 for the ATM traffic classes that have this characteristic). Furthermore, traffic in excess of the traffic contract may be carried when capacity is available, as mentioned previously. This can lead to congestion if this traffic is not walled off from guaranteed service traffic classes.

Congestion control in fast packet switches consists of the *drop policy*, that is, determining which packets to drop from which traffic classes or connections. The manner in which buffers are partitioned (and the occupancy measures used) are inputs to this policy [Giroux 1999]. A priority field in the packet header can be used to help make this determination (in ATM it is the cell loss priority CLP bit). It can either be set by the user to indicate the relative importance of packets within a flow [Turner 1988] or be set by internal network nodes when nonconforming traffic is allowed to pass a node with excess capacity, as previously described.

Distinct queueing per traffic class significantly improves the ability to apply distinct drop policies to each class and to isolate the effects from the best-effort traffic classes that are more likely to cause congestion. Distinct per VC queues further improve isolation and the granularity of control at the cost of significantly more queueing hardware. For example, TCP traffic over ATM can build very large queues in the case of bursty data traffic. Per connection (or flow) segregation prevents this bursty traffic from impacting traffic such as streaming media (which may or may not be carried in a guaranteed service class). The decreasing cost and density of memory brings per connection or flow queueing into the realm of consideration.

ATM cells that are part of an AAL-5 frame have a particular characteristic that is susceptible to congestion if frame discard policies are not used. Since individual cells do not have sequence numbers, it is not possible to retransmit an individual cell that is dropped due to congestion; the entire AAL frame must be retransmitted by the end system. The majority of cell loss in wireline networks is due to congestion, and the proper response should be to throttle the source, rather than retransmit a frame which may be many cells in length. The proper response is to discard an entire frame when a cell is dropped. This is partial packet discard (PPD) [Armitage 1993] when the remainder of cells in the frame are dropped, and early packet discard (EPD) [Romarow 1995] when all the cells in a frame are discarded when buffer occupancy exceeds a threshold, indicating impending congestion.

5.3.6　Functional Partitioning

A key issue in switch design is the determination of how to partition functionality among different technologies. The decisions include:

- Hardware versus software
- Fully custom VLSI versus semicustom (ASICs and gate arrays) versus standard hardware
- Implementation technology, for example, content addressable memory (CAM) versus random access memory (RAM), relatively fast expensive SRAM (static RAM) versus dynamic RAM (DRAM) and CMOS versus GaAs integrated circuit technology
- Electronic versus optical

Functional Partitioning and Assignment Principle　*Carefully determine what switch functionality is to be implemented in scarce or expensive technology.*

S-1C

While it might be possible to implement an entire system in the fastest technology, this is neither necessary nor meets Cost and Feasibility (III.4). An analysis of the critical path function determines datapath and transfer control functions on which performance depends. These are the operations that are candidates for fast implementation. Matching the processing rates and propagation delays of particular technologies to the bandwidth and latency requirements leads to the decisions on how to implement various parts of the critical path. For example, in a pipelined implementation, a particular pipeline stage might not be decomposable into substages. Thus, implementation of this stage in a faster technology (for example, GaAs and SRAM) may be warranted to keep the pipeline macrocycle short, even when the rest of the critical path is implemented in less expensive technology (for example, CMOS and DRAM). We will discuss two important examples of this decomposition.

5.3.6.1 *Hardware versus Software*

One of the first decisions that must be made is whether to implement a given function in hardware or software. High-speed switching places great demand on the datapath, and we can assume given the resource tradeoffs in the third- (1990s) and fourth- (2000s) generation networks that hardware implementation of the datapath (including switch fabric) is needed in high-speed networks. As discussed in Section 5.3.1, fast packet switching simplifies per packet processing, so that transfer control functions consist only of policing, direct lookup of connection ID, and the simple congestion control mechanisms described in Section 5.3.5. Output processing consists of simple buffer partitioning and traffic shaping strategies. Generally these are amenable to hardware processing as well.

Hardware implementation must be traded against the flexibility of software, which can be enhanced and upgraded more easily once network nodes have been deployed. In some cases, programmable hardware can be used to provide some of the speed advantages of hardware implementation (although not as fast as custom VLSI) and flexibility of software implementation. FPGAs (field programmable gate arrays) have dramatically increased in performance and reliability in the late 1990s, making them a candidate for such applications (for example, [Lockwood 2000]).

In Section 5.5.5, in the context of connectionless fast datagram switches, we discuss the more complex transfer control operations needed; an analysis is warranted for each of them.

5.3.6.2 *Electronic versus Optical*

We described the advantages of optical transmission in Section 5.1.1. A significant performance penalty occurs in the conversion of optical transmission to electronic signals for switching, which motivates switching in the optical domain. Optical switching technology (Section 5.4) provides a fast datapath, but optical logic and *control* circuits are beyond the ability of early fourth-generation (2000s) networking. This means that all-optical *packet switching* is impractical in the near future, since the packet header cannot be decoded and processed in the optical domain.[19] Optical burst switching [Turner 1999, Qiao 2000], as described in Section 4.1.5 is within the realm of technology in the early 2000s.

Thus, a common partitioning of functions is to switch in the optical domain with electronic control, as shown in Figure 5.24. A copy of incoming signaling control packets (TAG—Figure 4.10, RFD and IBT—Figure 4.12) or burst headers (IBT—Figure 4.11) are optically demultiplexed, converted to the electronic domain (o/e), and sent to the input processor. This performs the usual connection identifier lookup (TAG, RFD, JET) or forwarding lookup (IBT and

---

[19]Overviews of optical logic and packet switching research is given in [Hinton 1993], [Prucnal 1993], [Gambini 1997], and [Yao 2000].

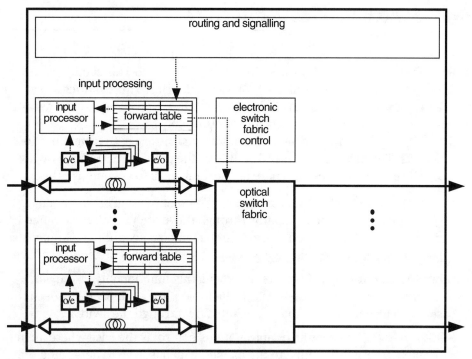

Figure 5.24 Electronic control of optical burst switch.

Section 5.5.2), and controls the path through the optical switch fabric. If necessary, a short fiber delay loop is used to allow the fabric path to be set before the data burst enters the fabric.

Buffering of data is also problematic. The only way to buffer data in the optical domain is through the use of fiber delay loops, which are extremely limited in the amount of data to be buffered. There are two strategies for dealing with this:

1. Use the nonblocking switch fabrics to circuit or burst switch so that there is little or no contention within the switch or at the output links. As described in Section 4.1.5, bursts can be scheduled to further reduce the probability of contention for an outgoing link. When there is contention, packets can either be dropped or *deflected* to an adjacent switch point for handling; this is called *deflection routing* [Baran 1964, Maxemchuck 1987, Borgonovo 1994, 1995].

2. Buffer in the electronic domain. In this case, the normal mode of operation is to pass packets in the optical domain, but in case a burst is blocked, it is demultiplexed, converted to the electronic domain (o/e), and stored in fast buffer memory. When the output is available, the data is converted back to the optical domain (e/o) and passed through the switch.

5.4   Switch Fabric Architecture

In the last section we described the architecture of fast packet switches, but did not delve into the core of the switch: the fabric itself. This section considers the architecture and alternatives for switch fabrics. These fabrics are at the center of fast packet and optical burst switches, as well as the fast datagram switches that will be discussed in Section 5.5.

Switch fabrics provide the mechanism for an arbitrary path from input to output links. The determination and setting of the path are performed by the switch fabric control function. There are several ways to accomplish this:

Centralized control.   Consists of a single point of control which makes a global decision on the best paths through the switch for all the connections and sets the position of the switch elements accordingly. It may also be used to rearrange existing switch paths when new connections arrive.

Distributed control.   Consists of moving this functionality to the *per* input port processing; the result of the lookup for each packet is used to set switch element position as packets flow through the switch.

Self-routing.   Self-routing or autonomous control is the case where an internal header is prepended to the packet, which is used to determine the route through each switch element as the packet flows through the fabric.

The advantage of distributed control and self-routing switches is that the control function is not an inherent limit to the scalability of the switch. The disadvantage is that global optimizations are more difficult to make. Note that in the switch architecture block diagrams (Such as Figure 5.16) we have explicitly shown a switch fabric control block, without implying how the fabric control function is implemented.

Another important aspect of switches is their blocking characteristics:

Strictly nonblocking switches are nonblocking under all conditions. Note that there still may be contention at the switch output due to multiplexing on the link often making the distinction from virtually nonblocking irrelevant.

Wide-sense nonblocking switches are nonblocking if an algorithm is used to set paths, rather than a random path being chosen.

Rearrangeably nonblocking switches always have a set of paths that are nonblocking, but existing connections may have to be rerouted through the switch to achieve this as new connections arrive. A centralized control function mechanism is needed to perform the rearrangement.

Virtually nonblocking switches have such a low probability of blocking that it is a second-order effect. For example, if the probability of blocking is so low that a packet is dropped once per hour on an OC-192 rate link, the loss rate will be orders of magnitude below other causes of loss that must be dealt with end-to-end. This is an important measure for multicast switches, whose blocking probability depends on the expected fanout of multicast traffic.

The goal is to have a nonblocking switch; the choice of the preceding characteristics is a tradeoff based on the inherent capabilities of a particular switch fabric and the complexity of path setup (wide sense) or rearrangement algorithm. Generally, strictly or wide-sense nonblocking switches are preferred to avoid the complexity and latency of switch rearrangement algorithms.

> **Nonblocking Switch Fabric Principle**   *A nonblocking switch fabric is the core of a high-performance switch. Avoid blocking by space-division parallelism, internal speedup, and internal pipelined buffering with cut-through. Strictly and wide-sense nonblocking avoids the complexity and delay of path rearrangement.*
>
> **S-II.4f**

In the rest of this section, we will explore the construction of switch fabrics. Section 5.4.1 considers the role of buffering with respect to the switch fabric (input, internal, output). Section 5.4.2 describes the design of single-stage switch elements, which can either be the switch fabric itself or be used as building blocks for the multistage switch architectures described in Section 5.4.3. Section 5.4.4 briefly describes switch architectures that support native multicast.

5.4.1   Buffering

Switch elements consist of an interconnection of input to output ports and perhaps buffers. Even when the switch itself is nonblocking, the egress links are a multiplexing point. Connection-oriented switches use admission control, discussed in Section 5.3.5, to avoid congestion on average; if all traffic were uniform, significant buffering would not be needed. When traffic is very bursty, however, the bursts destined for a particular output port will sometimes arrive at the same time, as shown in Figure 5.25.

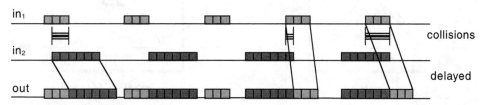

Figure 5.25   Burst collision.

In this example, bursts of packets (at peak rate = link rate) from input ports 1 and 2 are destined for a single output port. Note that although each of the flows is well behaved (regular burst and interburst lengths), since the burst lengths differ between the flows, burst overlap is inevitable. This happens even when the aggregate bandwidth can be handled on the output link.

Unless packets are to be dropped, buffers must be located *somewhere* in the switch to delay packets until the outgoing link is available. Note that once this is done, some of the flow characteristics will have changed. This motivates the provision of traffic shaping, as was discussed in Section 5.3.5.

5.4.1.1   Buffer Location

We can categorize the switch architecture in terms of the location of switching interconnections and buffers. In this discussion we are not concerned with the interconnection topology of the switch, and thus show a fully connected mesh.

An unbuffered switch fabric is shown in Figure 5.26a. While this is undesirable for fast packet switches, there are situations where unbuffered switches are employed. Optical components are suitable for transmission and switching, but there is no way to queue in the optical domain. Fiber delay loops are suitable only for very small delays. Thus, there are three alternatives for dealing with contention in an optical burst switch:

1. Schedule bursts using the mechanisms discussed in Section 4.1.5, such that the probability of burst collision is low enough that dropping bursts and retransmitting end-to-end are acceptable.

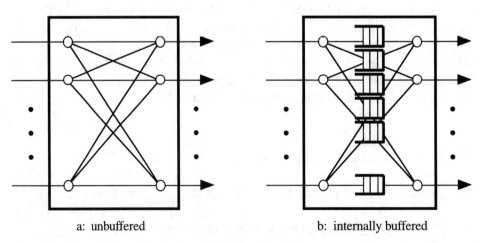

a: unbuffered   b: internally buffered

Figure 5.26 Unbuffered and internally buffered switches.

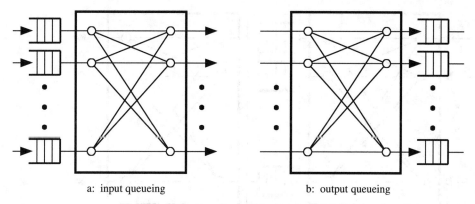

a: input queueing   b: output queueing

Figure 5.27   Input and output buffered switches.

2. Use deflection routing to deflect bursts to another switch with the hope that the bursts can be forwarded. Deflection routing can be used in conjunction with burst scheduling.

3. Convert bursts to the electronic domain for queueing, as described in Section 5.3.6.

A switch fabric can contain buffers in its internal structure (interconnection links and switch elements); this is shown in Figure 5.26b. This increases the complexity of the switch itself, while eliminating (or reducing) the need for external queueing.

There are two choices to external buffer placement: an input queued switch and an output queued switch, as shown in Figure 5.27.

It is also possible to partition the buffering function among the inputs and outputs, resulting in a combined input/output queued switch, as shown in Figure 5.28.

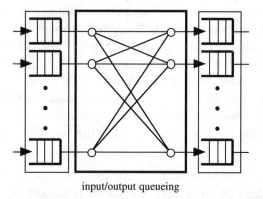

input/output queueing

Figure 5.28   Combined input/output buffered switch.

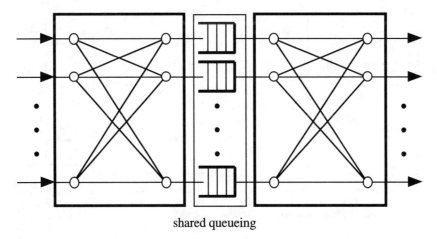

shared queueing

Figure 5.29 Shared buffer switch.

Finally, it may be the buffers themselves that are the core of the switch fabric, in which case interconnection is necessary on both sides, resulting in a centrally buffered switch, as shown in Figure 5.29. This is typically done to share buffer resources, and thus the queues are a logical partitioning of physical memory.

5.4.1.2 Head-of-Line Blocking

For externally buffered switch fabrics, the choice of input versus output buffers has significant impact on the overall blocking characteristic of the switch.

Input queueing, as shown in Figure 5.30a, holds packets until the switch is able to direct them to the appropriate output. The problem with this is that with FIFO queueing discipline, packets destined for *other* output ports that are free may be blocked; this is referred to as *head-of-line* blocking. In this example, the gray packet on the bottom port is blocked behind the black packet, although the gray packet is destined for a free port. Head-of-line blocking has been shown to limit switch throughput to $2 - \sqrt{2} = 58.6$ percent utilization [Karol 1987].

By moving the queues to the output side, the gray packet is not held up by the black packet, as shown in Figure 5.30b. Note that this does not come without cost. The switch has to be able to support the ability to pull packets off the input fast enough to allow the blocking packets to get out of the way. This can be accomplished in three ways:

Speedup. Packets can be accepted from the inputs without loss if the switch fabric runs at a data rate higher than the input links. The speedup S refers to the ratio of internal to external data rates. In general, a switch with n inputs and outputs will require a speedup of $S = n$, since it is possible that a packet will arrive for a given output port o_i at all of the inputs $i_0 \ldots i_{n1}$ simultaneously; unless all of these packets are accepted at an aggregate rate of n times the input link rate, a subsequent packet destined for a different output o_j will be blocked. Simulation studies and experimental data have shown that acceptable performance under realistic traffic patterns can be achieved with a speedup of several times [Turner 1998]. It is possible to provide strict nonblocking with a speedup of 2, but this requires an $O(n)$ scheduling algorithm to schedule the switch configuration [Chuang 1999].

Internal buffering.   Another way to accept packets from the incoming links is to remove them at the input link rate, but buffer them internally to the switch fabric, as shown by the second black packet in Figure 5.30a, rather than requiring that it make it all the way to the output queue immediately. An internally buffered switch fabric (Figure 5.26b) can provide this capability.

Internal expansion.   In the case of a space division switch, additional parallelism can be introduced by expanding the internal links and switch elements; an example of this is the Clos fabric [Clos 1953].

The choice of technique depends on the switch architecture, and they can be used in combination. For example, an internally buffered fabric with two packet buffers at each switch element can be combined with a modest speedup. As appropriate in Sections 5.4.2 and 5.4.3, we will note the feasibility of internal buffering in different switch fabric architectures.

A further motivation exists for output queueing in the case where output ports are attached to a shared medium network (for example, wireless RF). In this case the output processing function may require significant queuing due to contention from other network nodes for MAC. A single set of output queues can buffer for both switch link and MAC contention.

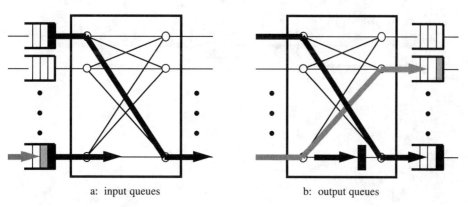

a: input queues   b: output queues

Figure 5.30   Input versus output queueing.

> **Head-of-Line Blocking Avoidance Principle** *Avoid head-of-line blocking. Output queuing requires internal speedup, expansion, or buffering. Virtual output queueing requires additional queues or queuing complexity. The two techniques must be traded against one another, and can be used in combination.*
>
> **S-II.4q**

5.4.1.3 *Virtual Output Queueing*

The impact of head-of-line blocking in input queues can be eliminated by replacing the FIFO queueing discipline with virtual output queues before the switch [Tamir 1988, Anderson 1993, McKeown 1996], such that packets destined for each output can be served whenever the corresponding egress link is available, as shown in Figure 5.31.

One mechanism is to stack n queues corresponding to the n outputs at *each* input (for a total of n^2), as shown in Figure 5.31a. Packets are removed in the

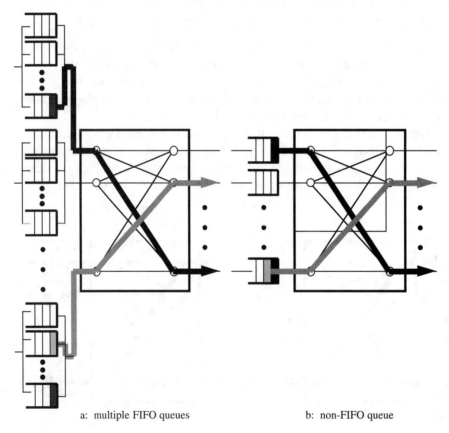

a: multiple FIFO queues   b: non-FIFO queue

Figure 5.31 Virtual output queueing.

order received, as output links are available. This scheme requires that packets be multiplexed and timestamped to determine the arrival order among the queues at each input. Alternatively, a scheduling algorithm can be applied to determine which packets to accept to match a set of nonconflicting output [McKeown 1999a]. The disadvantage of multiple queues is that it is more wasteful of buffer space, since *each* input buffer must be long enough to queue for worst-case bursty flows without dropping.

If the packets can be removed from the input queue in a non-FIFO manner, the extra buffers need not be used, as shown in Figure 5.31b. This requires more complexity in the buffers themselves, since linked lists of packets destined for each output must be maintained. It is also possible to combine input and output queuing (Figure 5.28) to reduce the speedup required [Chuang 1999].

Advances in hardware capabilities enable both of these schemes for virtual output queues. Increased memory density makes more queues practical; increased logic density makes more complex hardware queueing disciplines in hardware practical. The choice depends on the Resource Tradeoff Principle (2) at a particular point in time, and may involve a combination of techniques.

5.4.2 Single-Stage Shared Elements

We will now consider the construction of the basic elements of which switches are made. These single-stage elements can be deployed as switches in their own right or composed into larger multistage switches, as described in Section 5.4.4.

5.4.2.1 Bus Interconnects

The simplest switch design is a bus, as shown in Figure 5.32.

A bus is a shared medium, and thus bandwidth is limited by the physical characteristics of the bus, which does not scale as ports are added. For example, while the bus is occupied by the transfer from i_1, i_7 is blocked. Packets must wait in input queues until the bus is free. Assume that the clock rate of the bus is $1/t$ and the width is w bits. The aggregate throughput of the bus is

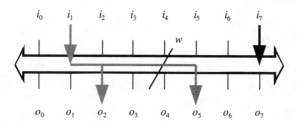

Figure 5.32 Bus switch.

then limited by $r < w/t$.[20] The bandwidth available to each of n ports is then limited by $r_i < w/nt$. Thus, for the bus to be nonblocking, it must scale either by speedup or in width with the number of ports added.

Generally, w will be at least 8 to match per byte transfers, providing a capacity of approximately 8 ports if the line rate matches the bus clock rate. Greater bus width is possible, but beyond 32 or 64 bits, unless the width matches the granularity of packet size, bandwidth is also lost due to idle time when the last part of a packet does not match the granularity of bus width. In the case of fixed size cells, this may not be a problem. Very wide buses become difficult from a physical design and layout perspective, as well.

Bus speedup is limited by the available electronic technology. If the line rate is fast enough to challenge the design of other parts of the switch (such as input processing and queueing), it is likely that the switching rate of the bus is limited to further speedup.

These effects result in a switch fabric with extremely limited scalability, suitable for only the smallest switches; perhaps 8 to 32 ports, but certainly not hundreds or thousands of ports. Furthermore, it is difficult to construct extremely large buses due to electromagnetic effects such as capacitive loading.

A primitive scaling technique is to provide several buses in parallel; in the general case this becomes a space division technique as discussed in Section 5.4.3.

5.4.2.1.1   Multicast

One of the nice properties about bus interconnects is that since they are a shared medium, the support for multicast is an inherent property. Multicast is accomplished by merely enabling multiple outputs simultaneously, for example, i_1 to o_2 and o_5 in Figure 5.32.

5.4.2.1.2   Ring Switches

Switches can also be constructed in a ring topology (for example, [Cidon 1993]). The scaling limitations are not quite as severe as in bus switches at the additional complexity of introducing a MAC protocol (time division or token) and packet insertion/removal logic on the ring. Throughput can be slightly higher due to better ring utilization of the MAC protocol and the isolation of electrical effects between ring insertion/removal logic units, at the cost of slight additional latency through the units.

5.4.2.2   *Shared Memory Fabrics*

Another way to switch is memory centric, in which a shared memory containing the buffers forms the core of the switch fabric (for example, Eng 1992), as shown in Figure 5.33.

---

[20]From which the overhead of contention and arbitration protocols must be subtracted.

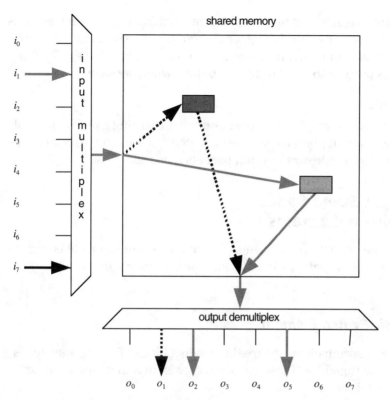

Figure 5.33 Shared memory switch.

Input ports are multiplexed into the read lines of the memory, and placed into a free buffer area. Packets are then sent back out the memory write lines and demultiplexed to the appropriate switch output port. As was the case for bus interconnects, the shared memory is a point of contention. The memory must be sped up to match the requirements of additional ports, with input queues delaying packets until write access is available to memory.

One of the difficulties in using shared memory switches for high-speed networking is that while memory density is increasing exponentially, memory access times are not. This makes it increasingly difficult to match the exponentially increasing link data rates in high-speed networks. Shared memory switches can be used as shared buffer building blocks in larger switches, however, using the bit-slice and multistage techniques described in Section 5.4.4.

A disadvantage of shared memory fabrics is that cut-through paths are not easily supported and packets must typically be completely read into memory before being output.

The input and output multiplexors can be viewed as degenerate cases of a bus, with a single output and input, respectively. This means that a shared memory switch is really a central shared buffer switch (Figure 5.29). By replacing the multiplexors with more sophisticated interconnects (such as a bus for low port count or a crossbar for higher port count), the shared memory section can be segregated into an array of buffer elements (as in [Chaney 97]. This technique allows packets to cut through the buffers when possible.

5.4.2.2.1 Multicast

Supporting multicast is simple, and consists of either writing a packet multiple times to different output ports (which requires multiple memory cycles) or designing the port demultiplexor to output packets in parallel.

5.4.3 Single-Stage Space Division Elements

A way to avoid the contention problems of shared medium elements is to construct a *space division* switch, which divides data transfers among parallel paths.

5.4.3.1 Basic Switch Element

Single-stage 2×2 switch elements are the building blocks for larger switches, as described in Section 5.1.4. These elements consist of either electronic or solid-state optical designs.

The basic switch element states are shown in Figure 5.34. The straight and cross states are used for normal point-to-point switching. The duplicate states shown in Figure 5.34c are used to support native multicast, as described in Section 5.4.5.

5.4.3.1.1 Electronic Switch Elements

We can construct a 2×2 switch element, as shown in Figure 5.35. The switch control logic provides signals that determine the routing of packets from the input lines i_0 and i_1 to the output ports o_0 and o_1, by setting the output multiplexor select lines.

If the switch element is not internally buffered, the packet buffers and associated multiplexors will not be present, and contention for an output port results in one of the packets being discarded. If the switch element is buffered, cut-through paths provide the ability to avoid the store-and-forward of pack-

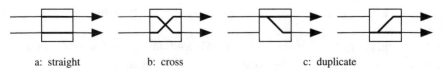

a: straight   b: cross   c: duplicate

Figure 5.34 Basic switch element states.

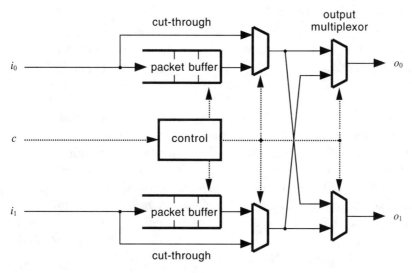

Figure 5.35 2 × 2 switch element.

ets, except when there is contention for an output. Multicasting is supported by enabling both output multiplexors for a given input. This design can be extended to support the *self-routing* of packets, as shown in Figure 5.36.

Recall that packets may have an internal header with output port p_{out} prepended (shown in Figure 5.17). This field is used to select the proper output port for the switch element (shown in Figure 5.41). An input per byte shift register delays the packets while the header is read and decoded.

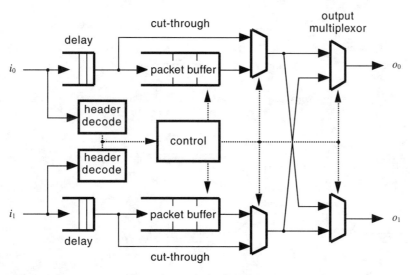

Figure 5.36 2 × 2 Self-routing switch element.

5.4.3.1.2   Optical Switch Elements

A basic optical switch element consists of a solid-state directional coupler [Ramamurthy 2000]. When two waveguides are in close proximity over the right distance, the signal is transferred between them, crossing back and forth an odd number of times. This results in the crossing of the signals between the waveguides, as shown in Figure 5.37a.

If a voltage is applied to an electrode near the waveguide, the signal is transferred an even number of times, and the signals exit on their own waveguides, shown in Figure 5.37b. Note that directional couplers are not wavelength sensitive; the same wavelength can be used on both waveguides.

In the early 2000s, $LiNbO_3$ directional couplers are capable of switching in 1 ns or less [Kartalopoulos 2000]. But their millimeter length limits the ability to construct switches much larger than 64×64 ports. There is also some crosstalk between the waveguides (due to imperfect coupling); this can be compensated for in the design of multistage switches, described in Section 5.4.4.

5.4.3.2   Crossbar

Switch elements larger than 2×2 are constructed by distributing the inputs along rows and expanding the output multiplexor along columns to form an array of crosspoints called a *crossbar*. Individual crosspoints consist of simple logic, as shown in Figure 5.38.

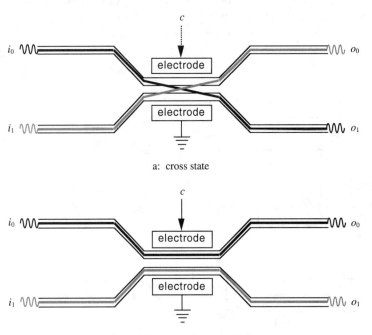

a: cross state

b: straight state (voltage applied)

Figure 5.37   Electro-optical switch element.

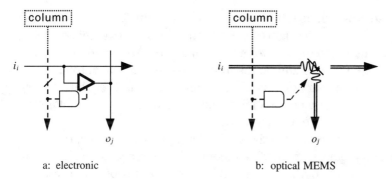

a: electronic   b: optical MEMS

Figure 5.38 Crosspoint.

Each crosspoint in the ith row has an input i_i in common with all other elements in the row. A *per* column register contains the row at which a switch element should transfer input to the jth output o_j, decoded by an and gate.

In the case of an electronic crosspoint (Figure 5.38a), this enables a column output driver. In the case of an optical micro-electronic mechanical system (MEMS) crosspoint (Figure 5.38b), this pivots a mirror in a gap in the row to reflect the beam into the column. In the early 2000s, MEMS crosspoints are capable of altering direction at microsecond rates [Kartalopoulos 2000, Neukermans 2001]. A challenge for MEMS switch elements is to switch with low loss, which requires a precision mirror surface and accurate aiming. Crosstalk can occur if light enters another row or column while the mirror is pivoting.

The resultant crosspoint states are shown in Figure 5.39. Data is crossed (Figure 5.39a), or when the switch point is enabled, turned (Figure 5.39b). Note that, for the electronic crosspoint, since the data passed along each row, a duplicate state (Figure 5.39c) comes for free with the turn, which is useful for multicast. This is not a case for the optical MEMS crosspoint, since the mirror blocks the signal from propagating from the rest of the row.[21]

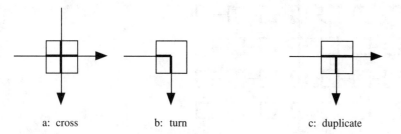

a: cross   b: turn   c: duplicate

Figure 5.39 Crossbar switch point states.

---

[21]If it were possible to use a MEMS beam-splitter instead, the split optical signal would have to be amplified to compensate for the loss at each split.

Arranging these crosspoints into an array of n^2 elements for n ports results in a crossbar switch, shown in Figure 5.40, which shows the example of switching input i_3 to output o_4 and input i_1 to outputs o_1 and o_6. Arbitration logic is needed to determine which of competing inputs transfers to the output.

The advantage of crossbar networks is their simplicity and regularity. Furthermore, they are internally nonblocking; that is, no path to a particular output will block another path to a different output.

The disadvantage of crossbars is the scaling complexity of $O(n^2)$; that is, a switch with n ports requires n^2 switch elements. While this is not a significant issue with small switches (perhaps up to 128 ports), it is a problem in very large switches. For example, a 1024 port switch requires over 1 million switch elements.

In the case of unbuffered crossbar switches, however, the m^2 scaling complexity is partially offset by the simplicity of the switch element design and the regularity of interconnect. This makes it cost effective to implement moderate size elements on a VLSI chip. Providing internal buffers at each crosspoint is possible, but greatly increases the complexity and reduces the number of elements that can fit on a single chip.

A simple model of the cost in chip area is $A = a_c + n(a_i + a_o) + n^2 a_x$. There is a single instance of area contributed to central control logic a_c, a linearly scaling component contributed by the input and output processing (and I/O to pins) $n(a_i + a_o)$, and the quadratically scaling component of the switch crosspoints

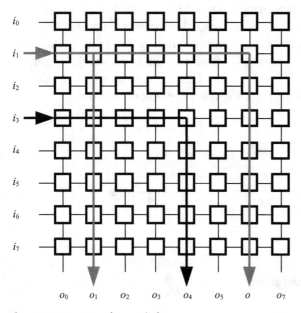

Figure 5.40   Crossbar switch.

n^2a_x. The simplicity in the switch point logic relative to the input and output processing (including packet buffers) keeps the total area manageable for moderate values of n; for moderate size switches $n(a_i + a_o)$ dominates the cost.

While multicast capability is inherently provided by electronic crosspoints, it considerably complicates the switch control, since at any particular time only a subset of outputs might be available. This issue is discussed in more detail in Section 5.4.5.

5.4.4   Multistage Switches

We have discussed the ways to design individual single-stage switch elements. In the case of crossbar elements, a single stage is sufficient to construct a small switch fabric (perhaps 32×32 to 128×128 ports). For large switches, however, switch elements must be interconnected to provide the desired number of ports.

Switch Scalability   *The construction of switches with a large port count requires scalable switch fabrics. Exploit regular structures for implementation in VLSI or optics as the basis for recursively constructed fabrics with logarithmic growth complexity.*

S-III.4

5.4.4.1   Tiling Crossbars

A simple way to interconnect switch elements is to tile them in a square array. This, in effect, makes a crossbar of crossbar switch elements. Since this suffers from quadratic scaling complexity in terms of the number of chips, this is generally not a cost-effective solution for large switches.

5.4.4.2   Multistage Interconnection Networks

Other interconnection topologies exist that have better scaling properties. It is possible to construct $O(n \log n)$ scaling multistage interconnection networks (MINs). There are a variety of isomorphic interconnection topologies, which have differing blocking and routing properties. These fabrics are generated by recursively interconnecting n stages of $\log n$ switch elements (note the dashed boxes). A 16 port delta network constructed from 2×2 switch elements is shown in Figure 5.41.

A nice property of the delta network is that it is self-routing. An internal header (as shown in Figure 5.17) containing the output port is prepended to the packet. As the packet reaches an element at the ith stage s_i, the packet is routed to the output of the ith bit of the header (top = 0, bottom = 1). As

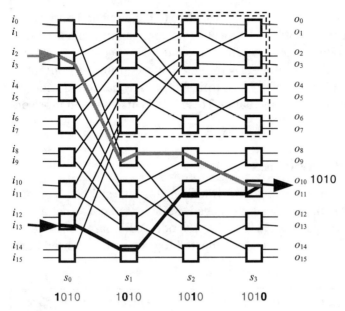

Figure 5.41 Delta switch.

shown by the heavy lines in Figure 5.41, the packet will be routed to o_{10} by routing to switch element outputs 1, 0, 1, and 0 in stages s_0, s_1, s_2, and s_3, respectively. This eliminates the need for central switch control to set the paths based on the table lookups, which can be distributed in large switches.

Since cells all follow the same path through the network, packet sequence is preserved. The disadvantage is that load is not distributed evenly across the links, requiring greater speedup for a given traffic pattern. An alternative is to dynamically route packets. This can be done by prepending switch stages, which randomly distribute the packets across the switch, either as an additional fabric [Turner 1988] or by using a fabric with additional stages, such as a Beneš fabric, as shown in Figure 5.42.

Note that the result of load balancing in the first stages is that packets can arrive out of order to the output port. In most cases, they must be reordered at the output in a resequencing buffer, by using a timestamp inserted into the internal switch header. Sequence must be preserved for ATM switches and for hop-by-hop SAR so that the frame can be reassembled from the internal switch cells before transmission on the outgoing link.

Multistage networks are also the technique used to scale larger switch fabrics, using shared memory and crossbar switch elements. An example of a multistage interconnection network constructed from 4 × 4 elements is shown in Figure 5.43.

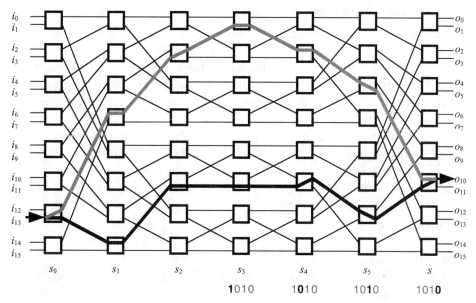

Figure 5.42   Beneš switch.

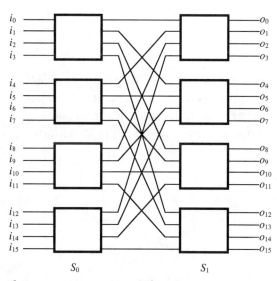

Figure 5.43   Banyan switch.

5.4.4.2.1 Optical Multistage Networks

Optical multistage networks can be generated from the optical switch elements, such as the directional couplers described in Section 5.4.3. Due to the optical insertion loss (~1 dB) entering a directional coupler, a switch fabric should ideally be constructed on a single substrate. This, however, limits the total size of a switch module due to the physical length of each coupler, as mentioned before.

There are two considerations that motivate different interconnection strategies from electronic switch fabrics. First, optical switch elements are incapable of buffering, and therefore, nonblocking bufferless interconnection fabrics are required. The Beneš fabric (Figure 5.42) is rearrangeably nonblocking with the minimum number of stages and is an appropriate candidate for optical switches.

Second, for directional coupler technologies that suffer from the crosstalk problem (for example, $LiNbO_3$) discussed in Section 5.4.3, dilation techniques are needed to ensure that only a single light path traverses a switch element at a time. These dilation techniques can be performed in space, time, or both [Pan 1999].

Figure 5.44 shows a 2×2 dilated Beneš fabric [Padmanabhan 1987]. Only one input and one output of each 2×2 switch element can be used at a time. When recursively constructed to generate a larger switch fabric, the total fabric contains roughly twice the number of switch elements, and the path must be chosen such that no switch element contains more than one lightpath.

In time division multiplexed (TDM) networks, it is also possible to dilate in time, ensuring that during a given time slot, only one of the two waveguides in a switch is active at a time.

5.4.4.3 Scaling Speed

We have discussed how to scale switch fabrics in size. To speed up a switch in excess of the practical limits of the logic or memory clock rate requires parallelism in the datapath, at a finer granularity than the space division path through the fabric. This can be accomplished by dividing the switch fabric datapath into slices, as shown in Figure 5.45.

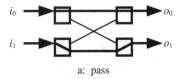
a: pass

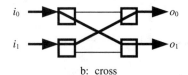
b: cross

Figure 5.44 Dilated Beneš switch.

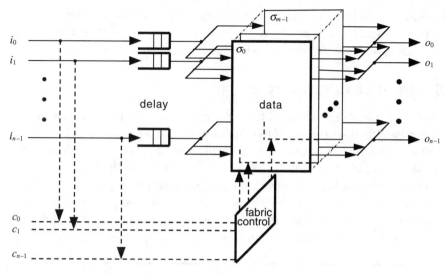

Figure 5.45 Parallel switch slices.

Switches typically (but not necessarily) have byte parallel datapaths, providing an $8\times$ speedup over line rate. This is important since the relatively complex protocol operations are harder to do at the clock rate of line rate bit serial operations (such as signal repeating and regeneration). In the case of space division switches, this is provided by byte-wide data paths through the fabric and switch elements. In the case of conventional shared memory switches, memory chips are byte parallel.

Further speedup is possible by dividing the switch fabric into a set of m slices ($\sigma_0 \ldots \sigma_{m-1}$), each of which operates on some portion of the packet in parallel. An additional speedup of m can be obtained by striping the packet through the fabric, at the cost of additional switch elements. For example, the complexity of MIN fabrics becomes $O(mn \log n)$ and crossbars $O(mn^2)$.

If the fabric is self-routing, the internal header must be sent to the fabric control slice rather than prepended to the packet. If the fabric has distributed control from the input processors, the control signals $c_0 - c_{n-1}$ from the n input ports are input to the fabric control slice.

The number of planes is dictated by the speedup desired, but is limited by packet size and must be balanced against input and output processing. In the case of fixed size cells, it is possible to have a slice per byte of the cell size (for example, 48 slices for ATM). If packets are of variable size, a number of slices exceeding the common small packet size is extremely wasteful of hardware resources, since extra slices will be unused much of the time. The other critical issue is that there is no benefit in speeding up the fabric beyond the capabilities of the input and output processing functions (such as CID lookup, traffic shaping, and output scheduling). This is less of an issue in the connection-oriented switches we have considered so far, but will be more so with the more complicated lookup and scheduling functions discussed with datagram switches in Section 5.5.

5.4.5 Multicast Support

A number of applications multicast information to multiple users simultaneously, for example, distribution of live multimedia content. Example 3.5 showed that the Network Should Provide Multicast Capabilities (2C) due to the considerable bandwidth savings on links. Part of this capability is network layer protocol support for multicast, for example, Internet group multicast protocol (IGMP) and ATM point-to-multipoint and leaf-initiated join connections. The other key piece is native multicast support in switches, so that packets do not have to be held and transmitted multiple times on egress switch ports.

> **Switches Should Provide Native Multicast**   *Switches should provide native multicast support to conserve bandwidth and avoid latency of repeated transmission.*
> **S-2C**

The mechanism to support multicast depends on the switch architecture; we have already shown that (electronic) crosspoints and 2×2 switch elements can duplicate packets. Optical waveguide splitters can also be used to construct multicast switch elements, but optical amplifiers such as semiconductor optical amplifiers (SOAs) are required to restore signal levels after the split.

5.4.5.1 Crossbar Switch Multicast

Crossbar switch elements pass data across the row, whether or not they are enabled to turn data, as shown in Figure 5.30. As indicated in Section 5.3, an arbiter is needed to determine a nonconflicting set of outputs among packets arriving at the input. When a packet is to be multicast to a set of outputs, the scheduling problem is significantly more difficult, since some, but not all, outputs may be available.

Service disciplines can be categorized based on whether all copies of a given input must be multicast at a time [Hayes 1991]:

No fanout spitting. Inputs are only allowed to discharge packets if the entire set of outputs are simultaneously available. If an output is blocked, the packet must wait for another scheduling cycle.

Fanout splitting. Inputs are allowed to pass packets to a subset of the outputs, and remain at the head of the input queue for multiple time steps until all of the remaining outputs are available. The output set that must be served in subsequent time step is the *residue*.

Assuming a random scheduling algorithm, fanout splitting results in higher throughput since it is work conserving, that is, packets will never be held (waiting for the full set of outputs to be available) when any output link is available [Hui 1994].

Fanout splitting can be visualized in a manner similar to the Tetris game [Prabhakar 1996], as shown in Figure 5.46.

Packets are held in input queues, with the head of each input queue eligible for output. Each packet has a bit vector (prepended by the input processor as part of the lookup process) indicating the output links to which it is destined. The goal is to schedule servicing such that

- Throughput is high.

- Some fairness measure is met, in particular packets should not be starved.

- The scheduling discipline can be implemented at high-speed (line rate).

The schedule consists of the ordering of packets above each output. For example, in Figure 5.46 (which follows the examples in [Prabhakar 1996, 1997]), the next cycle will output packets from i_1 to o_1, o_3, and o_5, allowing the next packet in the input queue for i_1 to progress to the head of the queue. Packets from i_2 will be output on o_2 and o_4, but the packet in the head of the queue for i_2 must remain for another cycle since o_3 and o_5 are not available.

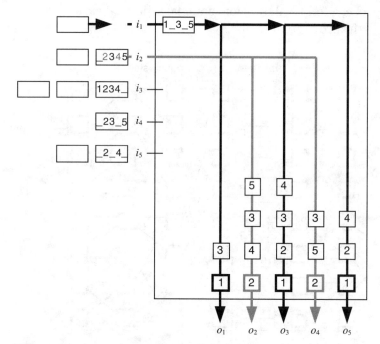

Figure 5.46   Crossbar multicast scheduling.

A variety of scheduling disciplines are possible, which trade these goals against one another, including [Prabhakar 1997]:

Concentrate. Concentrates residue among as few inputs as possible. Since this allows as many inputs to progress per time step as possible, it has the highest throughput, but inputs can be indefinitely starved.

Weight based. Each packet is assigned a weight, which determines the order of removal from the input queue: the longer it has been waiting at the head of an input queue, the higher the weight (this ensures fairness); the larger the fanout, the lower the weight (this concentrates residue so that more packets depart the input queue at each timestep.

The weight-based scheduling algorithm further allows weights to be varied based on differentiated service grades, and has a simple hardware implementation.

5.4.5.2　Multistage Fabric Multicast

The 2×2 switch elements shown in Figures 5.35 and 5.36 can easily be designed to support the *duplicate* states shown in Figure 5.34, in which an input is replicated to both outputs. These switch elements can be used to construct copy fabrics [Lee 1988, Turner 1988], as shown in Figure 5.47. A multicast switch can be constructed by the combination of a copy switch fabric stage, which replicates packets, followed by a conventional switch fabric stage that routes each copy to the proper output port.

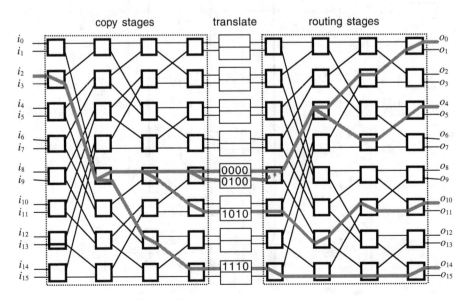

Figure 5.47　MIN multicast with copy stages.

In the self-routing version of this scheme, the internal packet header needs to carry the number of copies to be made through the copy stages. Copies are made as late as possible to reduce the load on internal links in the copy stages. Then each copy must have a distinct switch output port inserted into the internal header. Note that if the fabric is blocking, multiple copies of the same packet may block one another, as shown by the dashed line for the copies destined to o_0 and o_4 in Figure 5.47.

A number of alternatives are possible by connecting some to the switch outputs and *recirculating* packets back through the switches. For example, the first pass through the fabric can make copies to recirculation ports, and the second pass routes to the proper output port. Alternatively, a single copy can be made with each pass through the network, requiring $\log_2 c$ circulations to make c copies of a packet [Turner 1994]

5.5.   Fast Datagram Switches

In the third generation (1980s), the processing requirements to make full forwarding and scheduling decisions for individual datagrams were beyond the reach of feasible hardware to keep up with the link rate technology. Thus, the research community concentrated on connection-oriented fast packet switching technologies for high-speed networks. ATM infrastructure was widely deployed in the early 1990s, particularly in high-speed backbone networks. Additionally, the assumption was that connection-oriented video would be a dominant source of traffic, which would benefit from direct network layer support for QOS. Datagrams and transactions could be handled by running them over a permanent mesh of virtual circuits.

We described in Section 5.3 how connection-oriented fast packet switches enable high-speed networking by explicitly signaling hard state into the switches, thus substantially simplifying both input and output processing. Recall that input processing is reduced to a trivial connection ID lookup, with simple policing and congestion control hardware. Output processing may consist of traffic shaping of the packets on the outgoing links, but does not generally involve complex scheduling, unless hop-by-hop flow control schemes are employed (as described in Section 4.2.2), or it is desired to perform fair queuing within best-effort flows.

Two forces resisted the global deployment of a connection-oriented network layer, such as ATM. First, the explosion of the IP-based Internet and Web in the mid-1990s entrenched TCP as the end-to-end protocol, and IP as the single global network layer; the Hourglass Corollary (4D) indicates that there should only be one network layer. In the cases where connection-oriented network protocols were deployed in backbone networks (such as ATM or X.25), IP traffic was run over these other network layers in a kludge of inefficient layering and incompatible control mechanisms that resulted in the native network layer being used as if it were a link-layer. In the end, there was little motivation to create native ATM applications and transport protocols, or to use the ISO application protocols such as file transfer, access, and management (FTAM) or virtual terminal (VT).

Second, the limitations of shared medium link protocols, such as Ethernet and token ring, were overcome by the evolution of Ethernet to a switched point-to-point link protocol, with order-of-magnitude increases in data rate, as discussed in Example 5.2. This further reduced the motivation for adoption of ATM using scalable SONET links to increase the bandwidth on LAN links.

Therefore, much of the research community shifted their attention to speeding up connectionless datagram forwarding [Asthana 1992, Tantawy 1992, Koufopavlou 1994, Tantawy 1994c, Parulkar 1995, Newman 1997, Partridge 1998b]. Decreasing cost of processing hardware resulted in Resource Tradeoffs Change (2A) that made it feasible to consider datagram processing at line rate by the mid-1990s. A full ATM Layer 3 infrastructure became unnecessary, and deployments of IP over SONET (packet over SONET [POS] [Manchester 1998]) began, with research into IP directly over WDM (packets over wavelengths [POW] [Bannister 1999, Anderson 1999]). At the same time, the important characteristics of fast packet switching technologies began to be incorporated into the Internet, for example, IP switches based on the fast switch fabrics described in Section 5.4, and protocol optimizations such as MPLS (described in Example 5.5).

> **Fast Datagram Switch Principle**   *There is compelling reason to perform high-speed connectionless datagram switching. Apply connection-oriented fast packet switching techniques to fast datagram switching, and exploit technology advances to implement the additional input and output processing in the critical path.*
>
> **S-1B***d*

This section considers how to add the complexity to the switch input and output processing needed to support connectionless networks, while maintaining high performance. In the case of connectionless protocols, such as IP, ISO connectionless network protocol (CLNP) [ISO8473, Chapin 1981, Piscitello 1993, Perlman 2000], and IPX [Perlman 2000], hard state is not signaled into the switch, and complex *per* packet classification, forwarding, and scheduling decisions must be made.

Section 5.5.1 extends the basic fast packet switch architecture described in Section 5.3.1 to support datagram forwarding, with emphasis on worst-case packet processing rate as a performance metric. Section 5.5.2 considers how to replace the simple connection ID table lookup with a more complex lookup based on the destination address in each packet. Section 5.5.3 discusses the more general problem of packet classification in support of differentiated services and policy-based routing. Section 5.5.4 briefly describes the problem of more complex output scheduling.

5.5.1   Overall Architecture and Performance

At a high-level, the architecture of a fast connectionless datagram switch has the same functional blocks as the connection-oriented fast packet switch shown in Figure 5.16 in Section 5.3.

There is set of node control software, including routing, signaling, and management. The core of the switch is a switch fabric, whose architecture we described in Section 5.4. Input and output processing is present, and this is where the primary difference lies, as shown in Figure 5.48:

Input processing.   Considerably more complex, with an input processor (either a small fast RISC embedded controller [Spalink 2001] or processor specialized for network processing) performing address lookup using a prefix table, as well as packet classification.

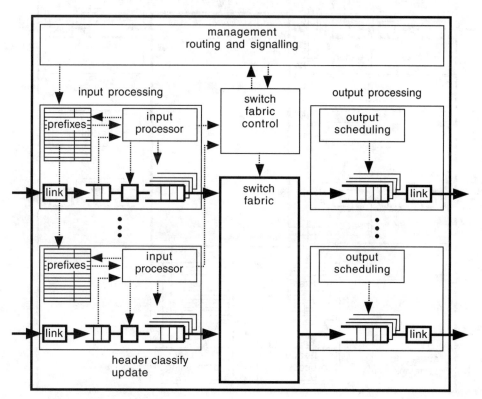

Figure 5.48   Fast datagram switch.

Output processing.　Also more complex, with packet scheduling (including traffic shaping) to meet QOS requirement for flows and to ensure fairness among best-effort flows.

This architecture can be characterized as a distributed packet processing architecture [Chan 1999], since each input and output interface processed packets completely autonomously. An alternative is to share a set of forwarding engines [Turner 1988, Asthana 1992, Partridge 1998b], as shown in Figure 5.49.

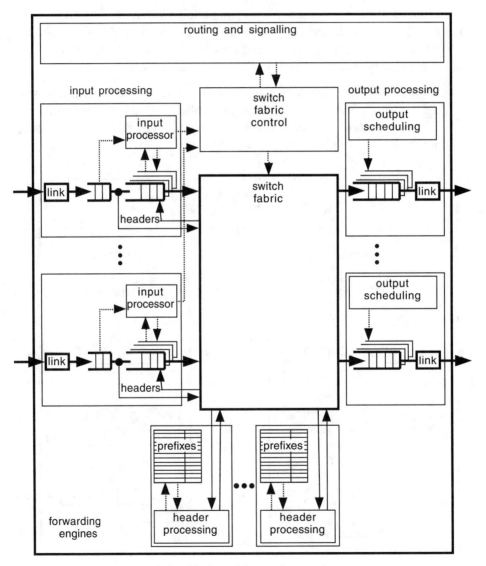

Figure 5.49　Datagram switch with shared forwarding engines.

This architecture has the advantage of allowing individual switches to be configured based on the needed packet processing rate. Rather than replacing all input port cards if the rate increases, the ratio of port cards to forwarding engines can be changed. The disadvantage is that the headers need to move through the switch fabric to the forwarding engines, and perhaps return to the input processors if the forwarding engines perform the header updates, such as TTL decrement and header checksum correction in IPv4. Furthermore, the problem of packet classification can be more difficult, if packets are to enter per class queues, the classification process must be complete before this happens (this is discussed in Section 5.5.3).

5.5.1.1   *Critical Path Analysis*

In Section 5.1 we introduced a division of protocol functionality by control, transfer control, and data transfer. Data transfer is part of the critical path, and must be optimized for high-speed processing. The transfer control functions, such as classification, forwarding, scheduling, and congestion control, need to be carefully analyzed to determine the frequency of operation and processing required (hardware delay or instruction count at a given clock cycle).

A careful analysis of the processing requirements for each of the operations [Koufopavlou 1994] can determine the technology required to support a given processing rate, and whether software processing by an embedded controller is sufficient or custom hardware is needed.

5.5.1.2   *Packet Processing Rates*

In connection-oriented fast packet switching, we are primarily concerned about the data rate. However, recall that we related this to the packet processing budget in Table 5.3, and considered the impact on hardware versus software implementation. Given the increased complexity of datagram forwarding and the wide variance in packet lengths for IP switches, we will reconsider this issue in the context of fast forwarding of Internet datagrams. The size of internet datagrams is largely between 40 B (TCP control messages such as acknowledgments) and 1500 B (Ethernet MTU), with almost half the packets at or near minimum size [Thompson 1997]. A common rule of thumb is that 1 megapacket per second of processing is needed for every gigabit per second of bandwidth, for 1,000-bit-long packets [Partridge 1998a]. This is based on an average measure of packet size rather than a minimum. We must also consider the minimum packet size of 40 B in designing a switch.

Whether of minimum or average size drives a design depends on whether packets are processed sequentially or in parallel. All processing that is done sequentially in the transmit or receive pipeline must be based on the *minimum* interarrival time. Otherwise, processing of a minimum size packet will delay the transfer of other subsequent packets. For example, a 40-B TCP packet carried in a 64-B Ethernet frame (including preamble) requires a processing rate in excess of 1.5 Mpkt/s on a gigabit Ethernet link.

Average packet size is sufficient if concurrent or parallel processing of packets can occur. The shared forwarding engine architecture of Figure 5.31 arbitrarily allocates forwarding engines to incoming packets in parallel. Thus, it is not necessary to perform forwarding decisions in the time required for the shortest packet, although a forwarding engine assignment policy may be necessary to segregate long packets from short ones.

There are reasons to avoid schemes that misorder and add jitter to the packet stream, however. First, adding significant jitter increases the need for traffic shaping, increases the buffering needed for shaping and output scheduling, and results in higher delay for flows. Second, while many end-to-end protocols are tolerant of misordering, application performance may be degraded, either causing packets to be dropped (for example, streaming media applications, Section 7.2.2), requiring additional resequence buffering capacity at the end system, or unneeded retransmissions from end-to-end protocols that infer packet loss from misordering (Section 7.4.3).

Packet Processing Rate   *The packet processing rate (packets per second) is a key throughput measure of a switch. Packet processing software and shared parallel hardware resources must be able to sustain the average packet processing rate. Functions in the serial critical path must be designed for the worst case packet processing rate of the path to avoid queueing and blocking of subsequent packets.*

S-II.4p

Thus, even though higher performance is required, it may be offset by simpler switch design and significant benefit at the end system. Note that the impact on this skewed TCP traffic distribution also motivates considering schemes that reduce the number of acknowledgments. This will be discussed in Section 7.4.3.

5.5.2   Fast Forwarding Lookup

In connection-oriented fast packet switching, the connection ID (CID) is *locally* negotiated between adjacent switches to keep the size of the CID small enough for a dense table storage of the number of simultaneous connections in each switch. Even though the *protocol* may support a particular number of connections (for example, $2^{28} = 256$ M in ATM), an individual *switch* can be engineered to support whatever makes sense in its context, and restrict the range of CIDs and resulting CID table size. CIDs are negotiated and assigned hop-by-hop between adjacent switches during connection setup. This allows the output port to be determined by a simple table lookup, as shown in Figure 5.17.

The problem of fast forwarding on destination addresses is conceptually similar to that of connection-oriented forwarding: When a packet arrives, extract the packet header field and use it to look into a forwarding table to determine the outgoing port that leads to the next hop toward the destination. The difference lies in the increased complexity and size of the destination address field. The number of possible entries in a forwarding table is based on the size of the destination address. A naïve directly addressed table would be an extremely large sparse structure. For example, an IPv4 table would need $2^{32} = 4$ G entries and an IPv6 table would need $2^{128} = 340 \times 10^{36} = 340$ EE (exa-exa) entries. Clearly, more complex data structures and algorithms are needed for lookup; the challenge is to optimize them to operate at line rate with reasonable cost. The solution depends on the address space size and use of hierarchy in the addressing scheme.

5.5.2.1   Flat Addressing

Unless the address space is very small, direct indexing of a table is not practical. A table capable of direct indexing of an n bit address needs 2^n entries. In general, the actual number of entries needed at a particular time will be much smaller. For example, an Ethernet MAC address is 48 bits, but a typical Ethernet switch will have only tens to hundreds of attached links. Clearly, it is not practical to have an addressing table with $2^{48} \approx 300 \times 10^{12}$ entries.

Two categories of address lookups can be considered: software search of the table and hardware matching using a content addressable memory (CAM), as shown in Figure 5.50.

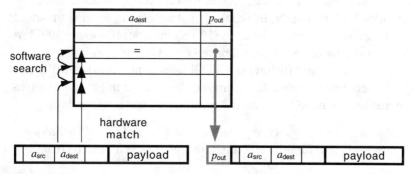

Figure 5.50   Address lookup.

5.5.2.1.1 Software Search

When address entries are not directly indexed, they must be searched to match addresses. We are concerned with several performance and cost measures:

Lookup time. The critical measure of performance that indicates whether the algorithm will be able to match desired line rate. The ideal is a single memory reference, as in the case of connection ID lookup. If this is a dynamic random access memory (DRAM) cycle, it translates to tens of RISC instruction cycles. If it is in a static random access memory (SRAM),[22] or within the on-chip Level 1 cache, it is reduced to several RISC CPU cycles. Given a processor with an instruction cycle of t sec, and a lookup algorithm that takes l instruction cycles, we get a packet processing rate constrained by $1/lt$ pkts/s. The relationship between packet processing rate and line rate depends on the packet size. For a packet size of b bits, the line rate supported is thus constrained by b/lt b/s. Clearly, the smaller the packet size, the more challenging the lookup. We are most concerned with the worst-case lookup time, as described in Section 5.5.1 This worst-case is manifest in two ways: the minimum packet size (as already described) and the worst-case lookup algorithm performance. The latter is important for the same reason as considering minimum size packets: Occasional worst-case lookup times may delay subsequent lookups, causing packets to back up in an input queue and be dropped due to buffer overrun.

Memory required. Indicates the amount of memory needed to hold the lookup data structures. All other things being equal, an algorithm with lower memory consumption is preferred, but the main concern is that the algorithm can operate using an amount of memory reasonable to contain in the switch input processing.

Update time. Indicates how long it takes to update the lookup data structure. Since this operation occurs on the granularity of routing decisions, it should be less critical than the lookup time performance. This parameter must be matched to the actual rate at which routing updates occur in real networks. Unfortunately, the routing instabilities in routing protocols deployed in the early third-generation (1990s) Internet [Labovitz 1997] require updates on the order of 10 ms, based on a possible update frequency of 100 per second [Srinivasan 1999]. While increased stability in routing protocols may reduce this number, the growth in mobile wireless nodes increases the need for dynamic routing and topology update.

A number of search techniques are possible, but generally used techniques are tree searches and hash functions. Tree searches maintain a tree structure

---

[22]SRAM is faster, less dense, and more expensive than DRAM; the ratios change as Resource Tradeoffs Change (2A).

in the memory, and approach a search time of $O(\log_B N)$ for N entries, where B is dependent on the branching factor of the tree. Increasing B reduces the search time at the expense of additional memory. A key issue in maintaining tree data structures is the overhead in inserting and reclaiming address entries in response to routing updates.

An alternative to tree searching is to use a hash function $H(a_{dest})$. Hashing allows a search with a single access, as long as there are no hash *collisions* that is, $H(a_{dest1}) = H(a_{dest2})$ for two distinct addresses a_{dest1} and a_{dest2}. Collisions require following linked lists, pointers to additional table cells, or sequential searches to find the appropriate match, and in the worst case can result in poorer performance than tree lookup. The performance of a hash function is dependent on how randomly the hash index is distributed. Unfortunately, functions that are simple to implement in hardware (such as an XOR) do not produce indicies that are as randomly distributed as more complex functions (such as a CRC). The larger the hash range, the less likely collisions will occur, assuming true random distribution of the indices.

Some of the complexity of hash resolution can be eliminated by use of *source hashing* [Chandranmenon 1995]. The transmitting end system computes a hash function and inserts it into a hash header field in the packet. The intermediate nodes no longer need to compute the index into the table, but rather simply extract it from the packet header. Collisions must still be resolved, however, and can occur across multiplexed data flows. The IPv6 flow label (shown in Example 5.6) is intended to be used as a source hash.

Since the update performance of hashing is also a single write (assuming no collision), hashing is suitable for very dynamic mobile addressing and routing topologies that have frequent forwarding table updates.

5.5.2.1.2 Content Addressable Memory

Content Addressable Memories (CAMs) [Kohonen 1980] consist of words that are addressed by content. Each word consists of a ⟨search-field, return-field⟩ tuple. When the search field is used to read the CAM, *all* words are checked in parallel in a single CAM cycle; the return-field portion of the word is the output of the CAM read. If the size of data to be matched is small, as is the case for lookup of a switch output port, it can be directly read from the return-field. In the case where the data to be returned is large, the return-field contains an index into a RAM module, requiring a two-cycle CAM/RAM read pair to retrieve the desired data.

In Figure 5.31, the destination address from the packet header a_{dest} is the search-field. The result of the CAM read is the output port p_{out}, which may be prepended as an internal switch header, as described in Section 5.3.2.

CAMs are more expensive and contain fewer memory cells for a given chip area than RAM, by about an order of magnitude, and consume considerably more power [McAuley 1993]. CAMs specifically designed for network address lookup can be significantly more efficient than general-purpose CAMs [Pei 1992], however. Conventional CAMs with fixed match fields and binary entries are appropriate when the number of words needed is relatively small, and the size of the search field is fixed, for example, in Ethernet switches.

5.5.2.2 *Hierarchical Addresses*

Recall that Hierarchy and Clustering Reduces State (5C); hierarchical addresses can be exploited to reduce the size of the forwarding tables. Instead of exact matching of full addresses, forwarding entries can be represented as *prefix addresses*, that is, a high-order bit portion of an address that must be matched to lead toward the destination. A simple example of hierarchical addressing is the public switched telephone network (PSTN), in which addresses are of the form ⟨country-code, area-code, exchange, station-number⟩.[23] A local telephone switch contains route information only about the station-numbers in exchanges that are directly attached to the same local switch. Telephone numbers with different exchanges are routed to the appropriate local switch without regard to the station-number portion. Telephone numbers with different area-codes are routed to the appropriate higher-layer switch (traditionally toll switch) for further routing to the exchange and then station-number.

If the address is divided into fixed length hierarchical portions, as for the PSTN, then hierarchical and incremental table lookup can be used, with each address portion indexing into a table that corresponds to the level in the hierarchy. This is similar in concept to the way in which processors map virtual addresses to real addresses (explained in Section 6.2.2). This requires a hierarchical address scheme matching the administrative clustering of the network [which we argued in the Network Hierarchy Principle (N-5C) is desirable].

Mobility of end-system addresses considerably complicates the ability to maintain small prefix tables, unless end systems are semipermanently assigned to home network nodes (as is the case for mobile IP). This presents problems with suboptimal routes and path lengths, however, as described in Example 4.3.

---

[23]This discussion is based on the historic PSTN addressing and routing hierarchy. Developments such as overlay area codes and number portability has made the situation more complex.

EXAMPLE 5.6: IP PACKET FORMATS

Since IP is the network layer protocol of the global Internet, the majority of activity in high-speed network node architecture and design in the late 1990s and early 2000s is targeted to supporting IP.

Addresses in the Internet are relatively flat, structured only by the per administrative domain structuring of subnets, which tends to cluster addresses with similar low-order bits. IP addresses originally were structured into a two-level class hierarchy, but the small address space necessitated abandoning fixed prefix boundaries with the adoption of classless interdomain routing (CIDR) [Rekhter 1993]. Thus, the forwarding prefixes installed by routing algorithms are variable length, depending on the number of address bits assigned to particular Internet administrative domains. Administrative domains can further cluster into subnets, resulting in ad hoc lower levels of addressing hierarchy.[24]

IP packets were designed long before current concern with high-speed processing; the version of IP that forms the basis of the fourth-generation (1990s) Internet is IPv4. The format of an IPv4 packet is shown in Figure 5.51a. When a packet is received, it may be classified for special treatment (for example, QOS or policy routing), as described in Section 5.5.3. The destination address is looked up in the forwarding data structure to determine the output port that leads to the next hop. The time to live (TTL) field is decremented, which prevents packets from looping indefinitely. To compensate for the decremented TTL, the header checksum must be corrected, which is a simple adjustment [Braden 1988, Mallory 1990] to the existing checksum, rather then a complete recalculation. The packet can then be sent through the switch fabric to the outgoing link.

Assuming fragmentation does not occur (MTU path discovery was performed) and there are no other options to process, IPv4 software forwarding can be done in about 20 lines of C code or approximately 200 RISC instructions, including device drivers [Partridge 1994a]. This assumes that the route is cached in a small table with a high hit ratio.[25] With the advent of CIDR in the mid-1990s, IP prefixes became variable in length, resulting in the need for longest prefix matching. The dramatic increase in the size of the Internet and the advent of large fast routers have significantly increased the number of prefixes to tens of thousands in a typical Internet router. The locality of addresses is dependent on a small number of long-lived flows. In backbone nodes with hundreds of thousands of simultaneous short-lived flows (for example, for Web transactions), the locality may be quite poor, and it is uncertain whether we can expect adequate level 1 cache hit ratios in forwarding processors using software lookups [Newman 1997].

(Continues)

[24]It is important to note that the DNS name hierarchy is *not* directly related to IP address hierarchy.
[25]A 90 percent hit ratio for a 200-table cache was observed in [Feldmeier 1988].

(*Continued*)

The impending exhaustion of IPv4 addresses (as well as other concerns) leads to calls for a new version of IP [Clark 1991, Partridge 1994a], with a working name of IP next generation (IPng).

Proposals included:

- TUBA (TCP and UDP with bigger addresses) [Callon 1992, Katz 1993], using ISO CLNP [ISO8473, Chapin 1981, 1983, Piscitello 1993] as the replacement for IP. The Internet Architecture Board (IAB) had endorsed CLNP as a basis for work on IPng in June 1992. Modifications to CLNP were deemed necessary, but the Internet community was not able to agree on whether this was possible without the blessing of the ISO standards process.[26]

- SIP (Simple Internet Protocol) [Deering 1993] and SIPP (SIP plus) [Hinden 1994], were based on a packet encapsulation similar to IPv4 but with a simpler packet header that included a flow label and 64-bit addresses.

- CATNIP (Common Architecture for the Next Generation Internet Protocol) [McGovern 1994] and TP/IX [Ullman 1993], proposed a convergence replacement of IP, CLNP, and IPX with a new protocol format similar in design philosophy to IPv4, but with 64-bit addresses. A forward cache identifier field in the header was used as a flow label for label swapping or for mobility. TP/IX further proposed longer fields in the TCP header to deal with high-bandwidth-×-delay product networks (discussed in Example 7.9).

- PIP [Francis 1993] proposed a significant departure from IP with variable length hierarchical addresses and routing, autoconfiguration of end-system addresses, and support for multicast and mobility.

- NIMROD [Chiappa 1994, Castineyra 1996] was designed as a hierarchical clustered routing architecture for IPng, with support for QOS, multicast [Ramanathan 1997a], and mobility [Ramanathan 1997b].

The protocol chosen was based on SIPP [Bradner 1995], with significantly longer 128-bit addresses; this is IPv6 [Deering 1998]. The specification of IPv6 was also targeted to more efficient processing to support high-speed networking and QOS. To this end, several important changes were made to the IPv4 packet format:

- The header has a simpler structure and fixed size (40 bytes), with options headers following the main header.

- An IPv6 flow is uniquely identified by the combination of the source address and a 20-bit flow label; the latter is randomly assigned by the

---

[26]In retrospect, it is clear that this would not have been an issue. Standards are irrelevant if they do not reflect reality, and a modified CLNP adopted by the IETF and deployed in the Internet would have quickly displaced ISO standard CLNP, which is now little used despite its status as an ISO and ITU standard.

source end system. This allows network nodes to use the flow label to hash into the forwarding table, and then further resolve by source address.[27] Note that not all IP packets need to be assigned flow labels. In particular, transactions, individual datagrams, and short-lived associations will not have flow labels explicitly assigned.

- There is no header checksum that must be checked and updated to correspond to the decrement in the 8-bit hop limit (previously TTL in IPv4) field. While this simplifies processing slightly, this comes at the cost of not protecting the header in lossy environments, such as wireless networks.

- An 8-bit traffic class field is provided to be used for provision of quality of service and to allow packet classification by service class, such as for differentiated services [Blake 1998, Kilkki 1999].

- Fragmentation of IPv6 packets is not permitted.

The future of IPv6 is uncertain; the impending exhaustion of addresses was initially ameliorated by CIDR and continues to be pushed out by the hack of using network address translators (NAT) [Hain 2000, Srisuresh 2001, Dutcher 2001] at the network edge.

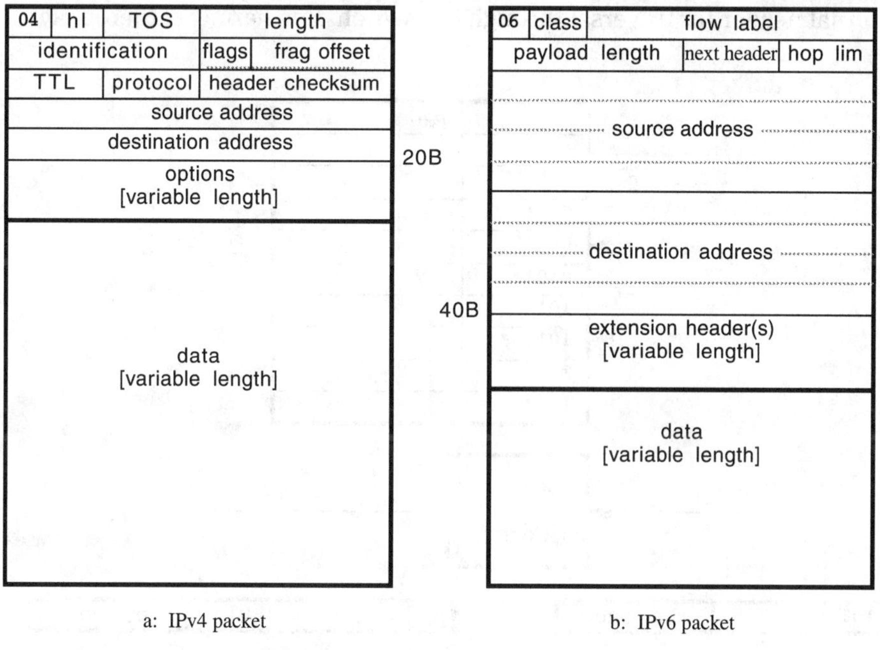

a: IPv4 packet   b: IPv6 packet

Figure 5.51   IPv4 and IPv6 packet formats.

[27]This is a weak form of source hashing, since there is not a distinct source hash field in the header reserved for the purpose.

5.5.2.3 *Software Prefix Matching*

We will first consider software techniques for matching address prefixes. In this case, the switch input processing contains an embedded processor that runs the matching algorithm in memory. The input processor performs the following functions:

Header processing. Decodes, computes new values for fields such as the TTL or hop count, and header checksum, and inserts them back into the header.

Address prefix lookup. Determines the outgoing port, and either sets the path in the switch fabric or prepends the packet with an internal header for self-routing switch fabrics (as described in Section 5.3.1 for connection-oriented fast packet switches).

Prefix table update. Update and maintenance in response to signals from the routing protocol in the switch control.

A small example set of prefixes that will be used throughout this section is shown in Figure 5.52.[28]

A brute force mechanism would be to search a prefix table for the longest match. As in other cases, the matching output port p_{out} may be prepended to an internal header for traversal through the switch. Furthermore, there may

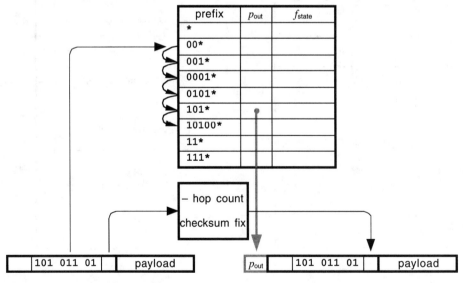

Figure 5.52 IP prefix matching.

---

[28]These prefixes correspond to the prefixes used in [Perlman 2000] Example 13.1; Chapter 13 summarizes fast matching techniques.

be entries for soft flow state f_{state} that assists in the determination of output port or scheduling (discussed in Section 5.5.3).

If the table is kept in sorted order, then the worst-case search time is $O(\log_2 N)$ operations, where N is the number of prefixes; for prefix tables with tens of thousands of entries (typical in the Internet), this is clearly unacceptable. Thus, we need to consider algorithms and data structures that perform better.

A basic prefix matching algorithm consists of traversing a *trie*, which is a sparsely populated binary tree that leads to all of the valid prefixes as leaves.[29] At each level i in the trie, the ith bit from the left of the address to be matched is used to drop to the next level in the tree. If a flag bit is set (represented by $*$ in the figure), a valid prefix has been found. An example trie is shown in Figure 5.53.

Matching the address `10101101` consists of first taking the right branch (`1`), then the left branch (`10`) then the right branch (`101*`), which is a valid prefix. However we are interested in finding the *longest* matching prefix, so an attempt is made to continue to traverse the trie looking for another valid prefix, until an appropriate branch does not exist, or a leaf node is reached. In this example, we take the left branch (`1010`), and then end, since the next digit is a `1` and there is no right branch. If the address to match had instead been `10100101`, we would have taken the left branch ending at the valid (and longer) prefix `10100*`.

This scheme requires worst-case $O(a)$ memory accesses to lookup, where a is the number of address bits and is the maximum depth of the trie, $O(Na)$ total table memory, and $O(1)$ memory accesses to update prefix entries. Thus, for 32-bit IPv4 and 128-bit IPv6 addresses, the worst case is 32 and 128 accesses, considerably worse than the one access desired.

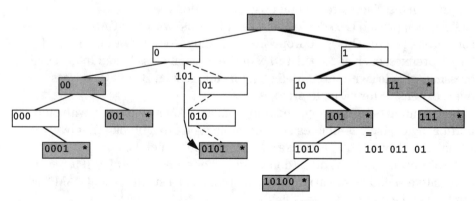

Figure 5.53 Trie prefix matching.

---

[29]*Trie* is pronounced as the word "try".

A simple improvement in search time is to collapse long paths in the tree that do not branch by adding multibit fields in the branching decision. For example, in Figure 5.53, the right branch of the 0 node can contain 101, indicating that the next entry down the right of the tree is 0101. This replaces the entries down the branch with dashed lines.

There are a variety of improvements possible (summarized in [Srinivasan 1999, Tzeng 1999, Perlman 2000]). An example is to search multiple bits at a time [Srinivasan 1999b], which reduces the depth of the tree, but requires all prefix entries to be multiple bits. This requires additional memory for prefixes that would otherwise not be needed. Another optimization is to search on prefix lengths, giving a worst-case lookup of $\log_2 a$ hashes [Waldvogel 1997].

5.5.2.4 Hardware Matching Support

The complexity of software algorithms, even with the optimizations described, motivates the consideration of hardware techniques for line rate lookup. There are two ways in which hardware can assist in the lookup process:

1. The assisting logic can be embedded in the memory, as is the case for CAMs.

2. Translation logic can be provided that assists the location of addresses in conventional memory.

We will consider each of these alternatives.

5.5.2.4.1 CAMs for Variable Prefixes

As described previously, CAMs have the ability to be searched in a single read cycle by a search-field, returning the appropriate match in a single access. The difficulty is that conventional CAMs do not provide direct support for variable length prefixes. There are several possible solutions.

A naïve approach is to deploy an array of CAMs, with one CAM element for each prefix length. This is appropriate to consider for a hierarchy of fixed length prefixes, such as for the PSTN or the original class-based Internet addressing scheme (with three prefix lengths for class A, B, and C addresses), but is expensive for variable prefixes.

One solution is to logically partition a binary CAM into blocks, with supporting logic which associates each possible prefix to a block [Tantawy 1994c]. Another solution is to use a *ternary CAM*, which has three possible states for each bit: 0, 1, and X (don't care) [Wade 1987, McAuley 1993]. This allows native encoding of variable length prefixes in a single logical CAM[30] without the need for separate mask fields.

---

[30]Which may be *implemented* as an array of multiple CAM chips.

Figure 5.54 shows a ternary CAM lookup structure. In this case, there may be multiple matches for a given search-field, and we need the longest match. Priority multiplexor logic is part of the CAM and is needed to select the longest matching return-field. Ternary CAMs are roughly double the cost of binary CAMs [McAuley 1993] per bit, but the overall cost compared to a binary scheme with separate mask fields is justified. The demand for large fast ternary CAMs has resulted in the development of multimegabit CAMs capable of operating at OC-192 (10 Gb/s) and OC-768 (40 Gb/s) rates in the early 2000s.

Whether the cost of a CAM-based lookup is justified compared to software lookups, or to hardware assisted lookup (described next) is based on the Resource Tradeoff Principle (2) at a particular time and the performance needed.

5.5.2.4.2 Multistage Lookup

A multistage lookup can be used when a majority of the prefixes are relatively short [Gupta 1998]; this is likely to be the case in backbone switches in the core of the network. For example, in the Internet of the late 1990s, a majority of prefixes do not exceed 24 bits in length, even though full IPv4 addresses are 32 bits long. The idea is to directly address a majority of the prefixes in a memory of manageable length, and handle the exceptions in a secondary memory, as shown in Figure 5.55.

A portion of the a bit address is used as a direct index into a short prefix table that is 2^p entries long, where the short prefix table can directly resolve longest match prefixes up to p bits long. A flag i indicates whether this entry is a complete prefix ($i = 0$), in which case short table entry contains the output port p_{out} that leads to the next hop (shown by the dashed arrow). If the longest

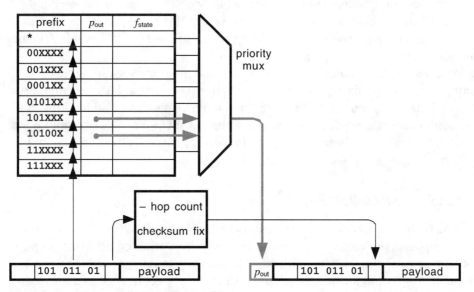

Figure 5.54 Ternary CAM prefix matching.

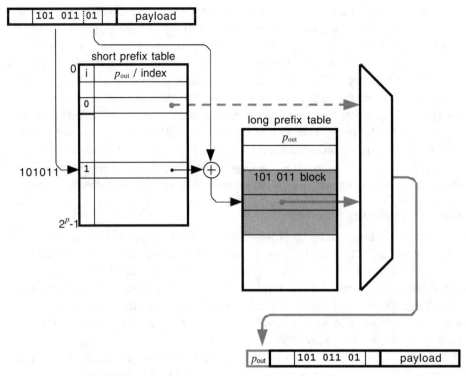

Figure 5.55 Multistage prefix match.

matching prefix is longer (i = 1), then the short table entry contains a pointer into a long prefix table, which contains a block of $2^{(a-p)}$ entries for each long prefix. The low-order $a - p$ bits is the index into this block, which provides the output port p_{out}. The size of the long prefix table is $P \cdot 2^{(a-p)}$, where P is the number of unique long prefixes.

This scheme is a tradeoff between speed and memory. Assuming that the number of long prefixes is relatively small, there is substantially less memory needed than a full direct index. Additional table levels can be added for some memory savings, but with diminishing returns. A memory cycle is required for each table level, but these can be pipelined to give an effective throughput of one read cycle *per* lookup.

5.5.2.5 *Source-Routing*

A final technique to consider is to eliminate the *per* hop address lookup by precomputing the route. This is done in connection-oriented networks as part of connection setup and maintained as VC state. It is also possible to do this for datagrams, and include the entire path in the packet header as a *source route*. This has long been supported (but little used) in IP, and been proposed in high-speed networks [Parulkar 1990a, Cidon 1993].

The transmitting end system or edge switch needs to compute the route for each datagram and insert the label stack in the packet header. In the case of a flow, the label stack can be stored as soft state at the flow ingress to avoid per packet route calculation. At each node in the network, the front label is popped off the stack (or rotated to the end) so that the next hop will see its forwarding decision at the top of the stack.[31]

Figure 5.56 shows a source-routed label stack example. At switch 1, the top entry is popped from the stack in the header, which indicates that the packet should be forwarded along outgoing port p_5, which leads to switch 2. Switch 2 pops the header stack and forwards the packet out port p_0, and so forth. It is possible to forward either based on outgoing link, as shown in this example, or on switch identifier, in which case a port table must be consulted that maps the switch ID to port number.

The problem with source routing is the difficulty in precomputing routes. End nodes are not likely to have access to internal network topology,[32] but the source route could be computed by an edge switch. Source routing does have application for some network control and management applications. It can also be useful for policy-based routing; in some cases, the source route may be at a high level (for example, service provider transit network or administrative domain), with forwarding through subnetworks handled in the conventional per packet manner.

Hardware versus Software Implementation of Input and Output Processing   *In determining the appropriate implementation of input and output processing, trade the cost and feasibility of hardware against the complexity and feasibility of embedded controller software.*

S-1C*h*

Datagram forwarding at gigabit per second rates had been considered an insurmountable problem in the mid-1990s. By the end of the 1990s, VLSI density,

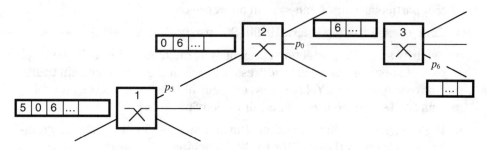

Figure 5.56   Source routed label stack.

---

[31]Note that, unlike MPLS, the label stack is *within* a single header.
[32]Network service providers do generally not expose internal topology to unauthorized users, considering it to be proprietary information.

embedded processing capability, and ternary CAM technology had increased so dramatically that datagram lookup is now generally considered a solved problem. The Resource Tradeoff Principle (2) will govern the best solution at a particular point in time.

5.5.3   Packet Classification and Filtering

We have described the input processing to determine where a packet is forwarded. The other key decision that must be made is how to treat the packet; this is called *packet classification*. In fact, address lookup is a type of classification that is important enough to warrant the separate treatment just given. Two other common forms of classification are the separation of control packets into the control path of the switch (for example, ICMP packets) and the separation of packets belonging to different traffic classes based on a well-defined field (for example, IPv4 TOS and IPv6 class). In connection-oriented fast packet switching, these routine classification functions are trivial, since connection ID lookup *is* classification and returns all needed state. Difficult decisions on route and traffic class are performed at connection setup. In datagram networks, these functions require relatively straightforward demultiplexing hardware in the input processing portion of the switch.

The general problem of classification is much more difficult, since it can involve complex and overlapping policy decisions based on multiple and arbitrary packet header fields and payload contents. Classification should not be limited to exact matches to fields, but also match based on inequalities (greater or less than a value), prefixes, and wildcards [Gupta 1999]. Examples of application for the general classification problem include:

- Classification into a QOS traffic class or differentiated service class to support a particular grade of service (GOS) based on criteria such as addresses and protocol types; for example, provision of a premium service to a particular pair of end-system addresses.

- Policy-based routing [Clark 1989b, Steenstrup 1993a, 1993b]

- Security and DOS protection (firewalls), for example, discarding of packets between particular addresses or when the rate of certain traffic (for example, TCP SYN packets) exceeds a threshold. Access control lists (ACLs) can be used to permit or deny packets.

- Higher-layer switching functions (layer 4 and 7 switching), such as redirection based on HTTP URLs for Web caching.

- Active network processing in which some packets are removed from the normal processing path into an active networking path (described in Section 5.6).

> **Bound Packet Classification Time**   *Packets that must be classified to potentially re-ceive delay-bounded service must be classified before any queuing at the input. The classification operation must have delay bounds that meet the most stringent service class.*
>
> **S-II.4c**

A key requirement if the classification is used for QOS or GOS differentia-tion is that this classification occur *before* queuing in the node. It does no good to classify a packet after it has been buffered for longer than the service class allows or if the classification itself exceeds this bound or a reasonable fraction thereof, since delays along a path are additive [Network Latency Prin-ciple (N-1A*l*)]. Thus, classification must be done at line rate at the input, and is clearly part of the critical path.

The general problem of classification can be viewed as the location of a point in n-dimensional space, where classification policies are overlapping n-dimensional rectangular prisms [Lakshman 1998].

A two-dimensional version of this is shown in Figure 5.57, based on source address and TOS fields in IPv4, each of which define one dimension. The pol-icy may be based on a single values, resulting in a point (R_5), or on a range of values resulting in a line (R_1) or rectangle (R_2, R_3, and R_4). Policies may be dis-joint (for example, R_2 and R_4) in which there is no question on how to resolve them or hierarchical (for example, R_5 in R_2), in which case the narrower rule should take precedence. In the case of overlapping policies (for example, R_3 and R_4), an explicit rule must determine the relative priority in the overlap

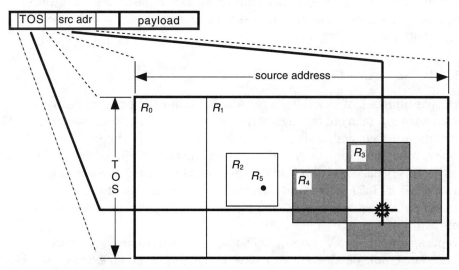

Figure 5.57   Packet filtering.

region. The default policy (R_0) is used when no other region matches. The classification algorithm must keep track of all distinct regions (shown as distinct shadings in Figure 5.57), including points, the intersection of two lines, and overlapping policies like the region $R_3 \cap R_4$.

The packet is represented by a particular point in the space corresponding to the values in the fields under consideration, shown by the star in the figure. The packet then falls in the region $R_3 \cap R_4$, and so the higher-priority rule must be used. The best known algorithms are either time or space efficient [Lakshman 1998, Overmars 1996] for n rules on F packet fields:

$$O((\log n)^{F-1}) \text{ time} \quad \text{and} \quad O(n) \text{ memory}$$

$$O(\log n) \text{ time} \quad \text{and} \quad O(n^F) \text{ memory}$$

As for the lookup problem, we can consider both hardware and software techniques.

5.5.3.1 Hardware Classification

Ternary CAMs can be used to match the rules in parallel, with the matches resolved by a priority multiplexor, similar to the address lookup in Figure 5.35. The disadvantage is the size of CAM needed for complex rule sets, and the difficulty in dealing with range values.

Parallel hardware can be exploited in custom matching hardware, as well. A naïve hardware approach is to provide a match unit for each rule [Baily 1994], which can perform classification in a single time step, but requires $O(n)$ processors. Another approach is to decompose the classification by dimension, and provide custom hardware to perform each dimension in parallel, followed by a combination step [Lakshman 1998]. This requires less hardware than per rule parallelism, but requires significant memory bandwidth, scaling linearly with the classifier size.

5.5.3.2 Software Classification

The naïve approach of searching n rules in $O(n)$ time is clearly inadequate. Not surprisingly, many of the high-performance software approaches and algorithms are a generalization of the techniques described in Section 5.1.1 for forwarding table lookup. A grid of tries [Srinivasan 1998] can be used to quickly classify based on two fields, by extending the trie data structure shown in Figure 5.53 to two fields. The scheme is extensible using cross-producting, but requires either $O(n^F)$ memory, or does not guarantee deterministic memory search time.

Tuple space search [Srinivasan 1999] maps filters to tuples, which are searched in a tuple database using a hash index. Tuple search exploits the observation that actual filters only use a smaller number of field lengths, particularly for IPv4 address prefixes. Thus even very large filter sets (thousands to millions) may only need several hundred tuples. The classification performance depends on the number of collisions and list length on tuple hashes.

5.5.3.3 Preprocessing Classifiers

One way to speed up the *per* packet classification is to preprocess all possible packet fields as an index into a class table. This would allow an $O(1)$ classification time, but for a packet header h bits long, 2^h entries are needed. It essentially reduces Figure 5.37 to an array of points. For example, the IPv4 header contains 10 B of address, TOS, and protocol fields; this would result in $2^{80} = 1.2 \times 10^{24}$ entries, which is clearly infeasible. It is reasonable to expect that only a small fraction of possible regions will be in use at a time; this has been verified by empirical evidence [Gupta 1999a]. By exploiting known classification structure, the memory requirement can be significantly reduced, resulting in an acceptable preprocessing to memory tradeoff, with fast classification time [Gupta 1999a, Gupta 1999b]. Hierarchical classification can introduce this structure, while increasing the efficiency of classification. Hierarchical classification can be related to subnetwork boundaries, or hierarchical link sharing, described in the next section.

5.5.4 Output Processing and Packet Scheduling

In connection-oriented fast packet switching, the scheduling of packets to outgoing links is a relatively simple exercise, consisting of FIFO queueing with traffic shaping to maintain the traffic contract, as described in Section 5.3.5. This is because connection admission control (CAC) was used to ensure that links and switch resources are sufficient to guarantee traffic contracts with a low probability of congestion, and policing is used to ensure that individual connections do not exceed their contract.

When congestion is impending, packets are discarded to avoid building queues, which are a sign of impending congestion (Section 7.5.4). Traffic classes can be isolated from one another by performing queueing, congestion control, and traffic shaping *per* class. For example, this can reduce the impact of bursty traffic on real-time constant bit-rate traffic, and allow less conservative admission control of the bursty traffic.

In cases where admission control and policing are not used to strictly limit the incoming traffic to a switch, more sophisticated output scheduling becomes essential. There is no a priori determination that flows will not interfere with one another when competing for a given egress link on a switch node. This is the case when best effort traffic (for example, ATM UBR in Example 7.7) is mixed with guaranteed service classes in a connection oriented fast packet switch. It is also the case in a datagram switches when resources are not reserved as a result of admission control or when only some flows have resource reservations using protocols such as resource reservation protocol (RSVP) [Zhang 1993].

Therefore, there are two reasons to perform output scheduling:

1. Guaranteed service classes need packets to be scheduled for transmission to the next hop at a rate sufficient to meet delay and bandwidth bounds of the traffic contract.

2. Best-effort traffic should be scheduled in a manner that maintains fair service among the best-effort flows. Relying on end-to-end reaction to congestion control mechanisms (described later) does not protect guaranteed service classes from the best-effort traffic. At best, a behaving source will react in a round-trip time (RTT); at worst, a misbehaving source will not throttle at all.

5.5.4.1   Fair Queueing

Packet fair queueing (PFQ) [Nagle 1984, Nagle 1987, Demers 1989] can be used to determine when packets are scheduled for transmission of a switch egress link, and it is essential the algorithms and mechanisms be efficient enough so that they can be implemented so that packets can be scheduled at line rate.

PFQ algorithms attempt to emulate generalized processor sharing (GPS), [Parekh 1993], which has the desired fairness and delay bound properties. Two things are required to implement PFQ. First the service order must be determined by computing and assigning packets a departure time. Second, the queues must be managed to dequeue packets in a non-FIFO manner (or be continuously rearranged so packets are in the proper order for FIFO departure).

Weighted fair queuing (WFQ) [Demers 1989] uses the virtual time function of GPS, but suffers from $O(N)$ complexity, where N is the number of flows, because the state of all flows is used to compute the virtual time function. Since switches must support thousands of simultaneous flows, this *per* packet algorithm is clearly unacceptable for large high-speed switches.

There are a number of techniques for reducing the state and algorithm complexity. Packets can be classified (Section 5.5.3) into a small number of traffic classes, by type (for example, real-time, best-effort), protocol (for example, TCP or UDP, with port numbers to separate higher layer protocols), administrative domains, or ranges of data rate. This allows much of the state to be maintained at the coarse traffic class granularity, even if flows are individually queued. The appropriate service disciplines can be used for each class, scheduling among multiple queues within the class when finer granularity queueing is desired.

Examples of hierarchical link sharing include:

- Virtual connections in virtual connection traffic classes in virtual path traffic classes for ATM [Giroux 1999].

- Flows in traffic classes in administrative domains [Floyd 1995], that is, each administrative domain gets a share of the traffic that it can subdivide as it wishes into traffic classes.

- Flows in administrative domains in traffic classes, that is, traffic classes are determined and partitioned at the top level, with individual administrative domains receiving differing shares of each class.

Algorithms which use only the state of packets currently queue in a switch further reduce the state required [Stiliadis 1998]. As for the case of a packet classification and lookup, the scheduling algorithm should have good scaling properties, at least $O(\log N)$ and preferably $O(1)$, and be implementable in software or hardware to operate at line rate (for example, [Shreedhar 1995], [Rexford 1996, 1997, Varma 1997, Stiliadis 1998, Briem 1998, Stephens 1999, Chao 1999]).

Output Scheduling and Queueing Granularity   *Output scheduling must operate at line rate to support the traffic classes required. Finer-grained queueing and scheduling provides greater isolation of flows and control at the cost of increased queueing complexity.*

S-II.4s

5.5.4.2 *Per-Flow Queueing*

The highest degree of isolation and control occurs when *per* flow queueing is used. This prevents extremely bursty flows from starving other flows. For example, long-lived TCP flows can be extremely bursty, in part due to the ACK aggregation and compression from window-based flow control (Section 7.5.5). Since it can be difficult to classify different types of TCP traffic (except perhaps by port number), bursty flows will impact short lived and response critical flows (for example, telnet and Web requests). Queueing *per* flow solves this problem [Suter 1998, Cam 1999].

The difficulty in *per* flow queueing lies in the complexity of shared queue management or the amount of memory required for distinct physical queues. The increasing density and decreasing cost of VLSI hardware has brought *per* flow queueing into the realm of feasibility, particularly when the aggregation techniques are used to simplify state.

5.5.4.3 *Congestion Control*

The goal of buffer management strategies should be to keep queues small. Large building queues increase delay, and are indicative of more traffic than the switch can handle, resulting in congestion.

> **Discard to Keep Queues from Building** *Queue length should reflect transient traffic conditions, and not be allowed to build in the steady state. Perform congestion avoidance and control, including packet discard, to keep queues small locally, and throttle the source for end-to-end congestion avoidance.*
>
> **S-6C***d*

If *per* flow input queueing is used with distinct physical queues, the delay impact of a building queue is limited to a single flow, but in all other cases other flows will be impacted. If the switch is output queued, then the flow building the queue is contending with other flows through the switch fabric. If queues are shared, buffer space is taken from other flows. If *per* flow queueing is not used, other traffic will be delayed behind the flow with the building queue.

Therefore, it is important that congestion control mechanisms be employed [Braden 1998] which:

1. Bound the steady state size of queues.

2. Notify applications to throttle when their traffic is causing queues to build.

Random early detection (RED) [Floyd 1993] randomly drops packets when a queue threshold is exceeded, and directly accomplishes the first objective. By keeping queue lengths short, the delay impact of cross traffic is minimized.

Explicit congestion notification (ECN) to applications is desirable, since it minimizes reaction time (particularly if ECN messages travel backward) as shown in Figure 4.15 and decouples end-to-end congestion control from error control as discussed in Section 7.5.4. However, protocols which use window-based flow, congestion, and error control (such as TCP) infer congestion from packet loss. By dropping packets from building queues, RED indicates congestion to the end-to-end protocol and causes it to throttle early enough to prevent congestion collapse, in which buffers are full and end systems continue to transmit at high rate.

5.6 Higher-Layer and Active Processing

In this section we provide a brief discussion on the higher-layer (4 to 7) and active processing in network nodes. Section 5.6.1 lays out the general problem and alternatives for such processing. Section 5.6.2 describes how active networking can be implemented on a high-speed switching node.

5.6.1   Alternative Strategies

There are a number of motivations to perform transport and application layer processing in network nodes. These include:

- Firewalls, which examine a number of transport and application layer protocol fields to pass or deny traffic.

- Web cache proxies, which examine HTTP headers to redirect requests, as described in Section 8.3.1.

- Active transcoders and protcol boosters [Feldmeier 1998, Marcus 1998] which determine content type of communicating users and splice the connection through the proper transcoding server.

- Multimedia stream mixing and merging, in support of multiparty, multi-media conferencing.

    There is a range of ways to implement this functionality:

- Application layer proxies implement a full protocol stack and terminate both sides of a multileg connection. While completely flexible, they are not a particularly high-performance solution. Optimizations can be applied, however, to increase the efficiency of multileg connection establishment [Maltz 1998, Spatscheck 2000].

- Active network nodes arbitrarily filter packets and are able to execute active applications that implement the desired functionality.

- Layer 4 [Srinivasan 1998, Buddikhot 1999] and layer 7 switches use the packet classification on layer 4 and layer 7 protocol fields, respectively, to determine packet forwarding (or rejection), as described in Section 5.1.3.

- Integration of application processing into layer 3 forwarding code is the least flexible solution.

We have already examined the classification solution, which can be viewed as a restricted case of active networking. Active networking uses general classification techniques to first identify packets for active processing, and then executes active applications in the network nodes on the identified packets, connections, or flows to provide the desired service.

This active processing can occur at the link and network layer to provide protocol functionality not part of the standard protocol stack, and at the higher transport, session, and application layers not normally part of network node processing.

5.6.2   Active Network Nodes

As discussed in Section 3.3.3, as Resource Tradeoffs Change (2A), we can consider the proper balance and placement of functionality in the network.

Relatively cheap processing (and memory) led us to consider active networking [Tennenhouse 1997, Battacharjeel 1998c]. In Section 5.6.1 we motivated active networking in the spectrum of solutions to provide layer 4 and layer 7 processing in network nodes. In this section, we discuss the organization and design of high-speed network nodes.

There are two additional motivations for active networking:

- Open flexible interfaces to allow provisioning of new protocols and services, without long protocol standardization and software design cycles; these are championed by the open architecture (OpenArch) and open signaling (OpenSig) initiatives.[33] If an active protocol extension or service shows long-lived and widespread applicability, it can later be incorporated into the standard protocol suite once the best implementation has been determined. This helps relieve the Standards Both Facilitate and Impede Dilemma (III.6).

- It is difficult to implement the high-layer protocol terminations, functionality, and switching described in the last section at high-speed. Active network processing moves this processing into the network layer switches, in conjunction with snooping and modifying on higher-layer protocol fields and manipulating data payloads. Systematic mechanisms are needed for accomplishing this in high-performance networks so that active processing does not impact the normal (nonactive) processing and so that the active processing itself can be done at high-speed.

The active networking community has defined a reference model that captures the essential functions that active nodes should support [Calvert 1999], as shown in Figure 5.58.

This model extends the architecture of a conventional Internet router to allow packets to be diverted from the normal forwarding path by packet filters, up through the NodeOS, and into execution environments (EEs) for active processing. EEs can be considered to be secure interpreters that provide the ability for active applications (AAs) to execute. A management EE (MEE) provides the management, monitoring, and control function of the active node [Jackson 2000].

This reference model indicates one of the keys to high-speed active networking: the separation of active processing from the normal forwarding path. It does not, however, reflect the implementation of the high-speed fast packet and datagram switches discussed in Sections 5.3 and 5.5, which distribute input and output processing. Just as lookup, classification, and scheduling are distributed among the switch ports, so should active processing [Decasper

---

[33]For which there are annual conferences.

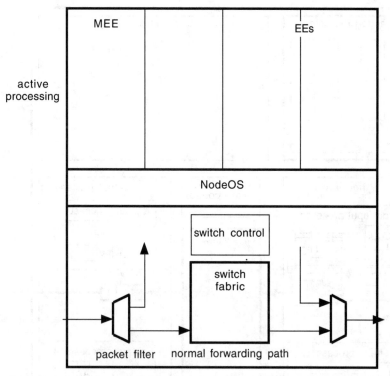

Figure 5.58   Active network node reference model.

1999]. Figure 5.59 overlays the active node reference model onto our high-speed switch architecture.

As in Figures 5.48 and 5.49, the processing is distributed along the ports or attached forwarding engines. Thus, the packet filtering function must occur per port in the input processing. There are then two places that active processing can occur: per port and globally to the switch. So, in addition to the active processing functional components shown in Figure 5.58, we add a capability of a portµOS and portEE that provides the environment necessary to allow the execution of per port active applications (portAAs).

Active Network Processing   *Active network processing should not impede the nonactive fast path; packet filters in the critical path must operate at line rate to pass nonactive packets. The ability to perform per packet active processing requires sufficient processing power to sustain the required active packet throughput.*

S-II.4a

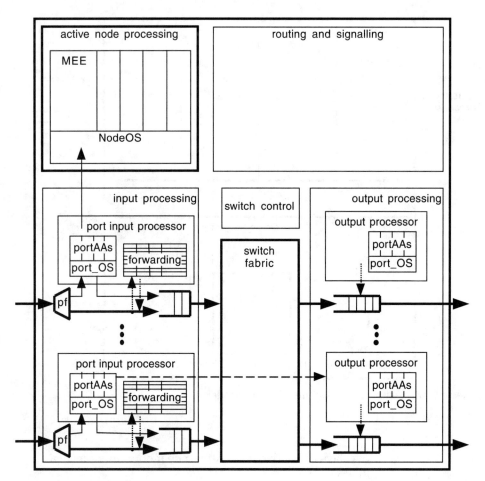

Figure 5.59   High-speed active router.

We can consider a range of active processing:

Global control plane functions.   Consist of processing that affects the node (and perhaps network) as a whole. An example of this is using traffic patterns to exert changes in the traffic management and forwarding functions on the node and exerting routing changes that propagate to other nodes. Clearly, this functionality can occur in the nodewide EEs. Similarly, network monitoring and control fit into this category.

***Per* flow control plane functions**.   Operate on the connection or flow state machine or control packets at the flow level. Examples of the former include modifying the behavior of the ATM connection or RSVP reservation state machines. This process can be generalized by defining a *connection model* or *flow model*, which has triggers that can fire to invoke active processing, in a manner similar to the IN (intelligent network) *call model* [Black 1988c]. In the case of connectionless datagram networks, individual control packets (network, transport, session, or application layer) must be filtered for active processing.

An example of this is an active caching algorithm that detects the destination IP address of a packet or URL in an HTTP request, and diverts the packet to a Web cache by replacing the destination IP address with the IP address of the best cached copy. In this particular example, the advantage of active router interaction is not only efficient examination and replacement of the URL and IP addresses, but the ability for the node to dynamically determine how to route the Web request based on current network connectivity and link state based on the ability to Exploit Local Knowledge (6B) and the Location of Data (7B). The forwarding redirection portion of the processing should operate within the *per* port active processing modules (or attached forwarding engines in the case of the shared forwarding engines shown in Figure 5.49). This will likely be done in concert with global control plane active processing, which uses the routing algorithms and knowledge of the cache location and properties to construct an active [Bhattacharjee 1998a] or adaptive [Zhang 1997] caching infrastructure (Section 8.3.1).

Per **packet control plane functions**.   Examine the contents of every packet in a flow. An example is active congestion control [Faber 1998], in which an active processing is used to perform intelligent discard when the node is congested. For example, high-frequency components in a wavelet encoding [Turner 1999b] or B and P frames in a MPEG-2 encoding [Bhattacharjee 1998b] can be dropped. This requires some custom processing at the switch port.

Per **packet data plane functions**.   Manipulate the contents of the packet in an significant manner, and may even sink and produce packets. This requires significant processing on the switch port. Examples include active transcoding which manipulates the payloads of every packet. This may be more effectively done by a separate transcoder, but it depends on the Resource Tradeoff Principle (2).

5.7   Summary

This chapter has described the components from which a high-speed network is constructed: links and switches. We first discussed the link characteristics that connect network nodes, and distinguished dedicated, multiplexed, and shared medium links. We then described link-layer components that perform layer 2 processing, such as optical regeneration, bridging, and MAC address switching.

Then, we moved up to the network layer, introducing the functionality required by layer 3 switches, and the performance problems with traditional store-and-forward packet switches. Connection-oriented fast packet switching was developed to meet the needs of high-speed networks, by using state to simplify the *per* packet forwarding decisions to a direct table lookup. The design of switch fabrics, which serve as the core of high-speed network nodes was then described. The desire to perform connectionless datagram forwarding, and the increased processing power available in VLSI circuits, has led to the implementation of the more complex *per* packet lookup, classification, and output scheduling functions at high-bandwidth link speed. Finally, we described the implementation of higher-layer functions and active network processing in high-speed network nodes.

5.7.1 Further Reading

The literature on link and switch technologies is vast, with extensive research performed over the last several decades. These sources can serve as a starting point by following their embedded references.

Link protocols and technologies are covered by the general networking texts referenced in Chapter 2. Specific sources also include [Spurgeon 2000] for Ethernet, [Goralski 2000] for SONET, and [Maxwell 1999, Abe 2000] for residential broadband including xDSL [Cioffi 1999a, 1999b] and HFC. The entire range of broadband access technologies is covered in [Gagnaire 1997, Papir 1992, and Modiano 1999]. Fiber optic transmission is covered in [Personick 1985], [Palais 1998]; optical free space transmission in [Karp 1988] and [Lambert 1995].

In depth treatments of interconnection networks and switching theory are provided in [Beneš 1965], [Reed 1987], [Ahmadi 1989], [Hui 1990], [Oie 1990], [Duato 1997], [Pattavina 1998], and [Turner 2000]. ATM switching systems, in particular, are covered in [Zegura 1993] and [Turner 1998]; a broader treatment of ATM, including the protocols, is in [dePrycker 1995], [Chen 1995], and [Händel 1998]. Switching systems from the telephony perspective, from electromechanical through electronic through photonic are covered in [Hills 1979], [Rey 1983], [McDonald 1983], [Noll 1998], [Bellamy 2000], and [Thompson 2000]. [Dhas 1991] contains a collection of many significant switching papers.

The field of optical networking made significant advances in the late 1990s, so it is important to use recent references for coverage of enabling components such MEMS switch elements, as well as science and technology increasing the bandwidth-$\times$-distance products such as dispersion management and control of nonlinear effects. Optical networking and photonic switching are comprehensively covered in [Hinton 1993], [Midwinter 1993a, 1993b], [Green 1993], [Kaminow 1997a, 1997b], [Prati 1997], [Ramaswami 1998], [Stern 1999], [Bononi 1999], [Kartalopoulos 2000], and [Sivalingam 2000]. [Mouftah 1999] contains a collection of significant papers on photonic switching. Special topics journal issues on optical networking and WDM include [Bala 1995a, 1995b], [Chlamtac 1995], [Choa 1999], and [IEEE 2000].

Wireless communications is covered in [Garg 1996] and [Rappaport 1996], with the emphasis on cellular telephony and [Geier 1999] with extensive coverage of IEEE 802.11. Satellite communications technology and systems are comprehensively covered in [Elbert 1997, 1999], [Hadjitheodosiu 1999], and [Richharia 1999].

A comprehensive treatment of both layer 2 and layer 3 network components is in [Minoli 1998] and [Perlman 2000]; the latter has a chapter of fast IP lookup. IP switching and MPLS are covered in [Davie 1998, 2000]. [Keshav 1998] and [Kumar 1998] provide good summaries of issues in modern IP switch design, with particular emphasis on scheduling and traffic. The tutorials [McKeown 1999b] and [Gupta 2000] provide broad coverage of fast IP switching, including address lookup, packet classification, buffering, and scheduling. [Srinivasan 1999b] provides a summary of lookup techniques and [Feldmann 2000] classification techniques. The requirements for IPv4 routers are specified in [Baker 1995]. [Bollapragada 2000] describes the architecture of several commercial IP routers. [Chao 1999a] is dedicated to fast datagram switching.

Quality of service and scheduling are covered in [Keshav 1997], and in depth treatment with an ATM perspective in [Giroux 1999].

NETWORK COMPONENT AXIOMS AND PRINCIPLES

L-II. Network Link Principle   *Network links must provide high-bandwidth connections between network nodes. Link-layer protocol processing should not introduce significant latency.*

L-8C. Link Protocol Scalability Principle   *Link protocols should be scalable in bandwidth, either variably or in discrete intervals (power-of-2 or order-of-magnitude). Header/trailer lengths and fields that relate to bandwidth should be long enough or contain a scale factor.*

L-II.2. Medium Access Control Principle   *The MAC protocol should efficiently arbitrate the shared medium, in either a fair manner or with the desired proportion.*

L-IIc. Link-Layer Components   *Link-layer components must sustain the data rate of the link, while not introducing significant delay.*

L-4F. Loss Characterization Principle   *Provide long-term and dynamic information on the reason for loss to higher layer protocols so that end-to-end mechanisms respond appropriately.*

L-4f. Early Filtering Principle   *Filter incoming data not destined for a node as early as possible and discard as much as possible at each layer.*

L-2C. Link-Layer Multicast Principle *Shared medium links provide native support for broadcast, essential for higher-layer control protocols and in support of multicast applications. Nonbroadcast point-to-point mesh LANs should provide broadcast and multicast support.*

S-II. Network Node Principle *Network nodes must support high-bandwidth, low-latency, end-to-end flows, as well as their aggregation. High-speed network nodes should provide a scalable number of high-bandwidth, low-delay interconnections.*

S-II.3. Store-and-Forward and Queueing Delay Minimization Principle *Store-and-forward delays should be avoided, and per-packet queuing should be minimized. In the ideal case, nodes should pipeline and cut-through packets with zero per packet delays.*

S-1Bc. Fast Packet Switch Critical Path Principle *Simplify and optimize per byte and per packet data manipulation and transfer control functions for implementation in the hardware critical path. State maintained per-connection streamlines per packet processing.*

S-5A. Connectionless versus Connection Tradeoff *The latency of connection setup must be traded against the increase in packet processing rate and resultant bandwidth increase achievable due to the less complex label swapping.*

S-8A. Packet Size and Variability Tradeoff *Packet size is a balance of a number of parameters that affect performance. Trade the statistical multiplexing and fine-grained control benefits of small packets against the efficiency of large packets. Trade the benefits to switch design of fixed cell size against the overhead of SAR and efficiency of variable packet size. Multiple discrete packet sizes increase flexibility at the cost of additional switch complexity. Hop-by-hop SAR localizes packet size optimizations a the cost of additional per hop delay and complexity.*

S-8B. Packet Control Field Structure *Optimize packet header and trailer fields for efficient processing. Fields should be simply encoded, byte aligned, and fixed length when possible. Variable, length fields should be prepended with their length.*

S-II.2. Switch Traffic Management *In a resource constrained environment, switches must support admission control with resource reservations to provide guaranteed service traffic classes and policing to prevent other traffic from interfering.*

S-6Cc. Congestion Avoidance and Control *Bound offered load by admission control, traffic policing, and traffic shaping. When impending congestion is detected by building queues, notify sources to throttle. When congestion occurs, drop end-to-end frames if larger than network packets.*

S-2B. Overengineering versus Optimality *Optimal traffic management policies use processing and memory, which also adds latency to connection establishment; trade these costs against the bandwidth wasted by overengineering and overprovisioning the network.*

S-1C. Functional Partitioning and Assignment Principle *Carefully determine what switch functionality is to be implemented in scarce or expensive technology.*

S-II.4f. NonBlocking Switch Fabric Principle *A nonblocking switch fabric is the core of a high-performance switch. Avoid blocking by space-division parallelism, internal speedup, and internal pipelined buffering with cut-through. Strictly and wide-sense nonblocking avoids the complexity and delay of path rearrangement.*

S-II.4q. Head-of-Line Blocking Avoidance Principle *Avoid head-of-line blocking. Output queuing requires internal speedup, expansion, or buffering. Virtual output queueing requires additional queues or queuing complexity. The two techniques must be traded against one another, and can be used in combination.*

S-III.4. Switch Scalability *The construction of switches with a large port count requires scalable switch fabrics. Exploit regular structures for implementation in VLSI or optics as the basis for recursively constructed fabrics with logarithmic growth complexity.*

S-2C. Switches Should Provide Native Multicast *Switches should provide native multicast support to conserve bandwidth and avoid latency of repeated transmission.*

S-1Bd. Fast Datagram Switch Principle *There is compelling motivation to perform high-speed connectionless datagram switching. Apply connection-oriented fast packet switching techniques to fast datagram switching, and exploit technology advances to implement the additional input and output processing in the critical path.*

S-II.4p. Packet Processing Rate *The packet processing rate (packets per second) is a key throughput measure of a switch. Packet processing software and shared parallel hardware resources must be able to sustain the average packet processing rate. Functions in the serial critical path must be designed for the worst case packet processing rate of the path to avoid queuing and blocking of subsequent packets.*

S-1Ch. Hardware versus Software Implementation of Input and Output Processing *In determining the appropriate implementation of input and output processing, trade the cost and feasibility of hardware against the complexity and feasibility of embedded controller software.*

S-II.4c. Bound Packet Classification Time *Packets that must be classified to potentially receive delay-bounded service must be classified before any queuing at the input. The classification operation must have delay bounds that meet the most stringent service class.*

S-II.4s. Output Scheduling and Queueing Granularity *Output scheduling must operate at line rate to support the traffic classes required. Finer-grained queueing and scheduling provides greater isolation of flows and control at the cost of increased queueing complexity.*

S-6C*d*. Discard to Keep Queues from Building   *Queue length should reflect transient traffic conditions and not be allowed to build in the steady state. Perform congestion avoidance and control including packet discard, to keep queues small locally, and throttle the source for end-to-end congestion avoidance.*

S-II.4*a*. Active Network Processing   *Active network processing should not impede the nonactive fast path; packet filters in the critical path must operate at line rate to pass nonactive packets. The ability to perform per packet active processing requires sufficient processing power to sustain the required active packet throughput.*

End Systems

We discussed how to achieve a high-performance path through the network in Chapters 3 and 4 and within the network nodes in Chapter 5. This chapter considers how end systems must be designed to enable end-to-end, low-latency, high-bandwidth communications between the edge of the network and applications. In particular, we will be concerned with implementation issues that affect the performance of all the protocol layers *inside* the end system in an integrated fashion. High-speed transport protocols and other end-to-end issues *between* end systems will be covered in Chapter 7 (which is why only one end system is highlighted in Figure 6.1). We will use the terms *end system* and *host* interchangeably in this chapter.

Without a low-latency, high-bandwidth pipe between a high-speed network and application memory, the host is the bottleneck in the end-to-end path. Thus, we first state the end system refinement of the High-Performance Paths Goal (II):[1]

End System Principle   *The communicating end systems are a critical component in end-to-end communications and must provide a low-latency, high-bandwidth path between the network interface and application memory.*

E-II

---

[1]A high-bandwidth, low-latency path must be provided between applications.

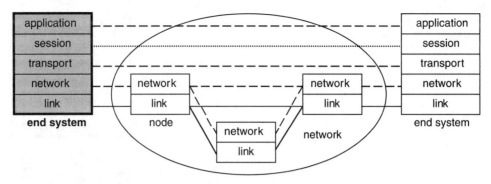

Figure 6.1   End system architecture and protocols.

To provide this high-performance path we must consider the host–network interface and host system hardware architecture (interconnect and memory system), as well as the software techniques to optimize protocol operation.

End system performance is concerned with supporting high-bandwidth, low-latency flows. This flow, however, is generally taking place in *support of* an application running on the end system, and thus it is vital that the communications do not consume so many resources that the application cannot perform useful work. Thus, a statement like "*This implementation of TCP runs at 1 Gb/s*" is not terribly useful unless it is accompanied by what sort of application workload is running that *utilizes* this bandwidth. An implementation of a protocol suite that utilizes so much of the CPU in support of a particular application that *other* applications cannot execute is not desirable.

A number of early end system and transport protocol performance studies did not consider this impact on applications. Therefore, it is particularly important to explicitly state the end system version of Application Primacy (I):

Application Primacy   *Optimization of communications processing in the end system must not degrade the performance of the applications using the network.*

E-I

This chapter is organized as follows: Section 6.1 describes the organization of the end system as a whole and introduces the hardware and software components of concern. It also discusses the traditional second-generation (1980s) layered I/O-based protocol implementation, and presents the ideal end system implementation model, based on the ideal network model from Chapter 2. Section 6.2 describes protocol software and the host operating system for high-speed networking. Principles and techniques such as critical path optimization, integrated layer processing (ILP), minimizing operating system context switches, and exploiting the virtual memory subsystem are discussed. Section 6.3 discusses host architecture and organization. Particular emphasis is placed on processor–memory interconnects to support a nonblocking high-bandwidth path between the network interface and application memory. Section 6.4 describes the implementation of high-speed host–network interfaces. Finally, Section 6.5 summarizes this chapter, reiterates the design principles, and provides some pointers for further reading.

6.1.   End System Components

We cannot overly stress the importance in considering the entire end system as a *system of subsystems*, consisting of all of the components involved in communications.

This section introduces the components and organization of traditional workstation class end systems, both from a hardware and software perspective. We then describe traditional I/O-based communications using a protocol stack and discuss the inefficiencies of this organization. Finally, we introduce an architectural model for an ideal high-performance end system. This will be used as a target when subsequent sections discuss the details and realities of various parts of the end system architecture.

6.1.1   End System Hardware

Figure 6.2 shows a generic hardware block diagram of a traditional workstation class system.

Host subsystems of interest to our pursuit of high-speed networking consist of

CPU.   An arithmetic and logic unit responsible for running user applications, communications protocols, and the operating system; there may be multiple CPUs in a single host.

Memory subsystem.   Stores programs and data.

Processor–memory interconnect.   Transfers instructions and data between the CPU, memory, and I/O subsystem.

I/O control.   Controls and moves data to and from a variety of differing format and data rate I/O devices; this may be a single general-purpose controller with a bus datapath or a sophisticated set of I/O processors with extensive buffering and caching capabilities.

Mass storage.   Generally magnetic and/or optical disks, which provide file system storage for programs and data, as well as secondary or auxiliary storage for virtual memory.

User I/O.   Interface to the user, for example, monitor, keyboard, mouse, and printers.

Network interface.   Connects the network to the host system, and may perform a range of protocol processing functions.

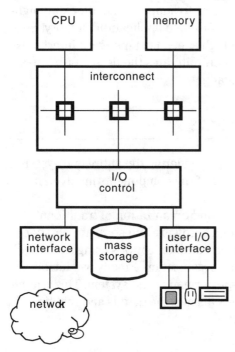

Figure 6.2 End system hardware.

6.1.2 End System Software

The other important decomposition of end system components is software based. The main software modules of interest to us for high-speed networking are shown in Figure 6.3:

Applications. The programs using communication services (covered in Chapter 8).

Protocol stack. The communication protocol processing (whether the protocols are located *within* operating system will be discussed in Section 6.2.2).

Operating system. Controls and manages host system resources, in particular:

Memory management. Manages physical and virtual memory and the virtual address translation tables.

Process scheduler. Manages and allocates CPU processing resources to threads, processes, and programs.

I/O subsystem. Translates user program I/O requests into the privileged system I/O instructions to the I/O controllers, and includes device-specific drivers.

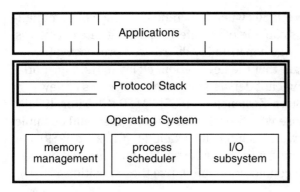

Figure 6.3 End system software.

The fact that the end system terminates *all* the layers in the protocol stack from physical up through application poses a particular challenge in optimizing the implementation of these layers; this is discussed in the next subsection. Note for now that the location of protocol processing can be in the end system software or in the network interface itself, or both.

6.1.3 End System Bottlenecks

Just as we emphasized the importance of the entire path through the network in Chapter 3, we must ensure that all the hardware components and software modules in the communications path between the network and application are of sufficiently high bandwidth $R = \min(r_i)$ and low latency $D = \Sigma\, d_i$ to provide an end-to-end high-performance path between communicating applications. This is particularly challenging in the end system, which is a complex set of hardware and software components interacting to perform protocol processing and run applications. Thus, we explicitly state the end system version of the Systemic Optimization Principle (IV):

Systemic Elimination of End System Bottlenecks   *The host organization, processor–memory interconnect, memory subsystem, operating system, protocol stack, and host–network interface are all critical components in end system performance, and must be optimized in concert with one another.*

E-IV

This can be viewed as a requirement to observe the End System Principle (E-II), that is, to have any hope of achieving Principle E-II we must apply Principle E-IV. Thus, in designing new high-performance end systems, it is vital to understand where the bottlenecks[2] are in existing systems by measurement and analysis, and in proposed systems by simulation.

[2]Technically, there can be only a single bottleneck at a time.

There was a period in the late 1980s when the grand challenge of communications was to design networks capable of transferring data at rates in excess of 1 Gb/s. Protocol processing was constraining distributed processing [Svobodova 1989], and it was thought that the key bottleneck lay in the transport protocols. This resulted in significant debate among the advocates of new transport protocols (such as Blast [Zwaenepoel 1985] VMTP [Cheriton 1986] and NETBLT [Clark 1987]), those who thought that protocols should be implemented in hardware in the network adapter (for example, [Chesson 1989], and those who thought that TCP would perform quite well if implemented properly. The following end system conjectures summarize these positions:

EC1. Designing a new transport protocol enables high-speed communication.

EC2. Implementing protocols on the host–network interface will enable high-speed networking.

EC3. Implementing protocol functionality in hardware speeds it up.

While there is some basis for each of these statements, the mere replacement of an existing transport protocol (such as TCP) by a new transport protocol and implementing it in hardware on the host–network interface does not *in itself* solve the problem.[3]

As we discussed in Chapter 2, it is critical to analyze existing end system architectures to determine where overhead and bottlenecks lie. It does little good to highly optimize operations that are not part of the bottleneck, or to create other bottlenecks as a side effect of an optimization. Thus, these conjectures *in isolation* violate the Selective Optimization Principle (1) and its corollaries, the Second-Order Effect Corollary (1A), and Functional Partitioning and Assignment Corollary (1C).

Considerations of the tradeoffs between hardware and software protocol functionality [Chesson 1989] and wide dissemination of the analysis of an existing protocol (TCP over IP) [Clark 1989a][4] provided needed perspective on where the bottlenecks *really* are, and what needed fixing. It was observed that the significant overheads were in the operating system and in per-byte operations such as checksumming and copying, as well as timer management. The approach shifted to systemic analysis and elimination of bottlenecks with emphasis on related operating system and protocol implementation efficiencies,

---

[3]This parallels the attempts to enhance the performance of specific operations by adding instructions to CPUs without properly considering the overall impact on instruction pipelines or the tradeoffs between processor complexity and the chip real estate available to 1st level caches, resulting in the wide application of RISC principles to even legacy processor architectures (such as the i86) in about the same time frame.

[4]However, this sort of analysis had been previously done in other contexts, albeit with more limited distribution, for protocols such as IBM SNA (systems network architecture).

as well as providing sufficient memory bandwidth to the network interface [Clark 1990, Sterbenz 1990a].

In the end, the transport protocol debate was irrelevant, due to the explosion of the Internet and pervasiveness of TCP. TCP is now the legacy data transport protocol of the global Internet, and for better or worse will be with us indefinitely. Since Backward Compatibility Inhibits Radical Change (III.7),a main thrust of research in the early 2000s is on how to optimize TCP for high-performance given the evolution of high-speed network infrastructure, and what changes can be made in the protocol without breaking previous implementations.

Optimize and Enhance Widely Deployed Protocols   *The practical difficulty in replacing protocols widely deployed on end systems indicates that it is important to optimize existing protocol implementations and add backward-compatible enhancements, rather than only trying to replace them with new protocols.*

E-III.7

6.1.4   Traditional End System Implementation

Traditional implementations of communications in the end system suffer from two important defects that limit performance: treating networked communication in the same way as general-purpose I/O and layered implementation of the protocol stack.

6.1.4.1   *Programmed versus Overlapped I/O*

Originally, all I/O processing was performed by the main CPU and operating system; this is called programmed I/O (PIO). The problem is that I/O operations are extremely slow relative to CPU computations and memory operations: Disk transfers are orders of magnitude slower than the CPU cycle time; character and unit-record I/O are orders of magnitude slower still. In PIO, the processor waits for each I/O operation to complete before resuming processing. In second computing generation systems,[5] I/O processing was moved off the host system to exploit parallelism and asynchrony, so that programs would not block on I/O operations.

Third computing generation mainframe processors continued this trend with sophisticated I/O processors (IOPs), typified by the IBM System/360

---

[5]Here we mean generations of computing systems rather than communications generations described in Chapter 2.

channels [Padegs 1964], Burroughs B5500 and 6500 series I/O processors [Enslow 1974, Doran 1979], and CDC 6600 PPUs (peripheral processing units) [Thornton 1970].[6] IOPs are attached directly to memory to completely overlap I/O and computations, to allow specialized hardware tuned to I/O processing, and to provide a configurable range of I/O bandwidths. This style of I/O processing was particularly amenable to block-mode I/O, and drove the architecture of intelligent terminal controllers over a decade before the advent of workstations and file servers.

In the 1980s a subset of this architecture became common in workstation class computers called *direct memory access* (DMA), in which a DMA controller is responsible for copying I/O data between memory and I/O controllers. We will discuss IOP and DMA host architectures in Section 6.3.

6.1.4.2 Overhead in I/O-Based Communications

Traditionally, network communication has been handled in the same manner as I/O to peripheral devices, with the network interface treated by the end system as just another I/O device. The performance implications of this, particularly when coupled with a layered implementation, are profound.

First, even with dedicated I/O processors or DMA engines, conventional I/O mechanisms are not well suited for high-speed communications. A significant problem is that I/O controllers are designed for the entire range of I/O devices, from fast disks to slow character devices, and are not generally capable of handling the bandwidth that high-speed applications require.[7] So just as CPU hardware and software are best not dedicated to I/O processing, general-purpose I/O mechanisms are not well suited to high-speed communications.

Second, I/O processing requires a context switch to the operating system to issue the I/O instructions, which are privileged. When coupled with a process per layer implementation, we get a data and control flow graph that looks something like Figure 6.4, which shows the transmission of a block of data block (with two protocol layers shown).

The top of the figure shows the division of processes, including the application program, two protocol layers, the operating system, followed by the I/O processor (or DMA controller) and network interface. When the application initiates a request to send data, a context switch occurs to the transport protocol, which performs fragmentation of the application data unit into multiple transport packets, and protocol encapsulation and processing to send each

---

[6]Many systems that pioneered new architectural concepts are documented in [Enslow 1974, Bell 1971, Bell 1978, Siewiorek 1982]; these are required reading for a historical perspective on computer and end system architecture.

[7]Nor should they; this would be a waste of unneeded high-performance hardware for low-performance I/O; graphics subsystems have developed their own special-purpose high-speed interfaces.

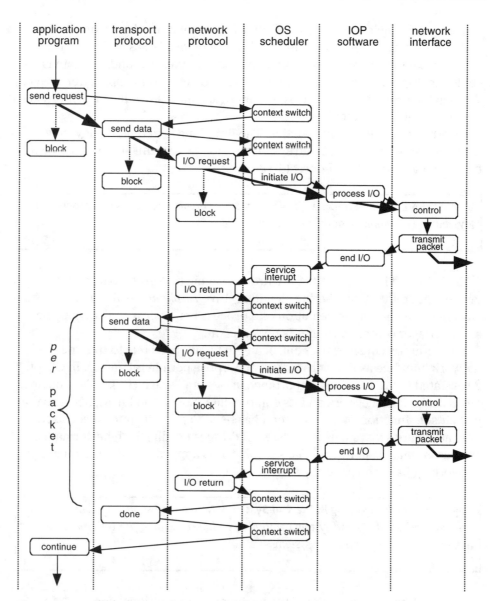

Figure 6.4   Layered I/O model communications flow.

packet. A context switch goes to the network layer for its encapsulation, and an I/O request is made to transmit the packet via the network interface. The operating system I/O subsystem software processes the I/O request, sends it to the I/O control hardware, which passes it to the network interface for transmission.[8] This transport layer / network layer / I/O loop occurs for *each* packet in the application data unit.

[8]And typically link layer an MAC processing, beginning with second-generation (1980s) networking.

Two inefficiencies can be seen. First, the control flow (thin arrows) is long and convoluted, jumping back and forth between processes and incurring multiple expensive operating system context switches. Second, the data is copied multiple times for each packet (thick arrows), from application space, through the protocol layer processes for encapsulation (or decapsulation) and then to the network interface.

Clearly we can do better than this. The first thing is to omit the layering overhead, so we restate the end system version of Layering as an Implementation Technique Performs Poorly (4A):

End System Layering Principle   *Layered protocol architecture does* not *depend on a layered process implementation in the end system.*

E-4A

As described in Section 2.3.4, we are not saying that protocols should not be layered, but rather that layering shouldn't drive *implementation* in an absurd way. In particular, implementation as a process per layer with data copying and interlayer context switches is not efficient.

Furthermore, consider the control and data overhead due to treating the network interface as if it were a general-purpose peripheral device. In Chapter 2 we stated the Networking Importance in System Design (I.4). This is obvious when designing a network and its components (nodes and links), because that is their sole function. While the trend has been to provide more specialized host hardware subsystems for classes of devices needing high-performance, such as graphic displays and mass storage, this application of the principle to networking has been painfully slow.

Importance of Networking in the End System   *Networking should be considered a first-class citizen of the end system computing architecture, on a par with memory or high-performance graphics subsystems.*

E-I.4

Now that we have considered the problems in a traditional approach for supporting communications in the end system, we are ready to consider the other extreme of an ideal end system architecture.

6.1.5   Ideal End System Architecture

In Chapter 2 we introduced an ideal end-to-end model for low-latency, high-bandwidth communication. Recall that two of the primary factors in designing low-latency systems are Store and Forward Avoidance (II.3) and Blocking Avoidance (II.4), by using such techniques as cut-through and pipelining. In

Chapter 5 we considered how to apply these principles to network nodes. In this chapter, we will do the same within the end system.

Figure 6.5 shows an end system view of the decomposed ideal network model (Figure 2.2). The network is shown as a cloud that is completely transparent to the end systems. The ideal end system supports the transfer of data between the *application* memory and network interface with unlimited bandwidth and no latency: $R = \infty$ and $D = 0$. Two end systems are shown because we will need to consider both transmission and reception of data, but we are concerned *only* within individual end systems in this chapter; end-to-end issues and transport protocols are the subject of Chapter 7.

The goal we will try to achieve is a *zero-copy* end system, in which packets move between application memory and the network without the latency of per packet store-and-forward hops or per byte manipulation loops of the entire packet [Sterbenz 1990a]. This is the end system version of Store and Forward Avoidance (II.3):

Copy Minimization Principle   *Data copying, or any operation that involves a separate sequential per byte touch of data, should be avoided. In the ideal case, a host–network interface should be zero copy.*

E-II.3

Note that we do not consider pipelining to be data copying or moving in this sense, although data moves through a pipeline. Parallelism can mask the effect of sequential data touching, copying, and moving. What we are trying to avoid is the case where data is manipulated, copied, or moved byte by byte (or word by word) by a processor exclusive of other operations, which contributes a latency of kbt/w, where k is the number of passes through a chunk of data b bits long, with w bits (byte or word) operated in parallel per time t.

Thus, we will discuss the host and network interface architectures that realize this ideal. In practice, existing protocols, operating system, and application semantics may not make zero-copy interfaces possible, in which case the goal is to minimize the number of copies. An example is the case where a transmission buffer must be held until reception can be acknowledged for transmission, requiring a one copy transmission interface.

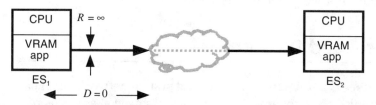

Figure 6.5   Ideal end system model.

Since we are concerned with interapplication communication, the end system model needs to support direct access between the network and the memory in which the application resides. We will model this as transferring data between the memory space of communicating applications, as if the memory modules were directly attached to the network. This is referred to as *memory as a network abstraction* [Delp 1985, 1988, 1991, Tam1 1990b]. There are two ways to do this (discussed in Section 6.3.2) but for now we will assume multiported memory, called VRAM (video RAM which is conventionally used for frame buffers). A pair of sequential ports (input and output) connect to the network for distributed application communication, and a conventional random access port connects to the CPU for local program execution, as shown in Figure 6.5. When an application wishes to send a chunk of data, it merely shifts it out of the sequential port, as shown for end system ES_1. When an application receives data, it merely shifts it into its memory space, as shown for ES_2. Thus, the end-to-end model is that of a zero-copy nonblocking pipe between application memory across the network.

Not surprisingly, the ideal model is too simplistic for implementation for several reasons. Physical memory is addressed in bytes or words, and we cannot expect processors to block for the speed of light latency through the network for every word transfer and to maintain end-to-end synchronization. Furthermore, the network is not a perfect medium: Data may be dropped, duplicated, or delivered out of order, and bits may be corrupted. We can't assume that just because we push a stream of bits out of one side that it will all be delivered properly and in order to the other side. Thus, link and transport protocols that do error and flow control are needed. Furthermore, although we may know what data to push out the transmitting end, the receiving end system needs to know what data has arrived at the receiving end, and *where* in memory it needs to reside for the application. Furthermore, the transmitting end may need to know when the receiving end had successfully received the data in case it needs to be modified or deleted. Thus, we need to understand the application semantics of when transmitted data is available to be overwritten, and received data needs to be mapped into the application address space. The transport protocol and operating system provide the needed support.

We will discuss host architectures that are amenable to zero and minimal copy in Section 6.3, host–network interface designs in Section 6.4, and the end-to-end transport protocol mechanisms in Chapter 7.

6.2   Protocol and OS Software

This section describes the software aspects of end system networking, in particular how to optimize protocol processing in software as well as issues related to the host operating system. We will be concerned with two major aspects of end system implementation: control and data. *Control* consists of the instruction processing within protocol software in support of such functions as error and flow control, the establishment of data flows, as well as the transfer of control between protocol functions. *Data* consists of the movement of data between the network interface, protocols, and the application using communications services.

First, we will examine ways to optimize protocol software. Then we will examine aspects of the operating system critical to communications performance: process and memory management. Finally, we will describe the important ways to accelerate the implementation of high-performance protocols in the host system: protocol bypass and integrated layer processing (ILP).

6.2.1   Protocol Software

The problem of optimizing communication software for high-performance is similar to other high-performance software optimizations: separate the normal critical path (defined in Section 2.3.1) processing and carefully optimize the critical path code.

> **Critical Path Principle**   *Optimize end system critical path protocol processing software and hardware, consisting of normal data path movement and the control functions on which it depends.*
>
> **E-1B**

Figure 6.6 shows an example execution flow graph for a piece of protocol software, which consists of a number of branches and loops. The critical path is shown by the thicker arrows within the graph. Note that the critical path itself may contain loops and branches.

The primary concern in optimizing code is to minimize the instruction path length I, measured by the time of execution, rather than the number of instructions.[9] Loops are of a particular concern, and a tight loop encoding can have a significant benefit on the overall instruction path. Furthermore, it is important that the instruction cache be large enough to hold the entire loop I_l to avoid the penalty of a cache miss per loop traversal. It may be better to unroll the loop into multiple parts rather than suffer a cache miss per loop. Data structures should be aligned and sized to fit in cache lines to avoid the severe effect of cache misses on every access. A similar effect can be a concern with other components in the memory hierarchy; for example,

---

[9]In modern RISC uniprocessors, these measures are similar, assuming all data is in cache. Care should be taken to include the stall overhead for any cross chip synchronization that must take place. A single read from off chip can take more time than the entire rest of the path. Superscalar processors introduce further parallelism within a single instruction thread.

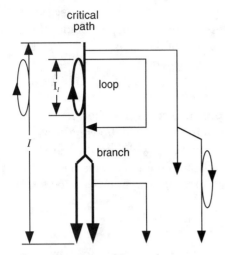

Figure 6.6 Instruction paths.

it is desirable that loops should be small enough and aligned to reside in a single virtual memory page. The consequences are not as severe as of cache misses, since the working set consists of multiple pages coresident in memory.

> **Consider the Side Effects**   *Optimizations frequently have unintended side effects to the detriment of performance. It is important to consider, analyze, and understand the consequences of optimization and difficulties in the end system due to the complex interaction of applications, operating system, and protocols.*
>
> **E-IV$_1$**

We can divide protocol processing functions into three classes: data manipulation, transfer control, and asynchronous control.

1. *Data manipulation* functions [Clark 1990] read and modify data:

   - Moving data to and from the network, including link and physical layer line coding (and decoding).
   - Bit error detection and correction.
   - Intermediate moving of data, for example, between the intermediate system buffers and application address space.
   - Buffering for retransmission; application and protocol semantics frequently require that a copy of transmitted data be retained until successful receipt is acknowledged from the receiving end.

- Encryption/decryption of data and control information.

- Presentation formatting of data for host or network encoding (such as ASN.1 or XDR).[10]

These core functions, if present, are part of the critical path. Moving data to and from the network is the essential datapath function that will always occur. Error detection is necessary for reliable protocols, which also may correct errors if an error correcting code is used. The need for intermediate moves of data and buffering for retransmission depends on the host–network interface architecture and application semantics; in a zero-copy interface, we completely eliminate these. Encryption and presentation formatting are present if needed for security and data format compatibility between end systems and the network.

2. *Transfer control* functions [Clark 1990] are control operations directly related to the *per* byte or *per* packet transfer of data:

- Flow/congestion control at the end system used to pace or rate control the entry of packets into the network, including scheduling and/or traffic shaping.

- Detecting lost or mis-sequenced packets at the receiving end.

- Acknowledgment of received packets to the sender.

- Multiplexing and demultiplexing of multiple application flows.

- Time-stamping and clock recovery of real-time packets.

- Framing/delineation, encapsulation/decapsulation, and fragmentation/reassembly[11] of protocol data units.

These functions are all candidates for the critical path, even though they may occur less frequently than data manipulation functions. As mentioned in Section 2.3.1, the determinant is whether the processing of subsequent packets depends on a particular function. This may be related to whether or not the control is in band or out of band. Out-of-band control runs asynchronously to the data flow and need not be part of the critical path. For example, the only in-band component of acknowledgments might be incrementing a counter in the connection state. The sequence of operations to build and send the acknowledgment message would be an out-of-band, relatively infrequent operation, not part of the critical path.

Careful analysis is needed to determine the dependency of data flow and frequency of these operations to determine if critical path optimization is necessary.

---

[10]ISO abstract syntax notation 1 and Sun Microsystems external data representation.
[11]In high-speed networking it is important to Avoid Hop-by-Hop Fragmentation (T-5F), but if it happens, it is a transfer control function.

3. *Asynchronous control* functions occur at connection or flow granularity, or are asynchronous to per packet data transfer:

- Connection setup and modification
- Per connection granularity flow and congestion control mechanisms
- Routing algorithms and link state updates
- Session control

These operations generally happen at significantly larger time granularity than data manipulation or transfer control functions, but we can't ignore them completely. While not candidates for critical path optimization, datagram transactions may have to wait on these, and applications typically have some requirements on connection establishment time.

6.2.1.1 Parallel Code

Another technique available for consideration is to parallelize protocol processing function. In general, parallelization of code is done for two reasons:

1. Reduce wait states by removing dependencies among parts to allow processing to continue, while another part of the processing is blocked waiting for an event, such as I/O.

2. Speed up protocols by dividing them into parts that can execute simultaneously on multiple processors: by send/receive, layer, function, or independent protocol data units.

For communications processing, the first case is handled at the system level by allowing I/O overlap and DMA [Xu 1995], as described in Section 6.1.4. The second case is not useful for the typical case of an application running on a uniprocessor; no speedup results from the parallel implementation of communications code. Limited speedup is possible on a multiprocessor end system but great care must be taken to actually achieve increased performance without interfering with application performance. It may be desirable to provide such implementations on nonshared memory, massively parallel machines to be able to keep individual processors busy and avoid communication hotspots in the interprocessor interconnects.

The ability to parallelize a particular protocol depends on several factors [Touch 1996]:

- The less interpacket state, the more easily a protocol can be parallelized.
- The maximum achievable parallelism is relatively independent of the type of decomposition (for example, by packet or by function).

- Intraconnection parallelism is limited by the tightness of coupling of state interactions; the more protocol functions that introduce dependencies (for example, reordering, loss recovery) [Feldmeier 1992], the less parallelism is achievable.

Finally, it is possible to consider parallel implementations of host–network interfaces; this will be discussed in Section 6.3.3.

6.2.2   Operating Systems

The operating system is the host control program, which provides an environment for application programs and user interfaces (such as command shells and the window managers, which are *not* part of the operating system itself in properly engineered systems). The operating system manages end system resources, such as processor cycles and memory, and allows them to be shared in a controlled manner by application programs and support activities, such as communications protocol processing.

We are primarily concerned with two components of the operating system: process management and memory management. These subsystems have a significant impact on, and offer opportunities to improve the performance of, communications protocols and applications.

6.2.2.1   Process Management

A process is an executing instantiation of a program, and consists of

- The locus of control through an instruction sequence.
- Data that is used and generated.
- Temporary data such as intermediate values and the program stack.
- Associated state that will allow the process to resume execution if interrupted and suspended.

The process state is stored in a data structure called a *process control block* (PCB) or *task control block* in some systems.[12] The PCB typically contains a process id and process state, state registers such as the program counter, program status word, and stack pointer, general and floating point registers, pointers to or identifiers of related processes, and address limits of the process.

---

[12]Unfortunately, PCB is also used for *protocol control block* for protocol state data structures; we will confine the use of PCB to the operating system sense to this section.

6.2.2.1.1   Scheduling and Context Switching

The switching between processes is referred to as a *context switch*. This is because the process to be suspended must have its context saved into its PCB,
and the context of the process to be executed must be restored from its PCB
into CPU registers. This is a relatively costly operation, on the order of hundreds of RISC instructions [Mogul 1991]. A context switch can occur for several reasons:

- A process will be suspended if a page fault occurs, with a switch to the
  OS page fault handler.

- A process blocks when it performs I/O and must wait for results.

- A process may get suspended by the CPU scheduler when it has exceeded its time quantum or when a higher-priority process is ready to
  execute.[13]

Context Switch Avoidance   *The number of context switches should be minimized,
and approach one per application data unit.*

                                                                    E-II.6a

---

For end system protocols, context switches occur for two reasons:

1. Transmission and reception of packets.
2. Switching between different processes in the protocol processing (for
   example, processes associated with different layers in the protocol stack
   or suboperations within a layer).

The first situation of a packet transmission or reception is generally necessary. In the case of a transmission, the sending of a packet involves privileged
system code to interact with the network interface to send the packet. In the
case of reception, once the packet has arrived, the application process must
be notified if it is blocked waiting.

The second situation, which we showed in Figure 6.4, can be avoided by
sensible protocol implementations. Thus, we should attempt to minimize the
number of context switches per packet sent or received to at most one for
each application data unit. It may be possible to do even better than this by
remapping, grouping data units, and interrupting a process only when a particular packet has not yet been received.

One way to reduce context switch overhead and maintain modularity of
protocol software is by the use of lightweight processes that share an address
space, typically called *threads*. This was recognized as a requirement for ap-

---

[13]Critical kernel processes may be *nonpreemptable*, indicating that they cannot be suspended.

plication performance in the 1960s, and implemented in a number of mainframe operating systems such as OS/360 (called tasks and subtasks).[14]

Multiple threads share an address space (code and data), as shown in Figure 6.7. While each needs some state (PCB and program stack), an interthread switch does not involve any memory management overhead. Sharing data between threads is naturally efficient, since threads have access to the same data segments. A conventional heavyweight process is simply a process that has only one thread. Thus, by implementing parts of a protocol suite as threads rather than (heavyweight) processes, the amount of overhead for context switches is reduced, as is the copying of data between processes. Protocols can still be modular, by implementing them as modules. Subroutine calls go down the stack and upcalls [Clark 1985] go up the stack.

6.2.2.1.2 Interrupts versus Polling

While it is possible to avoid many of the interrupts and context switches that result from poor distribution of protocol layers and functions among processes, a mechanism is still needed for processes to be aware of incoming data. Interrupts allow asynchronous notification, but are expensive by forcing a context switch to service the interrupt. An alternative technique is for a process to *poll* a data structure to determine if data has arrived into a buffer [Metcalfe 1978]. When the process has some knowledge of the arrival pattern, polling can be considerably more efficient.

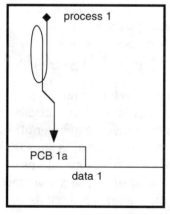

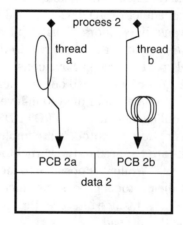

a: process   b: threads per process

Figure 6.7 Threads and processes.

---

[14]The term *thread* came into widespread use with the introduction of the Mach OS [Young 1987]. This highlights the dangers of not being aware of history; it is generally thought that Mach invented threads, when they had been in widespread use for two decades.

> **Interrupt versus Polling** *Interrupts provide the ability to react to asynchronous events, but are expensive operations. Polling can be used when a protocol has knowledge of when information arrives.*
>
> **E-4H**

The disadvantage with polling is getting the poll interval right. If the interval is too short, cycles are wasted on the poll that could be used by other activities in the same process, or by other processes. If the interval is too long, the receipt of data will be delayed, and more buffer memory may be required to avoid overwrite of subsequent incoming data.

Interrupts allow asynchronous overlap of other activities and processes until data has arrived, at the cost of interrupt servicing and context switching in the operating system.

Both of these schemes can coexist to reduce the overhead below an interrupt per packet. For example, when a burst of packets arrives (perhaps corresponding to an application data unit), polling can be used to handle the interburst packets, with an interrupt per burst.

6.2.2.1.3 Kernel versus User Space

Operating systems have at least two states of operation: user and kernel.[15] Applications run in user state, which has limited and controlled access to system level functions such as memory management, process scheduling, and I/O instructions. This is necessary to prevent accidental violations of other process spaces, unauthorized reading and writing data of other applications, manipulating the scheduler or I/O devices in a denial-of-service attack, and installing security bypass back doors. Thus, applications access system facilities via *system calls*, which perform the required authorization checks. These user/kernel space crossings have considerably more overhead than a simple subroutine call or interthread communication.

Protocols use a number of system-level facilities such as buffer management, scheduling, and access to I/O or DMA mechanisms for packet transmission and reception. If protocols are implemented in user space, a number of system calls are required to the kernel for each packet transferred, as shown in Figure 6.8a.[16] While it is possible to move some of these functions into user space with the protocol processing, such as buffer management, they will tend to be less efficient, since interuser protection mechanisms such as bounds checking, add overhead.

---

[15]The kernel is called *nucleus* or *supervisor* in some operating systems.
[16]If the transport protocol does all processing by calling the network layer, then the dotted arrows will not be present.

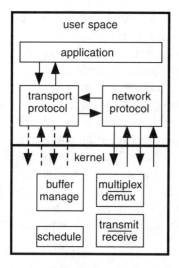

a: user space protocols

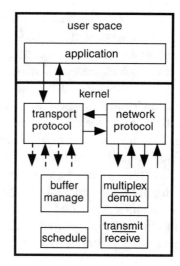

b: kernel protocols

Figure 6.8   Kernel and user space.

User/Kernel Crossing Avoidance   *The number of user space calls to the kernel should be minimized due to the overhead of authorization and security checks, the copying of buffers, and the inability to directly invoke needed kernel functions.*

E-II.6*k*

By implementing protocols in the kernel, this can be reduced to a single kernel crossing when the application calls and context switches to the kernel protocol routines, as shown in Figure 6.8b. As usual, this comes at some cost. If the kernel is not modular and well organized with open interfaces, it can be difficult to efficiently implement enhanced and new protocols. This is a significant issue for the research community in prototyping and analyzing new ideas. Thus, research protocols are sometimes implemented in user space, on which experiments and incremental improvements can take place. They are then moved to kernel space by operating system implementers. More commonly, research protocols are implemented in variants of Unix, which have open source code and loadable kernel modules, allowing experiments in performance as well as functionality. Keep It Simple and Open (IV$_2$) applies to operating systems to enable advancement in protocol science.

6.2.2.2   *Memory Management*

One of the most important functions of an operating system is to manage memory, which consists of allocating memory to processes and controlling the manner in which memory is shared between processes only when authorized. In the early days of computing, this consisted of policies for partitioning the available main memory between the operating system and processes. With increasing desire to multitask and timeshare computing systems, the amount of available memory became a bottleneck. The solution was in virtual memory: providing programs with a virtual address space decoupled from real (physical) memory.

In the context of networking, we are concerned with memory management for two reasons. First, we want efficient mechanisms for allocating and manipulating pools of memory that will be used for protocol data buffers. Secondly, to avoid extra copies we need mechanisms for sharing and remapping buffers between protocol processing and the application. Recall that one of the implementation techniques described in Chapter 2 to avoid copies was remapping (Figure 2.11). One of the ways to do this is by manipulating handles or pointers to buffers among protocol modules.

Avoid Data Copies by Remapping   *Use memory and buffer remapping techniques to avoid the overhead of copying and moving blocks of data.*

E-II.3m

Another way to remap buffers is to use virtual memory mechanisms provided by the operating system. In a typical virtual memory system, each process has its own address space. These address spaces may be linear with addresses starting at zero or they may be segmented, in which case each segment has a unique (per process) identifier with address beginning at zero. Segmented address spaces were introduced in the Burroughs systems and Multics [Organick 1972]. Segments have a number of useful properties, including application and object level sharing and protection, as well as providing a variable allocation unit that can correspond to application data units for distributed communications.[17]

Figure 6.9 shows a simple single-level address translation that maps virtual addresses v to real memory addresses r. The PCB points to the origin of a page table for a particular process. The virtual address is divided into a high-order set of bits $v.p$ which is the offset into the page table. This page table entry points to the location in real memory that contains the page. The low order bits $v.o$ are added to the page origin address to compute the real address r. In a segmented virtual memory, a second-level segment table is added; segments are normally divided into pages to simplify memory and secondary backing storage management with fixed size pages.[18]

---

[17]Segmented virtual memory should not *restrict* the programming model by forcing applications to artificially partition into small segments, as was the case with the Intel 80286.
[18]We have omitted many details of memory management, for example, the use of a hardware TLB to cache $v \rightarrow r$ mappings and avoid the overhead of software segment and page table traversal with every address reference.

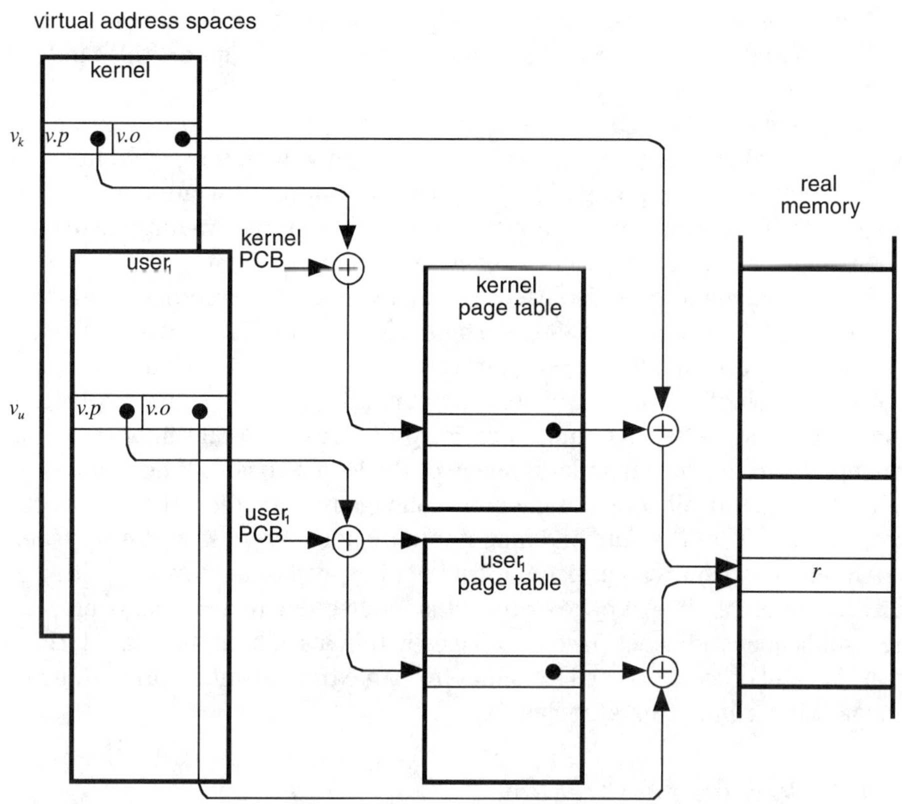

virtual address spaces

Figure 6.9   Virtual address translation.

Consider the case of a data received from the network. Figure 6.9 shows
two virtual address spaces: the kernel space and one of the user address
spaces for a particular application, user$_1$. The protocols, implemented in kernel space,[19] address a block of data *via* virtual addresses v_k. Once the data is
ready to be passed to the application, the protocol simply maps the block into
the user address space so that user addresses v_u point to the same real memory locations as v_k. This is done by inserting the entry into the user$_1$ page
table, without moving the data in real memory. The user process can then resume processing after a context switch. The reception of data has thus resulted in (at most) a single context switch and no copying of data.

There are overheads with this remapping, in excess of a single pointer
rewriting. Virtual address translation data structures, as well as the translation
lookaside buffer (TLB) contents, must be modified. Pages must be *pinned* or
nailed in physical memory and locked from other access during remapping,
and the corresponding control bits must be manipulated. For the reliable
transmission of data, the page must be pinned and locked until the receiving

---

[19]Or protocols implemented on the network interface, which addresses kernel space directly.

end has successfully acknowledged receipt, preventing the sending process from modifying it. The operating system semantics must support this mode of operation (unlike Unix sockets).

Remapping a page can be a very expensive operation in operating systems and processor hardware that have not been designed with this function in mind.[20] Furthermore, pinning of pages impacts resource allocation, by reducing the amount of memory available for other applications. Memory management policies must be carefully modified in this environment.

When virtual memory is also used as the mechanism to reference data objects across the network [Li 1990, Sterbenz 1990b, Tam 1990a], we refer to it as *distributed virtual shared memory* (DVSM), which is the virtual memory implementation of distributed shared memory (DSM). Rather than explicitly transferring data between communicating processes, data on remote systems is mapped into the virtual address space of the local process. When data is referenced but not locally present, memory management invokes the transport protocol to transfer the data and map it into the local process address space.

DVSM mechanisms can assist in masking the speed of light by exploiting locality to prefetch. When a page or object is fetched due to a memory reference, subsequent adjacent pages, all pages within a segment, or related program-level objects can be fetched at the same time in anticipation of use, to avoid extra round-trip latencies.

6.2.2.3 Resource Reservation

A primary function of the operating system is to mange resources. This generally consists of coarse-grained resource limits (for example, maximum CPU or memory utilization) per process or application. The desire to deliver live real-time streaming media has motivated the reservation of resources in the end system to individual communication flows to guarantee end-to-end performance of the stream [Campbell 1993, Leslie 1996].

> **Path Protection Corollary** *In a resource-constrained host, mechanisms must exist to reserve processing and memory resources needed to provide the high-performance path between application memory and the network interface and to support the required rate of protocol processing.*
>
> **E-II.2**

A similar motivation exists to guarantee high-performance to communicating applications in general, and can take the form of CPU and memory reserva-

---

[20]In some 1990s operating systems, the cost of remapping a page is as costly as copying all the data in the page.

tions. By reserving a certain rate or fraction of the CPU cycles, we can assure that high-performance communications can take place regardless of the load on the CPU by other processes. Similarly, memory reservation may be necessary to ensure that the required bandwidth is available between the host–network interface and memory subsystem. Sufficient memory should also be reserved for send and receive buffers, as well as in the application address spaces (the two are the same in zero copy systems). Finally, as part of the host–network to memory bandwidth, bandwidth on the processor memory interconnect may need to be guaranteed.

Whether or not reservations are needed, and how accurate the control, depends on the Optimal Resource Utilization versus Overengineering Tradeoff (2B). If the end system is not at all constrained in memory, processing, and interconnect bandwidth, there is no need for reservations. In an environment that is not severely resource constrained, simple reservations may be sufficient, and overall performance can actually be better in simple end systems.

If the high-speed applications have real-time constraints, such as for real-time process control, the scheduling algorithms will have to support this as well. Real-time operating systems provide the mechanisms to meet hard real-time constraints for processes.

Mobile computing systems have an additional reason to need resource reservation, since mobile networking blurs the distinction between end system and network node. Many mobile computing nodes perform both roles simultaneously, and in the ubiquitous computing environment (described in Section 9.1.2), we can expect at least one such node per individual. This is necessary to perform the density control optimizations described in Section 3.2.5 to construct a multihop wireless network in which user nodes forward traffic between *other* mobile nodes. Thus, not only do we need to perform resource reservations to protect the application flows from one another but also to protect the user's flows from transit traffic relayed between other users.

6.2.3   Protocol Software Optimizations

We have discussed the impact of operating system software on communications performance. We are now ready to discuss specific implementation techniques, the general protocol bypass technique, ILP to perform multiple layers in a single processing loop, and microprotocols.

6.2.3.1   Protocol Bypass

In Section 5.2.1 we introduced the concept of a critical path and its need for optimization; *protocol bypass* [Woodside 1990] is a general mechanism to accomplish this. The entire protocol stack is analyzed to determine frequent operations, which are put in the bypass path. The bypass consists of a single process without internal concurrency,[21] as shown in Figure 6.10.

Data in the bypass path is shared with the conventional protocol stack. When a data unit is to be sent or received, it is passed through a send or receive bypass filter respectively, and matched to a template in a manner similar to TCP header prediction [Jacobson 1990]. The template is used to build the packet on the transmitting side. The templates are state that can be created by connection setup or dynamically in a data-driven manner, as described in Sections 4.1.3 and 4.1.4. If the packet matches the template, it flows using the bypass path shown by the thick arrows; otherwise it uses the conventional protocol stack implementation.

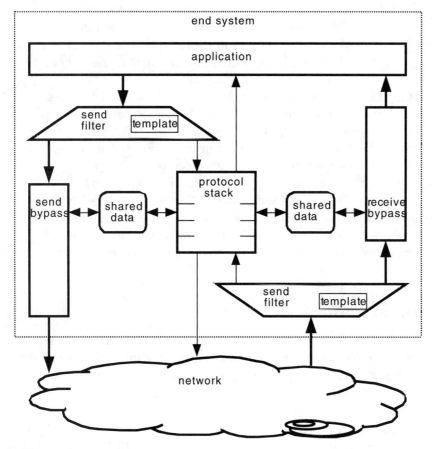

Figure 6.10   Protocol bypass.

[21]This does not preclude parallelism within the process across a multiprocessor system.

6.2.3.2 *Integrated Layer Processing*

Integrated layer processing (ILP) [Clark 1990] is a way to overcome the overhead of layered system implementations, and can be viewed as the way to efficiently implement the bypass path described earlier. Hardware versions of ILP are described in Section 6.4. ILP emphasizes the distinction between layering as a useful abstraction for communications systems and layering as an implementation technique based on the OSI standards.

ILP Principle   *All passes over protocol data units (including layer encapsulations/decapsulations) that take place in a particular component of the end system (CPU, network interface embedded controller, or network interface hardware) should be done at the same time.*

E-4E

In a conventional layered protocol implementation, the encapsulations/decapsulations are done as distinct steps, as described in Section 2.3.4. Even if we employ the software techniques described in this section to avoid context switches, user/kernel crossings, and remapping, we can do better by integrating the processing of the layers. For example, conventional transport and network layer processing of data would consist of multiple distinct loops, as shown in Figure 6.11a.

By employing ILP, all of the functions are processed in a single ILP code loop, as shown in Figure 6.11b. There are substantial savings in datapath processing by doing this. By leaving the data in place, copies between layers have been eliminated. Furthermore, joint code optimizations within a layer for per byte operations such as checksum and encryption may be possible. Additionally, by merging the processing loops for the various functions and putting them together, the overhead involved with transfer of control between the layers and functions has been reduced. A number of performance studies have shown the benefits of ILP [Abbott 1993, Braun 1995].

Modern end systems normally process the physical and link layers on the network interface card or chip. This is a result of a combination of several key factors: Technology has driven the ability to perform protocol processing in hardware, and it is natural to start with per bit processing (physical layer) and then move to the lowest layer of per packet processing (link framing and MAC—medium access control). The boundary between link and network layer processing has a clear division, making it a particularly good point at which to provide the abstraction.[22] This has driven common link layer network interfaces, such as Ethernet, to inexpensive commodity hardware.

---

[22]Shown in Figures 2.5 and 2.6.

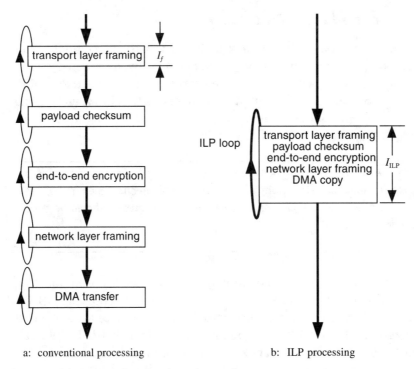

a: conventional processing   b: ILP processing

Figure 6.11   Conventional and ILP processing.

This generally limits the benefit of host-resident software ILP to the network and transport layers, as shown in Figure 6.11. Wireless RF (radio frequency) end systems, however, may perform more processing in software, particularly with the advent of software radios [Lackey 1995, Bose 1999]. Software radios allow flexibility and adaptability to varying channel conditions and diverse physical layers under program control. Only the analog signal path from the antenna (including frequency conversion) and the A↔D (analog–digital and digital–analog) conversion is performed in hardware. The rest of physical layer processing, including spectrum access, modulation, line coding, and channel coding, as well as the medium access control (MAC) and link layer framing are done in software, typically in a digital signal processor (DSP). We can expect fourth-generation (2000s) embedded nodes for ubiquitous computing to integrate the RF transceiver, DSP, and MCU (microcontroller unit—the embedded CPU) on a single chip (or perhaps analog and digital chips on a single carrier). In this case, we have the opportunity for ILP to do the entire protocol stack, from physical up to transport.

ILP does have limits, however, particularly where presentation processing changes the size or structure of the data, affecting the ability to process in place [Clark 1990]. The cache size required to avoid misses during protocol processing loops is dictated by the maximum required for each of the functions, $\max(I_f)$. If the entire ILP loop I_{ILP} does not fit into cache, performance can suffer significantly [Ahlgren 1996]. Thus, we must consider the limitations of optimizations in particular contexts, in this case the cache size of each processor on which the protocol suite will run.

6.2.3.3   *Microprotocols*

Another way to optimize implementation of protocols is to decompose them into small modular components called *microprotocols* [O'Malley 1990], which may be reused by different conventional macroprotocols. Microprotocols communicate with one another within an end system and across the network. For example, remote procedure call (RPC) can be composed by microprotocols, which perform fragmentation/reassembly, request/reply, and demultiplexing. A macroprotocol is created by a partial-order dependency graph of the microprotocols, as was shown in Figure 2.8.

Efficient implementation of microprotocols requires the same critical path optimizations we have been discussing. Microprotocols in the critical path need to be optimized and not suffer interprotocol context switching and user/kernel boundary crossings. For example, Unix System V streams [Bach 1986] provide a nice abstraction to compose protocols. The operating system implementation was so inefficient, however, that it was rarely used. Berkley Unix sockets [Stevens 1990] became the API in general use for network programming, in spite of less flexibility.

6.3.   End System Organization

We have considered how software-based protocols and operating systems must be designed to support the End System Principle (E-II); we are now ready to consider aspects of host architecture and organization that impact communications performance. These are primarily hardware concerns. We will defer the discussion of the host–network interface architecture to Section 6.4.

First, we will consider the overall architecture of the host system in general, including the evolution from single bus PIO to sophisticated high-performance processor–memory and I/O interconnects. This is related to the discussion of switch interconnects in Chapter 5. Then we will consider the alternative ways in which to connect the network into the processor–memory interconnect to provide a high-bandwidth path between the network and the memory modules in which application reside and the corresponding tradeoffs. Finally, we will discuss the relationship of the network interface to the memory hierarchy, integration of the host interconnect with the network itself, and the role of parallel host–network interfaces.

We should note that this discussion does not explicitly consider systems in which power is a constraint. This is reasonable for conventional fixed end systems, but is not for mobile nodes. In the ubiquitous computing environment, systems are generally self-powered, that is, power is drawn from batteries or the environment. This places significant constraints on system design and limits performance, since increasing hardware component count and clock rate increases the power required. This doesn't change the principles and design techniques we will discuss, but does mean that the power implications of decisions made must be carefully considered. Furthermore, this adds a power constraint function $\omega(W)$ to the objective function introduced in Section 3.3.1: $f(\beta(B), \mu(M), \pi(P) \mid \lambda(L), \omega(W))$. Generally, power is traded against performance, particularly in the frequency of a processor or bandwidth of a communication link.

6.3.1 Host Interconnects

A general computing system consists of one or more CPUs, memory modules, and I/O controllers. Two types of interconnection are required (which may or may not be the same physical interconnect):

Processor–memory.   Provides the CPU access to memory for program instructions and data. This interconnect can be highly optimized to the cycle times and cache line width of the CPU and memory word size, degree of interleaving, and cycle time.

I/O.   Provides a path between either the CPU or memory and the I/O subsystem. This interconnect typically serves a wide range in data rates and transfer sizes.

A variety of technologies and topologies can be used for these interconnections, ranging from a simple bus for low-end personal computers to a crossbar switch or multistage interconnection network (MIN) for high-end computing systems. We will discuss these in light of the End System Principle (E-II) to provide a high-bandwidth, low-latency path between the network interface and application memory.

This discussion is related to the one in Section 5.4 on switch fabric interconnects, but in the rather different context of end system architecture. In particular, there are two significant differences: First, the CPU and memory are tightly coupled such that queuing or blocking in the processor–memory interconnect would be a serious detriment to program performance. Second, the number of components on the interconnects is relatively small, indicating that these architectures need not scale to large numbers. Generally, the number is on the order of 10 to a 100, rather than thousands; for a small n, an $O(n^2)$ scaling complexity is acceptable.

6.3.1.1 Bus Interconnect

The simplest host interconnect is a single bus that shares both the processor–memory and I/O functionality, as shown in Figure 6.12. A bus is a parallel set of wires that carries data, address, and control signals.

A bus is a shared medium, and thus bandwidth is limited by the physical characteristics of the bus and does not scale as functional elements are added, as discussed in Chapter 5. Furthermore, if the bus supports multiple masters (units capable of initiating a communication) contending for the bus, a protocol must exist to arbitrate acquisition of the bus. The actual effective bus bandwidth r depends on the details of the protocol and the traffic characteristics of individual data flows, but is bounded by $r < w/nt$.

The clock rate of the bus is $1/t$. The wider the data path w, the greater the effective rate r; the more components n sharing the bus, the lower the effective rate r. The bus may have a faster clock cycle than the attached units, but unless the bus has a speedup factor of n (plus protocol overhead) for n units, the bus will be blocking.

Furthermore, if the units (memory and I/O devices) attached to the bus have a wide range of speed, faster units are likely to be blocked by the slower ones. A bus will block once it has been acquired, but the receiver (slave) is not yet ready to receive data. In this case, the bus master should time out and retry to the given slave later to avoid starvation of other transfers due to a misbehaving or failed device.

Fast I/O, such as for disk transfers and network traffic, can swamp the CPU if it must directly handle PIO (programmed I/O, described in Section 6.1.4). The first step is to add a direct memory access (DMA) controller to the bus, which is responsible for transferring data between I/O devices and memory, independent of CPU–memory interactions, as shown in Figure 6.13. The DMA architecture dates from the late 1950s and was present in the DEC PDP-1 [Bell 1978].

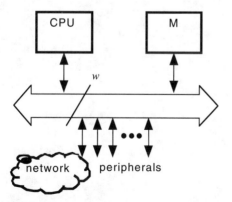

Figure 6.12   Simple bus architecture.

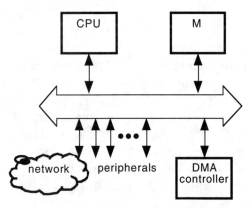

Figure 6.13 Bus architecture with DMA.

While this relieves the CPU of PIO transfers, two significant problems remain. The first is the contention between I/O and CPU–memory program execution and data access. The second is the requirement for asynchronous access of the CPU to memory, since both the DMA controller and CPUs are bus masters, which contend for the bus based on an arbitration protocol. The solution is to isolate I/O from CPU–memory interactions and provide a separate memory bus, as shown in Figure 6.14.

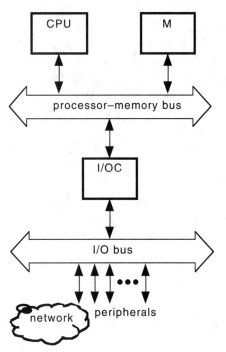

Figure 6.14 Separate memory and I/O bus.

An I/O controller (IOC) with DMA functionality sits between the buses and performs block transfers between memory and the I/O bus. This allows isolation and overlap of program execution with I/O transfers, even if I/O units are waiting and blocking transfer across the I/O bus. As a result of this, the CPU–memory bus can be synchronous, allowing fast transfers without the compromises on transfer unit size and overhead of arbitration protocols. The I/O bus can remain asynchronous with variable transfer units and a master timeout value longer than would be practical on the shared I/O–CPU–memory bus.

6.3.1.2 *Host–Network Interconnect*

While attaching the network interface to the I/O bus made sense for low communication data rates, high-performance communications motivates a distinct connection as for memory, as motivated in Section 6.1.4. An interconnect that is blocking and unable to keep up with the link data rate is not appropriate. While a more complicated multibus architecture could be considered (and is sometimes implemented to accelerate graphics processing), a better solution is a richer interconnect structure. The motivation is even stronger in multiprocessor systems and systems with high-performance interleaved memory.

High-performance multiprocessor systems consist of multiple CPUs, IOPs (I/O processors), and interleaved memory banks. This lead to more sophisticated processor–memory interconnects, beginning with the 1960s and 1970s mainframes, as discussed in Section 6.1.4. In the general case, a switch interconnect serves to connect memory to both CPUs and IOPs.

Figure 6.15 shows the datapath of a typical high-performance computing system consisting of multiple CPUs with cache ($), IOPs, and memory units.[23] The IOPs can range from relatively simple DMA engines, through more complex DMA engines with scatter/gather capabilities, to high-performance programmable I/O processors with embedded cache. In many cases, there are several IOP architectures to match the different characteristics of mass storage and character or unit record peripherals such as printers.[24] As long as the interconnect is nonblocking and memory is fast enough to handle the attached processors, we don't have the contention that existed with a single bus. While the interconnect shown is a crossbar switch, any appropriate topology could be used, such as the $O(n \log n)$ interconnects discussed in Chapter 5. Even though a crossbar is an $O(n^2)$ network, the constant is typically small enough that it is a cost-effective interconnect within a general-purpose computing platform. Massively parallel machines are more likely to have $O(n \log n)$ scaling interconnects.

---

[23]Control paths between CPUs and IOPs are not shown.
[24]These figures show a single IOP per I/O type, but a large system may have many IOPs.

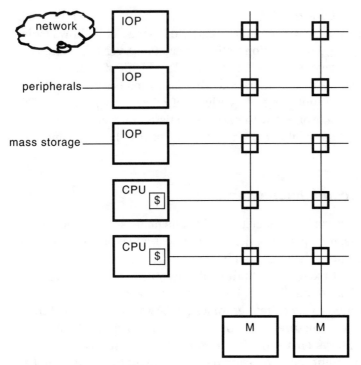

Figure 6.15   Crossbar interconnect.

6.3.2   Host–Network Interconnection Alternatives

We will now consider various ways to interface the network into the host architecture, without the constraint of treating communications as though it were merely another type of I/O. This includes the way in which we attach the network interface to the host memory or processor–memory interconnect, whether or not the network interfaces are singular or parallel, and the degree to which the host interconnect can be considered part of the network itself.

> **Nonblocking Host–Network Interconnect**   *The interconnect between the end system memory and the network interface should be nonblocking, and not interfere with peripheral I/O, and CPU–memory data transfer.*
>
> **E-II.4**

Recall that our fundamental goal of a host architecture supporting high-bandwidth, low-latency communications is to provide a high-performance pipe between the network and memory used by applications. There are two ways of doing this [Sterbenz 1990c]: interfacing the network to the processor–memory interconnect or to the back end of multiported memory [Dang 1987, Jansen 1988].

6.3.2.1   Processor–Memory Interconnect Interface

The obvious choice is to attach the network interface directly to the processor–memory interconnect, which treats the network interface as a first-class processing citizen, along with the IOPs. We refer to this as *interconnect interface architecture*, as shown in Figure 6.16.

In this case, the network communications processor (NCP) simply shares the same memory interconnect with the CPU(s) and IOP(s). Note that we could consider the NCP to be an extremely specialized IOP, but we want to emphasize that its role is *solely* to provide a high-bandwidth, low-latency path between the network and memory. Network link characteristics and protocols are quite different from local I/O device communication.

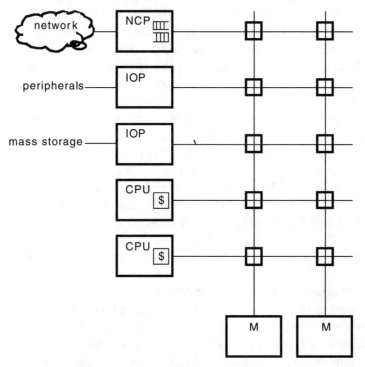

Figure 6.16   Interconnect interface architecture.

This architecture has the substantial advantage that all memory is uniform, that is, we don't have to worry about application data being in the proper type of memory for potential transmission. The network interface processor can transfer packets anywhere to or from physical memory. On the other hand, a significant concern is the possibility of contention for memory between CPU and network processors. If network traffic does not take priority over CPU access to memory, significant buffering will be required in the NCP (the whole point is to avoid a store-and-forward hop in the network interface). If network traffic does take priority, CPUs could be blocked for long periods of time while memory units are receiving data from the network interface. *Transmission* of data, on the other hand, can wait for access to the interconnect without resultant data loss. Thus, the system must be carefully engineered so that the interconnection network supports link rate communication without adversely affecting access to memory by the CPUs. Memory speedup and interleaving can ameliorate this challenge.

6.3.2.2   *Multiport Memory Interface*

The second way to provide high-performance access to memory is to provide backend access to the host–network interface. In this case some (or all) of the host memory is multiported VRAM-style memory, as introduced in Section 6.1.5 and shown in Figure 6.17. The communications memory module (CMM) has a conventional bidirectional random access port on the host interconnect side and a pair of sequential ports for input and output attached to the network interface processor.

This has the benefit of not suffering from the blocking effects of the interconnect interface architecture, since the memory serves to isolate the network traffic from the CPU–memory and I/O–memory traffic. The main drawback is that multiported memory is less dense and significantly more expensive than conventional RAM, and is unlikely to be the only memory technology used by a general-purpose end system. The size partitioning between main memory and CMMs must be predetermined. Furthermore, the system must ensure that the data to be transmitted resides in the *proper* memory module to avoid a copy from conventional main memory. Virtual memory mechanisms can be used to solve this problem by mapping received data into the application address space, but data that might possibly be transmitted to the network must be properly placed to avoid the extra copy between conventional memory and a CMM. In cases where protocol and application semantics require buffering for retransmission and a one-copy implementation is used, memory interface architecture is appropriate.

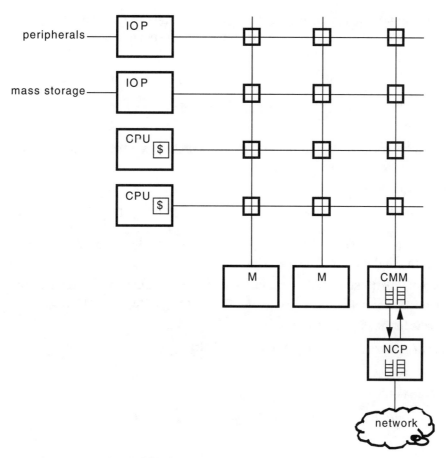

Figure 6.17   Memory interface architecture.

6.3.3   Host–Network Interface Issues

We have discussed alternative ways in which to connect the host interconnect and the network. We will now consider several related issues: the relationship of the network interface to the memory hierarchy, integration of the host interconnect with the network itself, and the role of parallel host–network interfaces.

6.3.3.1   Memory Hierarchy

Computing systems have long consisted of a multilevel memory hierarchy, which optimizes the speed and cost of different memory technologies and exploits locality in program execution and data access. The levels in the hierarchy range from expensive fast processor registers to cheap archival mass storage, covering many orders of magnitude in speed and cost:

CPU registers

Cache

> *1st level cache* on CPU chip with low intrachip delay, but constrained in size

> *2nd level cache* on separate chip (perhaps on the same chip carrier module as the CPU) memory

Main memory

Extended memory, relatively slower and less expensive than main memory; popular in the 1960s on mainframes when fast memory was very expensive with significant cost differential between different technologies such as semiconductor and ferrite core

Backing store (also called secondary memory or auxiliary store) for virtual memory that is paged or swapped out of main (or extended) memory

> *Cache* in the disk controller

> *Backing store*, typically fast magnetic disk

File storage

> *Cache* in the disk controller[25]

> *Mass storage* media, typically magnetic disk

Archival storage

> *Online archives*, for example, mechanical tape retrieval or optical jukebox

> *Offline archive* such as the conventional tape or optical disk library

Choosing the right storage hierarchy involves many of the optimizations and tradeoffs that we have been applying to high-speed network design. Over time the Resource Tradeoffs Change (2A), and levels come, go, or change role. Most systems have only a few of these levels.

We have been assuming that the target for data transfers to and from the network is main memory, but we should consider other possibilities in the hierarchy. In particular, in data-intensive distributed processing applications we may wish for the network interface to transfer directly to 2nd level cache; in this case, the network looks more like real memory, with the added benefit of not requiring any virtual address translation. Alternatively, when large

---

[25]There is no difference in cache used for backing store and files; the controller caches disk block without any knowledge of file structure. Disk modules may be divided between backing and file store, with more controller cache installed in backing store to improve performance.

amounts of data are being prefetched to reduce effective latency, we may wish to consider transferring directly to secondary storage. This is so that main memory is not swamped, forcing data within the application working set to be paged to secondary storage.

Similarly, there are instances where the target of the data shouldn't be in the conventional memory hierarchy at all. For example, in the case of high-resolution streaming video, it might be appropriate to place the data directly into the video frame buffer as it arrives. In support of high-bandwidth remote backup applications, the data should be sent directly to the disk via a SAN (storage area network) network interface.

As specialized networked devices become more common in the context of ubiquitous computing, the point of connection to the network must be evaluated for each type of specialized device interface.

6.3.3.2   Parallel Host–Network Interfaces

There are two ways in which we can consider parallelization of host–network interfaces: decomposition of protocol processing among multiple interface processors on a single network interface and multiple host–network interfaces per host. We will briefly discuss each of these cases.

6.3.3.2.1   Parallel Processing within a Network Interface

The ability to parallelize protocol functionality was discussed in Section 6.2.1. This could be exploited by mapping asynchronous processes that would execute in multiple microcontrollers on the host–network interface. This was an area of intense research in the late 1980s, with the INMOS Transputer a common implementation platform due to its message-passing primitives and relatively low cost [Zitterbart 1989]. While the research gave insight into the ability to parallelize protocol functionality and some speedup is possible, there are two problems to the wide-scale deployment of this approach.

First, the obvious speedup that can be obtained per flow is *two*, by assigning one processor each to transmit and receive processing (assuming decoupled send/receive state). Additional decomposition is possible: by protocol layer [Jansen 1988], microprotocol function (Section 6.2.3), or per packet for protocols that do not have tightly coupled interpacket state. Typically, the speedup obtainable is about a factor of 5 [Touch 1995a]. The benefits of assigning functions to distinct processors generally do not exceed the overhead in data movement or synchronization to shared memory among processors. Furthermore, Amdahl's law quickly limits the amount of additional speedup [Amdahl 1967]. Rather, there is far greater benefit in an ILP implementation, which keeps the data in place and in cache while the entire protocol stack is implemented in a single loop. Parallel decomposition by connection or flow scales well; the difficult issue is matching the granularity of parallel interface processing with the bandwidth requirements of individual flows.

Second, the cost of network interfaces that are general-purpose multiprocessors is significant. If the bandwidth requirements are such that an analysis indicates that hardware implementation is needed instead of host software, the cost is better spent on the other techniques described in this section, in particular, a pipelined hardware ILP implementation. A number of protocol functions, such as encryption, don't parallelize well (if at all), but may be amenable to pipelining, and benefit from carefully placed custom hardware.

6.3.3.2.2   Multiple Host–Network Interfaces

We have so far assumed that only one host–network interface is located on each host; this need not be the case. Conventionally, end systems that have multiple network interfaces are called *multihomed* hosts. Mobile wireless end systems that also serve as intermediate nodes in a multihop network are multihomed. Other reasons for doing this include performing research in routing on a conventional workstation, connecting a production and test network, during the transition while changing link layer technologies, and providing dynamic fail-over or crossover (for example, from intermittently connected high-speed to always connected low-speed interfaces).

We are interested in considering multiple host–network interfaces as a technique to support high-speed networking, which is quite different. One possibility is to stripe packets or bytes across interfaces, but this presents the misordering and skew problems discussed in Section 3.1.3. The best decomposition for multiple interfaces is to divide flows or connections across two or more host–network interfaces. These can either then be connected to parallel network access links or multiplexed to a single higher-speed network link. This technique can be cost-effective when a small incremental speedup is desired over a particular link technology, but the cost of the next increment is significantly more expensive. This assumes that technological increases are slow enough that a more complex multi-interface solution is justified. For example, Ethernet LAN bandwidths are increasing fast enough, and the interface cost is cheap enough, that multiple interfaces on conventional personal computers are generally not justified. On the other hand, increases in residential access rates have been much slower. In the 1980s, multiple analog modems were cheaper than the cost of a single ISDN link. In the late 1990s and early 2000s, multiple xDSL interfaces were cheaper then the cost of running fiber optics into the home.

A case where multiple host–network interfaces can significantly benefit performance is in nonuniform memory access (NUMA) multiprocessor systems, such as a hypercube in which each processor has local memory. In this case, a single host–network interface would cause the attached processor to be a bottleneck in distributing communications to all the other processors.

> **Nonuniform Memory Multiprocessor–Network Interconnect**   *Message passing multiprocessors need sufficient network interfaces to allow data to flow between the network and processor memory without interfering with the multiprocessing application.*
>
> **E-II.4m**

The highest-performance case would be to add a host–network interface to each processor. An example of a three-dimensional hypercube is shown in Figure 6.18.

This introduces other problems, however. While each processor has an interface to the network, incoming data must be addressed to the *proper* interface and processor; if it is not, the contention problems may be as bad as for the single interface architecture. For some distributed computations that have a clear (or random) partitioning, an interface per processor solution scales well.

Alternatively, the multiprocessor could be sparsely populated with network interfaces at the cost of some contention for the interprocessor interconnect and additional latency of communications between processors. The number of host–network interfaces that are appropriate depends on the relative cost of network interfaces to interprocessor interfaces, the relative costs of communication within and outside the multiprocessor, and the importance of high-bandwidth communications to the applications.

6.3.3.3   *Integration of Host Interconnect and Network*

The host interconnect is a network, but there are two significant differences from data networks that cover a wide area. First, it is reasonable to consider

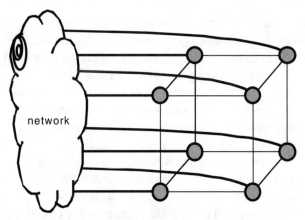

Figure 6.18   Fully interfaced hypercube multiprocessor.

the host interconnect to be error-free; this is typically guaranteed with error checking and correction (ECC) hardware for the processor–memory interconnect and memory subsystem. Second, the distances traversed are sufficiently low that network protocols are not needed to deal with latency and clock synchronization; synchronous interfaces and simple backpressure mechanisms generally suffice.

With care, we can consider integrating the processor–memory interconnect with the LAN (and thus the Internet at large). Conversely, we can consider breaking open and distributing the processor memory and I/O interconnect to a slightly larger area consisting of various peripherals such as an office. This network then becomes part of the LAN hierarchy. These are isomorphic views of the same architecture, originally proposed as desk area networks (DANs) [Finn 1991, Hayter 1991, Adam 1993]. This involves putting a network interface on each device, and requires the additional embedded processing intelligence to perform protocol processing.

SANs, are a first step in this direction, where large disk systems are directly networked with file servers. Ubiquitous networking takes this to the extreme case, in which home networks and body networks consist of intelligent devices, that are networked directly with one another.

The concept has seen deployment in connecting intelligent mass storage to processors in SANs [Sachs 1994, Watson 1995, Gibson 1998, 2000, Guha 1999, Carlson 2000], and shows promise for ubiquitous computing in the form of wearable personal area networks. In this case, all of the principles and trade-offs we have been considering must be carefully evaluated in the context of specialized devices, which may have limited power and processing capability, but still be participants in high-speed networked applications.

6.4 Host–Network Interface

We have considered how to optimize software processing of communication functionality and how to optimize the host architecture to support a high-bandwidth, low-latency path between the network interface and application memory. In this section, we cover the one remaining key part of the end system: the host–network interface itself. This is the end system component that terminates the link to the network, and performs some protocol processing. We have two major concerns. First, we must consider which protocol functionality should be implemented in the network interface and offloaded from the host CPU. Second, as with the rest of the end-to-end communications path, the host–network interface design and this protocol processing must done in a manner that provides a high-bandwidth, low-latency path between the network and host.

Following the End System Principle (E-II), Copy Minimization Principle (E-II.3), and Blocking Avoidance (II.4), our goal in the context of the host–

network interface will be to provide a high-bandwidth, low-latency pipeline between the host memory and the network. We will consider zero-copy and single-copy designs.

6.4.1 Offloading of Communication Processing

Originally, all communications were handled by software processing in the end host CPU, typically as application code using conventional I/O operations. As networking protocol suites were developed, it was realized that a tighter relationship with the operating system was desirable, and protocols were typically implemented in the operating system kernel, or at least as privileged system code. This decoupled applications from the protocol implementation, while allowing protocol processing direct access to privileged I/O and data management system routines and processor instructions, as described in Section 6.2.2.

Third computing generation mainframe processors had offloaded I/O to separate IOPs to overlap I/O and computations and to allow specialized hardware tuned to high-performance I/O processing. A logical extension to this was to also offload network processing into communication control processors, which implemented protocol suites such as SNA on the IBM 3705 communications processor attached to a System/360. Thus, the idea of offloading protocol processing onto specialized network interfaces dates from the 1960s.

6.4.1.1 Outboard Internet Protocol Processing

In conjunction with the 1980s challenge of communicating at 1 Gb/s, a number of proposals were made in the research community to offload protocol processing from the host CPU to a separate network interface card. While this resulted in significant debate in the research community, it was more a matter of pushing the envelope than proposing a radically new paradigm. While this had already been done in the mainframe environment, it was significantly different from the Unix-based minicomputer and workstation environment of the emerging Internet community, which unfortunately didn't tend to take the Not Invented Here Corollary ($\emptyset$-A) to heart. Furthermore, typical workstation class network interfaces were already performing some protocol function, in particular, link layer processing for Token Ring and Ethernet.

At this point, TCP was considered by many to be too complex to run at 1 Gb/s or to implement directly in hardware. Thus, this stage of offboard processing research prototypes was done in conjunction with the new transport protocols such as the PE (protocol engine) [Chesson 1989] for XTP, and NAB (network adapter board) [Kanakia 1988] for VMTP. While these were important research efforts, many of them predated a careful analysis of the bottlenecks in existing protocols, and assumed that merely implementing the transport protocol offboard would solve the problem. These correspond to the second and third conjecture we discussed in Section 6.1.3:

EC2. Implementing protocols on the host–network interface will enable high-speed networking.

EC3. Implementing protocol functionality in hardware speeds it up.

Following the more rigorous analysis discussed in Section 5.2 in the context of transport protocol bottlenecks, the next stage host–network interfaces in the late 1980s and early 1990s became concerned with a more systematic implementation of protocol processing [Sterbenz 1990a]. Many of these efforts frequently assumed that ATM would become a pervasive networking technology, and thus explored how to build a high-performance ATM network interface, for example, [Davie 1991 and Traw 1993]. The short interarrival time between ATM cells made it particularly challenging to design these high-speed interfaces. Other prototypes used HIPPI (high-performance parallel interface) [Watson 1990] and FDDI (fiber distributed data interface) [Banks 1993, Ramakrishnan 1993a]. The Nectar CAB [Cooper 1990] provided an off-board shared memory interface to LAN clustered processors.

EXAMPLE 6.1: THE XTP/PE INTERFACE

One of the most important early high-speed network interface efforts was the protocol engine (PE) [Chesson 1989]. This effort was significant not only in the novelty of the research for the time but also in its industrial backing by Silicon Graphics to produce working VLSI chips. A new transport protocol optimized for high-performance networking was designed: express transport protocol (XTP). XTP was fully specified and saw a number of host software implementations, particularly in Europe where quite a few high-speed networking research projects used XTP as the base protocol.

Unfortunately, few details on the PE implementation were published before the termination of the project. Certainly, the propensity to design new transport protocols in the late 1980s was replaced with the realization in the 1990s that any attempt to replace TCP as the de facto Internet transport protocol faced insurmountable barriers. Furthermore, optimizations to TCP in the early 1990s (Example 7.9) resulted in substantial improvements. XTP attempted to perform a balancing act between needed functions while remaining simple enough for VLSI implementation, and it is possible that it was just a bit too complex for hardware implementation circa 1990, given the Resource Tradeoff Principle (2).

6.4.1.2   Functionality to Offload

One of the fundamental questions to be answered in designing a host–network interface is *which* protocol processing function to offload from the host to the network interface. There are three motivations for implementing functionality on the host–network interface:

1. Processing that can be done most efficiently as the data is moved between the network and host memory.
2. Processing that can be done more efficiently in specialized hardware.
3. Processing that places a significant burden on the host CPU, in particular, due to the need to touch each byte (such as checksumming and encryption).

Host–Network Interface Functional Partitioning and Assignment   *Carefully determine what functionality should be implemented on the network interface rather than in end system software.*

E-1C*i*

It is very important to reiterate that merely moving processing from the CPU to the host–network interface does not increase performance; in fact, it may actually decrease overall system performance. The issues are analogous to the design of processor instruction sets. RISC research has shown us that merely increasing the number of functions implemented in a hardware set does not necessarily increase performance, unless the impact on the entire system is carefully analyzed.

Application layer framing (ALF), discussed in Section 7.3.1, suggests that at least some of this processing should occur in the host system. In particular, if a given function can be implemented as part of an ILP loop that must execute on the host anyway, and the function does not require extra touching of each data byte, there is minimal motivation to offload it to an external host–network interface. Furthermore, just as we try to match protocol processing to the characteristics of the network, we have the same problem matching to the application. As discussed in Section 2.3.4, this is the problem of matching end system and network formats. Thus, part of this assignment problem consists of trying to match application and network protocol data unit formats, control mechanisms, and determining where the protocol processing boundary should be.

Application Layer to Network Interface Synergy and Functional Division   *Application and lower-layer data unit formats and control mechanisms should not interfere with one another, and the division of functionality between host software and the network interface should minimize this interference.*

E-4C

ALF drives this from the application, but there are limits. For example, if the application data structure is larger than the network maximum transfer unit (MTU), it must be fragmented, which is an expensive operation. Another approach is to use a granularity of data that is matched to the host memory and operating system. For example, a packet can be page size, or power-of-2 fraction, if a page is larger than the MTU [Sterbenz 1990c]. If ATM had a somewhat larger cell size, this strategy could have been used without the overhead of adaptation layer segmentation and reassembly.

It is possible to implement some error and flow control mechanisms in very simple VLSI [Sterbenz 1992]. TCP is sufficiently complex, however, that full protocol operation is difficult to implement in custom hardware, but increases in VLSI technology have reduced this concern. Furthermore, standard Unix socket semantics prevent a zero-copy interface; transmitted data must remain in a buffer until acknowledged. Thus, conventional TCP using sockets dictates a single-copy transmit interface, rather than a zero-copy. Finally, pipelined operation requires cumulative fields such as a checksum to be located in the trailer so that they can be computed as the packet passes through the transmit pipeline and then inserted into the trailer. It is possible, however, to wrap the transport packet in with a performance optimized trailer, as is done in the Atomic transport protocol [Xu 1995].

Determining which functionality to implement on the network interface involves the usual application of the Systemic Optimization Principle (IV) and Functional Partitioning and Assignment Corollary (1C) constrained by Backward Compatibility Inhibits Radical Change (III.7) of the target protocols. If we had a free hand to start from scratch, the location of functionality would likely be somewhat different. Once we have determined the proper partition of functionality to offload to the host–network interface, we need to further optimize between microcontroller software and hardware on the network interface itself. This will be discussed shortly.

6.4.2   Network Interface Design

We will now discuss the principles in designing a high-performance host–network interface. There are two major areas of concern:

1. Architectures that support zero- or single-copy network interfaces and the host architectures described in Section 6.3.

2. Techniques to provide high bandwidth and low latency; a number of these will parallel the techniques covered in Section 6.2 in the context of software optimizations, in particular, the need for an optimized critical path and the hardware equivalent of ILP.

6.4.2.1 Hardware/Software Functionality Partitioning

The functional blocks in the host–network interface can be implemented either by an embedded controller operating on network interface memory or by custom hardware (which itself may range from programmable gate arrays to fully custom VLSI design). This decision is a tradeoff between cost and performance, and the choice is selected based on parameters such as bit rate and packet rate (driven by packet length).

> **Network Interface Hardware Functional Partitioning and Assignment** *Carefully determine what functionality should be implemented in network interface custom hardware, rather than on an embedded controller. Packet interarrival time driven by packet size is a critical determinant of this decision.*
>
> **E-1C*h***

The granularity of data unit determines whether function needs to be implemented in hardware or can be relegated to software. Clearly, as the bit rate increases, so does the need for sophisticated hardware to implement the data path. Similarly, as the packet rate increases (in packets/s), the interpacket arrival time decreases; this is a critical determinant of whether or not header processing and other transfer control functions must be performed by custom hardware (unless per packet parallelization can be applied). Some representative interpacket times are shown in Table 6.1. This table is based on Table 5.4, but includes the number of instructions I per packet[26] that can be processed for 100-MHz and 1-GHz processors. For high data rates and small packet sizes, the interpacket time t may be so short that an embedded controller isn't sufficiently fast to decode or build the header, and this must be done by custom hardware.

Solutions that are infeasible are shown in light font.[27] Table 6.1 indicates, for example, that at a data rate of 1 Gb/s, a 100-MHz processor is unlikely to be able to process small packets (40B in the Internet), but a 1-GHz processor can do so. If larger packets are used (1 KB), even a 100-MHz processor may be able to keep up with 10-Gb/s (OC-192) data rates.

Thus, as was the case for switch/router design covered in Chapter 4, packet size is a key determinant in the hardware/software tradeoffs in the host–network interface, as shown in Figure 6.19 [Sterbenz 1991].

This plot shows that for a given packet size, when the number of instruction cycles required to process each packet exceeds the capability of the network

---

[26]Assuming a RISC multiplier of 1 instruction/cycle.
[27]The 25 instruction cycle budget for packet processing is marginal, at best; 80 instructions is more likely to be feasible.

Table 6.1 Packet Processing Times and Instruction Budgets

		PACKET SIZE										
		1 B			32 B			128 B			1 KB	
		#INSTRUCTIONS			#INSTRUCTIONS			#INSTRUCTIONS			#INSTRUCTIONS	
RATE	t	100 MHZ	1 GHZ	t	100 MHZ	1 GHZ	t	100 MHZ	1 GHZ	t	100 MHZ	1 GHZ
1 Mb/s	8 µs	800	8,000	250 µs	25 k	250 k	1 ms	100 k	1 M	8 ms	800 k	8 M
10 Mb/s	800 ns	80	800	25 µs	2500	25 k	100 µs	10 k	100 k	800 µs	80 k	800 k
100 Mb/s	80 ns	8	80	2.5 µs	250	2500	10 µs	1000	10 k	80 µs	8000	80 k
1 Gb/s	8 ns	.8	8	250 ns	25	250	1 µs	100	1000	8 µs	800	8000
10 Gb/s	800 ps	.08	.8	2.5 ns	2.5	25	100 ns	10	100	800 ns	80	800

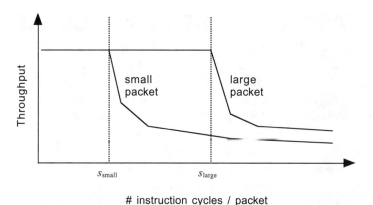

Figure 6.19   Software saturation.

interface processor for a given interarrival rate, the processor is driven into saturation. The saturation point for smaller dictates a smaller instruction cycle budget, s_{small}. For a given small packet size, the only alternative is to use a faster processor, and, when this is limited by the technology available, implement functionality directly in hardware.

6.4.2.2   Functional Partitioning and Assignment

As we did for host software, functionality in the host–network interface should be carefully analyzed to determine whether it is part of the critical path. The previous discussion of hardware/software partitioning applies to the routine processing of packets, and does not imply that *all* control and exception processing must be done in custom hardware, even at high data rates and small packet sizes.

At a high level, the functionality in the transmit and receive pipelines is similar, and we will now examine them in detail. As we did for host processing, we need to analyze functionality to determine if it is part of the critical path, and then determine whether the packet granularity and clock rate indicate that hardware implementation of packet-level processing is necessary.

The host–network interface will have a block that has overall control responsibility for the interface, as well as performing noncritical path processing. This may be an embedded microcontroller, and its ability to perform per packet processing depends on the line rate and packet size, discussed previously. For link-layer interfaces, the complexity of a custom VLSI controller may be less than that of a general-purpose embedded controller. If the interface is a commodity, as is the case for Ethernet, then the design cost of custom VLSI is justified.

EXAMPLE 6.2: THE FAILURE OF ATM TO THE DESKTOP

While ATM came from fast packet switching research in high-speed networking community (as discussed in Chapters 4 and 5), the choice of a small cell size actually had the opposite effect: It made high-speed network deployment *more* difficult, particularly at the end system. In the late 1980s and early 1990s, SONET OC-12 links (622 Mb/s) were just becoming available and were the target of research prototypes.[28] At 622 Mb/s the cell interarrival time is approximately 780 ns (the ATM cell rate in OC-12 is actually 544 Mb/s after SONET frame overhead; whether this additional 12 percent overhead time is usable for cell processing depends on how the network interface is designed and clocked). This was far too short to implement cell processing functions in the ~50-MHz microprocessors of the time, and forced the research community to design custom VLSI for the SONET link layer and ATM cell header operations. Commercial ATM/SONET user-network interface (UNI) chips for OC-12 were still several years in the future.

On the other hand, even though Ethernet was not originally designed as a scalable technology, Ethernet interfaces were far cheaper for a given data rate, and it became cheaper to scale Ethernet to 100-Mb/s than to build 155-Mb/s ATM interfaces, as described in Example 5.2. ATM forced processing to the worst case—the minimum packet size conceivably needed for any application—rather than the average case, which included a mix of larger packets.

Had the ATM community chosen a sensible cell size, research prototypes would have been much easier to produce, and commercial products would have come two or three years sooner. ATM might have been a more serious contender for networking to the desktop instead of languishing while the 100-Mb/s Ethernet standards settled.

The datapath pipelines consist of a set of functional units that process the critical data path. These certainly include physical layer coding, per byte transmit and receive operations, and link-layer processing. Low-level presentation layer functionality should also be performed here to eliminate excessive data manipulation by the host, such as formatting to a common network format (including byte ordering) and encryption/decryption.[29]

If the transport protocol and application semantics were designed for high-performance networking from the start, a number of features would be included

---

[28]622 Mb/s "rounds up" to 1 Gb/s, which was the measure used in the HPCC Gigabit testbeds of the early 1990s.

[29]Note that if encryption is performed in the network interface on an end system shared by multiple users, a secure OS is required to ensure *application-to-application* security; otherwise users will encrypt anyway, and redundantly. This is a strong version of the End-to-End Argument (3), in which the endpoints are the application rather than the network interface.

to optimize for pipelined processing and zero-copy semantics in the host–network interface. The packet consists of a header, payload, and trailer. The header and trailers contain information for the transport, network, and link layers, but these are built on transmission from a template, and decoded on receive in a single shot. This is the hardware version of ILP (proposed in Axon [Sterbenz 1990c] and HOPS [Haas 1990] but predating the use of the term).

Section 6.3.2 discussed two host architectures that support zero-copy (or reduced copy) interface: memory interface and interconnect interface. We will now consider the high-level design of the network interfaces for each of these host architectures, and then take a more detailed look at design of network interface pipelines.

The interconnect interface architecture introduced in Figure 6.15 requires a direct interface from the network interface. Thus the high-level architecture simply consists of data pipelines for transmit and receive, and control processing, as shown in Figure 6.20.

The memory interface architecture, introduced in Figure 6.16, brings multiport memory into the network interface, as shown in Figure 6.21. In both cases, the receive and transmit pipelines are where the data path portion of the critical path is implemented.

6.4.2.3   Data Path Pipelines

Data processing consists of moving the data payload between the network and host memory, and may involve transformation of the data (such as format conversion or byte order inversion). We will consider both the bandwidth and latency of data movement.

As we have previously discussed, the driving principle in data path design will be to avoid the latency of copying and blocking data, and thus we will

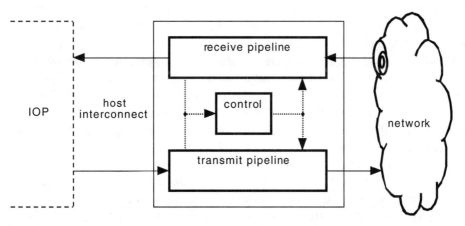

Figure 6.20   Interconnect interface architecture.

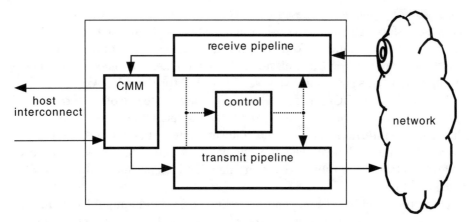

Figure 6.21 Memory interface architecture.

look to a pipelined implementation of the host–network interface datapath. We then have three concerns:

1. Implementation of pipeline at sufficiently high bandwidth
2. Implementation of pipeline at sufficiently low latency
3. Choosing pipelinable function

6.4.2.3.1 Bandwidth

The main determinant for bandwidth is the clock rate of the host–network interface, which is clearly related to the line rate of the network link. Network links are typically serial, for the reasons discussed in Section 3.1.3, and we will assume this here. High-bandwidth network links operate at high clock rate r_1 that challenges end system components. Fortunately, virtually all protocol operations are at least byte granularity, with the exception of physical layer coding. Thus, we get nearly an order-of-magnitude relief in the internal clock rate of the network interface, which is $r_8 = 8r_1$.

A higher degree of parallelism is possible, such as end system word or cache line, at the cost of some additional complexity to deal with per byte header field alignment and operations such as checksumming. The additional benefit $r_{32} = 4r_8$ is relatively small (four times speedup for 32-bit word width), and requires analysis to determine if the additional cost is justified in a particular case.

The next degree of parallelism to consider is packet width as was done for switches in Section 5.4.4. For all but very small packets (such as ATM cells), packet-level datapath width is far too large to even consider. For variable size packets, the datapath width must equal the *maximum* packet size, with hardware wasted much of the time for the (average) smaller packets.

6.4.2.3.2   Latency

The host–network interface needs to be low latency, but the question is how low is *sufficient*. Two factors drive the latency requirements:

1. The latency budget is determined by the application. The strictest latency budget we expect for interactive user applications is 100 ms, as will be discussed in Section 8.1.2. Distributed computing and control-feedback applications may require significantly lower-latency bounds, perhaps on the order of microseconds.

2. Latency of other components of the end-to-end system, in particular, the latency through the network *between* the end system interfaces. Recall that the speed-of-light propagation delay through a LAN is on the order of 10 μs, from Table 3.1, not including delays in the network nodes, which will be on the order of 1 ms per hop, as described in Chapter 5.

The Second-Order Effect Corollary (1A) tells us how much pipeline delay we can tolerate. There is no reason to take heroic measures to design a 1-μs latency interface if the latency through the network is 10 ms and the latency budget of the application is 100 ms. Thus, a host–network interface designed to operate in a conventional LAN or wide area network, and which needs to support a wide variety of applications, should be designed with a latency budget on the order of 100 μs. The design of a network interface for process control or distributed computing applications or in a DAN/SAN environment is significantly more challenging.

6.4.2.3.3   Datapath Pipelines

We will now consider the functionality and generic design of the datapath pipelines in the host–network interface. While the logical design of these components is beyond the scope of this book, we will discuss some of the issues involved in such design.

Figures 6.22 and 6.23 depict the design of typical transmit and receive pipelines, respectively. Not surprisingly, they are fairly symmetric to one another. We will proceed from the network side to the host in describing functionality.

For bit granularity operations:

Line coding. Physical layer processing is usually part of the host–network interface, and is responsible for converting between the network medium coding (electrical, optical, or wireless) and a bit stream on the network interface side.

Serial/byte conversion. The network link is most likely to be bit serial; in this case, a conversion is required between bit serial and the internal datapath width of the network interface. As discussed earlier, this is most likely to be byte wide, and may be wider if needed.

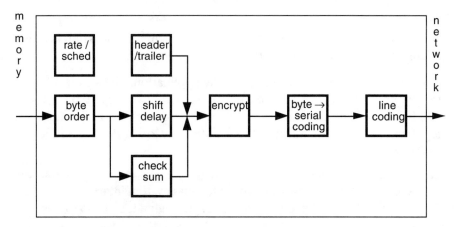

Figure 6.22 Transmit pipeline.

For byte/word granularity operations:

Encryption/Decryption. Two types of encryption can be considered for the network interface: per hop and end-to-end. Link-layer encryption may be needed for wireless access links to prevent eavesdropping. End-to-end encryption may be done in the network interface, but it is important to recall that this is *not* application-to-application encryption. The transport header may be end-to-end encrypted to hide user, application, and end system information from network nodes.

The performance benefit from hardware encryption may be substantial, and affect the decision on whether application-to-application encryption is

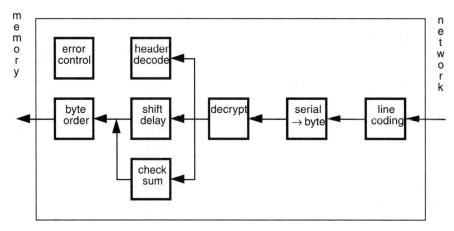

Figure 6.23 Receive pipeline.

justified, based on the security of the operating system and whether or not multiple users have access to the end system. Hardware-based pipelined encryption is an area that needs further research [Nechvatal 2000].

Error detection and correction. Packets need to have a check field to protect against bit errors in the payload and header fields. A zero-copy pipelined implementation requires that a payload check be at the end of the packet in the trailer for transmission, unless the pipeline is deep enough to hold an entire packet. The transmit pipeline logic computes the checksum as the packet flows by and then inserts it into the trailer. In a single-copy interface, the checksum can be performed in an ILP loop during the DMA copy from host to network interface.

The receive pipeline logic computes the checksum on the payload as the packet is received, and then compares it to the checksum field. In this case, the location of the check does not matter if, in the header, it is held until the packet is shifted through the pipeline. If the check fails (and does not have error-correction capabilities), an error signal is raised so that the proper error control can take place. The key issue here is that the application must not be able to use the packet until it has fully arrived and passed the check. In a zero-copy interface, this means that application memory cannot be unlocked until this has occurred.

Byte order. The network byte order must be converted to the host byte order, if they differ, and if the granularity of date unit from the host is word or greater. Unfortunately, widely deployed microprocessor architectures have reverse byte order with respect to IP network byte order. Some high-performance protocols allow the byte order to be negotiated on a per packet basis.

For packet granularity operations:

Header build. The transmit path builds and inserts the header in front of the payload and trailer at the end. The network interface is generally responsible for the link (and physical) layers, and may be responsible for the network and transport layers. All layers of protocol encapsulation may be performed based on a packet template in a single shot; this is the hardware equivalent of ILP.

Header decode. The receive path must be able to decode the packet header to determine how to process the packet and where the destination lies in the host. A small shift delay allows the header to be decoded before decisions are made that affect the handling and destination of the packet. Scatter/gather DMA functionality, or explicit destination information in the packet header, assists in the proper placement of the packet into host memory.

Rate scheduling. If rate-based flow control is used, a mechanism such as a leaky bucket scheduler can be used to determine the rate at which packets are read from host memory into the transmit pipeline. Hardware implementation of rate control can be simply done using counter-based timers [Sterbenz 1992].

6.5 Summary

This chapter has described the issues and design principles necessary for the end system to support high-bandwidth, low-latency communication between the application memory and network. We discussed the traditional host organization and bottlenecks in a layered I/O communications paradigm. We presented the ideal end system decomposition of the ideal network. The subsequent sections described how to approach the ideal in protocol software and its relationship to the operating system, host architecture and organization, and network interface design.

6.5.1 Further Reading

This chapter relies particularly heavily on operating system and computer architecture concepts. The literature in these area is vast, and relevant work goes back decades. We recommend [Blaauw 1997], [Hayes 1988], [Flynn 1995], [Kuck 1978], [Patterson 1998], and [Cragon 1996] as computer architecture textbooks, and [Stallings 1998b] and [Silberschatz 1998] as operating system textbooks. Given the pervasiveness of Unix as a networking research platform, [McKusick 1996], [Stevens 1990], and [Vahalia 1996] are essential references. A historical perspective on operating systems is still advisable, [Organick 1972] and [Johnson 1989] cover two pioneering systems (Mutics and MVS), the latter still in wide use.

In addition to the referenced papers, there have been several special journal issues specifically devoted to the topic of high-speed host–network interfaces: [Rudin 1989c, Haas 1993, Ramakrishnan 1993b]. [Krishnakumar 1989] gives an early summary of ULSI protocol implementations.

[Sterbenz 1991, Sterbenz 1993] explored what could be done by starting from scratch to design a new DVSM-based zero-copy network interface without the restrictions of any legacy protocols. [Steenkiste 1994] walks systematically through the optimizations that can be done for conventional host–network interfaces using TCP/IP. [Druschel 1993] examines work-station DMA and caching issues in the context of the x-kernel. [Chu 1996] describes the implementation of a zero-copy TCP in the Solaris variant of Unix.

END SYSTEM AXIOMS AND PRINCIPLES

E-II. End System Principle   *The communicating end systems are a critical component in end-to-end communications and must provide a low-latency, high-bandwidth path between the network interface and application memory.*

E-I. Application Primacy   *Optimization of communications processing in the end system must not degrade the performance of the applications using the network.*

E-IV. Systemic Elimination of End System Bottlenecks   *The host organization, processor–memory interconnect, memory subsystem, operating system, protocol stack, and host–network interface are all critical components in end system performance, and must be optimized in concert with one another.*

E-III.7. Optimize and Enhance Widely Deployed Protocols   *The practical difficulty in replacing protocols widely deployed on end systems indicates that it is important to optimizing existing protocol implementations, and add backward compatible enhancements, rather than only trying to replace them with new protocols.*

E-4A. End System Layering Principle   *Layered protocol architecture does not depend on a layered process implementation in the end system.*

E-I.4. Importance of Networking in the End System   *Networking should be considered a first-class citizen of the end system computing architecture, on a par with memory or high-performance graphics subsystems.*

E-II.3*m*. Copy Minimization Principle   *Data copying, or any operation that involves a separate sequential per byte touch of data, should be avoided. In the ideal case, a host–network interface should be zero copy.*

E-1B. Critical Path Principle   *Optimize end system critical path protocol processing software and hardware, consisting of normal data path movement and the control functions on which it depends.*

E-IV$_1$. Consider the Side Effects   *Optimizations frequently have unintended side effects to the detriment of performance. It is important to consider, analyze, and understand the consequences of optimization and difficulties in the end system due to the complex interaction of applications, operating system, and protocols.*

E-II.6*a*. Context Switch Avoidance   *The number of context switches should be minimized, and approach one per application data unit.*

E-4H. Interrupt versus Polling   *Interrupts provide the ability to react to asynchronous events, but are expensive operations. Polling can be used when a protocol has knowledge of when information arrives.*

E-II.6*k*. User/Kernel Crossing Avoidance   *The number of user space calls to the kernel should be minimized due to the overhead of authorization and security checks, the copying of buffers, and the inability to directly invoke needed kernel functions.*

E-II.3. Avoid Data Copies by Remapping *Use memory and buffer remapping techniques to avoid the overhead of copying and moving blocks of data.*

E-II.2. Path Protection Corollary *In a resource-constrained host, mechanisms must exist to reserve processing and memory resources needed to provide the high-performance path between application memory and the network interface and to support the required rate of protocol processing.*

E-4E. ILP Principle *All passes over protocol data units (including layer encapsulations/decapsulations) that take place in a particular component of the end system (CPU, network interface embedded controller, or network interface hardware) should be done at the same time.*

E-II.4. Nonblocking Host–Network Interconnect *The interconnect between the end system memory and the network interface should be nonblocking, and not interfere with peripheral I/O and CPU–memory data transfer.*

E-II.4*m*. Nonuniform Memory Multiprocessor–Network Interconnect *Message passing multiprocessors need sufficient network interfaces to allow data to flow between the network and processor memory without interfering with the multiprocessing application.*

E-1C*i*. Host–Network Interface Functional Partitioning and Assignment *Carefully determine what functionality should be implemented on the network interface rather than in end system software.*

E-4C. Application Layer to Network Interface Synergy and Functional Division *Application and lower-layer data unit formats and control mechanisms should not interfere with one another, and the division of functionality between host software and the network interface should minimize this interference.*

E-1C*h*. Network Interface Hardware Functional Partitioning and Assignment *Carefully determine what functionality should be implemented in network interface custom hardware, rather than on an embedded controller. Packet interarrival time driven by packet size is a critical determinant of this decision.*

CHAPTER 7

End-to-End Protocols

In Chapters 3 and 4 we discussed the topology and control of networks to provide high-bandwidth, low-latency paths between the network edges. In Chapters 5 and 6 we discussed how to design high-speed network components and end systems, respectively. This chapter describes the protocols and mechanisms that construct reliable, secure, high-performance end-to-end paths from one end system to another. These protocols and mechanisms operate at the transport layer in end systems, as shown in Figure 7.1, where per hop network services and local system functions are combined to create paths with end-to-end semantics. We will provide principles for deciding when to provide functions end-to-end or hop-by-hop.

The end-to-end version of the ideal network model introduced in Chapter 2 is shown in Figure 7.2. In this case the ideal path has unlimited bandwidth and no latency ($R = \infty$ and $D = 0$) through the network and the end systems from source application memory to destination application memory.

In this ideal case, the existence of a network is not seen by applications, which communicate by merely moving information between the memory modules. As usual, we will strive to get as close to this model as possible, but as we noted in the beginning of Chapter 6, real networks not only have constraints and variability on bandwidth and latency but also introduce errors in packet delivery, and have the need for end-to-end security. Thus an end-to-end *transport protocol* is required to deal with these issues. We will consider end-to-end issues and the resulting impact on high-speed transport protocol design.

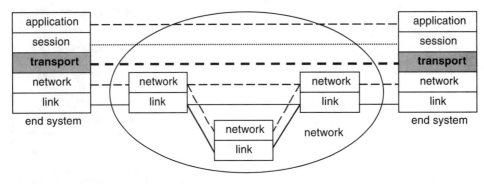

Figure 7.1   End-to-end protocols.

This chapter is organized as follows: Section 7.1 explains the semantics of "end-to-end," describes end-to-end functionality and mechanisms provided by transport protocols, and introduces the fundamental distinction between open-loop and closed-loop feedback control to manage transport protocol state. The remaining sections examine the different end-to-end mechanisms in more detail. Section 7.2 describes connection control and the management of state. Section 7.3 describes transport layer framing and multiplexing issues. Section 7.4 discusses alternative mechanisms for error control, and their ability to support high-speed networking. Section 7.5 describes open- and closed-loop flow and congestion control mechanisms. Section 7.6 briefly covers end-to-end security issues. Finally, Section 7.7 summarizes the chapter and provides suggestions for further reading.

7.1   Functions and Mechanisms

This section discusses the end-to-end arguments and their common misinterpretation. The various end-to-end mechanisms are then introduced, which will be the subject of subsequent sections in this chapter: framing and multiplexing, connection management, error control, flow and congestion control, and security. The service models and ways in which transport protocols are struc-

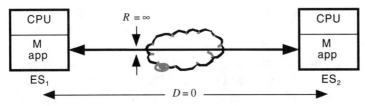

Figure 7.2   Ideal end-to-end network model.

tured are considered. Finally, two issues are introduced in a generic manner that will be of central importance in the remaining sections: open- versus closed-loop control and the effects of high bandwidth and large bandwidth-×-delay products on end-to-end mechanisms.

7.1.1   End-to-End Semantics

As introduced in Section 2.3.3, it is important to distinguish *end-to-end* (E2E) functions from *hop-by-hop* (HBH) functions. Hop-by-hop functions are performed locally without regard to the operations along all hops in the path. By contrast, end-to-end protocols cover the entire path of communication from source to destination, as shown in Figure 7.3.

Recall that the definition of E2E versus HBH is recursive, as noted in the Endpoint Recursion Corollary (3B). While we will be most concerned with *end system–to–end system* issues in this chapter, it is important to remember that end-to-end is a relative concept. Hop-by-hop protocols maintain state at the ends of links, subpaths, and/or subnetworks within the overall communication path. Examples of hop-by-hop functions include:

- Link layer protocols (such as SONET, HDLC, and PPP) (Section 5.1)

- Compression over low-bandwidth links and forward error correction over lossy wireless links

- Per hop network layer operations such as datagram forwarding and distributed routing protocols

- Link or subnetwork error control, including integrity checking, retransmission, and flow control

- Custom protocols for flow or error control, such as protocol boosters [Feldmeier 1998, Marcus 1998]

End-to-end functions manage state at the end system and often synchronize data or control between end systems. Examples include:

- Transport protocols such as TCP, TP4–OSI (transport protocol), and XTP, which provide framing, multiplexing, connection management, error control, and flow control.

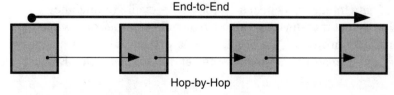

Figure 7.3   End-to-end versus hop-by-hop.

- Source routing [Sunshine 1977] for path determination.

- End-to-end encryption, which ensures the privacy of data through the *entire* communication path.

- Session protocols concerned with coordinating state between end systems and establishing other end-to-end associations.

- Application protocols such as the session initiation protocol (SIP) [Handley 1999], network time protocol (NTP) [Mills 1990] and distributed voting protocols [Gifford 1979].

7.1.1.1 The End-to-End Arguments

The End-to-End Arguments, which we introduced in Section 2.3.3, are the core determinant of what functionality needs to be provided by the transport layer. The most important goal of the ARPANET design was survivability in the face of node or link failures [Clark 1988]. This resulted in minimizing state inside the network and pushing functionality to the end systems. There had been other observations on the necessity to provide functionality end-to-end, particularly in the security domain[1]; the End-to-End Arguments [Saltzer 1984] formalized the reasoning.

End-to-End Argument *Functions required by communicating applications can be correctly and completely implemented only with the knowledge and help of the applications themselves. Providing these functions as features within the network itself is not possible.*

T-3

Hop-by-hop functional composition is not equivalent to end-to-end functionality. The reason for this is that hop-by-hop functionality provided at the edge of each link doesn't account for the behavior *within* the nodes that terminate the links. The canonical examples of end-to-end functions are data integrity and security. End users have no reason to trust per hop encryption mechanisms in which data is unencrypted at *any* point along the path. Link encryption does not prevent unauthorized access to data in the network nodes; encryption of data through a subnetwork does not guarantee privacy at the access link or between subnetworks.

In the case of data integrity, a checksum [or CRC—cyclic redundancy check] is used to detect transmission errors in a packet header or payload. While many link layer protocols, such as Ethernet, provide a link checksum on a per hop basis, this is insufficient to guarantee end-to-end integrity. Experi-

---

[1][Saltzer 1984] provides historical references.

ence has shown that a significant number of errors occur in between the protected links due to implementation bugs in widely deployed PC operating systems, poorly designed network interface cards, and memory bit errors in the routers [Stone 2000]. While we might hope that routers would never introduce errors,[2] an end-to-end checksum *ensures* that they are detected when they occur.[3] The issue of where to terminate the checksum in the end system is more subtle. In Section 6.4.2 we argued for performing the checksum in the network interface pipeline. Clearly, this is not the right thing to do if the network interface, interconnect to memory, and the memory itself are poorly designed or unreliable. Proper system design can extend this reliability, by protecting *all* data paths and memory location with parity checks at least, and error checking and correction (ECC) bits at best.

The original end-to-end arguments [Saltzer 1984] recognized that the performance of end-to-end functions might be enhanced by *also* providing hop-by-hop functions.

Hop-by-Hop Performance Enhancement Corollary   *It is beneficial to duplicate an end-to-end function hop-by-hop if the result is an overall (end-to-end) improvement in performance.*

T-3A

The example of data integrity is a good illustration of the Hop-by-Hop Performance Enhancement Corollary. For example, the ability of Ethernet to detect and recover from most link transmission errors improves overall (end-to-end) performance because the link-level recovery is very fast relative to the end-to-end delay of retransmission over a wide area network. This is particularly important in the case of poorly designed end system hardware interfaces, which are frequently installed on consumer personal computers.

Another example of a hop-by-hop performance enhancement is the provision of link layer reliability over lossy wireless links. Forward error correction (FEC) and per link retransmission can be used to reduce the effects of bit error rates to that of wireline links. In the absence of the hop-by-hop reliability, an entire end-to-end round-trip can be required to recover from such errors, resulting in significantly longer end-to-end latency over a long-haul network path that has a single short wireless access link.

---

[2]For robustness, ECC (error check and correction) memory should be used in network nodes and end systems for which economic value is associated with data integrity (for example, servers and nonhobby PCs).
[3]The probability that an error will be detected depends on the error model and error-detecting capability of the code.

On the other hand, an end-to-end protocol should *not* contain mechanisms that benefit some hops on the path, but are a performance degradation to other hops. For example, FEC is appropriate to lossy wireless links, as noted earlier, but trades bandwidth (FEC header bits) for latency of retransmission. This is the wrong thing to do on a low-speed (but reliable) modem access link. In this case, error control schemes should be optimized hop-by-hop, in conjunction with the required end-to-end retransmission. These per hop optimizations can be deployed as part of link protocols, where appropriate, or dynamic techniques such as *protocol boosters*.

7.1.1.2   Misinterpretations of the End-to-End Arguments

As often as the End-to-End Arguments (T-3) is invoked, the End-to-End Performance Enhancement Corollary (T-3A) is often forgotten. The following two conjectures summarize the most common misconceptions and overstatements of the End-to-End Argument:

E2E-Only. Do not replicate end-to-end services or features at the hop-by-hop level.

Everything-E2E. Implement as many services or features end-to-end as possible.

The E2E-Only conjecture suggests that hop-by-hop functions should *never* exist when the equivalent service is provided end-to-end. There are a number of examples of functions that *must* be provided end-to-end, but for which hop-by-hop provision enhances performance, such as the wireless link reliability case previously described. We should question whether an end-to-end function should also be performed hop-by-hop. If there is no performance benefit in doing so, it probably comes at the expense of performance, complexity, and reliability. This is why we questioned the need for SONET automatic protection switching (APS) in Example 5.3.

The Everything-E2E conjecture asserts that every function and service possible should be implemented end-to-end, and that hop-by-hop protocols should be minimal. This conjecture is an improper application of the Internet design philosophy [Clark 1988], which was based on keeping the network simple and stateless, with the majority of complexity and intelligence in the end systems. This design philosophy allowed the network to be robust in the presence of network failures and sabotage. This property was of primary concern to the initial ARPANET designers [McQuillan 1997, Cerf 1983b, Clark 1988, Carpenter 1996]. An additional benefit of moving complexity to the edges is that unexpected behavior and failures resulting from complexity are isolated to individual end systems and data transfers, rather than affecting the network at large. Unfortunately, the reasoned design principles of the ARPANET have been misinterpreted as justifying the Everything-E2E conjecture. On the other hand, the Internet transparency governed by the End-to-End Arguments is seriously threatened [Carpenter 2000].

Another application of the Everything-E2E conjecture was used by some proponents of optical networking in the late 1980s. The idea was that a large transparent optical WDM (wavelength division multiplexing) broadcast-and-select star network would allow *all* protocol functionality to be pushed to the edges. Senders broadcast data into the star with the only network layer protocol information consisting of the destination address, allowing the destination to tune to the appropriate wavelength. There is a flat address space, no routing protocol, and only a trivial wavelength contention resolution mechanism at the ingress point of the star. There are two problems with this scheme: aggregate bandwidth and power. First, the total aggregate bandwidth of a shared optical medium is on the order of 20 Tb/s (Section 5.1.1), but in the nearer term the usable aggregate is much less than 1 Tb/s, which happened to be similar to the estimated total aggregate bandwidth of the second-generation data networks of the 1980s. When this aggregate bandwidth of any shared medium is exceeded, however, we need to exploit the Scalability of Mesh Topologies (N-II.4) to employ spatial reuse; this now *requires* network routing protocols. Second, the amount of power required by the transmitter to drive a star coupler with millions or billions of ports is untenable. Thus, while optical stars may be useful as small to moderate size LAN switches, they cannot provide full end-to-end functionality. This means that they do not eliminate the need for hop-by-hop behaviors.

As the demands for high-speed networking increase and technology improves, there is continuous tension between the desire to keep the network simple and thus fast and the desire to augment the interior of the network with additional capabilities. This usually raises the End-to-End Argument (T-3), frequently in the form of the Everything-E2E conjecture. It is critical to apply the Systemic Optimization Principle (IV) to determine the *overall* effect of end-to-end versus hop-by-hop functionality. The fact that Resource Tradeoffs Change (2A) over time complicates our ability to properly determine where functionality should lie.

For example, connection-oriented fast packet switching aimed to enable significantly higher bandwidths by installing state in switches, so that packets could be quickly switched by a simple connection identifier table lookup, as described in Section 5.3. This pushed complexity to the edge of the network in the form of connection management and signaling. For the resource tradeoffs of third-generation networks (1990s), this had the intended effect: fast packet-switched networks were capable of supporting links at least an order of magnitude faster than conventional datagram-forwarding networks. In the fourth-generation (1990s), VLSI technology enabled complex processing operations, such as IP address lookup, to occur at high link bandwidths, and has reduced the need for hard connection state in switches, as discussed in

Section 5.5. The endpoints of fast packet switching have moved from the network edge to the switch fabric edge, with per switch segmentation and reassembly to allow cell switching in the fabric, as described in Section 5.3.3. Hop-by-hop segmentation and reassembly seemed absurd to many fast packet-switching researchers in the late 1980s, but has been enabled by changing resource tradeoffs, and required by the fact that Backward Compatibility Inhibits Radical Change (III.7). Performing segmentation and reassembly at each node allows fast IP switches to be dropped in the Internet as needed, rather than requiring entire (sub)networks be replaced.

Thus the end-to-end arguments *jointly* consist of End-to-End Argument and the Hop-by-Hop Performance Enhancement Corollary. Insisting on the plural use of the word *arguments* emphasizes the corollary and that the incorrect E2E-only and everything-E2E conjectures should not be applied.

7.1.1.3   *The Meaning of "In the Network"*

In this chapter (and Chapter 8) we will frequently be concerned with what functionality should be "in the network," so it is important to understand the various meaning that can be attributed to this statement. There are three distinct views [Sterbenz 1996]:

Functional. The functional view is based on the layer of the protocol stack; thus physical, link, and network layer functions are *in the network*; the session, transport, and application layers are not. An example of a function that is in the network is multicast; it is a native capability of ATM and IP with IGMP (Internet group multicast protocol) [Deering 1989]. Application layer multicast (Section 8.3.2) can be deployed when network layer multicast is not available.

Topological. The topological view has to do with whether or not functions and resources are colocated with network nodes or located with subscriber end systems. The motivation for Location of Data (7B) and servers topologically in the network is provided in Chapter 8. For example, locating caches throughout the network reduces response time and can also reduce aggregate bandwidth. Topologically in the network does *not* mean functionally in the network. Caching is an application layer service, even if a network layer enhancement like active networking is the enabler of this service.

Administrative. The administrative view relates to what entity has ownership and control of a particular function. For example, a network provider may own caches colocated with network nodes, or a third-party service provider may locate caches near backbone nodes. Administrative placement of functionality and services is frequently dictated more by business model than technical concerns.

EXAMPLE 7.1: EMAIL AND WEB CACHES

Both email and the Web are examples of where the application layer defines the endpoints for end-to-end functionality. In email, TCP is used to reliably transfer messages between mail servers. The use of TCP ensures that messages do not get corrupted in transit on these hops; however, mail can (and does) get lost at the servers themselves. Mail queues can back up or intermediate servers can be unavailable due to network outages or changes in configuration. The originating server cannot assume mail will get to its destination after successfully transmitting it on the first hop; an application-layer receipt is required from the ultimate destination to confirm delivery. It is this final receipt that establishes end-to-end delivery.

Email exemplifies the tradeoff between end-to-end and hop-by-hop reliability. TCP establishes hop-by-hop reliability with respect to the mail relays, and the application receipt establishes end-to-end reliability between the sending and receiving email client. Without the receipt, end-to-end delivery cannot be confirmed; without hop-by-hop reliability, an entire mail message would need to be retransmitted any time any packet of a message was lost between mail relays.

A similar case applies to the Web. Web caches reduce the latency, aggregate bandwidth, and server load, as described in Section 8.3.1. Multiple concatenated TCP connections can be involved between the client, a proxy, and the cache; TCP connections are hop-by-hop with respect to client-to-server end-to-end application layer association. It is possible to attempt to access a Web page at a remote site and to fail on an intermediate hop, without knowing whether the original server, a cache, a proxy, or link in between is down. The request might not make it to the cache or the reply might not return. If the requested page is static content to be viewed, it can be requested again by the user with minimal annoyance. If the failure occurs during an electronic commerce transaction, the user has no idea whether a purchase has been made, and may erroneously make multiple purchases by retrying. An out-of-band email confirmation is typically used to confirm the purchase, which is not in itself reliable.

In both cases the limitation of the hop-by-hop composition can only be overcome by the addition of a true end-to-end exchange at the application layer.

In this chapter, we will be primarily concerned with the *functional* distinction, and consider end system–to–end system transport layer mechanisms. But it is important to understand that the Endpoint Recursion Corollary (4B) applies at all levels. The high-speed application layer optimizations described in Chapter 8 frequently result in a concatenated sequence of transport layer connections or datagram flows. This means that the end-to-end recursion is *application to application*, rather than at the transport layer. The implication of this is that the *application layer* must be ultimately responsible for the end-to-end mechanisms in this case.

7.1.2 End-to-End Mechanisms

End-to-end mechanisms fall into six categories:

1. **Framing**. Responsible for the encapsulation of application data units (ADUs) into the transport protocol data units (TPDUs) that are transmitted end-to-end and recovering them back into ADUs at the receiving side. This may also consist of fragmenting and reassembling ADUs to TPDUs at the sending and receiving end, respectively, if the ADU is larger than the supported path maximum transfer unit (MTU).

2. **Multiplexing**. Responsible for interleaving data from applications into the shared network and matching incoming packets from the network to the proper receiving application. In the case of transport protocols, we need to be concerned with the matching of transport connections to underlying network flows and connections below, as well as to session and application associations above. Multiplexing can be done at multiple layers in the protocol stack, but this creates problems in high-speed networks, impacting latency, flow control, and buffering requirements.

3. **End-to-end state and connection management**. Responsible for establishing end-to-end state for a flow of packets between end systems. Connection management is typically required for service models that need reliable transport of data, or some assurance of traffic characteristics, and involves shared state. While many applications have these requirements, some do not. In the case of best-effort unreliable applications, connection management is not needed, and state is not explicitly shared between end systems. The relative latency contribution of control exchanges increases with bandwidth-$\times$-delay product.

4. **Error control**. Responsible for correcting transmission errors introduced in the network, including corrupted, lost, misordered, and duplicated packets, by retransmitting and resequencing packets as necessary. This is referred to as automatic repeat request (ARQ). Error control can also consist of FEC to correct bit errors without requiring retransmission. Error control is not needed for applications whose loss tolerance exceeds the loss characteristics of the network path. Providing end-to-end reliability in high bandwidth–delay product networks is challenging.

5. **Flow control**. Responsible for controlling the interval over which packets are transferred to meet application needs and for which the receiving

end system can accept.[4] A key function is to buffer data between the endpoint applications, controlling the flow of data into the network, and staging it up to the receiving end system. Choices in flow control are window-and rate-based mechanisms.

6. **Congestion control [Davies 1972].** Responsible for preventing and re-acting to network congestion; the former is more specifically called *congestion avoidance* [Jacobson 1988]. In general, congestion control uses information from the network to determine the proper timing of packet transmission. The feedback can be explicit information from the network nodes, or implicit, using a window-based mechanism that infers congestion from packet loss. The ability to prevent or react quickly to congestion is essential in high-speed networks.

The way in which the transport protocol implements these mechanisms is, in turn, dependent on the service model and mechanisms implemented in the network by the edge-to-edge network layer protocols and hop-by-hop link protocols.

We are concerned with what functions must be implemented end-to-end by the transport protocol, what functions are dependent on hop-by-hop functionality, and how these issues affect high-speed networking. It is critical that end-to-end mechanisms efficiently match the mechanisms provided by the network, and, in some cases, the network model has a profound effect on what must be done end-to-end. For example, in a connection-oriented network, multiplexing can be done at the network layer by assigning application flows directly to network connections. In a datagram network, multiplexing must be done at the transport layer. In other cases, such as error control, the End-to-End Argument (T-3) will directly indicate functionality that must be done end-to-end.

7.1.3 Transport Protocols

Now that we have described the set of orthogonal end-to-end mechanisms and functions, we will examine the way that transport protocols are organized and designed to use them. Transport protocols manage the transfer of data between end systems, providing the service needed by communicating applications. The service model consists of four major categories:

1. **Transfer mode.** Consists of the data transfer mode: connectionless datagram, connection-oriented, transaction, and continuous media streaming.

[4]The terminology used for flow and congestion control is overloaded, so in this chapter we will use the word *rate* solely to apply to open-loop rate control and the corresponding rate specification. The word *flow* will only be used in conjunction with flow control dictated by the receiver.

2. **Reliability.** Refers to whether or not data needs to be delivered in a reliable manner, or errors can be tolerated, and the degree of loss tolerance. Many applications (such as file transfer) are intolerant to data loss, but some applications (such as streaming video) may be tolerant to corrupted or lost data.

3. **Delivery order.** Refers to whether or not packets need to be delivered to the receiver in the same order transmitted. Some applications require ordered delivery, some are able to reorder, and some do not care about the order of data at all.

4. **Traffic characteristics.** Refers to the parameters to which the application is sensitive, such as data rate, jitter (variability in rate), and latency, including the need for real-time constraints.

The detailed specification of all the parameters of reliability and traffic characteristics are described as the QOS (quality of service) provided to the application. These are implemented by the transport protocol end-to-end control mechanisms, consisting of error and flow control, in conjunction with the characteristics of the path provided by the network.

7.1.3.1 Types of Transport Protocols

Another issue that will be of concern is how specifically a transport protocol is targeted to a particular application. We define a spectrum of specificity:

General-purpose transport protocols, such as TCP [Postel 1981d], OSI TP4, and XTP, which are designed to provide a full set of transport services to a wide variety of applications.

Functionally partitioned transport protocols, which provide a variety of service models, but are designed in a modular manner to efficiently provide a selectable menu of service models efficiently composed for a particular application. One approach to modularity is to provide a restricted combination of service options. For example, SNR [Netravali 1990] provides three modes of operation: mode 0—no error or flow control, mode 1—flow control but no error control, and mode 3—error and flow control. The OSI transport protocol suite contains five classes of transport protocols [Piscitello 1993, Jain 1993]: TP0—basic functionality with error reporting,[5] TP1—basic error recovery, TP2—basic functionality with error reporting and multiplexing, TP3—error recovery and multiplexing, and TP4—full error and flow control and multiplexing. The specification of classes was based on expected network layer functionality, but does not decree implementation as a single modular protocol.

---

[5]Error *reporting* from the network. The only ISO class that does its *own* end-to-end error detection and control is TP4.

A more modular approach is possible. TP++ [Feldmeier 1994] is designed as a set of orthogonal components, dictated by architectural features to support high-speed networking [Feldmeier 1993]. This allows selection and replacement of features in the protocol. The microprotocol concept [O'Malley 1990] allows construction of a partial-order dependency graph to compose arbitrary microprotocol elements into a (macro-) protocol. As discussed in Section 6.2.3, we need to be very careful that composition mechanisms are efficient, and that we don't introduce overheads such as context switching and data copies, as is the case for Unix System V streams [Bach 1986].

XTP [Chesson 1989, Strayer 1992] was designed to be modular for a different reason. As described in Section 6.4.1, XTP was designed for implementation in VLSI hardware. It was recognized that hardware may be limited in capacity, and which functions are implemented in hardware versus software may differ in separate implementations and as technology changes. In order to increase the efficiency of the hardware implementation, functions that are not required by a protocol are enabled or disabled as desired, resulting in a modular approach.

Application-oriented transport protocols [Parulkar 1990a, Sterbenz 1990d] are targeted to broad classes of applications such as message or object transfer, transactions (for example, VMTP [Cheriton 1986]) streaming media, and remote login. Note that while TCP was originally designed as a general-purpose transport protocol, the Internet protocol suite has shifted a bit toward the direction of being application-oriented, with TCP for reliable data transfer, UDP for unreliable transfer [Postel 1980b], T/TCP (TCP for transactions) [Braden 1992],[6] and RTP for real-time communications [Schulzrinne 1996].

Special-purpose transport protocols are designed for a specific application (such as NETBLT for bulk transfer [Clark 1987]).

Transport Protocol Functionality   *Transport protocols must be organized to deliver the set of end-to-end high-bandwidth, low-latency services needed by applications. Options and service models should be modularly accessible, without unintended performance degradation and feature interactions.*

T-IV

The proper specialization of a transport protocol is really more of a software engineering and deployment issue than a fundamental choice that matters. The important aspect is that unneeded services do not impair those that are needed by a particular high-speed application. There is no reason why a

---

[6]Although in practice, T/TCP has not been widely used for transactions such as Web browsing, in part due to security concerns with the current specification, as discussed on the IETF end-to-end mailing list.

modularly designed fully functional transport protocol cannot be efficient for high-speed networking [Watson 1987].

Transport protocols designed for high performance are frequently referred to as *lightweight*. While this is a term that does not have a precise definition, it generally refers to a protocol that has packet formats and control mechanisms designed to be simple, streamlined, and efficient, with a carefully optimized critical path. It is easier to design a special-purpose protocol to be lightweight, and indeed early transport protocol research concentrated on this approach. Careful functional partitioning of protocols can yield the same effect, as we have described.[7]

EXAMPLE 7.2: END-TO-END INTERNET PROTOCOLS

The Internet protocol suite was originally based on a single integrated transport and network layer protocol called network control program (NCP), later replaced with transmission control protocol (TCP) [Cerf 1974] in 1977. TCP was split in 1978 into a distinct transport and network layer: TCP over Internet protocol (IP). TCP provides connection-oriented reliable delivery. User datagram protocol (UDP) [Postel 1980b] was later added to provide (almost) direct access to IP datagram transfer, as shown in Figure 7.4.

More recently, two additional transport protocols have been added to the suite: T/TCP (TCP for transactions) and real-time transport protocol (RTP) [Schulzrinne 1996], which generally encapsulates UDP datagrams.

Above these transport protocols are a number of protocols that are conventionally called *application layer protocols*, simply because they are higher in the protocol stack than the transport protocol. A common selection is

- HTTP—hypertext transfer protocol for Web browsing
- SMTP—simple mail transfer protocol for the transfer of email between servers
- FTP—file transfer protocol for bulk transfer of files
- Telnet—for remote login to networked computers
- NFS—network file system for remote file access
- RTSP—real-time streaming protocol for the control of multimedia streaming

There is nothing fundamental about the distinction between transport and application protocols. It is really a matter of protocol reuse, efficiency, and software engineering that dictate where in the stack a new higher-layer protocol should reside. These protocols use the services of existing transport protocols to avoid the need to reinvent all of the functionality provided by TCP and UDP, even though it may not be the most efficient way to operate.

---

[7]Clearly, no one would admit to designing a new *heavyweight* protocol.

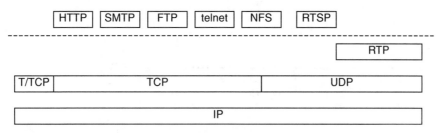

Figure 7.4   End-to-end Internet protocols.

7.1.4   Control of State

The maintenance of state is an essential factor in connection, flow, and error control mechanisms. The transport layer is the place where state must be coordinated for the *entire* communication path between end systems. State should be maintained in a stable manner, but may need to be changed in response to the dynamic behavior of the network below or the applications above.

7.1.4.1   *Open-Loop Control*

Control can be based on either open-loop or closed-loop feedback. Open-loop control, shown in Figure 7.5a, relies on state installed in the sender to regulate behavior. If there is to be any assurance of the quality of data delivery, this state must be based on some a priori knowledge of the network path characteristics, such as bandwidth, latency, and loss rates.

Examples of open-loop control are rate-based flow control (to be described in Section 7.5.2), and FEC (to be described in Section 7.4.4). If there is no a priori information about the path, there is no basis on which to set open-loop parameters, such as the bandwidth for rate control or the degree of forward error correction. Open-loop control does not adapt to dynamic network conditions, but may be adjusted at the coarse granularity of connection modification.

7.1.4.2   *Closed-Loop Control*

Closed-loop feedback control depends on ongoing feedback from the network layer protocols and components to adjust the behavior of the sender, as shown in Figure 7.5b. In the case of transport protocols, the feedback loop is terminated at the receiving end of a flow. It may be possible to use intermediate per hop state to close a shorter loop as shown in Figure 7.5c; this is an application of the Hop-by-Hop Performance Enhancement Corollary (T-3A).

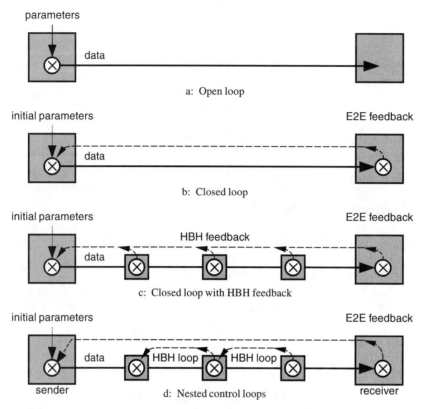

Figure 7.5   Open- and closed-loop feedback control.

An example is using backward explicit congestion notification, explained in Section 4.2.2, to reduce the latency of reacting to congestion. In this case, intermediate information is used for end-to-end control.

The composition of hop-by-hop loops that are nested within an end-to-end loop is shown in Figure 7.5d. Concatenated or nested feedback loops do not necessarily create stable end-to-end feedback. They are harder to control and may result in unpredictable or unstable behavior.

Determining the proper aggressiveness of the feedback mechanisms can be difficult. The two goals that are difficult to balance are fast convergence and stability. Aggressive fast convergence mechanisms (for example, exponential adjustment of parameters) may overreact to transient conditions; slow convergence mechanisms (for example, linear adjustment of parameters) take many round-trip times to converge. Additive increase/multiplicative decrease algorithms (AIMD) provide a good balance, and will be discussed in Section 7.5.4 in the context of congestion control.

> **Aggressiveness of Closed-Loop Control**   *The response to closed-loop feedback must be rapid enough so the system converges quickly to a new stable state—but not so aggressive that oscillations occur due to overreaction to transients.*
>
> **T-6D*a***

As a result of the convergence time, many closed-loop mechanisms are appropriate only for end-to-end associations lasting multiple round-trip times, where network properties, such as bandwidth, latency, and expected loss, are relatively stable over that period of time. When a connection is shorter than tens of round-trip times, or when network conditions fluctuate before the endpoints can react, open-loop control is indicated, or state sharing among connections as described in Section 7.2.3.

7.1.4.3   Hybrid Control

High-speed networks can use both open- and closed-loop control mechanisms. Closed-loop control is often required end-to-end (for example, for error correction), and open-loop can be used as a performance enhancement, either end-to-end or hop-by hop to reduce the frequency and degree of the closed-loop controls. For example, closed-loop control can be used for quick initial negotiation of parameters end-to-end, with subsequent open-loop control based on these parameters.

Another example of a hybrid mechanism is random early detection (RED) [Floyd 1993], introduced in Section 5.1.4. RED randomly discards packets when a queue length threshold is exceeded. This is an open-loop Congestion Avoidance (T-II.4*c*) mechanism, based solely on the queue state at a particular switch, which keeps queues from building, and helps reduce the impact of flows that are transmitting at a rate that would cause congestion. It also provides implicit notification to closed-loop control because sources that infer packet loss as congestion will throttle their transmission, as described in Section 7.5.4.

> **Open- versus Closed-Loop Control**   *Use open-loop control based on knowledge of the network path to reduce the delay in closed-loop convergence. Use closed-loop control to react to dynamic network and application behavior; intermediate per hop feedback can sometimes reduce the time to converge.*
>
> **T-6D**

Closed-loop control mechanisms are sensitive to both round-trip time and the bandwidth-$\times$-delay product; open-loop control is not. Thus, as network bandwidth increases, the relative time devoted to control increases for a given amount of data, and there is incentive to rely more heavily on open-loop control.

7.2 State Management

This section describes the end-to-end management of state in general, and connection control in particular. First the impact of high-speed networking is considered, consisting of the foreshortening of the data transmission without a corresponding decrease in the latency of control, and the increased difficulty in managing state. The next two subsections will discuss techniques to deal with these issues.

7.2.1 Impact of High Speed

High-speed networks have two significant effects on end-to-end state maintenance and connection control: the shortening of data transfer relative to end-to-end control operations and the increased state management between the end systems.

7.2.1.1 Connection Shortening

Even though it is common to talk about the *speed* of a link, we really mean the transmission data *rate* along a link. As data rates increase, packets don't really go faster in the network; the velocity of light governs the speed at which bits travel through the network. Recall from Chapter 4 that the time for a packet to traverse a link is the sum of the propagation and transmission delays $t_p + t_b$. The time for a bit to traverse a link is $t_p = x/kc$, where x is the distance traversed and kc is the velocity of light through a particular link medium.[8] At low rates, or for very long connections (for example, transfer of a large amount of data), the connection is dominated by the steady-state of data packet and acknowledgment packet exchanges [Heidemann 1997].

What does change with data rate, however, is the time to transmit (and receive) the block of data on the link, $t_b = b/r$ where b is the length of the data block and r is the bit rate. As r increases t_b decreases. This results in a shortening of the data transmission component proportional to the data rate [Touch 1994], as shown in Figure 7.6.

Assume a three-way handshake connection establishment by the sender of the data.[9] After approximately one round-trip time t_{RTT}, data can begin to flow. After a reliable data-transfer phase, ensured by the return of a final ACK mes-

---

[8]$1/k$ is the index of refraction of the medium.
[9]This is similar to the flow shown in Figure 4.7, except that we are hiding the intermediate hops (whose latency components are folded into t_p), and are not concerned about individual packets in the flow (all of which, including interpacket spacing are included in t_b). Similarly we are not concerned with the individual signaling delays in the network and it suffices to simplify to the granularity of t_{RTT}.

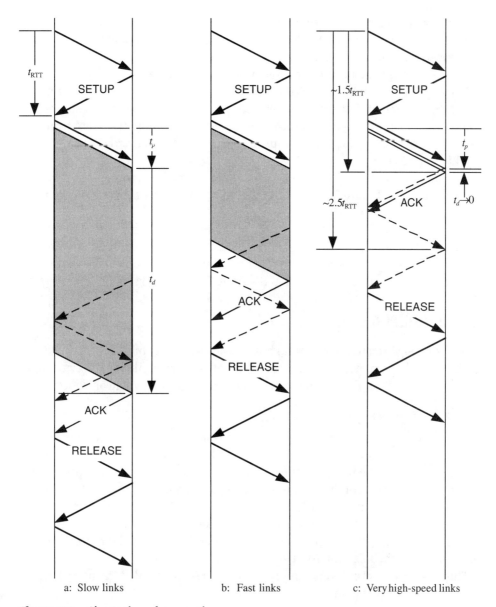

Figure 7.6 Shortening of connections.

sage to the sender, the connection can be released. As the data rate $r \to \infty$, $t_b \to 0$ and thus the time to ensure reliable delivery of the data $D \to 1.5\, t_{\mathrm{RTT}}$.

Furthermore, if any end-to-end control interactions are required during the transfer, they are less likely to complete within the data-transfer phase as the data rate increases. Consider the case of a retransmission request for a lost packet midstream, shown by the dashed arrows. In the slow link case of

Figure 7.6a, the retransmission may be able to occur during the normal data transmission phase. When the data rate is increased, it is virtually certain that the retransmission will significantly delay the delivery of the data D to 2.5 t_{RTT}, and increase the time before the connection can be released.

Finally, note that while the RELEASE of the connection does not directly affect the latency of data transfer for a particular connection, in a resource-constrained network it prevents *other* connections and data transfers from getting the resources they need. Thus, it is important to release resources as quickly as possible.

We can observe the same effect by lengthening the links for a given data rate, as shown in Figure 7.7. The effect of end-to-end latencies on control messages is dramatic as the distance increases.

Thus, it is important to adapt the control mechanisms to minimize unneeded latency. This will be the subject of Section 7.2.2 from an overall transfer and connection management perspective, with refinements specific to error and flow/congestion control discussed in Sections 7.4 and 7.5, respectively.

7.2.1.2   State Management

The second significant impact of high bandwidth-×-delay product networks is the increased complexity in state management. This is manifested in two ways: frequency of state updates and the amount of state out of synchronization.

7.2.1.2.1   Frequency of State Change

First, as the data rate increases, so does the *frequency* at which state must be updated. Both the network and the end-to-end transfer of a particular data flow drive this. In the network, the frequency of events and the rate of change in dynamic network conditions increase, requiring more frequent adjustment to end system state, particularly for congestion avoidance mechanisms. Furthermore, for a given packet size, the interpacket time decreases, requiring more frequent adjustments at both the sender and receiver, and more frequent end-to-end synchronization for a given data transfer flow.

This results in increased demand on the processing needed in end systems to keep up with the higher frequency of state change.

7.2.1.2.2   State out of Synchronization

Second, as the bandwidth-×-delay product increases, so does the amount of *state out of synchronization* [Clark 1987]. Whenever a packet is sent across the network that will affect the state of the remote side, it takes a one-way propagation delay before that state update can take place. Thus, the two ends of an end-to-end association are always at least a propagation delay out of sync and, in cases where state information is requested from the other end, an RTT out of date.

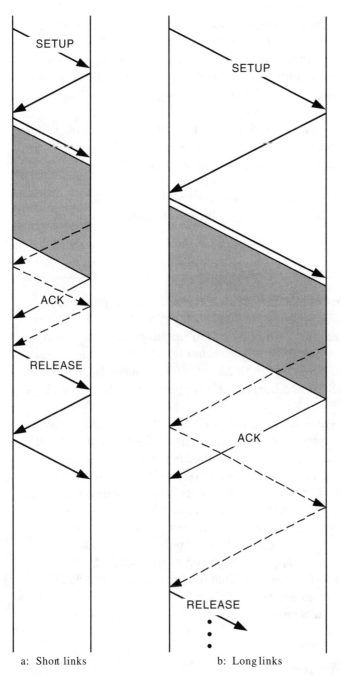

a: Short links   b: Long links

Figure 7.7 Long latency effects.

As the bandwidth-$\times$-delay product increases, state is increasingly out of synchronization for a given end-to-end latency, since more packets are in flight. This is the converse of the observation that the frequency of update needs to increase with bandwidth-$\times$-delay product. Long latencies limit the ability to keep the state synchronized end-to-end, even with more frequent updates.

This increases the memory required to maintain additional state out of synchronization, as well as processing needed to access and maintain the larger data structures. Furthermore, fields in packet headers may need to be larger to account for more packets in flight, for example, sequence numbers.

Techniques to manage the increased complexity in state management due to increased frequency and state out of synchronization are the topic of Section 7.2.3.

7.2.1.3   *Multipoint and Multicast*

A number of applications require associations between multiple simultaneous end systems and users. The network layer may provide a multipoint connection service, (for example, ATM point-to-multipoint and leaf-initiated join connections) or multicast forwarding (for example, IP IGMP). There is compelling reason to provide Support for Multicast (2C) to conserve bandwidth, as discussed in Section 3.3.1 and motivated by applications discussed in Chapter 8.

If total reliability is needed then multipoint connection state must be maintained end-to-end, as for point-to-point connections. While the total number of connections over which state must be maintained is less for multicast, the complexity of state for each reliable multicast connection is substantially greater than for a point-to-point connection. If careful state aggregation techniques are not employed, the amount of state and control messages for a $1:n$ point-to-multipoint connection can be $O(n)$, and for an $n:n$ multipoint-to-multipoint set $O(n^2)$, which is no better than individual point-to-point connections.

Fortunately, many multicast applications, such as multicast of entertainment video, do not need total reliability. This relaxes some of the requirements for complex state management and allows more reliance on open-loop control (to reduce the control message traffic) and soft state (described in Section 7.2.3).

7.2.2   Transfer Modes

The transport protocol is responsible for transporting data end-to-end, based on the service model required by the application. The information transfer type and reliability requirements determine the mode of information transfer. There are two fundamental modes to consider: connectionless datagram and connection-oriented, as shown Figure 7.8. There are also two variants that are important enough to warrant separate discussion in the context of high-speed networks: transactions and streaming of continuous media.

7.2.2.1   *Datagram Transfer*

In the case of unreliable datagram transfer, an ADU is encapsulated into a TPDU with no explicit end-to-end state coordination. The datagram carries all of the state that it needs (emphasized by the dark stripe in the beginning of the packet in Figure 7.8a), typically the destination end-system address and application port to which it is destined, along with a checksum for integrity checking on receipt. As for any end-to-end association, there is some implicit shared state, for example, knowledge about the global nature of addresses and the way in which application ports are demultiplexed. The latency of a datagram transfer consists only of the transmission delay based on the packet size t_b and the propagation delay through the network t_p; there is no overhead for connection SETUP.

A datagram transport protocol (such as UDP or TP0) has only framing and multiplexing functionality. The lack of end-to-end state establishment does not allow for any closed-loop control. Thus, reliability cannot be guaranteed (but can be statistically enhanced as described in Section 7.4.4), and the only QOS mechanisms possible are open-loop rate transmission with best-effort transfer.

Connectionless transfer makes sense where total reliability is not required, or where the reliability model is application specific or occurs at a large granularity. For example, if the application is periodically synchronizing state, and only requires a fraction of the messages to be reliably delivered, retransmission of information is best handled in application state machines.

7.2.2.2   *Connection-Oriented Transfer*

When reliable data transfer is needed, or when QOS guarantees are required, there is the need for end-to-end state installation and maintenance. This is performed by end-to-end connection control and may exploit the underlying capabilities of a connection-oriented network, as described in Section 4.1.3 and shown in Figure 7.8c.

7.2.2.2.1   **Transport and Network Connection**

If the network layer provides a connection service to the transport layer, the transport layer can simply pass setup-requests down to the network layer, as shown in Figure 7.9a. The network layer is then responsible for exchanging connection signaling messages (described in Section 4.1.3) and maintaining the connection state machines. This considerably simplifies the transport

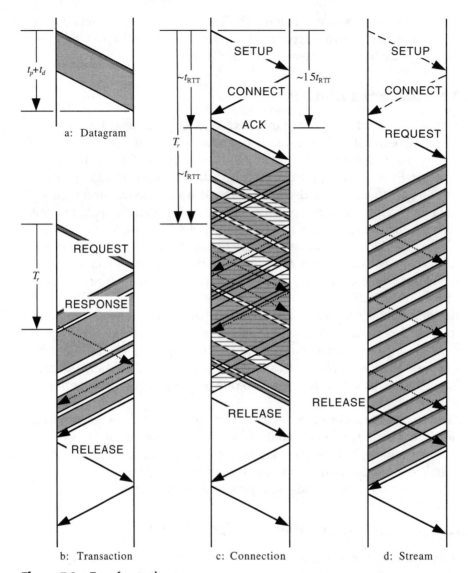

a: Datagram

b: Transaction

c: Connection

d: Stream

Figure 7.8   Transfer modes.

layer, as long as the connection model and parameters match that needed by the transport layer to provide the requisite service to the application. This is the model that the ATM protocol suite assumes. Note, however, that if the network layer provides *only* a connection-oriented service, then some mechanism must be in place to transfer transport layer datagrams without suffering the latency of connection setup.

On the other hand, if the network layer provides no support for connections, then the transport layer must manage the connections, as shown in

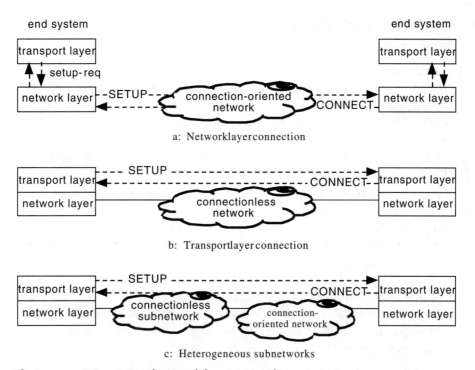

Figure 7.9 Transport and network layer connections.

Figure 7.9b. Since the network layer is connectionless, there is no connection state on which the transport layer can rely. The network layer may still accumulate and maintain internal soft state to increase the performance of packet switching, as described in Section 4.1.4. This is the model that the IP-based Internet uses.

The End-to-End Principle (T-3) tells us that if *any* part of the network traversed by a given data transfer is connectionless, then the transport layer *must* perform connection management, as shown in Figure 7.9c. The Hourglass Principle (4D) drives us toward a single global network layer protocol, which is IP. Although connection-oriented enhancements [Cranor 1993] and alternatives (such as ST2 [Delgrossi 1995]) have been proposed as performance enhancements, the fact that Backward Compatibility Inhibits Radical Change (III.7) indicates that the network layer must be assumed to be connectionless IP, and the transport layer must be prepared to provide connection management capabilities. In the cases where an end-to-end connection solely traverses a connection-oriented (sub)network, it may directly use the network layer connection capabilities; the transport layer connection establishment phase can perform this negotiation with the network layer.

7.2.2.2.2 Transport Connections

The life of a connection can be divided into four phases:

1. **Establishing.** This consists of signaling, initializing, and negotiating the end-to-end connection state. A connection is typically established by a three-way handshake [Tomlinson 1974, Sunshine 1978] consisting of SETUP, CONNECT, ACK messages (SYN, SYN, ACK in TCP). The establishing state is entered when a request comes from an application at the same endpoint. The requested state is entered when a connection SETUP message comes in from the network. Once both endpoints have agreed to the connection, data then can flow in one or both directions, as shown in Figure 7.8c. The initiator can start transferring data after approximately one RTT when the CONNECT is received; the called party can begin transfer after about 1.5 RTTs when the three-way handshake is complete.

   Establishment determines the static connection properties, such as the endpoint identifiers, path MTU, traffic class (including QOS and reliability requirements) and security associations. Establishment also initializes dynamic state, including traffic parameters and RTT estimates, which may vary as the connection progresses.

2. **Initializing.** Once the connection has been established, data can be transferred, but there may be a period of time before state converges. Examples of this include beginning to forward data before soft state is established (Figure 4.8), provisional best-effort transfer mode for optimistic connection establishment (Figure 4.9), and slow start for congestion avoidance (described in Section 7.5.4). Closed-loop feedback control has an initialization phase that lasts until steady-state stability has been reached; open-loop connection control may not have an initialization phase at all, because there is no mechanism to make changes from its settings determined by the establishment phase.

3. **Steady state.** The steady state[10] describes the long-term connection behavior after the end of the initialization phase. During steady state, the connection is stable, and state is updated at each end to reflect the status of the connection. This may be done by explicit state exchanges or based on information inferred from the incoming packet stream. It can also be affected by the local state of the endpoint (for example, end system CPU load or buffer availability) or by the state of other connections.

---

[10]*Steady state*, in the control theoretic sense, indicates that the transient response (initialization phase) has ended and the system has converged on stable behavior. During steady state, there can be variations and oscillations in the state, but they are bounded by negative feedback control in the case of closed-loop systems.

4. **Closing.** Once the data-transfer phase is completed, the state and resources held by the connection are no longer needed, and should be released for reuse by other data transfers. The closing phase performs this
function. It may be explicitly entered, for example, by the issuance of a
connection RELEASE signaling message, or may occur due to the time-
out of soft state.

Figure 7.10 shows a simple connection state machine that shows the
connection phases and their relationship to signaling messages. Each side
of the connection has its own state machine, and transitions can be triggered by requests from the application (transitions on the left side of the
figure) or messages coming from the network (transitions on the right side
of the figure).

Now that we have described connectionless datagrams and connections,
which are the fundamental transfer modes, we describe two important variants: transactions and continuous media streaming. Both of these variants can
be supported by either datagrams or fully reliable connections, but their mode
of operation is sufficiently different that optimizations in the end-to-end state
coordination are warranted in high-speed networks. In the case of transac-

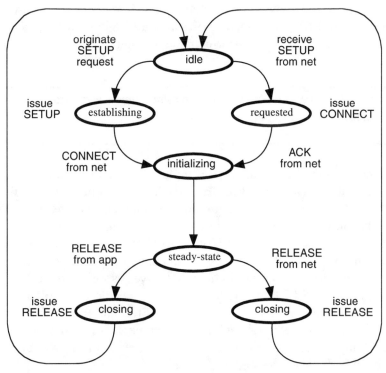

Figure 7.10 Connection state machine.

tions, we want to avoid the latency of connection setup, but still may need end-to-end state synchronization for the data response. In the case of continuous streaming media, the reliability and timing requirements are substantially different from conventional data connections.

7.2.2.3 Transactions

Transactions consist of a request (which is usually a short message) followed by a response, which can vary from a short response (for example, airline reservation transaction) to a large amount of data (for example, Web page). Transactions can be generated by interactive users, or by programs such as online transaction processing of databases and remote procedure calls in distributed processing.

Transactions generally require reliable transfer of data, and thus require connection state to be established, particularly for the response, which may involve many packets. The challenge is that transactions are frequently issued in interactive applications, and thus require interactive response bounds T_r of between 100 ms and 1 s, as described in Section 8.1.2.

Thus, the standard connection-oriented transfer model can be optimized so that data is received after a single RTT, as shown in Figure 7.8b, rather than the two RTTs required in the conventional connection-oriented case of Figure 7.8c. As in Figures 7.6 and 7.7, the dashed arrows indicate additional control mechanisms, such as acknowledgments (which might result in retransmissions for data in error).

Minimize Transaction Latency   *Combine connection establishment with request and data transfer to reduce end-to-end latency for transactions.*

T-6A

This can be accomplished by combining the application request and connection setup information in a single REQUEST packet. The connection response message and initial return of data are then combined into a single RESPONSE packet, after which subsequent data packets can flow, in the case of a long response. It is important to Structure the Data to Meet Interactive Response Bounds (A-7A) so that the application can begin processing and presenting the response to the user within the interactive response bound T_r; this is discussed in Section 8.1.2. While there have been specific protocol proposals (for example, VMTP [Cheriton 1986, 1988] and [Sterbenz 1990d]) for transaction protocols, as well as a transaction enhancement to TCP [Braden 1992, 1994], HTTP runs over standard TCP, requiring a new connection to be established for each Web page accessed.

7.2.2.4 *Continuous Media Streaming*

Another mode of transfer that warrants distinct treatment is continuous media streaming. The requirements for many streaming media applications are very different from conventional data applications, and are discussed in Chapter 8. In this chapter, we are concerned with the characteristics that affect the end-to-end maintenance of state: loss tolerance and delivery order and timeliness.

When a user plays multimedia streams, it is more important that timing and synchronization are correct than that all data is reliably delivered. It is better to have a loss in resolution or silence interval that lasts a few milliseconds when a packet is lost, rather than pausing for hundreds of milliseconds waiting for retransmission. Furthermore, it is important that the media be streamed at the required rate with bounds on jitter and that data is delivered in order to the application or user. A packet that is significantly out of order is no better than a lost packet.

Thus, hybrid control is appropriate for continuous media: open-loop error and per packet transmission rate control, with occasional closed-loop feedback to adjust sender bandwidth and stream rate to coincide with the receiver. The packet data rate is determined by a combination of the rate of stream creation (if live), the compression ratio and loss, the rate that the network can provide, and the rate the receiver can accept to process or display. Forward error correction may be applied to bound errors and increase quality over a high bandwidth, but lossy channel, and to correct for out-of-order delivery.

Thus, the full reliability of a conventional data transport connection is not needed; in fact, it is at odds with the needs of continuous media streaming. Whether or not a connection-oriented protocol is used depends on the needs of the application and the infrastructure available. For example, ATM provides connection-oriented traffic classes for continuous media: constant bit rate (CBR) and real-time variable bit rate (rt-VBR), depending on the burstiness of the coding. RTP is used for continuous media over IP, and is connectionless (usually running over UDP). This is the reason that the SETUP and CONNECT arrows are dashed in Figure 7.8d; their presence depends on whether they are used for connection setup or whether datagrams are streamed.

Continuous Media Streaming *Timeliness of delivery should not be traded for reliable transfer in real-time continuous media streams. Use a playback buffer to reorder and absorb jitter.*

T-I.2

For example, a REQUEST to begin playing with the receiver parameters can be sent in a datagram, and then the packets are returned in a sequence of datagrams with timing information, as shown in Figure 7.8d. RTP [Schulzrinne

1996] is a connectionless protocol whose state is augmented with timestamps. The timestamps enable resequencing of the packets at the receiver and playout based on the transmitted packet rate. Other connectionless protocols rate control the transmission of packets at the sender, establishing the rate of a series of packets using an out-of-band control protocol such as the real-time control protocol (RTCP) for RTP. Control protocols, such as RTSP (real-time streaming protocal) [Schulzrinne 1998] can be used for ongoing stream control.

There are several challenges to end-to-end synchronization of continuous media streams. First, sender and receiver clocks vary in precision. If the receiver clock is too slow, buffers will be overrun and packets will be lost, resulting in discontinuities in playback. If the receiver clock is too fast, gaps in the stream will result in drop-outs and silence intervals. This is solved by including explicit timing information in the packets, which allows the receiver to synchronize with the sender clock. Second, the network can introduce jitter in the stream, which must be absorbed in a *playback buffer*, which removes the jitter and may allow reordering of out-of sequence packets.

The *playout point*, shown in Figure 7.11, is the point in the stream that is currently being decoded and displayed at the receiver. By choosing a suitable playout point distinct from the latest received packet, the receiver can adapt to jitter introduced by the sender or the network. For example, in Figure 7.11 packet 6 has arrived before packet 5. Packets are placed in the playout buffer in the proper order (or equivalently read by the application in order). This allows packet 5 to arrive, and the application to play back 5 before 6. The playout point moves in the buffer toward the application if there are substantial packet drops due to out-of-order receipt or if the receiver frequently empties the buffer completely. The playout point should otherwise move toward the network side buffer, reducing the delay between transmission and playback.

The optimization of the playout point depends on the use of the stream and the number of receivers. If the stream is unidirectional and noninteractive, as in a live broadcast or on-demand video clip, then the playout point can be increased without significant impact. However, the requirement for interactive applications bound the size of the playout point. If the stream is a bidirectional telepresence application, an end-to-end real-time delay bound is required, as described in Section 8.2.2. Interactive controls on a stored media

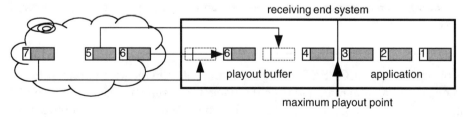

Figure 7.11   Playout point.

stream (for example, fast scan and pause) and interactive games also bound the playout point, and thus the jitter tolerable.

Real-time paths are a case where hop-by-hop optimizations can interfere with end-to-end mechanisms. The end-to-end protocol may wish to trade reliability for timeliness by permitting loss; reliable hop-by-hop link protocols can make this difficult. Retransmission of lost packets can result in misordering beyond the ability of the receiver to correct, and scrambling the stream if misordering is not expected.

7.2.3   State Establishment and Maintenance

As indicated in Section 7.2.1, high-speed networks significantly impact the establishment and maintenance of end-to-end state for two reasons: increased frequency of state updates and increased amount of state out of synchronization. This translates into the need for greater processing capability and more memory at the end system. While this is less of a concern in fourth-generation (2000s) networks that are characterized by powerful end systems and host–network interfaces, techniques to limit the complexity of state management are important. As the access bandwidth available to end systems increases in the fourth generation, the fact that Resource Tradeoffs Change (2A) will dictate the importance of managing state at a particular point in time.

The difference between hop-by-hop and end-to-end connection state is not always easily distinguishable. Some state is exclusively end-to-end, such as for transport protocols (for example, TCP). Some state is exclusively hop-by-hop, such as for network layer routing protocols and link-layer framing. Other mechanisms have the flavor of both hop-by-hop and end-to-end state. This is the case of connections provided by the network layer. Hop-by-hop signaling is required to establish an ATM connection or MPLS (multiprotocol label switching) path, but the result is an edge-to-edge connection that is transparent to the data that uses it.

The management of state is important through all phases of a transfer: during the establishment phase, state is installed and initialized; during the initialization phase, the state must quickly converge; during the steady-state phase, state must be maintained, synchronized, and evolved to adapt to changing conditions; and during the closing phase, the state must be properly removed so that resources can be reused.

7.2.3.1   Hard and Soft State

As discussed in the context of the network layer in Section 4.1.3, state can be hard or soft. Hard state is explicitly established and explicitly revoked. Soft state may either be explicitly established or implicitly accumulated, and is automatically revoked on a time-out. Periodic REFRESH messages maintain and (if necessary) modify soft state. Hard state allows a connection to be *maintained* with lower control message overhead; however, it requires the use of a signaling protocol to *establish* connections that can be complex.

Hard versus Soft State   *Balance the determinism and stability of hard state against the adaptability and robustness to failure of soft state.*

T-5A

Connection-oriented protocols, such as TCP, TP4, and the X.25 and ATM network layers, use hard state. Connectionless transfers may use soft state to enhance performance, and resource reservation protocols (such as RSVP—resource reservation protocol [Zhang 1993, Braden 1997]) can use soft state. Soft state can actually better reflect current network conditions, since it can be evolved as part of the refresh process. Hard state can be changed by the use of explicit MODIFY messages when conditions significantly change.

7.2.3.2   *State-Sharing*

One way to reduce the amount of state maintained and processed is to share state across end-to-end application associations. The ability to share information depends on the granularity over which particular characteristics and parameters are similar: per application, session, end-to-end transport association, end system, network path, network interface, or access link. State can also be shared across class of traffic, which is orthogonal to these other aggregations. State sharing can be spatial (across concurrent active data transfers) or temporal (reused from earlier transfers).

State Aggregation   *Spatially aggregate state to reduce complexity, but balance against loss in granularity. Temporally aggregate to reduce or eliminate establishment and initialization phase. State shared is fate shared.*

T-5B

A hierarchy of shared state can be maintained by the transport protocol, as shown in Figure 7.12, with per traffic class sharing orthogonal.

7.2.3.2.1   Spatial State Sharing

Within the transport protocol, state can be globally shared for the entire end system, for example, the data rate supported by the network interface. State can be shared over an aggregation of network paths; frequently much of the end-to-end state is dominated by only part of the path (a particular link or subnetwork). For example, the per network state partitioning might be divided among sets of connections that use a high-latency lossy satellite path versus

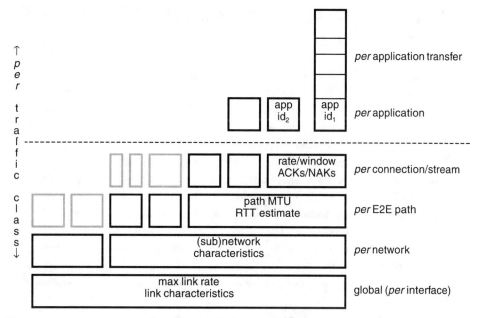

Figure 7.12 Transport and application layer state sharing.

sets of connections that use a low-latency reliable fiber optic link. Hierarchical addressing and routing domains can assist with this aggregation.

State can be most easily shared across pairs of end systems, since this reflects end-to-end path characteristics, such as the path MTU and RTT estimate, with substantial performance benefits [Touch 1997]. Parameters such as RTT can take multiple round-trips to estimate. By sharing these parameters, a data transfer can be established more quickly or have a shorter initialization phase. The frequency and mechanism can then be decoupled from the data transport. For example, more accurate probing techniques can be used to determine path characteristics (for example, packet-pair [Keshav 1991]).

Additional state can be aggregated at the transport layer, particularly when there is benefit from global end-system policies, for example, in congestion avoidance [Balakrishnan 1999]. This must be done with care, however, so that needed per connection granularity is not lost [Padma 1998, Eggert 2000].

7.2.3.2.2 Temporal State Sharing

Temporal state sharing refers to the reuse of state from previous data transfers or connections. The degree to which the previous state reflects the new transfer is based on the dynamicity of the network and the interval between transfers. Even if conditions have changed, this state reuse may result in initial conditions that provide a better estimate than no information at all, and reduce or eliminate the establishment and initialization phases.

EXAMPLE 7.3: TCP FOR TRANSACTIONS

The inefficiency of a general-purpose transport protocol for transactions has long been recognized [Braden 1985], and led to a number of proposals and implementations of transaction-oriented transport protocols (for example, [Cheriton 1988]) with the goal of limiting the end-to-end message exchange to a single request–response pair, as indicated in Section 7.2.2.

Another response to this problem was to modify TCP with temporal reuse of state to make it more suitable for transactions: T/TCP [Braden 1992, 1994]. T/TCP maintains a separate identification number per endpoint pair; this number is used to allow the early start of connections that reuse the pairwise endpoint state. If an identification doesn't exist in a particular end system, a conventional three-way handshake is used the first time to establish it.

This allows subsequent transactions to occur in the ideal single RTT. It is important to evolve dynamic state parameters over time however, in particular, the RTT estimate.

7.2.3.2.3 Application Layer State Sharing

Further sharing in state can occur by multiplexing applications into a single transport layer connection, as shown in the upper layers of Figure 7.12. While this allows the amortization of state management over multiple applications, it must be done with care so that individual applications do not interact with or impact one another in an undesired manner.

Furthermore, this adds an additional level of multiplexing, with resultant complexity (for example, the addition of application layer identifiers) and potential delay at the multiplexing point. It is important to Limit Layered Multiplexing (T-3A); Section 7.3.3 argues that multiplexing should be performed as few times as possible.

On the other hand, aggregation *within* an application can be very important. In Section 7.2.2 we discussed the difficulty of supporting transactions without suffering connection establishment latency. When an application issues a series of transactions to a single server, these can be shared within a single connection, eliminating the establishment phase latency, and perhaps the initialization phase as well.

7.2.3.2.4 Cost and Issues

While there are benefits to state sharing, they do not come without associated costs. The more the state is shared, the more the fate is shared; this can cause undesired and unintended interactions among the entities for which the sharing occurs. While state sharing can reduce the memory requirements, complex interrelationships of shared state can actually increase the processing requirements.

EXAMPLE 7.4: PERSISTENT HTTP

The original version of the hypertext transfer protocol (HTTP 1.0 [Berners-Lee 1996]) opened a *distinct* TCP connection not only for each Web page request but also for each object embedded in the page, even when located on the same server. This was inefficient due to the repeated connection establishment and initialization overhead, and was the major source of poor performance in the early Web [Mogul 1995].

The next version, HTTP 1.1 [Fielding 1999], allows HTTP persistence, both across objects in a given page, as well as across pages to a particular server. The implementation policy is browser and server specific, but a policy which balances the benefits of aggregation against the number of open connections is to keep the TCP connection open until a different server is referenced. This works well when the hyperlink tree resides on a single server, but it may not help when hyperlinks for embedded objects (including banner advertisements) come from other servers. More sophisticated policies are possible, including keeping the base page connection open while allowing a limited number of additional connections and by keeping some connections open until they time out and are displaced by new requests.

Furthermore, it can be difficult to determine when two hosts share path characteristics, and thus when their connections should share state. Connections between the same two hosts obviously share state. Connections between sets of hosts on the same LANs share path state, as do connections which share long-haul links. Discriminating between the important properties of the LAN and long-haul links can be difficult without explicit information from the network, however. Path characteristics change over time as well, indicating that some state needs to be decayed with age or refreshed.

There are also security implications to sharing state, whether reusing it between connections or sharing it among concurrent connections. Security concerns are particularly important when state is shared among a set of end systems.

7.2.4 Assumed Initial Conditions

Recall that one of the phases of a data transfer is initialization, which leads to steady state being achieved. Rapid convergence to steady state is desirable, for example, allowing a connection to use maximum bandwidth. One way to reduce the initialization phase is for the end system to start with parameters and assumptions that more accurately reflect steady state.

> **Use Initial Assumptions to Converge Quickly**   *The time to converge to steady state depends on the accuracy of the initial conditions, which depends on the currency of state information and the dynamicity of the network. Use past information to make assumptions that will converge quickly.*
>
> **T-5E**

By assuming initial conditions for a connection or transfer, the establishment and initialization overhead can be reduced [Watson 1989]. While this is related to the discussion on temporal sharing, in this case initial assumptions are derived from the past behavior of other transfers, rather than explicitly shared with them. Periodic end-to-end exchanges of state are used to keep state current, and need not be tied to per data packet transfers [Netravali 1990]. Evolving state can then be kept by the end system to be used by new data transfers and connections for their initial conditions.

7.3   Framing and Multiplexing

The most basic end-to-end service is multiplexing application data into the network and performing the framing and encapsulation necessary for end-to-end transport. Encapsulation must be done before a protocol data unit can be passed to the next lower layer of protocol processing. When multiple end-to-end associations share the network, the protocol data units must be multiplexed. First, we will discuss the framing mechanisms that include protocol encapsulation and may consist of fragmentation and reassembly. Then, we will consider multiplexing issues in high-speed end-to-end communications.

7.3.1   Framing and Fragmentation

As with any protocol layer interface, the encapsulation of ADUs into TPDUs requires framing of the data and determination of the proper fields in the TPDU header and trailer. It may also consist of fragmenting ADUs into multiple TPDUs, but this need not be the case. In the case of application layer framing (ALF will be discussed in Section 7.3.2), the ADU↔TPDU mapping is one-to-one. In other cases, efficiencies are gained by grouping multiple ADUs into a single TPDU.

7.3.1.1   *Packet Size and Control Overhead*

A significant issue in communications systems is the size of packets; we discussed this from a network node perspective in Section 5.3.3. In the case of switches and host–network interfaces, the interpacket arrival time dictates

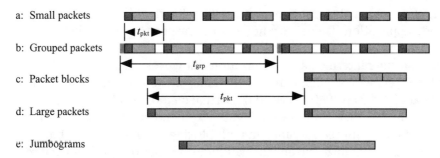

Figure 7.13   Packet size.

how quickly headers must be processed and decisions made on how to route the packet or where to place the payload in memory.

In the case of transport protocols, the interarrival time also dictates how quickly end-to-end operations must be done, in particular, the updating of end-to-end state and initiation of resulting action (for example, retransmission). For long-lived connections and continuous media streams, the maintenance and evolution of connection state are important.

Explicit information is carried in the TPDU header: whether it is data or control (for example, an acknowledgment), sequence number, payload size (if variable), destination, and QOS information. Implicit information includes arrival time (or rate) and inferred information about other packets, for example, due to a gap in sequence number or the failure of an expected ACK to arrive. This information is used to update the state of an individual connection, as well as shared state across connections. As the data rate increases for a given packet size, so does the frequency of state updates and resulting overhead in end-to-end state management.

One way to respond to this overhead is to increase the packet size, reducing the frequency of headers in the packet stream and thus reducing the frequency of per packet updates to connection and end system shared state [Touch 1995a]. This is possible in the cases of large data transfers, but is not useful when the semantic unit of transfer is small, for example, a transaction request or control packet. There is a spectrum of ways to group data into larger control units, as shown in Figure 7.13.

In the case of small packets, (Figure 7.13a) the interarrival time t_{pkt} is small, requiring fast decisions to be made and frequent control updates to connection state $1/t_{pkt}$. When packets are large (Figure 7.13d) t_{pkt} is long, reducing the frequency of state updates; extremely large packets are sometimes called *jumbograms* [Borman 1999], as shown in Figure 7.13e. In the limiting case, the entire data stream is sent as a single packet with one end-to-end state transaction. This is equivalent to turning off the data transfer control protocol, which is responsible for metering data transmission, retransmitting lost packets, and incrementally delivering the results to the receiver-side application. There are a number of reasons to limit packet size, however, as will be discussed shortly.

We can consider intermediate optimizations, however. Packets can be grouped into sets with similar state, for example, packets belonging to a single block of data [Cheriton 1986, Clark 1987], virtual memory segment [Sterbenz 1990b], Web page, or file, as shown in Figure 7.13b. Individual headers still allow packets to be spaced for efficient multiplexing and rate control, but header templates minimize the encapsulation/decapsulation overhead and reduce the state changes that occur intragroup at a frequency of $1/t_{pkt}$, limiting the full exertion of state control to a lower frequency $1/t_{grp}$. There may be a distinct group header attached to the first packet, or simply a begin group flag and length in the normal packet header at the beginning of each group.

Some of the benefits of interpacket state sharing can be performed implicitly, by filling in headers from templates for each end-to-end transmission, and by predicting and matching fields on receipt [Jacobson 1990]. TCP header prediction is included in Example 7.9 in Section 7.5.

Another optimization is to block ADUs within TPDUs, as shown in Figure 7.13c. This reduces the burden on the transport protocol to the long packet case, but requires application layer fragmentation and reassembly. An early example of this is the grouping of characters into a single TCP packet for Telnet [Nagle 1984], which had the additional advantage of not requiring an interrupt per character on the end systems.

Balance Packet Size   *Trade between control overhead and fine enough grained control. Choose size and aggregation methods that make sense end-to-end.*

T-8A

Thus, optimal packet size at the transport layer is a difficult balance, as it is in the network. Matching the network and end-to-end optimizations is even more challenging. We will now discuss some of the impacts of large and small packets to the transport layer and applications.

7.3.1.1.1   Large Packets

While increasing packet size reduces the frequency of end-to-end state updates, this has diminishing returns, and can actually be counterproductive to the control mechanisms. The receiver must be able to process data in very large chunks without intermediate information. The end-to-end connection state must not need to be adjusted more frequently, for example, in response to congestion notification from the network. By increasing the granularity of operation, applications may have to wait that could have used partial information.

Large packets also decrease the ability to multiplex efficiently at the network interface and within the network, as shown in Figure 7.14.[11]

When packets from two different sources in_1 and in_2, arrive at the same multiplexing point, one must be delayed until the output out is free. This causes some delay in the passing of individual packets. The longer the packet, the longer the delay imposed on other packets, which can impact the ability to meet real-time latency constraints. The difference between the minimum and maximum delay is the jitter, which impacts the playback buffer size required for streaming media. Note the relative impact that the large packets from in_2 have on the small packets from in_1 in Figure 7.14.

Finally, as mentioned previously, increasing the packet size beyond the semantic need of the operation does no good. Multiplexing small ADUs or control messages into a single larger packet can be difficult, and may cause unacceptable delay to wait to fill the packet.

7.3.1.1.2 Small Packets

On the other hand, packets should be small enough that sufficiently fine-grained control can be exerted on the end-to-end control mechanisms. In the case of error control for reliable transfer, a bit error in a large packet or congestion drop inside the network can affect far more data than if the packets were small, and use more bandwidth for the retransmission.

As discussed in Section 5.3.3, small packets decrease the fraction of bandwidth available for payload transport, but in environments where bandwidth is relatively inexpensive this is less important than generally recognized. In the transport protocol context, the primary disadvantage of small packets is the high rate at which per packet control must occur.

Small packets can be used to increase the sensitivity of the traffic control mechanisms, resulting in more effective rate control by scheduling inter-packet gaps and finer-grained adaptation to congestion control. Too large a granularity can cause either inefficiencies due to lack of precision or oscillation between parameters. Small packets also convey more implicit information state due to finer-grained arrival times. This can allow better

Figure 7.14   Delay and jitter imposed by large packets.

[11]Which is very similar to Figure 5.25.

resolution in traffic and RTT estimates. Information inferred from the other end of a connection can be more precise if packets are smaller and ACKs more frequent.

7.3.1.2 End-to-End Transfer and Fragmentation

Networks and links will impose a maximum packet size, either based on the limits of length fields, based on the design of the components that are switching them, or to reasonably bound delay and jitter. The concatenation of heterogeneous links and subnetworks increases the difficulty of optimizing end-to-end packet size. The overhead and latency associated with per hop fragmentation and reassembly in the network due to oversized packets can be significant [Kent 1987].

> **Avoid Hop-by-Hop Fragmentation** *The transport layer should be aware of or explicitly negotiate the maximum transfer unit of the path to avoid the overhead of fragmentation and reassembly.*
>
> **T-5F**

It is therefore important to avoid hop-by-hop fragmentation and reassembly by discovering and potentially negotiating the maximum transfer unit (MTU) end-to-end, so that the MTU is not exceeded by end-to-end TPDUs [Mogul 1990]. In IP networks, this is accomplished by probing the connection with increasing sized packets with the do not fragment bit turned on. The fragmenting node will instead send back an ICMP message indicating that the packet was dropped because it would have been fragmented. This allows IP fragmentation to simply be avoided. In cell-relay networks, such as ATM, fragmentation is fundamental to the design, as will be described in Section 5.3.3 and Example 7.5.

7.3.2 Application Layer Framing

Conventionally, when an application is ready to communicate, it issues a call to the transport layer with information on the location of the ADU and the destination. The transport protocol is then responsible for framing the data and using the error control mechanisms that will be discussed in Section 7.4 to ensure delivery to the destination with the required reliability model. If the ADU is larger than a TPDU (due to transport protocol limitations or MTU), it is fragmented, as shown in Figure 7.15a. If packet size is fixed, or has a limited number of sizes, there may be unused space within a packet.

In some cases, the application may be able to better determine the framing boundaries for TPDUs, and a one-to-one mapping ADU↔TPDU is justified.

This is called *application layer framing* (ALF) [Clark 1990], and is shown in Figure 7.15b. ALF is best done when the application can better deal with framing, sequencing, and loss, particularly when total reliability is not needed.

Application Layer Framing   *To the degree possible, match ADU and TPDU structure. In cases where the application can better determine structure and react to lost and misordered ADUs, ALF should be employed.*

T-4C

A good example motivating ALF is applications that have the ability to deal with out-of-order data. If the application is able to place data in its memory in the order received, or reconstruct missing data from FEC, it is not necessary to rely on transport protocol reordering mechanisms which may result in longer latency if retransmissions result. This requires explicit location information in the ADU header, implicit information that is easy to determine from the payload, or integration with the transport protocol [Sterbenz 1990d].

Another significant benefit of ALF is the ability for the application to perform selective protection, prioritization, and ordering of data. This allows the application to structure the packets so that it is possible for them to receive different treatment in the network. For example, the coding of video may produce some packets whose delivery is more important than others (for example, MPEG I frames). These packets should have a lower discard probability in the network, and may receive more aggressive FEC over lossy links. Lower-priority packets may be sent best effort, in excess of the traffic contract, with increased quality if they are not discarded. ALF provides the means for performing this discrimination, and network mechanisms can support such as the marking of nonconforming packets (rather than discard—described in Section 5.3.5) and intelligent dropping of layered codes (Section 8.3.2).

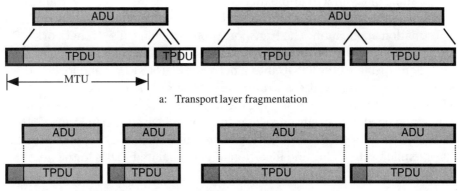

Figure 7.15   Application layer framing.

7.3.3 Multiplexing

A function that is required when applications share networks is the ability to *multiplex* application data into the network and *demultiplex* it at the other end to the appropriate receiving application. In the network, packets need to be routed to the appropriate end system. At the end system, we need additional information that indicates the application to which TPDUs are destined; this is an identifier typically called a *port*.[12]

There are a number of layers at which multiplexing may occur:

Application or session.   Interapplication coordination, for example, floor control of a multiparty conference.

Transport.   Applications sharing a network interface.

Network.   End systems sharing a network access point (edge multiplexor, router, or switch).

MAC and link.   Interfaces sharing a medium.

We are thus concerned with where multiplexing should take place to provide the necessary sharing, but should optimize based on high-speed networking concerns. Multiplexing has overhead in either scheduling the sending of a PDU, or buffering it for transmission, or both. Demultiplexing has overhead in determining where to send the data at the destination. Thus, *layered multiplexing*, in which multiplexing occurs at multiple layers, is a concern [Tennenhouse 1989, Feldmeier 1990a].

Limit Layered Multiplexing   *Layered multiplexing should be minimized and performed in an integrated manner for all layers at a single time.*

T-4A

An example of layered multiplexing is shown in Figure 7.16a. The transport layer encapsulates ADUs into TPDUs, and adds a port number p_i to identify the destination application. The transport protocol then calls the network layer protocol with the destination end system as a parameter. The network protocol encapsulates the TPDU into a network PDU (NPDU) and inserts the destination end system address a_j into the network packet header.

What we are really doing is sharing the network access link, and therefore multiplexing need only occur once, at a single point, as shown in Figure 7.16b. By multiplexing at a single time, back-pressure to higher layers can be used to replace explicit scheduling and insertion of encapsulated PDUs to the next

---

[12]The term *port* is used in the TCP/IP protocol suite, and is unfortunately overloaded with the usage for router port. ISO terminology is a transport service access point address (TSAPA), and SNA terminology is a logical unit.

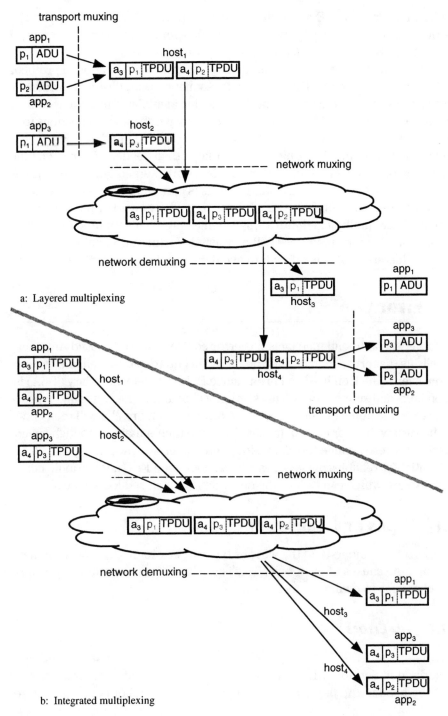

Figure 7.16 Layered multiplexing.

layer. The ILP Principle (E-4D—integrated layer processing) can be applied to perform the transport layer (port) and network layer (address) multiplexing at the same time, resulting in *integrated layer multiplexing.*

In connectionless networks, demultiplexing requires a combination of protocol identifier (which will do the demultiplexing) destination port, destination address, source address, and source port as the multiplexing identifier.[13] In a connection-oriented network, the transport layer can directly map transport connections to network layer connections to eliminate the need for layered multiplexing.

A disadvantage of multiplexing at a higher layer than needed is that each time multiplexing occurs the individual characteristics are merged into a larger granularity of control, resulting in fate sharing. This is particularly an issue when resources are reserved to provide QOS. If application flows with differing QOS requirements are multiplexed into a single connection that supports the most demanding application, resources will be wasted. Furthermore, unless the reservations are hierarchical, it is difficult to avoid interapplication QOS interference.

7.4 Error Control

The canonical end-to-end mechanism is error control; the End-to-End Argument (T-3) tells us that error control *must* be provided end-to-end for reliable transmission, even if the Hop-by-Hop Performance Enhancement Corollary (T-3A) is used on links and subnetworks. This section will examine the cause and types of errors and the impact of high-speed networking on errors. We will then consider the variety of error control mechanisms and their suitability to high-speed networking. These include the closed-loop retransmission mechanisms, which are essential for reliable transport, as well as open-loop FEC and periodic control exchanges, which can reduce the dependency on closed-loop control.

7.4.1 Types and Causes of Errors

It is important to understand the various types of errors that can occur in networks, and the causes of each type. This is the basis for determining appropriate mechanisms to deal with such errors.

7.4.1.1 Bit Errors

Bit errors are generated due to characteristics of the transmission medium, as described in Section 5.1.1. Bit errors are detected (and sometimes corrected) by header and payload check fields. When a packet is recognized to

---

[13]Source address and port are needed to ensure uniqueness and avoid the need for globally distinct port numbers. The BSD Unix socket is such a 5-tuple.

be corrupted (but is uncorrectable), it is discarded. It is important the check code be robust enough to make the probability of undetected multiple bit errors extraordinarily low, otherwise the result may be permanently corrupted data or a *packet insertion* into a different connection or to the wrong destination.

In the case of networks based on fiber optic links and properly designed network nodes and host–network interfaces, the probability of bit errors is extremely low, on the order of 10^{-12}. In the case of wireless links and analog modem access lines, the probability of errors can be high enough that bit errors are a significant source of packet loss. Adding structured redundancy to the bit stream, so that when some bits are lost the information can still be recovered, can measurably improve performance. This forward error correction can be applied to lower the probability of errors, but care must be taken due to the additional bandwidth required for the FEC field, as discussed in Section 7.4.4. Satellite links can have a loss rate on the order of 10^{-1}; links such as this require FEC to be able to operate at all.

7.4.1.2   Packet Errors

Packet-level errors are of concern in end-to-end communication; bit errors are manifested as packet loss or insertion at the transport layer. There are several types of packet errors that can occur.

Packet loss is the most significant error of concern. As indicated, detected bit errors result in packet loss, either due to intermediate discard by the link or (sub)network layer protocol, or by transport layer discard when the error is detected by the receiver. In wireline networks, the more significant cause of loss is due to buffer overrun resulting from congestion, or as a result of discard to avoid congestion, as described in Sections 4.2.2 and 5.5.4. If the fraction of bandwidth used by an individual data transfer is low, congestion loss is likely to be manifest as single packet losses.

Burst errors consist of a sequence of lost or corrupted packets, and may also be caused by long runs of bit errors on a very noisy wireless channel or channel fades. In wireline networks, burst errors are a common problem, particularly for high data rate transfers in networks operating near capacity. Congestion frequently results in multiple packets overflowing network node queues in a short interval of time. Congestion avoidance and control mechanisms can also result in multiple packet discards.

The mechanisms for dealing with packet loss will be discussed at length in the rest of this section. The difficulty in distinguishing losses due to channel errors from losses induced by congestion affects the flow and congestion mechanisms described in Section 7.5. There is substantial benefit in distinguishing the cause of the errors, resulting in the ability to decouple error from flow and congestion control.

Packet misordering occurs when packets do not follow one another on the same path. This can occur for a number of reasons, including the ability of individual packets to traverse different links, striping of packets along links and through switch planes where the interpacket skew is not contained hop-by-hop, or in switch fabrics that have multiple paths (such as Clos fabrics) or use recirculation to resolve output contention or to multicast (as described in Section 5.4.5). Packet reordering is common in the Internet [Bennett 1999].

An important (but often overlooked) cause of misordering over a large sequence of packets occurs when lost packets are retransmitted or when a link or connection reconfigures and automatically recovers along a new path. Misordering is detected using sequence numbers, whose sequence space requirement is dictated by the bandwidth-$\times$-delay product. This issue will be discussed in Section 7.4.2. Some error control schemes treat early arrivals as lost packets, avoiding the need to maintain state and buffering. In high-speed networks it is better to avoid the latency of retransmission with receiver reordering.

Packet duplication can happen whenever retransmissions occur for lost packets, in particular when a packet is retransmitted but the original is still in flight in the network. The more optimistic the retransmission mechanism, the greater the probability of duplication. Duplication is detected by observing duplicate sequence numbers, and the duplicates can be discarded. This requires maintenance of receiver state indicating which packets have already arrived.

Packet insertion is the introduction of spurious packets and can occur for three reasons:

1. When an undetectable header error occurs in the destination or connection identifier, a packet can appear at the wrong destination and be treated as valid. Proper header check fields should make the probability of this event extraordinarily low.

2. Insertion can occur if a packet is delayed so long in the network that it meets the validity criteria for a new connection or flow. Mechanisms such as limiting hop count and maximum packet lifetime minimize the possibility of this happening. Insertions can also be detected by grossly incorrect sequence number or a pattern match on other fields (such as incorrect source address in a point-to-point flow).

3. Faulty configurations and buggy software can be responsible for many errors [Stone 2000]. Layer and sanity checks are used to protect from this type of error.

7.4.1.3 *Fragment Loss and MTU*

Fragmentation of packets presents an additional challenge to error recovery. In addition to the latency overhead of fragmentation and reassembly discussed in Section 5.3.3, the overhead in error recovery can be multiplied. Generally, fragmentation is required whenever a link or transit subnetwork does not support a given packet size. An additional fragment sequence number is generally required in addition to the end-to-end (unfragmented) TPDU sequence number.

Error multiplication occurs because the loss of a fragment generally results in the need to retransmit the entire TPDU, unless the network or link layer buffers and retransmits fragments hop-by-hop. This is generally not practical due to the increased complexity and buffering needed. This error multiplication can lead to congestion collapse. If fragments of size b/f are being dropped due to congestion, which results in the retransmission of the entire TPDU of size b, the network is further driven into congestion. The fragment fraction f multiplies the retransmission load.

EXAMPLE 7.5: ATM SEGMENTATION AND FRAME DISCARD

The ATM protocol suite was designed to relay small fixed size cells, and due to the extremely small payload size (48 B), the cell header size was kept minimal, as shown in Figure 5.21. There was no space to consider a sequence number, and it was believed that it was not necessary if cells traversed the same path through the network and switches along a connection. Since the cells were so small relative to ADUs, an end-to-end ATM adaptation layer (AAL) was defined to segment higher-layer frames into ATM cells.

The initial proposal for the data AAL was needlessly complex, and contained a 4-bit sequence number in the AAL header (inside the ATM layer payload) that was not robust to the high bandwidth-$\times$-delay products in ATM networks. Furthermore it contained a per cell check (CRC-10), resulting in 44 remaining bytes of payload. A simple and efficient adaptation layer (SEAL) [Lyon 1991], which contains a single CRC-32 check for the entire TPDU, became the standard AAL5 for data transport and has sufficient error robustness [Greene 1992]. Had a native ATM transport protocol, for example, [Sharma 1994, Ahuja 1995], ever been adopted, AAL5 would have merely been its lower sublayer.

The performance of TCP on early ATM switches was abysmal for two reasons. First, switch queues were too small, by over an order of magnitude, to support the relatively bursty nature of TCP, compared to the TDM (time division multiplexed) traffic of the PSTN. Second, when the switches were congested, individual cells were dropped, resulting in the retransmission of entire AAL5 frames corresponding to TCP segments.

Studies showed the devastating effect of this naïve retransmission approach on *goodput* [Romanow 1995], which is defined as end-to-end throughput. Therefore ATM switch designs now implement frame discard policies such as PPD and EPD. Frame discard is *required* by the ATM GFR (guaranteed frame rate) traffic class most suitable to transport TCP.

If fragmentation must occur, the network should attempt to drop the entire TPDU rather than individual fragments, using policies such as partial packet discard (PPD) and early packet discard (EPD) described in Section 5.3.5. This effect can also occur if the transport protocol fragments ADUs into TPDUs, but the application layer is performing its own error control.

7.4.2 Impact of High Speed

Due to the need for a feedback control loop for reliable delivery guarantees, high-speed networking directly impacts error control. This is manifested by the influence that high bandwidth-×-delay product has on the ability to react to errors and on the size of packet header fields needed to account for the amount of data in flight.

7.4.2.1 Bandwidth-×-Delay Product

Error control is particularly challenging in high-speed networks due to high bandwidth-×-delay products,[14] for two significant reasons:

1. As the bit rate increases, the impact of a fixed-duration error event, such as a wireless channel fade or link failure and restoration, affects a larger amount of data. Thus, more packets are dropped. In the case of flows that use a significant fraction of link bandwidth, the length of burst errors increases. In the case of high aggregation of low individual bandwidth flows, what at low speed were single packet errors are spread as multiple errors over many flows.

2. The ability to react to conditions causing errors, such as congestion, is diminished with increasing bandwidth-×-delay product, since by the time end-to-end correction can take place, more bits in flight have been affected. Furthermore, as shown in Figure 7.6, the shortening of data transmission means that retransmissions of lost packets may occur well beyond when the data should have fully arrived. Finally, if hop-by-hop error control is employed, this can actually make a congestion condition *worse* by increasing the load on the error-controlled link before higher-layer mechanisms have compensated.

The latter item indicates that the Hop-by-Hop Performance Enhancement Corollary (T-3A) must be carefully applied. If the effect on hop-by-hop error control limits the scope of errors, for example, by dropping but not retransmitting lost packets or signaling ECN, the desired performance enhancement has occurred. On the other hand, hop-by-hop retransmission without

---

[14]It is also challenging for high bandwidth-×-delay products even when the data rate is low to moderate, such as in GEO satellites. Many of the error, flow, and congestion control mechanisms discussed in this chapter arose from, or have been applied to, satellite networks.

limiting the impact of increased load in the face of congestion is a positive feedback control mechanism that can drive the network into congestion collapse.

7.4.2.2 Sequence Numbers

Sequence numbers are typically used as the mechanism to ensure ordered delivery of packets and to request retransmission of lost packets. Too large a sequence number field consumes unnecessary overhead in the packet header. Too small a field doesn't serve the desired functionality if the sequence number wraps such that multiple packets with the same (or nearly adjacent) numbers may be in flight at the same time. The needed sequence number space in n bits can be expressed as [Watson 1981]:

$$2^n > (t_{\text{rexmit}} + 2t_{\text{MPL}} + t_{\text{ACK}})r_{\text{pkt}}$$

The time that a packet with a given sequence number can be retransmitted from the source is t_{rexmit}; this is dependent on the loss characteristics of the network. The maximum packet lifetime is t_{MPL}, and this term indicates how long the last instance of a sequence number could take to get to the receiver, as well as the how long the successful ACK takes to propagate back to the sender, allowing the number to be reused. The time to turn around the ACK at the receiver is t_{ACK}. The sum of these terms is multiplied by the rate at which packets can be generated r_{pkt}.

Packet Control Field Values *Optimize header control field values to trade efficiency against expected future requirements. Fields that are likely to be insufficient for future bandwidth-×-delay products should contain a scale factor.*

T-8C

The sequence number space chosen should consider the bandwidth-×-delay product of future network deployments.

7.4.3 Closed-Loop Retransmission

As with the other end-to-end control mechanisms, error control can be either open- or closed-loop. Open-loop control will be discussed in Section 7.4.4. For now it is sufficient to note that the absolute reliable delivery needed by most data application *requires* closed-loop feedback. An end-to-end feedback mechanism, typically part of the transport protocol, ensures reliable delivery by retransmitting lost (or errored) packets. This is called automatic repeat request (ARQ) and requires that the receiver inform the transmitter using *acknowledgments*. These may either be *positive acknowledgments* (ACKs), which explicitly acknowledge delivery, or *negative acknowledgments* (NAKs), which indicate lack of receipt of expected packets.

7.4.3.1   Go-Back-n

We will first describe a variant of the *go-back-n* retransmission scheme using positive acknowledgments and sender timers.[15] This scheme has been widely deployed in protocols such as TCP. Consider a sequence of numbered packets and a sliding retransmission window that indicates how many packets can be transmitted without acknowledgment. When a packet is acknowledged, the beginning of the window is advanced to the next sequence number. Packets can be transmitted as long as the window size is not exceeded; the end of the window is advanced to match the transmitted packet. Thus the window slides along the sequence number space, opening and closing slightly to correspond to the number of unacknowledged packets. This is shown in Figure 7.17a.

Note that as each packet *n* is correctly received in order, an acknowledgment A*n* is returned to the sender. When a packet is received that is not the

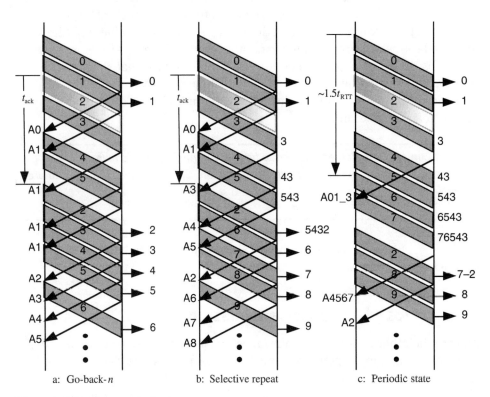

Figure 7.17   Error control schemes.

[15]Cumulative and window-based error and flow control schemes are quite complex and have many subtle variations. The goal in this section is to present simple representative examples of the major difference that impact high-speed networking. The go-back-*n* example uses the same sequence as [Kurose 2000], which is a good source for more information.

next expected sequence number (due to loss or reordering), it is discarded and the last acknowledgment is repeated. In this example, packet 2 is lost, and therefore acknowledgment A1 is repeated as packets 3, 4, and 5 are discarded. The sending side maintains acknowledgment timers for each packet. After a period of time t_{ACK} for packet 2, A2 is not received. The sending side then assumes that packet 2 is lost, backs up, and restarts the sequence at packet 2.

The key point is that a packet loss or misordering causes a significant delay, in excess of an RTT before the transmission can be restarted. Furthermore, bandwidth is wasted since all the packets following the loss must be retransmitted. For this scheme to be efficient, not only must the loss rate of the link be low, but also misordering must be uncommon; neither is the case in the Internet [Bennett 1999].

Part of the problem is that sliding window go-back-n integrates error and flow control in a single mechanism. Flow is restarted when there is an error, and as we will discuss in Section 7.5, flow control is exerted based on the smaller of the receiver window and network capacity. This capacity can be a congestion window determined by network probing, as described in Section 7.5.4, or by negotiation with the network, as described in Section 7.5.2. Decoupling these mechanisms is an important high-speed networking technique, proposed in the earliest high-speed transport protocols such as NETBLT [Clark 1987] and VMTP [Cheriton 1986].

7.4.3.2 Negative Acknowledgments

Negative acknowledgments have the potential to reduce the delay in go-back-n, since the receiver can request a retransmission as soon as it has inferred a packet loss, for example, with receipt of subsequent sequence numbers. Furthermore, if packets are generally transmitted successfully, negative acknowledgments result in fewer messages.

However, the receiver may not know when the end of the flow has occurred, and since the NAKs themselves may get lost, the sender may not know if the receiver is still alive. Thus, NAKs can supplement, but not easily replace, positive acknowledgments and must include a polling mechanism for receiver liveness, which has its own complexity in management. Note that NAKs are not the same as selective acknowledgments, which will be described later.

7.4.3.3 Fast Retransmit

Another optimization to reduce the dependency on the retransmission timer and latency of go-back-n is *fast retransmit*. If the bandwidth-$\times$-delay product is very high, many identical acknowledgments may arrive before the retransmission timer expires.[16] Fast retransmit exploits the fact that multiple identical ACKs probably indicate a packet loss, even before the retransmission timer has expired, and initiates the restart of the transfer at the packet just following the ACKs. In TCP, triple duplicate ACKs are used to trigger fast retransmit. This optimization is particularly important for window-based flow control, and is shown in Figure 7.26b.

7.4.3.4 Selective Repeat

An alternative to go-back-*n* is to *selective repeat*, which ACKs the last received packet, even if out of sequence. The receiver must buffer packets for resequencing, and the sender must maintain ACK state. This, along with open-loop rate-based flow control (described in Section 7.5.2), allows decoupling of error and flow control. An example of selective repeat is shown in Figure 7.17b. As in the previous example, packet 2 is lost, but subsequent packets are acknowledged and buffered until packet 2 is retransmitted. Packets 2 to 5 are then delivered to the application. It may be possible to deliver packets out of order into application space if the techniques described in Section 6.4.2 are employed, such as scatter/gather DMA when the location can be inferred from the sequence number or explicit destination address in the packet header [Sterbenz 1990c].

> **Decouple Error, Flow, and Congestion Control**   *Exploit selective acknowledgments and open-loop rate control to decouple error, flow, and congestion control mechanisms.*
>
> T-6E

7.4.3.5 ACK Aggregation

Acknowledgments can be sent per packet, as described. The granularity of per packet retransmission is related to the packet size. If packets are too large, more data may need to be retransmitted than necessary. The smaller the packet size, the higher the overhead of per packet acknowledgment. Smaller packets result in fewer and smaller retransmissions, as long as the packet is smaller than likely burst errors.

The granularity and resultant overhead of ACKs can be reduced by *ACK aggregation*. There are three mechanisms to accomplish this:

1. ACKs can be *piggybacked* onto data packets traveling in the reverse direction to reduce the message overhead. This was a common optimiza-

[16]This is not the case in Figure 7.17a, but imagine that the data rate is 10 times faster. In this case, the packet parallelograms will be one-tenth the thickness, and many A1 ACKs will arrive.

tion in second-generation networks, in which bandwidth was relatively expensive.

2. *Delayed ACKs* can be used, which delay ACKs for a short period of time, to send fewer aggregated acknowledgments. This has the additional advantage that packets received out of order within the delay time can be resequenced by the transport protocol without triggering a go-back-*n* restart of the data transfer.

3. Bit vectors can be used to aggregate a number of ACKs in a single control message. This allows selective acknowledgment of packets.

Since the bit vector provides both ACK and NAK information, acknowledgment aggregation can be arbitrarily tuned. The acknowledgments can be done on a per block [Zwaenepoel 1985, Netravali 1990] or per object [Sterbenz 1990d] basis, or at a given periodicity to tune the latency versus bandwidth tradeoff, as shown in Figure 7.17c. Furthermore, when an expected packet doesn't arrive, an early acknowledgment vector can be returned to the sender, allowing less periodic transmission of larger bit vectors in the normal case. Note that Figure 7.17c has only three ACKs.

7.4.3.6 *Multipoint Acknowledgments*

Reliable multicast requires some mechanism for triggering the retransmission of errored or lost packets, as does reliable point-to-point communication. If a naïve approach is used, in which all receivers individually ACK the sender, *ACK implosion* results, as shown in Figure 7.18a.

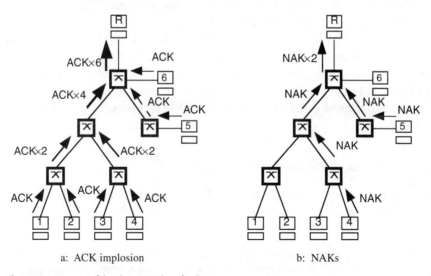

a: ACK implosion   b: NAKs

Figure 7.18 Multipoint ACK implosion.

Note that each of the six receivers sends ACKs back to the source (root R) of the multicast. As the ACKs progress toward the root of the tree, each link is subject to higher message load. If the multicast group is large, this overhead can drive the network into congestion collapse.

Thus, clever retransmission strategies are needed. If the network is relatively reliable, NAKs can be used instead of ACKs, but as indicated previously, this must be combined with a polling mechanism to determine liveness of the receiver. In large dynamic multicast groups, the overhead of the returned polls to the sender may be unacceptable and hierarchical management becomes necessary.

Some other form of ACK suppression is needed, either by combining ACKs at intermediate nodes in the multicast tree or by localizing retransmission. Both of these schemes require hop-by-hop ACK suppression, and the latter hop-by-hop buffering and retransmission [Levine 1996]. Just as efficient multicast requires support in the network for the replication of data to the leaves of the tree, support is also required in the network for the reduction of control messages back to the root of the tree.

7.4.3.7   Timer Estimation

Timers are used to estimate when retransmissions should occur. The selection of the timer value is critical [Zhang 1986, Karn 1987]—if too short, retransmissions will needlessly occur; if too long, the latency and bandwidth wasted will be even greater. The timer should be just large enough to account for the RTT of most packets. Accurate timer determination requires detailed knowledge about the characteristics of the network path. Thus, RTT estimation generally consists of a running average of previous RTTs with a variance term added.[17] The timer estimation itself is a closed-loop feedback control process at a longer granularity than the retransmission feedback loop. Explicit probing can also be used to estimate RTT, for example, using packet pair.

In the case of rate-controlled transmission (Section 7.5.2), and when the length of the data is signaled, the receiver can better estimate when data should arrive and request retransmission before the sender would time out [Clark 1987].

7.4.3.8   Complexity of Implementation

As with other protocol functions, it is important to consider the complexity of mechanism and the cost of implementation. Error control is a *transfer control*

---

[17][Keshav 1997] contains good coverage with references to different estimation schemes. Simple estimates of variability may be sufficient rather than an actual variance, which requires square root computations.

function (Section 6.2.1), and is a candidate for critical path optimization. Certainly error control must not adversely impact the critical path data transfer. Whether the error retransmission functions need to be similarly optimized depends on their frequency of occurrence. In the case of go-back-n, retransmission stalls the data flow, and is more critical to the delivery of the data stream. In the case of selective repeat, the data flow is less dependent on retransmissions, but the ability of the application to actually use data still depends on the arrival of the retransmitted data.

The important aspect is that the critical path portion of the error control schemes must be efficiently implemented in the end system. The Critical Path Corollary (1B) indicates that this error control functionality should be optimized for fast software implementation and, if appropriate, should fit within an ILP loop or be optimized for network interface microcontroller or hardware implementation [Chesson 1989, Sterbenz 1990c].

EXAMPLE 7.6: ERROR CONTROL IN SNA

SNA (Systems Network Architecture) is the networking protocol suite that evolved in the IBM enterprise computing environment, announced in 1974 with star connectivity to single mainframes and evolving to a full peer-to-peer mesh in 1976 [Gray 1979, Ahuja 1979]. Unlike the Internet, hop-by-hop reliability is provided in SNA by the link layer (*data link control*) and thus the network layer (*path control*) provides a reliable end-to-end path. Thus, error control was *not* provided at the transport layer (*transmission control*).

This seems to be at odds with the End-to-End Argument (T-3), but it is important to understand the environment in which SNA evolved. SNA was not intended to connect diverse subnetwork technologies, and was thus a homogeneous network technology. Thus, SNA network engineers could make strict assumptions on the reliability of the network nodes (mainframes and communications controllers), which provided ECC hardware on data paths and through memory.

In the early 1970s, data rates were sufficiently low, and the latency suffered by store-and-forward hops was such that hop-by-hop retransmission did not significantly affect the overall latency budget. Furthermore, SNA networks were carefully engineered to limit the number of hops.

Clearly, as the isolated enterprise networks of the first and second-generations (1980s) became subnets of the third-generation Internet (1990s), the data link reliability was no longer sufficient. In particular, the ability to extend SNA transmission control over non-SNA links was limited due to lack of end-to-end error control.

7.4.4 Open-Loop Error Control

Open-loop error control does *not* provide the absolute reliability of closed-loop retransmissions Open-loop error control assumes the degree of error control necessary to provide a statistical bound on errors. This is accomplished by introducing redundancy in the information sent—either intrapacket in the form of FEC (forward error correction) or interpacket by use of redundancy such as erasure codes [McAuley 1990] or repeated sending of information. Open-loop control is particularly appropriate when all of the following conditions are met:

- Applications are tolerant to some loss, expressed as a statistical measure (for example, probability of packet loss and burst error tolerance).

- Applications have real-time or near real-time latency requirements, such as interactive streaming of live-source multimedia (for example, teleconferencing and live video distribution), which challenges the ability to perform ARQ retransmissions in the latency bound.

- Networks paths have high latencies, in which the latency of retransmission challenges the application latency requirement, or networks have high bandwidth-$\times$-delay products, which require large playback or resequencing buffers for ARQ retransmission.

- Receivers can sink the additional data rate required by the redundancy, and have the processing capability to decode and correct the incoming stream.

Another situation where open-loop control is particularly effective is for lossy wireless links in general and satellite links in particular. Open-loop error control can raise the loss rate to an acceptable level for loss-tolerant applications (as discussed earlier), and minimize the use of closed-loop feedback retransmissions needed for loss-intolerant applications. Since open-loop control *always* uses bandwidth for redundancy on the assumption that data will be corrupted or lost, enough bandwidth must be available without constraining application requirements or driving the network into congestion.

Finally, open-loop error control can be used to reduce the ACK implosion problem in reliable multicast, enabling the use of NAKs with polling, as described in Section 7.4.3.

7.4.4.1 Forward Error Correction

FEC codes are the usual mechanism for providing open-loop error control on data [McAuley 1990, Shacham 1990, Rizzo 1997]. The principle behind FEC is that redundant information is placed on the transmission stream so that if some of the data is lost, the original information can be reconstructed from the structure of the remaining received data. Forms of FEC include the following:

Block codes.   Allow per block recovery if enough of the block arrives uncorrupted.

Convolutional codes.   Encode and decode continuously; a constraint length determines how many bits in the past are used for error correction bits.

For a given FEC code, the higher the redundancy, the greater the protection to bit errors, and the longer the block or constraint length, the more robust the code is to burst errors.

For a data block b bits long, h correction bits are added, resulting in a block $b + h$ bits long. There are two overheads that must be traded against the savings in acknowledgments for closed-loop control. First, the bandwidth required is increased by a factor of $(b + h)/b$. This must be compared to the additional forward link bandwidth required by the retransmissions of an ARQ scheme to deal with a similar loss rate, approximately nb where n is the probability of retransmission. If loss in a network is primarily due to congestion, then using FEC will *reduce* the goodput of the network [Biersack 1992].

Second, significant latency may be required to generate the FEC code at the transmitter and decode at the receiver to detect and correct errors. FEC becomes more advantageous in long-haul networks where the speed-of-light latency dominates. Hardware-based schemes [McAuley 1990] that can be inserted in the network interface pipeline with relatively low latency are particularly attractive.

Forward Error Correction   *Use FEC for low-latency, open-loop flow control when bandwidth is available and statistical loss tolerance bounds are acceptable to the application.*

                                                                T-6De

---

7.4.4.2 *Hybrid Schemes*

As indicated previously, open-loop control only provides statistical guarantees, and therefore is insufficient for the many loss-intolerant data applications. FEC can still be applied to lower the loss rate to that acceptable to loss-tolerant applications and to significantly reduce the rate of retransmission for loss-intolerant applications [Kallel 1988, 1994].

This results in a hybrid error control scheme, with open-loop providing a statistical reliability floor, and closed-loop feedback control providing total reliability to applications that need it. Hybrid schemes are particularly attractive in lossy high bandwidth-$\times$-delay networks, such as when satellite links are employed and to lower the need for ARQ, especially in reliable multicast.

7.4.4.3 Repetitive Coding and Periodic Updates

A naïve open-loop error control scheme is repetitive coding, which merely transmits packets a number of times. In this case, the efficiency is measured by the multiplicative transmission factor. Unless the repeated transmissions are spaced, or interleaved with other flows, repetitive coding is not robust to burst errors. Pure repetitive coding is rarely useful, since simple erasure codes provide equivalent protection with less overhead (for example, $1.5\times$ for a 2-out-of-3 code versus $2\times$ for a twice-duplicate repetition to correct a single packet loss). There are two variants, however, that are useful, particularly for control messages.

A number of control messages require periodic updates of state, but do not require total reliability in the delivery of individual messages. Examples include routing protocol messages that update forwarding tables and continuous media streaming synchronization (described in Section 7.2.1). In these cases, the loss of a single message merely means that the state will not converge as fast. A tradeoff can be made between the required convergence time and the required periodicity of the updates, given a particular error model.

The second way is to provide spatial redundancy in packets, either by *flooding* messages through the network [Boehm 1969, Farber 1986] or by more restricted spatial spreading, as in *spray routing* [Tchakountio 2000]. In these cases, control packets traverse multiple paths to reach a destination, which is robust to high error and loss rates, but mechanisms must be used to prevent unbounded propagation of packets. For example, in flooding, each node will send a packet to all its neighbors only the first time it is received.

7.5 Flow and Congestion Control

End-to-end flow and congestion control are used to control the rate at which an end system transmits packets destined for a receiving end system. Thus, they must be performed end-to-end and are commonly a transport layer function. The end-to-end mechanisms may be assisted by network or link layer functionality, justified by the Hop-by-Hop Performance Enhancement Corollary (T-3A). There are two important reasons to control the transmission of packets:

Receiver constraints. Communicating applications, and the end systems on which they run, are rarely perfectly matched in communication and processing power, memory available, and load due to other application processes. Thus, the interpacket transmission time is frequently constrained by the ability of the receiver to accept and process data. If these packets are transmitted faster, data will be lost at the receiving side of the path. *Flow control* allows applications to communicate while controlling the transmission so that data is not lost *end-to-end*.

Network path constraints. Many applications require a particular bandwidth, either to provide low Interapplication Delay (I.2) or to meet User Expectations of Continuous Media Quality (A-I.2e). If bandwidth is unlimited and free, transmission control is not needed; the sending application can inject data as fast as the receiving end system allows, and only flow control is needed. Network bandwidth generally is not unlimited, however, and if the transmission rate is not controlled, packets will be dropped in the network due to congestion (or congestion avoidance policies), which results from contention for links or paths through switches. In a network which provides QOS guarantees based on bandwidth reservations, packets may be intentionally dropped in excess of the agreed-upon traffic contract. Therefore, *congestion control* [Davies 1972] is a mechanism to match the application rate to the network path, and avoid loss in the network [Jain 1986].

Congestion induced by a given transfer has three effects: (1) it reduces the ability for other data transfers to use the network; (2) it reduces the ability for the given transfer to use the network, and, at least as importantly; (3) it impairs network control traffic such as for link state updates in routing algorithms.

It is important to understand that while flow and congestion control are exerted for different reasons, both mechanisms affect the timing of packet transmission and may be tightly coupled. In particular, there are two variants of congestion control: explicit and implicit. *Explicit* congestion control relies on information from the network nodes to indicate impending and current congestion, as described in Section 4.2.2. This makes is possible to Decouple Error, Flow, and Congestion Control (T-6E). *Implicit* congestion control infers congestion based on end-to-end packet loss. Generally, with window-based control this means that all the mechanisms (error, flow, and congestion) are coupled, since without explicit information the end system cannot determine whether packet loss is due to a bit error or congestion. This distinction is most important when some of the links in the network are lossy due to effects other than congestion (for example, wireless links).

In this section, we will first briefly discuss the impact of high-speed networks on congestion and flow control. Then, we will discuss open-loop rate control, which can serve both as a flow and congestion control mechanism. We will move to closed-loop control, first for flow control and then for congestion control. Finally we will indicate possible hybrid combinations of open- and closed-loop flow and congestion control.

7.5.1 Impact of High Speed

As we discussed for error control, the principal difficulty with flow and congestion control in high-speed networks arises due to high bandwidth-×-delay product and long-delay feedback control loops. There are two specific issues:

1. Traffic conditions that warrant exertion of control based on the *length of data* (the flow itself or cross-traffic in the network) change more quickly as the data rate increases. Due to the high bandwidth-×-delay product, network perturbations over a large amount of data may not be correctable within an end-to-end feedback control loop RTT.

2. The ability to respond to dynamic behavior that is based on a particular *interval of time* (for example, 100-ms interactive response latency budget) is reduced since the amount of data in flight increases with bandwidth. If the amount of data is short, a transfer may be complete before the path initialization phase is complete or before the network can react to traffic induced by the transfer.

7.5.1.1 Window Scaling

When a window is used to keep track of the amount of unacknowledged data, it must be large enough to scale with the bandwidth-×-delay product. There are two approaches that can be considered: (1) ensure that the window size field in packets is large enough to accommodate the largest possible window that is ever needed or (2) allow the size to be scaled by a negotiated factor.

If window adjustments are exchanged in control packets, it is not difficult for the field to be large enough for all possibilities. If the window is carried in the header of data packets traveling in the opposite direction, then the number of bits affects the header overhead, and is of more concern.

Window scaling allows the header field to be smaller, and allows a retrofit for protocols that didn't anticipate high bandwidth-×-delay products. As these offsets scale, it is assumed that the unit of acknowledgment and, correspondingly, the unit of retransmission, scales. Over a long, high-bandwidth pipe, this implies that using the window scale option necessarily increases the granularity of feedback. The effectiveness of window scaling is limited by the need for finer-grained control in window size in high bandwidth-×-delay product networks.

7.5.2 Open-Loop Rate Control

When the characteristics of a network path and receiver are known a priori and are relatively static, open-loop *rate control* can be used to control the source transmission, without requiring a feedback loop for adjustment. This has the significant advantage in high-speed networks of not being sensitive to the data rate or bandwidth-×-delay product.

> **Use Knowledge of Network Paths for Open-Loop Control**   *Exploit open-loop rate and congestion control based on a priori knowledge to the degree possible to reduce the need for feedback control.*
>
> **T-6Do**

The benefit of not relying on network and receiver feedback comes at the cost of determining a priori the set of rate parameters to be used by the sender. These parameters need to accurately reflect the needs and behavior of the application. In some cases, such as continuous streaming media, this is relatively simple, since it is dependent on the source rate and compression ratio. In many cases, such as interactive data and distributed computing applications, estimating the rate a priori can be extremely difficult.

The needs of the application and capabilities of the network path are used to construct a *rate specification*, which consists of a set of parameters, such as peak rate, average rate, and burstiness. This requires not only the network path characteristics to be known, but for them to remain stable over a long period of time. Generally, rate control is used in conjunction with a connection-oriented network that performs admission control, and guarantees the resources necessary to commit to a *traffic contract*, as described in Section 4.2.1. This couples the flow control and congestion avoidance mechanisms. The robustness of congestion avoidance is tied to how conservative the rate specification and traffic contract are. If some excess capacity is left in the network, it is less likely to become congested. Furthermore, excess capacity should be provisioned for overload resulting from link and node failures; such failures should not drive the network into congestion collapse.

7.5.2.1   Model

The model for an open-loop rate-controlled system is shown in Figure 7.19.

There are three ways in which an application can assume that the *network* will be able to support the data transfer:

1. Bandwidth is not constrained in the network.

2. A path is provisioned that supports a known rate. This can be done by assigning an end-system or application pair to a dedicated set of links through nonblocking switches or provisioning reserved resources, such as a dedicated lightpath, SONET TDM path, or permanent virtual circuit (PVC).

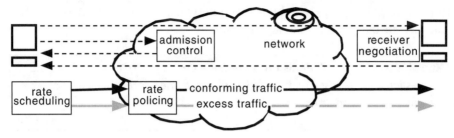

Figure 7.19   Open-loop rate control.

3. A request for bandwidth is signaled to the network. The network performs admission control to determine if the requested rate can be supported. Assuming that a traffic contract guarantees a QOS,
   corresponding resources will be reserved in the network.

Similarly, the transmitting end system needs to be able to assume that the
receiving end will be able to sink the data; there are two ways this can occur:

1. The application has a priori knowledge that the receiver is fast enough
   and will be able to sink the data.

2. The rate is negotiated with the receiver before the flow begins.[18]

In the case of a connection-oriented network, the signaling procedure described in Section 4.1.3 can be used. The transport protocol simply passes
the **setup-request** parameters to the network for connection establishment,
and the end-to-end negotiation occurs when the **SETUP** message propagates
to the receiver. If the sender can tolerate a range of QOS, this can be reflected by a range (or alternate) of parameter values in the **SETUP** message.
The parameters may be negotiated down to the minimum at any point in the
network, or at the receiving end system. If the minimum is not available, the
connection request is rejected. ATM natively supports this mechanism.
RSVP is an example of a protocol that negotiates resource reservation over
IP networks.

Once the data starts flowing, packets are scheduled out of the end system to
stay within the contracted rate specification. If packets are scheduled directly
out of memory, the scheduler assigns transmission times. If data is generated
by a program or continuous media source, the interface must buffer packets
that are generated before the schedule allows transmission. The source has an
incentive not to exceed the rate specification, since packets in excess of the

---

[18]Negotiation with the network and/or receiver is, of course, feedback, but it generally happens
once, after which the rate control is truly open-loop. It is possible to have an occasional renegoti-
ation of the traffic contract.

contract may be dropped by the network (shown by the light dotted line in Figure 7.19) or may overrun the receiver.

The network needs to ensure that packets are not injected at a rate faster than the traffic contract allows, and thus *polices* packets as they enter. The policing algorithm can be the same as the scheduling algorithm, except that arriving packets are not buffered, as described in Section 5.3.5. They are passed if conforming. They may be discarded if nonconforming or marked for later discard if excess capacity is available. This allows applications to send data in excess of the traffic contract on a best-effort basis. In many cases, it is better for the application to mark which packets should be measured against traffic contract conformance, so that high-priority packets are more likely to be passed.

Thus rate control can serve as a flow control mechanism by negotiating the rate specification with the receiver and scheduling packet transmissions. Rate control can serve as a congestion avoidance mechanism by negotiating the rate with the network. Admission control and policing of packets are the mechanisms that the network uses to enforce the agreed rate. If the network supports resource reservations, the flow and congestion control roles can be conveniently combined. If not, it is possible to use rate control for either flow or congestion control, in combination with closed-loop control. These variants are described in Section 7.5.5.

7.5.2.2 Rate Parameters

Data flow is measured as the *rate* in bits per second. The rate at which an application can send data is bounded by the bandwidth of the host–network interface link, and the bandwidth through the network link is bounded by the minimum bandwidth link, as described by the Network Bandwidth Principle (N-1A*b*).

The simplest measure is the *peak rate* r_p, which is the maximum instantaneous rate of the transmitter, as shown in Figure 7.20. In the case of fixed size packets, r_p can be measured, and packets scheduled for transmission, based on the minimum interpacket transmission time. In the case of variable size packets, the rate is measured over a time window. The problem with peak rate allocation is that it is generally an inefficient way to determine the resources needed for a transfer (fraction of link bandwidth and switch capacity and buffer allocation). Unless traffic is relatively uniform, peak rate allocation is

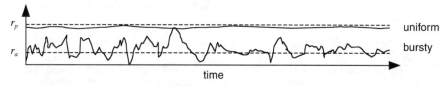

Figure 7.20 Peak and average rate.

EXAMPLE 7.7: ATM TRAFFIC CLASSES

ATM is a connection-oriented network layer with resources reserved, as described in Sections 4.1.3 and 5.3. This reservation allows open-loop rate control to be used by the source. A number of traffic classes are defined [Giroux 1999], as shown in Table 7.1.

Four traffic classes provide pure open-loop rate control: CBR allocates peak rate and has the corresponding adaptation layer AAL-1 that provides end-to-end time synchronization.

VBR allocates resources between peak and average rate based on a burst length parameter, and has two varieties, nonreal-time and real-time, which additionally specifies the maximum delay variance (jitter).

ABT[19] signals per block peak rate, average rate, and jitter. It is designed to be used with switches that support fast reservation. An optimistic mode is supported called immediate transmission (IT), in which the switch will attempt to accept data even if the rate increases and increase the reservation.

UBR provides no rate control at all, and is strictly a best-effort traffic class. In reality, there are few applications that are best effort, as described in Section 8.1.2.

In response to the desire to transport Internet traffic over ATM without the need for complex a priori rate specification, new traffic classes were proposed and adopted. ABR [Bonomi 1995] was designed as a traffic class that provided dynamic rate adjustment and congestion avoidance using a hybrid of open- and closed-loop control.[20] There are two ABR modes: Binary mode uses a forward ECN (FECN) bit to signal congestion. Explicit rate (ER) mode allows the switch to signal a rate at which the sender should transmit as conditions change. Thus, ER mode is a dynamic explicit rate scheme, as discussed in Section 7.5.5.

In response to criticism of the complexity that ABR flow control would impose on switch and host–network interfaces, the much simpler GFR[21] was standardized, which adds a *minimum* guaranteed rate to UBR and required AAL-5 frame discard policies.

---

extremely conservative, reserving far more resources than necessary. Traffic that is bursty has varying instantaneous bandwidth requirements with periods of low bandwidth, which could be used by other data transfers sharing parts of the network path.

The other rate measure of interest is the *average rate* r_a, which reflects

---

[19]ABT is part of the ITU traffic management specification I.371 but not specified by the ATM Forum [ATMF 1996t].

[20]A hop-by-hop credit-based scheme [Kung 1995] was considered, but lost in the standards battle to and end-to-end closed-feedback loop, as mentioned in Section 4.2.2.

[21]Originally called UBR+.

Table 7.1 ATM Traffic Classes

CLASS	NAME	CONTROL	TRAFFIC	PARAMETERS
CBR	Constant bit rate	Open loop	Real time	Peak rate
rt-VBR	Real-time variable bit rate	Open loop	Real time	Peak and average rate, burst jitter, latency
nrt-VBR	Nonreal-time variable bit rate	Open loop	Data	Peak and average rate, burst
ABT	ATM block transfer	Fast reservation open loop	Data	Per block peak and average rate, burst
ABR	Available bit rate	Hybrid	Data	Minimum rate*
GFR	Guaranteed framerate	Open loop	Data	Minimum rate*
UBR	Unspecified bit rate	None	Best effort	None*

*Peak rate is specified in the SETUP, but is not guaranteed for ABR, GFR, and UBR.

the average transmission rate over a time interval. If transmissions among different flows perfectly interleave or follow a distribution that aggregates (such as Poisson), average rate allocation would suffice. However, as shown in Figure 5.25, bursts can collide, requiring that packets contending for a link be queued. Thus, the actual allocation must lie between the peak and average rate.

The extremes of traffic type are *constant bit rate* (CBR), in which $r_p = r_a$, and highly bursty *variable bit rate* traffic, in which $r_p \gg r_a$. The burstiness of a flow can be characterized by a *burst factor*, which indicates the maximum burst tolerated. There are a number of ways this can be expressed, including peak/average ratio and maximum burst length at peak rate. The best possible scenario for the network is uniform traffic or perfect interleaving of bursts, allowing the network to allocate based on the aggregate average rate Σr_a. However, assuming random burst arrival, the burstier the traffic, the more resources (bandwidth and buffering) are required for a given average rate. This is because bursts destined for a particular switch output can collide, as was shown in Figure 7.14. The larger the bursts, the more buffers are required, which increases FIFO queueing latency.

Statistical multiplexing gains assume that burst arrivals are not correlated; if they are, then more resources will have to be allocated. For example, self-similar traffic [Leland 1993] reduces the statistical multiplexing gains. The actual bandwidth required by the network r lies between the average and peak aggregate rates: $\Sigma r_a < R < \Sigma r_p$.

7.5.3   Closed-Loop Flow Control

Closed-loop flow control relies on feedback information from the receiver and network to adjust its rate. The model for a closed-loop system is shown in Figure 7.21. The flow control aspects will be described in this subsection, and congestion control will be discussed in Section 7.5.4.

Closed-loop flow control is appropriate when the sending application has little knowledge about the receiver or the network. The feedback control loop allows the sender to transmit based on the changing ability for the receiver to accept data. Closed-loop congestion control allows the sender to adapt to the network, and will be discussed in Section 7.5.4.

The earliest flow control mechanisms consisted of on/off and stop-and-wait. On/off flow control relies on the receiver to inform the transmitter when to transmit or wait, and is only effective over low-latency links; an example is the XON/XOFF protocol for serial link computer peripherals. Stop-and-wait is the equivalent of go-back-1, and is inappropriate for even moderate-speed networks since only a single packet can be in flight at a time.

7.5.3.1   Window Flow Control

Window-based flow control uses a sliding window to determine the number of unacknowledged packets that a source can transmit. This was explained in Section 7.1.3, and couples the flow and error control mechanisms together. The simplest case is a static window. If the receiver is the bottleneck, then the window is chosen just large enough so that the receiver can buffer and process packets.

The source can adapt to changing receiver needs by changing the window size based on feedback. As the receiver buffers fill, the window is decreased in size; as the receiver buffers empty, the window is increased.

7.5.3.2   Window and Acknowledgment Granularity

For simplicity, we have been showing the granularity of windows and acknowledgments as the packet number, but this does not need to be the case. It is also

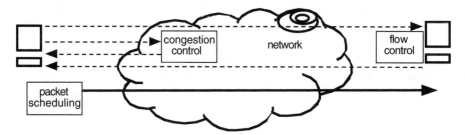

Figure 7.21   Closed-loop flow and congestion control.

possible to count in bytes or bits. If packets are a fixed size, there is little difference, other than the number of bits in fields. If packets are variable size, however, there are some differences.

Counting by byte (as is done in TCP) views the data transmission as an unstructured stream of bytes, rather than as a stream of packets. There are two advantages to this. First, flow and congestion control is concerned with the amount of data. It is less important to count the number of packets than the number of bytes of data. In particular, flow control is based on either the rate at which the receiver can accept data (measured in bytes per second) or the amount of free buffer space (measured in bytes). Congestion control is based on either the transmission rate (measured in bytes per second), or the number of bytes in flight. In both cases, counting bytes provides a direct measurement on the rate or amount of data, and thus a better estimate to the sender to determine when to transmit packets.

Second, even though it is best to Avoid Hop-by-Hop Fragmentation (T-5F) by end-to-end negotiation of MTU, byte counting allows this to happen when necessary on network nodes that support fragmentation. For example, a link failure might cause a rerouting to a link with a smaller MTU.

On the other hand, byte granularity can make error control more complex. In particular, selective acknowledgment cannot be done as a bit vector of packet numbers. A longer vector of byte counts (begin and end) must be exchanged in control packets, and the processing is more complex.

Finally, it is possible to count bits instead of bytes. There is little motivation for this in modern networks that generally connect byte-oriented end systems. Some protocols, such as Delta-t [Fletcher 1978, Watson 1989], used bit granularity to allow data to be exchanged between machines of different word lengths. In particular, 36-bit machines (Univac and DEC PDP-10) used a 9-bit byte and 60-bit machines (CDC) used a 9-, 12-, or 15-bit byte. The only difference to the protocol in bit granularity is three additional bits in control fields.

7.5.4   Closed-Loop Congestion Control

We have discussed the need to time the transmission of packets to match the ability of the receiver to accept them, which is flow control. The additional reason to control the transmission of packets is to avoid congesting the network; this is referred to as *congestion control* [Davies 1972]. The effect on increasing load offered to the network is shown in Figure 7.22.

The transmission of data into the network is the *offered load*; as this increases, the throughput of the network increases, which is the *carried load*. In the ideal case, carried load equals the offered load, as shown by the diagonal line with slope $= 1$ in Figure 7.22a. In reality, the network will begin to saturate, and the carried load will level off at the *knee* of the curve. Eventually, the network will be driven into congestion and no longer be able to carry the

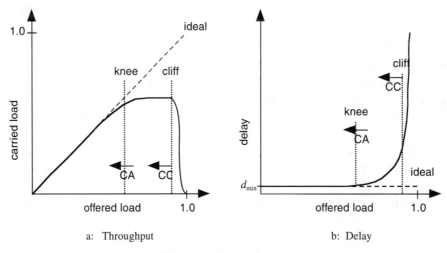

a: Throughput   b: Delay

Figure 7.22   Congestion avoidance and control regions.

traffic offered; at the *cliff* of the curve [Chiu 1989], the network goes into *congestion collapse*, and the throughput rapidly goes to zero. The main reason is that congestion causes packets to overrun queues in network nodes and be lost. If closed-loop error control mechanisms respond to this by retransmitting packets, they will make the congestion problem worse, when they should be backing off and restricting transmission.

The other impact of offered load is on the delay of the network, shown in Figure 7.22b. Once the traffic begins to saturate, queues begin to build, causing the delay d_q to increase beyond the propagation delay through the links and node d_{min}. Once the cliff of the throughput is reached, packets aren't getting through at all, and the delay curve increases without bound.

Thus, we have defined three operating regions partitioned by the knee and cliff of the throughput curve. The operating region that allows the network to meet the High-Performance Path Goal (II) is to the left of the knee, in which throughput increases to match the offered traffic and latency is low. Congestion control mechanisms operate at the cliff of the curve, when congestion is detected, and attempt to keep the operating point left of the cliff (shown by ←CC in Figure 7.22). To remain in the region to the left of the knee, congestion avoidance mechanisms must be used, which detect saturation of the network long before congestion actually occurs (←CA). As described in Section 4.2.2, network nodes can infer congestion by the building of queues, and issue ECN messages to throttle the transmission of packets. We are concerned with end-to-end congestion avoidance in this chapter. Mechanisms that use ECN messages are *explicit* congestion avoidance and control. Mechanisms that operate without information from the network are *implicit* congestion avoidance and control. In this case the node uses RED to drop packets so that the end systems will infer congestion less.

> **Congestion Avoidance**   *Congestion should be avoided before it happens. Keep queues from building and operate just to the left of the knee to maximize throughput and minimize latency.*
>
> **T-II.4c**

Recall that open-loop rate control is generally used in conjunction with an admission control mechanism that provides the ability to remain to the left of the knee. Connections are not admitted that would overcommit network resources; policing ensures that the transmitter lives up to the traffic contract. This congestion avoidance inherent to connection-oriented networks is described in Section 5.3.5.

On the other hand, closed-loop congestion control is based on the use of a window, as described for error and flow control. This ensures *conservation of packets* in the connection [Jacobson 1992b], since feedback is required before additional packets can enter. Further, it is a *self-clocking* mechanism, which reacts to congestion. In the operating range between the knee and cliff, packets are delayed, which causes ACKs to be delayed, which in turn slows the clocking of new packets into the network. Thus, the window feedback mechanism automatically performs some congestion avoidance, but with a reaction time in excess of an RTT.

If the network is the bottleneck, then the window is chosen to match the rate at which the network can pass data, rather than the receiver as described in Section 7.5.3. Thus, if windows are used for both flow and congestion control, the sending window must always be the minimum of the receiver and network window sizes. Performance is critically related to the choice of window size. If the window is not too small, data can be continuously transmitted, as shown in Figure 7.23a (with a window size of 4). If the window is too small, the rate is lower than necessary, as shown in Figure 7.23b.

However, if the window is too large, then the network can be driven into congestion at worst or will use congestion control mechanisms to discard packets. In either case, the effect is to reduce the end-to-end throughput, and increase the end-to-end latency due to the need to retransmit packets. Note that the appropriate window size is not necessarily that which fully uses capacity on the access link from the end system to the network.

> **Use Closed-Loop Congestion Control to Adjust to Network Conditions**   *Closed-loop feedback is needed to adjust to network conditions when there are no hard reservations.*
>
> **T-6Dc**

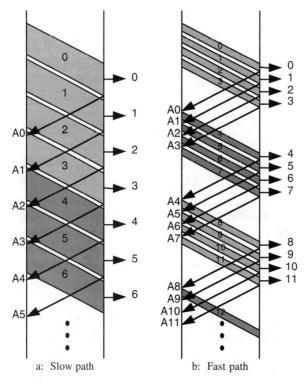

a: Slow path   b: Fast path

Figure 7.23 Effect of high bandwidth.

Thus, to better react to dynamic network conditions, the window must be dynamically adjusted to match network conditions. The goal is for the window to be large enough to use available bandwidth up to application requirements, but not so large as to drive the network into congestion. There are two concerns: (1) achieving the proper interpacket transmission timing in the initialization phase and (2) adapting to network conditions in a stable manner in the steady-state phase.

7.5.4.1 Initialization Phase

In the initialization phase, the window needs to approach the right size as quickly as possible. To avoid congesting the network, it should start at a value smaller than dictated by steady state, but discover and adapt to available capacity. If the initial window size is too large or the increase is too aggressive, the network will congest. If the initial window size is too small or increase too conservative, a short-lived data transfer will suffer significant latency, and may never reach steady-state data rate.

An example of dynamic window initialization is shown in Figure 7.24a. The window starts at a size of one packet, and is then incremented with

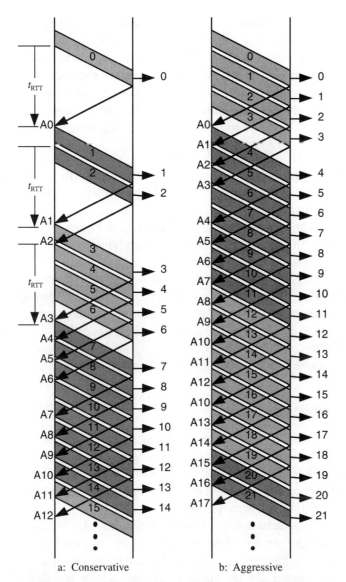

Figure 7.24 Slow start congestion window initialization.

each ACK received A*n*. This results in the doubling of the doubled with each round-trip time. This is the algorithm used in TCP, called *slow start* [Jacobson 1988],[22] and has proven to do a reasonable job of allowing applications to acquire bandwidth share in a connectionless network without resource reservations.

---

[22]TCP slow start isn't actually all that slow, since it is exponential. But it is a lot slower than instantaneous start would be.

This algorithm is relatively conservative in the initial window size, but aggressive in the rate of window increase; either can be adjusted. The problem in high bandwidth-×-delay product networks is generally getting the window to the steady-state *fast* enough, particularly for short-lived transfers such as transactions. Note that in the example of Figure 7.24a, it takes in excess of three RTTs to reach capacity; in extremely high bandwidth-×-delay product networks it may take tens of RTTs. The time to reach capacity is [Partridge 1997]

$$2(d_p + d_q)\,[1 + \log_{1.5} r(d_p + d_q)/b]$$

where $(d_p + d_q)$ is the one-way propagation + queuing delay through the network, and thus $2(d_p + d_q)$ is the RTT and $r(d_p + d_q)$ is the bandwidth-×-delay product and b is the packet length.

More aggressive initial conditions are needed for these cases. Figure 7.24b shows the effect of starting with a larger congestion probing window of four packets (which has been proposed for TCP [Allman 1998]). The available bandwidth is used more quickly, converging to the window size of 8 (there is no point in exceeding this value, and it will be adjusted to the optimum during the steady-state phase described next). Shared state from other connections sharing the same network path can be used for an initial estimate, as described in Section 7.2.3. However, if a number of connections simultaneously start in an aggressive manner, the risk of congestion is greater.

7.5.4.2   Steady-State Phase

In the steady-state phase, the goal is to keep the window the right size to stay on the knee of the throughput curve. There are two considerations. First, the window size should be relatively stable and not wildly oscillate between overshot and undershot values. Second, the offered load among connections sharing the network should be similar to ensure fairness.

A common mechanism is to use an *additive increase* in window size until the network explicitly throttles or the receiver detects loss and a *multiplicative decrease* in window size until the condition is ameliorated (AIMD), as shown in Figure 7.25. Note that both are linear, but the additive increase is slow and the multiplicative decrease is rapid. By carefully increasing and aggressively decreasing the window, the control loop is stable [Chiu 1989]. Furthermore, this scheme is fair among connections, since those receiving a larger share will be driven down multiplicatively and slowly recover bandwidth share. Other values of increase and decrease can provide similar behavior [Floyd 2000b].

The slow start exponential increase during the initialization phase is intended to get close to the steady-state value. AIMD not only maintains steady state, but converges to steady state from the end of slow start estimate, and corrects when dynamic network conditions require a change in the congestion window. Multiple round-trips are required to converge, linear in the number of packets that can be sent in a round-trip [Heidemann 1997].

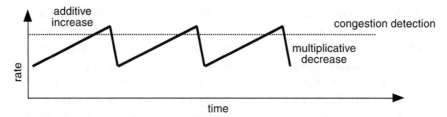

Figure 7.25 Additive increase multiplicative decrease.

Attempts to make the algorithm more reactive can reduce this convergence to logarithmic in the number of packets per RTT, but at the expense of stability. The window can grow more quickly in the early phases of a connection, or just after an idle connection restarts, in order to more rapidly converge on the final window size. But this rapid growth can more quickly overshoot the appropriate final value or result in slower reaction to detected packet losses.

When windows are used for error control in addition to flow and congestion control, the mechanisms can interfere with one another, as mentioned in Section 7.4.3. If the receiver does not know that a packet loss is due to a bit error, it will go into multiplicative decrease, rather than merely request retransmission of the packet. This is further motivation to Decouple Error, Flow, and Congestion Control (T-6E) for example, by using selective repeat error control or explicit congestion information from the network.

7.5.4.3 *Explicit versus Implicit Control*

As described before, congestion indication can either be explicit or implicit. If the network nodes provide explicit congestion notification (as described in Section 4.2.2) that is used to adjust the congestion window, an *explicit dynamic window* congestion control scheme can be realized. Early examples include DECbit [Ramakrishnan 1990], ATM (using a bit in the cell header shown in Figure 5.21), with later proposals to adapt IP [Ramakrishnan 1999] to notify TCP [Floyd 1994] and UDP/RTP [Medina 2000].

If the network does not directly participate in informing the transport layer, the receiving end system must infer a bottleneck in the network due to packet loss and reduce the window size; this is referred to as an *implicit dynamic window* congestion control scheme, as is used in TCP.

The disadvantage of implicit control is that error control and congestion control (and perhaps rate control) are combined into a single mechanism. The receiver does not know whether a packet was lost due to congestion, dropped due to a congestion avoidance policy, or dropped by a link due to a bit error. If the loss was due to an intermediate link discarding a packet with a bad link layer checksum, the congestion window will be needlessly reduced.

Figure 7.26a shows the case of a dropped packet due to congestion or a congestion avoidance policy in the network. Assume that packet 8 is dropped due to congestion. With go-back-n error control, it is not until the timer expires for packet 8 that the stream restarted and the window multiplicatively decreased (from 8 to 4 in this example). If the timer is based on too long an RTT estimate, the situation can be improved by fast retransmit, as introduced in Section 7.4.3. The stream is restarted after the receipt of the third A7 ACK, as shown in Figure 7.26b.

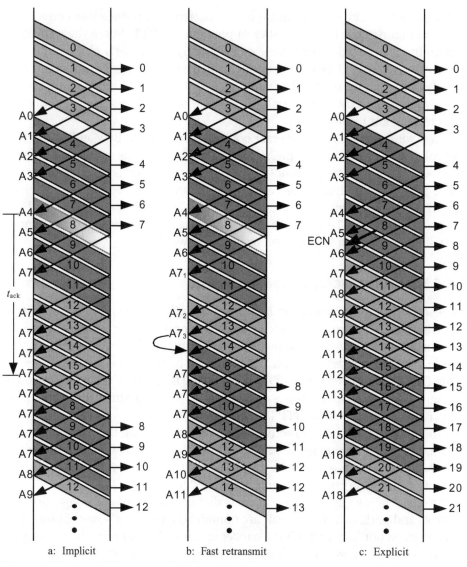

Figure 7.26   Explicit versus implicit dynamic window.

Explicit congestion notification from the network improves performance, as shown in Figure 7.26c. Instead of dropping packets when queues build in the network, an ECN control packet is sent to the sender (either directly in the case of backward ECN or via the receiving end system in the case of forward ECN). The packet does not need to be dropped, unless congestion is already occurring. When the sender receives the ECN packet, it decreases its window, but does not need to retransmit the dropped packet (nor restart the stream in the case of go-back-n error control). The window then additively increases (to 5 for packets 15 to 19), probing for the optimum.

7.5.5 Hybrid Flow and Congestion Control

It is possible to do pure open-loop rate control in connectionless networks only if the paths are sufficiently overprovisioned to avoid congestion and bound loss to acceptable values or path characteristics are known, as described in Section 7.5.2. Conversely, the performance of closed-loop feedback control can be enhanced by employing some open-loop control. We can thus consider hybrid schemes, which combine some of the benefits of both open- and closed-loop control. If the open-loop rate specification is adjusted by feedback, dynamic rate control results. Closed-loop feedback control can be augmented by pacing packets rather than bursting them back-to-back at maximum line rate.

7.5.5.1 *Dynamic Rate Control*

One of the difficulties with open-loop rate control is that even when resources can be committed by the network, application behavior can be too unpredictable for a reasonable a priori rate specification. In this case, *dynamic rate control* can be applied to adjust the rate to correspond to actual application data transfer requirements and adapt to network capacity and avoid congestion. This scheme is used by the ATM ABR traffic class (Example 7.7) in explicit rate mode [Bonomi 1995]. Periodic *resource management cells* are sent through the network. Switches compute the share of bandwidth available to the connection based on current load, and insert the rate in the cell. The cell passes through the network and is returned to the source, which adjusts its rate to match. Since the network provides rate information to the endpoints, this is an *explicit dynamic rate* control scheme. While it requires a fair amount of complexity to implement in the switches, advances in VLSI chip density have reduced the complexity concerns.

EXAMPLE 7.8: TCP CONGESTION CONTROL

End-to-end congestion control mechanisms have been added to TCP and evolved over its life. The basic mechanisms are an exponential initialization phase called *slow start* and an AIMD steady-state phase [Jacobson 1988], as shown in Figure 7.27.

A connection initially begins by sending a single packet, and then exponentially increases by incrementing the congestion window by one TCP segment (packet) with each received ACK, until congestion is detected. The window is then multiplicatively decreased by half, and the connection enters steady state.

During steady state, an AIMD algorithm maintains stability. The window increases linearly in size until congestion is detected, conventionally by packet loss. The congestion window is then multiplicatively decreased by half, and additively grows again. While the load for which congestion occurs changes over time, the AIMD algorithm tracks and maintains convergence.

Several optimizations to the basic algorithm have been implemented or proposed:

- Fast recovery allows a connection to keep transmitting after a fast retransmit, by waiting for a half-window quantity of duplicate ACKs, and continuing to send packets rather than going-back-*n*. This continued transmission of packets keeps the ACKs stream returning allowing a fast return to normal AIMD steady-state control.

- Partial acknowledgment response [Hoe 1996, Floyd 1999] is designed to recover more quickly from errors than the basic fast retransmit and fast recovery, by halving the window only once (rather than once per packet in the burst) and keeping the ACK clocking going.

- RED [Floyd 1993] is implemented in switches to discard packets when queues build. This serves to provide implicit congestion avoidance notification so that TCP sources back off before congestion actually occurs.

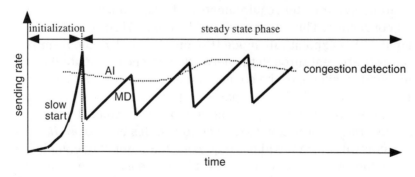

Figure 7.27 TCP slow start and steady-state control.

- ECN [Floyd 1994] allows TCP to exploit the proposed IP forward ECN capability [Ramakrishnan 1999] to trigger multiplicative decrease, better anticipating congestion without requiring discard to be used as an implicit congestion signal.

- Pacing [Visweswaraiah 1997, Partridge 1998] uses rate control to space the transmission of packets within the window to reduce the likelihood of congestion, as described in Section 7.5.5. Packets are spaced at the rate of W/RTT, where W is the window size, using a leaky bucket scheduler [Kulik 1999].

- Rate control based on equations that describe TCP behavior [Padhye 1998, Karandikar 1999, Floyd 2000a] provide for smaller oscillations in rate, which can also be applied to UDP traffic such as streaming media.

- Explicit transport error notification (ETEN) separates error from flow/congestion control mechanisms so that error losses are not misconstrued as congestion [Samaraweera 1997, 1999, Biaz 1998].

Various versions of TCP have implemented these optimizations:

- TCP Tahoe implements the original congestion control algorithms of slow start and AIMD, as well as fast retransmit error recovery.

- TCP Reno adds fast recovery, and is widely implemented.

- TCP NewReno [Floyd 1999] modifies the fast recovery to respond to partial acknowledgments.

- TCP Vegas [Brakmo 1995] proposed using an RTT estimate [Jain 1989, Wang 1991] to control the window size, rather than AIMD. It has been shown that the RTT estimate does not accurately enough reflect the queue lengths to be used as a predictor of congestion [Biaz 1999].

An early *implicit dynamic rate* scheme was implemented by NETBLT [Clark 1987], with the goal to decouple error and flow control. Flow control is rate-based with an adjustment per group of packets from the receiver; error control uses selective acknowledgments. NETBLT uses an implicit dynamic rate control scheme since information from the network is not used for rate adjustment.[23]

---

[23]Congestion control mechanisms are not considered in [Clark 1987].

TCP has shown a remarkable ability to adapt to high-speed networks by the addition of forward compatible options and modifications. Figure 7.28a shows fields in the TCP and IP headers that affect throughput [Partridge 1997]. The time to live field is an 8-bit field, which is decremented at each hop in the network until it reaches zero and is discarded. This limits the maximum packet lifetime (MPL) which is needed to determine the sequence number space in the TCP header for the packet sequence number (for the payload) and acknowledgment number (for a packet received), as described in Section 7.4.2. The IP identifier field is used to identify the fragment number if IP fragments TCP TPDUs in the network (which we try to avoid with MTU path discovery). The window size limits the number of unacknowledged packets, as described in Section 7.5.1.

Optimizations that have been applied to TCP include [Jacobson 1992a, Mathis 1996, Pink 1994]:

- Window scale option, which negotiates at connection setup (in a SYN option) a power-of-2 scale factor to be applied to the window size field, to a maximum of 2^{14} (the window is limited to half the sequence number space, from the formula in Section 7.4.2). For a GEO satellite link, this increases the throughput achievable from just under 1 Mb/s to approximately 15 Gb/s [Partridge 1997]; even this may be insufficient in the long term.

- RTTM (round-trip time measurement) adds a 32-bit timestamp in an option header to allow explicit measurement of RTT. This reduces the susceptibility of indirect estimates (such as [Karn 1987]) to interference from error control. It has been shown, however, that an estimate is not needed per packet, and that once per RTT is sufficient [Allman 1999a].

- PAWS (protection against wrapped sequence number), which uses the 32-bit timestamp to augment the 32-bit sequence number.

7.5.5.2 Pacing

An alternative hybrid approach is to augment window flow control to pace packets when the window allows transmission. Although a regular spacing of ACKs in window-based flow and congestion control ought to result in a relatively even spacing of packet transmissions, a number of conditions result in bursts of packets at full rate [Aggarwal 2000]. Examples include a burst transmission after packet loss, ACK aggregation (discussed in Section 7.4.3), and ACK compression (when ACKs are queued behind large data packets [Zhang 1991]). Pacing spaces packets in an attempt to reduce the

- SACK (selective acknowledgment), which allows negotiation for selective repeat operation at connection setup (in a SYN option), instead of the default go-back-*n*. A SACK option header is added to acknowledgment packets that contains a series of sequence number pairs ⟨first-byte,last-byte+1⟩ (TCP uses byte-oriented granularity).

- Fast retransmit [Jacobson 1990, Allman 1999b], which as described in Section 7.4.3 and shown in Figure 7.26, initiates retransmission on receipt of triple duplicate ACKs, even if the retransmission timer has not yet expired.

- Larger initial window [Allman 1998] to allow the rate to increase more quickly in high-bandwidth-×-delay product networks for transactions and short-lived connections, as shown in Figure 7.24b.

A number of end system implementation optimizations have also been made to TCP over its life. Figure 7.28b shows fields that either do not change within a TCP connection or change in a predictable manner [Partridge 1994a]. TCP header prediction [Jacobson 1990, Pink 1994] exploits this to simplify processing when the end system receives packets.

Furthermore, IP header fields that are also stable are highlighted. Invariant packet fields can be used in a template, which can be used to fill in headers for transmission or match on reception (as was described in Sections 6.2.3 and 6.4.2).

A trailer checksum option for TCP was proposed [Bridges 1994], which would allow pipelined implementation of the sender (as described in Section 6.4.2). After significant debate, the IETF community decided that potential benefits were not justified in the face of modifying TCP.[24]

A number of TCP optimizations have been proposed for high bandwidth-×-delay product networks [Allman 1999c, 2000a].

burstiness of transmission and reduce congestion. The pace is used to determine the *rate* at which to send, but the window still limits *how much* data can be sent.

Another form of pacing can be used with connection-oriented networks, which uses window-based flow control to allow the receiver to control the sender, in conjunction with rate control corresponding to the traffic reservation in the network [Gong 1994].

---

[24]This issue was debated on the IETF end-to-end mailing list.

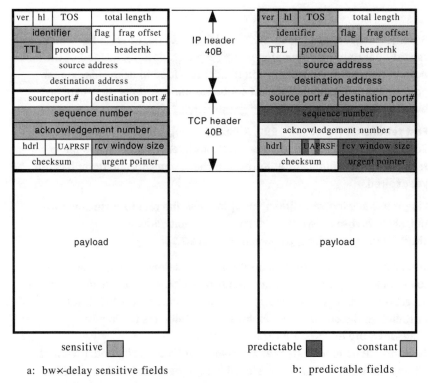

ver	hl	TOS	total length
identifier		flag	frag offset
TTL	protocol		headerhk
source address			
destination address			
sourceport #		destination port #	
sequence number			
acknowledgement number			
hdrl		UAPRSF	rcv window size
checksum		urgent pointer	

IP header
40B

TCP header
40B

payload

ver	hl	TOS	total length
identifier		flag	frag offset
TTL	protocol		headerhk
source address			
destination address			
source port #		destination port#	
sequence number			
acknowledgement number			
hdrl		UAPRSF	rcv window size
checksum		urgent pointer	

payload

sensitive ▢   predictable ■   constant ▢

a: bw×-delay sensitive fields   b: predictable fields

Figure 7.28   TCP fields affecting high performance.

7.6   Security and Information Assurance

Security is the one service that is arguably effective only on an end-to-end basis, although there are cases where hop-by-hop link enhancements are useful. Cryptography [Schneier 1996] is needed to solve some security problems, such as confidentially and data integrity; these are clearly high-speed issues. Other problems, such as infrastructure security, cannot be solved by cryptography.

A detailed description of security architectures is beyond the scope of this book,[25] but a brief discussion of high-speed end-to-end security issues is in order. First, we will discuss the need for end-to-end security, and its interaction with hop-by-hop security and other data transformation operations. Then, the high-speed networking issues will be discussed, including session establishment, encryption, and protocol infrastructure.

---

[25]Comprehensive coverage of the area is provided by [Kaufman 1995] and [Stallings 1995].

7.6.1   End-to-End Security

The End-to-End Argument (T-3) has strong application to the security and information assurance realm. If data is insecure at any point along the path, it is subject to compromise. Thus, hop-by-hop data integrity and encryption are not sufficient to guarantee these services end-to-end. This means that per link or per subnet security mechanisms are insufficient, and end users that need end-to-end security will perform their own data integrity, encryption, and authentication regardless of services provided in the network.

7.6.1.1   Hop-by-Hop Security

There are times, however, when strong end-to-end security mechanisms are not needed. There are varying levels of information assurance, and it may be sufficient to apply security mechanisms selectively to reduce the exposure along parts of a path. There are two examples of this:

1. Link-layer encryption can be applied to a wireless access or transit link to provide *wire equivalent protection* [IEEE802.11]. Wireless RF links are particularly subject to eavesdropping, since a physical tap into the line is not needed. By encrypting susceptible links, information assurance can be raised to the level of the less susceptible (wired) links.

2. Network edge-to-edge encryption and address authentication can be used to provide a secure virtual private network (VPN) infrastructure or reduce susceptibility in an insecure public network. It may be sufficient to provide a secure path among parts of an organization, without requiring high levels of intra-organization security.

It is important to reiterate that neither of these scenarios provides end-to-end security to the applications and users.

An additional reason to encrypt data over part of a path is to obscure user associations and traffic patterns. Even if the user data is encrypted, information can be gathered by snooping on packet headers, particularly end system addresses. By aggregating these flows into encrypted *tunnels*, and by the judicious use of traffic padding, the original traffic patterns can be obscured. It may be desirable in this case to encrypt *only* the header, so that recursion effects do not occur.

7.6.1.2   Recursion of Encryption

The type of protection afforded—end-to-end data confidentiality, selective field confidentiality, or traffic flow confidentiality—depend on the point of enforcement.

One of the problems of hop-by-hop encryption to raise the security of a susceptible link occurs when users need end-to-end information assurance. In this case, encryption will be recursive, since the link-layer encryption will occur on data that is already encrypted. This may compromise the strength of the end-to-end encryption unless the properties of the composed encryption are known.

Thus, hop-by-hop enhancement of encryption must be carefully applied. Its presence may be exposed to the end system, so that such links can either be avoided, or so lower-layer encryption can be selectively disabled (which, of course, must be done only with proper authentication).

In general, composition of security mechanisms can compromise overall security.

7.6.1.3   Composition with Data Transformation

Encryption algorithms transform data, and thus interact with other data transformation operations such as media encoding, FEC, and compression (discussed in Chapter 8). These other transformation operations must be done *before* encryption. The information characteristics of the data are obscured by encryption, rendering compression and coding algorithms useless. This has two significant consequences:

First, the order of encryption and other data transformation operations must be maintained in the end systems. If data transformation is done in the host–network interface, then encryption *must* also be done in the network interface, on the network side.

Second, since encryption obscures the properties of the coding, network-based transcoding is not possible without compromising end-to-end security by decrypting/encrypting at the transcoding point. This forces transcoding for compatibility to the end systems, rather than allowing it as a network service. Furthermore, application layer control information that is part of an encrypted network packet payload is obscured. An example is the URL in an HTTP request message; if it is encrypted, network-based caching cannot snoop on the URL to redirect the request to a cache.

Thus, many of the high-speed application adaptations that will be discussed in Section 8.3 are challenged (or eliminated) unless end-to-end encryption is selectively applied. Control information can be either kept in the clear or separately encrypted, so that network nodes with the proper authorization can decrypt. For example, in IPsec [Kent 1998, Kaufman 1999], some routing and segment offset information is duplicated in an insecure visible outer header, as well as inside an authenticated or encrypted inner header.

7.6.2   High-Speed Security

There are two significant high-speed security issues: (1) the time to authenticate end users, applications, and systems and establish secure associations and (2) the ability to perform high-speed encryption in the data path.

7.6.2.1   Session Establishment

An essential security operation is the establishment of sessions, which includes the initial secret exchange of keys. Key exchange protocols can be very complicated and often require multiple round-trips of messages. In addition, keys should only be used for a limited time before being discarded for new keys; rekeying overheads need to be considered as well.

As for other session and connection establishments, it is important that these operations occur within a reasonable time. For longer-lived associations, an establishment time on the order of a second or two may be an acceptable target. Performing such operations within a subsecond to 100-ms interactive latency bound is extremely challenging, and such operations should be amortized over multiple interactions when possible.

Unless the endpoints of a session have established mutual trust, a trusted third party is necessary, such as provided by a certificate authority (CA). The performance of public key infrastructure (PKI) operations is a concern, particularly for group communications. For example, when an individual certificate is revoked, all users in the group may have to be rekeyed. There is also the possibility for denial of service attacks, which specifically exploit their computational intensity. By flooding authentication requests to a server, a rogue cracker can deny legitimate users the ability to quickly establish secure sessions. Certificate revocation is also an operation subject to denial of service attacks. Implementations that perform Early Filtering (L-4f) to determine the legitimacy of requests can reduce the impact of such attacks.

7.6.2.2   Encryption

Encryption is a per byte or bit function, and thus must be optimized according to the Critical Path Principle (1B). If authentication is performed per session or connection, the time constraints are less severe. However, in connectionless networks such as the IPv4-based Internet, authentication is performed per packet and is thus a candidate for critical path optimization.

Both authentication and encryption are computationally very expensive [Nahum 1995]. Many algorithms require as many 32-bit arithmetic operations as there are bits in a message; typical software algorithms achieve only a fraction of the rate of other operations which operate per byte. For example, the

MD5 Internet authentication algorithm typically achieves only one half the processor clock rate, measured in megabytes per second (for example, 250 Mb/s on a 500-MHz CPU) [Touch 1995c]. Encryption algorithms are even more computationally intensive, by an order of magnitude. Performance was a key consideration in the choice of the advanced encryption standard (AES), with careful analysis of both software complexity and the ability to implement in fast hardware [Nechvatal 2000].

The key impediment to fast security algorithms is their need to touch every *bit* of data being protected, and the need to weave that bit's information throughout the other bits in a packet (or ADU). Standard data ordering is required to allow communicating end systems to agree on keyed information; this can require bit and byte reordering at the endpoints. Algorithms that are isomorphic to byte reordering (as is the Internet checksum) should be considered.

Critical Path Optimization of Security Operations   *Encryption and per packet authentication operations must be optimized for the critical path.*

T-1B

Encryption and per packet authentication are strong candidates for implementation in custom VLSI [Wilcox 1999] host–network interface hardware. To avoid store-and-forward and copy latencies, as well as buffer duplication, discussed in Section 6.4.2, pipelineable encryption and authentication algorithms are highly desirable. The entire operation can either be done in parallel or divided into a pipeline that matches the macrocycle pipeline clock of the network interface. The former can be considered for small fixed size packets (for example, ATM cells), but requires (at least) a linear increase in hardware as packet size scales.

7.6.2.3   Infrastructure Security

Network infrastructure consists of two pieces: (1) physical infrastructure (links and nodes) and (2) protocols (network, MAC, and link layers). The need to secure physical infrastructure from tapping and attack is well understood.

It is also essential to secure *all* network infrastructure and control protocols from attack. Infrastructure protocols and algorithms, including routing and signaling, are necessarily hop-by-hop between network nodes (for example [Kent 2000]). This has significant performance implications, since many of these operations occur frequently, for example, the link state updates of routing algorithms. Sufficient processing capability must be brought to bear so that network performance is not degraded when these protocols are secured. The provision of secure tunnels (for example, IPSec [Kent 1998]) between nodes engaged in an infrastructure protocol can provide information assurance *between* the nodes. However, it cannot provide overall protection from byzantine behavior of one of the nodes engaged in the infrastructure protocol.

7.7 Summary

End-to-end protocols tie the entire path of a communication together, binding it to the network below to realize the High-Performance Paths Goal (II), which provide the service model needed for Application Primacy (I) above. The service model provided to applications consists of the transfer mode (connectionless datagram, connection-oriented, transaction, and continuous streaming media), the degree of reliability, ordered delivery of data, and traffic characteristics.

The end-to-end arguments guide us in determining where to place protocol functions: The End-to-End Argument (T-3) tells us what functions *must* be provided by the transport layer (or above), such as error control for absolute reliability and end-to-end security. The Hop-by-Hop Performance Enhancement Corollary (T-3A) guides us in the placement of hop-by-hop functionality in the network and link layers, such as ECN and per hop FEC, to improve end-to-end performance.

The service model is supported by the basic end-to-end mechanisms, which are framing and multiplexing, state and connection management, error control, and flow control. Additionally, congestion control is performed in conjunction with the network to ensure that network paths are actually usable to applications and the network performance characteristics remain stable. In this chapter we described each of these mechanisms and the way in which they can provide high performance to applications. Chapter 8 will describe how high-speed networked applications use these transport layer services, and how applications adapt to and exert control on the network.

7.7.1 Further Reading

The general networking textbooks suggested in Section 2.5.1 have good coverage of transport protocols, including TCP. The basic mechanisms and issues in transport protocol design receive outstanding coverage in [Watson 1987]. A survey of a number of high-speed transport protocols is provided in [Doeringer 1990, 1994] and of high-speed protocol issues and research in [Feldmeier 1993]. Flow control is surveyed in [Gerla 1980] and high-speed error control in [Bhargaval 1998] and [Feldmeier 1990b]. A broad introduction to security mechanisms and protocols in general is provided in [Kaufman 1995], [Stallings 1995], and [Pfleeger 1996] and to IPsec in particular in [Kaufman 1999]. The broader issues surrounding security in the Internet are discussed in [Schneier 2000].

END-TO-END AXIOMS AND PRINCIPLES

T-3. End-to-End Argument *Functions required by communicating applications can be correctly and completely implemented only with the knowledge and help of the applications themselves. Providing these functions as features within the network itself is not possible.*

T-3A. Hop-by-Hop Performance Enhancement Corollary *It is beneficial to duplicate an end-to-end function hop-by-hop if the result is an overall (end-to-end) improvement in performance.*

T-IV. Transport Protocol Functionality *Transport protocols must be organized to deliver the set of end-to-end high-bandwidth, low-latency services needed by applications. Options and service models should be modularly accessible, without unintended performance degradation and feature interactions.*

T-6D*a*. Aggressiveness of Closed-Loop Control *The response to closed-loop feedback must be rapid enough so the system converges quickly to a new stable state—but not so aggressive that oscillations occur due to over-reaction to transients.*

T-6D. Open- versus Closed-Loop Control *Use open-loop control based on knowledge of the network path to reduce the delay in closed-loop convergence. Use closed-loop control to react to dynamic network and application behavior; intermediate per hop feedback can sometimes reduce the time to converge.*

T-6A. Minimize Transaction Latency *Combine connection establishment with request and data transfer to reduce end-to-end latency for transactions.*

T-I.2. Continuous Media Streaming *Timeliness of delivery should not be traded for reliable transfer in real-time continuous media streams. Use a playback buffer to reorder and absorb jitter.*

T-5A. Hard versus Soft State *Balance the determinism and stability of hard state against the adaptability and robustness to failure of soft state.*

T-5B. State Aggregation *Spatially aggregate state to reduce complexity, but balance against loss in granularity. Temporally aggregate to reduce or eliminate establishment and initialization phase. State shared is fate shared.*

T-5E. Use Initial Assumptions to Converge Quickly *The time to converge to steady state depends on the accuracy of the initial conditions, which depends on the currency of state information and the dynamicity of the network. Use past information to make assumptions that will converge quickly.*

T-8A. Balance Packet Size *Trade between control overhead and fine enough grained control. Choose size and aggregation methods that make sense end-to-end.*

T-5F. Avoid Hop-by-Hop Fragmentation *The transport layer should be aware of or explicitly negotiate the maximum transfer unit of the path to avoid the overhead of fragmentation and reassembly.*

T-4C. Application Layer Framing   *To the degree possible, match ADU and TPDU structure. In cases where the application can better determine structure and react to lost and misordered ADUs, ALF should be employed.*

T-3A. Limit Layered Multiplexing   *Layered multiplexing should be minimized and performed in an integrated manner for all layers at a single time.*

T-8C. Packet Control Field Values   *Optimize header control field values to trade efficiency against expected future requirements.*

T-6E. Decouple Error, Flow, and Congestion Control   *Exploit selective acknowledgments and open-loop rate control to decouple error, flow, and congestion control mechanisms.*

T-6De. Forward Error Correction   *Use FEC for low-latency, open-loop flow control when bandwidth is available and statistical loss tolerance bounds are acceptable to the application.*

T-6Do. Use Knowledge of Network Paths for Open-Loop Control   *Exploit open-loop rate and congestion control based on a priori knowledge to the degree possible to reduce the need for feedback control.*

T-II.4c. Congestion Avoidance   *Congestion should be avoided before it happens. Operate just to the left of the knee to maximize throughput and minimize latency.*

T-6Dc. Use Closed-Loop Congestion Control to Adjust to Network Conditions   *Closed-loop feedback is needed to adjust to network conditions when there are no hard reservations.*

T-1B. Critical Path Optimization of Security Operations   *Encryption and per packet authentication operations must be optimized for the critical path.*

CHAPTER 8

Networked Applications

This chapter discusses high-speed networked applications. All of the previous chapters have been leading to this, building an infrastructure for high-speed networking that finally finds a purpose as the medium for distributed application interaction. The axiom of Application Primacy (I) drives everything to this point.

> **Application Primacy**   *The sole and entire point of building a high-performance network infrastructure is to support the distributed applications that need it.*
>
> A-I

The relationship between applications and the network infrastructure through which they interact has two dimensions. The first relates the fundamental characteristics of an application to the semantics of high-performance networking—that an application requires "high performance" from the network. The second concerns the interface at which an application interacts with the network—how an application controls and reacts to the network. Underlying the first relationship is a progressive push-pull dynamic, whereby advances in network technology beget applications that exploit them, and the requirements of new applications drive the development of faster networks. The second relationship couples the application to network characteristics that are expressed in both the session and transport layers of the infrastructure, which is why these are highlighted in one of the end systems of Figure 8.1, in addition to the peer-to-peer application relationship.

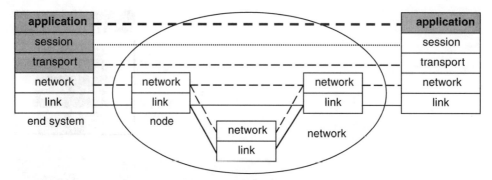

Figure 8.1 Applications and interface to lower layers.

Developing an application that depends on network capabilities that don't (yet) exist is both conceptually difficult and practically complicated. The awkwardness of creating applications "ahead of the network" is responsible for the fact that most of the work on high-speed networking has followed a "field of dreams" approach [Robinson 1989], in which new network capabilities precede the design of new applications. The Internet provides many examples of this: email, the Web, electronic commerce, and distributed games were not directly envisioned as target applications at the time of its design.

However, there are examples of application requirements directly driving the development of network capabilities. File-sharing protocols (such as Apollo Domain [Leach 1983] and NFS—network file system [Shepler 2000]) were developed in response to the demand for application access to distributed files. Multifolder mail protocols (such as Internet message access protocol—IMAP [Crispin 1996]) were designed after local mail programs provided a similar capability. This chapter examines both of these complementary driving characteristics of high-speed applications: how new capabilities enable new applications and how new applications drive the creation of new network services.

> **Field of Dreams versus Killer App Dilemma** *Advances in network technology create the "field of dreams" to which new applications are drawn, but are difficult to motivate without the tangible pull of a new "killer application"—which can't emerge in the absence of an adequate network infrastructure. This chicken-and-egg dilemma governs the supply-and-demand dynamic of high-speed networking.*
>
> **A-I.1**

The key to high-speed networked applications is the dynamic coupling between the application and the network, in which the application adapts to the network and the network adapts to the application. Applications can adapt to the network in different ways, including reducing perceived request–response latency, limiting bandwidth usage, scaling to support parallelization and distribution, and adapting to match specific network parameters. The network can similarly adapt to application cues synchronously, asynchronously, over the period of a session, or over intervals that are more frequent. These interactions require an interface at which the application can express its requirements to the network, and the network can inform the application about changing capabilities. In some cases, this can require one to make assumptions about the other, to accommodate legacy applications or networks that lack the ability to explicitly signal.

This chapter is organized as follows. Section 8.1 introduces the bandwidth and latency characteristics of high-speed applications, and describes the criteria by which we distinguish high-speed applications. The characteristics of best-effort, interactive, real-time, and deadline applications are considered. Section 8.2 discusses applications by category—information access, telepresence, and distributed computing—and their composition into more complex applications such as distributed collaboration. Section 8.3 considers how high-speed applications can adapt to mask latency or deal with less than ideal bandwidth. Section 8.4 describes the ways that applications can use feedback from, and exert control on, the network. Section 8.5 summarizes and lists the principles from this chapter.

8.1   Application Characteristics

This section introduces the characteristics that define high-speed applications. The measure of concern to applications is *delay*.

User Expectations of Interapplication Delay   *The performance metric of primary interest to the users of communicating applications is the total delay in completing the communication, including both the end-to-end delay and any delay introduced by the application itself.*

A-I.2

It is important to note that the applications themselves, as well as the network, must be designed and implemented to support high performance. When we talk about interapplication latency, we are concerned with the *top* of the application layer, at which the latency is visible to the user. In the case of an interactive user, it is the entry and presentation of data on the terminal. In the case of server information access, it is the reading of data in the server store. In the case of a distributed computation, it is measured by program progress as compared to a nondistributed version.

> **User Expectations of Continuous Media Quality** *The performance metric of primary interest to users of continuous media streams is quality of the stream such as frame rate and resolution for video and frequency range for audio.*
>
> **A-I.2c**

In the case of stored multimedia, delay is the performance metric of primary importance, since if the multimedia clip can be transported quickly enough, it can be played back by the user at the desired quality. In the case of live continuous media, data rate r is direct measure of the quality perceived by the user, since it is directly related to parameters such as frequency range, frame rate, frame resolution, and color depth.

The two key aspects of high-speed interapplication communication are bandwidth and latency, so it is sensitivity to these metrics that determines how speed is perceived by the application. As discussed before, delay consists of both the latency due to physical distribution and the bandwidth component to transmit a block of data at a rate r.

> **High-Speed Applications Need High Bandwidth and Low Latency** *Bandwidth and latency are the primary performance metrics governing interapplication delay. The latency requirements of an application depend on the expectations of the user. For data-intensive applications, delay sensitivity drives bandwidth requirements.*
>
> **A-I.3**

In the remainder of this section, we will discuss the bandwidth, latency, and error tolerance characteristics of high-speed applications, followed by a summary of characteristics by application flow type.

8.1.1   Bandwidth

High-speed applications can be classified by the bandwidth they require. Recall that the reason for this bandwidth is to provide sufficiently low delay between applications or users for data-intensive applications or to provide sufficient quality for streaming media applications. The bandwidth threshold is a constantly changing number, since it is relative to the network and end system technology available at a particular time. In the 1980s, megabit-per-second applications were considered high speed, but in the 1990s, it was gigabit-per-second applications.

> **Relative Magnitude of High Speed** *High speed is a relative term. Application requirements for high speed—alleged or actual—have historically grown to at least the limits of currently attainable link speeds and network capacity.*
>
> **A-2A**

8.1.1.1. Individual and Aggregate Bandwidth

As in the case for network bandwidth, there are two distinct ways to measure application bandwidth: per application instantiation and in aggregate.

Individual bandwidth. A single instance of an application that requires a significant fraction of the bandwidth available on a high-speed network link or high-performance end system interface can be considered a *high-speed application*. Supporting this sort of application requires high-bandwidth network infrastructure, high-speed transport protocols, and high-performance end systems. These applications are a primary focus of this chapter.

Aggregate bandwidth. An important measure of the impact of an application on the network infrastructure is the demand it places in aggregate. This is measured by the product of the per instance bandwidth × the number of simultaneous instantiations of the application [Lyles 1995]. Thus, an aggregate gigabit application might consist either of 100 simultaneous instances of a 10-Mb/s application or 10 simultaneous instances of a 100-Mb/s application. The aggregate bandwidth of the PSTN (public switched telephone network) is generally estimated at $O(1 \text{ Tb/s})$ as was the bandwidth of data networks in the mid-1990s (particularly the Internet, SNA, and X.25 packet networks). While it is expected that PSTN bandwidth will remain relatively flat, the aggregate bandwidth of the Internet continues to grow dramatically with no end in sight. In the early 2000s, bundles of fibers are being laid and switches deployed that exceed 1 Tb/s each.

An application that in aggregate consumes a significant fraction (1/100 to 1/1000) of the total available bandwidth of the network has significant impact on the network architecture, design, and engineering. By this measure, a gigabit-per-second aggregate qualified in the terabit-per-second infrastructure of the 1990s, and a terabit-per-second aggregate qualifies in the petabit-per-second infrastructure of the early 2000s. In this chapter we are concerned with the impact of applications in aggregate for two reasons. First, it is important to identify applications that drive the high-speed network infrastructure discussed in Chapters 3 through 5. Second, some of the techniques that enable high aggregate applications, such as caching and application layer multicast, are the subjects of this chapter.

Consider three example applications:

1. High-quality (for example, HDTV resolution) streaming video is a moderate-speed individual application, requiring on the order of 20-Mb/s bandwidth. During prime time (peak evening viewing hours) in the United States, in excess of 75 million households view television [US 1993]. If

each of these viewers received a 20-Mb/s stream, the aggregate bandwidth would be approximately 1.5 Pb/s [Nussbaumer 1995]. Clearly, this application demands high aggregate bandwidth infrastructure, and impacts application design, network protocol deployment, and network engineering to be deployable. Caching for stored content, multicast for live content, and engineering of the caching topology and multicast trees are required to support this application.

2. Interactive Web browsing is a high-speed individual application, requiring gigabit-per-second to browse pages incorporating high-resolution images. Web browsing also requires high aggregate bandwidth, with approximately the same number of users with Web access as prime-time television viewers in the United States [Nielsen 2000].[1]

3. Distributed supercomputing and scientific visualization are high-speed individual applications. Their use is restricted to a small group of scientists and engineers with the supercomputing and high-speed networking infrastructure needed to support them. Thus, as of the early 2000s, these can *not* be considered high-speed aggregate applications. The Field of Dreams versus Killer Application Dilemma (A-I.1) warns us that they may drive aggregate bandwidth in the future. Potential examples include engineers doing collaborative CADS (computer-aided design and simulation) and farmers doing remote weather visualization and crop-yield modeling.

8.1.1.2.   *Application Bandwidth Scaling*

The bandwidth that an application requires is generally not a fixed quantity; most applications operate over a range of bandwidths. Thus, it is important to understand how application utility scales with available bandwidth [Touch 1995b]. Some applications remain structurally unchanged, becoming only faster or perceptually better; other applications have difficulty keeping pace as bandwidths scale. The bandwidth scalability of applications can be described using the following taxonomy [Partridge 1994b]:

Bandwidth Enhanced. The application operates at various bandwidths. Although the application is functional at low bandwidths, it increases in utility given high-speed networking, and does not require fundamental restructuring. Streaming multimedia is the canonical example because high bandwidth increases the achievable resolution and frame rate, with an increased perceptual quality to users.

Bandwidth Challenged. The application is useful at various bandwidths, but either requires substantial revision, or operates in a different way at high speed. An example of a bandwidth-challenged application is distrib-

---

[1]Although not all users with Web access are simultaneously browsing.

uted computing. Some computations, such as Monte Carlo simulations, work with infrequent state exchange. As bandwidth increases, more sophisticated distributions of computation are possible, requiring greater control interaction and data exchange.

Bandwidth Enabled. The application is usable *only when* a high-bandwidth path is available. This may be dictated by particular bandwidth requirements of the application, for example, the high data rates of uncompressed video for networked studio production of movies. It may also be the case that without a base bandwidth, certain applications just don't make sense. Distributed scientific visualization and collaborative CAD/CAE (computer-aided design/engineering) are of this type.

In this chapter, we are most concerned with bandwidth-challenged and bandwidth-enabled applications. As mentioned earlier, we also generally require high individual bandwidth. For example, even though voice communications is bandwidth enabled, it is at such a low bandwidth (typically 56 or 64 Kb/s in the PSTN) that we do not consider it a high-speed application. Conversely, although multimedia streaming can benefit from high bandwidth, it is a bandwidth-enhanced application, and not considered high-speed in the general case. Specific applications that need high-bandwidth requirements for streaming media, such as telemedicine, are bandwidth enabled, and we do consider them to be high speed. While this is a useful taxonomy, it is important to note that the distinction between the types is not always as sharp as we would like.

8.1.1.3.   Application Partitioning

It is also important to consider the design and decomposition of an application to determine its bandwidth requirements. By definition, distributed applications must be partitioned across the network, determined in part by the location of users, data, and resources such as processors and servers. The manner in which the application is partitioned, however, can have a profound impact on the bandwidth required between the communicating parts.

Properly Partition Distributed Applications   *Carefully determine where to cut applications to distribute across the network. Some "high-speed" applications are simply poorly partitioned low-speed applications.*

A-IV₃

For example, the split between user display and image processing can be partitioned at the point where polygons, bytes, or pixels are communicated; this choice significantly impacts the bandwidth required (as well as where processing must reside). A distributed application demanding high bandwidth, but for which the pieces are not carefully grouped to avoid overhead and message latencies, is not inherently a high-speed application; rather it is a poorly implemented application.

8.1.2 Latency

High-speed applications are sensitive to latency in two fundamental ways: during startup and operating in the steady state.

The *startup* phase of an application consists of any signaling (session, transport, or network layer) required to initiate the data transfer, as well as the time for enough data to be accessed by the sending application, propagate through the network, and be received for the application to commence. The mechanism to transport the application flow need not be connection-oriented. However, if a connection is used to transport the data, the startup phase will include the connection establishment phase, and perhaps enough of the initialization phase to get data moving, as described in Section 7.2.1.

The *steady-state* phase consists of the behavior of long-lived application flows. During the application flow, however, actions may need to be performed which result in *transient* behavior, such as a request/response loop within the application, or adaptation to congestion in the network. Generally, the latency bounds required for startup and transient behavior are similar, and thus we will characterize applications by two sets of latency demands: startup/transient and steady state.

Some applications are characterized primarily by only one of the behaviors. For example, the latency measure of interest to short interactive transactions is startup; there is essentially no steady-state behavior. The latency measure of prime importance to live video interaction is steady state. For some applications, both latency measures are important. For example, *interactive* access to live video communication requires low latency for the interactive control loop to establish (startup) and modify (transient) the interaction, as well as low steady-state latency when video is flowing. We will indicate the applicable latency behavior as appropriate to the application classes discussed in the remainder of this section.

The utility of a particular latency is the measure of usefulness or desirability to the application. Applications have varying latency requirements, as shown in Figure 8.2 (and repeated as Figure 8.3), which measures application utility against latency. We will now describe the characteristics of best-effort, interactive, real-time, and deadline application classes.

8.1.2.1 Best-Effort Applications

The first category of applications to consider is those that have extremely loose latency budgets. In the networking community, these are typically called *best-effort*, but in the operating systems community they are traditionally

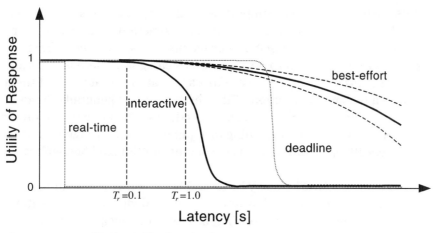

Figure 8.2   Application utility functions.

called *batch* or *background* applications. A best-effort application is one that has a very loose expectation on time of completion, with a gradually decreasing utility function. As time increases, the anticipated variance also increases, shown by the thin dashed lines in Figure 8.2. There are relatively few truly best-effort network applications; the canonical example is email. Users expect email to be delivered on the order of minutes, but are not surprised when the delivery time is much longer, and do not stall other activity waiting for email delivery. Network news has similar characteristics. Networked printing is another example of a best-effort application; while a user might walk to a printer after entering the command at a workstation, the expectation of the print being done depends on a number of factors, including the length of the print job and contention with other users. Document retrieval (for example, using FTP) has traditionally been considered best effort. While this may be appropriate for a large document retrieved to print for later reading, in the case of a document retrieved for immediate browsing, interactive response bounds are desirable.

In each of these cases, the best-effort networked application is seen by the user as a background operation that operates asynchronously and without blocking the foreground interaction with the local system. Email can be contrasted with chat, and noninteractive document retrieval with Web browsing, as foreground and background versions of the same applications, respectively.

Fair Service Among Best-Effort Applications   *In the absence of specific policy directives to favor some applications over others, network and end system resources should be allocated fairly (roughly equally) among competing best-effort applications.*

A-II.2*b*

The infrastructure required to support best-effort applications is minimal. Network and end-system resources allocated are generally what is left after all other applications that have QOS requirements, but some overall fraction of resources may be dedicated to best effort as a category. There is generally an expectation of *fairness* among best-effort applications, that is, all of them should receive a reasonable fraction of the service. This is generally implemented in end systems with a round-robin scheduling discipline by the operating system. In network nodes, queuing disciplines, such as weighted fair queuing [Demers 1989], ensure fair service among multiplexed best-effort flows.[2]

In a heavily loaded network, it may be desirable to reserve a minimum fraction of service (link bandwidth and switch resources) dedicated to best-effort applications in *aggregate*. This ensures that best-effort applications will always be able to make some progress, at the cost of denying admission or reducing quality of service to some other individual application flows.

8.1.2.2 *Interactive Applications*

Interactive applications have response time requirements that allow users to interact with the application without perceptible waiting between events. In the 1970s, the canonical interactive application was computer timesharing. In the 1980s, timesharing extended across the network, with distributed terminal access to mainframes and workstations remotely accessing file-and-compute servers. In the 1990s the canonical interactive application became Web browsing. The browser has become so pervasive that it is commonly used as a GUI (graphical user interface), whether for local data interaction or for browsing the Web proper. In this section, we will commonly use Web browsing as the example, with the understanding that the discussion applies to any interactive application, regardless of whether a browser is used for the GUI, or HTTP is used for the data transfer protocol.[3]

Response time T_r is the key performance metric for interactive applications, defined as the interval from the time a command is entered by the user (for example, key press or mouse click), until the data has returned and presented to the user. Unlike the measures for real-time and deadline, T_r is a round-trip measure rather than a one-way delay.

Response time consists of client, server, and network components:

$$T_r = d_c + 2[(1 + h + c)b/r + t_p] + d_s$$

[2]This does not mean that scheduling disciplines other than FCFS are trivial to implement in network node hardware, however, as discussed in Chapter 5.
[3]For example, even though a Web browser is frequently used as the GUI for streaming media, a streaming protocol such as RTSP–real-time streaming protocol [Schulzrinne 1998] is used to control the media stream.

The client component d_c consists of both request generation *and* response processing and presentation. The server component d_s consists of the time to process the request and serve the response to the network. The network component is the round-trip time $2[(1 + h + c)b/r + t_p]$, dominated by the delays presented in Section 2.2.1. The first term b/r is the transmission delay for a chunk of b bits long, and is dependent on the number of times that data must be forwarded h and copied c. We discussed techniques in Chapters 3 to 5 to reduce the multiplier $(1 + h + c)$ by Store-and-Forward Avoidance (II.3). This leaves the data rate r as the critical factor for transferring a chunk of data b bits long.

The second term t_p is due to the speed-of-light propagation through the network and components. Recalling network latencies in Table 3.1, a 100-ms response time can be achieved for all but the longest-haul terrestrial networks. In particular, the latency components of LANs and MANs are at least an order of magnitude below 100 ms. For intercontinental and satellite networks, the less strict subsecond response time must suffice only as a target, with latency masking techniques described in Section 8.4.2 employed to drive the response time toward 100 ms. Even the entire earth/moon system latency is at worst 2 or 3 seconds. For the interplanetary Internet, true request/response behavior is precluded by the speed of light; at this scale we must resort to other methods. To the degree that application cannot mask latency, application and user behavior must change.

Response time is a start-up phase measure; data in excess of that needed to satisfy the initial response (described in Section 8.2.1) is part of the steady-state phase.

Interactive Response Time   *Interactive applications should provide a response time ranging from an ideal of 100 ms to a maximum target of 1 second. Within this range, consistent response is better than high variance.*

A-I.2i

Human factors studies dating from the 1970s [Doherty 1982] provided the basis for a target of subsecond response time, $T_r < 1.0$ s. User productivity is dramatically reduced when response time is significantly longer, and becomes *point, click, and wait* rather than *point, click, point, click* for GUIs. Further productivity gains are realized when the response time decreases to the range of 100 ms, which is perceptually instantaneous, rather than 1 s, which is only perceptually fast. These points on the interactive utility function are shown in Figure 8.2. Human factors studies have also indicated that *consistent* response time is better for users than response with a significant variance, since users alter their behavior based on response time at a relatively slow rate.[4]

---

[4]For example, the MVS operationing system has a *minimum* response time parameter that delays responses to time-sharing applications, in order to provide a more uniform response characteristic.

Users may be more comfortable with a longer response time when they know that a more complex operation is taking place (such as a Web crawl or software installation). In this case, a status bar or countdown timer should be provided, as well as an option to do other operations in parallel. For example, downloading of a high-resolution image on a slow link should not block the browser, rather it should open a separate asynchronous window. As processing capabilities increase, user expectation for what can be done within interactive response bounds also increase.

A concrete example of this can be shown in file editing and Web browsing behavior. If response is essentially instantaneous, users can visually search for a string in a file or click quickly through Web pages looking for information. As response time approaches and exceeds subsecond, users are more careful in the manner in which information is located. Users are more likely to compose a string search command while editing or use a search engine while Web browsing. For example, if 100-ms responses are interspersed with periodic 800-ms responses, the user can become frustrated. It may be better to reduce the variance by setting a minimum response of 500 ms.

> **Structure Data to Meet Interactive Response Bounds**   *Structure and migrate data for interactive responses such that initially visible data is present at sufficient resolution within interactive response bounds.*
>
> **A-7A**

The response time measure is satisfied when *just enough* data is presented to the user to allow interaction. In the case of Web browsing, this is enough textual data from the page to fill the window visible on the screen, along with images in the same area to sufficient resolution. It is not necessary to have the entire Web page present in memory (which may be many sequential windows of text and images) within the response bound.[5] This means that the user interface must be capable of incrementally displaying the data. In general, data and applications should be structured so that incremental display is possible.[6]

> **Application Adaptation by Refinement**   *Quick and partial information is better than slow and complete information, particularly with refinement over time. Successive refinement can often be used to adapt a high-speed application to a low-speed network.*
>
> **A-5D**

---

[5]The next screen's worth of data should have arrived by the time another T_r has elapsed, anticipating that the user will scroll down the page.
[6]Some applications do not do this very well, particularly in the case of dynamically generated content.

It is often reasonable to provide a partial response quickly, and resolve it further while the initial response is being interpreted by the user. Consider the case of browsing through an image library. By displaying the image as it is received, the user has the ability to step through images before they have completely arrived. If the images are coded by scan line, they are painted from top to bottom. If they are progressively coded, however, the entire image comes into increasing focus. This generally allows the user to make decisions with less data displayed than for scan line coding, and thus requires lower bandwidth to display enough data in the interactive response time bound.

8.1.2.3   Real-Time Applications

Real-time applications have constraints on the synchronization and delivery of data. *Hard real-time* applications have an absolute requirement for data to be correctly delivered within the real-time bound T_{rt}. Examples of hard real-time applications include many process control systems (including robotic control), sensor and telemetry applications in which the data is lost if not collected by the receiving system, and some systems on which life depends (including medical and weapons systems). A few signal processing applications have extremely low latencies, with $T_{rt} < 1$ μs. As shown in Figure 8.3, the utility function drops from 1 to 0 as a step function at T_{rt}.

To provide guarantees on the bounded delivery of data, bandwidth must be reserved through the network, along with sufficient node and end-system resources to bound the latency.

Soft real-time systems have a somewhat less critical need for both time bound and guarantee of data delivery. The canonical example of a soft real-time application is multimedia teleconferencing, in which a tight bound on

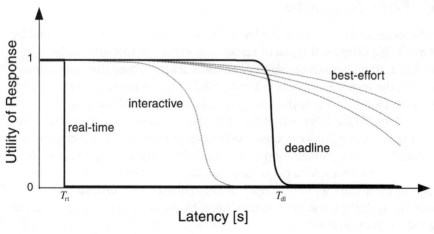

Figure 8.3   Application utility functions.

delay is required, but an occasional delayed or lost packet in the stream does not cause catastrophic failure, but rather a temporary degradation in perceptual quality. Audio delays in excess of 30 ms are perceived as echoes, and delays in excess of 500 ms impact the ability to converse in a normal manner.

Other applications with soft real-time constraints include many distributed computations, in which processes will be blocked if data isn't exchanged in time.

8.1.2.4   *Deadline Applications*

An example of a deadline application is remote backup, where the files should be transferred to the archives in bounded time. Technically, deadline applications are a subset of real-time applications, in which the time constraint is considerably longer than we typically expect for real-time applications: $T_{dl} \gg T_{rt}$, as shown in Figure 8.3.

This turns out to be a useful distinction, particularly in the way service to such applications is implemented. Deadline applications do not need the strict resource reservations required for real-time applications. The deadline can be met by reserving a minimum bandwidth through the network, computed as b/T_{dl}, where b is the size of the data that must be transmitted in the interval T_{dl}. In a best-effort network, the transmission rate is coupled with a deadline schedule; the transmission rate increases as the deadline is approached. This allows for short-term variance in the rate at which traffic can be offered, but only works if the network is not congested most of the time. This implementation precludes hard real-time constraints, resulting in an expected utility curve in Figure 8.3 that is not a sharp step function.

8.1.3   Error Tolerance

Applications are also characterized by their tolerance to errors introduced by the network. We discussed types of errors and error control mechanisms in Section 7.4, and the impact on high-speed networking. From the application perspective, the loss tolerance is critically tied to the performance measures of latency and bandwidth. Applications that are not loss tolerant need reliable delivery of data. To the degree that the underlying network infrastructure introduces errors (lossy links or congested nodes), error control mechanisms must compensate. The closed-loop error control mechanisms described in Section 7.4.3 add latency. The open-loop mechanisms described in Section 7.4.4 require more bandwidth. If these mechanisms are not provided at the transport layer, the application can use them, by requesting retransmission or adding redundancy to the data.

Applications that can tolerate some loss can better adapt to networks that introduce errors, while still meeting tight latency constraints. Fortunately, many applications that require (soft) real-time latency bounds are loss tolerant, such as streaming media.

8.1.4 Application Flow Characteristics

We can now summarize the bandwidth, latency, and error tolerance characteristics for a number of application flow types. Table 8.1 shows the characteristics for a number of types of application flows that comprise the application categories discussed in Section 8.2.

The first three columns indicate the relative magnitude of bandwidth required for each flow type. The next three columns describe the latency characteristics: the startup/transient and steady-state behavior, along with the latency budget. While the actual latency values are highly dependent on the actual application and scenarios using the streams, Table 8.1 gives an idea of the order-of-magnitude requirements. Distributed computing, process control, and telemetry are not characterized by the start-up latency since the requirement for how quickly the application starts is highly dependent on the particular application. The push aspect of information push and remote backup is described in Section 8.2.1. Web browsing and information push are transactional, and not particularly sensitive to steady-state latency. The distinction between stored (noninteractive) streaming video and stored *interactive* streaming video is that the former has no steady-state latency behavior. Interactive streaming video allows interactive stream control (pause, fast scan forward/reverse, and perhaps random access), and thus requires a control loop in the steady state that meets interactive latency bounds. Email is shown as an example of a best-effort application.

The fifth column indicates the loss tolerance of the application flow types; data applications (including distributed computing and process control) generally require reliable delivery, and multimedia applications are generally tolerant of some loss. Note, however, that a multimedia stream that is being delivered for archival purposes is a data application that may require reliable delivery. In the case of streaming media that is also being archived, the viewing can be loss tolerant, with errors retransmitted for the archival copy.

The last column indicates the ability of applications to adapt to bandwidth, latency, and errors for each flow type. Generally, applications that have the best ability to adapt are ones that are bandwidth enhanced (able to operate over a range of bandwidths), have loose latency constraints, or that are tolerant of errors. We will discuss a variety of adaptation mechanisms in Section 8.3.

Table 8.1 Application Flow Requirements

APPLICATION FLOW	INDIVIDUAL BANDWIDTH	CHARACTERISTIC		LATENCY BUDGET	LOSS TOLERANCE	ADAPTABILITY
		START-UP/ TRANSIENT DELAY CLASS	STEADY-STATE DELAY CLASS			
Distributed computing	Low–high	—	Real-time	1 μs–10 s	None	Low
Process control	Low	—	Real-time	1 μs–10 s	None	Low
Haptics (touch)	Very low	—	Real-time	10 ms	Low	Low
Live interactive voice	Low	Interactive	Real-time	30 ms	Low*	Limited
Live interactive video	Moderate	Interactive	Real-time	300 ms	Low	Moderate
Stored streaming video	Moderate	Interactive	—	1–10 s	Low	High
Stored interactive video	Moderate	Interactive	Interactive	100 ms	Low	Moderate
Web browsing	Moderate–high	Interactive	—	100 ms–1 s	None	Moderate
Information push	Low–moderate	Push	—	1 min–1 day	Moderate	High
Telemetry	Low–moderate	—	Varies	Varies	None	Limited
Remote backup	High	Push	Deadline	1 hour	None	High
Email	Low	Push	Best effort	1 min–1 hour	Very low	High

*People are more loss tolerant of video than audio.
Some data in this table is from [deSanti 1999].

446

8.2 Application Categories

Networked applications can be divided into three categories that characterize their behavior, as summarized in Table 8.2.[7] These can be considered *core* applications.

For each category, the relationship between the application endpoints is classified as client/server or peer-to-peer, and the symmetry of bandwidth in each direction is indicated. The transfer granularity is the amount of data transferred at a time; *continuous* means that a continuous stream of data is flowing. *End-to-end synchronization* refers to the need for time synchronization between the communicating applications. We will now discuss each category in more detail.

8.2.1 Information Access

Information access applications consist of a user accessing information on a remote server, in a transactional client/server mode. A user (or program) sends a request to a remote system for a particular piece of information, as shown in Figure 8.4. The server replies with the information requested, typically as a sequence of data packets.

Generally, information access applications are highly asymmetric in bandwidth consumption, with short requests and significant quantities of data returned.[8] Some transactional applications may have short replies, however, such as airline reservation systems. Examples of information access applications include Web browsing, digital library access, multimedia-on-demand, reservation systems, and GISs (geographical information systems).

Table 8.2 Core Application Categories

	CATEGORY		
CHARACTERISTIC	**INFORMATION ACCESS**	**TELEPRESENCE**	**DISTRIBUTED COMPUTING**
Application relationship	Client/server	Peer-to-peer	Varies
Bandwidth symmetry	Asymmetric	Symmetric	Symmetric
Transfer granularity	Large	Continuous	Varies
E2E synchronization	None	Real-time	Varies

[7]Similar to the taxonomy in [Partridge 1994b].
[8]Which does *not* mean that network infrastructure should be asymmetric, as will be discussed in Section 9.1.2.

request

response

Figure 8.4 Information access flow.

Response time T_r is the most important performance measure for information access. This requires bounding the network latency as well as supporting a data rate high enough to ensure delivery of enough data to satisfy the user request, as described in the previous section. In the case of a Web page, this consists of the first screen of data (text, images, and the applets that generate them). In the case of a multimedia stream, it consists of filling the playback buffer so that the media player can start, and provide interactive response to stream manipulation controls (such as pause and fast scan forward or reverse). In the case of a distributed VR (virtual reality) application, enough data must be present to satisfy likely navigation scenarios in addition to the initial VR image.

8.2.1.1 *Web Browsing*

The canonical information access application of the late 1990s is Web browsing. It is a challenging and ubiquitous high-speed networking application, not only in aggregate, but also for each individual user browsing. Web browsing has traditionally been considered a best-effort application, but this is point, click, and wait mode. For Web browsing to meet the requirements for interactive applications, a response time of 100 ms $\lesssim T_r \gtrsim 1$ s is required [Sterbenz 1994]. This latency bound drives the bandwidth requirement, especially for large Web objects such as those including embedded images. Medical and photographic-resolution images are particularly demanding.

Figure 8.5 [Touch 1996] shows the bandwidth requirements for different types of Web pages. The bottom horizontal band represents text-only Web pages, containing around 1 to 10 KB of data. The next band is the typical user or business Web page,[9] including embedded graphics and clickable maps, totaling 20 to 200 KB [Braun 1994, Mah 1997, Arlitt 1999, Ivory 2001]. The next band represents an image at typical screen (72 dots per inch) resolution, around 200 KB to 1 MB. The upper band represents photographic resolution digital images in the range of 10 MB (consumer) to 100 MB

---

[9]In the late 1990s; as network infrastructure and display technology evolves, the typical size increases [Alt 1998].

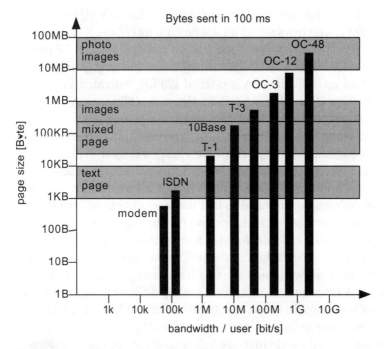

Figure 8.5   Web browsing bandwidth requirements.

(professional) [Kodak 2001]. The vertical bars indicate how much data can be transmitted over various link technologies in the 100-ms interactive response time budget, assuming the given link is the bandwidth bottleneck. Note how even modest Web pages can stress analog modem and ISDN rates; moderate quality pages require OC-3 (155-Mb/s) bandwidths. As Web page sizes increase with higher resolution and three-dimensional images (allowing local rotation), bandwidth requirements increase into the gigabit-per-second realm. This bandwidth demand is fueled in the consumer arena by high-resolution digital cameras and printers, coupled with the desire to deliver digital photographs on the Web.

This analysis only considers the propagation delay t_p, which assumes the entire 100 ms of response-time budget can be used for data transmission. Recall that client, server, and network node delays *also* contribute to the end-to-end interapplication delay: $d_c + d_s + 2(1 + h + c)b/r$. Consuming half the latency budget for these other factors doubles the required bandwidths. Servers outside a 100-ms propagation radius (around 5000 km) cannot be accessed within this latency bound at all with direct request–response techniques; this motivates the latency masking techniques discussed in Section 8.3.1.

Interactive medical imaging diagnosis has demands similar to Web browsing, and predates the use of a web browser as an application interface. X-ray images are typically 2K × 2K pixel × 12 bit deep, and may be as large as 4K × 5K pixel, resulting in images 8 to 40 MB in size. Magnetic resonance imaging (MRI) is typically 256 × 256 pixel for an individual image size of 128 KB, with an average of 100 images per study [Cox 1992, Blaine 1996]. Motion video clips are generated by fluoroscopy and ultrasonography. Radiation treatment planning is an example of a medical application that can benefit from distribution over the network [Bruner 1994]. The requirement for high-resolution images delivered in interactive response bounds makes telemedicine a bandwidth-enabled application.

Computer-generated holograms are already a reality in industrial manufacturing. For example, holograms are used to test the smoothness of curvature of a lens surface, by superimposing the hologram on the finished surface and looking for the appearance of any interference fringes that form if the two do not exactly match. It is thus desirable that the hologram-defining data set can be transferred in real time or near real time to a hologram generator, in a process control loop. A transfer rate of approximately 4 Gb/s is required for an uncompressed color holographic video of a small-volume object, and 4 Tb/s for an object 10 times larger in dimensions [Lucente 1993].

On-demand streaming audio and video are information access applications (as opposed to the telepresence category described in the next section). Streaming of the media to the client is not strictly required, but allows playback to begin before the entire clip is received. The latency requirements for streaming video depend on how the stream is manipulated. Streams that are not interactively manipulated (see stored streaming video in Table 8.1) need only send enough initial data to fill a playback buffer, which absorbs network jitter. The response time desired is to *begin* play, which allows users to "channel surf" in point-click-point-click mode, as for other interactive Web browsing. The latency bound to begin play of long movies is somewhat less tight (indicated by the 10-s number in Table 8.1), but the ability for the application to distinguish between long movies and short video clips is questionable. Interactively *manipulated* streams (see stored interactive video in Table 8.1) must keep enough data in the client playback buffer to allow the user to initiate the desired control operations, for example, pause and fast-scan forward/reverse, without incurring gaps in the processed stream. In this case, there are interactive requirements on the control loop during the steady-state phase. Some layered coding techniques (described in Section 8.3.2) match frame rates to the layers to enhance the fast scan capability. True random access within the stream requires a full request/response loop to jump between points in the video stream, with indexing to locate particular points in the content. The constituent delays in accessing stored video include the time to query, disk seek, disk access, packetize and frame, transmit through the network, shift through the playback buffer, depacketize, decode, and present to the user.

8.2.1.2   *Push Applications*

A variant of the basic information access category is *information push*. In this scenario, the server pushes data to the client *autonomously*,[10] as shown in Figure 8.6.

The information to be sent is based on server knowledge of the user. This knowledge may be determined from explicit user profile information, which is asynchronously sent by the user to a profile located near the server. The push may also be based on implicit information, such as an administrative domain name system (DNS) location pattern match or portion of the network address space. An example of this is an ISP or corporation pushing information to users on its network.

Client Pull versus Server Push   *The side that has the best knowledge of the client is the one that should initiate data transfer. Network load can be reduced by moving some of this knowledge to the server. Client demand fetch based on user requests; server push presend based on events the server knows about, assisted by user profiles.*

A-6B

This mode of operation is significantly less demanding of high-speed networks because a tight response time need not be met and information can be sent at a lower rate. It may still be important to deliver the information in a timely manner. For example, if the information to be pushed is a breaking news event, the latency budget is likely to be on the order of a minute, and may be classified as a deadline application.

There are some push applications, however, that require very large bandwidths to deliver the quantity of information required by the deadline. The canonical example is remote backup, which pushes data from the system to be backed up to the archive.

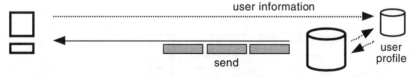

Figure 8.6   Information push flow.

---

[10]Autonomous behavior is a key determinant; many of the hyped "server push" applications of the late 1990s were actually just client browser event timers firing periodically to fetch information such as news or financial information, which is *not* a true push application.

8.2.2   Telepresence

Telepresence refers to creating a distributed virtual presence across the network.[11] This presence can consist of audio and video streams, changing images such as a shared white board, sharing control of a terminal screen, and collaborative work activities such as document editing. The canonical examples are teleconferencing and video conferencing. Once a session is established, data streamed between the participants, as shown in Figure 8.7.

The information exchanged typically consists of streaming multimedia data with control synchronization to update end-to-end state as necessary. The bandwidth needed is dictated by the quality of the stream (for example, audio frequency or video resolution and frame rate) and efficiency of compression. Unlike the case for stored streaming video (which is an information access application), live teleconferencing requires real-time constraints between the users. The audio and video components must keep perceptual delay within acceptable bounds, and be synchronized with one another if they are transported in distinct streams [Escobar 1994].

Furthermore, manipulation of the stream may involve changing the content by receiver action, such as asking a question during a distance learning session. This consists of switching among streams, and is a transient behavior that needs to occur in the interactive response latency bound.

Multimedia streams are not necessarily high bandwidth, and thus telepresence in general is a bandwidth-enhanced application. However, some telepresence applications such as telemedicine and distributed video production involve high-resolution images that need moderately high data rates, on the order of 100 Mb/s to 1 Gb/s. These may be classified as bandwidth-enabled applications to meet minimum requirements for user interaction. Teleimmersion applications that allow users to tightly interact in a high-resolution distributed multimedia virtual world [DeFanti 1999] also requires high bandwidth and the ability to integrate or synchronize multiple application flow types. Future telepresence/teleimmersion applications, such as a distributed holographic virtual reality, could involve extremely high data rates, and would unquestionably qualify as high-speed network applications.

data streams with embedded synchronisation

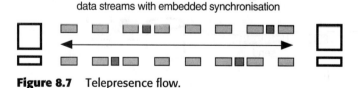

Figure 8.7   Telepresence flow.

[11]We use *telepresence* in the weakest sense of the word, in which a POTS (Plain Ordinary Telephone System) phone call qualifies; we use *teleimmersion* in the higher bandwidth and multiple stream sense, in which users are immersed in a shared environment.

The main challenge with telepresence applications is providing sufficiently low end-to-end latency to meet the end-to-end real-time synchronization requirements, as discussed in Section 8.1.2. This latency consists not only of the communication latency, but also that of the codecs (which code/compress and decode/decompress the stream) and jitter absorption and stream synchronization buffers. These latencies can be substantial, which reduces the latency budget left for the speed-of-light transmission delay.

8.2.3   Distributed Computing

Distributed computing applications involve the distribution of computations beyond a room (at least LAN distances), and involve an arbitrary exchange of data, as shown in Figure 8.8. This can consist of control and state synchronization, as well as very large blocks of data.

In some cases, the partitioning of the computation can be optimized to account for network bandwidth and latency characteristics. This is normally the case when distributing across common computing platforms to achieve overall application speedup, as in the case of networks of workstations (NOWs) [Anderson 1995].

Constraints on Partitioning of Distributed Computations   *The ability to efficiently partition a distributed computation may be limited by the physical distribution of scarce computing and storage resources.*

A-III.5

In other cases, for example, distributed modeling and visualization, the computation may be between fixed scarce supercomputers, data archives, and special-purpose processors. In this case, the computation must adapt to the location of fixed computing and network infrastructure.

8.2.4   Composed Applications

Other networked applications consist of the composition of the core application categories. For example, distance learning contains multiple components. The telepresence component consists of the telelecture multicast and video

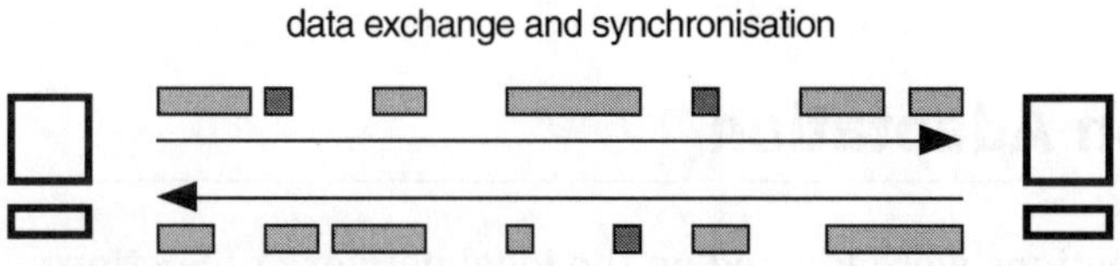

data exchange and synchronisation

Figure 8.8   Distributed computing flow.

conferencing of remote students into the classroom. The information access component consists of Web browsing and multimedia on demand to provide remote students with supplementary materials, as well as related email lists and newsgroups. These activities may be either pushed by the instructor, requested by individual students, or collaboratively accessed by a collection of students. A similar example is that of computer supported collaborative work (CSCW), which also has telepresence and information access components.

8.2.5 Nonhigh-Speed Applications

Finally, some applications and enabling infrastructure cannot be classified as high speed, although they are sometimes considered as such. Multimedia applications, in the general case, are not high speed. Audio is a particularly low-bandwidth application, and video operates and scales over the range of $O(10$ Kb/s) through $O(1$ Gb/s). Thus, video is a bandwidth-enhanced application that *may* require high bandwidth in a particular case. As indicated previously, specific examples include telemedicine and networked studio production.

Similarly, QOS mechanisms are needed for a variety of applications, ranging from low speed to high speed. The need for QOS is based on how scarce resources are, rather than on any absolute measure of the bandwidth and latency QOS metrics.

Telemetry is largely a low- to moderate-bandwidth application. Satellite sensors can download terabytes of data each day, accumulating huge volumes of information, but typically at a moderate sustained data rate. Generally, data must be sent as produced with little ability to adapt bandwidth, since satellites and remote-sensing devices tend to have little on-board storage. Local sensors, such as are used in robotics or human interactions, are generally very low data rate, but if used in a process control loop may have extremely tight real-time latency bounds on the order of 10 ms. Large dense sensor arrays can produce high-aggregate bandwidth, but data fusion within the sensor net can dramatically reduce the bandwidth requirement, and may be necessary to conserve power in individual elements. This is an example of the need to Properly Partition Distributed Applications (A-IV$_3$).

Although the human eye is a high-bandwidth input device, most other human interaction is very low bandwidth, including audio and haptic (pressure/touch). Many video applications may appear to require moderate to high bandwidth, but compression techniques can decrease the bandwidth required, as discussed in Section 8.3.2.

8.3 Application Adaptation

If communicating applications were located on the ideal network of Section 2.2.2, with no latency and unlimited bandwidth, there would be no need for adaptation. In reality, applications must deal with significant latencies and constrained bandwidth. There are a number of techniques applications use to mask latency or to apparently support high-bandwidth interaction over low-bandwidth links. While some application adaptations are very static, for example, image compression using standard compression techniques such as JPEG, many useful adaptations are dynamic and require knowledge of the communication path.

> **Application Adaptation Depends on Network Feedback**   *Application adaptation techniques involve the application reacting to information about the network, and are dependent on knowledge about the communication path. Some adaptations benefit from active cooperation from the network.*
>
> **A-4F*f***

These techniques are generally done at the application layer, either because they require application control or because they are based on the semantics of the data stream. Some adaptations can be moved into common libraries on end systems or moved down to the transport layer to reduce redundancy, provide increased coordination, and amortize implementation effort. As noted in Section 7.1.2, the difference between the functionality placed in application protocols (for example, as HTTP or RTSP) and that provided by transport protocols (for example, TCP or RTP) is largely based on practical deployment concerns; both the application and transport layers operate end-to-end.

Other adaptations can be performed in the network by active networking techniques, as described in Chapters 3 and 5; examples include active caching and content transcoding. Note that whether adaptations are performed at the end systems or in an active network node does not alter the fact that they are *application layer* adaptations. Active network nodes have the capability to snoop on high-layer protocol headers and ADUs (applications data units) to perform transport, session, and application layer processing in the network to increase efficiency and resource utilization.

> **User Feedback to Adaptive Applications**   *Adaptive applications benefit from user controls: either an explicit feedback loop, or implicit controls based on past behavior or a user profile.*
>
> **A-6B*u***

Just as application adaptations can benefit from network feedback, they can also benefit from user control. For example, a user may wish to control the tradeoff between resolution and frame rate in a videoconference for a given bandwidth connection. In the case of a stationary talking head, higher resolution and lower frame rate result in better perceptual quality. In the case of an individual walking around a room, the frame rate becomes more important. In cases where it is difficult for the application to unambiguously determine the optimal set of parameters for user quality, direct user input becomes important.

Application Adaptation Synergy   *Many application adaptation techniques are mutually exclusive; some can occur only at the expense of others. They must be carefully implemented and coordinated to avoid interference.*

A-IV$_1$

Finally, while some of the adaptation techniques discussed in this section are compatible with one another, it is important to understand that many are not. For example, data that is coded can be cached as long as the units over which coding and caching occur are compatible. If coding at a large granularity removes the distinction among smaller granularity objects, caching becomes difficult (or at least more expensive requiring multiple code/decode cycles). Different techniques for implementing coding are likely to be incompatible with one another. Different techniques for latency masking, such as demand caching, push sending, and datacycle may interfere with one another if not implemented carefully.

8.3.1   Latency Reduction

Latency reduction is very challenging, particularly since we can't beat the Speed of Light (III.1) when applications are physically separated.

Application Latency Principle   *Interapplication delays are the sum of all the constituent delays that cannot be parallelized. User-perceived delay is the ultimate measure of the performance of a high-speed system.*

A-IA*l*

In Chapters 3 and 6, we used the Network Latency Principle (N-1A*l*), Network Link Principle (L-II), Network Node Principle (N-II), and the End System Principle (E-II) to consider how to design and engineer a low-latency path through the network and end systems. The delay that end users see also consists of the delay through the application itself. Just as network protocols must be designed in an efficient manner to support low latency, so must the application. In Section 8.1.1 we noted that it is important to Properly Partition Distributed Applications (A-IV$_3$). By engineering the application so that the Location of Data (7B) programs are as close to one another as possible, many latencies can be avoided.

Some operations must be distributed; the whole point of networking is to support distributed applications. Beyond these straightforward optimization techniques, techniques must be brought to bear which *mask* latency. These techniques include mirroring and caching, which exploit spatial and temporal locality, respectively, and anticipatory techniques which move data *before* it is referenced.

8.3.1.1   *Mirroring and Caching*

The obvious way to reduce latency in distributed applications is to bring data closer to the consuming application or user. These techniques also reduce aggregate network bandwidth at the cost of increased memory, as indicated in Section 3.3.1.

8.3.1.1.1   Mirroring

A simple technique for latency reduction is to replicate data and distribute copies throughout the network. *Mirror* servers are loaded with copies of the data and located throughout the network.

Exploit Spatial Locality to Reduce Latency   *Reduce the latency of access by locating data physically close to the users and applications that need it.*

A-7Bs

Replication can be done manually in the case of very static data or automatically based on a periodic timer or driven by changes to the data that needs to be propagated. Multicast delivery to the mirrors is a useful bandwidth conserving technique. Mirroring is a trivial form of anticipation, since the data is already at a mirror site when the client request is made (more sophisticated anticipatory techniques will be described in the next section). The idea is to direct the request to a mirror that is across a lower-latency path than the original server. In the case of the request latency, this is primarily due to the propagation (and queuing) delay of the path. In the case of the response, which may be data intensive, the bandwidth of the path also affects the latency.[12]

There are five broad techniques for fetching data from the best server, shown as different request paths in Figure 8.9:

1. **Manual selection**. The user is presented with a list of mirrors indicating geographical location (city or country), from which one must be chosen. This is the simplest technique, but except for very coarse-grained replications (for example, location by continent) it does not perform particularly well and requires a manual user selection step.

---

[12]As described in Section 8.1.2, we are concerned with the portion of the data that needs to be displayed within the interactive response bound, with subsequent data arriving as necessary for further interaction.

2. **Proxy redirection**. The user communicates with a proxy that translates requests to an appropriate mirror server, based on knowledge about the user and mirror locations.

3. **Anycast**. The target address is an *anycast* group [Partridge 1993a] of caches, to which any one need respond. The anycast address may be inserted by the proxy (as shown in Figure 8.9), by the client, or by server redirection. IPv6 provides explicit support for anycast address groups.

4. **Server redirection**. The server relays the request to an appropriate mirror server. The server is less likely to have good knowledge of user location, but better knowledge of its mirrors.

5. **Active mirroring**. Active network nodes redirect requests to the best mirror server, by snooping on and replacing the destination location or address. This scheme has the advantage that the chosen mirror server can be based on current network traffic characteristics, allowing load balancing and optimization of network resources, in addition to reducing latency to the user or application. While there is some delay in the active path processing of the redirection, it is likely to be less than incurred by a server, and perhaps less than a proxy.

In some of these cases, the request path can be considerably longer than the response path (particularly server redirection). The transfer of embedded and subsequently referenced objects can be optimized by rewriting the pointers[13]

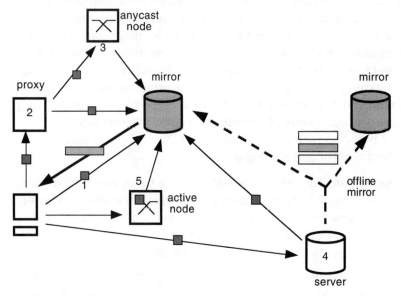

Figure 8.9   Mirroring.

[13]Hyperlink URLs in the case of Web pages.

to reference the mirror (rather than the original server) for these objects. All subsequent requests will then go directly to the mirror without the need for relay or redirection.

8.3.1.1.2   Local Caching

Another technique to reduce latency is to *cache* data on the user end system once it has been referenced, with the expectation that it will be used again.

Exploit Temporal Locality to Reduce Latency   *Reduce the latency of access by retaining data locally (or nearby) that is likely to be referenced in the future.*

A-7B*t*

The first time a data object is referenced, a cache miss occurs, and the request propagates to the server. Subsequent requests result in a cache hit, and are satisfied without the RTT latency to the server, as shown in Figure 8.10.

A *replacement policy* is used to determine which objects to remove from the cache when it fills. Data that has been modified must be returned to the server; read-only objects are simply removed. The most common replacement policy is least recently used (LRU), which removes objects that haven't been referenced for the longest time. This policy may be weighted by considering the cost and latency of replacement and refetching. Cached objects should be removed asynchronously, ensuring that there is always some empty space in the cache such that individual requests don't stall on object removal.

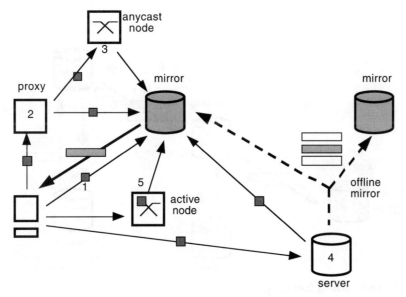

Figure 8.10   Local caching.

8.3.1.1.3   Network Caching

It is possible to combine the dynamic behavior of local caching with the benefits of network mirroring by putting caches in the network [Danzig 1993, Glassman 1994]. Network caching is demand driven, as for local caching, and is invoked when there is a local cache miss. However, instead of going directly to the server, a local miss is directed to the network caching hierarchy [Chankhunthod 1995, Wessels 1998], as shown in Figure 8.11.

At each level in the cache hierarchy, a miss results in sending the request up the tree to the *root cache*; a root cache miss results in a request to the original server. This hierarchical aggregation allows the distribution of content based on locality of request, distributing the request load across multiple caches on branches of the tree. The capacity of the tree is limited by the ability of cache nodes to handle miss requests from below. Increasing the tree breadth and depth reduces the load on a particular node; multiple trees spread the load across root caches. The caching infrastructure should be placed to optimize resources [Krishnan 2000] but does not need to be statically configured; it can adaptively adjust the topology to meet traffic demands [Zhang 1998].

> **Balance Network Resources by Hierarchical Caching**   *Balance aggregate network bandwidth against storage required by hierarchical caching.*
>
> **A-5C**

The VOD content Example 3.5 gave us an idea how the tradeoffs between bandwidth and memory can be used to engineer the hierarchy. Further considerations that push the caching down the tree include the maximum request rate a

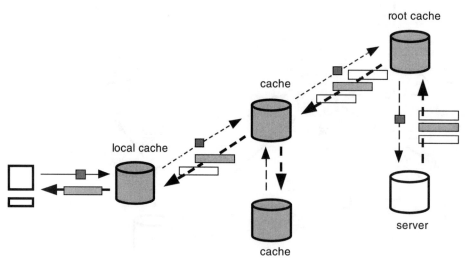

Figure 8.11   Network caching hierarchy.

server can handle and bounding the request latency. The number of levels in the cache hierarchy must be low enough to so that the sum of the per level request processing overhead delays does not exceed the interactive latency bound.

As for mirroring, anycast can be used to direct requests to the proper leaf node in the caching hierarchy. Similarly, *active caching* [Bhattacharjee 1998a] is a more general mechanism in which active network nodes participate in redirecting requests to the proper cache, with the sorts of dynamic network optimizations described for active mirroring.

8.3.1.1.4   Dynamic Content and Multiple Writers

Dynamic content creation by the server from a large database for each user can significantly limit the ability to cache, unless care is taken to properly structure the data and partition the application.

Structure Data and Migrate Code for Dynamic Content   *Structure data from which content is dynamically generated into cacheable units. Cache the programs that generate the content along with the data.*

A-7Ac

There are two issues to consider: the structure of the data and the location of the code.

The first issue is whether the data can be structured into smaller units, and if so, whether there is sufficient spatial locality in the reference patterns to allow *parts* of the database to be cached near users. For example, the tables in a relational database can be cached as independent units, but if the majority of queries involve JOINs over all of the tables, there is little benefit to this partitioning; the entire database must be cached.

Secondly, in cases where the data can be structured into cacheable units, the program code that creates the dynamic content should be cached along with the data. This allows the dynamic content to be generated at the right depth of the tree; optimizing the cached location of data while preventing more data than necessary to be pushed all the way to the client.

Caching is relatively straightforward when read-only access is needed for static data. Caching is more challenging when there are multiple writers, that is, when multiple applications need to modify the same data. This requires a cache coherence protocol (for example, [Li 1989]).

8.3.1.1.5   Policy Constraints

Caching is an example of how externalities can change the utility or feasibility of an application adaptation technique. Policy and Administration (III.6) affect the ability to implement performance enhancements. For example, content publishers may attempt to exert intellectual property rights by restricting copies of content; the distinctions between a stored copy, mirrored copy, network cached copy, locally cached copy, and Web browser in-memory copy are subtle. Another example is that advertising revenue may depend on hit rates of Web pages and click-through URLs; this information is substantially more difficult to track from cached copies. Thus, there may be objections to caching that have nothing to do with its intended purpose.[14]

The benefit of caching is linked to how and when the cache is loaded with remote content. In addition to the demand-fetch loading of caches, it is possible to load data in advance of its first use. Anticipatory techniques will be discussed next.

8.3.1.2   *Anticipation*

Mirroring and caching are latency (and aggregate bandwidth) reduction techniques that exploit locality. Mirroring replicates data anticipating that it will be closer to the consumer (spatial locality), and caching keeps data anticipating that it will be used again (temporal locality). We can consider more sophisticated techniques that anticipate future behavior. The goal is to predict which data will be accessed and move it so that it is in place before the request is made to eliminate the request/response latency. These techniques generally trade bandwidth for latency, since it is not possible to perfectly anticipate which data should be transferred.

> **Use Bandwidth to Reduce Latency**   *Bandwidth can be utilized to reduce latency by anticipatory prefetching and presending.*
>
> **A-2**

8.3.1.2.1   Prefetching

By predicting future reference patterns, an application can *prefetch* data and code so that it will be resident before needed. This is a technique long used in virtual memory systems to reduce the probability of a page fault and the resulting disk access latency [Aho 1971, Coffman 1973]. Prediction of future behavior can be difficult, and the effectiveness depends on the type of hints available in the application and the way in which data is structured [Touch 1992, 1993]. Examples of prefetching based on application semantics include fetching linked objects in a Web page [Padmanabhan 1994, Touch 1996, Markatos 1998], files in an FTP directory [Touch 1994], or pages in a virtual memory segment and related segment objects [Sterbenz 1990b].

As an example, if the response time to fetch a Web page from a server is T_r = 900 ms at 10 Mb/s, but we desire a response time of 300 ms, we can meet

---

[14]As is often the case, attempts to artificially draw these distinctions and exert undue control are likely to be futile.

this bound if we fetch hyperlinks to a depth of three. In the steady state, there will always be a complete set of Web pages present to the next two levels. This comes at the cost of the bandwidth of fetching the branches in parallel. If each Web page contains 10 hyperlinks, an additional 100 Mb/s will be used to fetch the second level and 1 Gb/s to fetch the third level. This results in a total of 1.11 Gb/s, two orders of magnitude above the 10 Mb/s required for a single page. On the other hand, rate controlling the prefetches can reduce the burstiness of traffic [Salchi 1006, Crovella 1998].

While parallel communication can be used to reduce latency at the cost of available bandwidth, the bandwidth available for this technique not likely to be unlimited. To fetch to a given depth in the tree, the breadth of the fetch must be limited. In some cases, restructuring the application can help. For example, a Web page that is a long list of documents can be restructured as a hierarchical index, limiting the breadth and amortizing the user search overhead over the fetching down the tree, rather than scanning a long list.

Beyond this, additional application semantics are needed to provide the hints of what to fetch. In the case of Web pages, parameters ranking the expected probability of access can be added to each hyperlink in the page to be used by the Web browser to determine which pages to prefetch. Locally stored user history can augment this to determine what to prefetch based on past behavior.

8.3.1.2.2   Application Prediction

Some distributed applications periodically exchange state information. When processing is relatively cheap, it may be possible for the application to spend additional CPU cycles running algorithms that approximate the state of the other parts of the system, for example, motion vectors in a VR application or interpolation/extrapolation of changing sensor data. In cases where the prediction is likely to match the actual state, or where the short-term consequences of imprecision are small, the application can tolerate longer latencies in state exchange, while periodically catching up.

8.3.1.2.3   Preloading and Presending

Recall in Section 8.2.1 the discussion of Client Pull versus Server Push (A-6B). Sometimes the server side can better anticipate which data to *presend* rather than waiting for the client to prefetch [Touch 1995b]. An example is the event-driven change of dynamic data that the server knows about, such as breaking news and sports, or data generated by a program on the distributed system.

This is also a case of making the proper tradeoff in choosing Interrupt versus Polling (4H) control. The client would need to poll the server for changed information, but it is better for the server to push data and interrupt the client based on the event. By doing so, the overheads of the polling requests are eliminated, and lower bandwidth suffices since the latency bound is more relaxed. In the case of Web pages, there is no need for the client to send prefetching requests to the server that has the page; a one-way latency can be saved.

Note that this is a case where two mechanisms may work against one another if not implemented carefully. There is no benefit to presend data already prefetched, consuming bandwidth that could be used to presend other data not already resident in the local cache.

8.3.1.2.4   Datacycle

Another form of anticipation consists of repeatedly sending an entire data set, in anticipation of access; this is called *datacycle* [Bowen 1992], as shown in Figure 8.12b.

A conventional request/response time takes T_r, and includes the round-trip latency between the client and server, as shown in Figure 8.12a. If the time to cycle through the data T_c is a fraction of the latency, then the mean time to wait for the desired data to appear in the stream is smaller: $t_c < T_r$. It is quicker for a client to sip from this stream of repeating transmissions than to request a specific entry and wait for a specific response. Note that this is another case where we are trading bandwidth for latency, since data is constantly being transmitted that is not actually used. On the other hand, if the datacycle is multicast, the bandwidth required in the backbone network may actually decrease. The target of the datacycle may be an intermediate system near the user, rather than the end system, balancing this tradeoff. Datacycle architectures become more challenging when there are multiple writers to the data [Banerjee 1993], but can still be an important latency masking technique. A further refinement of this technique is to use Tornado coding to allow reliable dissemination of the data without requiring the client to wait multiple cycles; this is called a *digital fountain* [Byers 1998].

8.3.1.3   Data Transformation

Data transformation operations, such as compression and encoding, may contribute substantially to end-to-end latency. In some cases, support in the network interface pipeline may eliminate the per byte overhead of a store-and-forward operation at the cost of additional pipeline stages, as discussed

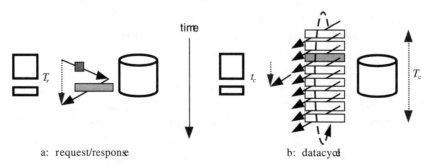

a: request/response   b: datacycle

Figure 8.12   Datacycle versus request/response.

in Section 5.4.2. At best, this is only practical for a small set of frequently used compression and coding schemes, and only if they are pipelineable. There are a number of reasons to support a variety of application and device-specific coding and compression schemes.[15] Thus, in many cases, these operations must be done by the application in the end system or in transcoding gateways in the network.

8.3.1.3.1 Encoding

Encoding, formatting, and alignment can be eliminated only by agreement of both the sending and receiving application, and in some cases the network that transports the data. Most networks have standards for data formats, such as byte order and word alignment. Heterogeneous networking relies on these standards to abstract application implementation from details of the underlying hardware. This encoding can result in avoidable latencies. If all parties of a communications association agree, however, alternative data representations can be selected, especially where they avoid encoding and formatting altogether.

The Internet relies on *network standard* byte order, where data larger than a single byte is sent from most-significant byte first, also called *big-endian* order. Unfortunately, the majority of end systems use *little-endian* byte order, requiring the format conversion. This is due to the problem that Backward Compatibility Inhibits Radical Change (III.7), since the Intel x86 microprocessor family is little-endian.

Active transcoding can be used as a means by which active network nodes determine the content and format encoding requirements of the end systems. Network-based transcoding gateways can then be selected that dynamically minimize latency, meet user bandwidth requirements, and perform network load balancing.

8.3.1.3.2 Compression

Compression is a memory and bandwidth conserving technique that may contribute to latency as a store-and-forward operation. As before, the latency of transferring a block of data (one way) can be expressed as

$$D = d_c + [(1 + h + c)b/r + t_p] + d_s$$

We can explicitly express the delays in encoding and compressing for transmission t_e and decoding and decompressing for reception t_d, as well as the compression ratio $0 < q < 1$, rewriting the delay equation as

$$D = (d_c + t_e) + [(1 + h + c)b/rq + t_p] + (t_d + d_s)$$

As shown in Figure 8.13, the end-to-end latency depends on whether or not the additional delays $t_e + t_d$ are offset by the reduced transmission delay bq/r. For high compression gains with relatively low compression/decompression

---

[15]However, the presence of an efficient pipelined codec should be considered as a tradeoff in determining which is the best scheme an application should use.

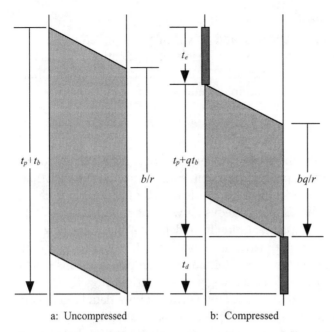

a: Uncompressed   b: Compressed

Figure 8.13 Compression latency.

latency, end-to-end latency is decreased. If the object is stored in compressed form, t_e is eliminated from individual transmissions.

> **Compression of Data** *Compression of data reduces bandwidth at the expense of the processing complexity and delay of the compression/decompression algorithms.*
>
> **A-2B**

8.3.1.3.3 Pipelining

Pipelining overlaps the processing or transmission of data blocks, as discussed in Section 2.4.4, and can be applied to various network and end-system components, as discussed in Chapter 5 and Section 6.4.2. At the application layer, pipelining overlaps compression, coding, and transmission; at the receiving side decoding, decompression, and presentation can be overlapped, as shown in Figure 8.14.

Figure 8.14b shows the effect of using smaller ADUs (application data units), and pipelining their processing. This is only effective if the processing of the pipeline stages can be done in *parallel*: in multiple functional units on a superscalar or vector processor, spread across a multiprocessor, or overlapped between the CPU and processing on the network interface (as described in Section 6.4.2). Concurrent but nonparallel pipeline operations on a uniprocessor result in no speedup, as shown in Figure 8.14a

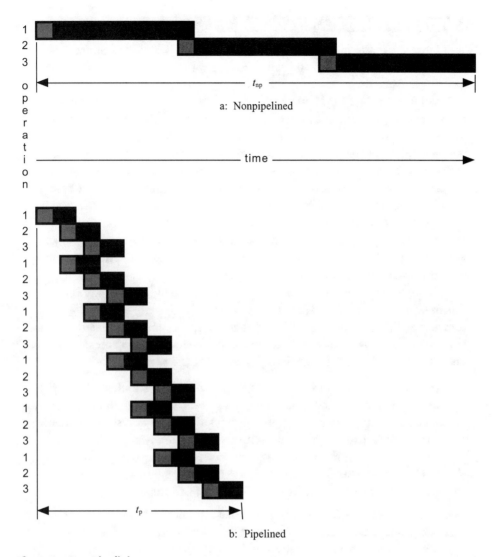

a: Nonpipelined

b: Pipelined

Figure 8.14 Pipelining.

8.3.2 Bandwidth Improvement

The fundamental goal of high-performance applications of interest to us is low Interapplication Delay (I.2), which is constrained by Network Bandwidth and Latency (I.3). Some applications are not capable of delivering the bandwidths desired because they are located across a low-bandwidth path or because they have difficulty using the available high-speed path. There

EXAMPLE 8.1: INTERPLANETARY WEB

Web browsing in the Interplanetary Internet is an application that must deal with extremely long latency, and serves to illustrate the range of techniques we have been discussing.

Recall from Table 2.1 that all distances in the earth/moon system have round-trip speed-of-light latencies, of at most, several seconds. Thus, Web browsing between the earth and moon is practical in its current form with judicious use of the caching and presending techniques we have described. The penalty for a cache miss results in response times of several seconds, which misses the subsecond target, but does not necessitate a fundamental change in the Web.

The latencies between planets is significantly longer, and requires rethinking not only the way that protocols are designed but also the way in which applications behave. For example, the RTT between Earth and Mars is 6 to 45 minutes, depending on planetary alignment; the RTT between Earth and Jupiter is on the order 1 to 1.5 hours.

Web browsing between planets requires a combination of techniques, as shown in Figure 8.15. Although near-term Mars missions will be highly constrained by bandwidth, for this example we will assume an infrastructure of free-space laser links providing the bandwidth needed for Web access. Assume that an individual on a Martian colony is browsing the Web.

Caching, presending, and prefetching. Clearly, caching should be heavily utilized to mask latency. Due to the long latencies, caches should be push loaded by servers that expect their information to be accessed frequently. Furthermore, user profiles can be used to intelligently prefetch and preload pages for particular users, increasing the probability of a hit. As the latency increases, we can prefetch deeper in the HTML (hypertext markup language) anchor tree, at the cost of additional bandwidth.

Request processing. If a page is not cached intraplanet, it is critical that the address resolution and HTTP request direction go to the closest location. DNS will need to be split between planetary systems with partial resolution, that is, we do not want to fully resolve the IP address of www.jpl.nasa.gov.earth on Mars, but rather recognize that the request should go to Earth for further incremental resolution.[16] Furthermore, the distance to multiple cached versions of a page changes as planetary bodies and spacecraft move. Fortunately, these will be predictable trajectories,

[16]In the short term the interplanetary Internet is likely to be deployed as a set of planetary Internets interconnected by gateways, with split routing domain and local DNS name; a bundle layer sits over conventional transport layer with bundles store-and-forwarded between planetary Internets. This is due to initial low-bandwidth deep space links, low degree of connectivity, and intermittent links due to planetary rotation and occultation [Cerf 2001].

and the proxy server should have hints as to where pages might be cached, and the current relative distances to these caches.

Latency aware applications. QOS metrics are generally not part of the information used to rank search engine queries and responses. In the interplanetary Web, users may wish to specify an acceptable response time or have responses sorted by expected response time, based on dynamic computed distances to Web pages or cached copies. On a cache miss, the browser should provide an estimate of the delay to fetch the page, as well as information on how stale the data is.

User feedback. Interplanetary latencies are long enough that user behavior will depend on whether or not a particular page is cached within a particular planetary system. For example, on a Mars cache miss, the user should determine whether to wait the RTT to Earth to get the page (fetched as a background task). The answer may be different depending on whether or not the RTT is 6 minutes or 45 minutes due to planetary alignment. The Web browser should provide direct feedback to the user allowing a choice to be made (perhaps assisted by defaults). It may also be useful to provide feedback on the currency of the information that is likely to change. A user may choose to get a stale cached copy from a .earth cache in 10 minutes, rather than wait for the definitive copy from the .jupiter server in 1 hour.

There are more down-to-earth applications for these techniques. Episodic connectivity can occur in a number of terrestrial situations. Examples include a military vessel that must maintain radio silence for a long period of time or an individual with a wireless Internet access spending periods of time in a cave or mine.

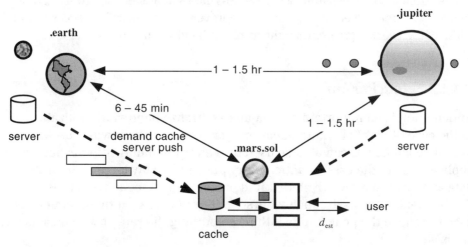

Figure 8.15   Interplanetary Web browsing.

are a number of techniques that can increase the apparent bandwidth available to an application.

> **Application Bandwidth Principle**   *The bandwidth perceived by the user is the minimum of all bandwidths along a path, including through the application itself.*
>
> **A-1A***b*

Many of the bandwidth improvement techniques have already been discussed in Section 8.3.1 in the context of latency improvement.

8.3.2.1   *Mirroring and Caching*

As in the case of latency reduction, mirroring and caching are important bandwidth reduction techniques. By pushing data closer to the consumer, load is reduced on the server, since a large number of common requests are being handled by the caches. The server then has increased capacity to handle its remaining load.

As described in Section 3.3.1, aggregate bandwidth is reduced when data is pushed closer to the edge of the network. This helps to increase the bandwidth available to individual applications. Furthermore, when the client is located on a high-speed LAN or access link, more effective bandwidth is available by locating the cache in the same high-speed subnetwork.

Furthermore, the benefit of caching continuously is that when data is pushed, it can be moved throughout the cache hierarchy at lower bandwidth than if it were demand fetched.

It is possible to apply parallelism to access data simultaneously from multiple caches or mirrors [Byers 1999]; this can improve performance if the access bandwidth of the client is greater than the available bandwidth at the server end.

8.3.2.2   *Anticipation*

Anticipation is an important technique to optimize bandwidth utilization. In the case of parallel communication it is increasing bandwidth utilization to reduce latency. It can also be used to *reduce* the bandwidth needed by applications. In the case of anticipatory pushing, it may be used to preload data at a lower bandwidth so that it is present when needed. In cases where client requests are highly bursty but predictable, anticipation can be used to reduce the peak bandwidth by smoothing the rate at which caches are preloaded.

8.3.2.3   Data Transformation

Data compression is the most common bandwidth (and memory) reducing technique, at the cost of processing and perhaps latency, as described in section 8.3.1. There are two motivations for this: Compression of a chunk of data reduces the bandwidth required to transfer within a given latency bound. This is particularly important for interactive information access applications, such as Web browsing, as long as the compression and decompression delays $t_e + t_d$ don't dominate.

For streaming multimedia applications, compression reduces the bandwidth required to stream. In this case the issue is what level of quality can be supported for a link of given bandwidth. In some cases, compression consists of direct coding of the bit stream, for example, run length encoding or discrete cosine transform (DCT) frame encoding. Differences between higher granularity structure can be exploited, for example, sending only the difference between periodic key frames in a video stream, as in MPEG-2 B-frames. Application-level interaction, such as transmitting vector and polygon coordinates, can further improve compression ratios.

8.3.2.4   Multicast and Stream Merging

As introduced in Section 3.3.1, multicast is a key way to reduce aggregate bandwidth. In section 8.3.1 we noted that multicast can be an effective way to load mirrors and caches. Multicast is such a fundamental service that the Network Should Provide Support for Multicast Capabilities (2C). While multicast is supported in IPv4 with IGMP, IPv6, and ATM, the actual deployment of multicast by network providers has significantly lagged the protocol standards.

Thus, applications may be faced with a situation where the network does not provide this needed service. As a result, *application layer multicast* [Cooperstock 1996] can be used to ameliorate the situation. For example, when a mirror or cache needs to push information down the tree, it sends a single copy to all of its immediate children. These children then continue the process to their descendents. While this reduces aggregate bandwidth, it still incurs significant load on the servers, which must sequentially send multiple copies. The server load is considerably reduced when multicast is enabled as a network layer service.

The multicast of stored streaming media is challenging, since even in the case of very popular content, individual users will be viewing different points in the video clip. To allow the merged transmission of streams to multiple users, a variety of techniques, such as *interval caching* [Dan 1996] and *rate adaptive merging* [Krishnan 1997, 1999], can be used to match users to intervals of a stream and adjust their rates to overlap.

EXAMPLE 8.2: MPEG-2 COMPRESSION

MPEG (Motion Picture Experts Group) [ISO13818] is a compression technique widely used for the compression of video content. MPEG was intended for high compression ratios, and consists of a stream consisting of a *group of pictures*, each of which contains three types of encoded frames:

- I-frames are DCT-encoded video frames, similar to JPEG (Joint Photographic Experts Group) [ISO10918], and contain the information for an entire frame.

- P-frames are motion-predicted frames coded from the previous I or P frame.

- B-frames are bidirectionally interpolated from the closest previous and subsequent I or P frame.

Thus an MPEG stream consists of a sequence of I, B, and P frames (the relative number of each frame type in a group of pictures is one of the variable parameters of the coding process):

IBBPBBPBB IBBPBBPBB IBBPBBPBB...

The computation of I frames is relatively straightforward. The computation of the motion prediction vectors for P and B frames is computationally intensive, but the decoding is relatively simple. MPEG was intended for offline compression of movies that would be decompressed in real time as accessed by VOD (video on demand) clients. High compression ratios were desired to support the streaming of movies over moderate rate residential access lines, such as ADSL (on the order of 2 Mb/s).

Unfortunately, this is a case where a narrow point solution doesn't apply well to the broader context of streaming media in the Internet, where asymmetric assumptions on computational complexity don't hold, and bandwidth is not extremely scarce. Furthermore, the compression ratios engineered for the 2-Mb/s residential access lines of the late 1990s become irrelevant with the deployment of higher-speed lines, such as cable modems, VDSL (very high-speed digital subscriber lines), and FTTH (fiber to the home).

8.3.2.5 Rate Adaptation and Layered Coding

An important application adaptation is to gracefully adapt to the bandwidth available [Diot 1995]. This is easiest to do for bandwidth-enhanced applications, which operate over a range of bandwidths with no structural change. For example, a streaming multimedia client can adapt to the data rate by dynamically adjusting the frame rate and resolution. Rate adaptation is more difficult for bandwidth-challenged applications, which may require different modes of operation over varying bandwidths. Bandwidth-enabled applications simply cannot operate below their required bandwidth.

Multilayer encoding is a mechanism to help the application to dynamically adapt to variations in network bandwidth. Section 8.1.2 discussed successive refinement, where rough, rapid information can suffice to meet interactive response bounds, with sequential transmission of refining data. The transmission of successive refinements can also be *concurrent*, resulting in multilayer encoding [McCanne 1996]. This allows the application to adjust stream quality to match available bandwidth.

Cooperation from the application is required because semantics of the data stream are required to generate a multilayer encoding, and the layers must be labeled by the application. The application can adjust which subsets of layers are sent based on loss feedback, as can the transport layer, but it is most effective if the network itself performs the adjustment at the point of congestion. Cooperation of the network is required to drop low-priority (very fine) layers in deference to high-priority (coarse) layers appropriately. This can be accomplished by active network nodes, as described in Chapters 3 and 5. For example, dropping B and P frames in an MPEG stream first [Bhattacharjee 1998b] or the high-resolution components of a wavelet encoding [Decasper 1999b], significantly improves image quality at the applications.

8.3.2.6   ADU Size

As discussed in Section 7.3.1 (and shown in Figure 7.13), the granularity of data units impacts usable bandwidth; larger ADUs have less header overhead and processing overhead per unit of data.

Increasing ADU size increases staging delays incurred by different operations such as compression, as well as the latency of store-and-forward operations. Large ADU size also limits the effectiveness of pipelining, which reduces ADU size to exploit overlap, as shown in Figure 8.14b. This overlap is only effective if speedup is available by performing the pipelined operations in parallel, as described in Section 8.3.1.

8.3.2.7   Striping

Occasionally, more bandwidth is needed than can be provided on a single link, but multiple parallel links are available. In this case, the links can be used in parallel. The use of parallel links between network nodes is a common network engineering technique. In this context, we are concerned with the use of parallel end-to-end links by the application. This is most likely to be necessary in the case of low-to-moderate residential bandwidth access links, for example, the use of two xDSL lines or ISDN channels by a single user. PPP (point-to-point protocol) is sometimes used to bundle parallel channels in this manner.

A single block of data is split into a set of components, each of which is *striped* across the different channels and reassembled at the other end (for example, [Traw 1995]), as shown in Figure 8.16.

The granularity of striping can range from per byte, through per cell, to per packet. The critical issue is whether the receiving end can properly demultiplex the stripes. If the interstripe skew can be contained to less than the time to transmit a stripe unit, the receiving end can simply demultiplex the stripes in the order received. The smaller the data unit, the more difficult to control skew. If the actual skew exceeds the tolerance, the stripes may be incorrectly reassembled, as shown in Figure 8.16. Simply counting the arriving stripe units isn't sufficient unless there are guaranteed to be no losses. While this technique is frequently used within systems, it is difficult to maintain across a network.

Alternatives are to support the striping in the link protocol across the striped link or end to end in the transport protocol using sequence numbers to maintain order. Another option is for the application to stripe over multiple transport-layer flows. As with ALF, it may be more efficient to allow the application to determine this labeling and reordering, especially in cases where the receiver can accept the component blocks out of order, simplifying operation [Feldmeier 1992].

8.3.3   Scaling and Aggregation

We have already noted the Relative Magnitude of High-Speed (A-2A); applications must scale and aggregate to continue to use and challenge network capabilities. The ability of an application to accommodate these scale changes is critical to its adaptation. We have already discussed bandwidth and latency. Additionally, applications need to be able to scale in the size of associations. In particular, multiparty applications must be able to scale in group size. This results in scaling of addressable endpoints, as well as in the number of connections or flows.

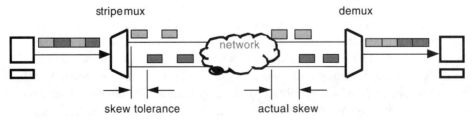

Figure 8.16   Striping and skew tolerance.

Additional clients increase the load on individual servers in a client/server system; mirroring and caching can reduce or distribute the load. Where this is not possible, an individual server can offload or distribute its load after receiving a request. Servers generally benefit from *precomputing* responses, just as caches benefit from preloading responses. One-to-many interactions benefit from distributing processing and state away from the one toward the many.

Solutions to the scale problem are difficult to achieve, especially because of the dynamic range of parameters over which the applications must operate. Latency compensation needs to scale from microseconds to seconds (6 orders of magnitude); bandwidths from bits per second to terabits per second (12 orders of magnitude), and group membership from 1 to millions or billions (6 to 9 orders of magnitude). Solutions spanning 2 or 3 orders of magnitude are relatively easy to devise, but larger orders often require hierarchical solutions.

A hierarchical scaling solution allows aggregates to themselves aggregate, most usefully using the same mechanism as the base aggregation. Several such recursive applications of aggregation suffice to cover the orders discussed here; there should be no limit to the recursion, at best.

Aggregation of Application Operations   *Reduce the cost of all per connection or per application operations by aggregation. Support ways to aggregate requests and responses between the application and network, and for the application, to control the frequency of response and size of aggregation.*

A-5B

Aggregation is one way to handle scale. Caches aggregate requests, resulting in a single server response satisfying a large number of client requests. Small transactions can be aggregated into larger ones to reduce per transaction or per message overheads.

Application-level multiplexing uses a single connection for multiple concurrent or sequential transactions [Feldmeier 1990a, Gettys 1998, Rose 2000], and is attractive because it can be deployed with new applications. Application multiplexing can complicate high-performance systems, however. Applications must organize blocks of data from separate streams into a single flow and coordinate their prioritized interleaving; this can interfere with transport and network layer multiplexing, and must be done carefully to Limit Layered Multiplexing (T-3A) performance degradation. For example, it can be difficult for ADU boundaries to be maintained by underlying transport protocols.

Aggregation techniques complicate the implementation of applications, Similar benefits can be achieved by amortizing connection state at the transport layer [Touch 1997, Padmanabhan 1998, Balakrishnan 1999, Eggert 2000].

> **Partitioning of Application versus Protocol Functionality** *Keep the network impact of application design choices in mind. Not all functions are best deployed within an application.*
>
> **A-1C**

It is thus important to understand the performance tradeoffs between application and transport protocol implementation of functionality.

8.3.4 Application Layer Framing

Application layer framing (ALF) [Clark 1990] matches the size of ADUs to that of transport, network, and link PDUs, as discussed in Section 7.3.1 in the context of end-to-end issues.

> **Application–Network Synergy Principle** *Increase performance by matching application characteristics to the network. Use ALF to decrease the overhead of protocol encapsulation, control transfer, and decapsulation.*
>
> **A-4C**

When ADU and PDU sizes differ, applications incur unnecessary fragmentation and reassembly latencies because portions of a single ADU are contained in separate PDUs. If an ADU is larger than the MTU (maximum transfer unit) of the network path, multiple PDUs are required per ADU transfer. When ADUs are not treated as a unit by the transport protocol, spurious latencies can result from acknowledgment gaps or retransmissions. If the ADU is smaller than the path MTU, protocol overhead is greater.

Implementing ALF is complicated by the fact that we need to consider the end-system data structures that are involved in the communication process, such as memory buffers, virtual memory pages, and cache lines. In this case, it is important that the operating system support flexible and efficient buffer management to allow ADUs to be manipulated and encapsulated/decapsulated to PDUs. For large blocks of data, the virtual memory data structures may be utilized, for example, matching ADU to segment and page to PDU [Sterbenz 1990b].

8.3.5 Mobile and Wireless Applications

Applications that are mobile and use wireless networks deserve special consideration. Wireless links and networks present characteristics that are particularly challenging to applications. Mobility visible to the application requires adaptation to changing conditions.

8.3.5.1   Wireless Applications

Wireless networks have two unique characteristics that place increasing demand on application adaptation: channel fades (due to moving obstructions and weather) and dynamic bandwidth (due to power adaptation, distance, and interference), as described in Sections 3.2.5 and 5.1.1. In general, this means that applications that run over wireless links must be even more adaptive and must be able to rapidly adapt to changing path characteristics.

Channel fades present an error model intermediate between a bit or short burst error and a link failure requiring reconfiguration. The application may have to react as it would if there were an underlying link failure and rerouting, tolerating silence intervals and retransmitting lost data if necessary. For applications like Web browsing, this may increase the response time; for noninteractive streaming media, the playback buffer size must be increased to account for retransmission time. Supporting real-time applications over a very lossy channel is challenging and may require users to adapt when the application cannot. FEC (forward error correction described in Section 7.4.4) can help mask lossy channels.

The dynamic bandwidth characteristics of wireless channels simply means that applications must be prepared to readapt to bandwidth at a rate that is perhaps greater than for wireline networks. Layered coding naturally adapts to such changes, by providing varying resolution to the application as the channel bandwidth varies. Applications that set adaptation parameters need to be prepared to dynamically adjust them as necessary, perhaps by renegotiating application-to-application.

8.3.5.2   Mobility across Subnetworks

Mobility within a particular network technology requires support from the network and, in the case of wireless networks, adaptation as just described. Mobility *across* diverse network technologies requires additional adaptations.

Consider a scenario in which a member of a CSCW session is traveling. Initially, the member is plugged into the same wired subnetwork as the other local participants in a conference room. When it is time to return home, she unplugs from the wired net and establishes wireless connectivity, initiates a videoconference, and attaches to the shared whiteboard application on her notebook computer. On the plane, she switches to the Airphone and then back to a wireless connection for the train trip back to her office. She then decides to go to a conference room, plug back into a high-speed wired connection, and use a large flat panel display for the videoconference.

This sort of scenario requires both session control across subnetworks and applications, and application adaptation to significant differences in the bandwidth between the wireless and wired network, and latency between the local environment and wide area Internet. We can't expect the subnetworks themselves to provide transparency over the discontinuities caused by subnetwork handoff. Rather, the session control mechanisms and applications will have to adapt.

While we desire as much functional transparency to the application as possible, QOS and content encoding types may not be transparent to applications, based on access network constraints and technology. We may be able to increase the transparency by utilizing resources in the Internet such as content transcoders.

8.4 Application–Network Interaction

We have discussed a number of ways in which applications can adapt to network latency and bandwidth. In Section 8.3 we indicated that Application Adaptation Depends on Network Feedback (A-4c). In some cases the insufficient bandwidth or high latency is a persistent condition for which static adaptations suffice. In other cases, network conditions dynamically change, and applications can benefit from dynamic adaptation and active cooperation from the network. The interactions that support dynamic adaptation are the focus of this section.

An application programming interface (API) is required to support and coordinate application interaction with the network. This includes ways for the application to control the network (knobs) and ways for the network to provide status for application adaptation (dials),[17] as shown in Figure 8.17.

The goal is to allow applications to be developed independently of particular network technologies to enable the application to adapt to network characteristics and control network properties in real time (for example, [Belot 1996a, 1996b, Turletti 1996]). Furthermore, these interfaces should degenerate appropriately to support applications that cannot adapt or networks that cannot be configured.

Furthermore, an important function is to translate between user or application QOS measures and the network parameters that are necessary to deliver the desired QOS. Users generally understand QOS in relative terms and coarse granularity, for example, fast versus slow response and low versus high resolution. These must be translated to network parameters, such as peak and average bandwidth, burst length, jitter, latency, reordering tolerance, and error rates.

API Scalability Principle *All interfaces between an application and network should scale with respect to bandwidth, latency, and number (nodes, end systems, and users). Parameters should have a scale factor (order of magnitude exponent), a precision factor (multiplier), and a variance.*

A-4l

---

[17]David D. Clark used the terms *levers and dials* in the early 1990s, which later appeared in [Partridge 1994b] and in a figure in [Clark 1995].

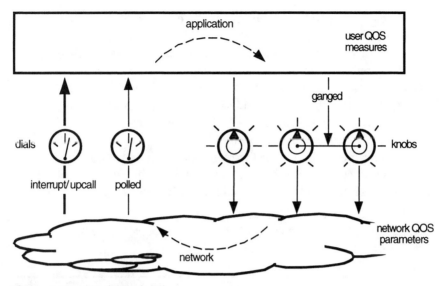

Figure 8.17 Knobs and dials.

These interfaces need to support a variety of applications and network technologies, either in different instances or concurrently in a single end system. It is critical that interface parameters scale, not only with a multiplier, but also with an exponential factor to indicate over what order of magnitude they are operating. It is also crucial that the precision of information be included in the interface; each parameter, whether a network control or feedback, must indicate its expected variance and time scale over which the variance holds. This stability information is required for the application to adjust its feedback loops, and properly determine whether and how to adapt to changes.

In some cases, knobs and dials may be presented directly to the user as part of the GUI (graphical user interface) for the application allowing User Feedback to Adaptive Applications (A-6Bu). For example, a user may have a bandwidth knob on a videoconferencing application that allows direct control, and allows the user to immediately understand the effect of the exerted control. This can assist in the problem of translating coarse-grained application QOS to fine-grained network parameters.

8.4.1 Network Control (Knobs)

Network control is performed by *knobs* (or levers), which exert control on the network by conveying application requests to alter network parameters and behavior. This allows the network to provide the requisite service and continuously adapt its own resource utilization and control mechanisms. Some network parameters may be set at session establishment or connection setup.

Knobs allow these parameters to be dynamically changed over the life of a session or connection.

Not all knobs correspond directly to network parameters, services, or capabilities. Some knobs are compositional, resulting in requests to a constellation of network capabilities. Some knobs translate via heuristics. Other knobs are cross-linked (ganged), such that manipulating one automatically changes others, even if each is also configurable explicitly. For example, peak bandwidth and burst rate combine to determine buffer allocations at network switches, but these same parameters can be individually tuned. Knobs should, however, correspond to a real control on the network; otherwise they may be used to no effect at the expense of a knob which would actually improve performance.

Knobs Should Correspond to Network Actions   *A knob should not be built into the network that does not correspond to a real controllable action.*

A-4Ck

Note, however, that this may be tempered by legacy applications and intended future capabilities. For example, a knob may be provided at an API for a control function that is expected to be placed in the network. The performance implications of this must be weighed very carefully.

Knobs have varying effects on the underlying system depending on the granularity of control, the frequency of their change, and how rapidly changes are incorporated into the network. Some network parameters should not be rapidly changed; for example, rapid decrease of buffer capacity may result in burst losses, whereas gradual decreases can minimize or spread losses, while other individual buffers are freed or end-to-end feedback controls compensate.

8.4.2   Network Feedback (Dials)

Application adjustment can be enhanced by explicit feedback from the network. Some parameters are constant for the life of a session or connection, such as MTU (maximum transmission unit). Other parameters change over the life of the flow, either slowly (for example, latency) or rapidly (for example, bandwidth or loss). Measurement of these parameters can require probes of the network, or alarms in response to programmed triggers. They can also occur once at the start of a connection or be refined and refreshed periodically.

Applications determine network state over the life of a session by accessing *dials*. Dials, like knobs, need to provide both multiplier and exponential values to scale over orders of magnitude. Dials may be context sensitive, reporting different values based on the application, user, properties of other network parameters, or time of day. The most key aspect is that these dials be flexible; no predetermined set of dials (or knobs) suffices for all applications.

As for knobs, dials should correspond to real parameters or properties of the network.

Dials Should Correspond to Observable Properties   *A dial should not be provided that does not correspond to a real observable parameter.*

A-4Cd

Dials can operate either synchronously or asynchronously.

8.4.2.1   *Synchronous and Asynchronous*

Applications need to acquire accurate information about the state of the communication path to enable appropriate adaptation. Applications invoke interfaces to the transport, network, and link layers to request the current status of this data, via synchronous or asynchronous interfaces. Synchronous interfaces stall the application while the information is determined and responded; asynchronous interfaces configure a way for the lower layers to contact the application by unsolicited responses.

Support Synchronous and Asynchronous Dials   *Network instrumentation should support both asynchronous (interrupt-driven) and synchronous (polled) feedback mechanisms.*

A-4H

Synchronous interfaces are useful where status information is kept locally or where it can be computed quickly. These interfaces allow an application to trigger a recalculation and explicit response, and cause the application to react only when called. The tradeoff is that they stall the invoking application during the exchange, and expect the application to know the appropriate time to make requests. Thus, the number of synchronous operations should be kept low enough to minimize overhead, while providing the granularity of feedback needed. Synchronous interfaces are limited when network conditions change unpredictably and when such changes are needed rapidly by the application.

Asynchronous interfaces allow an application to configure lower layers with a persistent request, where responses are generated by the lower layers automatically. This includes both upcalls[18] and interrupts to the application. As little time should be spent on the asynchronous operations as possible; upcalls are less expensive than interrupts. Multiple outstanding partial responses must also be supported.

The benefit of asynchrony is that network parameters are more accurately known because changes can trigger the interrupt or upcall. This mode is ap-

---

[18]An upward procedure call [Clark 1985].

propriate when network state changes unpredictably and infrequently, and synchronous polling would be inefficient on short time scales.

Part of adapting to the network is predicting the future state of the network. Proper adaptation involves judicious balancing of synchronous and asynchronous dials and adjustment of the period over which state is considered valid. Variability is important in considering the utility of state. For example, if RTT varies widely, then the application reaction to RTT should consider how seriously to use individual samples of the RTT value, or whether it is more appropriate to operate on the basis of the maximum, minimum, or mean value over a longer interval. Even the period over which such statistics are gathered can be varied to adjust the reactance of the application [Faber 1992].

Consider the Network Time Protocol, (NTP), an application protocol that adjusts the clock of an end host in order to synchronize it with other network-based clocks. Initially, NTP supplied the operating system (and thus other applications) only the precise local time; newer interfaces include variance bounds on the time report [Mills 1991]. Similar interfaces inside of TCP's RTT estimation algorithm now include RTT and RTT variance; actions depend on the RTT augmented by this variance. As a result, application behavior can depend on both the value of a network parameter and the confidence to which the value is known.

Provide Variance Values to Imprecise Values   *The quality of feedback depends on the stability and precision of the information provided. If information is approximated or aggregated and the application does not know the degree of imprecision a priori, provide an explicit variance to the value.*

A-5Av

In both the synchronous and asynchronous case, there is substantial benefit from aggregation. Applications rarely react to very specific or detailed network status; it is sufficient to present coarse or aggregate information and let the application make further demands if refinement is required. Thus, it is important to support the Aggregation of Application Operations (A-5B) and allow the application to control the frequency of response and size of aggregation.

8.4.3 Transparency and Dependence

The combination of knobs and dials presents a model of the network to the application and a model of the application to the network. The interface between the two provides an abstraction that allows a single network to support different applications or an application to adapt to different networks. There is a fine line between abstraction and hiding, which transparent interfaces attempt to mitigate.

Interfaces provide an abstraction which simplifies interaction. In this simplification, some of the details are deliberately abstracted or combined. The key issue for high-performance applications is that their need to adapt be supported, without incurring unnecessary detail in their interface to the network, while not hiding essential information. The challenge is to provide an abstraction that presents scale in dimensions that are likely to change in the network, or for which the application can adapt, while providing functional transparency.

Functional Transparency and Abstraction Should Not Result in Hiding   *Layering is designed around abstraction, providing a simpler representation of a complicated interface. Abstraction can obscure a necessary property or parameter, resulting in hiding. Hiding is not a desirable property of layering.*

A-4Fh

For example, consider a networked file system as an abstraction of a variety of local file systems. The convention in Unix file systems is that /tmp refers to temporary workspace local to the machine. However, in many cases it is less critical that a temporary file be physically on the same machine than that the access be low latency and high bandwidth. Network attached storage might provide lower latency and higher bandwidth than the local hard disk. The application uses a suboptimal service if the filesystem interprets /tmp as meaning 'local filesystem'; /tmp has hidden the different alternatives from the application. A better interface is to allow the application to specify properties, such as expected size, frequency of access, persistence, bandwidth, and latency. Based on these parameters, a networked file system could determine the appropriate workspace location, with sufficient simplicity in the application interface.

Location Independent Interfaces Should Not Hide Latency   *Interfaces should be provided to access data independent of physical location, but latency and other QOS measures should be available to applications that can benefit from this knowledge.*

A-4Fl

Web uniform resource locators (URLs) give no indication of the bandwidth and latency between the user and the page, nor the size of the page. While the transparency of the Web provides a powerful abstraction, some translucency using metadata can be useful. This allows users to make choices in which set of pages to fetch or whether to request a large page over a slow access link with images, without images or not at all. The only way a user can determine whether to load a large page is if the size is explicitly given on the referring page, and the user has knowledge about the data rate of the bottleneck link.

Networked DSM (distributed shared memory) and DVSM (distributed virtual shared memory) systems [Sterbenz 1990b, Delp 1991] provide geographic and topologic transparency to the location of a memory object. While this has benefits, programs that are oblivious to the possibility that memory references might take in excess of 100 ms over a wide area network cannot deliver predictable performance. Programs should be aware of the latency penalty, and exploit hints and feedback from the end system and network.

8.4.4　Legacy Issues

Not all applications are adaptive, and not all networks support application control. For example, Ethernet, the most widely deployed LAN technology, lacks resource reservation and real-time capabilities.[19] Legacy applications continue to run decades after they were designed, many of which predate commodity networking altogether.

> **Default to Support Legacy Applications** *Networks should provide a meaningful degenerate behavior to support legacy applications or applications whose capabilities are outside the scope of the system.*
>
> **A-III.7**

Support for legacy applications requires reasonable defaults and the ability of the network API to operate in the absence of application control. For example, it may require only synchronous interactions because upcalls are either not supported by the end system or because the application has not been compiled or linked to appropriate libraries. Similarly, some applications may support network interaction, but only over limited scales. When network parameters exceed these ranges, or when control is absent, reasonable degenerate behavior is required.

Current applications will eventually become legacy, as will network interfaces. Design decisions intended to simplify APIs, abstract parameters, or facilitate implementations may have unintended consequences. Every fixed parameter may eventually require variation, but it is not feasible to expose every parameter in a single, compact interface. These issues apply not only to the parameters of an interface but their semantics as well. For example, Unix has imposed a copy-on-write semantics to the send interface, so that send calls are synchronous and the application can reuse the buffer immediately on return. Such an interface can require additional copy operations, where an asynchronous interface with upcalls to release buffers after network writes would be more efficient [Brustoloni 1996].

---

[19]Although they are being considered in newer versions of the Ethernet standard.

8.5 Summary

This chapter has considered the issues important to high-speed networked applications. High-speed applications can be characterized by their individual or aggregate bandwidth requirements and the degree to which high bandwidth enhances, challenges, or enables the application. We discussed categories of applications and the different latency characteristics of real-time, interactive, deadline, and best-effort applications. Understanding these characteristics helps us prepare for future high-speed applications, without knowing exactly what the applications will be.

It is critical that high-speed applications and supporting network infrastructure be adaptive in latency, bandwidth, and group membership size. Mirroring, caching, anticipation, and data transformation are all key techniques to mask latency and adapt to available bandwidth. It is important to match the application and network through such techniques as ALF and layered encoding.

These adaptations require an interface between the application and network; knobs and dials provide this control and feedback. A variety of interface mechanisms should be supported to optimize the application–network interaction. Functional transparency is desirable, but performance parameters such as latency and bandwidth should be exposed to applications and users that can exploit them.

We need to do our best to Prepare for the Future ($\varnothing_4$) by building applications whose capabilities span a wide dynamic range of network characteristics and can deal with heterogeneity.

8.5.1 Further Reading

There are numerous sources for descriptions of high-speed applications. This chapter has indicated that we need to be critical in accepting whether or not an application is *really* high speed, regardless of its description. Many high-speed applications appear first in the supercomputing community, since they have the high-speed computing and communications infrastructure on which to research and prototype new applications. Many of these applications eventually find their way into wider use. For example, distributed simulation and visualization applications prototyped in supercomputing centers eventually find application in industrial engineering design tools and weather forecasting for farmers, as infrastructure becomes cheap enough. A short list of readings on applications for high-speed networks includes [Lyles 1995] (which is devoted to applications requiring high-speed networks), [McGarty 1992] (which is devoted to medical applications), [Catlett 1992], [Johnson 1992], [Lyles 1992], [NRC 1993], [Pehrson 1992] and the Applications part of *The Grid* [Foster 1999]: [Messina 1999, Johnston 1999, Moore 1999, and DeFanti 1999] (whose references should be followed for further information). A discussion on high-speed middleware is presented in [Sterbenz 1995]. Multimedia applications and networking are comprehensively covered in [Kuo 1998] and [Crowcroft 1999].

APPLICATION AXIOMS AND PRINCIPLES

A-I. Application Primacy   *The sole and entire point of building a high-performance network infrastructure is to support the distributed applications that need it.*

A-I.1. Field of Dreams versus Killer App Dilemma   *Advances in network technology create the "field of dreams" to which new applications are drawn, but are difficult to motivate without the tangible pull of a new "killer application"—which can't emerge in the absence of an adequate network infrastructure. This chicken-and-egg dilemma governs the supply-and-demand dynamic of high-speed networking.*

A-I.2. User Expectations of Interapplication Delay   *The performance metric of primary interest to the users of communicating applications is the total delay in completing the communication, including both the end-to-end delay and any delay introduced by the application itself.*

A-I.2c. User Expectations of Continuous Media Quality   *The performance metric of primary interest to users of continuous media streams is quality of the stream such as frame rate and resolution for video and frequency range for audio.*

A-I.3. High-Speed Applications Need High Bandwidth and Low Latency   *Bandwidth and latency are the primary performance metrics governing interapplication delay. The latency requirements of an application depend on the expectations of the user. For data–intensive applications, delay sensitivity drives bandwidth requirements.*

A-2A. Relative Magnitude of High Speed   *High speed is a relative term. Application requirements for high speed—alleged or actual—always grow to at least the limits of currently attainable link speeds and network capacity.*

A-IV₃. Properly Partition Distributed Applications   *Carefully determine where to cut applications to distribute across the network. Some "high-speed" applications are simply poorly partitioned low-speed applications.*

A-II.2b. Fair Service among Best-Effort Applications   *In the absence of specific policy directives to favor some applications over others, network and end-system resources should be allocated fairly (roughly equally) among competing best-effort applications.*

A-I.2i. Interactive Response Time   *Interactive applications should provide a response time ranging from an ideal of 100 ms to a maximum target of 1 second. Within this range, consistent response is better than high variance.*

A-7Ai. Structure Data to Meet Interactive Response Bounds   *Structure and migrate data for interactive responses such that initially visible data is present at sufficient resolution within interactive response bounds.*

A-5D. Application Adaptation by Refinement   *Quick and partial information is better than slow and complete information, particularly with refinement over time. Successive refinement can often be used to adapt a high-speed application to a low-speed network.*

A-6B. Client Pull versus Server Push   *The side that has the best knowledge of the client is the one that should initiate data transfer. Network load can be reduced by moving some of this knowledge to the server. Client demand fetch is based on user requests; server push presend based on events the server knows about, assisted by user profiles.*

A-III.5. Constraints on Partitioning of Distributed Computations   *The ability to efficiently partition a distributed computation may be limited by the physical distribution of scarce computing and storage resources.*

A-4Ff. Application Adaptation Depends on Network Feedback   *Application adaptation techniques involve the application reacting to information about the network, and are dependent on knowledge about the communication path. Some adaptations benefit from active cooperation from the network.*

A-6Bu. User Feedback to Adaptive Applications   *Adaptive applications benefit from user control: either an explicit feedback loop or implicit controls based on past behavior or a user profile.*

A-IV$_1$. Application Adaptation Synergy   *Many application adaptation techniques are mutually exclusive; one can occur only at the expense or inhibition of another. They must be carefully implemented and coordinated to avoid interference.*

A-IAl. Application Latency Principle   *Interapplication delays are the sum of all the constituent delays that cannot be parallelized. User-perceived delay is the ultimate measure of the performance of a high-speed system.*

A-7Bs. Exploit Spatial Locality to Reduce Latency   *Reduce the latency of access by locating data physically close to the users and applications that need it.*

A-7Bt. Exploit Temporal Locality to Reduce Latency   *Reduce the latency of access by retaining data locally (or nearby) that is likely to be referenced in the future.*

A-5C. Balance Network Resources by Hierarchical Caching   *Balance aggregate network bandwidth against storage required by hierarchical caching.*

A-7Ac. Structure Data and Migrate Code for Dynamic Content   *Structure data from which content is dynamically generated into cacheable units. Cache the programs that generate the content along with the data.*

A-2. Use Bandwidth to Reduce Latency   *Bandwidth can be utilized to reduce latency by anticipatory prefetching and presending.*

A-2B. Compression of Data   *Compression of data reduces bandwidth at the expense of the processing complexity and delay of the compression/decompression algorithms.*

A-1A*b*. Application Bandwidth Principle   *The bandwidth perceived by the user is the minimum of all bandwidths along a path, including through the application itself.*

A-5B. Aggregation of Application Operations   *Reduce the cost of all per connection or per application operations by aggregation. Support ways to aggregate requests and responses between the application and network, and for the application, to control the frequency of response and size of aggregation.*

A-1C. Partitioning of Application versus Protocol Functionality   *Keep the network impact of application design choices in mind. Not all functions are best deployed within an application.*

A-4C. Application–Network Synergy Principle   *Increase performance by matching application characteristics to the network. Use ALF to decrease the overhead of protocol encapsulation, control transfer, and decapsulation.*

A-4I. API Scalability Principle   *All interfaces between an application and network should scale with respect to bandwidth, latency, and number (nodes, end systems, and users). Parameters should have a scale factor (order of magnitude exponent), a precision factor (multiplier), and a variance.*

A-4C*k*. Knobs Should Correspond to Network Actions   *A knob should not be built into the network that does not correspond to a real controllable action.*

A-4C*d*. Dials Should Correspond to Observable Properties   *A dial should not be provided that does not correspond to a real observable parameter.*

A-4H. Support Synchronous and Asynchronous Dials   *Network instrumentation should support both asynchronous (interrupt-driven) and synchronous (polled) feedback mechanisms.*

A-5A*v*. Provide Variance Values to Imprecise Values   *The quality of feedback depends on the stability and precision of the information provided. If information is approximated or aggregated and the application does not know the degree of imprecision a priori, provide an explicit variance to the value.*

A-4F*h*. Functional Transparency and Abstraction Should Not Result in Hiding   *Layering is designed around abstraction, providing a simpler representation of a complicated interface. Abstraction can obscure a necessary property or parameter, resulting in hiding. Hiding is not a desirable property of layering.*

A-4F*l*. Location Independent Interfaces Should Not Hide Latency   *Interfaces should be provided to access data independent of physical location, but latency and other QOS measures should be available to applications that can benefit from this knowledge.*

A-III.7. Default to Support Legacy Applications   *Networks should provide a meaningful degenerate behavior to support legacy application or applications whose capabilities are outside the scope of the system.*

CHAPTER 9

Future Directions and Conclusion

Now that we have completed our tour of the principles of high-speed network design, it is time to step back as we did in Chapter 2, but this time with a focus on the future. Section 9.1 does this, starting from the discussion in Section 2.1: *A Brief History of Networking*. We consider the directions we can predict and those that we can't, and some areas that promise to enable and challenge high-speed networking in the fourth generation. Section 9.2 provides a brief conclusion to this chapter and the book.

9.1   Looking toward the Future

In Chapter 2, our fundamental axiom set consisted of Know the Past, Know the Present, Know the Future, and Prepare for the Future ($\emptyset$). At the end of the book, it is time to reflect on the future parts of this axiom:

> **Know the Future**   *The future hasn't happened yet, and is guaranteed to contain at least one completely unexpected discovery that changes everything.*
>
> $\emptyset_3$

The one thing we can know about the future is that there will be surprises. Some will be twists on what we expect, and some will come completely out of the blue. Consider the situation if we were pondering the future just 10 years before this writing, at the beginning of the third networking generation (1990).

489

The Internet was solidly entrenched as the network infrastructure that bound universities and industrial researchers by email and FTP to share documents and software, but few expected the universal consumer access that would be the norm 10 years later. Those who did assumed that it would be (only) email. While email was an important driver to get businesses and consumers online, it was not the killer app.

The Web didn't exist, although the pieces did; some of them had existed for a long time. Hypertext [Bush 1945, Nelson 1965] was well established, and DVSM (distributed virtual shared memory) mechanisms existed to provide transparency to program objects over a wide area network. There was a URL-like convention for expressing remote files (`ftp:/<host-name>/<directory-path>`), and GUIs (graphical user interfaces) existed for remote file access, such as XFTP [Smith 1991]. Time Berners-Lee invented the Web [Berners-Lee 1989] by putting these ideas together to solve a practical problem, and his invention has fundamentally changed the way in which we use information and network technology. While HTTP is not substantially different from FTP in most uses, the missing piece was to *open* the retrieved file, and present clickable hypertext links to other files. This closed the loop between filenames and file contents and allowed seamless access. The Web browser has become not only the way in which we access content remotely across the Web, but also the GUI platform of choice for all sorts of applications, independent of the need to access remote information.

Integrated services were anticipated, but it was just becoming clear in 1990 to a large number of people that it would be the *Internet* that would ultimately deliver this vision, and not the PSTN.[1] The PSTN was optimized for traditional analog voice traffic, and the efforts to enhance it, including deployments of ISDN (integrated services digital networks) and the AIN (advanced intelligent network), failed.[2] The fundamental architecture and protocols were not adaptable to data-driven intelligence in end systems. Thus, the PSTN is destined to do little more than carry voice, and serve as an access bit pipe from residences to the Internet for the remaining analog modems. When the Internet fully evolves to support the quality of service needed for high-quality real-time voice and video, the PSTN will simply be a legacy subnet for voice, which connects the remaining POTS (plain ordinary telephone service) infrastructure.

Laptop computers and mobile telephones were a novelty that only a few road warriors carried in 1990, and wireless networking was not something that most of us thought about very much. Laptop computers were heavy, expensive, and had significantly less capability than their desktop equivalents. The functionality gap has narrowed considerably[3] (except for screen

---

[1]The statement that "the Internet *is* the global information infrastructure" still provoked arguments in the early 1990s.
[2]Integrated services digital network and advanced intelligent network.
[3]Subject to power and heat constraints discussed in Section 9.1.1.

size). Wireless telephones, Palm Pilots, and notebook computers are now commonplace.

Therefore, we shouldn't overestimate our ability to predict how the fourth generation (2000s) of networking will evolve, and what the fifth generation holds in store. What we *can* do, however, is to understand the forces at work, and prepare for the future given the uncertainty we cannot remove.

Prepare for the Future   *Simply knowing the past does not prepare us to understand the future. We must constantly reevaluate tradeoffs in the face of emerging technology, and question the basic assumptions of the present.*

$\varnothing_4$

We can ponder what the future will hold in three fundamental areas. The first two, developments in enabling technology and application demand, are obvious. It is the tension between these two that results in the Field of Dreams versus Killer App Dilemma (I.1). The third area should be clear now that we are at the end of this book: changing resource tradeoffs. We will examine this one first.

9.1.1   Changing Resource Tradeoffs

Ultimately, it is the cost and availability of network infrastructure that allow the widespread deployment of high-speed applications. The *balance* between the cost and availability of processing, memory, and bandwidth resources, constrained by latency and power, determines the shape of the solution; this is the Resource Tradeoff Principle (2). Thus, we restate the corollary that is important in preparing for the future:

Resource Tradeoffs Change   *The relative cost of resources and the impact of constraints change over time, due to nonuniform advances in different aspects of technology.*

2A

Minor relative changes in the cost of resources result in incremental growth and deployment of network infrastructure. They affect network engineering and the placement of resources, as described in Section 3.3. Significant changes in the relative cost of resources, however, have more dramatic impact.

9.1.1.1   Shifts in Resource Tradeoffs

Significant changes in the relative cost of resources alter the way in which networks are deployed and used. In the first generation (through 1970s), bandwidth was relatively scarce and expensive. Users accessed computers remotely using 110- and 300-baud modems, but this resulted in long response times even for text pages. Users interacted with computers in different ways than they did when locally attached, being more careful of input because it was more costly to suffer the delay of a mistake. Real full-screen interaction was not practical, although full-screen forms were used for transactional systems. In this case, cursor movement was best handled locally by intelligent terminals and controllers such as the IBM 3270 series. Protocols were optimized to conserve bandwidth with little concern for the processing cost on the host computer.

By the early third generation (1990s), the tradeoff between bandwidth and processing had changed; fiber optic cable made bandwidth cheap relative to processing, and the bottlenecks lay in store-and-forward routers and end-system servers, workstations, and personal computers. Fast packet switching enabled high-speed networks, and optimizations made to conserve bandwidth were now significantly less important than optimizations made to reduce processing requirements in end systems. Although there was talk of bandwidth being "free," this was not the case; when bandwidth is abundant, new applications emerge to take advantage of it, and the demand quickly expands to meet or exceed the supply. The balance is shifting again, with the Web and multimedia streaming consuming available bandwidth.

The Web not only drove bandwidth, but also changed the interaction mode and traffic demands. Internet infrastructure had been optimized for infinite-source TCP, and discounted the per connection costs. Long-transfer TCP connections had been the majority of the traffic for telnet, FTP, and batched email. Transactional systems were still running on disconnected enterprise networks tuned for the purpose. Web browsing shifted the balance of Internet load toward short transactional traffic. The majority of traffic was on the order of 10 packets, of which nearly half are connection setup and teardown. This requires optimization of connection establishment, and we must now consider applying congestion control to the control packets as well as the data. Whole new ways of handling the control, for example, connection aggregation, are coming to the fore, and old techniques, such as multiplexing within the stream, are being rediscovered.

We live in a precarious balance as the processing, memory, and bandwidth curves slip back and forth relative to one another. Commodity microprocessors in the early 2000s have clock cycles in excess of 1 GHz; there are things we can do at these rates that didn't make sense at 10 MHz, such as loading and interpreting applets within 100-ms response time budgets. CPUs require power, however, and it is a challenge to provide services to the mobile wireless world, where power constraints and heat dissipation push back against the shift toward using increasing processor functionality. The prospect of processors embedded in memory chips [Patterson 1997] further complicates the balance.

Before we had a chance to optimize for the transactional model, streaming media entered the scene, providing a mix of long-lived multimedia traffic mixed in with the transactions. Multicast was needed to conserve bandwidth, and service providers resisted, afraid that the floodgates would open—but they already had.

About all we can do is be flexible and vigilant. Since we *know* resource tradeoffs will change, we shouldn't be *surprised* when they do. Network protocols should be designed with the flexibility to adapt to changing resource tradeoffs. This is hardest to do with IP, which is the waist of the hourglass, but routing protocols and traffic management can change somewhat while the IP packet format and forwarding protocols remain stable. It is slightly easier to do at layers above and below because it is less disruptive to add a new transport protocol, such as RTP, to satisfy the requirements of a new class of applications or to add new application protocols such as HTTP and RTSP.

9.1.1.2 *Fundamental Changes*

A more drastic question is raised when the balance shifts so fundamentally that *one* resource is essentially free and unlimited. This might occur if something made a resource several orders of magnitude cheaper with respect to the others, for example, 10 Gb/s to the desktop and home (OC-192 or 10-Gb Ethernet), 1-THz processors, or terabyte main memory in the early 2000s.[4] We have already discussed some of the techniques that would come to bear.

We can easily imagine current applications using a couple of orders more bandwidth for faster response in Web browsing of pages with photographic resolution images and streaming of higher-resolution video. There would be no need to cache and load balance for bandwidth reduction, but caching would still need to take place due to latency concerns. Bandwidth would be burned to reduce delay, for example, by deep prefetching in the Web hyperlink tree (assuming that memory is cheap enough at the end system to serve as a temporary cache).

If memory were to become significantly cheaper, compression wouldn't be needed to conserve memory, but would still be employed to the degree necessary to conserve bandwidth and keep interactive latency low. Far more local demand-based caching would be done, but prefetch- and presend-based caching would still be constrained by bandwidth.

It is difficult to imagine what we would do in a world where one of the resources was essentially *free*, since our ability to use a particular resource still depends on the availability of other resources. For example, the ability to prefetch in the face of free bandwidth is still constrained by the cost of memory to hold the data.

---

[4]But not all at the *same* time; this would merely be an acceleration of the existing curves.

9.1.2   Technology and Applications

It is difficult to separate advances that will be enabled by technology from those that will be driven by user and application demand, due to the Field of Dreams versus Killer App Dilemma (I.1). The Web was invented to fill a need for the exchange of scientific information; the current pervasiveness of the Web is due to the discovery of all the things that could be done once it was there. The Web is a wonderful example of how an application can blossom if only a small amount of infrastructure is needed to get started. The infrastructure was provided by the Internet; the barrier to deployment of a new application on the Internet is small. Other applications, such as those requiring mobility, require a more significant investment in the infrastructure. In this case we really need the wireless field of dreams before we know what the mobile killer app will be. If the field of dreams is not built right, we may never know. The only thing about a killer app we can predict with certainty is that we never know it until *after* it's arrived.

It is useful to examine the perils of improper assumptions in the infrastructure. Video-on-demand was touted as a killer app throughout much of the third generation (1990s). Numerous VOD trials were planned by service providers. The dedicated infrastructure to provide such services was expensive, not only on the server side, but also on the consumer side since sufficient bandwidth into the home was not extant. A few of the trials actually took place but were not considered a success. This is not an indictment to VOD as an application, but rather to the limited trials that were done. We know that streaming media is blossoming on the Internet, and when the bandwidth and QOS into the home are sufficient to allow high-resolution movie viewing, this will merely be yet another type of content fetched from the Web.

A second example is in the assumption of asymmetry. Web browsing has highly asymmetric traffic characteristics: small requests from user to server, high bandwidth responses from server back to user. As long as consumers are not also content providers, an asymmetric infrastructure would suffice. Unfortunately, service providers looked at traffic patterns in the third generation, made assumptions about what the future would be, optimizing for, and explicitly provisioning[5] asymmetric bandwidth with central servers. The ISP industry was surprised when Napster [Napster 1999] shattered their model,[6] but those of us who were thinking about the future weren't the slightest bit sur-

---

[5]In particular, with ADSL and asymmetric CATV modem services.
[6]Napster is a web site that allows users to upload digital music tracks for others to download, and has an estimated 2 million music exchanges per hour and 20 million users in mid-2000 after less than a year in existence. As was the case for audio and cassettes it is under legal challenge from the Recording Industry Association of America (RIAA) in a futile attempt to control the direction of the future.

prised. We *didn't* know that it would be *music* that would first turn so many of the world's consumers into content providers. We *did* suspect that there were all sorts of reasons that consumers would want to provide content, including family photo archives, videoconferencing, personal Web servers, and video content production [Davis 1997]. The fact that Napster automated the process and didn't require knowledgeable users to serve content accelerated the shift. So knowing the exact application didn't matter, but questioning the traffic patterns of the day would have better prepared for the future.[7]

While we can't perfectly predict the future, we can consider some areas that promise to enable and challenge high-speed networking in the fourth generation (beginning roughly in 2000). We will begin with advances in network infrastructure and then consider application scenarios.

9.1.2.1   Network Infrastructure

While we can't predict exactly what advances in technology will enable new high-speed network infrastructure in the fourth and fifth generations, there are a few areas that show promise. We discussed some of these technologies as applicable in Chapters 3, 4, and 5, but now consider the impact that these technologies may have on the future Internet.

9.1.2.1.1   All Optical Networking

Optical fiber links became the infrastructure of choice for wide area networks in the third generation (1980s). The advent of EDFAs (Er-doped fiber amplifiers) enabled long WDM links, almost overnight. Optical switches, after many years of research, appear poised to make an impact in the fourth generation, due to rapid advances in optical, microelectronic, and MEMS (microelectromechanical systems) technology. All-optical networking, in the sense of optical lightpaths through the switch optically coupled to WDM links may become a significant fourth-generation technology. As described in Chapter 5, optical switches are not capable of packet switching in the conventional sense, but rather perform burst or fast circuit switching. This requires new protocol research, particularly in routing, for widespread deployment in the Internet. The discovery of small, dense, cheap wavelength converts could have an impact as significant as EDFAs. All-optical networking in the strict sense, with optical control paths for packet header decoding and switch control, is further off—perhaps a fifth-generation technology. On the other hand, these advances will only take place if the relative cost of optical switching technology decreases

---

[7]We also had some history to draw on, since the peer-to-peer opportunities of the Internet were explicitly recognized by the early developers, and considered by them to be at least as important as the opportunities for client-server applications.

with respect to the continuing decrease in electronic switching technology. We can't predict exactly how the cost curves will track one another, but need to be prepared for either case.

Free space photonic links have the potential to deliver the high-bandwidth capacity of wired networks to the mobile wireless environment. While only suitable for line-of-sight applications, there is a significant application space within buildings, in dry climates, for switched satellite networks, and the interplanetary Internet.

9.1.2.1.2   Mobile Wireless Networking

Applications and users of mobile wireless networking area are already entrenched in the fourth generation, but the technology is still in its infancy. We have discussed some of the issues in Chapters 3 and 5, but this is a case where the Field of Dreams versus Killer App Dilemma (I.1) is waiting for the construction of the infrastructure. Fortunately, the demand for wireless connectivity is so high that there are business cases for commercial deployment. We must be careful, however, to avoid disasters due to product and service deployments that have not looked toward the future. The disaster of Iridium (Example 3.1) and the shortsighted three-bit address space in Bluetooth[8] [Mettala 1999] should give us pause for thought.

We will talk about the application side of this technology in the next subsection.

9.1.2.1.3   Active Networking

Active networking (AN) is a field that was born from questioning what could be done with changing resource costs [Tennenhouse 1996], as described in Section 3.3.4. While the decreasing cost of computing and memory provides new opportunities to provide services in the network, it is not yet clear how it will play out. Moderate AN is likely to be a fourth-generation technology, since the difficult performance and security issues are in tighter control by the network service provider. There is still considerable work to be done, however, on how to gain the benefits of AN in high-speed networks. Control plane AN is not a significant performance issue due to the long granularity of operation, but how to do data plane AN, requiring the active processing of packets at line rate, is more challenging. This will depend on the delicate balance between the cost of bandwidth (which dictates line rate) and the cost of processing (which dictates if the active processing can be fast enough to keep up).

Strong AN, in which end users of the network inject and execute code in network nodes, is further off, at best. The security and resource management

---

[8]Allowing only 8 devices to actively participate in the lowest-level cluster, called a *piconet*

issues require significantly more research, and are terrifying to network service providers. If the problems are solved, however, it may be a way for network service providers to sell CPU cycles in addition to bandwidth.

9.1.2.2 Application Scenarios

We will now consider several broad application scenarios that promise to push our ability to support high-performance applications to extreme limits, ranging from those that will impact many of us directly, to those somewhat less down to earth.

9.1.2.2.1 Ubiquitous Computing and Smart Spaces

Ubiquitous computing [Weiser 1991, 1999, Abowd 2000], *smart spaces* [Englebart 1962, Akyol 1999, Mark 1999], and *pervasive computing* [Birnbaum 1997] refer to an emerging interdisciplinary field in which numerous embedded mobile wireless computing nodes interact with one another, as well as with stationary nodes in the environment. An individual's computing platform consists of a number of distributed processing nodes, I/O devices, and sensors. Individuals communicate with one another, with the fixed resources in smart rooms (such as display devices and printers), and with resources providing various services on the Internet. These nodes must become aware of one another, self-organize into federations, and maintain secure, private sessions among groups.

Ubiquitous computing environments may have thousands or millions of devices within range of one another. The scaling and density techniques discussed in Section 3.2 will be critically important and will need to deal with many orders of magnitude more nodes than in the wired Internet. The aggregate bandwidth demands on wireless channels vastly exceed our current understanding of the channel capacity available, driving research in new ways to use radio spectrum, as well as free space photonic links, as described in the last section. While many embedded nodes (such as sensors) will not need high individual bandwidth connections, many others will. The link between an individual's personal node [Finn 1998] and a flat panel display will require moderate to high bandwidth; the link to the Web will require the same sorts of bandwidth we have been describing for conventional wired end systems. While we understand some of the issues, we will have to see how the fourth generation unfolds to know the answers and the way in which ubiquitous computing and communication are actually deployed.

Amorphous computing [Abelson 2000], may take us to the next level (perhaps in the fifth generation), with thousands or millions of embedded processors self-organizing and self-specializing into amorphous computing and sensor nets. We may see smart paint on the walls of rooms, smart blood in our bodies, and smart dust [Kahn 1999] dropped from the sky.

It is not hard to imagine a global tera- and petanode network for ubiquitous computing and a zetta- and yottanode network with amorphous computing.

9.1.2.2.2   Teleimmersion and Distributed Virtual Reality

Teleimmersion and distributed virtual reality (VR) are extreme cases of telepresence, where users distributed across the network are immersed in a shared VR world. Early prototypes such as the cave automatic virtual environment (CAVE) project [Cruz-Neira 1992] are interesting, but give us only a glimpse of what might be possible. While we understand the bandwidth requirements driven by the resolution and frame rate that the human eye can comprehend, this may not be sufficient. We can imagine groups of individuals physically interacting with one another in a projected holographic VR space, which is shared across the network with other groups of individuals. This may require bandwidth many orders of magnitude higher than current teleimmersion prototypes.[9]

9.1.2.2.3   Distributed Computing

Although distributed computing was one of the application classes described in Section 8.2.3, it is the least mature, except for very special network deployments. Distributed computing applications have generally been limited to clusters of supercomputers connected by high-speed LANs, further connected by dedicated long-haul links when necessary. Moving distributed computing to the mainstream over the Internet has many of the same challenges that are required for high-quality video streaming and telepresence: sufficient bandwidth with the QOS guarantees needed for real-time and near real-time synchronization and data exchange among distributed processes.

Networked distributed computing is motivated for two reasons: (1) access to computing and data resources not available locally and (2) utilization of excess computing and memory resources on other end systems attached to the network. The first scenario is needed when expensive limited resources, such as a massively parallel supercomputer or large shared database, are needed to solve a problem across the network. The second scenario is of greater interest for wide-scale deployment. It is highly dependent on the balance between end-system and network resources. Processing and memory must be abundant enough so that end systems have more than they need much of the time, but not so cheap that the distribution of processing is not necessary. Bandwidth

[9]Imagine the *Star Trek Enterprise* holodeck distributed across the Internet.

must be plentiful enough that it is reasonable to distribute a task among networked end systems. Early efforts in this direction include NOWs (networks of workstations) and the SETI@home project (search for extraterrestrial intelligence) [SETI 1998], in which volunteers run processes on their personal computers to search for patterns in radio signals. It will be interesting to see how the development of QOS in the Internet and the shifting balance of resource cost enables the development of such applications.

9.1.2.2.4   Interplanetary Internet

We hope to see significant progress in planetary exploration during the time frame of the fourth generation, particularly to Mars. The Mars missions require communication among spacecraft, planetary rovers, and Earth-based mission control. We can already see the need to extend the Internet beyond the Earth and its artificial satellites to the rest of the solar system: the interplanetary Internet [Cerf 1998]. While fourth-generation deployments will be limited in scope and restricted to the Mars missions, now is the time to start thinking for the future. We don't want to deploy a point solution for Mars and have to start from scratch when we go to the Jupiter system.

The interplanetary Web (Example 8.1) indicated some of the challenges we will face. Current deep space links are of moderate bandwidths, and the bandwidth-×-delay product is on the same order of magnitude as high-speed terrestrial optical fiber links. The development of free space photonic links, however, provides us with the possibility of intrasolar system links with truly staggering bandwidth-×-delay products of petabits or exabits between planetary systems and spacecraft.

Our high-speed networking architectures will be challenged to scale to these extremely long latencies and high bandwidth-×-delay products, as we attempt to extend applications and infrastructure like the Web to the entire solar system. The intergalactic Internet will have to wait for developments in faster-than-light propagation (for example, [Wang 2000]) and wormhole routing[10] that are further in the future, but we shouldn't assume that it will not eventually be an issue.

9.2   Conclusion

At the beginning of this book, we laid out the fundamental axioms and design principles for high-speed networks. We then refined these principles to network architecture, the components in the network, end systems, and the applications that motivate high-speed networks. We avoided extensive cover-

---

[10]In the transdimensional sense rather than traditional network usage.

age of any particular technology because while technologies change, the fundamental design principles do not. We expect these principles to be just as applicable at the beginning of the fifth generation as at the beginning of the fourth.

While we can't predict the future, we can strive to understand the past, question the assumptions of the present, and think about the potential future impact of changing resource tradeoffs. We hope that the systemic approach of this book will help you to adapt to the changes that we cannot foresee.

References

Note: Internet RFCs (requests for comments) and unexpired Internet Drafts are available from http://www.rfc-editor.org. Internet drafts are *work in progress*, and it is at the sole discretion of the authors whether they are made available for historical reference past the expiration date; expired Internet Drafts can generally be found by searching on the file name (without the version number). In some cases Web URLs are the best way to cite technical reports, tutorials, and papers in obscure proceedings; these URLs are provided for convenience but are not necessarily stable.

[Abbott 1993] M.B. Abbott and Larry L. Peterson, "Increasing Network Throughput by Integrating Network Layers," *IEEE/ACM Transactions on Networking*, vol.1, no.5, IEEE/ACM, New York, October 1993, pp. 600–610.

[Abe 2000] George Abe, *Residential Broadband* 2nd ed., Cisco Press, Indianapolis, IN, 2000.

[Abelson 2000] Harold Abelson, Don Allen, Daniel Coore, Chris Hanson, George Homsy, Thomas F. Knight, Jr., Radhika Nagpal, Erik Rauch, Gerald Jay Sussman, and Ron Weiss, "Amorphous Computing," *Communications of the ACM*, vol.43, no.5, ACM, New York, May 2000, pp. 74–82.

[Abowd 2000] Gregory D. Abowd and James P.G. Sterbenz, "Final Report on the Inter-Agency Workshop on Research Issues for Smart Environments," *IEEE Personal Communications*, vol.7, no.5, IEEE, New York, October 2000, pp. 36–40.

[Abramson 1970] N. Abramson, "The ALOHA System – Another Alternative for Computer Communications," *Proceedings of the Fall Joint Computer Conference*, vol.36, AFIPS, 1970, pp. 295–298.

[Acosta 1999] Roberto J. Acosta, Robert Bauer, Richard J. Krawczyk, Richard C. Reinhart, Michael J. Zernic, and Frank Gargione, "Advanced Communications Technology Satellite (ACTS): Four-Year System Performance," *IEEE Journal on Selected Areas in Communications*, vol.17, no.2, IEEE, New York, February 1999, pp. 193–203.

[Adam 1993] J. F. Adam, H. H. Houh, and D. L. Tennenhouse, "Experience with the VuNet: A Network Architecture for a Distributed Multimedia System," *Proceedings of the IEEE 18th Conference on Local Computer Networks*, IEEE, New York, September 1993, pp. 70–76.

[Agrawal 1996] P. Agrawal, B. Narendran, J. Sienicki, and S. Yajnik, "An Adaptive Power Control and Coding Scheme for Mobile Radio Systems," *Proceedings of International Conference on Personal Wireless Communications* (New Delhi), IEEE, New York, February 1996, pp. 283–288.

[Aggarwal 2000] Amit Aggarwal, Stefan Savage, and Thomas Anderson, "Understanding the Performance of TCP Pacing," *Proceedings of INFOCOM 2000* (Tel Aviv IL), vol.3, IEEE, New York, March 2000, pp.1157–1165.

[Ahlgren 1996] Bengt Ahlgren, Mats Björkman, and Per Gunningberg, "Integrated Layer Processing Can Be Hazerdous to Your Performance," *Protocols for High Speed Networks V*, IFIP/IEEE PfHSN'96 (Sophia-Antipolis, FR), October 1996, Wallid Dabbous and Christophe Diot, eds., 1997 Chapman & Hall, London/Kluwer Academic Publishers, Norwell, MA, pp. 167–181.

[Ahmadi 1989] Hamid Ahmadi, and Wolfgang E. Denzel, "A Survey of Modern High-Performance Switching Techniques," *IEEE Journal on Selected Areas in Communications*, vol.7, no.7, IEEE, New York, September 1989, pp. 1091–1103.

[Aho 1971] Alfred V. Aho, Peter J. Denning, and Jeffrey D. Ullman, "Principles of Optimal Page Replacement," *Journal of the ACM*, vol.18, no.1, ACM, New York, January 1971, pp. 80–93.

[Ahuja 1979] Vijay Ahuja, "Routing and Flow Control in Systems Network Architecture," *IBM Systems Journal*, vol.18, no.2, IBM, Armonk, NY, 1979, pp. 298–314.

[Ahuja 1996] R. Ahuja, S. Keshav, and H. Saran, "Design, Implementation, and Performance Measurement of a Native-Mode ATM Transport Layer," *IEEE/ACM Transactions on Networking*, vol.4, no.4, IEEE/ACM, New York, August 1996, pp. 502–515.

[Akyol 1999] Bora A. Akyol, Matt Fredette, Alden W. Jackson, Rajesh Krishnan, David Mankins, Craig Partridge, Nicholas Shectman, and Gregory D. Troxel, "Smart Office Spaces," *Proceedings Usenix Workshop on Embedded Systems*, March 1999.

[Allman 1998] Mark Allman, Sally Floyd, and Craig Partridge, *Increasing TCP's Initial Window*, RFC 2414 (experimental), September 1998.

[Allman 1999a] Mark Allman and Vern Paxon, "On Estimating End-to-End Network Path Properties," *Proceedings of ACM SIGCOMM'99*, (Cambridge, MA), *Computer Communication Review*, vol.29, no.4, ACM, New York, August 1999, pp. 263–274.

[Allman 1999b] Mark Allman, Vern Paxon, and W. Richard Stevens, *TCP Congestion Control*, RFC 2581 (standards track), April 1999.

[Allman 1999c] Mark Allman, Daniel R. Glover, and Luis Sanchez, *Enhancing TCP Over Satellite Channels using Standard Mechanisms*, RFC 2488/BCP 28, January 1999.

[Allman 2000] Mark Allman, ed., *Ongoing TCP Research Related to Satellites*, RFC 2760 (informational), February 2000.

[Alt 1998] Paul M. Alt and Kohki Noda, "Increasing Electronic Display Content: An Introduction," *IBM Journal of Research and Development*, vol.42, no.3/4, IBM, Armonk, NY, May/July 1998, pp. 315–320.

[Amdahl 1967] Gene Amdahl, "Validity of Single Processor Approach to Achieving Large Scale Computing Capabilities," *Proceedings of the Spring Joint Computer Conference*, Reston, VA, AFIPS, April 1967, pp. 483–485.

[Amstutz 1983] Stanford R. Amstutz, "Burst Switching—An Introduction," *IEEE Communications*, vol.21, no.8, IEEE, New York, November 1983, pp. 36–42.

[Anderson 1993] Thomas E. Anderson, Susan S. Owicki, James B. Saxe, and Charles P. Thacker, "High Speed Switch Scheduling for Local-Area Networks," *ACM Transactions on Computer Systems*, vol.11, no.4, ACM, New York, November 1993, pp. 319–352.

[Anderson 1995] Thomas E. Anderson, David E. Culler, David A. Patterson, et al., "A Case for NOW (Networks of Workstations)," *IEEE Micro*, vol.15, no.1, IEEE, New York, February 1995, pp. 54–64.

[Anderson 1999] Jon Anderson, James S. Manchester, Antonio Rodriguez-Moral, and Malathi Veeraraghavan, "Protocols and Architectures for IP Optical Networking," *Bell Labs Technical Journal*, vol.4, no.1, Lucent Technologies, Murray Hill, NJ, January–March 1999, pp. 105–123.

[Anderson 2000] Loa Anderson, Paul Doolan, Nancy Feldman, Andre Fredette, and Bob Thomas, *LDP Specification*, Internet Draft draft-ietf-mpls-ldp-11.txt, work in progress, August 2000.

[Arlitt 2000] Martin Arlitt and Tai Jain, "A Workload Characterization Study of the 1998 World Cup Web Site," *IEEE Network*, vol.14, no.3, IEEE, New York, May/June 2000, pp. 30–37.

[Armitage 1993] Grenville J. Armitage and Kieth M. Adams, "Packet Reassembly During Cell Loss," *IEEE Network*, vol.7, no.5, IEEE, New York, September 1993, pp. 26–34.

[Asthana 1992] A. Asthana, C. Delph, H.V. Jagadish, and P. Krzyzanowski, "Towards a Gigabit IP Router," *Journal of High Speed Networks*, vol.1, no.4, IOS Press, Amsterdam, 1994, pp. 281–288.

[Atkins 1980] James D. Atkins, "Path Control: The Transport Network of SNA," *IEEE Transactions on Communications*, vol.com-28, no.4, IEEE, New York, April 1980, pp. 527–538.

[ATMF 1996p] ATM Forum Technical Committee, *Private Network-Network Interface Specification (PNNI)*, version 1.0, March 1996.

[ATMF 1996t] ATM Forum Technical Committee, *Traffic Management Specification*, version 4.0, af-tm-0056.0000, April 1996.

[Awduche 2000] Daniel O. Awduche, Lou Berger, Der-Hwa Gan, Tony Li, Vijay Srinivasan, and George Swallow, *RSVP-TE: Extensions to RSVP for LSP Tunnels*, Internet Draft draft-ietf-mpls-rsvp-lsp-tunnel-07.txt, work in progress, August 2000.

[Bach 1986] Maurice J. Bach, *The Design of the Unix Operating System*, Prentice-Hall, Englewood Cliffs, NJ, 1986.

[Baker 1995] F. Baker, ed., *Requirements for IP Version 4 Routers*, RFC 1812 (standards track), June 1995.

[Bailey 1994] Mary L. Baily, Burra Gopal, Michael Pagels, Larry L. Peterson, and Prasenjit Sarkar, "PATHFINDER: A Pattern-Based Packet Classifier," *Proceedings of the First Symposium on Operating Systems Design and Implementation OSDI'94* (Monterey, CA), Usenix, Berkeley, CA, November 1994.

[Bala 1995a] Krishna Bala and Biswanath Mukherjee, eds., WDM Networks special issue (part 1) of *Journal of High Speed Networks*, vol.4, no.1, IOS Press, Amsterdam, 1995.

[Bala 1995b] Krishna Bala and Biswanath Mukherjee, eds., WDM Networks special issue (part 2) of *Journal of High Speed Networks*, vol.4, no.2, IOS Press, Amsterdam, 1995.

[Balakrishnan 1999] Hari Balakrishnan, Hariharan S. Rahul, and Srinivasan Seshan, "An Integrated Congestion Management Architecture for Internet Hosts," *Proceedings of ACM SIGCOMM'99*, (Cambridge, MA), *Computer Communication Review*, vol.29, no.4, ACM, New York, August 1999, pp. 175–188.

[Banerjee 1993] Sujata Banerjee, Victor O.K. Li, and Chihping Wang, "Distributed Database Systems in High-Speed Wide-Area Networks," *IEEE Journal on Selected Areas in Communications*, vol.11, no.4, IEEE, New York, February 1993, pp.191–202.

[Banks 1993] David Banks and Michael Prudence, "A High-Performance Network Architecture for a PA-RISC Workstation," *IEEE Journal on Selected Areas in Communications*, vol.11, no.2, IEEE, New York, May 1993, pp.617–630.

[Bannister 1999] Joseph Bannister, Joseph D. Touch, Alan Willner, and Stephen Suryaputra, "How Many Wavelengths Do We Really Need in an Optical Backbone Network?," *Protocols for High Speed Networks VI*, IFIP/IEEE PfHSN'99 (Salem, MA), August 1999, Joseph D. Touch and James P.G. Sterbenz, eds., Kluwer Academic Publishers, Norwell, MA, 2000, pp. 43–60.

[Baran 1964] Paul Baran, "On Distributed Communications Networks," *IEEE Transactions on Communications Systems*, vol.cs-12, no.3, IEEE, New York, March 1964, pp. 1–9.

[Basturk 1999] E. Basturk, A. Birman, G. Delp, R. Guérin, R. Haas, S. Kamat, D. Kandlur, P. Pan, D. Pendarakis, V. Peris, R. Rajan, D. Saha, and D. Williams, "Design and Implementation of a QOS Capable Switch-Router," *Computer Networks*, North-Holland/Elsevier, Amsterdam, vol.31, no.1–2, January 1999, pp. 19–32.

[Bell 1971] C. Gordon Bell and Allen Newell, *Computer Structures: Readings and Examples*, McGraw-Hill, New York, 1971.

[Bell 1978] C. Gordon Bell, J. Craig Mudge, and John E. McNamara, *Computer Engineering: A DEC View of Hardware Systems Design*, Digital Equipment Corporation Press, Bedford, MA, 1978.

[Bellamy 2000] John C. Bellamy, *Digital Telephony*, John Wiley, New York, 2000.

[Beneš 1965] V.E. Beneš, *Mathematical Theory of Connecting Networks*, Academic Press, New York, 1965.

[Bennett 1999] Jon Bennett, Craig Partridge, and Nicholas Shectman, "Packet Reordering is Not Pathological Network Behavior," *IEEE/ACM Transactions on Networking*, vol.7, no.6, IEEE / ACM, New York, December 1999, pp. 789–797.

[Berners-Lee 1989] Tim Berners-Lee, *Information Management: A Proposal*, CERN, 1989, www.w3.org/History/1989/proposal.html.

[Berners-Lee 1996] Tim Berners-Lee, Roy T. Fielding, and Henrik Frystyk, *Hypertext Transfer Protocol—HTTP/1.0*, RFC 1945 (informational), May 1996.

[Bernet 1998] Yoram Bernet, "The Complementary Roles of RSVP and Differentiated Services in the Full-Service QOS Network," *IEEE Communications*, vol.38, no.2, IEEE, New York, February 2000, pp. 154–162.

[Bernet 2000] Yoram Bernet, Peter Ford, Raj Yavatkar, Fred Baker, Lixia Zhang, Michael Speer, Robert Braden, Bruce Davie, John Wroclawski, and Eyal Felstaine, *A Framework for Integrated Services Operation over Diffserv Networks*, RFC 2998 (informational), November 2000.

[Bertsekas 1992] Dimitri Bertsekas and Robert Gallager, *Data Networks*, 2nd ed., Prentice Hall, Englewood Cliffs, NJ, 1992

[Beshai 1995] Maged Beshai and Ernst Münter, "Multi-Tera-bit/s Switch Based on Burst Transfer and Independent Shared Buffers," *Proceedings of GLOBECOM'95* (Singapore), vol.3, IEEE, New York, November 1995, pp. 1724–1730.

[Bhargava 1988] Amit Bhargava, James F. Kurose, Don Towsley, and Guy Vanleemput, "Performance Comparison of Error Control Schemes in High-

Speed Computer Communication Networks," *IEEE Journal in Selected Areas in Communications*, vol.6, no.9, IEEE, New York, December 1988, pp. 1565–1575

[Bhattacharjee 1998a] Samrat Bhattacharjee, Kenneth L. Calvert, and Ellen W. Zegura, "Self-Organizing Wide-Area Network Caches," *Proceedings of IN-FOCOM '98* (San Francisco), vol.2, IEEE, New York, April 1998, pp. 600–608.

[Bhattacharjee 1998b] Samrat Bhattacharjee, Kenneth L. Calvert, and Ellen W. Zegura, "Congestion Control and Caching in CANES," *Proceedings of ICC '98 Workshop on Active and Programmable Networks*, (Atlanta), IEEE, New York, June 1998.

[Bhattacharjee 1998c] Samrat Bhattacharjee, Ken L. Calvert, Ellen W. Zegura, and James P.G. Sterbenz, "Directions in Active Networks," *IEEE Communications*, vol.36, no.10, October 1998, IEEE, New York, pp. 72–78.

[Biaz 1998] Saâd Biaz and Nitin H. Vaidya, "Distinguishing Congestion Losses from Wireless Transmission Losses: A Negative Result," *Proceedings of 7th International Conference on Computer Communications and Networks (IC^{3}N)* (Lafayette, LA), IEEE, New York, October 1998, pp. 722–731.

[Biaz 1999] Saâd Biaz and Nitin H. Vaidya, *Is the Round-Trip Time Correlated with the Number of Packets in Flight?*, Texas A&M University Dept. of Computer Science Technical Report 99–006, March 1999.

[Biersack 1992] Ernst W. Biersack, "Performance Evaluation of Forward Error Correction in ATM Networks," *Proceedings of ACM SIGCOMM'92*, (Baltimore), *Computer Communication Review*, vol.22, no.4, ACM, New York, August 1992, pp. 248–257.

[Bing 2000] Benny Bing, *High-Speed Wireless ATM and LANs*, Artech House, Norwood, MA, 2000.

[Birnbaum 1997] Joel Birnbaum, "Pervasive Information Systems," *Communications of the ACM*, vol.40, no.2, ACM, New York, February 1997, pp. 40–41.

[Blaauw 1997] Gerrit A. Blaauw and Frederick P. Brooks, Jr., *Computer Architecture: Concepts and Evolution*, Addison-Wesley, Reading, MA, 1997.

[Black 1998a] Uyless Black, *ATM: Signaling in Broadband Networks*, vol. 2, Prentice Hall, Upper Saddle River, NJ, 1998.

[Black 1998b] Uyless Black, *ATM: Internetworking with ATM*, vol. 3, Prentice Hall, Upper Saddle River, NJ, 1998.

[Black 1998c] Uyless Black, *The Intelligent Network: Customizing Telecommunication Networks and Services*, Prentice-Hall, Upper Saddle River, NJ, 1998.

[Black 1999] Uyless Black, *ATM: Foundation for Broadband Networks*, vol. 1, 2nd ed., Prentice Hall, Upper Saddle River, NJ, 1999.

[Blaine 1996] G. James Blaine, Jerome R. Cox, and R. Gilbert Jost, "Networks for Electronic Radiology," *Radiologic Clinics of North America*, vol.43, no.3, Harcourt Health Sciences, St. Louis, MO, May 1996, pp. 505–524.

[Blake 1998] Steven Blake, David L. Black, Mark A. Carlson, Elwyn Davies, Zheng Wang, and Walter Weiss, *An Architecture for Differentiated Services*, RFC 2475 (informational), December 1998.

[Boggs 1988] David R. Boggs, Jeffrey C. Mogul, and Christopher A. Kent, "Measured Capacity of an Ethernet: Myths and Reality," *Proceedings of ACM SIGCOMM'88*, (Stanford, CA), *Computer Communication Review*, vol.18, no.4, ACM, New York, August 1998, pp. 222–234.

[Bohem 1969] B.W. Bohem and R.L. Mobley, "Adaptive Routing Techniques for Distributed Communications Systems," *IEEE Transactions on Communication Technology*, vol.com-17, no.3, IEEE New York, June 1969, pp. 340–349.

[Bohm 1996] Christer Bohm, Markus Hidell, Per Lindgren, Lars Ramfelt, and Peter Sjödin, "Fast Circuit Switching for the Next Generation of High Performance Networks, *IEEE Journal on Selected Areas in Communications*, vol.14, no.2, IEEE, New York, February 1996, pp. 298–305.

[Bollapragada 2000] Vijay Bollapragada, Curtis Murphy, and Russ White, *Inside Cisco IOS Software Architecture*, Cisco Press, Indianapolis, IN, 2000.

[Bolot 1996a] Jean-Chrysostome Bolot and Andrés Vega-García, "Control Mechanisms for Packet Audio in the Internet," *Proceedings of INFOCOM'96* (San Francisco), vol.1, IEEE, New York, March 1996, pp. 232–239.

[Bolot 1996b] Jean-Chrysostome Bolot and Thierry Turletti, "Adaptive Error Control for Packet Video in the Internet," *Proceedings of International Conference on Image Processing'96* (Lausanne), IEEE, New York, September 1996, pp. 25–28.

[Bonomi 1995] Flavio Bonomi and Kerry W. Fendick, "The Rate-Based Flow Control Framework for the Available Bit Rate ATM Service," *IEEE Network*, vol.9, no.2, IEEE, New York, March/April 1995, pp. 25–39.

[Bononi 1999] Alberto Bononi, *Optical Networking*, 11th International Tyrrhenian Workshop on Digital Communications, September 1999 (Santa Margherita, IT), Springer, London, 1999.

[Borgonovo 1994] Flaminio Borgonovo, Luigi Fratta, and Joseph A. Bannister, "On the Design of Optical Deflection-Routing Networks," *Proceedings of INFOCOM'94* (Toronto), IEEE, New York, June 1994, pp. 120–129.

[Borgonovo 1995] Flaminio Borgonovo, "Deflection Routing," in *Routing in Communications Networks*, Martha Steenstrup, ed., Prentice Hall, Englewood Cliffs, NJ, 1995, pp. 263–305.

[Borman 1999] David A. Borman, Stephen E. Deering, and Robert M. Hinden, *IPv6 Jumbograms* (standards track), RFC 1883, May 1997.

[Bose 1999] Vanu Bose, David Wetherall, and John Guttag, "RadioActive Networks," *Proceedings of ACM/IEEE MobiCom'99*, ACM, New York, 1999, pp. 242–248.

[Bosse 1998] John G. van Bosse, *Signaling in Telecommunication Networks*, John Wiley, New York, 1998.

[Bowen 1992] Thomas F. Bowen, Gita Gopal, Gary E. Herman, Takako M. Hickey, K. C. Lee, William H. Mansfield, John Raitz, and Abel Weinrib, "The Datacycle Architecture," *Communications of the ACM*, vol. 35, no.12, ACM, New York, December 1992, pp. 71–792.

[Boyer 1992] Pierre E. Boyer and D.P. Tranchier, "A Reservation Principle with Applications to ATM Traffic Control," *Computer Networks and ISDN Systems*, vol.24, no.4, North-Holland/Elsevier, Amsterdam, May 1992, pp. 321–334.

[Boyer 1994] Pierre E. Boyer, "Fast Resource Management in ATM Networks," in *Architecture and Protocols for High-Speed Networks*, Otto Spaniol, André Danthine, and Wolfgang Effelsberg, eds., Kluwer Academic Publishers, Norwell, MA, 1994, pp. 51–68.

[Braden 1985] Robert Braden, *Towards a Transport Service for Transaction Processing Applications*, RFC 955, September 1985.

[Braden 1988] Robert Braden, David A. Borman, and Craig Partridge, *Computing the Internet Checksum*, RFC 1071, September 1998.

[Braden 1992] Robert Braden, *Extending TCP for Transactions—Concepts*, RFC 1379, November 1992.

[Braden 1994] Robert Braden, *T/TCP—TCP Extensions for Transactions Functional Specification*, RFC 1644 (experimental), July 1994.

[Braden 1997] Robert Braden, ed., Lixia Zhang, Steve Berson, Shai Herzog, and Sugih Jamin, *Resource ReSerVation Protocol (RSVP—Version 1 Functional Specification*, RFC 2205 (standards track), September 1997.

[Braden 1998] Robert Braden, David D. Clark, Jon Crowcroft, Bruce Davie, Stephen E. Deering, Deborah Estrin, Sally Floyd, Van Jacobson, Greg Minshall, Craig Partridge, Larry L. Peterson, K.K. Ramakrishnan, Scott Shenker, John Wroclawski, and Lixia Zhang, *Recommendations on Queue Management and Congestion Avoidance in the Internet*, RFC 2309 (informational), April 1998.

[Braden 2000] Robert Braden, David D. Clark, Scott Shenker, and John Wroclawski, *Developing a Next-Generation Internet Architecture*, July 2000, available from www.isi.edu/newarch.

[Bradner 1995] Scott Bradner and Allison Mankin, *The Recommendation for the IP Next Generation Protocol*, RFC 1752 (standards track), January 1995.

[Brakmo 1995] Lawrence S. Brakmo and Larry L. Peterson, "TCP Vegas: End to End Congestion Avoidance on the Global Internet," *IEEE Journal on Selected Areas in Communications*, vol.13, no.8, IEEE, New York, October 1995, pp. 1465–1480.

[Braun 1994] Hans-Werner Braun and Kimberly Claffy, "Web Traffic Characterization: An Assessment of the Impact of Caching Documents from the NCSA's Web Server," *Proceedings of the 2nd World Wide Web Conference* (Chicago), IW^{3}C^2, Geneva, October 1994.

[Braun 1995] Torsten Braun and Christophe Diot, "Protocol Implementation using Integrated Layer Processing," *Proceedings of ACM SIGCOMM'95* (Cambridge, MA), *Computer Communication Review*, vol.25, no.4, ACM, New York, August 1995, pp. 151–161.

[Bray 2001] Jennifer Bray and Charles F. Sturman, *Bluetooth: Connect Without Cables*, Prentice Hall, Upper Saddle River, NJ, 2001.

[Bridges 1994] M. Bridges, S. Subramaniam, and D. Edwards, *TCP Embedded Trailer Checksum*, Internet Draft draft-bridges-tcp-checksum-01.txt, work in progress, December 1994.

[Briem 1998] Uwe Briem, Eugen Wallmeier, Christophe Beck, and Fred Matthiesen, "Traffic Management for an ATM Switch with Per-VC Queueing: Concept and Implementation," *IEEE Communications*, vol.36, no.1, IEEE, New York, January 1998, pp. 88–93.

[Brustoloni 1996] José Carlos Brustoloni and Peter Steenkiste, "Effects of Buffering Semantics on I/O Performance," *Proceedings of the Second Symposium on Operating Systems Design and Implementation (OSDI'96)* (Seattle, WA) Usenix, Berkeley, CA, October 1996, pp. 277–291

[Bruwer 1994] William A. Bruwer, John D. Loop, James A. Symon, and B. G. Thompson, "VISTAnet and MCIA: Medical Applications Leading to the NCIH," *IEEE Network*, vol.8, no.6, IEEE, New York, November/December 1994, pp. 24–31.

[Bush 1945] Vannever Bush, "As We May Think," *The Atlantic Monthly*, vol.176, no.1, Boston , July 1945, pp. 101–108.

[Byers 1998] John W. Byers, Michael Luby, Michael Mitzenmacher, and Ashutosh Rege, "A Digital Fountain Approach to Reliable Distribution of Bulk Data," *Proceedings of ACM SIGCOMM'88*, (Vancouver, BC), *Computer Communication Review*, vol.28, no.4, ACM, New York, August 1998, pp. 56–67.

[Callon 1992] Ross Callon, *TCP and UDP with bigger Addresses (TUBA), A Simple Proposal for Internet Addressing and Routing*, RFC 1347, June 1992

[Calvert 1999a] Kenneth L. Calvert, James Griffioen, Amit Sehgal, and Su Wen, "Concast: Design and Implementation of a New Network Service," *Proceedings of the International Conference on Network Protocols 1999* (Toronto), IEEE, New York, October 1999, pp. 335–344.

[Calvert 1999b] Ken L. Calvert, ed., *Architectural Framework for Active Networks* version 1.0,DARPA Active Network architecture document, July 1999, available from www.dcs.uky.edu/~calvert/arch-docs.html.

[Campbell 1993] Andrew Campbell, Geoff Coulson, Francisco García, and David Hutchinson, "Orchestration Services for Distributed Multimedia Syncronisation," *IFIP High Performance Networking IV* 1994 (Liège BE), André Danthine and Otto Spaniol, ed., North-Holland Elsevier, Amsterdam, 1992, pp. 153–168.

[Carlson 2000] Mark A. Carlson, Satish Mali, Milan Merhar, Charles Monia, and Murali Rajagopal, *A Framework for IP Based Storage*, Internet Draft draft-ietf-ips-framework-00.txt, work in progress, November 2000.

[Carpenter 1996] Brian E. Carpenter, *Architectural Principles of the Internet*, RFC 1958 (informational), June 1996.

[Carpenter 2000] Brian E. Carpenter, *Internet Transparency*, RFC 2775 (informational), February 2000.

[Castineyra 1996] Isidro Castineyra, Noel Chiappa, and Martha Steenstrup, *The Nimrod Routing Architecture*, RFC 1992 (informational), August 1996.

[Catlett 1992] Charles E. Catlett, "In Search of Gigabit Applications," *IEEE Communications*, vol.30, no.4, IEEE, New York, April 1992, pp. 42–51.

[Cerf 1974] Vinton G. Cerf and Robert Kahn, "A Protocol for Packet Network Interconnection," *IEEE Transactions on Communications Technology*, vol. com-22, no.5, IEEE, New York, May 1974, pp. 627–641.

[Cerf 1983a] Vinton G. Cerf and Edward Cain, "The DoD Internet Architecture Model," *Computer Networks*, vol.7, no.5, Elsevier Science/North-Holland, Amsterdam, October 1983, pp. 307–318.

[Cerf 1983b] Vinton G. Cerf and Robert E. Lyons, "Military Requirements for Packet-Switched Networks and Their Implications for Protocol Standardization," *Computer Networks*, vol.7, no.5, Elsevier Science/North-Holland, Amsterdam, October 1983, pp. 293–306.

[Cerf 1998] Vinton G. Cerf, "Interplanetary Internet," presentation at *INET'98* (Geneva), Internet Society, Reston, VA, July 1998.

[Cerf 2001] Vinton G. Cerf, Scott C. Burleigh, Adrian J. Hooke, Leigh Torgerson, Robert C. Durst, Keith L. Scott, Eric J. Travis, and Howard S. Weiss, *Interplanetary Internet (IPN): Architectural Definition*, Internet Draft draft-irtf-ipnrg-arch-00.txt, work in progress, February 2001.

[Chan 1999] Henry C. B. Chan, Hussein M. Alnuweiri, and Victor C.M. Leung, "A Framework for Optimizing the Cost and Performance of Next-Generation Routers," *IEEE Journal on Selected Areas in Communications*, vol.17, no.6, IEEE, New York, June 1999, pp. 1013–1029.

[Chandranmenon 1995] Girish P. Chandranmenon and George Varghese, "Trading Packet Headers for Packet Processing," *Proceedings of ACM SIGCOMM'95*, (Cambridge, MA), *Computer Communication Review*, vol.25, no.4, ACM, New York,, August 1995, pp. 162–173.

[Chankhunthod 1995] A. Chankhunthod, P.B. Danzig, C. Neerdaels, M.F. Schwartz, and K.J. Worrell, *A Hierarchical Internet Object Cache*, USC technical report 95–611, University of Southern California, Los Angeles, CA, catarina.usc.edu/danzig/cache.ps.

[Chao 1999a] H. Jonathan Chao, Michael Degermark, Nick McKeown, and Henry Hong-Yi Tzeng, Next Generation IP Switches and Routers special issue of *IEEE Journal on Selected Areas in Communications*, vol.17, no.6, IEEE, New York, June 1999.

[Chao 1999b] H. Jonathan Chao, Yau-Ren Jenq, Xiaolei Guo, and Cheuk H. Lam, "Design of Packet-Fair Queueing Schedulers Using a RAM-Based Searching Engine," *IEEE Journal on Selected Areas in Communications*, vol.17, no.6, IEEE, New York, June 1999, pp. 1105–1126.

[Chapin 1981] A. Lyman Chapin, *Connectionless Data Transmission*, RFC 787, ANSI X3 working paper X3S33/X3T56/81–85 X3T5/81–71 X3T51/81–44 X3S37/81–71R, May 1981.

[Chapin 1983] A. Lyman Chapin "Connections and Connectionless Data Transmission," *Proceedings of the IEEE*, vol.71, no.12, IEEE, New York, December 1983, pp. 1365–1371.

[Chen 1995] Thomas M. Chen and Stephen S. Liu, *ATM Switching Systems*, Artech House, Norwood, MA, 1995.

[Cheriton 1986] David Cheriton, "VMTP: A Transport Protocol for the Next Generation of Computer Systems," *Proceedings of ACM SIGCOMM'86* (Stowe, VT), *Computer Communication Review*, vol.16, no.3, ACM, New York, August 1986, pp. 406–415.

[Cheriton 1988] David Cheriton, *VMTP: Versatile Message Transaction Protocol Specification*, RFC 1045, February 1988.

[Chesson 1989] Greg Chesson, "XTP/PE Design Considerations," in *Protocols for High-Speed Networks*, IFIP PfHSN'89 (Zürich), May 1989, Harry Rudin and Robin Williamson, eds., Elsevier/North-Holland, Amsterdam, 1989, pp. 27–33.

[Chiappa 1994] Noel Chiappa, *IPng Technical Requirements of the Nimrod Routing and Addressing Architecture*, RFC 1753 (informational), December 1994.

[Chiu 1989] Dah-Ming Chiu and Raj Jain, "Analysis of the Increase and Decrease Algorithms for Congestion Avoidance in Computer Networks," *Computer Networks and ISDN Systems*, vol.17, no.1, North-Holland/Elsivier, Amsterdam, June 1989, pp. 1–14.

[Chlamtac 1995] Imrich Chlamtac and Andrea Fumagalli, eds., Optical Networks special issue of *Journal of High Speed Networks*, vol.4, no.4, IOS Press, Amsterdam, 1995.

[Chandhok 2000] N. Chandhok, A. Durresi, R. Jagannathan, Raj Jain, S. Seetharaman, and K. Vinodkrishnan, *IP over Optical Networks: A Summary of Issues*, Internet Draft draft-osu-ipo-mpls-issues-00.txt, work in progress, July 2000.

[Choa 1999] Fow-Sen Choa, ed., Optical Networking special issue of *Journal of High Speed Networks*, vol.8, no.1, IOS Press, Amsterdam, 1999.

[Chraplyvy 1990] Andrew R. Chraplyvy, "Limitations on Lightwave Communications Imposed by Optical-Fiber Nonlinearities," *IEEE Journal on Lightwave Technology*, vol.8, no.10, October 1990, IEEE, New York, pp. 1548–1557.

[Chu 1996] Hsiao-Keng Jerry Chu, "Zero-Copy TCP in Solaris," *Proceedings of Usenix 1996*, (San Diego, CA), Usenix, Berkeley, CA, 1996.

[Chuang 1999] Shang-Tse Chuang, Ashish Goel, Nick McKeown, and Balaji Prabhakar, "Matching Output Queueing with a Combined Input/Output-Queued Switch," *IEEE Journal on Selected Areas in Communications*, vol.17, no.6, IEEE, New York, June 1999, pp. 1030–1039.

[Cidon 1990] Israel Cidon, Inder Gopal, and Adrian Segall, "Fast Connection Establishment in High Speed Networks," *Proceedings of ACM SIG-COMM'90* (Philadelphia, PA), *ACM Computer Communication Review*, vol.20, no.4, ACM, New York, September 1990, pp. 287–296.

[Cidon 1993] Israel Cidon, Inder Gopal, P. Madan Gopal, Roch Guérin, Jim Janniello, and Marc Kaplan, "The plaNET/Orbit High Speed Network," *Journal of High Speed Networks*, vol.2, no.3, IOS Press, Amsterdam, 1993, pp. 171–208.

[Ciciora 1999] Walter Ciciora, James Farmer, and David Large, *Modern Cable Television Technology: Video, Voice, and Cable Television Technology*, Morgan Kaufmann, San Francisco, 1999.

[Cioffi 1999a] John M. Cioffi, Vladimir Oksman, Jean-Jacques Werner, Thierry Pollet, Paul M.P. Spruyt, Jacky S. Chow, and Krista S. Jacobsen, "Very-High-Speed Digital Subscriber Lines," *IEEE Communications*, vol.37, no.4, IEEE, New York, April 1999, pp. 72–79.

[Cioffi 1999b] John M. Cioffi, P. Silverman, T. Starr," "Digital Subscriber Lines," *Computer Networks*, vol.31, no.4, North-Holland/Elsevier, Amsterdam, February 1999, pp. 283–311.

[Clark 1985] David D. Clark, "The Structuring of Systems Using Upcalls," *Proceedings of ACM SIGCOMM Ninth Data Communications Symposium* (Whistler British Columbia, *ACM Computer Communications Review*, vol.15, no.4, ACM, New York, September 1985, pp. 171–180.

[Clark 1987a] David D. Clark, Mark L. Lambert, and Lixia Zhang, "NETBLT: A High Throughput Transport Protocol," *Proceedings of ACM SIGCOMM'87* (Stowe, VT), *Computer Communication Review*, vol.17, no.5, ACM, New York, August 1987, pp. 353–359.

[Clark 1987b] David. D. Clark, Mark L. Lambert, and Lixia Zhang. "NETBLT: A Bulk Data Transfer Protocol," RFC 998, March 1987.

[Clark 1988] David D. Clark, "Design Philosophy of the DARPA Internet Protocols," *Proceedings of ACM SIGCOMM'88* (Stanford, CA), *Computer Communication Review*, vol.18, no.4, ACM, New York, August 1988, pp. 186–114.

[Clark 1989a] David D. Clark, Van Jacobson, John Romkey, and Howard Salwen, "An Analysis of TCP Processing Overhead," *IEEE Communications*, vol.27, no. 6, IEEE, New York, June 1989, pp. 23–29.

[Clark 1989b] David D. Clark, *Policy Routing in Internet Protocols*, RFC 1102, May 1989.

[Clark 1990] David D. Clark and David L. Tennenhouse, "Architectural Considerations for a New Generation of Protocols," *Proceedings ACM SIG-COMM'90* (Philadelphia, PA), *Computer Communication Review*, vol.20, no.4, ACM, New York, September 1990, pp. 200–208.

[Clark 1991] David D. Clark, A. Lyman Chapin, Vinton G. Cerf, Robert Braden, and Russell Hobby, *Towards the Future Internet Architecture*, RFC 1287, December 1991.

[Clark 1992] David D. Clark, Bruce S. Davie, David J. Farber, Inder S. Gopal, Bharath K. Kadaba, David W. Sincoskie, Jonathan M. Smith, and David L. Tennenhouse, "The Aurora Gigabit Testbed," *Proceedings of INFOCOM'92* (Florence, IT), IEEE, New York, May 1992, pp. 569–581.

[Clark 1995] David D. Clark, *Protocol Design and Performance*, tutorial notes, IEEE INFOCOM'95, Boston, April 1995.

[Clos 1953] C. Clos, "A Study of Non-Blocking Switching Networks," *Bell System Technical Journal*, vol.32, no.3, March 1953, pp. 406–424.

[CNRI 1996] *The Gigabit Testbed Initiative Final Report*, Corporation for National Research Initiatives, Reston, VA, December 1996, available from www.cnri.net/gigafr.

[Coffman 1973] Edward G. Coffman, Jr. and Peter J. Denning, *Operating Systems Theory*, Prentice Hall, Englewood Cliffs, NJ, 1973.

[Comer 1991] Douglas E. Comer and David L. Stevens, *Internetworking with TCP/IP: Design, Implementation, and Internals*, vol. II, Prentice Hall, Englewood Cliffs, NJ, 1991.

[Comer 1993] Douglas E. Comer and David L. Stevens, *Internetworking with TCP/IP Volume III: Client-Server Programming and Applications*, vol. III, Prentice Hall, Englewood Cliffs, NJ, 1993.

[Comer 2000] Douglas E. Comer, *Internetworking with TCP/IP: Principles, Protocols, and Architectures*, vol. 1, 4th ed., Prentice Hall, Englewood Cliffs, NJ, 1991.

[Cooper 1990] Eric C, Cooper, Peter A. Steenkiste, Robert D. Sansom, and Brian D. Zill, "Protocol Implementation on the Nectar Communication Processor," *Proceedings of ACM SIGCOMM'90* (Philadelphia, PA), *Computer Communication Review*, vol.20, no.4, ACM, New York, September 1990, pp. 135–144.

[Cooperstock 1996] "Why Use a Fishing Line When You Have A Net?: An Adaptive Multicast Data Distribution Protocol," *Proceedings of Usenix 1996* (San Diego), Usenix, Berkeley, CA, 1996.

[Coudreuse 1987] J.-P. Coudreuse and M. Servel, "Prelude: An Asynchronous Time-Division Based Network," *Proceedings of ICC'87*, Seattle, vol. 2, IEEE, New York, 1987, pp. 769–773.

[Cox 1992] Jerome R. Cox, Jr., Edward Muka, G. James Blaine, Stephen M. Moore, and R. Gilbert Jost "Considerations in Moving Electronic Radiography into Routine Use," *IEEE Journal on Selected Areas in Communications*, vol. 10, no.7, IEEE, New York, September 1992, pp. 1108–1120.

[Cragon 1996] Harvey G. Cragon, *Memory Systems and Pipelined Processors*, Jones and Bartlett, Boston, 1996.

[Cranor 1992] Charles D. Cranor and Gurudatta M. Parulkar, "An Implementation Model for Connection-Oriented Internet Protocols," *Journal of Internetworking: Research and Experience*, vol.4, John Wiley, New York, pp. 133–157.

[Crispin 1996] Mark R. Crispin, *Internet Message Access Protocol*, version 4, rev 1, RFC 2060 (standards track), December 1996.

[Crocker 1969] Steve Crocker, *Host Requirements*, RFC 1, April 1969.

[Crovella 1998] Mark Crovella and Paul Barford, "The Network Effects of Prefetching," *Proceedings of INFOCOM'98* (San Francisco), vol.3, IEEE, New York, April 1998, pp. 1232–1239.

[Crowcroft 1992] John Crowcroft, I. Wakeman, Z. Wang, and D. Sirovica, "Is Layering Harmful?," *IEEE Network*, vol.6, no.1, IEEE, New York, January 1992, pp. 20–24.

[Crowcroft 1999] John Crowcroft, Mark Handley, and Ian Wakeman, *Internetworking Multimedia*, Taylor and Francis, London/Morgan-Kaufmann, San Francisco, 1999.

[Cruz-Neira 1992] D. Cruz-Neira, D. Sandin, T. DeFanti, R. Kenyon, and J. Hart, "The CAVE: Audio Visual Experience Automatic Virtual Environment," *Communications of the ACM*, vol.35, no.6, ACM, New York, June 1992, pp. 65–72.

[Cypser 1991] R.J. Cypser, *Communications for Cooperating Systems: OSI, SNA, and TCP/IP*, Addison-Wesley, Reading, MA, 1991.

[Dabbous 1997] Wallid Dabbous and Christophe Diot, eds., *Protocols for High Speed Networks V*, IFIP, Chapman & Hall, London/Kluwer Academic Publishers, Norwell, MA, 1997.

[Dalal 1978] Yogen K. Dalal and Robert Metcalfe, "Reverse Path Forwarding of Broadcast Packets," *Communications of the ACM*, vol.21, no.12, ACM, New York, December 1978, pp. 1040–1048.

[Dang 1987] M. Dang, P. Rolin, L. Sponga, and G. Votsis, "Some Effects of High Speed LANs on the Design of MAC Communicating Circuits," *IFIP High Speed Local Area Networks*, 1987 (Aachen, DE), Otto Spaniol and André Danthine, eds., North-Holland, Amsterdam, 1987, pp. 37–51.

[Danzig 1993] Peter B. Danzig, Richard S. Hall, and Michael F. Schwartz, "A Case for Caching File Objects Inside Internetworks," *Proceedings of ACM SIGCOMM'93* (San Francisco), *Computer Communication Review*, vol.23, no.4, ACM, New York, September 1993, pp. 239–248.

[Davie 1991] Bruce S. Davie, "A Host–Network Interface Architecture for ATM," *Proceedings of ACM SIGCOMM'91* (Zürich), *Computer Communication Review*, vol.21, no.4, ACM, New York, September 1991, pp. 307–315.

[Davie 1998] Bruce S. Davie, Paul Doolan, and Yakov Rechter, *Switching in IP Networks*, Morgan Kaufmann, San Francisco, 1998.

[Davie 2000] Bruce S. Davie and Yakov Rekhter, *MPLS: Technology and Applications*, Morgan Kaufmann, San Francisco, 2000.

[Davies 1972] Donald Watts Davies, "The Control of Congestion in Packet-Switching Networks," *IEEE Transactions on Communications*, vol.com-20, no.3, IEEE, New York, June 1972, pp. 546–550.

[Davies 1979] Donald Watts Davies, D.L.A. Barber, W.L. Price, and C.M. Solomonides, *Computer Networks and Their Protocols*, John Wiley, Chichester, UK, 1979.

[Davis 1997] Marc Davis, "Garage Cinema and the Future of Media Technology," *Communications of the ACM*, vol.40, no.2, ACM, New York, February 1997, pp. 42–48.

[Dawkins 2000] Spencer Dawkins, Gabriel E. Montenegro, Markku Kojo, Vincent Magret, and Nitin Vaidya, *End-to-End Performance Implications of Links with Errors*, Internet Draft draft-ietf-pilc-link-error-06.txt, work in progress, November 2000.

[Day 1983] John D. Day and Hubert Zimmerman "The OSI Reference Model," *Proceedings of the IEEE*, vol.71, no.12, IEEE, New York, December 1983, pp. 1334–1340.

[Decasper 1999a] Dan S. Decasper, Bernhard Plattner, Guru M. Parulkar, Sumi Choi, John D. DeHart, and Tilman Wolf, "A Scalable, High-Performance Active Network Node," *IEEE Network*, vol.13, no.1, IEEE New York, January/February 1999, pp. 8–19.

[Decasper 1999b] Dan S. Decasper, John D. DeHart, Ralph Keller, Jonathan S. Turner, Sumi Choi, and Tilman Wolf, *Demonstration of a High Performance Active Router*, DARPA Active Networks Demonstration Workshop, September 1999, available from www.arl.wustl.edu/arl/projects/ann.

[Deering 1989] Stephen E. Deering, *Host Extensions for IP Multicasting*, RFC 1112/STD 5, August 1989.

[Deering 1991] Stephen E. Deering, "Multicast Routing in Internetworks and Extended LANs," *Proceedings of ACM SIGCOMM'88* (Stanford, CA), *Computer Communication Review*, vol.18, no.4, ACM, New York, August 1988, pp. 55–64.

[Deering 1993] Stephen E. Deering, "SIP: Simple Internet Protocol," *IEEE Network*, vol.7, no.3, IEEE, New York, May 1993, pp. 16–28.

[Deering 1998] Stephen E. Deering and Robert M. Hinden, *Internet Protocol, Version 6 (IPv6) Specification*, RFC 2460 (standards track), December 1998.

[DeFanti 1999] Tom DeFanti and Rick Stevens, "Teleimmersion," in *The Grid: Blueprint for a New Computing Infrastructure*, Ian Foster and Carl Kesselman, eds., Morgan Kaufmann, San Francisco, 1999, pp. 131–155.

[Delgrossi 1995] Luca Delgrossi and Louis Berger, eds., *Internet Stream Protocol Version 2 (ST2): Protocol Specification—Version ST2+*, RFC 1819 (experimental), August 1995.

[Delp 1985] Gary S. Delp and David J. Farber, *Memnet: An Experiment in High Speed Memory Mapped Local Network Interfaces*, University of Delaware Dept. of EE technical report, no.85–11–1, Newark, DE, November 1985.

[Delp 1988] Gary S. Delp, Adarshpal S. Sethi, and David J. Farber, "An Analysis of Memnet: An Experiment in High-Speed Shared-Memory Local Networking," *Proceedings of ACM SIGCOMM'88* (Stanford, CA), *Computer Communication Review*, vol.18, no.4, ACM, New York, August 1988, pp. 165–174.

[Delp 1991] Gary S. Delp, Ronald S. Minnich, David J. Farber, Jonathan M. Smith, and Ming-Chit Tam, "Memory as a Network Abstraction," *IEEE Network*, vol.5, no.4, IEEE, New York, July 1991, pp.34–41.

[Demers 1989] Alan Demers, Srinivasan Keshav, and Scott Shenker, "Analysis and Simulation of a Fair Queueing Algorithm," *Proceedings of ACM SIGCOMM'89* (Austin, TX), *Computer Communication Review*, vol.19, no.4, ACM, New York, September 1989, pp. 1–12.

[dePrycker 1995] Martin de Prycker, *Asynchronous Transfer Mode: Solution for Broadband ISDN*, 3rd ed., Prentice Hall International, London, 1995.

[Devault 1988] Michel Devault, Jean-Yves Cochennec, and Michel Servel, "The 'Prelude' ATD Experiment: Assessments and Future Prospects," *IEEE Journal on Selected Areas in Communications*, vol.6, no.9, IEEE, New York, December 1999, pp. 1528–1537.

[Dhas 1991] Chris Dhas, Vijaya K. Konangi, and M. Sreetharan, eds., *Broadband Switching Architectures: Protocols, Design, and Analysis*, IEEE Computer Society Press, Washington, DC, 1991.

[Diot 1995] Christophe Diot, Christian Huitema, and T. Turletti, "Multimedia Applications Should be Adaptive," *Proceedings of Architecture and Implementation of High Performance Communications Subsystems HPCS'95* (Mystic, CT), IEEE, New York, August 1995, pp. 117–125.

[Diot 1997] Christophe Diot, Walid Dabbous, and Jon Crowcroft, "Multipoint Communication: A Survey of Protocols, Functions, and Mechanisms," *IEEE Journal on Selected Areas in Communications*, vol.15, no.3, IEEE, New York, April 1997, pp. 277–290.

[Dixit 2000] Sudhir Dixit and Philip J. Lin, eds., Optical Networks Come of Age special issue of *IEEE Communications*, vol.38, no.2, IEEE, New York, February 2000.

[Dixit 2001] Sudhir Dixit and Philip J. Lin, eds., Advances in Packet Switching/Routing in Optical Networks special issue of *IEEE Communications*, vol.39, no.2, IEEE, New York, February 2001.

[Doeringer 1990] Willibald A Doeringer, Doug Dykeman, Matthias Kaiserwerth, Bernd Werner Meister, Harry Rudin, and Robin Williamson, "A Survey of Light-Weight Transport Protocols for High-Speed Networks," *IEEE Transactions on Communications*, vol.38, no.11, IEEE, New York, November 1990, pp. 2025–2039.

[Doeringer 1994] Willibald A Doeringer, Doug Dykeman, Matthias Kaiserwerth, Bernd Werner Meister, Harry Rudin, and Robin Williamson, "A Survey of Light-Weight Transport Protocols for High-Speed Networks," in *High Performance Networks: Technology and Protocols*, Ahmed N. Tantawy, ed., Kluwer Academic Publishers, Norwell, MA, pp. 3–28.

[Doherty 1982] Walter J. Doherty and Ahrvind J. Thadani, *The Economic Value of Rapid Response Time*, IBM, GE20–0752–00, 1982, available from www.vm.ibm.com/devpages/jelliott/evrrt.html.

[Doran 1979] R.W. Doran, *Computer Architecture: A Structured Approach*, Academic Press, London, 1979.

[Doshi 1993] Bharat T. Doshi, Arun N. Netravali, and Krishnan K. Sabnani, "Error and Flow Control Performance of a High Speed Protocol," *IEEE Transactions on Communications*, vol.41, no.5, IEEE, New York, May 1993, pp. 707–720.

[Druschel 1993] Peter Druschel, Mark B. Abbott, Michael A. Pagels, and Larry L. Peterson, "Network Subsystem Design," *IEEE Network*, vol.7, no.4, IEEE, New York, July 1993, pp. 8–17.

[Duato 1997] José Duato, Sudhakar Yalamanchili, and Lionel Ni, *Interconnection Networks: An Engineering Approach*, IEEE Computer Society Press, Los Alamitos, CA, 1997.

[Dube 1999] Rohit Dube, "A Comparison of Scaling Techniques for BGP," *ACM SIGCOMM Computer Communication Review*, vol.29, no.3, ACM, New York, July 1999, pp. 44–46.

[Durham 1999] David Durham and Raj Yavatkar, *Inside the Internet's Resource reSerVation Protocol*, John Wiley, New York, 1999.

[Easton 1982] R. L. Easton, P. T. Hutchison, R.W. Kolor, R.C. Mondello, and R.W. Muise, "TASI-E Communications System," *IEEE Transactions on Communication*, vol.30, no.4, IEEE, New York, April 1982, pp. 803–807.

[Eggert 2000] Lars Eggert, John Heidemann, and Joseph D. Touch "Effects of Ensemble-TCP," *ACM SIGCOMM Computer Communication Review*, vol.30, no.1, ACM, New York, January 2000, pp. 15–29.

[Eichler 2000] G. Eichler, H. Hussnman, G. Mamais, T. Venieris, C. Prehofer, and S. Salsano, "Implementing Integrated and Differentiated Services for the Internet with ATM Networks: A Practical Approach," *IEEE Communications*, vol.38, no.1, IEEE, New York, January 2000, pp. 132–141.

[Elbert 1997] Bruce R. Elbert, *The Satellite Communication Application Handbook*, Artech House, Norwood, MA, 1999.

[Elbert 1999] Bruce R. Elbert, *Introduction to Satellite Communication*, 2nd ed., Artech House, Norwood, MA, 1999.

[Eng 1992] Kai Y. Eng, Mark A. Pashan, R.A. Spanke, and Mark J Karol, "A Prototype Growable 2.5 Gb/s ATM Switch for Broadband Applications," *Journal of High Speed Networks*, vol.1, no.3, IOS Press, Amsterdam, 1992, pp. 237–253.

[Engelbart 1962] D. C. Engelbart, *Augmenting Human Intellect: A Conceptual Framework*, SRI project report AFOSR-3233, SRI, Menlo Park, CA, available from http://sloan.stanford.edu/mousesite/EngelbartPapers/B5_F18_ConceptFrameworkInd.html.

[Enslow 1974] Phillip H. Enslow, *Multiprocessors and Parallel Processing*, John Wiley, New York, 1974.

[Esaki 1995], H. Esaki, K.-I. Nagami, and M. Ohta, "High Speed Datagram Switching over Internet Using ATM Technology," *Proceedings of Networld + Interop '95* (Las Vegas), E-12-1, March 1995.

[Escobar 1990] Julio Escobar, Gregory Lauer, and Martha Steenstrup, "Performance Analysis of a Rate-Based Congestion Control Algorithm for Receiver-Directed Packet-Radio Networks," *Proceedings of MILCOM'90* (Monterey, CA), vol.2, IEEE, New York, September 1990, pp. 615–621.

[Escobar 1994] Julio Escobar, Craig Partridge, and Debra Deutsch, "Flow Synchronization Protocol," *IEEE/ACM Transactions on Networking*, vol.2, no.2, IEEE/ACM, New York, April 1994, pp. 111–121.

[Escobar 1995] Julio Escobar, "Run-Away Dynamics of CDMA Channels in an Adaptive Packet Radio Network," *Wireless Networks*, vol.1, no.1, Baltzer Science Publishers BV, Bussum, Netherlands, February 1995, pp. 37–46.

[Faber 1992] Theodore Faber, Lawrence H. Landweber, and Amarnath Mukherjee, "Dynamic Time Windows: Packet Admission Control with Feedback," *Proceedings of SIGCOMM'92* (Baltimore), *Computer Communication Review*, vol.22, no.4, ACM, New York, August 1992, pp. 124–135.

[Faber 1998] Theodore Faber, "ACC: Using Active Networking to Enhance Feedback Congestion Control Mechanisms," *IEEE Network*, vol.12, no.3, IEEE, New York, May/June 1998, pp. 61–65.

[Farber 1986] David J. Farber and Gurudatta M. Parulkar, "A Closer Look at Noahnet," *Proceedings of ACM SIGCOMM'95* (Stowe, VT), Computer Communication Review, vol.16, no.3, ACM, New York, August 1986, pp. 204–213.

[Feldmann 2000] Anja Feldmann and S. Muthukrishnan, "Tradeoffs for Packet Classification," *Proceedings of INFOCOM 2000* (Tel Aviv), vol.3, IEEE, New York, March 2000, pp.1193–1202.

[Feldmeier 1988] David C. Feldmeier, "Improving Gateway Performance with a Routing Table Cache," *Proceedings of INFOCOM'88* (New Orleans), IEEE, New York, March 1988, pp. 298–307.

[Feldmeier 1990a] David C. Feldmeier, "Multiplexing Issues in Communication System Design," *Proceedings of ACM SIGCOMM'90* (Philadelphia PA), *Computer Communication Review*, vol.20, no.4, ACM, New York, September 1990, pp. 209–219.

[Feldmeier 1990b] David C. Feldmeier and Ernst W. Biersack, "Comparison of Error Control Protocols for High Bandwidth-Delay Product Networks." *Protocols for High-Speed Networks II*, IFIP PfHSN'90 (Palo Alto, CA), November 1990, Marjory Johnson, ed., Elsevier/North-Holland, Amsterdam, 1991, pp. 271–298.

[Feldmeier 1992] D. Feldmeier and Anthony J. McAuley, "Reducing Protocol Ordering Constraints to Improve Performance," *Protocols for High Speed Networks III*, IFIP PfHSN'92 (Stockholm), May 1992, Per Gunningberg, Björn Perhson, and Stephen Pink, eds., Elsevier/North-Holland, Amsterdam, 1993, pp. 3–18.

[Feldmeier 1993] David C. Feldmeier, "A Framework of Architectural Concepts for High-Speed Communications Systems," *IEEE Journal on Selected Areas in Communications*, vol.11, no.4, IEEE, New York, May 1993, pp. 480–488.

[Feldmeier 1994] David C. Feldmeier, "An Overview of the TP++ Transport Protocol Project," in *High Performance Networks*, Ahmed N. Tantawy, ed., Kluwer Academic Publishers, Norwell, MA, 1994.

[Feldmeier 1998] David C. Feldmeier, Anthony J. McAuley, Jonathan M. Smith, Deborah S. Bakin, William S. Marcus, and Thomas M. Raleigh, "Protocol Boosters," *IEEE Journal on Selected Areas in Communications*, vol.16, no.3, IEEE, New York, April 1998, pp. 437–444.

[Fielding 1999] Roy T. Fielding, James Gettys, Jeffrey C. Mogul, Henrik Frystyk Nielsen, Larry Masinter, Paul J. Leach, and Tim Berners-Lee, *Hypertext Transfer Protocol—HTTP/1.1*, RFC 2616 (standards track), June 1999.

[Finn 1991] Gregory G. Finn, "An Integration of Network Communication with Workstation Architecture," *ACM Computer Communication Review*, vol.21, no.5, ACM, Washington, DC, October 1991, pp. 18–29.

[Finn 1998] Gregory G. Finn and Joseph D. Touch, "The Personal Node," *Proceedings Usenix Workshop on Embedded Systems*, (Cambridge, MA), March 1999, Usenix, Berkely, CA, also ISI Research Report, ISI/RR-98–461, July, 1998.

[Fletcher 1978] John G. Fletcher and Richard W. Watson, "Mechanisms for a Reliable Timer Protocol," *Computer Networks*, vol.2, no.4–5, North-Holland, Amsterdam, September–October 1978, pp. 271–290.

[Floyd 1993] Sally Floyd and Van Jacobson, "Random Early Detection Gateways for Congestion Avoidance," *IEEE/ACM Transactions on Networking*, vol.1, no.4, IEEE/ACM, New York, August 1993, pp. 397–413.

[Floyd 1994] Sally Floyd "TCP and Explicit Congestion Notification," *Computer Communication Review*, vol.24, no.5, ACM, New York, October 1994, pp. 10–23.

[Floyd 1995] Sally Floyd and Van Jacobson, "Link Sharing and Resource Management Models for Packet Networks," *IEEE/ACM Transactions on Networking*, vol.3, no.4, IEEE/ACM, New York, August 1995, pp. 365–386.

[Floyd 1999] Sally Floyd and Tom Henderson, *The NewReno Modification of TCP's Fast Recovery Option*, RFC 2582 (experimental), April 1999.

[Floyd 2000a] Sally Floyd, Mark Handley, Jitendra Padhye, and Jörg Widmer, "Equation-Based Congestion Control for Unicast Applications" *Proceedings of ACM SIGCOMM 2000* (Stockholm, SE), *Computer Communication Review*, vol.30, no.4, ACM, New York, August 2000, pp. 43–56.

[Floyd 2000b] Sally Floyd, Mark Handley, and Jitendra Padhye, "A Comparison of Equation-Based and AIMD Congestion Control," *Workshop on the Modeling of Flow and Congestion control Mechanism* (École Normale Supérieure, Paris), available from www.aciri.org/tfrc/aimd.pdf.

[Flynn 1995] Michael J. Flynn, *Computer Architecture: Pipelined and Parallel Processor Design*, Jones and Bartlett, Boston, 1995.

[Folts 1983] Harold C. Folts and Richard desJardins, eds., Open Systems Interconnection (OSI)—Standard Architecture and Protocols special issue of *Proceedings of the IEEE*, vol.71, no.12, IEEE, New York, December 1983.

[Foster 1999] Ian Foster and Carl Kesselman, eds., *The Grid: Blueprint for a New Computing Infrastructure*, Morgan Kaufmann, San Francisco, 1999.

[Francis 1993] Paul Francis, "A Near-Term Architecture for Deploying Pip," *IEEE Network*, vol.7, no.3, IEEE, New York, May 1993, pp. 30–37.

[Fraser 1989] A.G. Fraser, "The Universal Receiver Protocol," *Protocols for High-Speed Networks*, IFIP PfHSN'89 (Zürich), May 1989, Harry Rudin, ed., Elsevier/North-Holland, Amsterdam, 1989, pp. 19–28.

[Gagnaire 1997] Maurice Gagnaire, "An Overview of Broadband Access Technologies," *Proceedings of the IEEE*, vol.85, no.12, IEEE, New York, December 1999, pp. 1958–1972.

[Gambini 1997] Piero Gambini, "State of the Art of Photonic Packet Switched Networks, in *Photonic Networks: Advances in Optical Communications*, Giancarlo Prati, ed., 8th International Tyrrhenian Workshop on Digital Communications, September 1996 (Lerici, IT), Springer, London, 1997.

[Garg 1996] Vijay K. Garg and Joseph E. Wilkes, *Wireless and Personal Communications Systems*, Prentice Hall, Upper Saddle River, NJ, 1996.

[Geier 1999] *Wireless LANs: Implementing Interoperable Networks*, Macmillan, Indianapolis, IN, 1999.

[Geisel 1963] Dr. Seuss, *Hop on Pop*, Beginner Books, New York, 1963.

[Gerla 1980] Mario Gerla and Leonard Kleinrock, "Flow Control: A Comparative Study," *IEEE Transactions on Communications*, vol.com-28, no.4, IEEE, New York, April 1989, pp. 553–574.

[Gettys 1998] J. Gettys and H.F. Nielsen, "SMUX Protocol Specification," W3C Technical Report WD-mux-19980710, World-Wide Web Consortium (W3C), July 10, 1998.

[Gibson 1998] Garth A. Gibson, David F. Nagle, Khalil Amiri, Jeff Butler, Fay W. Chang, Howard Gobioff, Charles Hardin, Erik Riedel, David Rochberg, and Jim Zelenka, "A Cost-Effective, High-Bandwidth Storage Architecture," *Proceedings of the 8th International Conference on Architectural Support for Programming Languages and Operating Systems (ASPLOS)* (San Jose, CA), ACM, New York, October 1998, pp. 92–103.

[Gibson 2000] Garth A. Gibson and Rodney Van Meter, "Network Attached Storage Architecture," *Communications of the ACM*, vol.43, no.11, ACM, New York, November 2000, pp. 37–45.

[Gifford 1979] D. K. Gifford, "Weighted Voting for Replicated Data," *Proceedings of ACM Symposium on Operating Systems Principes SOSP'79*, Pacific Grove, CA, ACM, New York , December 1979, pp. 150–162.

[Giroux 1999] Natalie Giroux and Sudhakar Ganti, *Quality of Service in ATM Networks*, Prentice Hall, Upper Saddle River, NJ, 1999.

[Glassman 1994] Steven Glassman, "A Caching Relay for the World Wide Web," *Proceedings of the 1st World Wide Web Conference* (Geneva), IW^3C^2, Geneva, May 1994, pp. 69–76.

[Glover 1998] I. Glover and P. Grant, *Digital Communications*, Prentice Hall, Upper Saddle River, NJ, 1998.

[Gong 1994] Fengmin Gong and Gurudatta Parulkar, "A Two-Level Flow Control Scheme for High-Speed Networks," *Journal of High Speed Networks*, vol.3, no.3, 1994, pp. 261–284.

[Goralski 2000] Walter J. Goralski, *SONET*, 2nd ed., McGraw-Hill, New York, 2000.

[Gray 1979] James P. Gray and Tony B. NcNeill, "SNA Multiple-System Networking," *IBM Systems Journal*, vol.18, no.2, IBM, Armonk, NY, 1979, pp. 263–297.

[Green 1980] Paul E. Green, Jr., Alexander A. McKenzie, Carl A. Sunshine, and Stuart Wecker, eds., Computer Network Architectures and Protocols special issue of *IEEE Transactions on Communications*, vol.com-28, no.4, IEEE, New York, April 1980.

[Green 1982] Paul E. Green Jr., ed., *Computer Network Architectures and Protocols*, Plenum Press, New York, 1982 (extended book version of [Green 1980]).

[Green 1993] Paul E. Green, Jr., *Fiber Optic Networks*, Prentice Hall, Englewood Cliffs, NJ, 1993.

[Green 2000] Paul Green, "Progress in Optical Networking," *IEEE Communications*, vol.39, no.1, IEEE, New York, January 2000, pp. 54–61.

[Greene 1992] Daniel H. Greene and J. Bryan Lyles, "Reliability of Adaptation Layers," *Protocols for High Speed Networks III*, IFIP PfHSN'1992 (Stockholm, SE), May 1992, Per Gunningberg, Björn Perhson, and Stephen Pink, eds., Elsevier/North-Holland, Amsterdam, 1993, pp. 185–200.

[Guha 1999] Aloke Guha, "The Evolution to Network Storage Architectures for Multimedia Applications," *Proceedings of IEEE Multimedia Computing and Systems'99* (Florence), vol.1, IEEE, New York, June 1999, pp. 68–73.

[Gupta 1998] Pankaj Gupta, Steven Lin, and Nick McKeown, "Routing Lookups in Hardware at Memory Access Speeds," *Proceedings of INFOCOM'98* (San Francisco), IEEE, New York, March 1998, pp. 1240–1247.

[Gupta 1999a] Pankaj Gupta and Nick McKeown, "Packet Classification on Multiple Fields," *Proceedings of ACM SIGCOMM'99* (Cambridge, MA), *Computer Communication Review*, vol.29, no.4, ACM, New York, August 1999, pp. 147–160.

[Gupta 1999b] Pankaj Gupta and Nick McKeown, "Packet Classification Using Hierarchical Intelligent Cuttings," *IEEE Hot Interconnects 7* (Stanford, CA), August 1999, available at *www.hoti.org/hoti7—wednesday.html.*

[Gupta 2000a] Pankaj Gupta, *Routing Lookups and Packet Classification: Theory and Practice* [McKeown 1999b], IEEE Hot Interconnects 8 (Stanford, CA) tutorial, August 2000, available from klamath.stanford.edu/~pankaj/talks/hoti_tutorial.ppt.

[Gupta 2000b] Pankaj Gupta, Balaji Prabhakar, and Stephen Boyd, "Near-Optimal Routing Lookups with Bounded Worst-Case Performance," *Proceedings of INFOCOM 2000* (Tel Aviv), vol.3, IEEE, New York, March 2000, pp. 1184–1192.

[Haas 1990] Zygmunt Haas, "A Communication Architecture for High Speed Networking," *Proceedings of IEEE INFOCOM'90* (San Francisco), IEEE, New York, June 1990, pp. 433–441.

[Haas 1993] Zygmunt Haas, Danny Cohen, Gurudatta M. Parulkar, and Ahmed N. Tantawy, eds., "Protocols for Gigabit Networks," *IEEE Journal on Selected Areas in Communications*, vol.11, no.4, IEEE, New York, May. 1993.

[Hadjitheodosiou 1999] Michael H. Hadjitheodosiou, Anthony Ephrimedes, and Daniel Friedman, "Broadband Access via Satellite," *Computer Networks*, vol.31, no.4, North-Holland/Elsevier, Amsterdam, February 1999, pp. 353–378.

[Hain 2000] Tony Hain, *Architectural Implications of NAT*, RFC 2993 (informational), November 2000.

[Händel 1998] Rainer Händel, Manfred N. Huber, and Stefan Schröder, *ATM Networks: Concepts, Protocols, and Applications*, 3rd ed., Addison-Wesley Longman, Harlow, UK, 1998.

[Handley 1999] Mark Handley, Henning Schulzrinne, Eve Schooler, and Jonathan Rosenberg, *SIP: Session Initiation Protocol*, RFC 2543 (standards track), March 1999.

[Hari 2000] Adiseshu Hari, Subbash Suri, and Guruddata M. Parulkar, "Detecting and Resolving Packet Filter Conflicts," *Proceedings of INFOCOM 2000* (Tel Aviv), vol.3, IEEE, New York, March 2000, pp. 1203–1212.

[Hayes 1988] John P. Hayes, *Computer Architecture and Organization*, McGraw-Hill, New York, 1988.

[Hayes 1991] J.F. Hayes, R. Breault, and M. Mehmet-Ali, "Performance Analysis of a Multicast Switch," *IEEE Transactions on Communications*, vol. 39, no.4, April 1991, IEEE, New York, pp. 581–587.

[Hayter 1991] M. Hayter and D. McAuley, "The Desk Area Network," *ACM Operating Systems Review*, vol.25, no.4, October 1991, pp. 14–21.

[Heidemann 1997] John Heidemann, Katia Obraczka, and Jospeh D. Touch, "Modeling the Performance of HTTP Over Several Transport Protocols," *IEEE/ACM Transactions on Networking*, vol.5, no.5, IEEE/ACM, New York, October 1997, pp. 616–630.

[Hills 1979] M.T. Hills, *Telecommunications Switching Systems*, MIT Press, Cambridge, MA, 1979.

[Hinden 1994] Robert M. Hinden, *Simple Internet Protocol Plus White Paper*, RFC 1710, October 1994.

[Hinton 1993] H. Scott Hinton, *An Introduction to Photonic Switching Fabrics*, Plenum Press, New York/Kluwer Academic Publishers, Norwell, MA, 1993.

[Hinton 1988] H. Scott Hinton, "Architectural Considerations for Photonic Switching Networks," *IEEE Journal on Selected Areas in Communications*, vol.6, no.7, IEEE, New York, August 1988, pp. 1209–1226.

[Hluchyj 1988] Michael G. Hluchyj and Mark J. Karol, "Queueing in High-Performance Packet Switching," *IEEE Journal on Selected Areas in Communications*, vol.6, no.9, December 1988, pp. 1587–1597.

[Hoberecht 1980] Verlin L. Hoberecht, "SNA Function Management," *IEEE Transactions on Communications*, vol.com-28, no.4, IEEE, New York, April 1980, pp. 594–603.

[Hoe 1996] Janey C. Hoe, "Improving the Start-up Behavior of a Congestion Control Scheme for TCP, *Proceedings of ACM SIGCOMM'96* (Palo Alto, CA), *Computer Communication Review*, vol.26, no.4, ACM, New York, August 1996, pp. 270–280.

[Hoffnagle 1995] Gene F. Hoffnagle, ed., Network Broadband Services special issue of *IBM Systems Journal*, vol.34, no.4, IBM, Armonk, NY, 1995.

[Hopper 1991] Andy Hopper, "Design and Use of High-Speed Networks in Multimedia Applications, *IFIP High Speed Networking III* 1991 (Berlin, DE), André Danthine and Otto Spaniol, eds., North-Holland/Elsevier, Amsterdam, 1991, 25–38.

[Hui 1988] Joseph Y. Hui, "Resource Allocation for Broadband Networks," *IEEE Journal on Selected Areas in Communications*, vol.6, no.9, IEEE, New York, December 1988, pp. 1598–1608.

[Hui 1990] Joseph Y. Hui, *Switching Theory for Integrated Broadband Networks*, Kluwer Academic Publishers, Norwell, MA, 1990.

[Hui 1994] Joseph Y. Hui and Thomas Renner, "Queueing Analysis for Multicast Packet Switching," *IEEE Transactions on Communications*, vol. 42, no.2/3/4, February/March/April 1994, IEEE, New York, 1994, pp. 723–731.

[Huitema 2000] Christian Huitema, *Routing in the Internet*, 2nd ed., Prentice Hall, Upper Saddle River, NJ, 2000.

[IEEE802.2] ANSI/IEEE Standard 802.2, 1998 Edition, ISO/IEC 8802–1:1998, Information technology—Telecommunications and information exchange between systems—Local and metropolitan are networks—Specific requirements—*Part 2: Logical Link Control*, IEEE, New York, 1998.

[IEEE802.3] IEEE Standard 802.3, 2000 Edition, Information technology—Telecommunications and information exchange between systems—Local and metropolitan are networks—Specific requirements—*Part 3: Carrier Sense Multiple Access with Collision Detection (CSMA/CD) Access Method and Physical Layer Specifications*, IEEE, New York, 2000.

[IEEE802.5] IEEE Standard 802.5, 1998 Edition, ISO/IEC 8802–5:1998, Information technology—Telecommunications and information exchange between systems—Local and metropolitan are networks—Specific requirements—*Part 5: Token Ring Access Method and Physical Layer Specifications*, IEEE, New York, 1998.

[IEEE802.11] IEEE Standard 802.11, 1997 Edition, Information technology—Telecommunications and information exchange between systems—Local and metropolitan are networks—Specific requirements—*Part 11: Wireless LAN Medium Access Control (MAC) and Physical Layer(PHY) Specifications*, IEEE, New York , 1997.

[IEEE802.11a] IEEE Standard 802.11a, Supplement to IEEE Standard for Information technology—Telecommunications and information exchange between systems—Local and metropolitan are networks—Specific requirements—*Part 11: Wireless LAN Medium Access Control (MAC) and Physical Layer(PHY) Specifications: High-Speed Physical Layer in the 5 GHz Band*, IEEE, New York, 1999.

[IEEE802.11b] IEEE Standard 802.11b, Supplement to IEEE Standard for Information technology—Telecommunications and information exchange between systems—Local and metropolitan are networks—Specific requirements—*Part 11: Wireless LAN Medium Access Control (MAC) and Physical Layer(PHY) Specifications: High-Speed Physical Layer in the 2.4 GHz Band*, IEEE, New York, 1999.

[IrDA 1998] Infrared Data Association, *Serial Infrared Physical Layer Specification*, version 1.3, October 1998, available from www.irda.org/standards/specifications.asp.

[IrDA 1999] Infrared Data Association, *Serial Infrared Physical Layer Specification for 16 Mb/s Addition (VFIR)*, January 1999, available from www.irda.org/standards/specifications.asp.

[ISO3309] ISO/IEC 3309:1993, *Information technology – Telecommunications and Information Exchange Between Systems – High-Level Data Link Control (HDLC) Procedures – Frame Structure*, 1993.

[ISO10918] ISO/IEC 10918-1:1994, *Information technology – Digital Compression and Coding of Continuous-Tone Still Images: Requirements and Guidelines* (Ed. 1, 182 p, XD), 1994.

[ISO13818] ISO/IEC 13818-1:2000, *Information Technology – Generic Coding of Moving Pictures and Associated Audio Information: Systems*, 2000.

[ISO7498] ISO/IEC Standard 7498:1983, *Information Technology—Basic Reference Model for Open Systems Interconnection*, 1983.

[ISO8473] ISO/IEC Standard 8473:1998 2nd, *Information Technology—Protocol for Providing the Connectionless-Mode Network Service: Protocol Specification*, 1998.

[ITUX.25] ITU-T Standard X.25, *Interface between Data Terminal Equipment (DTE) and Data Circuit-Terminating Equipment (DC) for Terminals Operating in the Packet Mode and Connected to Public Data Networks by Dedicated Circuit*, ITU-T standard X.25, October 1996.

[Ivory 2001] Melody Y. Ivory, Rashmi R. Sinha, and Marti A. Hearst, "Empirically Validated Web Page Design Metrics," *Proceedings of ACM SIGCHI 2001* (Seattle), ACM, New York, March 2001.

[Jackson 2000] Alden W. Jackson, James P.G. Sterbenz, Matthew N. Condell, Joel Levin, and David J. Waitzman, *SENCOMM Architecture* version 1.1, BBN Technical Memorandum, no.1278, Cambridge, MA, Jan 2001, available from www.ir.bbn.com/projects/sencomm/doc/architecture.ps.

[Jacobson 1988] Van Jacobson, "Congestion Avoidance and Control," *Proceedings of ACM SIGCOMM'88* (Stanford, CA), *ACM Computer Communication Review*, vol.18, no.4, ACM, New York, August 1988, pp. 314–329.

[Jacobson 1990] Van Jacobson, "4BSD Header Prediction," tutorial presentation foils, *ACM Computer Communication Review*, vol.20, no.1, ACM, New York, April 1990, pp. 13–15.

[Jacobson 1992a] Van Jacobson, Robert Braden, and David A. Borman, *TCP Extensions for High Performance*, RFC 1323 (standards track), May 1992.

[Jacobson 1992b] Van Jacobson and Mike Karels. "Congestion Avoidance and Control," ftp.ee.lbl.gov/papers/congavoid.ps.Z, revision of [Jacobson 1988].

[Jain 1986] Raj Jain, "A Timeout-Based Congestion Control Scheme for Window Flow-Controlled Networks," *IEEE Journal on Selected Areas in Communications*, vol.sac-4, no.7, IEEE, New York, October 1986, pp. 1162–1167.

[Jain 1989] Raj Jain, "A Delay-Based Approach for Congestion Avoidance in Interconnected Heterogeneous Networks," *ACM Computer Communication Review*, vol.19, no.5, ACM, New York, October 1989, pp. 56–71.

[Jain 1991] Raj Jain, *The Art of Computer Systems Performance Analysis*, John Wiley, New York, 1991.

[Jain 1993] Bijendra N. Jain and Ashok K. Agrawala, *Open Systems Interconnection*, McGraw-Hill, New York, 1993.

[Jajszczyk 1993] Andrzej Jajszczyk and H. T. Mouftah, "Photonic Fast Packet Switching," *IEEE Communications*, vol.31, no.2, IEEE, New York, February 1993, pp. 58–65.

[Jansen 1988] Mogens Nordberg Jensen and Morten Skov, "VLSI-Architectures Implementing Lower layer Protocols in Very High Data Rate LANs," *IFIP High Speed Local Area Networks II*, HSLAN'88 (Liège, BE), Otto Spaniol and André Danthine, eds., North-Holland, Amsterdam, 1990, pp. 187–205.

[Joel 1996] Amos E. Joel, Jr., Peter O'Reilly, and Richard A. Thompson, "Circuit Switching for Broadband ISDN and Beyond" guest editorial, *IEEE Journal on Selected Areas in Communications*, vol.14, no.2, IEEE, New York, February 1996, pp. 289–292.

[Johnson 1989] Robert H. Johnson, *MVS: Concepts and Facilities*, McGraw-Hill, New York, 1989.

[Johnson 1991] Marjory J. Johnson, ed., *Protocols for High Speed Networks II*, IFIP, North-Holland/Elsevier, Amsterdam, 1991.

[Johnson 1992] Marjory J. Johnson, "Using High-Performance Networks to Enable Computational Aerosciences Applications," *Protocols for High Speed Networks III*, IFIP PfHSN'1992 (Stockholm, SE), May 1992, Per Gunningberg, Björn Perhson, and Stephen Pink, eds., Elsevier/North-Holland, 1993, pp. 137–152.

[Johnston 1999] William E. Johnston, "Realtime Widely Distributed Instrumentation Systems," in *The Grid: Blueprint for a New Computing Infrastructure*, Ian Foster and Carl Kesselman, eds., Morgan Kaufmann, San Francisco, 1999, pp. 75–103.

[Kadaba 1983] Bharath-Kumar Kadaba and Jeffrey M. Jaffe, "Routing to Multiple Destinations in Computer Networks," *IEEE Transactions on Communications*, vol.com-31, no.3, IEEE, New York, March, 1983, pp. 343–351.

[Kahn 1978] R.E. Kahn, S. Gronemeyer, J. Burchfiel, and R. Kunzelman, "Advances in Packet Radio Technology," *Proceedings of the IEEE*, vol.66, no.11, IEEE, New York, November 1978, pp. 1468–1496.

[Kahn 1999] J.M. Kahn, R.H. Katz, and K.S.G. Pister, "Mobile Networking for Smart Dust," *Proceedings of ACM/IEEE MobiCom'99* (Seattle, WA), ACM, New York, 1999, pp. 271–278.

[Kallel 1988] Samir Kallel and David Haccoun, "Sequential Decoding with ARQ and Code Combining: A Robust Hybrid FEC/ARQ System," *IEEE Transactions on Communications*, vol.36, no.7, IEEE, New York, July 1988, pp. 773–780.

[Kallel 1994] Samir Kallel, "Efficient Hybrid ARQ Protocols with Adaptive Forward Error Correction," *IEEE Transactions on Communications*, vol.42, no.2/3/4, IEEE, New York, February/March/April 1994, pp. 281–289.

[Kam 1999] Anthony C. Kam and Kai-Yeung Siu, "Linear-Complexity Algorithms for QOS Support in Input-Queued Switches with No Speedup," *IEEE Journal on Selected Areas in Communications*, vol.17, no.6, IEEE, New York, June 1999, pp. 1040–1056.

[Kaminow 1997a] Ivan P. Kaminow and Thomas L. Koch, eds., *Optical Fiber Telecommunications IIIA*, Academic Press, San Diego, CA, 1997.

[Kaminow 1997b] Ivan P. Kaminow and Thomas L. Koch, eds., *Optical Fiber Telecommunications IIIB*, Academic Press, San Diego, CA, 1997.

[Kanakia 1988] Hamant Kanakia and D.R. Cheriton, "The VMP Network Adapter Board (NAB): High Performance Communication for Multiprocessors," *Proceedings of ACM SIGCOMM'88* (Stanford, CA), *Computer Communication Review*, vol.18, no.4, ACM, New York, August 1988, pp.175–187.

[Karandikar 2000] Shrikrishna Karandikar, Shivkumar Kalyanaraman, Prasad Bagal, and Bob Packer, "TCP Rate Control," *ACM SIGCOMM Computer Communication Review*, vol.30, no.1, ACM, New York, January 2000, pp. 45–58.

[Karn 1987] Phil Karn and Craig Partridge, "Improving Round-Trip Time Estimates in Reliable Transport Protocols," *Proceedings of ACM SIGCOMM'87* (Stowe, VT), *Computer Communication Review*, vol.17, no.5, ACM, New York, August 1987, pp. 2–7.

[Karn 2000] Phil Karn, Aaron Falk, Joseph D. Touch, Marie-Jose Montpetit, Jamshid Mahdavi, Gabriel Montenegro, Dan Grossman, and Gorry Fairhurst, *Advice for Internet Subnetwork Designers*, Internet Draft draft-ietf-pilc-link-design-04.txt, work in progress, November 2000.

[Karp 1988] Sherman Karp, Robert M. Gagliardi, Steven E. Moran, and Larry B. Stouts, *Optical Channels: Fibers, Clouds, Water, and the Atmosphere*, Plenum Press, New York/Kluwer Academic Publishers, Norwell, MA, 1988.

[Kartalopoulos 2000] Stamatios V. Kartalopoulos, *Introduction to DWDM Technology: Data in a Rainbow*, SPIE Optical Engineering Press, Bellingham, WA/IEEE Press, New York, 2000.

[Katz 1993] Dave Katz and Peter S. Ford, "TUBA: Replacing IP with CLNP," *IEEE Network*, vol.7, no.3, IEEE, New York, May 1993, pp. 38–44.

[Kaufman 1995] Charlie Kaufman, Radia Perlman, and Mike Speciner, *Network Security: PRIVATE Communication in a PUBLIC World*, Prentice Hall, Englewood Cliffs, NJ, 1995.

[Kaufman 1999] Elizabeth Kaufman and Andrew Newman, *Implementing IPsec*, John Wiley, New York, 1999.

[Kent 1987] Christopher A. Kent and Jeffrey C. Mogul, "Fragmentation Considered Harmful," *Proceedings of ACM SIGCOMM'87* (Stowe, VT), *Computer Communication Review*, vol.17, no.5, ACM, New York, August 1987, pp. 390–401.

[Kent 1998] Stephen Kent and Randall Atkinson, *Security Architecture for IP*, RFC 2401 (standards track), November 1998.

[Kermani 1979] Parviz Kermani and Leonard Kleinrock, "Virtual Cut-Through: A New Computer Communications Switching Technique," *Computer Networks*, vol.3, no.4, North-Holland, Amsterdam, September 1979, pp. 267–286.

[Keshav 1991] Srinivasan Keshav, "A Control-Theoretic Approach to Flow Control," *Proceedings of ACM SIGCOMM'91* (Zürich), *ACM Computer Communication Review*, vol.21, no.4, ACM, New York, September 1991, pp. 3–15.

[Keshav 1997] Srinivasan Keshav, *An Engineering Approach to Computer Networking: ATM Networks, the Internet, and the Telephone Network*, Addison-Wesley, Reading, MA, 1997.

[Keshav 1998] S. Keshav and Rosen Sharma, "Issues and Trends in Router Design," *IEEE Communications*, vol.36, no.5, IEEE, New York, May 1998, pp. 144–151.

[Kilkki 1999] Kalevi Kilkki, *Differentiated Services for the Internet*, Macmillan Technical Publishing, Indianapolis, IN, 1999.

[Kleinrock 1961] Leonard Kleinrock, "Information Flow in Large Communication Nets," RLE Quarterly Progress Report, July 1961, available from www.lk.cs.ucla.edu/LK/Bib/REPORT/PhD.

[Kleinrock 1977] Leonard Kleinrock and Farouk Kamoun, "Hierarchical Routing for Large Networks: Performance Evaluation and Optimization," *Computer Networks*, vol.1, no.3, North-Holland, Amsterdam, January 1977, pp. 155–174.

[Knox 1993] D. Knox and S. Panchanathan, "Parallel Searching Techniques for Routing Table Lookup," *Proceedings of INFOCOM'93* (Florence), IEEE, New York, 1993, pp. 1400–1405.

[Kodak 2001] *Kodak Photo CD Frequently Asked Questions*, Eastman Kodak Company, Rochester, NY, www.kodak.com/global/en/service/faqs/faq1001a.shtml.

[Kohonen 1980] Teuvo Kohonen, *Content Addressable Memories*, Springer-Verlag, Berlin, 1980.

[Koufopavlou 1994] Odysseas G. Koufopavlou, Ahmed N. Tantawy, and Martina Zitterbart, "A Comparison of Gigabit Router Architectures," *IFIP High Performance Networking V* 1994 (Grenoble, FR), S. Fdida, ed., North-Holland Elsevier, Amsterdam, 1994, 107–121.

[Krishna 1999b] Pattabhiraman Krishna, Naimish S. Patel, Anna Charny, and Robert J. Simcoe, "On the Speedup Required for Work-Conserving Crossbar Switches," *IEEE Journal on Selected Areas in Communications*, vol.17, no.6, IEEE, New York, June 1999, pp. 1057–1066.

[Krishnakumar 1989] A.S. Krishnakumar and Krishnan Sabnani, "VLSI Implementations of Communications Protocols—A Survey," *IEEE Journal on Selected Areas in Communications*, vol.7, no.7, IEEE, New York, September 1989, pp. 1082–1090.

[Krishnan 1997] Rajesh Krishnan, Dinesh Venkatesh, and Thomas D. Little, "A Failure and Overload Tolerance Mechanism for Continuous Media Servers," *Proceedings of ACM Multimedia* (Seattle, WA), ACM, New York, November 1997, pp. 131–142.

[Krishnan 1999a] Rajesh Krishnan, "Timeshared Video-on-Demand: A Workable Solution to VOD)," *IEEE Multimedia*, vol.6, no.1, IEEE, New York, January–March 1999, pp. 77–79.

[Krishnan 1999b] Rajesh Krishnan, Ram Ramamathan, and Martha Steenstrup, "Optimization Algorithms for Large Self-Structuring Networks," *Proceedings of INFOCOM'99* (New York), vol.1, IEEE, New York, March 1999, pp. 71–78.

[Krishnan 2000a] P. Krishnan, Danny Raz, and Yuval Shavitt, "The Cache Location Problem," *IEEE/ACM Transactions on Networking*, vol.8 no.5, IEEE/ACM, New York, October 2000, pp. 568–582.

[Krishnan 2000b] Rajesh Krishnan, James P.G. Sterbenz, and A. Lyman Chapin, "Routing Issues in Interconnecting IP Networks with the PetaWeb," *International Telecommunication Network Planning Symposium (Networks 2000)* (Toronto), September 2000, available from www.ir.bbn.com/projects/petaweb/papers/networks2000.pdf.

[Kuck 1978] David J. Kuck, *The Structure of Computers and Computations*, John Wiley, New York, 1978.

[Kulik 1999] Joanna Kulik, Robert Coulter, Dennis Rockwell, and Craig Partridge, *A Simulation Study of Paced TCP*, BBN Technical Memorandum, no.1218, BBN Technologies, Cambridge, MA, August 1999.

[Kulzer 1984] John J. Kulzer and Warren A. Montgomery, "Statistical Switching Architectures for Future Services," *Proceedings of the International Switching Symposium (ISS'94)*, Florence, May 1984, pp. 1–6.

[Kumar 1998] Vijay P. Kumar, T.V. Lakshman, and Dimitrios Stiliadis, "Beyond Best Effort: Router Architectures for the Differentiated Services of Tomorrow's Internet," *IEEE Communications*, vol.36, no.5, IEEE, New York, May 1998, pp. 152–164.

[Kümmerle 1978] Karl Kümmerle and Harry Rudin, "Packet and Circuit Switching: Cost/Performance Boundaries," *Computer Networks*, vol.2, no.1, North-Holland, Amsterdam, February 1978, pp. 2–17.

[Kung 1993] H.T. Kung and Alan Chapman, "The FCVC (Flow-Controlled Virtual Channels) Proposal for ATM Networks: A Summary," *Proceedings of ICNP'93* (San Francisco), IEEE, New York, October 1993, pp. 116–127.

[Kung 1995] H.T. Kung and Robert Morris, "Credit-Based Flow Control for ATM Networks," *IEEE Network*, vol.9, no.2, IEEE, New York, March/April 1995, pp. 40–48.

[Kuo 1998] Franklin F. Kuo, Wolfgang Effelsberg, and J.J. Garcia-Luna-Aceves eds., *Multimedia Communications: Protocols and Applications*, Prentice Hall, Upper Saddle River, NJ, 1998.

[Kurose 2000] James F. Kurose and Keith W. Ross, *Computer Networking: A Top-Down Approach Featuring the Internet*, Addison-Wesley, Reading, MA, 2000.

[Kwok 1999] Timothy C. Kwok, "Residential Broadband Architecture Over ADSL and G.Lite (G.992.2): PPP Over ATM," *IEEE Communications*, vol.37, no.5, IEEE, New York, pp. 84–89.

[Labovitz 1998] Craig Labovitz, G. Robert Malan, and Farnam Jahanian, "Internet Routing Instability," *IEEE/ACM Transactions on Networking*, vol.6, no.5, IEEE/ACM, New York, October 1998, pp. 515–528.

[Labovitz 2000] Craig Labovitz, Abha Ahuja, Abhijit Bose, and Farnam Jahanian, "Delayed Internet Routing Convergence," *Proceedings of ACM*

SIGCOMM 2000 (Stockholm, SE), *Computer Communication Review*, vol.30, no.4, ACM, New York, August 2000, pp. 175–187.

[Lackey 1995] Raymond J. Lackey and Donald W. Upmal, "Speakeasy: The Military Software Radio," *IEEE Communications*, vol.33, no.5, IEEE, New York, May 1995, pp. 56–61.

[Lakshman 1998] T.V. Lakshman and Dimitrious Stiliadis, "High-Speed Policy-Based Packet Forwarding Using Efficient Multi-Dimensional Range Matching," *Proceedings of ACM SIGCOMM'98*, (Vancouver, British Columbia), *Computer Communication Review*, vol.28, no.4, ACM, New York, August 1998, pp. 203–214.

[Lambert 1995] Stephen G. Lambert and William L. Casey, *Laser Communications in Space*, Artech House, Norwood, MA, 1995.

[Leach 1983] Paul J. Leach, et al., "The Architecture of an Integrated Local Network," *IEEE Journal on Selected Areas in Communications*, vol. sac-1, no.5, IEEE, New York, November 1983, pp. 842–856.

[Lee 1988] Tony T. Lee, "Non-Blocking Copy Networks for Multicast Packet Switching," *IEEE Journal on Selected Areas in Communications*, vol.6, no.9, IEEE, New York, December 1988, pp. 1609–1616.

[Lee 1994] Tony T. Lee and Soung C. Liew, "Broadband Packet Switches Based on Dilated Interconnection Networks," *IEEE Transactions on Communications*, vol.42, no.2/3/4, IEEE, New York, February/March/April 1994, pp. 732–744.

[Leiner] Barry M. Leiner, Vinton G. Cerf, David D. Clark, Robert E. Kahn, Leonard Kleinrock, Daniel C. Lynch, Jon Postel, Larry G. Roberts, and Stephen Wolff, *A Brief History of the Internet*, www.isoc.org/internet/history/brief.html.

[Leiner 1988] Barry M. Leiner, ed., *Critical Issues in High Bandwidth Networking*, RFC 1077, November 1988.

[Leland 1993] W.E. Leland, Murad S. Taqqu, Walter Willinger, and Daniel V. Wilson, "On the Self-Similar Nature of Ethernet Traffic," *Proceedings of ACM SIGCOMM'93* (San Francisco), *Computer Com-munication Review*, vol.23, no.4, ACM, New York, September 1993, pp. 183–193.

[Lemme 1999] Peter W. Lemme, Simon M. Glenister, and Alan W. Miller, "Iridium Aeronautical Satellite Communications," *IEEE Aerospace and Electronic Systems*, vol.14, no.11, IEEE, New York, November 1999, pp. 11–16.

[Leslie 1996] Ian M. Leslie, Derek McAuley, Richard Black, Timothy Roscoe, Paul Barham, David Evers, Robin Fairbairns, and Eoin Hyden, "The Design and Implementation of an Operating System to Support Distributed Multimedia Applications," *IEEE Journal on Selected Areas in Communications*, vol.14, no.7, IEEE, New York, 1996.

[Levine 1996] Brian Neil Levine and J.J. Garcia-Luna-Aceves, "A Comparison of Known Classes of Reliable Multicast Protocols," *Proceedings of ICNP'96* (Columbus, OH), IEEE, New York, October 1996, pp. 112–121.

[Li 1989] Li, K., Hudak, P., "Memory Coherence in Shared Virtual Memory Systems," *ACM Transaction on Computer Systems*, vol.7, no.4, ACM, New York, November 1989, pp. 321–359.

[Lindgren 1994] Per Lindgren and Christer Bohm "Fast Connection Establishment in the DTM Gigabit Network, IFIP *High Performance Networking V*, 1994 (Grenoble, France), S. Fdida, ed., North-Holland Elsevier, Amsterdam, 1994, pp. 285–296.

[Livermore 1998] Eric Livermore, Richard P. Skillen, Maged Beshai, and Marek Wernik, "Architecture and Control of an Adaptive High-Capacity Flat Network," *IEEE Communications*, vol.36, no.5, IEEE, New York, May 1998, pp. 106–112.

[Lockwood 2000] John W. Lockwood, Jonathan S. Turner, and David E. Taylor, "Field Programmable Port Extender (FPX) for Distributed Routing and Queuing," *ACM International Symposium on Field Programmable Gate Arrays FPGA'2000* (Monterey, CA), ACM, New York, February 2000, pp. 137–144.

[Lyles 1992] J. Bryan Lyles and Daniel C. Swinehart, "The Emerging Gigabit Environment and the Role of Local ATM," *IEEE Communications*, vol.30, no.4, IEEE, New York, April 1992, pp. 52–58.

[Lyles 1995] J. Bryan Lyles, Ira Richer, and James P.G. Sterbenz, "Applications Enabling the Wide Scale Deployment of Gigabit Networks" (editorial), *IEEE Journal on Selected Areas in Communications*, vol.13, no.5, IEEE, New York, June 1995, pp.765–767.

[Lyon 1991] Tom Lyon, *Simple and Efficient Adaptation Layer*, ANSI T1S1.5/91–292, August 1991.

[Mah 1997] Bruce A. Mah, "An Empirical Model of HTTP Network Traffic," *Proceedings of INFOCOM'97* (Kobe, Japan), vol.2, IEEE, New York, April 1997, pp. 592–600.

[Mahanti 2000] Anirban Mahanti, Carey Williamson, and Derek Eager, "Traffic Analysis of a Web Caching Hierarchy," *IEEE Network*, vol.14, no.3, IEEE, New York, May/June 2000, pp. 16–23.

[Malis 1999] Andrew G. Malis and William Allen Simpson, *PPP over SONET/SDH*, RFC 2615 (proposed standard), June 1999.

[Mallory 1990] Tracy Mallory and A. Kullberg, *Incremental Updating of the Internet Checksum*, RFC 1141, January 1990.

[Maltz 1998] David A. Maltz and Pravin Bhagwat, "MSOCKS: An Architecture for Transport Layer Mobility," *Proceedings of INFOCOM '98* (San Francisco), vol. 3, IEEE, New York, March 1998, pp. 1037–1045.

[Manchester 1998] James Manchester, Jon Anderson, Bharat Doshi, and Subra Dravida, "IP over SONET," *IEEE Communications*, vol.36, no.5, IEEE, New York, May 1998, pp. 136–141.

[Mankin 1997] Allison Mankin, ed., *Resource ReSerVation Protocol (RSVP) Version 1 Applicability Statement—Some Guidelines on Deployment*, RFC 2208 (informational), September 1997.

[Marcus 1998] William S. Marcus, Ilija Hadzic, Anthony J. McAuley and Jonathan M. Smith, "Protocol Boosters: Applying Programmability to Network Infrastructures," *IEEE Communications*, vol.36, no.10, IEEE, New York, October 1998, pp. 79–83.

[Mark 1999] William Mark, "Turning Pervasive Computing into Mediated Spaces," *IBM Systems Journal*, vol.38, no.4, IBM, Armonk, NY, 1999, pp. 677–692.

[Markatos 1998] Evangelos P. Markatos and Catherine E. Chronaki, "A Top-10 Approach to Prefetching on the Web," *Proceedings of INET'98* (Geneva), Internet Society, Reston, VA.

[Mathis 1996] Matt Mathis, Jamshid Mahdavi, Sally Floyd, and Allyn Romanow, *TCP Selective Acknowledgement Options*, RFC 2018 (standards track), October 1996.

[Maufer 1988] Thomas A. Maufer, *Deploying IP Multicast in the Enterprise*, Prentice Hall, Upper Saddle River, NJ, 1998.

[Maxemchuck 1987] Nicholas F. Maxemchuk, "Routing in the Manhattan Street Network," *IEEE Transactions on Communications*, vol.com-35, no.5, IEEE, New York, May 1987, pp. 503–512.

[Maxwell 1999] Kim Maxwell, *Residential Broadband: An Insider's Guide to the Battle for the Last Mile*, John Wiley, New York, 1999.

[Mazraani 1990] Tony Y. Mazraani and Gurudatta M. Parulkar, "Specification of a Multipoint Congram-Oriented High Performance Internet Protocol," *Proceedings of INFOCOM'90* (San Francisco), IEEE, New York, June 1990, pp. 450–457.

[McAuley 1990] Anthony J. McAuley, "Reliable Broadband Communication Using a Burst Erasure Code," *Proceedings of ACM SIGCOMM'90* (Philadelphia, PA), *Computer Communication Review* vol.20, no.4, ACM, New York, September 1990, pp. 297–306.

[McAuley 1993] Anthony J. McAuley and Paul Francis, "Fast Routing Table Lookup Using CAMs," *Proceedings of INFOCOM'93* (Florence), IEEE, New York, 1993, pp. 1382–1391.

[McCanne 1996] Steven McCanne, Van Jacobson, and Martin Vetterli, "Receiver-Driven Layered Multicast," *Proceedings of ACM SIGCOMM'96* (Palo Alto, CA), *Computer Communication Review*, vol.26, no.4, ACM, New York, August 1996, pp. 117–130.

[McDonald 1983] John C. McDonald, *Fundamentals of Digital Switching*, Plenum Press, New York/Kluwer Academic Publishers, Norwell, MA, 1983.

[McGarty 1992] Terrence P. McGarty, G. James Blaine, and Morris Goldberg, eds., "Medical Communications," *IEEE Journal on Selected Areas in Communications*, vol.10, no.7, IEEE, New York, September 1992.

[McGovern 1994] Michael McGovern and Robert Ullman, *CATNIP: Common Architecture for the Internet*, RFC 1707 (informational), October 1994.

[McKeown 1996] Neck McKeown, Venkat Anantharam, and Jean Walrand, "Achieving 100% Throughput in an Input-Queued Switch," *Proceedings of INFOCOM'96* (San Francisco), IEEE, New York, March 1996, pp. 296–302.

[McKeown 1997] Nick McKeown, Martin Izzard, Adisak Mekkittkul, William Ellersick, and Mark Horowitz, "Tiny Tera: A Packet Switch Core," *IEEE Micro*, vol.17, no.1, January/February 1997, pp. 26–33.

[McKeown 1999a] Nick McKeown, "The *i*SLIP Scheduling Algorithm for Input Queued Switches," *IEEE/ACM Transactions on Networking*, vol.7, no.2, IEEE/ACM, New York, April 1999, pp. 188–201.

[McKeown 1999b] Nick McKeown and Balaji Prabhakar, *High Performance Switches and Routers: Theory and Practice*, ACM SIGCOMM'99 (Cambridge, MA) tutorial, August 1999, available from tiny-tera.stanford.edu/~nickm/talks.

[McKusick 1996] Marshall Kirk McKusick, *The Design and Implementation of the 4.4BSD Operating System*, Addison-Wesley, Reading, MA, 1996.

[McQuillan 1977] John M. McQuillan and David Walden, "The ARPA Network Design Decisions," *Computer Networks*, vol.1, no.5, North-Holland, Amsterdam, August 1977, pp. 243–289.

[Medina 2000] Octavio Medina, Francis Dupont, and Laurent Toutain, *A Proposal for the Use of ECN Bits with UDP Flows*, Internet Draft draft-medina-ecn-udp-00.txt, work in progress, July 2000.

[Mei 1997] Yousong Mei and Chunming Qiao, "Efficient Distributed Control Protocols for WDMA-Optical Networks," *Proceedings of International Conference on Computer Communication and Networks (IC³N)* (Las Vegas), IEEE, New York, September 1997, pp. 150–153.

[Meijer 1982] Anton Meijer and Paul Peters, *Computer Network Architectures*, Computer Science Press, Rockville, MD, 1982.

[Messina 1999] Paul Messina, "Distributed Supercomputing Applications," in *The Grid: Blueprint for a New Computing Infrastructure*, Ian Foster and Carl Kesselman, eds., Morgan Kaufmann, San Francisco, 1999, pp. 55–73.

[Metcalfe 1976] Robert M. Metcalfe and David R. Boggs, "Ethernet: Distributed Packet Switching for Local Computer Networks," *Communications of the ACM*, vol.19, no.5, ACM, New York, July 1976, pp.395–404.

[Mettala 1999] Riku Mettala, *Bluetooth Protocol Architecture*, available from www.bluetooth.com.

[Midwinter 1993a] John E. Midwinter, ed., *Photonics in Switching, Volume I: Background and Components*, Academic Press, San Diego, CA, 1993.

[Midwinter 1993b] John E. Midwinter, ed., *Photonics in Switching, Volume II: Systems*, Academic Press, San Diego, CA, 1993.

[Miller 2001] Brent A. Miller and Chatschik Bisdikian, *Bluetooth Revealed*, Prentice Hall, Upper Saddle River, NJ, 2001.

[Mills 1987] David L. Mills and Hans-Werner Braun, "The NSFNET Backbone Architecture," *Proceedings of ACM SIGCOMM'87* (Stowe, VT), *Computer Communication Review*, vol.17, no.5, ACM, New York, August 1987, pp. 191–196.

[Mills 1990] David L. Mills, "On the Accuracy and Stability of Clocks Synchronized by the Network Time Protocol in the Internet System," *ACM Computer Communication Review*, vol.20, no.1, ACM, New York, January 1990, pp. 65–75.

[Mills 1991] David L. Mills, "Internet Time Synchronization: The Network Time Protocol," *IEEE Transactions on Communications*, vol.com-39, no.10 IEEE, New York, October 1991, pp. 1482–1493.

[Minoli 1998] Daniel Minoli and Andrew Schmidt, *Network Layer Switched Services*, John Wiley, New York, 1998.

[Mishra 1992] Partho P. Mishra and Hemant Kanakia, "A Hop by Hop Rate-Based Congestion Control Scheme," *Proceedings of ACM SIGCOMM'92*, (Baltimore, MD), *Computer Communication Review*, vol.22, no.4, ACM, New York, October 1992, pp. 112–123.

[Modiano 1999] Eytan Modiano and Sedat Ölçer, eds., Broadband Access Networks special issue of *Computer Networks*, vol.31, no.4, North-Holland/Elsevier, Amsterdam, February 1999.

[Mogul 1990] Jeffrey C. Mogul and Stephen E. Deering, "Path MTU Discovery," RFC 1191, November 1990.

[Mogul 1991] Jeffrey C. Mogul and Anita Borg, "The Effects of Context Switches on Cache Performance," *Proceedings of the 4th International Conference on Architectural Support for Programming Languages and Operating Systems (ASPLOS)* (Santa Clara, CA), ACM, New York, April 1991, pp. 75–84.

[Mogul 1995] Jeffrey C. Mogul, "The Case for Persistent-Connection HTTP," *ACM Computer Communication Review*, vol.25, no.4, ACM, New York, October 1995, pp. 299–313.

[Moldklev 1994] Kjersti Moldklev and Per Gunningberg, "Deadlock Situations in TCP over ATM," IFIP/IEEE PfHSN IV, 1994 (Vancouver, British Columbia), Gerald Neufeld and Mabo Ito, eds., Chapman and Hall, New York, 1995, pp. 244–259.

[Molle 1994] Mart M. Molle, *A New Binary Logarithmic Arbitration Method for Ethernet*, University of Toronto Computer Systems Research Institute technical report CSRI-298, Toronto, July 1994.

[Moore 1999] Reagan W. Moore, Chaitanya Baru, Richard Marciano, Arcot Rajasekar, and Michael Wan, "Data-Intensive Computing," in *The Grid: Blueprint for a New Computing Infrastructure*, Ian Foster and Carl Kesselman, eds., Morgan Kaufmann, San Francisco, 1999, pp. 105–129.

[Mouftah 1999] Hussein T. Mouftah and Jaafar M.H. Elmirghani, eds., *Photonic Switching Technology: Systems and Networks*, IEEE Press, New York, 1999.

[Mukherjee 1997] Biswanath Mukherjee, *Optical Communication Networks*, McGraw-Hill, New York, 1997.

[Nagle 1984] John Nagle *Congestion Control in IP/TCP Internetworks*, RFC 896, January 1984.

[Nagle 1987] John Nagle, "On Packet Switches with Infinite Storage," *IEEE Transactions on Communications*, vol. com-35, no.4, April 1987, IEEE, New York, pp. 435–438.

[Nahum 1995] Eric Nahum, Sean O'Malley, Hilarie Orman, and Richard Schroeppel, "Toward High Performance Cryptographic Software," *Proceedings of Architecture and Implementation of High Performance Communications Subsystems HPCS'95* (Mystic, CT), IEEE, New York, August 1995, pp 69–72.

[Napster 1999] www.napster.com.

[Nechvatal 2000] James Nechvatal, Elaine Barker, Lawrence Bassham, William Burr, Morris Dworkin, James Foti, and Edward Roback, *Report on the Development of the Advanced Encryption Standard (AES)*, NIST Information Technology Laboratory, Computer Security Division, Washington, DC, October 2000, availble from http://csrc.nist.gov/encryption/aes.

[Nelson 1965] Theodor H. Nelson, "A File Structure for the Complex, The Changing and The Indeterminate," *Proceedings of the ACM 20th National Conference*, ACM, New York, 1965.

[Netravali 1990] Arun N. Netravili, Willian D. Roome, and Krishnan Sabnani, "Design and Implementation of a High-Speed Transport Protocol," *IEEE Transactions on Communications*, vol.38, no.11, IEEE, New York, November 1990, pp. 2010–2024.

[Neufeld 1995] Gerald Neufeld and Mabo Ito, eds., *Protocols for High Speed Networks IV*, IFIP, Chapman & Hall, London/Kluwer Academic Publishers, Norwell, MA, 1995.

[Neukermans 2001] Armand Neukermans and Rajiv Ramaswami, "MEMS Technology for Optical Networking Applications, *IEEE Communications*, vol.39, no.1, IEEE, New York, January 2001, pp. 62–69.

[Newman 1992], Peter Newman , "ATM Technology for Corporate Networks," *IEEE Communications*, vol.30, no.4, IEEE, New York, April 1992, pp. 91–101.

[Newman 1996] Peter Newman, Tom Lyon, and Greg Minshall, "Flow Labeled IP: A Connectionless Approach to ATM," *Proceedings of INFOCOM'96* (San Francisco), vol.3, IEEE, New York, March 1996, pp. 1251–1260.

[Newman 1997] Peter Newman, Greg Minshall, and L. Huston, "IP Switching and Gigabit Routers," *IEEE Communications*, vol.35, no.1, IEEE, New York, January 1997, pp. 64–69.

[Nielsen 2000] Nielsen//NetRatings, www.nielsen-netratings.com.

[Noll 1998] A. Michael Noll, *Introduction to Telephones and Telephone Switching Systems*, Artech House, Norwood, MA, 1998.

[Nordbotten 2000] Agne Nordbotten, "LMDS Systems and their Application," *IEEE Communications*, vol.38, no.6, IEEE, New York, June 2000, pp. 150–154.

[NRC 1993] *Applying Information Technology for Scientific Research*, National Research Council, National Academy Press, Washington, DC, 1993.

[NRC 1994] *Realizing the Information Future: The Internet and Beyond*, Computer Science and Telecommunications Board, National Research Council, National Academy Press, Washington, DC, 1994, p. 53.

[Nussbaumer 1995] Jean-Paul Nussbaumer, Baiju V. Patel, Frank Schaffa, and James P.G. Sterbenz, "Networking Requirements for Interactive Video on Demand," *IEEE Journal on Selected Areas in Communications*, vol.13, no.5, IEEE, New York, June 1995, pp.779–787.

[O'Keefe 1998] Matthew T. O'Keefe, "Shared File Systems and Fibre Channel," *Proceeding of the 6th NASA Goddard Space Flight Center Conference on Mass Storage and Technologies* (College Park, MD), NASA Goddard Space Flight Center, Greenbelt, MD, March 1998.

[O'Malley 1990] Sean W. O'Malley and Larry L. Peterson, "A Highly Layered Architecture for High-Speed Networks," *Protocols for High Speed Networks II*, IFIP PfHSN'90 (Palo Alto, CA), November 1990, Marjory Johnson, ed., Elsevier/North-Holland, Amsterdam, 1991, pp. 141–156.

[O'Reilly 1987] Peter O'Reilly, "Burst and Fast Packet Switching: Performance Comparisons," *Computer Networks and ISDN Systems*, North-Holland, Amsterdam, vol.13, no.1, 1987, pp. 21–32.

[Obraczka 1997] Katia Obraczka, "Multicast Transport Protocols: A Survey and Taxonomy," *IEEE Communications*, vol.36, no.1, IEEE, New York, January 1998, pp. 94–103.

[Ohnishi 1988] Hirokazu Ohnishi, Tadanobu Okada, and Kiyohiro Noguchi, "Flow Control Schemes and Delay/Loss Tradeoff in ATM Networks," *IEEE Journal on Selected Areas in Communications*, vol.6, no.9, IEEE, New York, December 1988, pp. 1609–1616.

[Oie 1990] Yuji Oie, Tatsuya Suda, Masayuki Murata, David Kolson, and Hideo Miyahara, "Survey of Switching Techniques in High-Speed Networks and Their Performance," *Proceedings of INFOCOM'90* (San Francisco), IEEE, New York, June 1990, pp. 1242–1251.

[Onvural 1997] Raif O. Onvural and Rao Cherukuri, *Signaling in ATM Networks*, Artech House, Norwood, MA, 1997.

[Organick 1972] Elliot I. Organick, *The Multics System: An Examination of Its Structure*, MIT Press, Cambridge, MA, 1972.

[Overmars 1996] M.H. Overmars and A.F. van der Stappen, "Range Searching and Point Location Among Fat Objects," *Journal of Algorithms*, vol.21, no.3, Academic Press, San Diego, 1996, pp. 629–656.

[Padegs 1964] A. Padegs, "The Structure of the System/360, Part IV: Channel Design Considerations," *IBM Systems Journal*, vol.3, no.2, IBM, Yorktown Heights, NY, 1964, pp. 165–180.

[Padhye 1998] Jitendra Padhye, Victor Firoiu, Don Towsley, and Jim Kurose, "Modeling TCP Throughput—A Simple Model and its Empirical Validation," *Proceedings of ACM SIGCOMM'98* (Vancouver, British Columbia), *Computer Communication Review*, vol.28, no.4, ACM, New York, October 1998, pp. 303–314.

[Padmanabhan 1994] Venkata N. Padmanabhan and Jeffrey C. Mogul, "Improving HTTP Latency," *Proceedings of the 2nd World Wide Web Conference* (Chicago), IW^{3}C^2, Geneva, October 1994.

[Padmanabhan 1998] Venkata N. Padmanabhan and Randy H. Katz, "TCP Fast Start: a Technique for Speeding up Web Transfers," *Proceedings of Globecom Internet Mini-Conference* (Sydney), November 1998.

[Palais 1998] Joseph C. Palais, *Fiber Optic Communications*, 4th ed., Prentice Hall, Upper Saddle River, NJ, 1998.

[Pan 1999] Yi Pan, Chunming Qiao, and Yuanyuan Yang, "Optical Multistage Interconnection Networks: New Challenges and Approaches," *IEEE Communications*, vol. 37, no.2, IEEE, New York, February 1999, pp. 50–56.

[Papir 1999] Zdzislaw Papir and Andrew Simmonds, "Competing for Throughput in the Local Loop," *IEEE Communications*, vol.37, no.5, IEEE, New York, May 1999, pp. 61–66.

[Parekh 1993] A. Parekh and R. Gallager, "A Generalized Processor Sharing Approach to Flow Control—The Single Node Case" *IEEE/ACM Transactions on Networking*, vol.1, no.3, IEEE/ACM, New York, June 1993, pp. 344–357.

[Partridge 1990a] Craig Partridge, "How Slow is One Gigabit per Second?," *ACM Computer Communication Review*, vol.20, no.1, January 1990, pp. 44–53.

[Partridge 1990b] Craig Partridge, *Internet Research Steering Group Workshop on Very-High-Speed Networks*, RFC 1152 (workshop report), April 1990.

[Partridge 1993a] Craig Partridge, Trevor Mendez, and Walter Milliken, *Host Anycasting Service*, RFC 1546 (informational), November 1993.

[Partridge 1993b] Craig Partridge, "Protocols for High-Speed Networks: Some Questions and a Few Answers," *Computer Networks and ISDN Systems*, vol.25, no.9, North-Holland/Elsevier, Amsterdam, April 1993, pp. 1019–1028.

[Partridge 1994a] Craig Partridge, *Gigabit Networking*, Addison-Wesley, Reading, MA, 1994.

[Partridge 1994b] Craig Partridge, ed., *Report of the ARPA/NSF Workshop on Research in Gigabit Networking*, Washington, DC, July 1994, available from www.cise.nsf.gov/anir/giga/craig.txt.

[Partridge 1994c] Craig Partridge and Frank Kastenholz, *Technical Criteria for Choosing IP The Next Generation (IPng)*, RFC 1726 (informational), December 1994.

[Partridge 1997] Craig Partridge and Timothy J. Shepard, "TCP/IP Performance over Satellite Links" *IEEE Network*, vol.11, no.5, IEEE, New York, September/October 1997, pp. 44–49.

[Partridge 1998a] Craig Partridge, Philip P. Carvey, Ed Burgess, Isidro Castineyra, Tom Clarke, Lise Graham, Michael Hathaway, Phil Herman, Allen King, Steve Kolhami, Tracy Ma, John Mcallen, Trevor Mendez, Walter C. Milliken, Ronald Pettyjohn, John Rokosz, Joshua Seeger, Michael Sollins, Steve Storch, Benjamin Tober, Gregory D. Troxel, David Waitzman, and Scott Winterble, "A 50-Gb/s IP Router," IEEE/ACM Transactions on Networking, vol.6, no.3, IEEE/ACM, New York, June 1998, pp. 237–248.

[Partridge 1998b] Craig Partridge, Sally Floyd, and Mark Allman, *Increasing TCP's Initial Window*, RFC 2414 (experimental), May 1998.

[Parulkar 1990a] Gurudatta M. Parulkar and Jonathan S. Turner, "Towards a Framework for High-Speed Communication in a Heterogeneous Networking Environment," *IEEE Network*, vol.4, no.2, IEEE, New York, March 1990, pp. 19–27.

[Parulkar 1990b] Gurudatta M. Parulkar, "The Next Generation of Internetworking," *ACM SIGCOMM Computer Communication Review*, vol.20, no.1, ACM, New York, January 1990, pp. 18–43.

[Parulkar 1995] Guru Parulkar, Douglas C. Schmidt, and Jonathan S. Turner, "a^{l}t^{P}m: A Strategy for Integrating IP with ATM," *Proceedings of ACM SIGCOMM'95* (Cambridge, MA), *Computer Communication Review*, vol.25, no.4, ACM, New York, August 1995, pp. 49–57.

[Pattavina 1998] Achille Pattavina, *Switching Theory: Architecture and Performance in Broadband ATM Networks*, John Wiley, Chichester, UK, 1998.

[Patterson 1997] David A. Patterson, Thomas Anderson, Neal Cardwell, Richard Fromm, Kimberly Keaton, Christoforos Kozyrakis, Randi Thomas, and Katherine Yelick, "A Case for Intelligent RAM," *IEEE Micro*, vol.17, no.2, IEEE, New York, March/April 1997, pp. 34–44.

[Patterson 1998] David A, Patterson and John L. Hennessy, *Computer Organization and Design: The Hardware/Software Interface*, 2nd ed., Morgan Kaufmann, San Francisco, 1998.

[Pehrson 1992] Björn Pehrson, Per Gunningberg, and Stephen Pink, "Distributed Multimedia Applications on Gigabit Networks," *IEEE Network*, vol.6, no.1, IEEE, New York, January 1992, pp. 26–35.

[Pehrson 1993] Björn Pehrson, Per Gunningberg, and Stephen Pink, eds., *Protocols for High Speed Networks III*, IFIP, North-Holland/Elsevier, Amsterdam, 1993.

[Pei 1992] Tong-Bi Pei and Charles Zukowski, "Putting Routing Tables in Silicon," *IEEE Network*, vol.6, no.1, IEEE, New York, January 1992, pp. 42–50.

[Perkins 1998] Charles E. Perkins, *Mobile IP: Design Principles and Practices*, Addison-Wesley, Reading, MA, 1998.

[Perkins 1999] Stephen Perkins and Alan Gatherer, "Two-Way Broadband CATV-HFC Networks: State-of-the-Art and Future Trends," *Computer Networks*, vol.31, no.4, North-Holland/Elsevier, Amsterdam, February 1999, pp. 313–326.

[Perkins 2001], Charles E. Perkins, ed., *Ad Hoc Networking*, Addison-Wesley, Boston, 2001.

[Perlman 2000] Radia Perlman, *Interconnections: Bridges and Routers, Switches, and Internetworking Protocols*, Addision-Wesley, Reading, MA, 2000.

[Personick 1985] Stewart D. Personick, *Fiber Optics: Technology and Applications*, Plenum Press, New York/Kluwer Academic Publishers, Norwell, MA, 1985.

[Peterson 2000] Larry L. Peterson and Bruce S. Davie, *Computer Networks: A Systems Approach*, Morgan Kaufmann, San Francisco, 2000.

[Pink 1994] Stephen Pink, "TCP/IP in Gigabit Networks," in *High Performance Networks: Frontiers and Experience*, Ahmed N. Tantawy, ed., Kluwer Academic Publishers, Norwell, MA, 1994, pp.135–156.

[Piscitello 1993a] David M. Piscitello and A. Lyman Chapin, *Open Systems Networking: TCP/IP and OSI*, Addison-Wesley, Reading, MA, 1993.

[Piscitello 1993b] David M. Piscitello, *Use of ISO CLNP in TUBA Environments*, RFC 1561 (experimental), December 1993.

[Postel 1980a] Jonathan B. Postel, "Internetwork Protocol Approaches," *IEEE Transactions on Communications*, vol.com-28, no.4, IEEE, New York, April 1980, pp. 604–611.

[Postel 1980b] Jonathan B. Postel, ed., *User Datagram Protocol*, RFC 768 / STD 006, August 1980.

[Postel 1981a] Jonathan B. Postel, Carl A. Sunshine, and Danny Cohen, "The ARPA Internet Protocol," *Computer Networks*, vol.5, no.4, North-Holland, Amsterdam, July 1981, pp. 261–271.

[Postel 1981b] Jonathan B. Postel, ed., *Internet Protocol*, RFC 793/ STD 005, September 1981.

[Postel 1981c] Jonathan B. Postel, ed., *Internet Control Message Protocol*, RFC 792 / STD 005, September 1981.

[Postel 1981d] Jonathan B. Postel, ed., *Transmission Control Protocol*, RFC 793/ STD 007, September 1981.

[Prabhakar 1996] Balaji Prabhakar, Nick McKeown, and Jean Mairesse, "Tetris Models for Multicast Switches," *Proceedings of the 30th Conference on Information Science Systems*, Princeton, NJ, 1996.

[Prabhakar 1997] Balaji Prabhakar, Nick McKeown, and Ritesh Ahuja, "Multicast Scheduling for Input-Queued Switches," *IEEE Journal on Selected Areas in Communications*, vol.15, no.5, IEEE, New York, June 1997, pp. 855–866.

[Prati 1997] Giancarlo Prati, ed., *Photonic Networks: Advances in Optical Communications*, 8th International Tyrrhenian Workshop on Digital Communications, September 1996 (Lerici, IT), Springer, London, 1997.

[Prucnal 1993] Paul R. Prucnal, "Photonic Fast Packet Switching" in *Photonics in Switching, Volume II: Systems*, John E. Midwinter, ed., Academic Press, New York, 1993.

[Pursley 1999] Michael B. Pursley and Clint S. Wilkins, "Adaptive-Rate Coding for Frequency Hop Communications over Raleigh Fading Channels," *IEEE Journal on Selected Areas in Communications*, vol.17, no.7, IEEE, New York, July 1999, pp. 1224–1232.

[Qiao 1996] Chunming Qiao and Yousong Mei "Wavelength Reservation under Distributed Control," *IEEE/LEOS Broadband Optical Networks*, 1996, pp. 45–46.

[Qiao 1999] Chunming Qiao and Myungsik Yoo, "Optical Burst Switching—A New Paradigm for an Optical Internet," *Journal of High Speed Networks*, vol.8, no.1, 1999, pp. 69–84.

[Qiao 2000] Chunming Qiao and Myungsik Yoo, "A Taxonomy of Switching Techniques," in *Optical WDM Networks: Principles and Practice*, Krishna M. Sivalingam and Suresh Subramaniam, eds., Kluwer Academic Publishers, Norwell, MA, 2000, pp. 103–125.

[Quartermann 1989] John S. Quarterman, *The Matrix: Computer Networks and Conferencing Systems Worldwide*, Digital Press, Maynard, MA, 1989.

[Rajagopalan 2000] Bala Rajagopalan, James Luciani, Daniel Awduche, Brad Cain, Bilel Jamoussi, and Debanjan Saha, *IP over Optical Networks: A Framework*, Internet Draft draft-many-ip-optical-framework-02.txt, work in progress, May 2000.

[Ramakrishnan 1990] K.K. Ramakrishnan and Raj Jain, "A Binary Feedback Scheme for Congestion Avoidance" *ACM Transactions on Computer Systems*, vol.8, no.2, ACM, Washington, DC, May 1990, pp. 158–181.

[Ramakrishnan 1993a] K.K. Ramakrishnan, "Performance Considerations in Designing Network Interfaces," *IEEE Journal on Selected Areas in Communications*, vol.11, no.2, IEEE, New York, February 1993, pp. 203–219.

[Ramakrishnan 1993b] K.K. Ramakrishnan, ed., End-System Support for High-Speed Networks special issue of *IEEE Network*, vol.7, no.4, IEEE, New York, July 1993.

[Ramakrishnan 1999] K.K. Ramakrishnan and Sally Floyd, *A Proposal to Add Explicit Congestion Notification (ECN) to IP*, RFC 2481 (experimental), January 1999.

[Ramamurthy 2000a] Byrav Ramamurthy, "Switches, Wavelength Routers, and Wavelength Converters," in Krishna M. Sivalingam and Suresh Subramaniam, eds., *Optical WDM Networks: Principles and Practice*, Kluwer Academic Publishers, Norwell, MA, 2000, pp.27–50.

[Ramamurthy 2000b] Byrav Ramamurthy and Jason P. Jue, "Fiber, Lasers, Receivers, an Amplifiers," in Krishna M. Sivalingam and Suresh Subramaniam, eds., *Optical WDM Networks: Principles and Practice*, Kluwer Academic Publishers, Norwell, MA, 2000, pp. 51–75.

[Ramanathan 1996] Ram Ramanathan and Martha Steenstrup, "A Survey of Routing Techniques for Mobile Communications Networks," *Mobile Networks and Applications*, vol.1, no.2, Baltzer Science Publishers BV, 1996, pp. 89–104.

[Ramanathan 1997a] Ram Ramanathan, *Multicast Support for Nimrod: Requirements and Solution Approaches*, RFC 2102 (informational) February 1997.

[Ramanathan 1997b] Ram Ramanathan, *Mobility Support for Nimrod: Challenges and Solution Approaches*, RFC 2103 (informational) February 1997.

[Ramanathan 1998] Ram Ramanathan and Martha Steenstrup, "Hierarchically-Organized, Multihop Mobile Wireless Networks for Quality-of-Service Support," *Mobile Networks and Applications*, vol.3, no.1, Baltzer Science Publishers BV, January 1998, pp. 101–119.

[Ramanathan 2000] Ram Ramanathan and Regina Roslaes-Hain, "Topology Control of Multihop Wireless Networks using Transmit Power Adjustment," *Proceedings of IEEE INFOCOM 2000* (Tel Aviv), vol.2, IEEE, New York, March 2000, pp.404–413.

[Ramaswami 1996] R. Ramaswami and A. Segall, A, "Distributed Network Control for Wavelength Routed Optical Networks," *Proceedings of IEEE INFOCOM'96* (San Francisco), vol.1, IEEE, New York, March 1996, pp. 138–147.

[Ramaswami 1998] Rajiv Ramaswami and Kumar N. Sivarajan, *Optical Networks: A Practical Perspective*, Morgan Kaufmann, San Francisco, 1998.

[Rappaport 1996] Theodore S. Rappaport, *Wireless Communications: Principles and Practice*, Prentice Hall, Upper Saddle River, NJ, 1996.

[Reed 1987] Daniel A. Reed and Richard M. Fujimoto, *Multicomputer Networks: Message-Based Parallel Processing*, MIT Press, Cambridge, MA, 1987.

[Rekhter 1993] Yakov Rekhter and Tony Li, *An Architecture for IP Address Allocation with CIDR*, RFC 1515 (standards track), September 1993.

[Rekhter 1997], Yakov Rekhter, Bruce S. Davie, Eric Rosen, George Swallow, Dino Farinacci, and Dave Katz, "Tag Switching Architecture Overview," *Proceedings of the IEEE*, vol.82, no.12, IEEE, New York, December 1997, pp. 1973–1983.

[Rexford 1996] Jennifer L. Rexford, Albert L. Greenberg, and Flavio G. Bonomi, "Hardware-Efficient Fair Queueing Architectures for High-Speed Networks," *Proceedings of INFOCOM'96* (San Francisco), IEEE, New York, March 1996, pp. 638–646.

[Rexford 1997] Jennifer L. Rexford, Flavio G. Bonomi, Albert L. Greenberg, and Albert Wong, "A Scalable Architecture for Fair Leaky Bucket Shaping," *Proceedings of INFOCOM'97* (Kobe JP), IEEE, New York, April 1997, pp. 1054–1062.

[Rey 1983] R.F. Rey, ed., *Engineering and Operations in the Bell System*, 2nd ed., AT&T Bell Laboratories, Murray Hill, NJ, 1983.

[Richer 1992] Ira Richer and Geoffrey Baehr, eds., Gigabit Networks special issue of *IEEE Communications*, vol. 30, no. 4, IEEE, New York, July 1993.

[Richharia 1999] Madhavendra Richharia, *Satellite Communications Systems*, McGraw-Hill, New York, 1999.

[Rizzo 1997] Luigi Rizzo, "Effective Erasure Codes for Reliable Computer Communication Protocols," *ACM Computer Communication Review*, vol.27, no.2, ACM, New York, April 1997, pp. 24–36.

[Robinson 1989] Phil Alden Robinson, director, *Field of Dreams* (movie), Gordon Company/Universal Studios, Hollywood, CA, 1989, based on the book *Shoeless Joe*, by W.P. Kinsella, Houghton Mifflin/Mariner, Boston, 1982/1999.

[Romanow 1995] Allyn Romanow and Sally Floyd, "Dynamics of TCP Traffic over ATM Networks," *IEEE Journal on Selected Areas in Communications*, vol.1, no.6, IEEE, New York, May 1995, pp. 633–641.

[Rose 2000] Rose, M., *The Blocks eXtensible eXchange Protocol Framework* Internet Draft draft-ietf-beep-framework-08.txt, work in progress, November 2000.

[Rosen 2000a] Eric C. Rosen, Arun Viswanathan, and Ross Callon, *Multiprotocol Label Switching Architecture*, Internet Draft draft-ietf-mpls-arch-07.txt, work in progress, July 2000.

[Rosen 2000b] Eric C. Rosen, Yakov Rekhter, Daniel Tappan, Guy Fedorkow, Dino Farinacci, Tone Li, and Alex Conta, *MPLS Label Stack Encodings*, Internet Draft draft-ietf-mpls-shim-08.txt, work in progress, July 2000.

[Rudin 1976] Harry Rudin, "On Routing and 'Delta Routing': A Taxonomy and Performance Comparison of Techniques for Packet-Switched Networks," *IEEE Transactions on Communications*, vol.com-24, no.1, IEEE New York, 1976, pp. 43–59.

[Rudin 1989a] Harry Rudin, "Preface," *Protocols for High Speed Networks*, Harry Rudin and Robin Williamson, eds., IFIP, North-Holland/Elsevier, Amsterdam, 1989, p. v.

[Rudin 1989b] Harry Rudin and Robin Williamson, eds., *Protocols for High Speed Networks*, IFIP, North-Holland/Elsevier, Amsterdam, 1989.

[Rudin 1989c] Harry Rudin and Robin Williamson, eds., High Speed Network Protocols special issue of *IEEE Communications*, vol.27, no.6, IEEE, New York, June 1989.

[Russell 2000] Travis Russell, *Signaling System, #7*, 3rd ed., McGraw-Hill, New York, 2000.

[Sachs 1994] Martin W. Sachs, Avraham Leff, and Denise Sevigay, "LAN and I/O Convergence: A Survey of the Issues," *IEEE Computer*, vol.27, no.2, IEEE, New York, December 1994, pp. 24–32.

[Saltzer 1981] J.H. Saltzer, D.P. Reed, and D.D. Clark, "End-to-End Arguments in System Design," *Proceedings of the Second International Conference on Distributed Computing Systems (ICDCS)*, IEEE, New York, 1981, pp. 509–512 (earlier version of [Saltzer 1984]).

[Saltzer 1984] J.H. Saltzer, D.P. Reed, and D.D. Clark, "End-to-End Arguments in System Design," *ACM Transactions on Computer Systems*, vol.2, no.4, ACM, New York, November 1984, 227–288.

[Salus 1995] Peter H. Salus, *Casting the Net: From ARPANET to Internet and Beyond*, Addison-Wesley, Reading, MA, 1995.

[Samaraweera 1997] N.K.G. Samaraweera and G. Fairhurst, "Explicit Loss Indication and Accurate RTO Estimation for TCP Error Recovery using Satellite Links, *IEEE Proceedings—Communications*, vol.144, no.1, IEEE, London, February 1997, pp. 47–53.

[Samaraweera 1999] N.K.G. Samaraweera, "Non-Congestion Packet Loss Detection for TCP Error Recovery using Wireless Links, *IEE Proceedings—Communications*, vol.146, no.4, IEE, London, August 1999, pp. 222–230.

[Sari 1999] Hikmet Sari, "Broadband Radio Access to Home and Businesses: MMDS and LMDS," *Computer Networks*, vol.31, no.4, North-Holland/Elsevier, Amsterdam, February 1999, pp. 379–393.

[Schneier 1996] Bruce Schneier, *Applied Cryptography*, 2nd ed., John Wiley, New York, 1996.

[Schneier 2000] Bruce Schneier, *Secrets and Lies: Digital Security in a Networked World*, John Wiley, New York, 1996.

[Schulzrinne 1996] Henning Schulzrinne, Stephen L. Casner, Ron Frederick, and Van Jacobsen, *RTP: A Transport Protocol for Real-Time Applications*, RFC 1889 (standards track), January 1996.

[Schulzrinne 1998] Henning Schulzrinne, Anup Rao, and Robert Lanphier, *Real Time Streaming Protocol (RTSP)*, RFC 2326 (standards track), April 1998.

[Scudder 1999] John G. Scudder and Rohit Dube, "BGP Scaling Techniques Revisited," *ACM SIGCOMM Computer Communication Review*, vol.29, no.5, ACM, New York, October 1999, pp. 22–23.

[Semke 1998] Jeffrey Semke, Jamshid Mahdavi, and Matthew Mathis, "Automatic TCP Buffer Tuning," *Proceedings of ACM SIGCOMM'98* (Vancouver, British Columbia), *Computer Communication Review*, vol.28, no.4, ACM, New York, August 1998, pp. 315–323.

[SETI 1998] *The SETI@home Sky Survey*, setiathome.ssl.berkeley.edu/sciencepaper.html.

[Shacham 1990] Nachum Shacham and Paul McKenny, "Packet Recovery in High-Speed Networks Using Coding and Buffer Management," *Proceedings of INFOCOM'90* (San Francicso), vol.1, IEEE, New York, June 1990, pp. 124–131.

[Sharma 1994] R. Sharma and S. Keshav, "Signaling and Operating System Support for Native-Mode ATM Applications," *Proceedings of ACM SIGCOMM'94* (London), *Computer Communication Review*, vol.24, no.4, ACM, New York, August 1995, pp. 149–157.

[Shenker 1995] Scott Shenker, "Fundamental Design Issues for the Future Internet," *IEEE Journal on Selected Areas in Communications*, vol.13, no.7, IEEE, New York, 1995, pp. 1176–1188.

[Shepler 2000] Spencer Shepler, Brent Callaghan, David Robinson, Robert Thurlow, Carl Beame, Mike Eisler, and David Noveck, *NFS Version 4 Protocol*, RFC 3010 (standards track), December 2000.

[Shreedhar 1995] M. Shreedhar and George Varghese, "Efficient Fair Queueing using Deficit Round Robin," *Proceedings of ACM SIGCOMM'95* (Cambridge, MA), *Computer Communication Review*, vol.25, no.4, ACM, New York, August 1995, pp. 231–242.

[Siewiorek 1982] Daniel P. Siewiorek, C. Gordon Bell, and Allen Newell, *Computer Structures: Principles and Examples*, McGraw-Hill, New York, 1982.

[Silberschatz 1998] Avi Silberschatz and Peter Galvin, *Operating Systems Concepts*, 5th ed., Addison-Wesley, Reading, MA, 1998 [commonly called "the dinosaur book"].

[Sivalingam 2000] Krishna M. Sivalingam and Suresh Subramaniam, *Optical WDM Networks: Principles and Practice*, Kluwer Academic Publishers, Norwell, MA, 2000.

[Smith 1991] Neale Smith, xftp (X-windows file transfer program), Lawrence Livermore National Laboratory, www.llnl.gov/ia/xftp.html (first prototype written 1991).

[Smith 1993] Jonathan M. Smith, Eric C. Cooper, Bruce S. Davie, Ian M. Leslie, Yoram Ofek, and Richard W. Watson, eds., High-Speed Computer/Network Interfaces *IEEE Journal on Selected Areas in Communications*, vol.11, no.2, IEEE, New York, February 1993.

[Soltis 1996] Steven R. Soltis, Thomas M. Ruwart, and Matthew T. O'Keefe, "The Global File System," *Proceeding of the 5th NASA Goddard Space Flight Center Conference on Mass Storage and Technologies* (College Park, MD), NASA Goddard Space Flight Center, Greenbelt, MD, September 1996.

[Somani 2000] Arun K. Somani and Byrav Ramamurthy, eds., Optical Communication Networks for the Next-Generation Internet special issue of *IEEE Network*, vol.14, no.6, IEEE, New York, November/December 2000.

[Spalink 2001] Tammo Spalink, Scott Karlin, and Larry L. Peterson, *Evaluating Network Processors in IP Forwarding*, technical report TR-626-00 (revised), Princeton University Department of Computer Science, Princeton, NJ, January 2001.

[Spaniol 1994] Otto Spaniol, André Danthine, and Wolfgang Effelsberg, eds., *Architecture and Protocols for High-Speed Networks*, Kluwer Academic Publishers, Norwell, MA, 1994.

[Spatscheck 2000] Oliver Spatscheck, Jørgen S. Hansen, John H. Hartman, and Larry L. Peterson, "Optimizing TCP Forwarder Performance," *IEEE/ACM Transactions on Networking*, vol.8, no.2, IEEE, New York, April 2000, pp. 146–157.

[Spurgeon 2000] Charles E. Spurgeon, *Ethernet: The Definitive Guide*, O'Reilly, Sebastopol, CA, 2000.

[Srinivasan 1998] V. Srinivasan, George Varghese, Subhash Suri, and Marcel Waldvogel, "Fast and Scalable Layer Four Switching," *Proceedings of ACM SIGCOMM'98* (Vancouver, British Columbia), *Computer Communication Review*, vol.28, no.4, ACM, New York, August 1998, pp. 191–202.

[Srinivasan 1999a] V. Srinivasan, Subhash Suri, and George Varghese, "Packet Classification using Tuple Space Search," *Proceedings of ACM SIG-*

COMM'99 (Cambridge, MA), *Computer Communication Review*, vol.29, no.4, ACM, New York, August 1999, pp. 135–146.

[Srinivasan 1999b] V. Srinivasan and George Varghese, "A Survey of Recent IP Lookup Schemes," *Protocols for High Speed Networks VI*, IFIP/IEEE PfHSN'99 (Salem, MA), August 1999, Joseph D, Touch and James P.G. Sterbenz, eds., Kluwer Academic Publishers, Norwell, MA, 2000, pp. 9–23.

[Srisuresh 2001] Pyda Srisuresh and Kjeld Borch Egevang, *Traditional IP Network Address Translator (Traditional NAT)*, RFC 3022 (informational), January 2001.

[Stallings 1995] William Stallings, *Network and Internetwork Security: Principles and Practice*, Prentice Hall, Englewood Cliffs, NJ, 1995.

[Stallings 1998a] William Stallings, *High-Speed Networks: TCP/IP and ATM Design Principles*, Prentice Hall, Upper Saddle River, NJ, 1998.

[Stallings 1998b] William Stallings, *Operating Systems: Internals and Design Principles*, 3rd ed., Prentice Hall, Upper Saddle River, NJ, 1998.

[Stallings 2000a] William Stallings, *Data and Computer Communications*, 6th ed., Prentice Hall, Upper Saddle River, NJ, 2000.

[Stallings 2000b] William Stallings, *Local and Metropolitan Area Networks*, 6th ed., Prentice Hall, Upper Saddle River, NJ, 2000.

[Steenkiste 1994] Peter A. Steenkiste, "A Systematic Approach to Host Network Interface Design for High-Speed Networks," *IEEE Computer*, vol.27, no.3, IEEE, New York, March 1994, pp. 47–57.

[Steenstrup 1993a] Martha Steenstrup, *An Architecture for Inter-Domain Policy Routing*, RFC 1478 (proposed standard), June 1993.

[Steenstrup 1993b] Martha Steenstrup, *Inter-Domain Policy Routing Protocol Specification: Version 1*, RFC 1479 (proposed standard), July 1993.

[Steenstrup 1995], Martha Steenstrup editor, *Routing in Communications Networks*, Prentice Hall, Englewood Cliffs, NJ, 1995.

[Steenstrup 2001] Martha Steenstrup, "Cluster-Based Networks," in *Ad Hoc Networking*, Charles E. Perkins, ed., Addison-Wesley, Boston, 2001, pp. 75–138.

[Stephens 1999] Donpaul C. Stephens, Jon C.R. Bennett, and Hui Zhang, "Implementing Scheduling Algorithms in High-Speed Networks," *IEEE Journal on Selected Areas in Communications*, vol.17, no.6, IEEE, New York, June 1999, pp. 1145–1158.

[Sterbenz 1990a] James P.G. Sterbenz and Gurudatta M. Parulkar, "Axon: A Distributed Communication Architecture for High-Speed Networking," *Proceedings of IEEE INFOCOM'90* (San Francisco), June 1990, pp 415–425.

[Sterbenz 1990b] James P.G. Sterbenz and Gurudatta M. Parulkar, "Axon Network Virtual Storage for High Performance Distributed Applications," *Proceedings of 10th International Conference on Distributed Computing Systems ICDCS* (Paris), IEEE, New York, June 1990, pp 484–492.

[Sterbenz 1990c] James P.G. Sterbenz and Gurudatta M. Parulkar, "Axon Host–Network Interface for Gigabit Communications," *Protocols for High Speed Networks II*, IFIP PfHSN'90 (Palo Alto, CA), November 1990, Marjory Johnson, ed., Elsevier/North-Holland, Amsterdam, 1991, pp. 211–236.

[Sterbenz 1990d] James P.G. Sterbenz and Gurudatta M. Parulkar, "Axon: Application-Oriented Lightweight Transport Protocol Design," *Proceedings of Tenth International Conference on Computer Communication (ICCC'90)* (New Delhi) ICCC, Narosa Publishing House, New Delhi, 1990, pp. 379–387.

[Sterbenz 1991] James P.G. Sterbenz, *Axon: A Host–Network Interface Architecture for Gigabit Communications*, D.Sc. dissertation, Washington University in St. Louis, 1991, University of Michigan, Ann Arbor, 9223579.

[Sterbenz 1992] James P.G. Sterbenz, Anshul Kantawala, Milind Buddhikot, and Gurudatta M. Parulkar, "Hardware Based Error and Flow Control in the Axon Gigabit Host–Network Interface," *Proceedings of IEEE INFOCOM'92* (Florence), IEEE, New York, May 1992, pp 282–293.

[Sterbenz 1993] James P.G. Sterbenz and Gurudatta M. Parulkar, "Design of a Gigabit Host–Network Interface," *Journal of High Speed Networking*, vol.2, no.1, IOS Press, Amsterdam, 1993, pp. 27–62.

[Sterbenz 1994] James P.G. Sterbenz, "Protocols for High Speed Networks: Life After ATM?," *Protocols for High Speed Networks IV*, IFIP/IEEE PfHSN'94 (Vancouver, British Columbia), August 1994, Gerald Neufeld and Mabo Ito, eds., Chapman & Hall, London/Kluwer Academic Publishers, Norwell, MA, 1995, pp. 3–18.

[Sterbenz 1995] James P.G. Sterbenz, Henning G. Schulzrinne, and Joseph D. Touch, "Report and Discussion on the IEEE ComSoc TCGN Gigabit Networking Workshop 1995," *IEEE Network*, vol.9, no.4, IEEE, New York, July/August 1995, pp. 9–21.

[Sterbenz 1996a] James P.G. Sterbenz, "What Belongs *in* the Network, and What Does *in* the Network Mean?," animation session presentation, *Protocols for High Speed Networks*, IFIP/IEEE PfHSN'96 (Sophia-Antipolis, FR), October 1996.

[Sterbenz 1996b] James P.G. Sterbenz and Gregory S. Lauer, "Issues in Session Control for Broadband Network Services," *IEEE Gigabit Networking Workshop (GBN)* (San Francisco), March 1996.

[Sterbenz 2000] James P.G. Sterbenz and Joseph D. Touch, "Preface," *Protocols for High Speed Networks VI*, IFIP/IEEE PfHSN'99 (Salem, MA), August 1999, Kluwer Academic Publishers, Boston, 2000, pp. ix–xii.

[Stern 1999] Thomas E. Stern, T. and Krishna Bala, *Multiwavelength Optical Networks: A Layered Approach*, Addison-Wesley, Reading, MA, 1999.

[Stevens 1988] J. Stevens, *Spatial Reuse through Dynamic Power and Routing Control in Common-Chanel Random-Access Packet Radio Networks*, SURAN program technical note SRNTN 59, August 1988, available from the Defence Technical Information Center (DTIC).

[Stevens 1990] W. Richard Stevens, *UNIX Network Programming*, Prentice Hall, Englewood Cliffs, NJ, 1990.

[Stevens 1994] W. Richard Stevens, *TCP/IP Illustrated, Volume 1: The Protocols*, Addison-Wesley, Reading, MA, 1994.

[Stevens 1995] W. Richard Stevens, *TCP/IP Illustrated, Volume 2: The Implementation*, Addison-Wesley, Reading, MA, 1995.

[Stevens 1996] W. Richard Stevens, *TCP/IP Illustrated, Volume 3: TCP for Transactions, HTTP, NNTP, and the Unix® Domain Protocols*, Addison-Wesley, Reading, MA, 1996.

[Stevenson 1992] Daniel S. Stevenson and Julian G. Rosenman, "The VISTAnet Gigabit Testbed," *IEEE Journal on Selected Areas in Communications*, vol.10, no.9, IEEE, New York, December 1992, pp. 1413–1420.

[Stiliadis 1998a] Dimitrios Stiliadis and Anujan Varma, "Rate-Proportional Servers: A Design Methodology for Fair Queueing Algorithms," *IEEE/ACM Transactions on Networking*, vol.6, no.2, IEEE/ACM, New York, April 1998, pp. 164–174.

[Stiliadis 1998b] Dimitrios Stiliadis and Anujan Varma, "Efficient Fair Queueing Algorithms for Packet-Switched Networks," *IEEE/ACM Transactions on Networking*, vol.6, no.2, IEEE/ACM, New York, April 1998, pp. 175–185.

[Stone 2000] Jonathan Stone and Craig Partridge, "When the CRC and TCP Checksum Disagree," *Proceedings of ACM SIGCOMM 2000* (Stockholm), *Computer Communication Review*, vol.30, no.4, ACM, New York, August 2000, pp. 309–319.

[Strayer 1992] W. Timothy Strayer, B. Dempsey, and A. Weaver, *XTP: The Xpress Transfer Protocol*, Addison-Wesley, Reading, MA, 1992.

[Sunshine 1977] Carl A. Sunshine, "Source Routing in Computer Networks," *ACM Computer Communication Review*, vol.7, no.1, ACM, New York, January 1977, pp. 29–33.

[Sunshine 1978] Carl A. Sunshine and Yogen K. Dalal, "Connection Management in Transport Protocols," *Computer Networks*, vol.2, no.6, North-Holland, Amsterdam, December 1978, pp. 454–473.

[Sunshine 1989] Carl A. Sunshine, *Computer Network Architectures and Protocols*, 2nd ed., Plenum Press, New York/Kluwer Academic Publishers, Norwell, MA, 1989 (significant revision of [Green 1982] with many different chapters).

[Suter 1998] Bernhard Suter, T.V. Lakshman, Dimitrios Stiliadis, and Abhijit K. Choudhury, "Design Considerations for Supporting TCP with Per-Flow Queuing," *Proceedings of INFOCOM'98* (San Francisco), IEEE, New York, March 1998, pp. 299–306.

[Suzuki 1992] Hiroshi Suzuki and Fouad A, Tobagi, "Fast Bandwidth Reservation Scheme with Multi-Link and Multi-Path Routing in ATM Networks, *Proceedings of INFOCOM'92* (Florence), IEEE, New York, May 1992, pp. 2233–2240.

[Svobodova 1989] L. Svobodova, "Measured Performance of Transport Service in LANs," *Computer Networks and ISDN Systems*, vol.17, no.1, North-Holland/Elsevier, Amsterdam, 1989, pp. 31–45.

[Tam 1990a] Ming-Chit Tam and David J. Farber, "CapNet—An Approach to Ultra-High Speed Network," *Proceedings of ICC'90*, IEEE, New York, April 1990, pp 955–961.

[Tam 1990b] Ming-Chit Tam, Jonathan M. Smith, and David J. Farber "A Taxonomy-Based Comparison of Several Distributed Shared Memory Systems," *ACM SIGOPS Operating Systems Review* vol.24, no.3, ACM, New York, July 1990, pp. 40–67.

[Tamir 1988] Yuval Tamir and Gregory L. Frazier, "High Performance Multi-Queue Buffers for VLSI Communication Switches," *Proceedings of ISCA'88*, ACM, New York, June 1988, pp. 343–354.

[Tannenbaum 1996] Andrew S. Tannenbaum, *Computer Networks*, 3rd ed., Prentice Hall, Upper Saddle River, NJ, 1996.

[Tantawy 1992] Ahmed N. Tantawy and Martina Zitterbart, "Multiprocessing in High Performance IP Routers," *Protocols for High Speed Networks III*, IFIP PfHSN'92 (Stockholm), May 1992, Per Gunningberg, Björn Perhson, and Stephen Pink, eds., Elsevier/North-Holland, Amsterdam, 1993, pp. 235–254.

[Tantawy 1994a], Ahmed N. Tantawy, *High Performance Networks: Technology and Protocols*, Kluwer Academic Publishers, Boston, 1994.

[Tantawy 1994b], Ahmed N. Tantawy, *High Performance Networks: Frontiers and Experience*, Kluwer Academic Publishers, Boston, 1994.

[Tantawy 1994c] Ahmed N. Tantawy, Odysseas Koufopavlou, Martina Zitterbart, and Joseph Alber, "On the Design of a Multigigabit IP Router," *Journal of High Speed Networks*, vol.3, no.3, IOS Press, Amsterdam, 1994.

[Tchakountio 2001] Fabrice Tchakountio and Ram Ramanathan, *Routing To Highly Mobile Endpoints: A Theoretical and Experimental Study of Limits and Solutions*, BBN Technical Memorandum no. 1280, 2001.

[Tennenhouse 1989] David. L. Tennenhouse, "Layered Multiplexing Considered Harmful," *Protocols for High-Speed Networks*, IFIP PfHSN'89 (Zürich), May 1989, Harry Rudin and Robin Williamson, eds., Elsevier/North-Holland, Amsterdam, 1989, pp. 143–148.

[Tennenhouse 1996] David L. Tennenhouse and David J. Wetherall, "Toward an Active Network Architecture," *ACM Computer Communication Review*, vol.26, no.2, ACM, New York, April 1996, pp. 5–18.

[Tennenhouse 1997] David L. Tennenhouse, Jonathan M. Smith, W. David Sincoskie, David J. Wetherall, and Gary J. Minden, "A Survey of Active Network Research," *IEEE Communications*, vol.35, no.1, IEEE, New York, January 1997, pp. 80–86.

[Terstriep 1996] Jeffrey A. Terstriep, Ronald J. Menelli, and Thomas T. Kwan, "Experiences with a Wide Area Gigabit Network," *Proceedings of the 15th*

International Phoenix Conference on Computers and Communications (Phoenix), IEEE, New York, March 1996, pp. 179–187.

[Thompson 1996] Richard A. Thompson, "Operational Domains for Circuit- and Packet-Switching," *IEEE Journal on Selected Areas in Communications*, vol.14, no.2, IEEE, New York, February 1996, pp. 293–297.

[Thompson 1997] Kevin Thompson, Gregory J. Miller, and Rick Wilder, "Wide-Area Internet Traffic Patterns and Characteristics," *IEEE Network*, vol.11, no.6, IEEE, New York, November/December 1997, pp. 10–23.

[Thompson 2000] Richard A. Thompson, *Telephone Switching Systems*, Artech House, Norwood, MA, 2000.

[Thornton 1970] J.E. Thornton, *Design of a Computer: The Control Data 6600*, Scott, Foresman and Co., Glenview, IL, 1970.

[Tomlinson 1974] Raymond S. Tomlinson, "Selecting Sequence Numbers," *Proceedings of ACM SIGCOMM/SIGOPS Interprocess Communications Workshop* (Santa Monica, CA), *ACM SIGOPS Operating Systems Review*, vol. 9, no.3, ACM, New York, July 1975, pp. 11–23.

[Touch 1989] Joseph D. Touch and David J. Farber, "MIRAGE: A Model for Ultra-High-Speed Protocol Analysis and Design," *Protocols for High Speed Networks*, IFIP PfHSN'89 (Zürich), May 1989, Harry Rudin and Robin Williamson, eds., Elsevier/North-Holland, Amsterdam, 1989, pp. 115–133.

[Touch 1992] Joseph D. Touch, *Mirage: A Model for Latency in Communication*, Ph.D. dissertation, Dept. of Computer and Information Science technical report MS-CIS-92–42/DSL-11, University of Pennsylvania, 1992.

[Touch 1993] Joseph D. Touch, "Parallel Communication" *Proceedings of INFOCOM'93* (San Francisco), IEEE, New York, March 1993, pp. 506–512.

[Touch 1994] Joseph D. Touch and David J. Farber, "An Experiment in Latency Reduction," *Proceedings of INFOCOM'94* (Toronto), IEEE, New York, June 1994, pp. 175–183.

[Touch 1995a] Joseph D. Touch, "Protocol Parallelization," *Protocols for High Speed Networks IV*, IFIP/IEEE PfHSN'94 (Vancouver, British Columbia), Gerald Neufeld and Mabo Ito, eds., Chapman and Hall, London/Kluwer Academic Publishers, Norwell, MA, 1995, pp. 349–360.

[Touch 1995b] Joseph D. Touch, "Defining 'High Speed' Protocols : Five Challenges and an Example That Survives the Challenges," *IEEE Journal on Selected Areas in Communications*, vol.13, no.5, IEEE, New York, June 1995, pp. 828–835.

[Touch 1995c] Joseph D. Touch, "Performance Analysis of MD5," *Proceedings of ACM SIGCOMM'95* (Cambridge, MA), *Computer Communication Review*, vol.25, no.4, ACM, New York, August 1995, pp. 77–86.

[Touch 1996] Joseph D. Touch, "High Performance Web," animation session, *Protocols for High-Speed Network*, IFIP/IEEE, PfHSN'96 (Sophia-Antipolis, FR), October 1996.

[Touch 1997] Joseph D. Touch, *TCP Control Block Interdependence*, RFC 2140 (informational), April 1997.

[Touch 2000] Joseph D. Touch and James P.G. Sterbenz, eds., *Protocols for High Speed Networks VI*, IFIP, Kluwer Academic Publishers, Norwell, MA, 2000.

[Traw 1993] C. Brandan S. Traw, and Jonathan M. Smith, "Hardware/Software Organization of a High-Performance ATM Host Interface," *IEEE Journal on Selected Areas in Communications*, vol.11, no.2, IEEE, New York, February 1993, pp.228–239.

[Traw 1995] C. Brendan S. Traw, and Jonathan M. Smith, "Striping within the Network Subsystem," *IEEE Network*, vol.9, no.4, IEEE, New York, July/August 1995, pp. 22–33.

[Turletti 1996] Thierry Turletti and Christian Huitema, "Videoconferencing on the Internet," *IEEE/ACM Transactions on Networking*, vol.4, no.3, IEEE/ACM, New York, June 1996, pp. 340–351.

[Turner 1986a] Jonathan S. Turner, "New Directions in Communications (or Which Way to the Information Age)," *IEEE Communications Magazine*, vol.24, no.10, IEEE, New York, October 1986, pp. 8–15.

[Turner 1986b] Jonathan S. Turner, "Design of an Integrated Services *Packet* Network," *IEEE Journal on Selected Areas in Communications*, vol.sac-4, no.8, IEEE, New York, November 1986, pp. 1373–1380.

[Turner 1988] Jonathan S. Turner, "Design of a Broadcast Packet Switching Network," *IEEE Transactions on Communications*, vol.36, no.6, IEEE, New York, June 1988, pp. 734–743.

[Turner 1991] Jonathan S. Turner, *A Proposed Bandwidth Management and Congestion Control Scheme for Multicast ATM Networks*, Washington University Computer and Communications Research Center technical report wuccrc-91–1, May 1991.

[Turner 1994] Jonathan S. Turner, "An Optimal Nonblocking Multicast Virtual Circuit Switch," *Proceedings of INFOCOM'94* (Toronto), IEEE, New York, Jun 1994, pp. 298–305.

[Turner 1997] Jonathan S. Turner and Naoaki Yamanaka, *Architectural Choices in Large Scale ATM Switches*, Washington University Department of Computer Science Technical Report WUCS-97–21, www.cs.wustl.edu/cs/techreports/1997/wucs-97–21.ps.Z, May 1997.

[Turner 1998] Jonathan S. Turner and Naoaki Yamanaka, "Architectural Choices in Large Scale ATM Switches, *IEICE Transactions*, vol.E81-B, no.2, 1998, pp.120–137; also available as Washington University Department of Computer Science Technical Report WUCS-97–21, www.cs.wustl.edu/cs/techreports/1997/wucs-97–21.ps.Z, May 1997.

[Turner 1999] Jonathan S. Turner, "Terabit Burst Switching," *Journal of High Speed Networks*, vol.8, no.1, IOS Press, Amsterdam, 1999, pp. 3–16.

[Turner 2000] Jonathan S. Turner, *Design and Analysis of Switching Systems*, presentation foils and draft book chapters, www.wucs.wustl.edu/~jst/cs/577.

[Tzeng 1999] Henry Hong-Yi Tzeng and Tony Przygienda, "On Fast Address-Lookup Algorithms," *IEEE Journal on Selected Areas in Communications*, vol.17, no.6, IEEE, New York, June 1999, pp. 1067–1082.

[Ullman 1993] Robert Ullman, *TP/IX: The Next Internet*, RFC 1475, June 1993.

[US 1993] *Statistical Abstract of the United States*, U.S. Bureau of the Census, 113th ed., 1993.

[Vahalia 1996] Uresh Vahalia, *Unix Internals: The New Frontiers*, Prentice Hall, Upper Saddle River, NJ, 1996.

[Varma 1997] Anujan Varma and Dimitrios Stiliadis, "Hardware Implementation of Fair Queueing Algorithms for Asynchronous Transfer Mode Networks, *IEEE Communications*, vol.35, no.12, IEEE, New York, December 1997, pp. 54–68.

[Vickers 1988] Richard Vickers and Marek Wernik, "Evolution of Switch Architecture and Technology," *Proceedings of the 1988 Zürich Seminar on Digital Communications*, IEEE, New York, March 1988, pp. 185–190.

[Vickers 1991] Richard Vickers and Marek Wernik, "The Role of SDH and ATM in Broadband Access Networks," *Proceedings of Globecom'91* (Phoenix), vol.1, IEEE, New York, December 1991, pp. 212–216.

[Vickers 1993] Richard Vickers, "The Development of ATM Standards and Technology: A Retrospective," *IEEE Micro*, vol.13, no.6, December 1993, pp. 62–73.

[Viswanathan 1998] Arun Viswanathan, Nancy Feldman, Zheng Wang, and Ross Callon "Evolution of Multiprotocol Label Switching," *IEEE Communications*, vol.36, no.5, IEEE, New York, May 1998, pp. 165–172.

[Visweswaraiah 1997] Vikram Visweswaraiah and John Heidemann. "Improving Restart of Idle TCP Connections," Technical Report 97–661, University of Southern California, November, 1997.

[Wade 1987] J.P. Wade and C.G. Sodini, "Dynamic Cross-Coupled Bitline Content Addressable Memory Cell for High Density Arrays," *IEEE Journal of Solid State Circuits*, vol.22, no.2, IEEE, New York, February 1987, pp. 119–121.

[Waldvogel 1997] Marcel Waldvogel, George Varghese, Jonathan Turner, and Bernhard Plattner, "Scalable High Speed IP Routing Lookups," *Proceedings of ACM SIGCOMM'97* (Cannes FR), *Computer Communication Review*, vol.27, no.4, ACM, New York, September 1997, pp. 25–35.

[Wang 1991] Zheng Wang and Jon Crowcroft, "A New Congestion Control Scheme: Slow Start and Search (tri-s)," *ACM Computer Communication Review*, vol.21, no.1, ACM, New York, January 1991, pp. 32–43.

[Wang 2000] Lijun Wang, A Kuzmich, and A. Dogariu, "Gain Assisted Superluminal Light Propagation," *Nature*, vol. 406, July 2000, pp. 277–279.

[Watson 1981] Richard W. Watson, "Timer-Based Mechanisms in Reliable Transport Protocol Connection Management," *Computer Networks*, vol.5, no.1, North-Holland, Amsterdam, February 1981, pp. 47–56.

[Watson 1987] Richard W. Watson and Sandy A. Mamrak, "Gaining Efficiency in Transport Services by Appropriate Design and Implementation Choices," *ACM Transactions on Computer Systems*, vol.5, no.2, May 1987, pp. 97–120.

[Watson 1989] Richard W. Watson, "The Delta-t Transport Protocol: Features and Experience," *Protocols for High-Speed Networks*, IFIP PfHSN'89 (Zürich), May 1989, Harry Rudin, and Robin Williamson, eds., 1989, pp. 3–17.

[Watson 1990] Greg Watson and Stanley Ooi, "What *Should* a Gbit/s Network Interface Look Like?," *Protocols for High Speed Networks II*, IFIP PfHSN'90 (Palo Alto, CA), November 1990, Marjory Johnson, ed., Elsevier/North-Holland, Amsterdam, 1991, pp. 237–250.

[Watson 1995] Richard W. Watson and Robert A. Coyne, "The Parallel I/O Architecture of the High-Performance Storage System (HPSS)," *Proceedings of the 14th IEEE Symposium on Mass Storage* (Monterey, CA), IEEE, New York, 1995, pp. 27–44.

[Waxman 1988] Bernard M. Waxman, "Routing of Multipoint Connections" *IEEE Journal on Selected Areas in Communications*, vol.6, no.9, IEEE, New York, December 1988, pp. 1617–1622.

[Wecker 1980] Stuart Wecker, "DNA: The Digital Network Architecture," *IEEE Transactions on Communications*, vol. com-28, no.4, IEEE, New York, April 1980, pp. 510–526.

[Weiser 1991] Mark Weiser, "The Computer For the 21st Century," *Scientific American*, New York, vol. 256, no. 3, September 1991, pp. 94–104.

[Weiser 1999] Mark Weiser, Rich Gold, and John Seely Brown, "The Origins of Ubiquitous Computing Research at PARC in the Late 1980s," *IBM Systems Journal*, vol.38 no.4, IBM, Armonk, NY, 1999, pp. 693–696.

[Weiss 1994] Shlomo Weiss and James E. Smith, *POWER and PowerPC: Principles, Architecture, Implementation*, Morgan Kaufmann, San Francisco, 1994.

[Wessels 1998] Duane Wessels and K. Claffy, "ICP and the Squid Web Cache, April 1998, pp. 345–357.

[Williams 2000] Stuart Williams, "IrDA: Past, Present, and Future," *IEEE Personal Communications*, vol.7, no.1, IEEE, New York, February 2000, pp. 11–19.

[Wittmann 2001] Ralph Wittmann and Martina Zitterbart, *Multicast Communication: Protocol and Applications*, Morgan Kaufmann, San Francisco, 2001.

[Woo 2000] Thomas Y.C. Woo, "A Modular Approach to Packet Classification: Algorithms and Results," *Proceedings of INFOCOM 2000* (Tel Aviv), vol.3, IEEE, New York, March 2000, pp. 1213–1222.

[Woodside 1990] C.M. Woodside, K. Ravinadran, and R.G. Franks, "The Protocol Bypass Concept for High Speed OSI Data Transfer." *Protocols for High-Speed Networks II*, IFIP PfHSN'1990 (Palo Alto, CA), October 1990, Marjory Johnson, ed., Elsevier/North-Holland, Amsterdam, 1991, pp. 107–122.

[Wroclawski 1997] John Wroclawski, *Use of RSVP with Internet Integrated Services*, RFC 2210 (standards track), September 1997.

[Wu 1987] L.T. Wu, S.H. Lee, and T.T. Lee, "Dynamic TDM—A Packet Approach to Broadband Networking, *Proceedings of ICC'87*, Seattle, IEEE, New York, pp. 1585–1592.

[Xu 1995] Hong Xu and Tom W. Fischer, "Improving PVM Performance Using the ATOMIC User-Level Protocol," *High-Speed Network Computing Workshop* at *International Parallel Processing Symposium'95*, available from www.isi.edu/div7/atomic2/pubs.html.

[Yao 2000] Shun Yao and Biswanath Mukherjee, "Advances in Photonic Packet Switching: An Overview," *IEEE Communications*, vol.38, no.2, IEEE, New York, February 2000, pp. 84–94.

[Yoo 1997] Myungsik Yoo and Chunming Qiao, "Just-Enough-Time (JET): A High Speed Protocol for Bursty Traffic in Optical Networks," *Proceedings of IEEE/LEOS Conference on Technologies For a Global Information Infrastructure*, Montreal, IEEE, New York, August 1997, pp. 26–27.

[Young 1987] Michael Young, Avadis Tevanian, Jr., Richard Rashid, David Golub, Jeffrey Eppinger, Jonathan Chew, William Bolosky, David Black, and Robert Baron, "The Duality of Memory and Communication in the Implementation of a Multiprocessor Operating System," *Proceedings of the 11th Symposium on Operating Systems Principles* (Austin, TX), November 1987, *ACM SIGOPS Operating Systems Review*, vol.21, no.5, pp. 63–76.

[Yuan 2001] Ruixi Yuan and W. Timothy Strayer, *Virtual Private Networks: Technologies and Solutions*, Addison-Wesley, Reading, MA, 2001.

[Zegura 1993] Ellen Witte Zegura, "Architecture for ATM Switching Systems," *IEEE Communications*, vol.31, no.2, IEEE, New York, February 1993, pp. 28–37.

[Zhang 1986] Lixia Zhang, "Why TCP Timers Don't Work Well," *Proceedings of ACM SIGCOMM'86* (Stowe, VT), *ACM Computer Communication Review*, vol.16, no.3, ACM, New York, August 1986, pp. 397–405.

[Zhang 1991] Lixia Zhang, Scott Shenker, and David D. Clark, "Observations on the Dynamics of a Congestion Control Algorithm," *Proceedings of ACM SIGCOMM'91* (Zürich), *Computer Communication Review*, vol.21, no.4, ACM, New York, September 1990, pp. 133–147.

[Zhang 1993] Lixia Zhang, Stephen E. Deering, Deborah Estrin, Scott Shenker, and Daniel Zappala, "RSVP: A New Resource reSerVation Protocol," *IEEE Network*, vol.9, no.5, IEEE, New York, September 1993, pp. 8–18.

[Zhang 1997] Lixia Zhang, Sally Floyd, and Van Jacobson, "Adaptive Web Caching," *Proceedings of the 2nd Web Cache Workshop* (Boulder CO US), June 1997, available from irl.cs.ucla.edu/AWC.

[Zhang 1998] Lixia Zhang, Scott Michel, Khoi Nguyen, Adam Rosenstein, Sally Floyd, and Van Jacobson, "Adaptive Web Caching: Towards a New Global

Caching Infrastructure," *Third International WWW Caching Workshop* (Manchester, UK), June 1998, available from irl.cs.ucla.edu/AWC.

[Zitterbart 1989] Martina Zitterbart, "High-Speed Protocol Implementations Based on a Multiprocessor Architecture," *Protocols for High Speed Networks*, IFIP PfHSN'89 (Zürich), May 1989, Harry Rudin and Robin Williamson, eds., Elsevier/North-Holland, Amsterdam, 1989, pp. 151–164.

[Zwaenepoel 1985] Willy Zwaenepoel, "Protocols for Large Data Transfer over Local Area Networks," *Proceedings of ACM SIGCOMM Ninth Data Communications Symposium* (Whistler, British Columbia), *ACM Computer Communications Review*, vol. 15, no. 4, ACM, New York, September 1985, pp. 22–32.

Axioms and Principles

This appendix lists all of the axioms and principles from the entire book, sorted in the order presented in Chapter 2, followed by the page number on which they appear. Axioms and principles that have a letter prefix indicate their applicability:

N—network architecture and topology (Chapters 3 and 4)

L—links and link layer components (Chapter 5)

S—switch (network layer component) (Chapter 5)

E—end system (Chapter 6)

T—end-to-end and transport layer (Chapter 7)

A—application (Chapter 8)

Axioms

The five axioms provide the highest level guidance for the content of this book, and are numbered with Ø followed by roman numerals. Axioms that are split or have additional corollaries at the highest level have subscripts; refinement corollaries contain the principal axiom number followed by an Arabic numeral.

Ø KNOW THE PAST, PRESENT, AND FUTURE

Ø₁. Know the Past   *Genuinely new ideas are extremely rare. Almost every "new" idea has a past full of lessons that can either be learned or ignored.*   *[14]*

Ø₂. Know the Present   *Ideas look different in the present because the context in which they have reappeared is different. Understanding the difference tells us which lessons to learn from the past and which to ignore.*   *[14]*

Ø₃. Know the Future   *The future hasn't happened yet, and is guaranteed to contain at least one completely unexpected discovery that changes everything.*   *[15, 489]*

Ø₄. Prepare for the Future   *Simply knowing the past does not prepare us to understand the future. We must constantly reevaluate tradeoffs in the face of emerging technology, and question the basic assumptions of the present.*   *[20, 491]*

Ø-A. Not Invented Here Corollary [1980s version]   *Operating systems didn't begin with Unix, and networking didn't begin with TCP/IP.*   *[17]*

Ø-B. Not Invented Here Corollary [1990s version]   *Operating systems didn't begin with Windows, and host architecture didn't begin with the PC and the x86 architecture.*   *[18]*

I APPLICATION PRIMACY

I. Application Primacy   *The sole and entire point of building a high-performance network infrastructure is to support the distributed applications that need it.*   *[20]*

E-I. Application Primacy   *Optimization of communications processing in the end system must not degrade the performance of the applications using the network.*   *[286]*

A-I. Application Primacy   *The sole and entire point of building a high-performance network infrastructure is to support the distributed applications that need it.*   *[431]*

I.1. Field of Dreams versus Killer App Dilemma   *The emergence of the next "killer application" is difficult without sufficient network infrastructure. The incentive to build network infrastructure is viewed as a "field of dreams" without concrete projections of application and user demand.*   *[21]*

A-I.1. Field of Dreams versus Killer App Dilemma   *Advances in network technology create the "field of dreams" to which new applications are drawn, but are difficult to motivate without the tangible pull of a new "killer application"—which can't emerge in the absence of an adequate network infrastructure. This chicken-and-egg dilemma governs the supply-and-demand dynamic of high-speed networking.*   *[432]*

I.2. Interapplication Delay   *The performance metric of primary interest to communicating applications is the total delay in transferring data. The metric of interest to users includes the delay through the application.*   *[21]*

T-I.2. Continuous Media Streaming   *Timeliness of delivery should not be traded for reliable transfer in real-time continuous media streams. Use a playback buffer to reorder and absorb jitter.   [371]*

A-I.2. User Expectation of Interapplication Delay   *The performance metric of primary interest to the users of communicating applications is the total delay in completing the communication, including both the end-to-end delay and any delay introduced by the application itself.   [433]*

A-I.2c. User Expectations of Continuous Media Quality   *The performance metric of primary interest to users of continuous media streams is quality of the stream such as frame rate and resolution for video and frequency range for audio.   [434]*

A-I.2i. Interactive Response Time   *Interactive applications should provide a response time ranging from an ideal of 100 ms to a maximum target of 1 second. Within this range, consistent response is better than high variance.   [441]*

I.3. Network Bandwidth and Latency   *Bandwidth and latency are the primary performance network metrics important to interapplication delay.   [22]*

A-I.3. High-Speed Applications Need High Bandwidth and Low Latency   *Bandwidth and latency are the primary performance metrics governing interapplication delay. The latency requirements of an application depend on the expectations of the user. For data-intensive applications, delay sensitivity drives bandwidth requirements.   [434]*

S-I.3. Packet Processing Rate   *The packet processing rate (packets per second) is a key throughput measure of a switch. Packet processing software and shared parallel hardware resources must be able to sustain the average packet processing rate. Functions in the serial critical path must be designed for the worst-case packet processing rate of the path to avoid queueing and blocking of subsequent packets.   [254]*

I.4. Networking Importance in System Design   *Communication is the defining characteristic of networked applications, and thus support for communication must be an integral part of systems supporting distributed applications.   [22]*

E-I.4. Importance of Networking in the End System   *Networking should be considered a first-class citizen of the end system computing architecture, on a par with memory or high-performance graphics subsystems.   [294]*

II   HIGH-PERFORMANCE PATHS GOAL

II. High-Performance Paths Goal   *The network and end systems must provide a low-latency high-bandwidth path between applications to support low interapplication delay.   [24]*

N-II. Network Path Principle   *The network must provide high-bandwidth, low-latency paths between end systems.   [80]*

N-IIo. Network Overlay Principle *Overlay networks must provide the same high-performance paths as the physical networks. The number of overlay layers should be kept as small as possible, and overlays must be adaptable based on end-to-end path requirements and topology information from the lower layers.* *[92]*

L-II. Network Link Principle *Network links must provide high-bandwidth connections between network nodes. Link-layer protocol processing should not introduce significant latency.* *[167]*

L-IIc. Link-Layer Components *Link-layer components must sustain the data rate of the link, while not introducing significant delay.* *[188]*

S-II. Network Node Principle *Network nodes must support high-bandwidth, low-latency, end-to-end flows, as well as their aggregation. High-speed network nodes should provide a scalable number of high-bandwidth, low-delay interconnections.* *[195]*

E-II. End System Principle *The communicating end systems are a critical component in end-to-end communications and must provide a low-latency, high-bandwidth path between the network interface and application memory.* *[285]*

II.1. Path Establishment Corollary *Signaling and routing mechanisms must exist to discover, establish, and forward data along the high-performance paths.* *[24]*

N-II.1. Network Path Establishment *The routing algorithms and signaling mechanisms must be capable of forwarding datagrams or establishing connections on sufficiently high-performance paths and with low latency to meet application demands.* *[134]*

II.2. Path Protection Corollary *In a resource-constrained environment, mechanisms must exist to arbitrate and reserve the resources needed to provide the high-performance path and prevent other applications from interfering by congesting the network.* *[25]*

N-II.2. Network Path Protection *QOS mechanisms must be capable of guaranteeing bandwidth and latency bounds, when needed.* *[151]*

L-II.2. Medium Access Control Principle *The MAC protocol should efficiently arbitrate the shared medium in either a fair manner or with the desired proportion.* *[182]*

S-II.2 Switch Traffic Management *In a resource-constrained environment, switches must support admission control with resource reservations to provide guaranteed-service traffic classes and policing to prevent other traffic from interfering.* *[215]*

E-II.2. Path Protection Corollary *In a resource-constrained host, mechanisms must exist to reserve processing and memory resources needed to provide the high-performance path between application memory and the network interface and to support the required rate of protocol processing.* *[308]*

A-II.2*b*. Fair Service Among Best-Effort Applications   *In the absence of specific policy directives to favor some applications over others, network and end system resources should be allocated fairly (roughly equally) among competing best-effort applications.   [439]*

II.3. Store-and-Forward Avoidance   *Store-and-forward and copy operations on data have such a significant latency penalty that they should be avoided whenever possible. [25]*

S-II.3. Store-and-Forward and Queueing Delay Minimization Principle   *Store-and-forward delays should be avoided, and per packet queuing should be minimized. In the ideal case, nodes should pipeline and cut through packets with zero per packet delays.   [201]*

E-II.3. Copy Minimization Principle   *Data copying, or any operation that involves a separate sequential per byte touch of data, should be avoided. In the ideal case, a host–network interface should be zero copy.   [295]*

E-II.3*m*. Avoid Data Copies by Remapping   *Use memory and buffer remapping techniques to avoid the overhead of copying and moving blocks of data.   [306]*

II.4. Blocking Avoidance   *Blocking along paths should be avoided, whether due to the overlap of interfering paths or due to the building of queues.   [26]*

N-II.4. Avoid Congestion and Keep Queues Short   *Avoid congestion by network engineering, traffic management with resource reservation, and by dropping packets. Buffers should be kept as empty as possible, with queuing only for transient situations, to allow cut-through and avoid the latency of FIFO queueing.   [156]*

S-II.4*f*. Nonblocking Switch Fabric Principle   *A nonblocking switch fabric is the core of a high-performance switch. Avoid blocking by space-division parallelism, internal speedup, and internal pipelined buffering with cut-through. Strictly and wide-sense nonblocking avoids the complexity and delay of path rearrangement.   [227]*

S-II.4*q*. Head-of-Line Blocking Avoidance Principle   *Avoid head-of-line blocking. Output queuing requires internal speedup, expansion, or buffering. Virtual output queueing requires additional queues or queuing complexity. The two techniques must be traded against one another, and can be used in combination.   [232]*

S-II.4*c*. Bound Packet Classification Time   *Packets that must be classified to potentially receive delay-bounded service must be classified before any queuing at the input. The classification operation must have delay bounds that meet the most stringent service class.   [269]*

S-II.4*s*. Output Scheduling and Queueing Granularity   *Output scheduling must operate at line rate to support the traffic classes required. Finer-grained queueing and scheduling provides greater isolation of flows and control, at the cost of increased queueing complexity.   [273]*

S-II.4a. Active Network Processing *Active network processing should not impede the nonactive fast path; packet filters in the critical path must operate at line rate to pass nonactive packets. The ability to perform per packet active processing requires sufficient processing power to sustain the required active packet throughput.* *[277]*

E-II.4. Nonblocking Host–Network Interconnect *The interconnect between the end system memory and the network interface should be nonblocking, and not interfere with peripheral I/O, and CPU–memory data transfer.* *[318]*

E-II.4m. Nonuniform Memory Multiprocessor–Network Interconnect *Message passing multiprocessors need sufficient network interfaces to allow data to flow between the network and processor memory without interfering with the multiprocessing application.* *[325]*

T-II.4c. Congestion Avoidance *Congestion should be avoided before it happens. Keep queues from building and operate just to the left of the knee to maximize throughput and minimize latency.* *[411]*

II.5. Contention Avoidance *Channel contention due to a shared medium should be avoided.* *[26]*

N-II.5. Scalability of Mesh Topologies *Mesh network technologies scale better than shared medium link technologies.* *[82]*

II.6. Efficient Transfer of Control *Control mechanisms on which the critical path depends should be efficient. High overhead transfer of control between protocol-processing modules should be avoided.* *[26]*

E-II.6c. Context Switch Avoidance *The number of context switches should be minimized, and approach one per application data unit.* *[302]*

E-II.6k. User/Kernel Crossing Avoidance *The number of user space calls to the kernel should be minimized due to the overhead of authorization and security checks, the copying of buffers, and the inability to directly invoke needed kernel functions.* *[305]*

II.7. Path Information Assurance Tradeoff *Paths have application-driven reliability and security requirements that may have to be traded against performance.* *[26]*

III LIMITING CONSTRAINTS

III. Limiting Constraints *Real-world constraints make it difficult to provide high-performance paths to applications.* *[27]*

N-III. Administrative Constraints Increase the Importance of Good Design *Policy and administrative constraints distort the criteria that govern the application of many high-performance network design principles. The importance of good (principled) design is elevated when these constraints are present.* *[108]*

III.1. Speed of Light   *The latency suffered by propagating signals due to the speed of light is a fundamental law of physics, and is not susceptible to direct optimization.*   *[27]*

III.2. Channel Capacity   *The capacity of communication channels is limited by physics. Clever multiplexing and spatial reuse can reduce the impact, but not eliminate the constraint.*   *[27]*

III.3. Switching Speed   *There are limits on switching frequency of components, constrained by process technology at a given time, and ultimately limited by physics.*   *[28]*

III.4. Cost and Feasibility   *The relative cost and scaling complexity of competing architectures and designs must be considered in choosing alternatives to deploy.*   *[28]*

S-III.4. Switch Scalability   *The construction of switches with a large port count requires scalable switch fabrics. Exploit regular structures for implementation in VLSI or optics as the basis for recursively constructed fabrics with logarithmic growth complexity.*   *[241]*

III.5. Heterogeneity   *The network is a heterogeneous world, which contains the applications and end systems that networks tie together, and the node and link infrastructure from which networks are built.*   *[29]*

A-III.5. Constraints on Partitioning of Distributed Computations   *The ability to efficiently partition a distributed computation may be limited by the physical distribution of scarce computing and storage resources.*   *[453]*

III.6. Policy and Administration   *Policies and administrative concerns frustrate the deployment of optimal high-speed network topologies, constrain the paths through which applications can communicate, and may dictate how application functionality is distributed.*   *[29]*

III.7. Backward Compatibility Inhibits Radical Change   *The difficulty of completely replacing widely deployed network protocols means that improvements must be backward compatible and incremental. Hacks are used and institutionalized to extend the life of network protocols.*   *[30]*

E-III.7. Optimize and Enhance Widely Deployed Protocols   *The practical difficulty in replacing protocols widely deployed on end systems indicates that it is important to optimizing existing protocol implementations and add backward compatible enhancements, rather than only trying to replace them with new protocols.*   *[291]*

A-III.7. Default to Support Legacy Applications   *Networks should provide a meaningful degenerate behavior to support legacy applications, or applications whose capabilities are outside the scope of the system.*   *[484]*

III.8. Standards both Facilitate and Impede Dilemma   *Standards are critical to facilitate interoperability, but standards that are specified too early or are overly specific can impede progress. Standards that are specified too late or are not specific enough are useless.*   *[30]*

Design Principles

The last major axiom is the Systemic Optimization Principle (IV), on which all of the major design principles are based. Design principles are numbered with Arabic numerals, omitting the IV roman numeral for brevity, for example, 2A rather than IV-2A, and N-2A rather than N-IV-2A (for the network architecture version). Refinements of similar principles are suffixed with an italic letter.

IV   SYSTEMIC OPTIMIZATION

IV. Systemic Optimization Principle   *Networks are systems of systems with complex compositions and interactions at multiple levels of hardware and software. These pieces must be analyzed and optimized in concert with one another.*   *[31]*

E-IV. Systemic Elimination of End System Bottlenecks   *The host organization, processor–memory interconnect, memory subsystem, operating system, protocol stack, and host–network interface are all critical components in end system performance, and must be optimized in concert with one-another.*   *[289]*

T-IV. Transport Protocol Functionality   *Transport protocols must be organized to deliver the set of end-to-end high-bandwidth, low-latency services needed by applications. Options and service models should be modularly accessible, without unintended performance degradation and feature interactions.*   *[355]*

IV$_1$. Consider Side Effects   *Optimizations frequently have unintended side effects to the detriment of overall performance. It is important to consider, analyze, and understand the consequences of optimizations.*   *[32]*

E-IV$_1$. Consider the Side Effects   *Optimizations frequently have unintended side effects to the detriment of performance. It is important to consider, analyze, and understand the consequences of optimization and difficulties in the end system due to the complex interaction of application, operating system, and protocols.*   *[298]*

A-IV$_1$. Application Adaptation Synergy   *Many application adaptation techniques are mutually exclusive; some can occur only at the expense of others. They must be carefully implemented and coordinated to avoid interference.*   *[456]*

IV$_2$. Keep it Simple and Open   *It is difficult to understand and optimize complex systems, and virtually impossible to understand closed systems, which do not have open published interfaces.*   *[32]*

IV$_3$. System Partitioning Corollary   *Carefully determine how functionality is distributed across a network. Improper partitioning of a function can dramatically reduce overall performance.*   *[33]*

A-IV$_3$. Properly Partition Distributed Applications   *Carefully determine where to cut applications to distribute across the network. Some "high-speed" applications are simply poorly partitioned low-speed applications.*   *[437]*

IV₄. Flexibility and Workaround Corollary   *Provide protocol fields, control mechanisms, and software hooks to allow graceful enhancements and workarounds when fundamental tradeoffs change.   [34]*

1   SELECTIVE OPTIMIZATION

1. Selective Optimization Principle   *It is neither practical nor feasible to optimize everything. Spend implementation time and system cost on the most important contributors to performance.   [34]*

1A. Second-Order Effect Corollary   *The impact of spatially local or piecewise optimizations on the overall performance must be understood; components with only a second-order effect on performance should not be the target of optimization.   [34]*

N-1A*l*. Network Latency Principle   *The latency along a path is the sum of all its components. The benefit of optimizing an individual link is directly proportional to its relative contribution to the total end-to-end latency.   [83]*

A-1A*l*. Application Latency Principle   *Interapplication delays are the sum of all the constituent delays that cannot be parallelized. User-perceived delay is the ultimate measure of the performance of a high-speed system.   [456]*

N-1A*h*. Network Diameter Principle   *The number of per hop latencies along a path is bounded by the diameter of the network. The network topology should keep the diameter low.   [87]*

N-1A*b*. Network Bandwidth Principle   *The maximum bandwidth along a path is limited by the minimum bandwidth link or node, which is the bottleneck. There is no point in optimizing a link that is not a bottleneck.   [89]*

A-1A*b*. Application Bandwidth Principle   *The bandwidth perceived by the user is the minimum of all bandwidths along a path, including through the application itself.   [470]*

1B. Critical Path Corollary   *Optimize implementations for the critical path, in both control and data flow.   [35]*

N-1B. Network Monitoring   *Network monitoring functions must be built into the critical path to provide nonintrusive local filtering and aggregation of statistics.   [161]*

S-1B*c*. Fast Packet Switch Critical Path Principle   *Simplify and optimize per byte and per packet data manipulation and transfer control functions for implementation in the hardware critical path. State maintained per connection streamlines per packet processing.   [203]*

S-1B*d*. Fast Datagram Switch Principle   *There is compelling motivation to perform high-speed connectionless datagram switching. Apply connection-oriented fast packet switching techniques to fast datagram switching, and exploit technology advances to implement the additional input and output processing in the critical path.   [250]*

    E-1B. Critical Path Principle *Optimize end system critical path protocol processing software and hardware, consisting of normal data path movement and the control functions on which it depends.* *[297]*

    T-1B. Critical Path Optimization of Security Operations *Encryption and per packet authentication operations must be optimized for the critical path.* *[426]*

1C. Functional Partitioning and Assignment Corollary *Carefully determine what functionality is implemented in scarce or expensive technology.* *[36]*

    S-1C. Functional Partitioning and Assignment Principle *Carefully determine what switch functionality is to be implemented in scarce or expensive technology.* *[223]*

    S-1C*h*. Hardware versus Software Implementation of Input and Output Processing *In determining the appropriate implementation of input and output processing, trade the cost and feasibility of hardware against the complexity and feasibility of embedded controller software.* *[267]*

    E-1C*i*. Host–Network Interface Functional Partitioning and Assignment *Carefully determine what functionality should be implemented on the network interface rather than in end system software.* *[329]*

    E-1C*h*. Network Interface Hardware Functional Partitioning and Assignment *Carefully determine what functionality should be implemented in network interface custom hardware, rather than on an embedded controller. Packet interarrival time driven by packet size is a critical determinant of this decision.* *[331]*

    A-1C. Partitioning of Application versus Protocol Functionality *Keep the network impact of application design choices in mind. Not all functions are best deployed within an application.* *[476]*

2   RESOURCE TRADEOFFS

2. Resource Tradeoff Principle *Networks are collections of resources. The relative composition of these resources must be balanced to optimize cost and performance.* *[37]*

    N-2. Network Resource Tradeoff and Engineering Principle *Networks are collections of resources. The relative composition of these resources must be balanced to optimize cost and performance and to determine network topology, engineering, and functional placement.* *[110]*

    A-2. Use Bandwidth to Reduce Latency *Bandwidth can be utilized to reduce latency by anticipatory prefetching and presending.* *[462]*

    2A. Resource Tradeoffs Change *The relative cost of resources and the impact of constraints change over time due to nonuniform advances in different aspects of technology.* *[37]*

N-2A. Resource Tradeoffs Change and Enable New Paradigms *The relative cost of resources and constraints changes over time due to nonuniform advances in different aspects of technology. This should motivate constant rethinking about the way in which networks are structured and used.* *[115]*

A-2A. Relative Magnitude of High Speed *High speed is a relative term. Application requirements for high speed—alleged or actual—have historically grown to at least the limits of currently attainable link speeds and network capacity.* *[434]*

2B. Optimal Resources Utilization versus Overengineering Tradeoff *Balance the benefit of optimal resource utilization against the costs of the algorithms that attempt to achieve optimal solutions.* *[38]*

N-2B. Network Resource Tradeoff and Engineering Principle *Balance the tradeoff of optimal resource utilization and its associated complexity and cost against the cost of suboptimal resource utilization resulting from oveengineering the network.* *[152]*

N-2Bc. Congestion Control Fairness versus Complexity *The lack of fairness in simple congestion control and avoidance mechanisms must be traded against the complexity of fair implementations.* *[156]*

N-2Br. Dynamic Path Rerouting *Dynamic behavior can require adjustments to topology to maintain a high performance path. The overhead and frequency of topology maintenance must be traded against the lack of optimality.* *[159]*

S-2B. Overengineering versus Optimality *Optimal traffic management policies use processing and memory, which also adds latency to connection establishment; trade these costs against the bandwidth wasted by overengineering and overprovisioning the network.* *[222]*

A-2B. Compression of Data *Compression of data reduces bandwidth at the expense of the processing complexity and delay of the compression/decompression algorithms.* *[466]*

2C. Support for Multicast *Multicast is an important mechanism for conserving bandwidth and supporting network control protocols, and should be supported by the network.* *[39]*

L-2C. Link-Layer Multicast Principle *Shared medium links provide native support for broadcast, essential for higher-layer control protocols and in support of multicast applications. Nonbroadcast point-to-point mesh LANs should provide broadcast and multicast support.* *[194]*

S-2C. Switches Should Provide Native Multicast *Switches should provide native multicast support to conserve bandwidth and avoid latency of repeated transmission.* *[246]*

3   END-TO-END ARGUMENTS

3. End-to-End Argument   *Functions required by communicating applications can be correctly and completely implemented only with the knowledge and help of the applications themselves. Providing these functions as features within the network itself is not possible.*   *[39]*

> **T-3. End-to-End Argument**   *Functions required by communicating applications can be correctly and completely implemented only with the knowledge and help of the applications themselves. Providing these functions as features within the network itself is not possible.*   *[346]*

3A. Hop-by-Hop Performance Enhancement Corollary   *It may be beneficial to duplicate an end-to-end function hop-by-hop, if doing so results in an overall (end-to-end) improvement in performance.*   *[40]*

> **N-3A. Congestion Control in the Network Improves Performance**   *Even though the end-to-end protocols must perform congestion control, there is substantial performance benefit in assistance from the network.*   *[153]*

> **T-3A. Hop-by-Hop Performance Enhancement Corollary**   *It is beneficial to duplicate an end-to-end function hop-by-hop, if the result is an overall (end-to-end) improvement in performance.*   *[347]*

3B. Endpoint Recursion Corollary   *What is hop-by-hop in one context may be end-to-end in another. The End-to-End Argument can be applied recursively to any sequence of nodes in the network, or layers in the protocol stack.*   *[41]*

4   PROTOCOL LAYERING

4. Protocol Layering Principle   *Layering is a useful abstraction for thinking about networking system architecture and for organizing protocols based on network structure.*   *[42]*

> **L-4f. Early Filtering Principle**   *Filter the incoming data not destined for a node as early as possible, and discard as much as possible at each layer.*   *[194]*

4A. Layering as an Implementation Technique Performs Poorly   *Layered protocol architecture should not be confused with inefficient layer implementation techniques.*   *[45]*

> **E-4A. End System Layering Principle**   *Layered protocol architecture does not depend on a layered process implementation in the end system.*   *[294]*

> **T-4A. Limit Layered Multiplexing**   *Layered multiplexing should be minimized, and performed in an integrated manner for all layers at a single time.*   *[384]*

4B. Redundant Layer Functionality Corollary   *Functionality should not be included in a layer that must be duplicated in a higher layer, unless there is tangible benefit in doing so.*   *[45]*

4C. Layer Synergy Corollary   *When layering is used as a means of protocol division, allowing asynchronous processing and independent data encapsulations, the processing and control mechanisms should not interfere with one another. Protocol data units should translate efficiently between layers.*   *[46]*

    E-4C. Application Layer to Network Interface Synergy and Functional Division   *Application and lower-layer data unit formats and control mechanisms should not interfere with one another, and the division of functionality between host software and the network interface should minimize this interference.*   *[329]*

    T-4C. Application Layer Framing   *To the degree possible, match ADU and TPDU structure. In cases where the application can better determine structure and react to lost and misordered ADUs, ALF should be employed.*   *[383]*

    A-4C. Application–Network Synergy Principle   *Increase performance by matching application characteristics to the network. Use ALF to decrease the overhead of protocol encapsulation, control transfer, and decapsulation.*   *[476]*

    A-4C*k*. Knobs Should Correspond to Network Actions   *A knob should not be built into the network that does not correspond to a real controllable action.*   *[480]*

    A-4C*d*. Dials Should Correspond to Observable Properties   *A dial should not be provided that does not correspond to a real observable parameter.*   *[481]*

    A-4C*v*. Provide Variance Values to Imprecise Values   *The quality of feedback depends on the stability and precision of the information provided. If information is approximated or aggregated and the application does not know the degree of imprecision a priori, provide an explicit variance to the value.*   *[482]*

4D. Hourglass Corollary   *The network layer provides the convergence of addressing, routing, and signaling that ties the global Internet together. It is essential that addressing be common and that routing and signalling protocols be highly compatible.*   *[46]*

4E. Integrated Layer Processing (ILP) Corollary   *When multiple layers are generated or terminated in a single component, all encapsulations/decapsulations should be done at once, if possible.*   *[47]*

    E-4D. ILP Principle   *All passes over protocol data units (including layer encapsulations/decapsulations) that take place in a particular component of the end system (CPU, network interface embedded controller, or network interface hardware) should be done at the same time.*   *[311]*

4F. Balance Transparency and Abstraction versus Hiding   *Layering is designed around abstraction, providing a simpler representation of a complicated interface. Abstraction can hide necessary properties or parameters, which is not a desirable property of layering.*   *[47]*

    N-4F. Session–Connection Interlayer Awareness   *Session control awareness of network layer control parameters allows the overlap of session and control signaling to reduce overall latency.*   *[147]*

L-4F. Loss Characterization Principle   *Provide long-term and dynamic information on the reason for loss to higher-layer protocols so that end-to-end mechanisms respond appropriately.   [193]*

A-4F*f*. Application Adaptation Depends on Network Feedback   *Application adaptation techniques involve the application reacting to information about the network, and are dependent on knowledge about the communication path. Some adaptations benefit from active cooperation from the network.   [455]*

A-4F*h*. Functional Transparency and Abstraction Should Not Result in Hiding   *Layering is designed around abstraction, providing a simpler representation of a complicated interface. Abstraction can obscure a necessary property or parameter, resulting in hiding. Hiding is not a desirable property of layering.   [483]*

A-4F*I*. Location-Independent Interfaces Should Not Hide Latency   *Interfaces should be provided to access data independent of physical location, but latency and other QOS measures should be available to applications that can benefit from this knowledge.   [483]*

4G. Support a Variety of Interface Mechanisms   *A range of interlayer interface mechanisms should be provided as appropriate for performance optimization: synchronous and asynchronous; interrupt-driven and polled.   [48]*

4H. Interrupt versus Polling   *Interrupts provide the ability to react to asynchronous events, but are expensive operations. Polling can be used when a protocol has knowledge of when information arrives.   [48]*

E-4H. Interrupt versus Polling   *Interrupts provide the ability to react to asynchronous events, but are expensive operations. Polling can be used when a protocol has knowledge of when information arrives.   [304]*

A-4H. Support Synchronous and Asynchronous Dials   *Network instrumentation should support both asynchronous (interrupt-driven) and synchronous (polled) feedback mechanisms.   [481]*

4I. Interface Scalability Corollary   *Interlayer interfaces should support the scalability of the network and parameters transferred among the application, protocol stack, and network components.   [48]*

A-4I. API Scalability Principle   *All interfaces between an application and network should scale with respect to bandwidth, latency, and number (nodes, end systems, and users). Parameters should have a scale factor (order of magnitude exponent), a precision factor (multiplier), and a variance.   [478]*

5 STATE MANAGEMENT

5. State Management Principle   *The mechanisms for installation and management of state should be carefully chosen to balance fast, approximate, and coarse-grained against slow, accurate, and fine-grained.   [50]*

5A. Hard State versus Soft State versus Stateless Tradeoff   *Balance the tradeoff between the latency to set up hard state on a per connection basis versus the per data unit overhead of making stateless decisions or of establishing and maintaining soft state.   [51]*

    N-5A. Connectionless versus Connection Tradeoff   *The latency of connection setup must be traded against the reduction in end-to-end data transfer delay due to the elimination of store and forward delay and faster transmission due to nodes capable of increased bandwidth.   [132]*

    S-5A. Connectionless versus Connection Tradeoff   *The latency of connection setup must be traded against the increase in packet processing rate and resultant bandwidth increase achievable due to the less complex label swapping.   [205]*

    T-5A. Hard versus Soft State   *Balance the determinism and stability of hard state against the adaptability and robustness to failure of soft state.   [374]*

5B. Aggregation and Reduction of State Transfer   *Aggregation of state reduces the amount of information stored. Reducing the rate at which state information is propagated through the network reduces bandwidth and processing at network nodes, which comes at the expense of finer-grained control with more precise information.   [51]*

    T-5B. State Aggregation   *Spatially aggregate state to reduce complexity, but balance against loss in granularity. Temporally aggregate to reduce or eliminate establishment and initialization phase. State shared is fate shared.   [374]*

    A-5B. Aggregation of Application Operations   *Reduce the cost of all per connection or per application operations by aggregation. Support ways to aggregate requests and responses between the application and network and for the application to control the frequency of response and size of aggregation.   [475]*

5C. Hierarchy Corollary   *Use hierarchy and clustering to manage complexity by abstracting and aggregating information to higher levels, and to isolate the effects of changes within clusters.   [53]*

    N-5C. Network Hierarchy Principle   *Use hierarchy and clustering to manage network scale and complexity and reduce the overhead of routing algorithms.   [100]*

    N-5C*b*. Hierarchy to Aggregate and Isolate Bandwidth   *Use hierarchy to manage bandwidth aggregation in the core of the network, and to isolate clusters of traffic locality from one another.   [102]*

    N-5C*l*. Hierarchy to Minimize Latency   *Use hierarchy and cluster size to minimize network diameter and resultant latency.   [103]*

    N-5C*w*. Density Control to Optimize Degree and Diameter   *Use density control and long link overlays to optimize the tradeoff between dense low-diameter and sparse high-diameter wireless networks.   [106]*

A-5C. Balance Network Resources by Hierarchical Caching *Balance aggregate network bandwidth against storage required by hierarchical caching.* *[460]*

5D. Scope of Information Tradeoff *Make quick decisions based on local information when possible. Even if you try to make a better decision with more detailed global state, by the time the information is collected and filtered, the state of the network may have changed.* *[53]*

A-5D. Application Adaptation by Refinement *Quick and partial information is better than slow and complete information, particularly with refinement over time. Successive refinement can often be used to adapt a high-speed application to a low-speed network.* *[442]*

5E. Assumed Initial Conditions *Use reasonable assumptions based on past history or related associations to establish initial conditions for the installation of new state.* *[53]*

T-5E. Use Initial Assumptions to Converge Quickly *The time to converge to steady state depends on the accuracy of the initial conditions, which depends on the currency of state information and the dynamicity of the network. Use past information to make assumptions that will converge quickly.* *[378]*

5F. Minimize Control Overhead *The purpose of a network is to carry application data. The processing and transmission overhead introduced by control mechanisms should be kept as low as possible to maximize the fraction of network resources available for carrying application data.* *[54]*

T-5F. Avoid Hop-by-Hop Fragmentation *The transport layer should be aware of or explicitly negotiate the maximum transfer unit of the path, to avoid the overhead of fragmentation and reassembly.* *[382]*

6   CONTROL MECHANISM LATENCY

6. Control Mechanism Latency Principle *Effective network control depends on the availability of accurate and current information. Control mechanisms must operate within convergence bounds that are matched to the rate of change in the network, and latency bounds to provide low interapplication delay.* *[54]*

6A. Minimize Round Trips *Structure control messages and the information they convey to minimize the number of round trips required to accomplish data transfer.* *[55]*

N-6A. Overlap Signaling Messages with Data Transfer *To reduce unneeded end-to-end latency, signaling messages should be overlapped with data transfer.* *[137]*

T-6A. Minimize Transaction Latency *Combine connection establishment with request and data transfer to reduce end-to-end latency for transactions.* *[370]*

6B. Exploit Local Knowledge *Control should be exerted by the entity that has the knowledge needed to do so directly and efficiently.* *[57]*

N-6B. Root versus Leaf Multicast Control *Root multicast control is appropriate when a single entity has knowledge of the multicast group. Leaf-controlled multicast is needed for large dynamic groups.* *[145]*

A-6B. Client Pull versus Server Push *The side that that has the best knowledge of the client is the one that should initiate data transfer. Network load can be reduced by moving some of this knowledge to the server. Client demand fetch based on user requests; server push presend based on events the server knows about, assisted by user profiles.* *[451]*

A-6B*u*. User Feedback to Adaptive Applications *Adaptive applications benefit from user controls: either an explicit feedback loop or implicit controls based on past behavior or a user profile.* *[455]*

6C. Anticipate Future State *Anticipate future state so that actions can be taken proactively, before repair needs to be performed on the network that affects application performance.* *[59]*

S-6C*c*. Congestion Avoidance and Control *Bound offered load by admission control, traffic policing, and traffic shaping. When impending congestion is detected by building queues, notify sources to throttle. When congestion occurs, drop end-to-end frames if larger than network packets.* *[221]*

S-6C*d*. Discard to Keep Queues from Building *Queue length should reflect transient traffic conditions, and not be allowed to build in the steady state. Perform congestion avoidance and control, including packet discard, to keep queues small locally, and throttle the source for end-to-end congestion avoidance.* *[274]*

6D. Open- versus Closed-Loop Control *Use open-loop control based on knowledge of the network path to reduce the delay in closed-loop convergence. Use closed-loop control to react to dynamic network and application behavior.* *[59]*

T-6D. Open- versus Closed-Loop Control *Use open-loop control based on knowledge of the network path to reduce the delay in closed-loop convergence. Use closed-loop control to react to dynamic network and application behavior; intermediate per hop feedback can sometimes reduce the time to converge.* *[359]*

T-6D*a*. Aggressiveness of Closed-Loop Control *The response to closed-loop feedback must be rapid enough so the system converges quickly to a new stable state—but not so aggressive that oscillations occur due to overreaction to transients.* *[359]*

T-6D*c*. Use Closed-Loop Congestion Control to Adjust to Network Conditions *Closed-loop feedback is needed to adjust to network conditions when there are no hard reservations.* *[411]*

T-6D*o*. Use Knowledge of Network Paths for Open-Loop Control *Exploit open-loop rate and congestion control based on a priori knowledge to the degree possible to reduce the need for feedback control.* *[403]*

T-6De. Forward Error Correction   *Use FEC for low-latency, open-loop flow control when bandwidth is available and statistical loss tolerance bounds are acceptable to the application.   [399]*

6E. Separate Control Mechanisms   *Control mechanisms should be distinct, or the information conveyed explicit enough, so that the proper action is taken.   [60]*

T-6E. Decouple Error, Flow, and Congestion Control   *Exploit selective acknowledgments and open-loop rate control to decouple error, flow, and congestion control mechanisms.   [395]*

7   DISTRIBUTED DATA

7. Distributed Data Principle   *Distributed applications should select and organize the data they exchange to minimize the amount and latency of data transferred and to allow incremental processing of data.   [60]*

7A. Partitioning and Structuring of Data   *Whenever possible, data should be partitioned and structured to minimize the amount of data transferred and the latency in communication.   [61]*

A-7A. Structure Data to Meet Interactive Response Bounds   *Structure and migrate data for interactive responses such that initially visible data is present at sufficient resolution within interactive response bounds.   [442]*

A-7Ac. Structure Data and Migrate Code for Dynamic Content   *Structure data from which content is dynamically generated into cacheable units. Cache the programs that generate the content along with the data.   [461]*

7B. Location of Data   *Data should be positioned close to the application that needs it to minimize the latency of access. Replication of data helps accomplish this.   [61]*

A-7Bs. Exploit Spatial Locality to Reduce Latency   *Reduce the latency of access by locating data physically close to the users and applications that need it.   [457]*

A-7Bt. Exploit Temporal Locality to Reduce Latency   *Reduce the latency of access by retaining data locally (or nearby) that is likely to be referenced in the future.   [459]*

8   PROTOCOL DATA UNITS

8. Protocol Data Unit Principle   *The size and structure of PDUs are critical to high-bandwidth, low-latency communication.   [61]*

8A. PDU Size and Granularity   *The size of PDUs is a balance of a number of parameters that affect performance. Trade the statistical multiplexing benefits of small packets against the efficiency of large packets.   [62]*

S-8A. Packet Size and Variability Tradeoff   *Packet size is a balance of a number of parameters that affect performance. Trade the statistical multiplexing and fine-grained control benefits of small packets against the efficiency of large packets. Trade the benefits to switch design of fixed cell size against the overhead of SAR and efficiency of variable packet size. Multiple discrete packet sizes increase flexibility at the cost of additional switch complexity. Hop-by-hop SAR localizes packet size optimizations at the cost of additional per hop delay and complexity.*   *[209]*

T-8A. Balance Packet Size   *Trade between control overhead and fine enough grained control. Choose size and aggregation methods that make sense end-to-end.*   *[380]*

8B. PDU Control Field Structure   *Optimize PDU header and trailer fields for efficient processing. Fields should be simply encoded, byte aligned, and fixed length when possible. Variable length fields should be prepended with their length.*   *[62].*

N-8B. Efficiency of Signaling   *Signaling messages should be simple in coding and format and fit in a single packet to minimize the latency in processing. The signaling protocol should be robust to lost messages.*   *[133]*

S-8B. Packet Control Field Structure   *Optimize packet header and trailer fields for efficient processing. Fields should be simply encoded, byte aligned, and fixed length when possible. Variable-length fields should be prepended with their length.*   *[215]*

8C. Scalability of Control Fields   *PDU header and trailer fields and structure should be scalable with data rate and bandwidth-×-delay product.*   *[63]*

L-8C. Link Protocol Scalability Principle   *Link protocols should be scalable in bandwidth, either variably or in discrete intervals (power-of-2 or order-of-magnitude). Header/trailer lengths and fields that relate to bandwidth should be long enough or contain a scale factor.*   *[176]*

T-8C. Packet Control Field Values   *Optimize header control field values to trade efficiency against expected future requirements. Fields that are likely to be insufficient for future bandwidth-×-delay products should contain a scale factor.*   *[391]*

Acronyms

2R	regeneration and reshaping (physical layer)
3R	regeneration with retiming and reshaping (physical layer)
AAL	ATM adaptation layer
ABR	available bit rate (ATM traffic class for data)
ACK	acknowledgment
A↔D	analog-to-digital and digital-to-analog conversion
ADM	add/drop multiplexor (SONET ring component)
ADSL	asymmetric digital subscriber line
ADU	application data unit
AIMD	additive increase/multiplicative decrease (feedback control)
ALF	application layer framing
AN	active network
API	application programming interface
APS	automatic protection switching (for SONET)
ARP	address resolution protocol
ARPANET	Advanced Research Projects Agency network (Internet precursor)
ARQ	automatic repeat request (closed-loop error control)
ASIC	application-specific integrated circuit
ASN.1	abstract syntax notation 1 (ISO presentation layer data format)
ATM	asynchronous transfer mode (statistical multiplexing technique)[1]

[1]Common use, followed in this book, is for the layer 3 protocol suite and technology using ATM statistical multiplexing.

ATMF	ATM forum (industry consortium that generates ATM standards)
BECN	backward explicit congestion notification
BGP	border gateway protocol (Internet routing protocol)
B-ISDN	broadband integrated services digital network
BNA	Burroughs Network Architecture (Unisys)
BSD	Berkeley software distribution (Unix)
CA	certificate authority
CAC	connection admission control
CAD	computer-aided design
CADS	computer-aided design and simulation
CAE	computer-aided engineering
CAM	content addressable memory
CATV	community antenna television[2]
CBR	constant bit rate (traffic class)
CID	connection identifier
CIDR	classless interdomain routing
CDMA	code division multiple access (multiplexing technique)
CLNP	connectionless network protocol (ISO)
CMM	communications memory module
CMOS	complementary metal oxide semiconductor (silicon technology)
CPU	central processing unit
CRC	cyclic redundancy check
CSCW	computer-supported cooperative work
CSMA	carrier sense multiple access
CSMA/CD	carrier sense multiple access with collision detection
DAN	desk area network
DCA	Distributed Communications Architecture (Unisys–Sperry Univac)
DCT	discrete cosine transform (used in JPEG and MPEG compression)
DHCP	dynamic host configuration protocol (for automatic IP address assignment)
DMA	direct memory access
DNA	Digital Network Architecture (DEC)
DNS	domain name system
DRAM	dynamic RAM
DSL	digital subscriber line
DSM	distributed shared memory
DSP	digital signal processor
DVSM	distributed virtual shared memory
DWDM	dense wavelength division multiplexing (100s to 1000s of wavelengths)
E2E	end to end
ECC	error checking and correction
ECN	explicit congestion notification
EDFA	erbium-doped fiber amplifier

---

[2]As originally defined; common use is *cable television*.

EPD	early packet discard
ER	explicit rate mode (ATM ABR traffic class)
FA	foreign agent (mobile IP)
FCC	Federal Communications Commission (U.S. government)
FCS	fibre channel standard (link technology and protocol)
FDDI	fiber distributed data interface (LAN/MAN technology)
FEC	forward error correction; forwarding equivalence class (MPLS)
FECN	forward explicit congestion notification
FIFO	first-in first-out (queueing discipline)
FTP	file transfer protocol
FTTH	fiber to the home
FWM	four wave mixing (fiber optic nonlinearity)
GaAs	gallium arsenide (semiconductor technology)
GEO	geosynchronous earth orbiting (satellite)
GFR	guaranteed frame rate (ATM traffic class for data)
GIS	geographical information system
GOS	grade of service
GUI	graphical user interface
HA	home agent (mobile IP)
HBH	hop by hop
HDLC	high-level data link control (ISO link protocol)
HDTV	high-definition television (with 16:9 aspect ratio)
HFC	hybrid fiber/coax (CATV link technology)
HIPPI	high-performance parallel interface (data link protocol)
HLR	home location register (for cellular telephony)
HPCC	High-Performance Computing and Communications[3]
HTML	hypertext markup language
HTTP	hypertext transfer protocol (for Web request/response)
IBT	in-band terminator (OBS protocol)
ICMP	Internet control message protocol
IEEE	Institute of Electrical and Electronics Engineers
IGMP	Internet group management protocol
ILP	integrated layer processing
IMAP	Internet message access protocol
IN	intelligent network
INX	Internet network exchange (public peering point)
I/O	input/output
IOC	I/O controller
IOP	I/O processor
IP	Internet protocol
IPng	Internet protocol, the next generation (early name for IPv6)

[3]U.S. government program responsible for widespread development and deployment of the Internet into the public sector, frequently called the *Gore Bill* in the late 1980s.

IPv4	Internet protocol version 4
IPv6	Internet protocol version 6
IPX	Internetwork Packet Exchange (Novell)
ISDN	integrated services digital network
ISM	industrial, scientific, and medical (U.S. frequency spectrum)
ISO	International Organization for Standardization
ITU	International Telecommunication Union (standards body)
IWU	interworking unit
JET	just enough time (OBS protocol)
JPEG	Joint Photographic Experts Group
LAN	local area network
LDP	label distribution protocol (MPLS)
LEO	low earth orbiting (satellite)
LINO	last-in never-out (tail-drop queueing discipline)
LMDS	local multipoint distribution services
LLC	logical link control (IEEE 802.3)
MAC	medium access control
MAN	metropolitan area network
MCU	microcontroller unit
MD	message digest
MDn	Internet message digest algorithm n
MPEG	Motion Picture Experts Group
MPLS	multiprotocol label switching
MPλS	multiprotocol lambda switching
MRI	magnetic resonance imaging
MTU	maximum transmission unit
NAK	negative acknowledgment
NAS	network attached storage
NAT	network address translator
NCP	network communications processor; network control program (early name for TCP and IP)
NFS	network file system
NI	network interface
NNI	network node interface (generally ATM)
NOW	network of workstations
NPDU	network protocol data unit (packet)
NRZI	nonreturn to zero, invert on ones (line code)
NSFNET	National Science Foundation network (early 1990s U.S. Internet backbone)
NTP	network time protocol
NUMA	nonuniform memory access
OBS	optical burst switching
OC	optical carrier (SONET)
OS	operating system
OSI	open systems interconnection

PAM	pulse amplitude modulation (line code)
PAWS	protection against wrapped sequence numbers (TCP)
PC	personal computer
PCB	process control block
PCM	pulse code modulation (line code)
PDU	protocol data unit
PE	protocol engine (research project)
PIO	programmed input/output
PKI	public key infrastructure
P-NNI	private NNI (ATM)
POP	point of presence (access to network service provider)
POS	packet over SONET (IP over SONET)
POTS	plain ordinary telephone service[4]
POW	packet over wavelength
PPD	partial packet discard
PPM	pulse position modulation (line code)
PPP	point-to-point protocol (link)
PPU	peripheral processing unit (CDC 6600 series I/O processor)
PSTN	public switched telephone network
PVC	permanent virtual circuit (provisioned rather than signaled); permanent virtual connection (ATM)
QAM	quadrature amplitude modulation (line code)
QOS	quality of service
RAM	random access memory
RED	random early detection (congestion avoidance)[5]
RF	radio frequency
RFD	reserve a fixed duration (OBS protocol)
RISC	reduced instruction set computing
RPC	remote procedure call
RSVP	resource reservation protocol
RTCP	real-time control protocol (for RTP)
RTP	real-time transport protocol
RTSP	real-time streaming protocol (streaming media control)
RTT	round-trip time
RTTM	round-trip time measurement (TCP)
S-AAL	signaling ATM adaptation layer
SACK	selective acknowledgment
SAN	storage area network
SAR	segmentation and reassembly (ATM)
SEAL	simple and efficient adaptation layer (AAL5)
SETI	search for extraterrestrial intelligence

[4]As originally defined; common use is also *plain old telephone system.*
[5]Frequently used as *random early discard.*

SIP	session initiation protocol
SMTP	simple mail transfer protocol
SNA	Systems Network Architecture (IBM)
SNAP	subnetwork access protocol (IEEE 802.3)
SOA	semiconductor optical amplifier
SONET	synchronous optical network (MAN and WAN link layer)
SRAM	static RAM
STM	synchronous transfer mode (deterministic multiplexing technique)
SS7	signaling system number 7 (PSTN)
STS	synchronous transport signal (SONET electronic domain)
SVC	switched virtual connection (ATM)
TAG	tell-and-go (OBS protocol)
TCP	transmission control protocol
TDM	time division multiplexing
TDMA	time division multiple access (multiplexing technique)
TLB	translation lookaside buffer (caches virtual to real address mappings)
TPDU	transport protocol data unit
TPn	transport protocol class $n=\{0 \ldots 4\}$ (OSI)
TSAPA	transport service access point address (ISO equivalent of TCP port)
TSI	time slot interchange (interchanges TDM channels)
T/TCP	transaction TCP
UBR	unspecified bit rate (ATM best-effort traffic class)
UDP	user datagram protocol
UNI	user–network interface (generally ATM)
URL	uniform resource locator
UTP	unshielded twisted pair (cable)
VBR	variable bit rate (bursty traffic class)
VBR-nrt	nonreal-time VBR (ATM traffic class)
VBR-rt	real-time VBR (ATM traffic class)
VC	virtual circuit; virtual connection
VDSL	very high-speed digital subscriber line
VLR	visitor location register (for cellular telephony)
VMTP	versatile message transaction protocol
VOD	video on demand
VP	virtual path (ATM)
VPN	virtual private network
VR	virtual reality
VRAM	video RAM (multiported memory with random and sequential ports)
WAN	wide area network
WDM	wavelength division multiplexing
XC	cross connect (link layer switch with provisioned interconnections)
XDR	external data representation (presentation layer)
xDSL	digital subscriber line (x indicates various types: ADSL, VDSL, etc.)
XTP	express transport protocol

INDEX

Page references followed by italic *t* indicate material in tables. References followed by italic *n* indicate material in footnotes.

A

Abstraction, Balance
  Transparency and, versus
  Hiding (4F), 47–48
Abstraction and Functional
  Transparency and Should
  Not Result in Hiding (A-
  4F), 483
acknowledgments, 391–394
  aggregation, 394
  granularity, 408–409
  hop-by-hop, 55
  implosion, 395–396
  multiple, 395–396
  negative, 393
  selective, 394
  TCP in ATM, 70
active caching, 461
active mirroring, 458
active network management,
  162
Active Network Processing (S-
  II.4a), 277–279
active networking, 19,
  496–497
  architecture, 115–116
  management, 161–162
  moderate, 115, 496
  monitoring, 161–162
  node architecture, 275–279
  processing types, 278–279
  strong, 115, 496–497
active probes, 162

adaptation of applications,
  454–478
  bandwidth improvement,
  470–474
  latency reduction,
  456–469
  mobile, 476–478
  scaling, 475–476
  wireless, 477
Adaptation, Application by
  Refinement (A-5D),
  442–443
Adaptation, Application
  Depends on Network
  Feedback (A-4Ff), 455
Adaptation, Application
  Synergy (A-IV$_1$), 456
add-drop multiplexor, 190
address lookup, 254–268
Administrative Constraints
  Increase the Importance
  of Good Design (N-III),
  108
advanced encryption standard
  (AES), 436
aggregate bandwidth, 3
  applications, 435, 470
Aggregate and Isolate
  Bandwidth, Hierarchy to
  (N-5Cb), 102
aggregation of bandwidth, 95
  applications, 474–476
  and isolation, 101–102

Aggregation and Reduction of
  State Transfer (5B), 51–52
Aggregation of Application
  Operations (A-5B), 475
all-optical networking, 495–496
Amdahl's law, 323
America Online, 16
amorphous computing, 497–498
amplifiers, 188–189
  erbium doped fiber (EDFA),
  171, 188, 495
antennas, 173, 176
Anticipate Future State (6C), 59
anticipation
  for bandwidth improvement,
  470–471
  for latency reduction, 462–464
anycast, 458
API (application programming
  interface), 478
API Scalability Principle (A-4I),
  478
Apollo Domain, 432
Application Adaptation by
  Refinement (A-5D),
  442–443
Application Adaptation
  Depends on Network
  Feedback (A-4Ff), 455
Application Adaptation Synergy
  (A-IV$_1$), 456
Application Bandwidth
  Principle (A-1Ab), 470

Components, Link Layer (L-IIc), 188
composed applications, 453–454
compression (of data), 465–466
Compression of Data (A-2B), 466
CompuServe, 16
Computer-supported collaborative work (CSCW), 454
concast, 162
concatenated data networks, 177
congestion, 401, 409–411
  cliff, 409–410
  collapse, 410
  knee, 409–410
  signaling, 154–155
Congestion, Avoid and Keep Queues Short (N-II.4), 156
congestion avoidance, 353
  datagram switch, 274
  network based, 155–156
  random early detection, 156, 274, 359
  switch, 221–222
Congestion Avoidance (T-II.4c), 411
Congestion Avoidance and Control (S-6Cc), 221
congestion control, 353
  closed-loop, 409–419
  datagram switch, 274
  defined, 401
  end-to-end, 353, 409–423
  high-speed impact, 402
  hop-by-hop, 156–157
  hybrid, 417–422
  network-based, 152–156
  switch, 222–223
Congestion Control and Avoidance (S-6Cc), 221
Congestion Control, Decouple from Error and Flow (T-6E), 395
Congestion Control Fairness versus Complexity (N-2Bc), 156
Congestion Control in the Network Improves Performance (N-3A), 153–154
Congestion Control, Use Closed-Loop to Adjust to Network Conditions (T-6Dc), 411–412
Connectionless versus Connection Tradeoff (N-5A, S-5A), 132, 205

connection management, 352
connection-oriented networks, 121
connection-oriented transfer and signaling
  network layer, 129–132
  transport layer, 365–370
connections, 120
connection shortening, 360–362
constant bit rate (CBR), 407
Constraints, Administrative Increase the Importance of Good Design (N-lll), 108
Constraints, Limiting (III), 27
constraints limiting high-speed networking, 27–31, 94–95, 107–110
Constraints on Partitioning of Distributed Applications (A-III.5), 453
content addressable memories (CAMs), 257–258
  for variable prefixes, 264
content cache location, 113
Content, Dynamic, Structure Data and Migrate Code for (A-7Ac), 461
contention, See buffering; blocking; store-and-forward
Contention Avoidance (II.5), 26
Context Switch Avoidance (E-II.6c), 302–303
context switching, 302–303
continuous data transfer, 447
Continuous Media Quality, User Expectations of (A-I.2c), 434
Continuous Media Streaming (T-I.2), 371
continuous media streaming, 355, 371–373
  mixing and merging, 275
  on-demand, 450
  stream merging, 471
  video, 435–436
control. See network control and signaling
control-driven soft state accumulation, 135
Control, Efficient Transfer of (II.6), 26
Control Mechanism Latency Principle (6), 54
control mechanisms, 26, 54–60
  closed- and open-loop, 59–60
Control Mechanisms, Separate (6E), 60

Control, Open- versus Closed-Loop (6D), 59–60, 359
Control Overhead, Minimize (5F), 54
convergence of networking, 15t, 17–19
convolutional codes, 399
copper wire, 16, 17, 169–170
Copy Minimization Principle (E-II.3), 295–296
copy operations, 25
Copies, Avoid Data by Remapping (E-II.3m), 306–308
Cost and Feasibility (III.4), 28–29
CPU, 287
credit balance, 157
credit-based hop-by-hop flow control, 157
critical path, 34–36
Critical Path Corollary (1B, E-IB), 35–36, 297
Critical Path, Fast Packet Switch Principle (S-1Bc), 203
Critical Path Optimization of Security Operations (T-1B), 426
crossbars, 238–241
  end system, 317–318
  multicast switch, 246–248
  switch fabric, 238–241
  tiling, 241
cross-connects, 190
crosspoint, 238–240
cryptography, 422
CSNET, 17
cut-through paths, 71
cyclic redundancy check (CRC), 346

D

data communications, 16
data compression. See compression
datacycle, 464
Data, Distributed Principle (7), 60
data-driven soft state accumulation, 135
data encoding, 465
Data, Location of (7B), 61
datagram overlay meshes, 91
datagram switches. See fast datagram switches
datagram transfer, 365
data integrity, 346